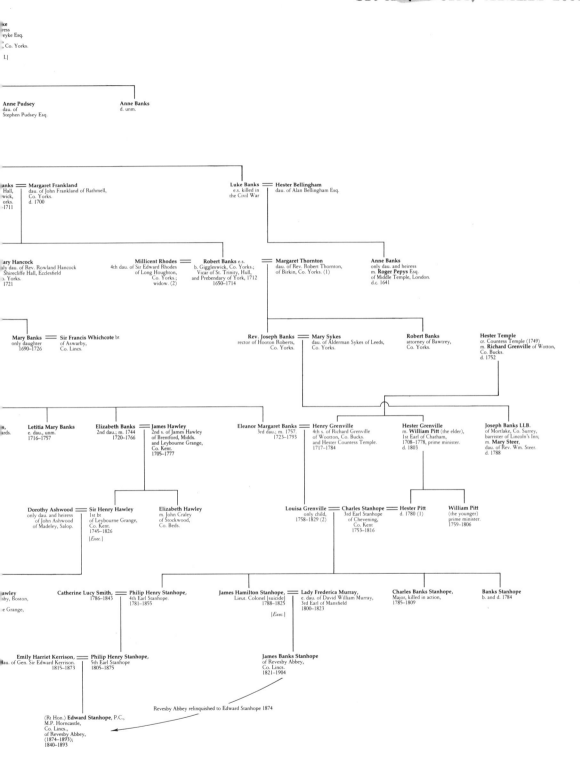

SIR JOSEPH BANKS

The first authentic portrait of Sir Joseph Banks, *aet.* 29, painted by Benjamin West,
PRA *c.* December 1771, 4 to 5 months after the return of HMS *Endeavour*.

SIR

JOSEPH BANKS

1743–1820

HAROLD B. CARTER

BRITISH MUSEUM (NATURAL HISTORY)

'. . . wide as the world is, traces of you are
to be found in every corner of it'

Robert Hobart, Lord Hobart, 4th Earl of
Buckinghamshire to Banks, 18 October 1793
Lincolnshire Archives Office, Hill Colln. 2. 28

© Harold B. Carter 1988
First published 1988, reprinted 1991
British Museum (Natural History)
Cromwell Road
London SW7 5BD

British Library Cataloguing in Publication Data
Carter Harold B.
  Sir Joseph Banks, 1743–1820.
  1. Banks, *Sir* Joseph   2. Scientists –
Great Britain ·– Biography
  I. Title
  581.092'4   Q143.33

ISBN 0 565 00993 1

Photoset by Waveney Typesetters, Norwich
Printed by Bookcraft (Bath) Ltd.

CONTENTS

PART THREE

1797–1820

HM MINISTER OF PHILOSOPHIC AFFAIRS

The Rt Hon., Sir Joseph Banks, BT, PC, GCB, PRS, FSA

FOREWORD

Unravelling the multifarious threads of the life of Sir Joseph Banks has occupied Mr H. B. Carter for over 25 years. Banks's name is intimately connected with the origins and history of the British Museum (Natural History) and for this reason my predecessors and I encouraged and supported Mr Carter's work.

Significantly, in consequence of Mr Carter's researches, there is now in the Museum Library a repository of microfilms, photocopies and transcripts of all the major holdings of Banksian correspondence which is a resource of international importance.

Banks was the 'Father of Australia'. It was he who, as a naturalist aboard HMS *Endeavour* under Captain James Cook, recognized the potential for European settlement of Botany Bay. It is fitting, therefore, that this biography is published as the bicentenary of the founding of the European settlement of Australia approaches.

Banks himself published little. He inspired, encouraged and supported others, and in consequence he has been a shadowy figure in the annals of British science. I welcome this comprehensive study which goes some way toward establishing Banks's real contribution to the advancement of British science.

R. H. Hedley, CB, DSc, FIBiol
Director

Preface

The figure of Sir Joseph Banks is still only faintly etched on the historic records of the past two centuries. His established place as the man who emerged from the class of wealthy landed gentlemen in Georgian England to be President of the Royal Society for an unbroken span of 42 years does not sufficiently explain his part in the world of national and international affairs. The circle of his associates was perhaps more extensive and various than that of any of his more obviously notable contemporaries. Wherever he was, in London or in the counties, his house was a centre to which men of all races and social ranks came or wrote from within the furthest limits of the world as it was known to the western European of his time. He was certainly sure of his own stature among the great men of his own period and not unmindful of the interest which his posterity might have in his life and achievements. His papers were kept in some order for this end, but not greatly beyond what was needed for the daily round of his complex activities. There is no doubt, however, that he was sincere in conserving his own affairs within the privacy of his own household and the security of his own study. There was never at hand any industrious Boswell to record the detail of his opinions or the flavour of his conversation. Nor did he indulge his vanity with a diary beyond those youthful sheets penned under pressure from an admiring sister or the later desultory notes kept for practical use. He sought neither an inflated place in history nor the role of host to the literary parasites of his own or later times.

He remains to this day, therefore, a sort of historic ghost – a spectre that even at its best has been sensed only as a disarticulated mass and out of perspective. For this he was himself more responsible than anyone. He took few steps to ensure that his real shape and substance would survive. Not even the organized mass of his working correspondence and other papers secure in his study at 32 Soho Square and in his county houses, had they remained intact, would have rounded out the semblance of the man. They would have done more, certainly, than most such relics that survive for other men – but where are they now? Scattered by slow degrees under the terms of a will not urgent with concern for their survival, they have been dispersed with much gone beyond recovery. But enough survive, it now seems, to make possible the evocation of some measure of historical justice.

The view of Sir Joseph Banks conveyed by the miscellany of short biographies, memoirs, and literary references in the lives of other men, is thus fragmentary and distorted. The shifting image invoked ranges from the romantic young man of wealth in the guise of a dilettante botanist who stooped to sail with Captain Cook as a supernumerary infliction on board the *Endeavour* to that other character – the gouty President of the Royal Society, the autocrat of the 'philosophers' who never quite shed the mud which was flung during the 'dissensions' within that august body and who was finally to achieve pejorative distinction as 'the great Panjandrum of British science'. Between these apparently disparate beings drifts the shadow of a latter-day

Maecenas who, as a patron of this and that, was content 'to swallow gross flattery' and said to have made his house 'too like a court'. Between the image of the wealthy young dilettante traveller who seemed never to have grown old and that of the domineering old baronet and PRS who seemed never to have been young there is an evident void. This has been only occasionally and then very tenuously bridged.

Not, indeed, for nearly 90 years after his death was there a moderately successful gathering of the pieces into some order as a separate printed volume. This emerged in 1909 from the distant enthusiasms of a colonial botanist, the English expatriate J. H. Maiden, FRS who, from the antipodean limits of the Banksian world, had every stimulus and reason to attempt to see the image clear. During those 90 years only a part of the central mass of papers had been tossed and turned by many hands in the process of selecting and transcribing what seemed to be the choice items fit for the conventions of nineteenth-century biography. No such biography, however, came into public view. All that appeared was the occasional memoir and the odd encyclopaedia or dictionary entry culled from a mere portion of the surviving manuscripts or from the limited resources of personal knowledge. One by one those who had known the man himself themselves had grown old, forgetful, or even disdainful, and in their turn had died bequeathing little beyond a few faint traces in their own biographies or other literary relics. The linking strands between the eighteenth and nineteenth centuries in the lives of men successively frayed and broke. Since then the awakening concern of the twentieth century with the social and scientific roots of the modern world has done something to repair these bonds. For all that remains to be done, enough has now been gathered into one place to re-compose the fragments of a life, too long neglected among historical studies, into a skeletal structure on which the flesh of more particular academic themes may now be hung.

This volume is intended to offer the elements of such a frame. It is intended also as a partial resolution of my debt to the British Museum (Natural History) for working hospitality over many years in the long and continuing task of gathering the scattered Banks papers, in one guise or another, under its mantle to form an organized research archive of general utility. Implicit also in this is my debt to successive generous grants for just this purpose from the American Philosophical Society, the Royal Society, and the State Library of New South Wales at intervals between 1965 and 1983. Over this period these resources – copies of Banksian documents in various forms – have been brought together from many collections and arranged in a chronological order as far as this has been practicable. From this assembly of more than 15 000 items, the general pattern of the life of Banks emerged to cover a span of the 55 adult years which ended with his death in 1820. On this base the present version has been composed.

Any biography is, of course, only one view of the subject from among innumerable angles as various as there are hopeful authors seeking an art form for their own self-expression or serious historians in scholarly pursuit of evanescent truth. In 1909 J. H. Maiden, as a botanical FRS, presented the fruits of some ten years' searching in a volume which he defined as *matériaux pour servir* toward a life of Banks. Now, a long life-time later, I have the temerity to offer a condensation of my own gatherings as an outline drafted from more extensive sources than writers in the interim years have used. Clearly, this is not a work of professional biography. In one sense it is a deviation from the main task of putting the Banks's *reliquiae* into sufficient order for modern scientific and historical research. It is also merely one personal sampling of the documentary mass and, in the broken time at my disposal, one personal sifting of the evidence to deduce the essential pattern of the life within the circumstances of its time.

It will be evident that in the process I have not given either references or notes in relation to the text itself nor to any of the passages cited. At an early stage it became apparent that to do so would be supererogant when so many clues to the origins of the material used were embedded in the body of the text, the select bibliography, the appendices, and the captions to the illustrations. The decision to keep a clear page in the main text was strengthened by the present intention of the British Museum (Natural History) to publish as a concurrent volume · a separate guide to bibliographical and biographical sources from my material, fulfilling thereby the terms of a special grant to the author for this purpose from the Royal Society. In this way, with other Banksian volumes already published by the Museum in the *Historical Series* of its *Bulletin*, it is hoped that a path will have been cleared toward the further publication of surviving papers, especially the correspondence, such as those already in print under the terms of the Sir Joseph Banks Memorial Act of 1945 in the jurisdiction of New South Wales, continuing the first intentions of the original Memorial Fund set up in May 1905.

The publication of this particular volume is due in the first instance to the Trustees of the British Museum (Natural History) by whom it was commissioned and to whom I am especially indebted for much working hospitality during its preparation. That this has come about owes a very great deal to the steady support of Mr M. J. Rowlands during his long term as Chief Librarian under whom the present Banks archive at the Museum with which I am concerned was assembled for studies such as this. My gratitude for this collaboration must be extended also to the present Head of Library Services, Mr A. P. Harvey, and his Deputy, Mr R. E. R. Banks, under whom the later stages of production have been managed. Throughout I have had the great benefit of regular help from Miss Dorothy Norman in coping with archival and related problems. It is pleasant also to acknowledge my debt over the years to the encouragement received in many forms from those others in the Museum who have been concerned in setting straight the Banksian record by their own studies, notably: Dr P. J. P. Whitehead, Mr A. C. Wheeler, Dr W. T. Stearn, Mr J. B. Marshall, Mr E. W. Groves, Dr C. J. Humphries, the late Miss P. I. Edwards and Mrs. J. A. Diment.

The present version of the life of Banks requires also a warm acknowledgement of the generosity and freedom with which the many public and private holders of origina sources have made them available to me in various ways. Those on whom I have drawn are listed in the select bibliography and I am grateful for the permissions granted to me in the use of this material. Among those who have made this possible I must acknowledge particularly: the late Miss P. Mander-Jones, former Mitchell Librarian, and her successors Mr. G. H. Richardson and Miss Suzanne Mourot; Mr R. H. Dillon, the first Sutro Librarian; the late Dr G. W. Corner, former Secretary/ Director of the American Philosophical Society; Mr D. R. Watkins, Chief Reference Librarian, and Miss Judith Schiff at the Sterling Memorial Library, Yale University; Mr S. Parks and Mrs John C. Reily at the Beinecke Rare Book and Manuscript Library of the same University; Mr H. W. Robinson, Librarian of the Royal Society; Mr G. D. R. Bridson, former Librarian of the Linnean Society of London; and Mr R. F. Doust, State Librarian and Secretary to the Library Council of New South Wales.

More recently in the later stages of this work I have had much benefit from the special knowledge of Mr S. R. Band of Ashover, Derbyshire, in relation to the lead mines of that area, and that of Dr W. M. Hunt of Boston, Lincolnshire, on the canals and navigations of that county. I owe a particular debt to Mr John Sambrook, former Senior Illustrator, Survey of London, for his drawing of the premises at 32 Soho Square making architectural sense as a reconstruction from my own gathering of data for such a purpose.

Finally I am most grateful to Mrs F. E. Warr for her help in my library pursuits; to Miss Valerie Jones for setting my maps in order; and to Mr R. C. Driver for the many tasks of copying which my original typescripts have required.

Harold B. Carter

Yeo Bank
Congresbury
Co. Avon
May 1987

PART ONE
1630–1779

THE TRAVELLER
MR JOSEPH BANKS,
DCL, FRS, FSA

CHAPTER 1

THE FAMILY FROM RIBBLESDALE
1630–1740

Few families can trace their origins with much certainty further back than two or three hundred years from their own day, and in this the Banks family is no exception. On the north-western watershed of the Pennines in Ribblesdale lies the small town of Giggleswick. Here the parish registers show that the name of Banks was common enough but from which particular Banks of the many recorded there emerged the ancestors of the future Sir Joseph the choice can only be tenuous. On the evidence of local historians we must exclude any connection with the Bankes family of Bank Newton near Gargrave, a claim somewhat hazardously devised in the search for a source of coat armour in the baronetcy to come. The true progenitor seems to be Robert Banks, possibly a lawyer, born in the late sixteenth century, a younger son of Thomas Banks of Bankwell in the parish of Giggleswick. He married Anne, daughter and heiress of Joseph Creyke of Beck Hall, which from 1615 appears in the ownership of Robert Banks himself. By this marriage there were three sons. Luke, the eldest, was killed as a royalist soldier in the Civil War. Robert, the second son, also fought for the King leading a troop of horse in 1642 in the regiment of the Duke of Newcastle. He survived the war and lost much of his fortune but seems to have earned a claim for compensation under the Restoration. Joseph, the third son, was apparently a lawyer and one of the six clerks of Chancery in his day.

Only the second son, Robert Banks II, continued the line. He married Anne, daughter of Stephen Pudsey, and their son, Robert Banks III was born on 27 March 1630. This third Robert, a soldier, is the first reasonably clear figure to emerge from the cluster of ancestors to whom Sir Joseph could reasonably lay claim. Robert Banks III (1630–1711) seems to have adopted as a profession what his father had taken up briefly as a task of loyalty to the Crown in a great civil crisis. For some 18 years he seems to have served, again like his father, as an officer in the regiment of William Cavendish, first Duke of Newcastle. At one period he is reputed to have been one of the garrison of the fort at Bridlington under Sir John Reresby and set there for the protection of colliers and other shipping along the east Yorkshire coast. Beyond this not much is known of Robert Banks III.

It was probably in 1649, the year of the trial and execution of Charles I, that Robert Banks III, not yet 20, married Margaret, daughter of John Frankland of Rathmell, a village south of Giggleswick. From the same roots would descend the Franklands of Thirkleby, of whom the sixth baronet would become a Fellow of the Royal Society and a close associate of the Banks who would be its President for so long. By contrast, Margaret's brother, Richard Frankland emerged from Christ's College, Cambridge, to be expelled from his living under the Uniformity Act of 1662 and to found at Rathmell one of the most famous dissenting academies in Giggleswick.

3

The marriage was fruitful but fated. It was fruitful in the family of sons born to the young couple at Beck Hall; Robert Banks IV, born in 1650, sometime Vicar of Hull and Prebend of York who died in 1714; John, born in 1653, who died in 1662 and Joseph, born in 1665. Above all it was fruitful in this last event, for here was that Joseph Banks whose sturdy abilities would found the fortune which would lead the family out of the Yorkshire dales to join the rising gentry of Lincolnshire and to colonize the undeveloped fens with their rich potential. The marriage was fated when, after nearly 40 years, the union withered. In 1688 Robert Banks sold Beck Hall for £700 and moved to Leven in Westmorland, separated for ever from his wife. Margaret herself, probably in 1689, moved back again to Rathmell where, after years of hunted migrations, her non-conforming brother had at last re-established his academy. Somewhat grudgingly 'tabled' there, she endured the Calvanist discipline of the academy household until Richard's death in 1698. He was buried at Giggleswick and two years later, on 5 April 1700, his sister joined him there, recorded in the parish register simply as 'Margareta Banks de Rathmell'.

The product of the cross-fertilization of these seventeenth-century emnities was now embodied in the rising young attorney, Joseph Banks I of Shiercliffe Hall, Sheffield. His father Robert Banks III lived on far enough into the eighteenth century to enjoy a little of the material fruits which the energies of his youngest son had gleaned from the exercise of his profession and business common sense. The old professional soldier died peacefully enough at 81. He lies buried by the church at Scofton in the county of Nottinghamshire within the boundary of the first major advance in the landed estate forming under the hand of Joseph Banks I.

II

The early education of the first Joseph Banks is obscure. Successive generations of the Banks family of Bankwell were governors of Giggleswick grammar school and his maternal uncle, the Revd Richard Frankland had certainly been educated there. He too may have entered this famous school which now incorporates as one of its houses the Beck Hall rebuilt on the site of the building where he was born, transformed in other hands after the Glorious Revolution in an elegant William and Mary style. It is sure, however, that in 1681, as a boy of 16, he was sent to Sheffield and that in 1684 he was articled to Thomas Chappell, possibly a relative but certainly a busy attorney there. The practice was a thriving one in a town of fast-growing business, founded essentially on the smoking iron forges of Hallamshire and the trading opportunities of a central corn market. As master to an eager and ambitious young man, Thomas Chappell was well placed to set his feet on a sure path to professional success. He was a town trustee and agent to the Duke of Norfolk within whose manor the town of Sheffield lay.

Joseph's articles duly expired and soon after, in 1689, he married Mary Hancock, daughter of another non-conforming minister the Revd Rowland Hancock, the displaced Vicar of Ecclesfield, more recently pastor of a Congregational church near Shiercliffe Hall of which he was a tenant in part. Joseph, now 24, was clearly not dissuaded from union with the dissenting world by the recent separation of his parents and the retreat of his mother to the bleak household at the Rathmell academy. Nor was his own conformity to the established church a bar to the generosity of his father-in-law. Mary Hancock brought with her a marriage portion of £400, enough to form a solid foundation for an enterprising young man.

Here then, in the first year of the new reign of William and Mary began effectively the rise to affluence of the original Yorkshire family whose last notable figure by direct descent in the male line would be Joseph Banks IV, otherwise Sir Joseph Banks, 1st Baronet, and the last in that creation. By the time of the accession of Anne in 1702 the fortune of the family was secure and Joseph Banks I could retire to the ranks of the landed gentry. In this metamorphosis the course of his life was typical of the period, an example of the upward social mobility always possible wherever a stable compound of reasonable intellect, good sense and driving energy appeared in a family.

In the summer of 1690 the eldest child of Joseph I, Mary, was born and in the same season five years later his second and last child, his son and heir, Joseph Banks II – both at Shiercliffe Hall of which the young couple occupied only a part. Here they lived, about a mile from the centre of Sheffield, at the end of a steep ascent on the road to Penistone, a slope which Joseph I had lessened with the approval of the Duke of Norfolk. It is a mark of his growing affluence that this piece of road improvement stemmed from his ownership of a private carriage, one of the few near Sheffield at that time. In 1692 he was Under-Sheriff of the county of Yorkshire and on the death of his old master Thomas Chappell he succeeded to the post of Town Trustee in Sheffield. His prospects ripened further when he became agent to the Dukes of Norfolk, of Leeds, and of Newcastle. By 1704 he had become collector for the Trustees and in 1706 Clerk of the Peace for Nottinghamshire, an office under the patronage of the Duke of Newcastle and held, mostly by deputy, until he died in 1727. These posts were the reward of a busy man well-regarded in his profession of attorney as contemporary references confirm. Nor was he slow in putting his professional skills to work in his own interest. Much of his money was made by shrewd property speculation and the whole course of his patient building toward the ultimate investment in Lincolnshire land clearly charts the process which changed the Yorkshire lawyer into the landed gentleman of a county that presented the challenges of a new frontier.

At some time before 1702 Joseph Banks I had left Shiercliffe Hall and moved to Scofton, near Worksop in Nottinghamshire, among the quiet meadows which still border the sleepy River Ryton. At the age of 37 he had at last acquired an estate of sufficient competence to which he could retire from the smoke and noise of Sheffield. The estate of Scofton, merged now with that of Osberton Hall, fell into his hands through his work as agent for the Duke of Newcastle and his contact with the Duke's man of business, William Jessop of Broomhall, also a client of Banks. Scofton Hall was at that time one of the homes of the Jessop family and it was from William, otherwise Judge, Jessop that Joseph Banks I acquired it.

He was also preparing for his first entry into the broad and marshy acres of Lincolnshire, negotiating during 1701 for the Holland estate south of the Wash. This, rather more than 3000 acres, he bought from Sir George Humble for the sum of £9000. With this long stride away from the dales and factories of Yorkshire into the undeveloped fens of south Lincolnshire, with the half-way house at Scofton, there followed a period of more than ten years consolidation. There was for example, his purchase in 1710 of Towarth Grange near Scofton, much out of repair, bought with 110 acres of land for £270. In 1718 he sold it profitably to Major-General Sutton and his brother Sir Robert Sutton, KB, Ambassador to the Porte. It was to the General also that he had already sold Scofton the previous year.

The social progress of Joseph Banks I may be well observed about this time in his marriage negotiations on behalf of his daughter Mary, now 20. In the pursuit of a treaty of marriage to George Vane, heir of Lionel Vane of Long Newton, County Durham, Mary was to have offered £4000 as her fortune with a jointure of £400. The matter came to nothing. Joseph I felt he had been 'bit' by Mr Vane but he was not discouraged by this wound from trying again a little later that year. This was a more protracted business with two intermediaries in action – the Revd William Steer who had married Mary's first cousin Anne Banks, and Henry Frankland, second son of the 1st Baronet of Thirkleby. The target in this engagement was Roger, son and heir of Colonel Talbot of Wood End, Thornton le Street, in the North Riding. The Colonel expected Mary to bring with her a fortune now of £5000, while Joseph I for his part expected the settlement of the Talbot estates to be greater than was proposed. Again, for all the complicated diplomacy and plain horse-trading by Cos. William Steer on behalf of his Cos. Mally, nothing was resolved for the very human reason that Mally did not like the man:

> . . . I cannot for my life think him agreeable, nor I don't expect a longer
> acquaintance will make him appear more taking; and I think that man and woman
> must run a great hazard of living misserably all their lives where there is not a
> mutual inclination before hand . . .

Joseph I recognized the sense of this with his stolid good humour and the affair ended with polite regrets on all sides.

In the keen competition of the marriage market of that period Mary and her father had to wait another seven years before the right bargain was found and struck. When she married Sir Francis Whichcote, Baronet of Aswarby in Lincolnshire, her marriage portion was £8000 with a further £4000 to accrue on the death of her father whom she was to predecease in 1726. The refurbishment of her tombstone at Chesham in Buckinghamshire in time became a task for her grand-nephew.

Almost in step with the marriage problems of Mary and illuminating the social advance of the family were those touching the education of her young brother, Joseph II. At the age of 13 he had been judged worthy by his father to have a tutor in the person of John Balguy, son of the master of Sheffield Grammar School, Thomas Balguy. From the summer of 1708, for the next three years, this recently fledged graduate of St John's, Cambridge, gave Joseph II the benefit of his romantic and classical studies by the Cam. This was spiced with a touch of worldly paternalism when Joseph I carried John Balguy and young Jo to the capital and left them there together for a while – 'They both want a little of London' was the father's theory. Then in 1711, after his ordination as a priest, John Balguy gave up his tutoring and retired to a small living at Durham. The further education of his young protégé was thus a matter of some concern for the family.

William Steer was another ornament of the same academic generation at St John's, Cambridge as John Balguy. He felt deeply enough on the subject of his young kinsman's future to speak firmly to his wife's formidable uncle. Hints of a Grand Tour under the eye of a certain Mr D— raised many doubts in the mind of the young Vicar of Ecclesfield. A guardian on such a tour, said he, was intended to introduce young gentlemen into good, and keep them out of bad company. Mr D— was likely to do neither for, apart from his questionable principles, he loved

> ... not to go sober to bed and birds of a feather will flock together ... A great many wonder at the first step you are going to make, and if Jo should prove a rake, the Vicar of Ecclesfield thinks he will be able to give you the reason of it ...

Indeed the vicar was prepared to go much further with his advice:

> ... I wish I could persuade you (but theirs little hopes) to give him a year's run at one of the universities: this would furnish him with that learning which would be serviceable to him all his life after ... and when he had been there some time he might meet with a better opportunity of travelling, and I believe the universities are of that repute abroad, that it would be of some credit to him to have been of one of 'em ...

The good sense of Joseph I conceded the first point at least for, as far as we know, young Jo did not make the Grand Tour under the dubious guidance of Mr D— or indeed ever. Neither, on reflection, did he go so far as to expose his heir to the scarcely less dubious seductions of Cambridge or Oxford, but he thanked the well-meaning vicar for his advice. So in the end Joseph II, from the little we know, did not become a rake. Instead, at the age of 19, he settled down dutifully enough, after some further moulding by his father and William Steer, as a married man and the first young master of Revesby Abbey. On 11 April 1714 he married Anne Hodgkinson, only child and heiress of William Hodgkinson, merchant, of Overton Hall in the parish of Ashover and the county of Derbyshire. By this matrimonial bargain, accomplished within one month of the purchase of Revesby Abbey estate on 14 March 1714, Joseph Banks I had established the framework of the family assets for more than a century to come. He could now turn to the embellishment of all that he had so shrewdly gathered as property and to the enjoyment of all those social perquisites which their ownership ensured.

III

The fortune of Joseph Banks I reached fruition in the first decades of Hanoverian England. But the pressure of external events prevented the occupation of the Revesby Abbey estates until 22 August 1715, a year after its purchase. Queen Anne died on 1 August 1714 and on 18 September George I landed in England from Hanover. Soon after came the elections to the first dominantly Whig Parliament of the new regime wherein Joseph I sealed his aspirations by his election as the second member for Grimsby, qualifying by his purchase of the freedom for £20. Then came the upheavals of the Jacobite rising of 'the Fifteen'. In this Joseph I, still a landholder at Scofton, was charged with furnishing a horseman and arms for the militia, and the defence of the realm was reinforced by the commission of young Joseph II, at 20, as lieutenant in the second troop of horse of the Nottinghamshire militia. By the spring of 1716 the Jacobite scare was over, and Joseph Banks I had established his home in London at Boswell Court while Joseph Banks II, with his young bride, had begun the

7

slow evacuation of goods and chattels from Scofton Hall to the new Lincolnshire base of the family at last. Meanwhile, at Overton Hall another generation had appeared in the form of Joseph Banks III who was born there on 27 February 1715 (o.s.).

The steady movement to the south-east from the dales of Yorkshire to the edge of the Lincolnshire fens by Joseph Banks I was the march of a pioneering entrepreneur, and the last touch was the purchase of the manor of Revesby, Wilksby and Kirkby Park with the associated closes, and the woodlands of Tumby, Fulsby and Sherwood. It followed the same line of shrewd investment as his earlier transactions where his eye was sharply focused on the prospect of gains in the rent roll and capital value in both the short and the long view. It was doubtless the long view that informed his approach to the bleak landscape surrounding the Wash with its rich brown soil already showing its potential. He was himself aware of this but it was to be under his great-grandson that the fens were at last to yield some of their final acres to become the vast garden of intensive agriculture they are today.

Leaving the refurbishment of Revesby Abbey and the development of the estate to his son and daughter-in-law, Joseph Banks I retired to exercise management from a distance. The London house in Boswell Court, within the site of the present Law Courts on the Strand, was his residence in town as Member of Parliament during the extended sitting from 1715 to 1722, and visible evidence of a lifetime's ambition. During this period he came close also to the searing breath of public scandal when, in the bursting of the South Sea Bubble in the autumn of 1720, he was only narrowly cleared before the Committee of Secrecy from suspicion of malpractice with this contentious stock. Here, strangely, the evidence of his own son, Joseph II apparently had decisive weight. There was no such escape, however, for his fellow member for Grimsby, Sir Robert Chaplin, a director of the South Sea Company, who was judged guilty and expelled from the House. Some of this mud may have rubbed off on Joseph I, for at the next election of 1722 he lost his Grimsby seat. Nevertheless he was returned as a Treasury nominee for Totnes in Devon and remained a Member of Parliament until the last year of his life. He did not stand again in the elections of 1727.

As he had grown in lands and fortune so too had he developed in bodily shape and substance, a strong family trait. For his last ten years it was difficult to find a horse which could safely bear his weight. His wife, Mary Hancock, had predeceased him in February 1722. As a widower his last years were spent alone, largely in Boswell Court, practising a little law spiced with a little politics until in 1726 his health began to trouble him. After an illness in the winter, he returned in 1727 to Revesby Abbey where he had apparently long intended to retire, to live in St Sythe's Hall, which once stood within the present park, while his son occupied the large house itself. Active and alert to the end, in spite of his cumbrous weight, he rounded off a lifetime of sound business by acquiring the estates of Fulstow and Marsh Chapel for 22 years' purchase. Then, on 27 September 1727, he died a victim of his own unflagging energy. By the evidence of his great-grandson

> . . . it is traditionally receivd in the family that the large room on the east side of the house was built this year, and that the immediate cause of his death was a broken shin got by falling among the rafters of the ceiling . . .

8

Buried in the chancel of the church at Revesby, which by his will was to be rebuilt by his son, his earthly presence was commemorated by the marble bust finished by John Nost in 1730. This was based apparently on the half-length portrait which once hung in the dining room of the big house. The semblance of his strong north-country features survive to remind us of their affinity with those of his last and great direct male descendant whose life ended the line he had founded. There were to be four Joseph Banks's in this particular branch of the original Yorkshire family in successive generations but only Joseph I and Joseph IV have any strong claim on the attention of posterity. The first Joseph as the founding patriarch was the creator of the wealth and the great estates which the last Joseph was to bend to the service of the wider interests of the nation and humanity by that combination of qualities which they both shared – honesty, shrewdness and ambition; a sense of business, hard but fair; a ceaseless activity of body and of mind, forceful and autocratic as the need arose but tempered by an innate kindness and general good humour.

IV

By the will of Joseph Banks I the estate at and about Revesby Abbey was settled on Joseph Banks II and his descendants and with this was confirmed the settlement of the South Holland lands as part of the marriage portion with Anne. So too were the manors of Cheadle and Kingsley in Staffordshire and all the far-flung lesser freehold, copyhold and leasehold estates in the counties of York, Nottingham, Middlesex and Essex; the investments in the South Sea Company stock after the settlement of his personal debts and legacies to be laid out in further lands in Lincolnshire, Nottinghamshire, Derbyshire, Rutlandshire, Hampshire, Bedfordshire and Hertford-shire to be settled in the same fashion as the manor of Revesby and other lands in Lindsey and Kesteven. There was also a list of those to whom mourning rings valued at two guineas apiece were to be given. There was, of course, ample provision for the family reaching into remote corners of the living relationships and for three generations into the future which allowed for most contingencies.

Well in advance of the building of the Foundling Hospital there was also that bequest, under certain conditions, of

> ... Five hundred pounds to the Lord Mayor and Aldermen of London towards raising a fund and erecting a Hospital for Foundling children within the City and Suburbs thereof to prevent the innocent infants from being destroyed by Parish Nourses or otherways ...

There were too, as evidence of the good master, the bequests to faithful servants and his intention to build on Revesby Green

> ... an Hospital or Almshouse for Ten poor decayed Farmers who are come to poverty by loss of Cattle or other inevitable accidents and not by Idleness Drunkedness or other Extravagance and each of them to have £5 a year a piece yearly a good Room to dwell in to be paid monthly by equal portions and none to be admitted till Sixty Years of Age and the Widdowes to such Farmers as before described to be equally entitled to the Charity ...

9

There was, moreover, an authoritative command to future generations from the patriarch whose will in more senses than one was imposed for the next century. It was a matter which reflected some of the rivalries to be found in the marriage market between self-made men of robust individuality. This touched the Derbyshire estate of Overton Hall which had been a prize in the marriage of Anne Hodgkinson to Joseph Banks II. Here was a tussle of family names, not uncommon, but likely at times to confuse posterity.

Joseph I made his feelings very clear on the subject:

> ... AND WHEREAS my said Brother Hodgkinson hath settled or devised or promis'd or intends so to do all his estate Real and Personal upon my Grandson William Banks and his heirs he changeing his surname to Hodgkinson which estate is computed to be in the value Twenty thousand pounds and upwards Now in case the Issue Male of my said Grandson Joseph fails so that the Estate thereby devised to him and them come to my said Grandson William in such case I hereby Order that he and his Issue shall not have or enjoy the same unless he continue the surname of Banks and settle all the Estate given him by my Brother Hodgkinson or the full value thereof on his Brother Robert by the Act of Parliament or pursuant to a Decree of Chancery If such can be obtained which I hope will not be difficult But if Denyed I hereby order the whole value of my said Brother Hodgkinson's Estate to be setled on the said Robert out of my said Lincolnshire or other Estate and on his sons and Issue as I have already setled my Lincolnshire Estate and in case my Brother Hodgkinson settle or devise his Estate as aforesaid on my Grandson William in such case I hereby Revoke the Legacy of Four thousand Pounds herein before given him ...

But grand old men, even when they are able attorneys in the affairs of other men, are not always without errors of their own. The will of Joseph I had its ambiguities and alterations in his own script which suggest that he intended to make a new one. At least one further detail seems to have been intended, for Joseph II was under the impression that his father had in mind an additional provision for John Norton, above what he had received in common with the other servants named, and had omitted this by mistake. So, dutiful to what he believd was his father's intention toward one who was thought to be a natural son, Joseph II gave John Norton £300 out of the personal estate. This is not the only hint of extra-marital episodes among the men of the Banks family.

The importance of this will was clear enough to his immediate descent, but to clarify and establish the entail beyond future legal doubt, Joseph II found it necessary to apply to Parliament for a private Act which became statutory in 1736 as 'An Act for Explaining the Will of Joseph Banks, Esquire, deceased, and for impowering several Persons claiming under the said Will to make Jointures and Leases in such manner as is therein mentioned'. So it remained for nearly 100 years, until the will of his last direct male descendant, the fourth Joseph required another private Act of Parliament to confirm the division of the estates when the entail lapsed. The details of the Act of 1736, with the rent roll to Lady Day of 1735, give us, taken together, a succinct account of the material achievement of Joseph I. By his ability and character, the young attorney of 24 in 1689, aided by the modest marriage settlement of £400 from his non-conforming father-in-law, had by the time of his death, 38 years later, raised himself to the upper bracket of the wealthy landed gentry among those who emerged from post-Restoration England. In 1735 the total income from the estates in Lincolnshire and Staffordshire was about £3275. This was derived mainly from more than 200 tenants in both counties, the returns from the annual felling on 1100 acres of woodland in the parishes of Revesby and Tumby and the profits from the small collieries and cottage tenants near Cheadle and Kingsley. This was the burden of responsibility accepted by Joseph Banks II at the age of 32 and by then the father of six young children – three sons and three daughters.

The burden had come to rest on the younger Joseph by slow degrees. His honeymoon year seems to have been spent largely at Overton Hall until after the birth of Joseph III when the alarms of the 'Fifteen' rebellion called him to arms until the end of 1715. The decrepitude of the house at Revesby could have had few attractions for a young bride reared in the social warmth of the Amber Valley. So it was from the spring of 1716 that Joseph II found himself fully engaged with the alterations at Revesby Abbey, supervising the work of John Sherlock, the master carpenter from Boston. By the autumn the young couple was in residence and already in a fair way to taking up the social round of Lincoln city and the surrounding county. There was still much to be done about the roof above and much excavating and reconstruction in the cellars beneath. A good cook had yet to be found. Moreover the family was now augmented by the birth of a daughter Letitia Mary, in March of that year. But in spite of all, Joseph II felt sufficiently established to throw open the doors of Revesby Abbey and to report to his father in London with subdued satisfaction:

> . . . I expect to-day to see the Duke of Ancaster which is an honour he has paid to
> none except Captain Short. He often enquires very kindly after you, and on
> Thursday the Dutchess and the neighbouring gentlemen and ladies come to dance
> here, we haveing done the same at all their houses. So that we could no ways avoid
> it, haveing made use of much less rooms than our own . . .

Nor by this time was Anne Banks afraid to raise her own sensible objections to her formidable father-in-law's plans. She, and others also, had fears about the arrangement of the new wing 'so much nearer the front of the house will make the building look irregeler' as well as causing inconvenience inside. This display of firmness from 'his obedient and dughtyfull daughter' was treated with respect by Joseph I, who sent a long explanation of the reasoning behind the alterations to her with instructions for John Sherlock before anything further was done. The Hodgkinson character was well able to match the forceful Banksian ability.

In April 1717 the estate at Scofton was sold while Joseph II and Anne were staying with the Hodgkinson family at Overton. This was approved by all the family, notably in what followed from the sale – a generous offer to the young Banks's of furniture and fitments from Scofton Hall for Revesby Abbey according to their own choice, reserving especially for them the two marble chimney pieces. On their return to Revesby later that month, Joseph II and Anne spent two nights at Scofton making an exact catalogue of the contents of the house and a list of the particular items 'pitched on' for Revesby. Some goods were immediately sent off in a drover's cart with some sheep which Joseph II had brought with him from Overton. By 1 July 1717 Joseph II was able to declare to his father: 'I thank God we've gott all our goods safe home'. The Banks family from Giggleswick, Yorkshire, was now truly established for posterity as the Banks's of Revesby Abbey, Lincolnshire.

Although the refurbished manor house at Revesby had now become the county seat and power base of the family, no Banks was ever born there and for none was it ever a home for long. To the man who had acquired it, it was essentially a capital asset to be managed from his London home and visited occasionally when his presence was needed. For the man who first received it as an inheritance, Joseph II, his occupation of the house was more an irksome filial duty, a family commitment. He had no real taste for the country scene. He supervised and managed more or less to his father's satisfaction during the first five years of the family's ownership, the period of restoration and reconstruction, but there was a restless element in his being which kept him from settling long in any one place. This had almost the character of a sad search for an identity which is often the lot of those born to ambitious and forceful parents with dynastic visions.

His eldest daughter, Letitia Mary, was born in London in March 1716, apparently at Boswell Court. So also was his second son, William, in 1719 – a troubled entry, for his mother Anne 'had the Small Pox out upon her when brought to bed & narrowly Escaped with life'. This was in March, and later that year Joseph II seems to have taken the first of many steps away from Revesby Abbey when he occupied a house of the Burghersh Chantry in Lincoln, at first probably as a sub-tenant, but which later in 1724 he leased from the Dean and Chapter of Lincoln Cathedral. Here his next two children were born – his second daughter, Elizabeth, in 1720 and his third son, Robert, in 1722. For more than ten years Joseph II seems to have preferred this house in a secluded part of the cathedral precincts to the hall in the park at Revesby 25 miles away. In February 1722 his mother died at Boswell Court and, most probably at the same house in the following year, his sixth child and youngest daughter, the handsome Eleanora Margaret was born. Joseph II had at last fulfilled the expectations of Joseph I.

His procreative duty done and his pioneering tasks by the fens well advanced, Joseph II gradually eased himself free from the curbing hand of a father, whom he respected but may not have much loved, into the somewhat aimless enjoyment of his patrimony as the delights of county and more distant urban society at last seemed to open for him. He still faced his duty as a man of county responsibilities becoming to his status as an extensive landowner. He entered Parliament as a Whig for Peterborough in a by-election of 1728, but this was more flirtation than fulfilment. He attended to the education of his children according to his lights, advancing that of his sons beyond his own but no less mindful for that of his daughters. Indeed he bought a house at Grimsthorpe conveniently near Calverley's school there for the three girls and near enough to the Duke of Ancaster's for their social advancement. As a Member of Parliament, like his father, he sought a house in London and found it in 1728 on the south side of St James's Square with a stable yard opening into Charles II Street. He found an outlet for his sporting pursuits also by leasing Quickswood in Hertfordshire from the Earl of Salisbury. Here he kept a pack of deer hounds from the kennels of the 8th Earl of Exeter at Burghley near Stamford. He moved also in the company of learned men of his time and neighbourhood. Dr William Stukeley, FR & AS was his friend. He was sponsor at the baptism of Stukeley's daughter at Stamford in June 1731. Stukeley himself marked the relationship by dedicating his plan of the Roman Banovallum, which is the town of

Horncastle near Revesby, to Joseph Banks II. In 1730 he was elected a fellow of the Royal Society of London with the support of Roger Gale, FRS with whom he shared an interest in Roman coins. Inevitably he was a member of the Spalding Gentlemen's Society. In due time he served his term as High Sheriff of Lincolnshire in 1735.

His life was interrupted about the time of his election to Parliament in 1728 when his wife's health began to fail. For some months she visited Bristol, no doubt for the purpose of seeking help in the chalybeate waters of the Hot Wells. With some relief from this source, she lived on for another two years, to die on 7 September 1730. She had survived long enough to see her initials added to those of her husband on the lead piping of the completed east and west wings at Revesby.

It is expressive of the pattern of Joseph II's life, as much as of the times, that scarcely a year later he had found another wife in the young widow of Newcomen Wallis, his sub-tenant in the Burghersh Chantry. Catherine Wallis at 23 was already the mother of a son Thomas. On 30 October 1731 she became Catherine Banks, receiving as part of her marriage settlement the house in St James's Square which for the rest of her short life was for the most part her home. For more than two years after Anne's death it had been let to Count Dagenfeldt, the Prussian Ambassador until December 1732. In the interim Joseph II had leased Quickswood and another house in Ormond Street, Queen's Square. However, it was in the Chantry house that little Catherine Banks was born on 10 October 1732 but she died 11 days later. Without Catherine the mother was alone, for Joseph was at Quickswood, engaged perhaps with his field sports there.

The brief second marriage continued, as it was to end, at the house in St James's Square. Here Collingwood Banks was born on 20 August 1734. Less than two years later George Banks was born on 17 March 1736, followed within the hour by the death of his mother in her thirtieth year. Both sons had been conceived and born between periods of gout which had first afflicted Joseph II in the winter of 1733 when he was 38 years old. As far as we know he was the first of his family to be so attacked, the price perhaps of its rise to affluence and high feeding. It also led him to seek relief from the waters at Bath fairly regularly from 1733 to 1736 under the care of Dr William Oliver, FRS. His second marriage was thus a fragmentary affair.

At the elections of 1734 Joseph II did not succeed again as Member for Peterborough. It is not known whether he was actually a candidate but he certainly did not show much concern in the defence of his seat. On the whole he seems to have been happy enough to do his duty as High Sheriff of Lincolnshire the following year and thereafter to lapse into the role of husband and father to his eight surviving children. He had been diligent in executing Joseph I's wishes in building the almshouses on Revesby Green finished in 1729 at a cost of £350, with silver badges made for the coats of the beneficiaries of this charity. He had rebuilt Revesby Church according to his father's will, completed in 1730 for £700, and for which his eldest daughter Letitia Mary had laid the foundation stone. As a crowning act of filial piety he raised within the new edifice the massive 'monument of Jos: Banks the 1st'.

He had duly given the sum of £300 to John Norton believing that this was the intention of his father toward his natural son. John, however, died in 1730, still in his apprenticeship, and the debt of conscience fell void. But Joseph II had his own reparation to make. After the death of his second wife in March 1736 he too followed his father's example with a less sanctified relationship with another woman. Hence we have the codicil to his will, dated 8 February 1737, which provided from his personal estate for

> ... my servant Elizth Buckley for and during the term of her natural life ... And if she shall be with child at my death or shall be delivered of a child within 9 months after my death I charge all my estates with £10 a year which I give to the said child for its maintenance till twelve years old and after that I give it in like manner £20 a year till sixteen years old and then £100 to put it out apprentice and after such apprenticeship I give the child £500 to set up with to be raised by my Executors or Administrators ...

The witness to this enlightened provision was his second daughter 'Eliza Banks'.

Troubled more or less by gout until he died on 10 April 1741, within a year of the tragically early death of his eldest son, Joseph III, he too was buried in the precincts of the church at Revesby. A further codicil had had to be added to his will acknowledging the ample provision made for his two surviving sons of the first marriage, William and Robert, under the terms of the entail and thereby devising the remainder of his real estate

> ... in the Parts of Kestevan in the County of Lincolnshire with my house and furniture in Ancaster (except plate and jewels) also my copyhold estate at Deeping being in the whole about £200 a year ...

to his two sons of the second marriage, Collingwood and George.

V

We come now to the grandchildren of the patriarch Joseph I, those nine children born to Joseph II into whose hands the widespread estates had so swiftly come. Little is known of the eldest son Joseph III. Born in the year of the Old Pretender's rising, at his mother's home among the Derbyshire hills, his education is obscure. Tutored perhaps in his early youth at Revesby Abbey he appears to have broken new ground by finishing his education at Geneva and then, as a hardening experience, to have served briefly as a volunteer with the British Fleet in the Mediterranean. Returning home as a young man of 20 he was struck by smallpox about which his cousin Diana Turnor expressed a certain cousinly detachment when she wrote to his stepmother on 19 March 1735:

> ... I can't say I condole with you upon the loss of Mr Jo Banks beauty for [I] fancy that ... distemper could not have robbed him of so much, but he has enough remains for a man, for certainly that is a perfection that is the least missed in that sex, but am mighty glad to hear that he has got over it so well ...

She may have erred in the matter of 'Mr Jo Banks' and his beauty, for in the next two years he was twice unsuccessful in his search for a bride. Then he suddenly died of an acute but nameless fever at Revesby Abbey on 12 May 1740, attended by his three young sisters and his very young stepbrother George. He was the second Joseph Banks to be buried at Revesby.

The weight of this emergency was carried by the eldest sister, Letitia Mary, now in her twenty-fifth year and evidently well-established in her role as Miss Banks of Revesby Abbey. Under her care for a few years the Park and its environs were alive with the sound of childrens' voices, those of 'leetle Georgy' and 'dear Coll.', gathered there after the death of Catherine Banks at George's birth. When her brother Jo died so suddenly she was supported in her distress by Mrs Henry Collingwood, the maternal grandmother of her two small stepbrothers, and by the professional kindnesses of the doctors Wallis and Dymoke from Lincoln who stayed briefly with the bereaved girls after the event. Otherwise this feminine household was void of any masculine help in the family crisis. Their father was away in London having taken young Coll. to his first school at Glatton on the way. 'Brother Hodgkinson', otherwise William Banks, was immured at Overton Hall himself severely ill. Robert was far away at Bristol in his apprenticeship as a merchant venturer there. The three daughters combined to write a concerned and thoughtful letter of solace to their father in London the day after Jo's death, assuring him that everything possible had been done to save him.

Letitia Mary lived on as a dutiful and obedient daughter and eldest sister to die at Grantham on 10 September 1757, a spinster of 41. She was buried near her brother at Revesby church, the very building whose foundation stone she had laid as a child of 14. The two younger sisters, however, when the flurries and complications of the inheritance of the entailed family estates had been settled after the deaths of their brother and father in such quick succession, resumed a social life that ensured their marriages and the eventual partition of the estates themselves in the next century.

Elizabeth, the middle sister, at 24, and during her brother William's brief sojourn as a young married man in Argyle Street, slipped quietly away from that other short-lived Banks abode in Bruton Street on 8 November 1744 to marry, at Gray's Inn chapel, Dr James Hawley, MD, FRS, of Leybourne Grange, Kent. Henry, her only son, born the following year on 12 November 1745 was the first of the long line of Hawley baronets. On 27 November 1766 she died at 46, pre-deceasing her much older husband by 11 years. She now lies buried among the Hawleys at Leybourne in Kent.

Eleanora Margaret, the youngest sister, much lauded as one of the great beauties of her period, kept her spinsterhood secure to the ripe age of 34. In October 1757, at Revesby church, just one month after the burial of her sister Letitia Mary there, she married the Hon. Henry Grenville. This marriage was potent in strengthening the social chain of the Banks family of Revesby Abbey. Henry Grenville was the youngest brother of Richard, later the 2nd Earl Temple, and also, by the marriage of his only sister Hester, the brother-in-law of William Pitt, 1st Earl of Chatham. There was again only one child from the marriage of Eleanora Margaret, a daughter Louisa, born on 28 July 1758. Thereafter Margaret Grenville, as her family knew her, entered the world of diplomacy when her husband was appointed Ambassador to the Porte at Constantinople and in later years Governor of the Barbados.

Louisa Grenville, an only child, is at first glance a frail link between the generations in that century of short and uncertain female lives. For the family she was in fact one of the most significant of them all, if only by her mere existence. Through her mother she was first cousin to Joseph IV whose life we are about to pursue. Through her father she was also first cousin to William Pitt the Younger, her junior by one year, and also to William Wyndham Grenville, both Prime Ministers of later years. Louisa was thus a nodal point in a network of power and influence by her birth alone. Through her marriage, as the second wife of Charles, 3rd Earl Stanhope, FRS on 19 March 1781, she became mother and grandmother of future earls but, through her youngest son, James Hamilton Stanhope, she established the other line of descent through which would pass one part of the divided estates of her first cousin, Joseph Banks IV.

Eleanora Margaret Grenville herself lived long enough not only to enjoy the pleasure of the youthful Joseph IV's company as a favourite nephew but also that of the mature and scholarly Sir Joseph Banks, PRS he was to become. She died aged 70, on 19 June 1793, at Hampton Court, and now lies buried among the Stanhopes at Chevening.

In this way the granddaughters, not the grandsons, of the first Joseph Banks perpetuated the inheritance of the Lincolnshire estates which he had founded, kept more or less as they were but divided under the two families into which they married. However, after the premature deaths of his brother and father in rapid succession in the year 1740–1, it was William Banks-Hodgkinson of Overton Hall who found himself vested with the Lincolnshire inheritance under the inexorable terms of the will of Joseph Banks I.

The education of William Banks for this task seems to have differed little from that of his father in that it was not obviously extensive. He was tutored at home by the Revd Henry Shepherd and later more formally polished at the Queen Elizabeth Grammar School in Horncastle six miles away. For him there was no excursion into foreign parts as for his brother Joseph III. When he was 17 on 24 April 1736 he was matriculated at Christ Church, Oxford, and in the same year entered at the Middle Temple, London, but with what further progress in the law we do not know. By the death of his maternal grandfather in 1732 he had already inherited the Overton estate and with it had taken the name of Hodgkinson with that of Banks, obedient to the terms of the Hodgkinson will. He had thus become involved in Derbyshire rather than Lincolnshire society by the time of his father's death. So when he came to relinquish both the name and the estate of the Hodgkinson inheritance to his younger brother Robert under the Banksian will, it is not surprising that he had already found the prospect of a Derbyshire bride.

Sarah Bate, a girl of about his own age from the southern verge of the county, was the eldest daughter of William Bate of Foston, the surviving son of Richard Bate, merchant of London. Arabella Bate, his wife, was the eldest daughter and heiress of Thomas Chambers, citizen and also merchant of London. Here again are links of some weight in the extending social base of the Banks's of Revesby Abbey for Sarah Bate's maternal aunt, Hannah-Sophia Chambers, was the wife of Brownlow Cecil, 8th Earl of Exeter. Thus it is not surprising that when William Banks and Sarah Bate were married on 26 September 1741 the ceremony took place in the chapel at Burghley House, Stamford. Three days later, at Michaelmas, William Banks paid the rates on what may have been the first London home of the young couple. This was one of the group of four houses known as Argyll Buildings, each with a rateable value of £40, in Bruton Street on the south side close to the corner with Berkeley Square and the more opulent house of James, 4th Duke of Argyll. It was, however, at the house, No.30 in Argyll Street (west side) in the next parish of St James's, that their two children were born: Joseph IV on 13 February 1743 and his sister Sarah Sophia on 28 October 1744.

Mrs William Banks (née Sarah Bate). Pastel by John Russell, RA.

In 1741 William Banks had also launched himself on the wider world by contesting the seat of Grampound in Cornwall where he had been defeated. The victors, however, were unseated on a petition and he was then declared elected into the third Parliament of George II. His status in Lincolnshire was sealed by his appointment as Deputy-Lieutenant in 1743. To match his public dignity the big house at Revesby was redecorated and to some extent refurnished over the period October 1743 to November 1744. Then the young family returned to Revesby Abbey for a brief period before disease again intruded to strike down and shorten the life of the young husband and father. At some time during 1745, at the age of 26, William incurred a mysterious fever that left him paraplegic and confined to his chair – except for a few months in 1752 when he enjoyed an inexplicable remission and briefly had the use of his legs again. During this short phase he was able to ride and 'attend to his Favorite business of drainage' but all too soon fell back to his former helpless state. This was, said the medical fraternity, 'in consequence of [his] using more riding exercise than was prudent'. Thereafter his activities were restricted by the necessity of being carried either to his chaise for travel or to his bed for rest. He rarely visited abroad according to his son Joseph IV who, in his turn but much later in life, would spend his last years as helpless as his father, the victim of no less crippling gout. However, the few glimpses of William Banks that survive give the impression of a man with the same indomitable good humour and stoic endurance that his son was to show in like circumstances.

His active interest in agriculture and the problems of fen drainage and land reclamation was sufficient to attract much like-minded company to Revesby Abbey. He was also diligent in improving the surroundings of the house and park; planting elms, planning the gardens, excavating the Long Pond to the north of the house, and establishing the menagerie. Nor was he unmindful of other more distant and less bucolic affairs such as establishing the fair at Horncastle in his role as lessee from the Bishop of Carlisle, lord of the manor in which that town lay. He it was also who saved the stained glass from the old Tattershall church by securing its removal to that of St Martin's at Stamford Baron.

On 23 September 1761 at the age of 42 he died at Revesby Abbey after a short and deceptive illness which caused no immediate alarm to his doctors but which was later attributed to 'the bursting of an impostume in his breast'. On 1 October 1761 he was buried among the other members of his family in Revesby church where the register records him, quite simply, for posterity: 'A most worthy gentleman and Lord of this Mannour'. He left his heir, Joseph IV, still a minor, a youth of 18 in his first year at Oxford. He had, however, left affairs in the hands of two guardians until Joseph IV should come of age in 1764: his wife Sarah and his brother Robert Banks-Hodgkinson. It was the latter who, during the undergraduate years of his nephew and the last three years of his minority, was to supervise and educate him in the practical world of affairs.

Robert Banks was born on 8 March 1722. His early years are even less distinct than those of his elder brother William but probably followed a similar path until he too reached the age of 17. He was matriculated at Christ Church, Oxford, on 8 June 1741 at the age of 19, but for him there was no Middle Temple entry. Instead, reaching out toward the open sea and distant places, he had been indentured as an apprentice under the mantle of The Society of Merchant Venturers in Bristol. The fact is recorded in the minutes of a General Meeting of the Society on 12 October 1739, when Robert was 17:

> Memorandum that Robert Banks, son of Joseph Banks of Revesby Abbey in the County of Lincoln, Esquire, was bound apprentice to William Jefferis Esquire, a member of this Society and Mary his wife, by Indenture of Apprenticeship dated 18th April last, and enrolled at the Tolzey according to custom.

Just one week after this entry orders were received by Admiral Edward Vernon 'to destroy the Spanish settlements in the West Indies and to distress their shipping by every method whatever'. The niggling hostilities of the decade had erupted in the War of Jenkins's Ear and the Bristol Merchant Venturers were well placed to reap mercantile advantages from it. Young Robert Banks certainly heard much on this subject at the Tolzey. Although he never served his full term to become a merchant venturer he risked small sums of his own often enough in the privateering craft that in those days passed down the Avon gorge to tease and plunder the Spaniards. Before he could enjoy these vicarious adventures in the Caribbean his life was turned to a different course by the sudden death of his eldest brother. The news came to him from yet another Joseph Banks, evidently his cousin the lawyer of Chancery Lane. So, after less than a year in Bristol, he found it necessary to spend much of 1740 at Revesby Abbey with William and his sisters dealing with the personal affairs consequent upon Jo's untimely death.

The important turn in his life had come with his succession to the Overton estate. At 18 he too, in the best Banksian manner, had become a landed gentleman. Later in the summer he returned to Bristol 'after a long and troublesome journey of 4 days and a piece', as he told his father, and settled down again in the society of its merchant venturers. Life in the midst of the Bristol trade was more heady now with war in and about the Spanish main and the Spanish colonies of America. Here we have the first young Banks effectively to extend the family activities beyond the limits of county society, the pleasures of a town house in the purlieus of St James's or the Strand, or the speculative temptations of South Sea stock.

His father's occasional visits to Bath during his second marriage, and his mother's earlier pilgrimage to the rather less salubrious environs of the Hot Wells at Bristol almost certainly laid the social foundations for much of Robert's future. Gout and similar middle-class ailments were a potent social flux in the West Country centres of fashion, frivolity, quasi-scientific medicine and hard-headed business. Joseph II was certainly known to such merchant families of Bristol society as the Eltons, the Wraxhalls and the Jefferis with others whose daily trade centred on the small ships threading the tricky navigation of the Severn estuary from the tidal muddiness of the Avon to the open Atlantic.

With a modest allowance from his father, Robert was soon engaged on his own account in the business of merchant venturing. A small sum laid out in herrings and tobacco pipes succeeded well enough. More to the point though was his request to his father in September 1740 for £30 in bills

> . . . the properest time now drawing on in fitting out ships for the Christmas market in Jamaica . . .

19

Heston House, Heston (demolished 1937). Purchased at auction in 1775 by Robert Banks-Hodgkinson, FRS who enlarged and re-fronted the house (as shown) in 1783.

There was also the harvest of the open sea to be gathered:

> ... We have now going out a schooner called *Vernon,* mounts twenty guns and is to carry 100 or 110 men to go out solely upon privateering. We are in expectations of great matters from the above vessell ...

However, as a counter to this optimism, ships returning from the American coasts brought sobering news of unsuccessful forays against the Spanish colony of Florida in the abortive seige of St Augustine, as an example, with the implied threat of Indian raids and Negro insurrection among the plantations of neighbouring South Carolina.

In March 1743 Robert came of age and, by the conveyance from his brother William, was transformed into Robert Banks-Hodgkinson of Overton Hall. After four years among the merchant venturers, he turned his back on Bristol about the same time that his nephew Joseph Banks IV was baptized in the church of St James's in London. For another 14 years Robert remained single as the master of Overton Hall. In 1751 he was elected to Parliament as the member for Wareham. On 1 October 1757 he married Bridget, the elder daughter of Thomas Williams of Edwinsford, near Tally in Carmarthenshire. A few years later when his father-in-law died he took charge of the Edwinsford estate which had been settled on his wife at her marriage.

When in the autumn of 1761 Robert became his nephew's guardian, a relationship was established which was to last for more than 30 years. Their close friendship was marked from the first by the high respect in which the uncle held his young nephew, and their mutual regard emphasized over the years by the closeness of their London and Middlesex abodes. For his London house Robert Banks-Hodgkinson took residence in

> ... the desirable leasehold estate consisting of an excellent Dwelling House and Offices, spacious back court, double coach house, and stabling for six horses, eligibly situate at No.2 New Burlington Street, Saville Row ...

in 1767, the same year in which his nephew entered the somewhat larger No.14 nearly opposite. For his Middlesex home he acquired at auction in 1775

> ... a valuable and very desirable Freehold and Copyhold Estate pleasantly situate at Heston, near Hounslow, in the County of Middlesex; Comprising an excellent modern-built Villa with numerous and detached Offices, Coach houses, Stabling, Fore Court, Gardens, beautiful Lawn and Pleasure Ground, Orchard rich Meadows, and Arable Land nearly contiguous; The Whole containing by Admeasurement, Twenty-one Acres Two Roods and Thirty-four Perches ...

Robert's villa, Heston House, lay just '2 miles 2 furlongs and 7 perches' as measured by his nephew's 'way-wiser' from

> ... that capital Messuage and Tenement called Spring Grove House, situate and being at Smallbury Green ...

occupied by Joseph IV from the first year of his married life in 1779. In the final disposal of these two Banks-Hodgkinson properties in 1793 Robert's executors were his two nephews, Sir Joseph Banks and Henry Hawley.

On 30 April 1778 Robert Banks-Hodgkinson was elected a Fellow of the Royal Society on a certificate drafted and signed by his nephew. In support were the names of 16 other Fellows. The signatories all testified 'from personal knowledge' in the usual form that he was 'a gentleman well vers'd in many branches of Classical and Philosphical literature'. They included a due proportion of gentleman landowners like himself – Benjamin Way, Robert Shuttleworth, William Perrin, John Lloyd – but also men of science such as Daniel Solander, James Lind, Sir George Shuckburgh, Alexander Aubert, Colonel William Roy, in the fields of botany, experimental physics, mathematics, astronomy and surveying. With these also were linked the names of Richard Kaye, Charles Morton, Ralph Willett, Thomas Morell and William Musgrave, reflecting the bibliophile, classical and antiquarian elements, underlined by his Fellowship also of the Society of Antiquaries – a combination common enough at the time. In 1781 he was admitted a member of the Royal Society dining club at the *Mitre* in Fleet Street and so, as it were, entered a final state of grace in the academic society of London. He had indeed for several years already dined as a periodic 'stranger' with the 'rebellious club' of which his nephew Joseph IV had been elected 'perpetual Dictator'. Thus the last 15 years of his life were spent perhaps more as the gentleman-scholar of London and Middlesex than as the landed gentleman of Derbyshire and South Wales – punctuated only by his year as High Sheriff of Carmarthenshire in 1784.

When Robert died early on Sunday morning 11 November 1792 in his seventy-first year there is no doubt he was deeply mourned by his nephew who had posted back fast from Revesby Abbey to attend him at the last. This almost filial grief however was no curb to a scientifically detached curiosity in the autopsy which revealed a splendid urinary calculus in his uncle's bladder. For some weeks after the event Banks carefully recorded the loss in weight of the stone from an initial '2 ounces 2 Pennyweights 7 grains Troy' 61 hours after its removal from the body, to a final '2 ounces all but 2 grains' on 26 January 1793 when he delivered this notable specimen 'at 10 at night' to Dr Everard Home, assistant to the eminent John Hunter at St George's Hospital. This was surely beyond the call of an executor's duty – or even that of a fond ward for his former guardian. Meanwhile the body of Robert himself had been laid to rest in Battersea beside his wife Bridget, who had predeceased him on 14 July 1792.

Robert's town house at No. 2 New Burlington Street on the north side still survives not so many yards from the more commodious No. 14 on the south side where his famous nephew in the years of his bachelor heyday from 1767 to 1777 gathered and displayed his collections to the scholars and curiosos of Western Europe.

There remain now to be noted the brief lives of those other young Banks's – Collingwood and George. Collingwood, the elder, carrying his maternal family name, was born in St James's Square on 20 August 1734. After his mother's death two years later he seems to have spent the next few years at Revesby Abbey under the care of Letitia Mary, supported from time to time by his maternal grandmother, Mrs Henry Collingwood. Then in 1740 as a six-year old he was confided by his father to the care of Mr Joseph Devereux at his boarding school at Glatton. Between this date and his death and burial at Christ Church, Oxford, as an undergraduate in 1755, there is apparently nothing more to record.

George born in the hour of his mother's death on 17 March 1736, also in St James's Square, spent his toddling years about the house and park at Revesby Abbey. Then he followed his brother to school at Glatton. Nothing is known of the years which transformed the attractive 'leetle Georgy' who so delighted his three stepsisters into the unattractive Captain in the Coldstream Regiment of Foot Guards. He died otherwise undistinguished at the end of February 1773 in Boyle Street, Savile Row. With the bouts of wild drinking that seem to have hastened his end at the age of 37, he had been the plague of his nearest relatives, his stepbrother Robert Banks-Hodgkinson, Joseph IV as he prepared for his voyage in the *Endeavor,* and that other Joseph Banks of Lincoln's Inn.

Here then is enough of the immediate family history to make intelligible the actual origins, sifted from the myths and legends, of that last Joseph Banks to inherit the fortune and estates accumulated by his great-grandfather. There is perhaps little enough to portend the man of science and erudition who was to emerge. He was favoured certainly by the comfortable estate whose income ensured the nucleus of a good education and with it the great vacuum of uncommitted leisure as a challenge to his talent and energy. Of his period he was not alone in these advantages, but he must rank high among those whose wealth from the land was used less for power and profit than as a benefaction of service to mankind within the frame of contemporary social perspectives.

22

CHAPTER 2

A GENTLEMAN'S EDUCATION
1743–1766

William Banks, now a 24-year old Member of Parliament with his wife Sarah moved from the honeymoon house in Bruton Street early in 1743, in time for the birth of their first child, Joseph Banks IV, on 13 February at No.30 Argyle Street. Two weeks later the heir was baptized at the parish church in Piccadilly by the Revd Mr Cox, where in October the following year his sister Sarah Sophia was christened by the same hand. Then, before Christmas that year, the young family left London for the refurbished Revesby Abbey. Here for the next few years the two children grew out their infancy in the care of a young and healthy mother for whom life was burdened also with a young husband crippled and chair-bound at 26 within a year of their homecoming.

The kindergarten years of young Joseph IV were divided between an active 'conformity to the precepts of a mother void of all imaginary fear', as in old age he recalled to the Revd Samuel Hopkinson of Bourn, and submission to the more academic precepts of the Revd Henry Shepherd, rector of Moorby and once the youthful tutor of his father. Then, in April 1752, at the age of nine, in the same year that William Banks enjoyed a brief remission from paralysis, young Joseph entered Harrow as his preparatory school. Here he was not far from the avuncular eye of Robert Banks-Hodgkinson the incumbent, during parliamentary sessions, of the house at No. 2 New Burlington Street. Within ten miles or so there was also his maternal aunt Arabella and her husband George Aufrere, another Member of Parliament, settled at Gough House by the Thames in Chelsea. The parkland and broad acres of Revesby Abbey and the mysteries of the nearby fens, no longer daily delights for the boy Joseph, were to become mere intermittent pleasures of the school holidays.

Then in the greater maturity of his early teens he was moved from Harrow-on-the-Hill and sent to Eton on 11 September 1756. Here he was fortunate in the headmaster, Dr Edward Barnard, a disciplinarian in classics, 'the Pitt of masters', and the more genial Dr Thomas Dampier, Usher of the Lower School. As an oppidan in the house of Edward Young he struggled with the prevailing regimen of a dominantly classical education in which Harrow had ill-prepared him. Entered in the third form, his deficiencies had become obvious by the Christmas holidays of 1756. The hard winter and bad roads of early 1757 delayed his return to school. This brought a concerned letter from Edward Young, dated 6 February, enquiring why, and analysing for William Banks the dubious performance of his son in his first Eton term. Young emphasized the great importance of gaining facility in turning English into Latin and in the use of Greek grammar. This was necessary to the forming of 'an Habit of Attention and Diligence' useful in the stricter regime of the Upper School and it was an area where 'Master Banks' was somewhat lagging. There was another cause for concern – 'a great Inattention in Him, and an immediate Love of Play – something to be mastered as 'a constant Obstacle to His Improvement' and calling for a fatherly reprimand.

This may have taken place in the Easter vacation of 1757, for it would appear, again from the conversation of his old age, that in the summer of that year a notable change in his attitude to formal study was observed. If the evidence of Everard Home is to be accepted, it was then that his lifetime engagement with the study of nature and the plant world in particular began, coincident with a determination to obey his father's injunctions on the more earnest pursuit of Latin and Greek. The discipline and creative teaching of Dr Barnard ensured progress in the latter during the last two years of his time at Eton, but it was apparently an old copy of Gerard's *Herball* and his own strong initiatives that established the slender grounding in the natural sciences on which his life's work grew. This found visible expression in his first collection of plants, insects and shells gathered in the byways and hedges along the Thames in the ample red-letter days and other free time during the term, augmented by ramblings at home among the fens and wolds of Lincolnshire.

As a senior in the fifth and what little he had of his sixth form year he was part of the headmaster's division of some 50 boys in a school population that had risen to well over 300 since Barnard had taken office in 1754. Under this regime there were 14 lesson periods in the week devoted to the study of a range of classical authors, among which seven periods were given to construing, Homer and the Greek dramatists, Virgil, Horace, Lucian, Ovid and Cicero. In English literature the reading list included Milton, Pope and Addison's *Spectator*. In history, the ancient included such texts as John Potter's *Archaeologia Graeca* and for the modern White Kennet's *Compleat History*. In addition there were three exercises in composition every week to be done in free time – an original prose theme of 20 lines, not less than ten elegaic couplets and five or six stanzas of lyrics on the same theme, rising to Greek hexameters in the sixth form. In the fifth form geography and algebra were the only diversions from the classical curriculum with Euclid for those who stayed long enough at school. French was an optional extra and, from the evidence of later years, Banks may have given this some attention. Over all, during his Eton schooldays, there hung the power of Barnard's verbal rebuke, more effective than the corporal punishment he was generally reluctant to apply. To this was added his strong aversion to the wearing of long hair by the boys.

Among his contemporary oppidans most were like Banks himself – the sons of landed gentlemen or of the rising merchant class of whom Henry Brougham, William Perrin and Valentine Morris were among his closer friends. Of the titled aristocracy or their sons and younger brothers, there were at this period comparatively few in the school – between 20 and 30. Of these the Hon. Constantine John Phipps was Banks's most particular friend.

II

Early in 1760, when he was 17, mindful of the smallpox disfigurement of his dead uncle Joseph Banks III, Joseph was brought home to undergo a 14-day course of inoculation devised by the Suttons. He did not return to Eton to complete his last term until after his recovery from the second attempt by this method. Instead he enjoyed his longest period of untrammelled freedom at Revesby Abbey and its surrounding countryside.

Then, on 16 December 1760, he was matriculated at Christ Church, Oxford, the college intended for his father and his uncle Robert and where his step-uncle Collingwood Banks had died and had been buried in 1755. His Oxford residence began on 24 December 1760 though not, apparently, in the college itself. It was not, indeed, until 24 June 1762 that he acquired the dignity of occupying Rooms 6 and 8 on stair 8 in Peckwater Quadrangle.

As a gentleman-commoner he was again fortunate in entering Christ Church during an upsurge in its fortunes under Dean David Gregory, the first Professor of History and Modern Languages at Oxford. As canon he had repaired Christ Church hall and as dean had finished the upper rooms of the college library and raised the terrace in the great quadrangle. Within his deanship had also come the benefactions of Matthew Lee, an old graduate of the college, with stipends for the Lee's Readers in chemistry, physics and anatomy, and funds enough for the building of an anatomy school. By contrast, in botany this element of scientific stimulus was in abeyance. The vigour which John Dillenius, the first Sherardian professor of the subject, had infused was now languishing under his successor in the chair, Dr Humphrey Sibthorp, who had nevertheless purchased the manuscripts, drawings and collections of his predecessor for the Sherardian Museum. In this quarter the young Banks found no dynamic teaching but a more passive scientific hospitality with freedom to follow his self-determined way. In this, as in most other aspects of his Oxford years, there is little enough to record from direct evidence. As at Eton so here within the university and on through the after years Banks was self-educated in the natural sciences as far as we can judge. His dedicated response to his father's wish and the classical discipline of Dr Edward Barnard had turned the inattentive boy with an inordinate love of play into the enquiring student with a burning taste for knowledge.

Before his first university year was out, the premature death of his father, on 23 September 1761, took him back to Revesby Abbey and to his inheritance under the joint guardianship of his mother and his uncle Robert. For him the family centre now moved south as his mother made her home in Chelsea, near her sister Arabella, taking the Turret House at 22 Paradise Row close by the Apothecaries' Physic Garden with all its attractions for her son. However, for the widow herself, proximity to Arabella Aufrère was perhaps more important than botany or the Physic Garden. For the bereaved heir, Robert Banks-Hodgkinson, as the practical manager of his financial affairs, now became an emphatic influence in his life. Through the uncle's hands passed all the funds from the account at Snow and Denne in the Strand allotted to his ward for his college bills, his allowance, and for various expenses, notably his vacation travelling to Revesby Abbey, to Overton Hall and to Edwinsford. These disbursements amounted to some £400-£450 a year until the young man came of age and took command of his own affairs on 19 April 1764. In these last two and-a-half years of his minority he seems to have served a sort of practical apprenticeship in estate management during vacations from Oxford in Wales, Staffordshire, Derbyshire and Lincolnshire under the combined tutelage of his uncle Robert, John Gilbert and Benjamin Stephenson, a powerful combination of good sense and wide experience. He seems to have spent little enough time now in the feminine company of his mother and sister at Chelsea.

His attendance at Oxford was a flexible compromise between keeping terms and

25

Joseph Banks's room 6 on stair 8 in Peckwater Quadrangle Christ Church, Oxford,
top right-hand windows on the corner just below the parapet.

studying the complexities of his inheritance with his uncle. Indeed, during 1763, the
summer and Michaelmas terms were sacrificed to more than six months continuous
absence from college on the estates at Revesby Abbey, Overton Hall and
Edwinsford, almost as though this were a last intensive course in property
management before he grasped the reins entirely for himself. Christ Church,
however, was clearly his independent base of operations for nearly five years from
December 1760 to the late summer of 1765, those years of education which in
retrospect he counted as a time of true happiness. No reading lists nor even the
names of his tutors survive to enlighten us about the detailed course it actually
followed, only a stray myth of college gossip and occasional latter-day anecdote.

As an Etonian with modest Latin and less Greek (by some standards) but an
obsession with natural history, he was inevitably an oddity of the Junior Common
Room, as he was to remain an exception all his life in the council rooms and
gatherings of his academic friends. But he was always a respected oddity. So there
are perhaps traces of his leadership to be found in the sudden appearance at Oxford
in 1762, in the summer term, of three new clubs which together reflect the range of
the young Banks's developing interests: the Botanical Club to meet at Cabbage Hall;
the Fossil Club at Tittup Hall near Headington Quarries, not far from Shotover Hill;
and the Antiquarian's Club to meet in the Trotter Room at the Hole-in-the-Wall, a
former haunt of Thomas Hearne, another Oxford oddity, second keeper of the
Bodleian Library. How far Banks was a moving spirit in these things can only be
surmised but such things were certainly close to his taste.

More definite and indicative is the association he formed with John Parsons, his senior at Christ Church, whose preference for natural history seems to have matched that of Banks but which led him on to medicine. His special interest in botany gained him the Hope medal for the best *hortus siccus* at Edinburgh in 1766, but his zoological studies brought him in 1767 to the Lee Readership in anatomy at Christ Church as its first incumbent and, with it, the task of building the first anatomy school at Oxford. Banks had evidently found in Parsons a stimulating kindred spirit and perhaps a tutor whose standards he could profitably accept, especially in zoological studies. Then, with Parsons following medicine in London and Scotland, Banks, with the agreement of Dr Humphrey Sibthorp as the compliant Sherardian professor, brought the younger Israel Lyons at his personal expense from Cambridge to Oxford to deliver a short summer course in July 1764 as a touch of botanical cross-pollination. With this last entrepreneurial gesture Banks effectively left Oxford for fresh academic pastures in Bloomsbury even though for several years he kept an access to his rooms in Peckwater Quadrangle.

III

His entry into the intellectual world of London was well marked by his first reader's ticket at the British Museum, Montagu House, dated 3 August 1764. For the fuller enjoyment of this privilege he had taken lodgings in Ormond Street nearby. Here he began his lifelong association with the Museum just over five years from its opening to public use. Here, too, he took his first steps toward his fellowship of the Royal Society by his association with the company he found there.

The Reading Room at this stage was a narrow, dark and damp room, No. 90 in the south-west corner of the 'base story' or ground floor, with only two windows overlooking the well-kept gardens on the west side, poorly lit except in summer. For the readers, of whom there were few, there was a single wainscot table covered with green baize affording space for 20 chairs, a capacity almost never filled. It was not until September 1765 that the bare boards of the floor were covered with a rush matting and the frames of the two windows repaired and made weather-tight. The Revd Richard Penneck was in the first years of his long curacy as Keeper of the Reading Room and through him Banks negotiated the tedious process of tapping the library resources. As company at this time he may have had that of Dr William Stukeley, a link with his grandfather Joseph Banks II and the antiquities of Lincolnshire. But in 1767 he must also have shared the intimacy of this modest room with Phillip Stephens, Secretary of the Admiralty, with whom he was granted a six-month's ticket in March of that year. Other companions in these early years whom Banks may have met were Thomas Gray, the poet, William Blackstone, the jurist, and David Hume, the Scottish philosopher and historian, for the Reading Room then was primarily the haunt of those with a literary rather than a scientific bent. However, upstairs among the collections on display, was the man with whom Banks was to form a symbiosis in natural history with effects ranging far beyond the vision of the Trustees.

In the west wing in two rooms on the first floor were the collections based on the original Sloane nucleus and, since March 1763, Daniel Solander had been working among them as an assistant in the Department of Natural and Artificial Productions preparing a systematic catalogue of the 'natural' specimens. By September 1764 he

The British Museum in Montagu House, 1780, guarded by the York Regiment during the Gordon Riots. Drawing by Paul Sandby, RA.

had listed and described the greater part of the animal collections; the insects, amphibia, birds and quadrupeds, with some of the fossils. However, being frequently disturbed by the small conducted parties of visitors, he asked the Trustees to provide him with a separate room away from such annoyance in 'the base story'. By 13 February 1765 he was established in his own separate room on the ground floor. He was now able to report the cataloguing in fair copy of some 3000 specimens of animals in the Sloanian Collection, and in excess of 1500 plant specimens from about 700 Linnaean species in the *hortus siccus* volumes of Hermann, Oldenlands, Desmarest, Kiggelaers and Meerseveens, mostly from Africa. Solander had now laid the foundations of a system of record and description on the small octavo sheets or 'slips' with which his name has ever since been associated, to be stored in the small boxes that in principle were the basic design of the Solander case in such varied use today.

Without any other firm evidence beyond the chances of sheer propinquity, it is probable that it was here on the ground floor of Montagu House in the autumn of 1764 that Joseph Banks and Daniel Solander began to forge that working partnership and lasting friendship from which so many advances in natural history were to evolve. But Banks was not alone in drawing pleasure and information from the presence of the Swede. Other men, older and already productive in several fields, had been attracted to the company and instruction of this pleasant and articulate disciple of Linnaeus, by now a welcome figure in the Bloomsbury scene. There was John Ellis FRS with his *Natural History of the Corallines* already behind him and soon to help

28

Dr Daniel Charles Solander, FRS. Painting by Johan Zoffany, RA.

Solander arrange John Greg's collections from the ceded islands of the West Indies and that of Lord Hissborough from the same region. There was the Revd John Lightfoot, librarian and chaplain to the Dowager-Duchess of Portland, as curator of the Bulstrode collections seeking light on matters of conchology and botany. James Lee, the Scottish nurseryman and partner of Lewis Kennedy at The Vineyard, Hammersmith, eager to graft the Linnaean system on to the practicalities of commercial horticulture was of the company. Inevitably there was Thomas Pennant seeking leave from the Trustees for Peter Mazell to copy drawings in the Museum collections as plates for his *British Zoology*. Soon there was also William Perrin, junior to Banks both at Eton and Christ Church, and already the young master of the family plantations in Jamaica, an estate at West Farleigh near Maidstone and a house close by in Bloomsbury Square. It was probably with Perrin that Banks went botanizing along the Weald of Kent in the summer of 1765 after a winter of discipline under Solander at the Museum in the rigours of botanical diagnosis and Latin description. But it was from the spring of this year that the earliest evidence of a serious foreign correspondence can be dated in the Latin reply of 21 March 1765 from Louis Guillame Le Monnier, physician and botanist at Versailles, responding to Banks in his first probings abroad.

Montagu House and its adjacent garden had more to offer than the first fumblings in organized natural history and hours of antiquarian browsing in the Reading Room. For some 18 months Banks had many occasions, social and academic, in which to meet men whose company could bear other fruit for an intelligent and personable young man, especially one of enterprise and an instinctive negotiating skill. Banks had already taken a first step into the world of London societies and clubs in his membership, within a month of his father's death, of the Society for the Encouragement of Arts, Manufactures and Commerce on 21 October 1761, as an Oxford undergraduate. Now at the age of 23, his Fellowship of the Society of Antiquaries and of the Royal Society, so speedily attained, seem to owe more to the cluster of relationships formed in and about the British Museum and the impact of his own personality on that small academic group than to elements of social power and influence arising from his fortune as a wealthy landed gentleman. The list of his sponsors on the certificates submitted to both societies is short, and notable only for a certain academic weight and an antiquarian mould so common among the eighteenth-century middle class.

No name of any aristocratic significance occurs among the seven sponsors whose signatures appear. Elected to the Society of Antiquaries on 27 February 1766 he was recommended as

> . . . a Gentleman of great Merit, Learning & other Accomplishments, &
> particularly well versed in the Antiquities of this and other Nations . . .

by four sponsors only. First, there was Dr Charles Lyttelton, the ailing Bishop of Carlisle, elected President of the Society of Antiquaries in 1765, a man of Eton and Oxford but also, as Bishop, Lord of the Manor of Horncastle in Lincolnshire from whom the Banks family held property in the town. Socially the Bishop stood highest among the seven. Next, there was Dr Charles Morton, the easy-going physician and scholarly under-librarian and keeper of Manuscripts at the Museum, through whom

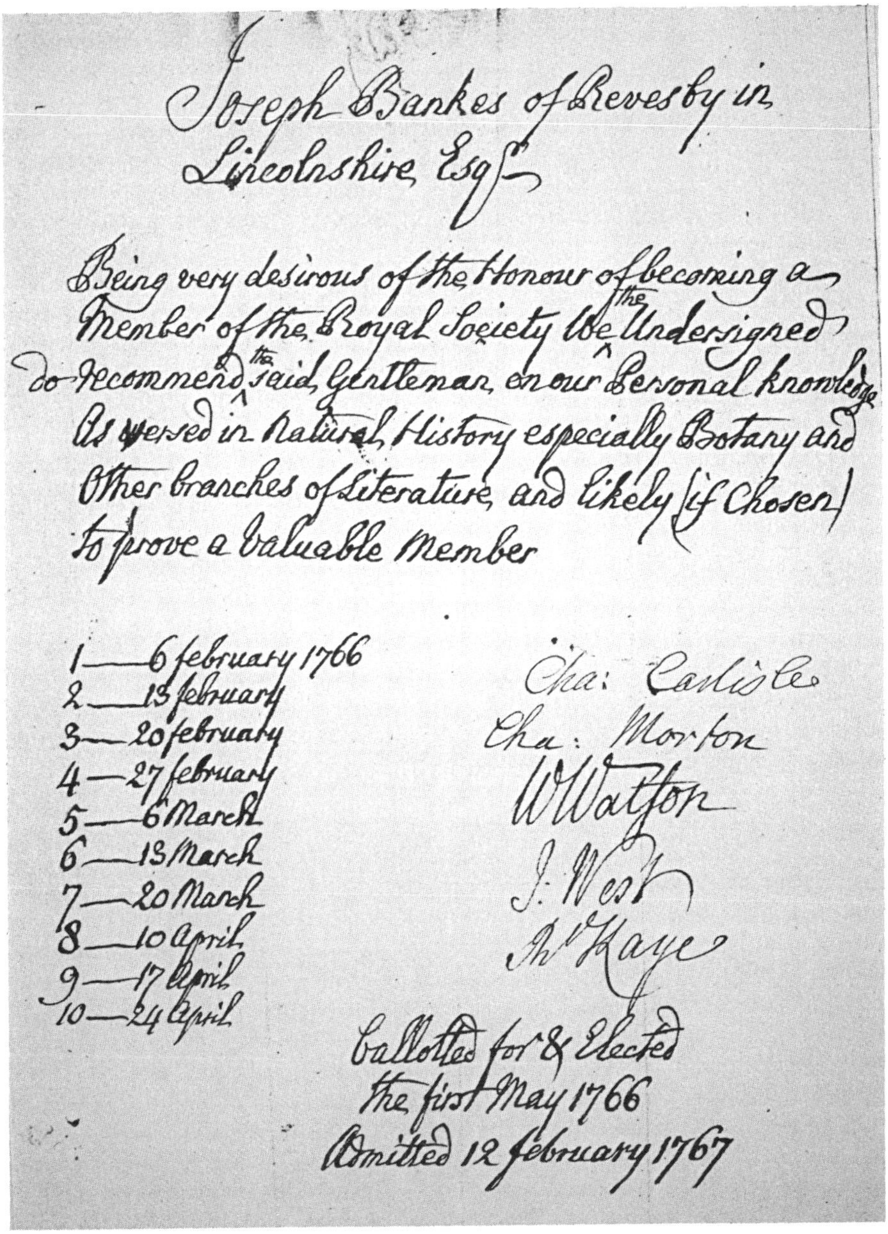

Joseph Bankes of Revesby in
Lincolnshire, Esqr

Being very desirous of the Honour of becoming a
Member of the Royal Society We the Undersigned
do recommend the said Gentleman, on our Personal knowledge
As versed in Natural History especially Botany and
Other branches of Literature, and likely (if Chosen)
to prove a Valuable Member

1 ——— 6 february 1766
2 ——— 13 february
3 ——— 20 february
4 ——— 27 february
5 ——— 6 March
6 ——— 13 March
7 ——— 20 March
8 ——— 10 April
9 ——— 17 April
10 ——— 24 April

Cha: Carlisle
Cha: Morton
W Watson
J West
R Kaye

Ballotted for & Elected
the first May 1766
Admitted 12 february 1767

Joseph Banks's certificate of election to the Royal Society.

Banks probably met the Bishop and the other antiquaries. Morton was also Secretary of the Royal Society. Third, there was William Norris of Merton, Oxford, the hard-working Secretary of the Society of Antiquaries. Last, came Thomas Astle, Keeper of the State Papers in Whitehall and a palaeographer.

In his election to the Royal Society on 1 May 1766 there were five signatures on his certificate. Of these, two had already appeared for his Fellowship of the Society of Antiquaries – the Bishop of Carlisle and Dr Charles Morton. The remaining three were led by James West, Treasurer of the Royal Society, a Balliol man, politician and lawyer, an antiquary with a leaning to science and a deep love of typography, later and briefly PRS. But perhaps the greatest weight was the name of Dr (later Sir) William Watson, physician, naturalist, experimenter in electricity, friend and correspondent of Peter Kalm and Peter Simon Pallas, an active trustee and frequent presence among the natural history collections of the British Museum. Finally there was the name of Richard Kaye, later Sir Richard Kaye, Dean of Lincoln, an FRS of 1765 and a botanizing friend of Banks. With this sponsorship, then, was elected on 1 May 1766 the Fellow who was to become the longest serving President of the Royal Society

> ... as versed in Natural History especially Botany and Other branches of Literature, and likely (if Chosen) to prove a Valuable Member.

His election was an act of faith and hope based not on evidence of scientific performance but on the incipient glint of a keen intelligence, some evidence of a critical mind and an apparent capacity for investigative study. With his admittance on 12 February 1767, two weeks after his return from Newfoundland and Labrador, the Society had ample evidence that its judgement had not been misplaced.

IV

Apart from a brief return to Oxford for six weeks in July and August 1765, perhaps for some botanizing and animal dissections with John Parsons after his field excursion with William Perrin in Kent, the year seems to have passed for Banks in studious exploration of London and its academic society. This included no doubt the company of Phillip Miller at the Chelsea Physic Garden so easily achieved from the proximity of his mother's house. But how much time he spent with his mother and sister at Chelsea at this period, or ever, is not clear. Later, during his married life, the Turret House and his uncle George Aufrère's Gough House served for brief and occasional visits as the family passed to and fro between Soho Square and Spring Grove. However, in these early years of his majority and post-graduate freedom, Chelsea was too far west of the evolving society of clubs and taverns between the City and St James's, the British Museum and Whitehall, when from lodgings in Great Ormond Street he could encompass so many of these attractions on foot. Bloomsbury and St James's, Oxford and Wales, rather than the market garden suburbia of Chelsea held more to engage his intellect and physical energies. Into the world of opportunity after the Seven Years War the person of an old school friend, already wise in its dangers and delights, was now to enter his life.

Lt the Hon. Constantine John Phipps, Commander of HMS *Terpsichore* from June 1765, had left Eton in the winter of 1758–9 to serve as a midshipman under his uncle

Augustus John Hervey (later 3rd Earl of Bristol) in the Channel and the West Indies against the French. Now after seven years of active service in the Royal Navy he was seeking relief but not absolute rest from its rigours.

Banks also, after seven years of increasingly concentrated academic discipline, crowned by the stimulating months of more or less scientific bench work at the British Museum, was ready for a period of investigative field work. Daniel Solander had already established himself as the tutor and soul-mate of Banks the scholar. In Phipps at this point, there entered the intelligent man of action calling, in effect, to Banks the man of adventure and practical enterprise as his tutor in seamanship and the vagaries of the sea. Between them, though quite how we do not know, Banks and Phipps were entered as supernumeraries on board HMS *Niger* Captain Sir Thomas Adams, a 32-gun frigate, bound on fisheries protection duty for the next season off Newfoundland in the new climate of Anglo-French relations after the Treaty of Paris. For Phipps this was a period of official leave combining patrol experience without the burden of command. For Banks this, his first voyage beyond coastal waters, was a first expedition in field natural history and foreign travel on any scale. It was a final stage in his apprenticeship to the biological sciences by the standards of his day, a test of his abilities in many ways but not least that of his capacity to act and work alone as the young scientist he had in truth become.

Guided by the field experience of Solander from his Lapland tour and that of John Ellis from his West Indies visits, Banks set off in April 1766 well equipped for the purposes of botanical and zoological collecting, with his servant Peter Briscoe as assistant. With him he carried an array of written questions from Thomas Pennant, primarily devoted to the mammals and birds he might encounter, as future grist for the Pennant literary machine.

At Salisbury on 7 April he met Phipps and on the 9th they arrived at Plymouth where the *Niger* lay. For nearly two weeks the sailing was delayed, mostly by unfavourable winds. Banks profitably filled the time collecting plant and animal life along the foreshores, exploring the estate of Mount Edgecombe, botanizing inland, fishing in the harbour. With William Cookworthy, the Quaker pioneer of the English porcelain industry in which Banks kept a lifelong interest, he explored the china clay area of Cornwall and mulled over the nature of the geological strata involved.

At last, with a wind at ENE, the *Niger* set sail on 22 April to anchor in the harbour of St John's on 11 May. In this 19-day passage across the north Atlantic Banks not only tried the possibilities of marine biology, fishing with line and net from the quarter cabin windows, but discovered his own limitations as a sailor during the gales of the first week of May when seasickness left him unable to write, in spite of heroic measures of attempted self-control. Apart from brief entries in his journal, he had managed to finish at least one letter to his uncle Robert at Edwinsford which, sent perhaps by returning supply ships from St John's to the port of Bristol, reached Wales by the end of May. Back came a reply, dated 31 May, acknowledging a letter 'from the main ocean' with news of a run of '900 miles in six days which is pretty good work' and repeating home news in a letter of 10 May already on its way. With the spring traffic of the fisheries' supply fleets to the Newfoundland Grand Banks from the West Country ports, a moderate flow of correspondence was sustained even as far as the south coast of Labrador.

For a month the *Niger* was anchored in the harbour at St John's. With the ship as his base, Banks and Peter Briscoe roamed the countryside collecting plants, shooting

33

bird specimens, fishing with rod and line and trawling from a ship's boat for a variety of marine life. Ashore he noted the strata exposed in the building of a fort on the south shore and collected geological specimens.

On 11 June the frigate moved to Croque Harbour near the north-east tip of the island for one week; then north by stages, touching at Conche, to Hare Bay on 11 July where the ship anchored for over three weeks. From leaving Conche on 22 June until the end of July at Hare Bay, Banks lay ill on the ship, his diary and his specimens neglected. From his letter of 11 August to William Perrin a brief picture of this ordeal emerges:

> . . . We have had the wettest & worst season here almost that ever was known which laid Poor Pilgarlick up with a fever the most of the month of July to the Great detriment of his Collections as that is the very hight of the Season here for Plants however thank god he has got upon his Legs again by the assistance of a Bottle of Bark which always stands at his Elbow he has made one Excursion to Bellisle de Groias & returnd not ill Paid for his trouble . . .

For the 'Bottle of Bark' he had his sister Sarah Sophia to thank, as he wrote on the same day to her, without any details of his illness, but extolling the virtues of the remedy:

> . . . it has one merit however I think for if it would not cure an ague I am sure it would kill a horse . . .

What this fever was we can only surmise. Its apparent response to the 'bark', a decoction of cinchona from Peruvian bark, suggests malaria in the benign tertian form appropriate to the northern latitude of Newfoundland. His use of the term 'ague' applied also to the similar condition in the fens of Lincolnshire at that time. Certainly the mosquito population ashore was in great activity as Banks had already experienced at Croque and Phipps also, as he built his 'Crusoe Hall' ashore there, working in Banks's words

> . . . night & day & Lets the Mosquetos eat more of him than he does of any Kind of food all through Eagerness . . .

On 6 August the *Niger* sailed for Chatteaux Bay on the south Labrador mainland at the strategic entrance to the Strait of Belle Isle. Here, for obvious reasons in defence of the new Canadian possessions, a blockhouse and stockaded fort was to be erected on the point covering the entrace to Pitt's Harbour on a plan devised by the Governor of Newfoundland, Commodore Hugh Palliser. As the ship left Hare Bay it ran into a severe gale, 'the deuce of a rough one', said Banks as he wrote to Perrin on the passage, such a one that

> . . . I can not Keep my seat without being moord head & Stern as *we* Sea men call it that is my Legs against the Ledge & my Back against the Mizzen Mast . . .

But otherwise he had the happiness of having gained, for the first time, a mastery over the seasickness which had so much plagued him in the 'Least Degree of Rough

Weather', a weakness which he attributed to his having been before at sea mostly in small boats with a motion different from that of a larger vessel. In the euphoria of the moment he wrote not only to Perrin but also to Solander, Pennant and to his sister Sarah Sophia, to whom he gossiped lightly. He hoped that James Lee had given her nosegays on her visits to The Vineyard. If she had not received this courtesy, he threatened, then Lee could expect no insects from his Newfoundland collection when he returned. He shed some light for her upon his amusements:

> . . . How do you think I have spent my Leisure Time since I have been here Very Musically I can assure you I have learnt to Play upon a new Instrument as I have Forswore the Flute I have tried my hand upon strings What do you think it is now not a fiddle I can assure [you] but a Poor innocent Guittar which Lay in the Cabbin on which I can play Lady Coventries minuet & in Infancy &c: with Great success . . .

These letters he sent home from Chatteaux Bay soon after their arrival on 10 August when he went on shore. There on the nearby bogs he collected little botanically but saw, for the first time, great flocks of the Eskimo curlew, *Numenius borealis* Forster, some of which he had broiled for dinner that day.

For nearly two months the *Niger* lay in Chatteaux Bay while the ship's company laboured in the building of York fort, a task finished by the end of September to the surprise of everyone in the speed at which it was done. In this period Banks ranged as far as he could, exploring the islands in the bay and east to St Peter's Island on several excursions, hoping to make contact with the Esquimos of that part of the coast, but without success. Neither the Beothuk Indians of the main island of Newfoundland nor the Esquimos of the Labrador tundra were at any time seen by Banks but he was able to gather enough information at second hand for a general account. In this process he obtained the scalp of Sam Fry, a fisherman who had fallen victim to the Beothuks. Their rough surgery differed from that of the mainland Indians as they skinned the whole face down to the upper lip. Sam had been killed the year before and the scalp preserved his features well enough for recognition. But otherwise Banks viewed the stories he heard and noted with cautious scepticism. By contrast he was able to compound a full account of the operations of the cod fishermen, both English and French, as he saw them at work himself. This general account was included by Pennant later in his *Arctic Zoology*, but without explicit acknowledgement as in so much else he acquired from Banks.

During the stay in Chatteaux Bay Banks learned by direct experience a sobering lesson in the power of the wind and wave. On 2 September he and the master of the *Niger*, with the permission of Sir Thomas Adams, planned a voyage of a week or ten days along the coast in a sturdy shallop. As they turned out of the Bay past Castle Island a head wind blocked their progress to the north and they returned cautiously to harbour and tied up beside an anchored snow to await fairer weather. Instead a furious gale developed overnight blowing down the strait, destroying a number of small vessels like the shallop itself, especially among the French who lost about 100 men. Several brigs were driven ashore and broken to pieces. With Sir Thomas Adams in hearty agreement, Banks, suitably chastened, laconically recorded:

... as the blowing Season was Come in I was Easily Persuaded that I was Safer on board the *Niger* than on any Boat in the Country ...

For the remaining weeks on the station he worked within closer and safer confines until the departure on 3 October. Presented with a live porcupine, *Erithizon dorsatum* (L.) by the sergeant of marines, who was among the 20 men remaining at the new Fort York, he returned the courtesy by leaving his last thermometer with the lieutenant [Walters] in command. Walters in turn promised to send Banks an account of the weather for the next year.

On 4 October the *Niger* was anchored again at Croque where Banks now found the climate more agreeable, free from the plagues of gadflies and mosquitoes on shore. For a week he explored more deeply inland than he had been able to do before when both he and Sir Thomas Adams were struck down with fever:

> ... Sir Thomas & I were both Very Ill here Especialy me who at one time they did not Expect to recover I know not whether that gave a disgust but we both Joind in Pronouncing the Place the Least agreable of any we had Seen in the Countrey ...

It was under these circumstances that his friendship began with William Monkhouse, surgeon of the *Niger*, and two years later to be surgeon of the *Endeavour* and to die at Batavia of a more virulent malaria than Banks had suffered at Croque. But at Croque now in the autumn Banks was able to observe more closely the operations of the English sealers and the New England whalers while the ship replenished its stores with fresh vegetables and poultry from the garden established there during the summer. On 11 October the *Niger* came to anchor again in St John's harbour near the *Guernsey* to report to Commodore Hugh Palliser and to prepare for sea.

Banks now had more than three weeks to savour the unsavoury precincts of the town and its prevailing fishiness, unrivalled for filth and dirt, in his opinion, by any fishing town he knew in England. From this squalor there was relief only in the society and hospitality of the Governor on the *Guernsey*, of which the highlight was the surprisingly elegant supper, replete with wines and Italian liqueurs, in celebration of the coronation anniversary on 25 October.

Two days later HMS *Grenville* under the command of its master, James Cook, entered harbour, coming in for refreshment at the end of its period of hydrographic survey along the southern coast of Newfoundland from St Mary's Bay to Cape Ray. Now for two days only, 27 and 28 October, there may have been a chance that Banks and Cook met for the first time; if so, it would most probably have been on board the *Guernsey* but of this there is no record.

On 29 October HMS *Niger* sailed on her return voyage by way of Lisbon, exploiting the south-west trades in the customary passage. But less than a week out, on 5 November, a heavy gale struck to remind Banks once more of the hazards of scientific adventure:

> ... we had a very hard Gale ... which has almost ruind me in the Course of it we shipp'd a Sea which Stove in our Quarter & almost Filld the Cabbin with water in an instant where it washd backward & forward with such rapidity that it broke in Peices Every chair & table in the place among other things that Sufferd my Poor Box of Seeds was one which was intirely demolish'd as was my Box of Earth with Plants in it which Stood upon deck ...

The Hon. Constantine John Phipps, FRS, later 2nd Baron Mulgrave. Painting by
Thomas Gainsborough, RA, 1785.

Seeds and living plants may have been lost but enough of the scientific harvest survived as dried specimens in the *hortus siccus*, spirit specimens and skins in the glass rounds, the casks and the kegs, to leave a notable record and evidence of the young man's worth as a new Fellow of the Royal Society.

V

Three weeks at sea brought the *Niger* to the mouth of the Tagus and an anchorage in the river off Lisbon on 18 November 1766. After the rigours of an autumn among the 'ice islands' of Labrador, Banks now had six weeks of more clement weather but somewhat restricted social pleasure among the Portuguese and members of the resident English 'factories' in that city. Though the Portuguese were wary of admitting personable young men into their homes, the English community of merchant families, especially that of Gerard Devisme, offered a society pleasant enough, with diverting female company, as later correspondence reveals. Lisbon probably seldom saw such engaging young Englishmen as the two Etonians, the amiable Banks and the witty Phipps. Neither saw the interior of a Portuguese home but both left a warm afterglow in the memories of those they met.

For Banks there was botanical profit in the company he found, not only that of Devisme but also of the Abbé João de Loureiro and the botanist Domingo Vandelli. Through the Abbé a thread of communication would eventually lead to south-east Asia and the *Flora Cochinchinensis*. Through Vandelli and Devisme would grow the plant accretions from the Peninsula, the Azores and South America and, by their collaboration with Banks, Lisbon would gain its first botanic garden. But, in spite of these distractions, it is clear that Banks, from the moment of his arrival in Portugal, was probing the future for his collections with plans for his settlement in London again. In an exchange of letters by the Lisbon packet, Perrin from Bloomsbury told him of his impending two years abroad on the Continent. Still with 'the Fire of Botany' burning in his soul, he had hopes of seeing Banks again before he himself left for Paris. At the Museum, he said, Solander was well and had named a plant after Banks. From Downing, Thomas Pennant belatedly acknowledged letters from Chatteaux Bay and Lisbon, condoled with Banks over his losses of specimens on the passage home, but voiced a pre-emptive eagerness to lay hands on the bird collection for his 'American Zoology' in the making.

On 30 December the *Niger* sailed from Lisbon but it was not until 26 January 1767, after a stormy passage home, that the ship was able to anchor at Spithead. From Portsmouth evidently Banks wrote direct to Benjamin Stephenson calling for his horses to be sent to London from Revesby Abbey. It had been a bitter and snowbound winter on the edge of the fens but Stephenson had already prepared the horses and young James Roberts for their journey south as soon as the roads were clear. The first stages of a new life for the returning voyager in the metropolis were taking shape, but a safe haven for the collections themselves had yet to be found.

Banks had been away from London for nearly ten months of which four had been spent at sea under sail. About six months had been spent at anchor with a cabin on board the *Niger* as his home throughout except for some few weeks of comfort ashore in Lisbon. His main collecting sites had been round Plymouth (about ten days); St John's, Newfoundland (about six weeks in all); Croque (about two weeks); Canada Bay and Conche (about a week); Hare Bay (a week); Chatteaux Bay, South Labrador and its environs (about seven weeks); and Lisbon, Portugal (nearly six weeks). For at least one month, July 1766, he was severely ill in his cabin, inactive and disorganized, at Croque and Hare Bay. A further check on his hopes lay in the sea damage to his collections on the Atlantic voyage home. Nevertheless, what he brought home, as far as we can tell now, was a worthy gathering for the time he could spend under the circumstances.

As practical experience in the hazards as well as the opportunities of fieldwork in natural history and geographical exploration it was thoroughly profitable in the foundation laid for the years to come in the south Pacific. In the immediate future, however, at home in London it afforded material for exercising the recording art of Georg Dionysius Ehret in his last years on some of the plants; for the burgeoning skill of young Sydney Parkinson on the birds, fishes and insects; and for that of the more obscure Peter Paillou with the birds, largely for the benefit of Thomas Pennant in the sequence of his zoological books, with Peter Mazell as the occasional engraver.

CHAPTER 3

The 'vinyard of natural history'
1767–1768

Banks returned from his Newfoundland and South Labrador journey at the end of January 1767 without a London address of his own. The voyage had enhanced his innate sense of independence for he avoided his mother's house and also that of his uncle Robert. Instead he took lodgings at a Mr Loisel's in Conduit Street while he sought a solution for the longer term. The first weeks of February were occupied with the problems of gathering and securing his collections but there was time enough for him to settle on No. 14 New Burlington Street before setting out on – an 'excursion' he termed it – of two weeks' duration to the naval establishments at Chatham, Rochester, Sheerness and the Isle of Sheppey. One reason may have been some unfinished business related to equipment and collections on HMS *Niger*. Another may have been a response to an invitation from Sir Thomas Adams with whom he had become firm friends. He set out by chaise from London on 21 February through the new housing development at Shooter's Hill where he botanized a little before changing horses at Dartford to reach Chatham at half-past-three. On his way he condemned Strood and Rochester as the dirtiest towns in England. For nearly three days he divided his time between a close study of the Chatham naval shipyard, where he learned much about construction and armament, and the castle at Rochester which he observed with an antiquarian eye of some acuity. In the same spirit he assessed the cathedral and compared it with Christ Church at Oxford, bemoaning the almost complete loss of its ancient 'Painted Glass . . . broke by the mistaken Zeal of the Oliverian Soldiers' he supposed, but more completely than any other such case that he knew. In all these pursuits he kept an alert botanical eye on the vegetation. He visited the vitriol works at Gillingham next day but found no one able to answer his questions on the process. Returning through Strood he watched boys making gun flints and at both places enquired about fossils.

At Gillingham he succeeded in finding some good specimens of the 'Piped waxen vein of Grey' but nothing from the flint knappers although they told him of occasional 'Echini'. Later that day he was joined by the Banks-Hodgkinsons and a Miss Henley and next morning with his uncle inspected Best's Brewery. Although the rain was unceasing he showed the ladies the dockyards to their considerable interest but not to the well-being of their dresses. This diversion ended on the 27th when the Hodgkinsons returned to London leaving Banks and Sir Thomas Adams to their more technical and less social activities. For Banks there were Mr Tomlin's and Mr Milton's shell collections to be seen and assessed as well as the 'great Hawk' shot in that part of the country. There was the gift of a well-dried specimen of the Bohemian chatterer to be accepted from Mr Tomlin but a ring with a fly in amber to be refused, as too valuable 'if genuine' to receive on so short an acquaintance. He learned also from the dockyard commissioner, Mr Hanway, that Sheerness harbour was now heavily infested with 'the worm' brought in from warmer latitudes.

So to Sheerness he and Sir Thomas sailed in the passage boat on 28 February where they inspected the fortifications and the half-moon battery of some 30 42-pounders commanding the Thames and Medway junction just below the Isle of Grain. In the evening they examined the township of ship's hulls set in rows to house the artificers and their families. Early next morning at seven a.m. he set off to walk round the Isle of Sheppey with Mr Allchurch, the master-caulker of the shipyard, on a collecting expedition for fossils and seaweeds finding great quantities of feather and herring-bone corralines on the way. Here too, along the cliffs, they saw the copperas stone, 'a decayd Pyrites' which the Sheppey poor collected and sold to the vitriol works at the rate of one penny a gallon, from which some earned as much as £15 a year. Banks thought a similar encouragement might induce the local people to gather fossils from the cliffs as they were otherwise scarce upon the foreshore. But Banks himself during one tide collected a few good specimens of the 'piped waxen vein', the *Ludus helmotii*, the 'starry waxen vein' and some pyrites 'of the blisterd sort' known to him from the similar nodules to be found at the Ecton copper mine in Staffordshire where they were profuse. They then went over the hill to East End where he hoped the copperas workers might have something to sell but with little result. After dinner at East Church he and Allchurch went to Shellness hunting roots of the great sea cudweed [*Gnaphalium* spp.] which William Hudson had found there the previous year. Again they were disappointed, for the exceptional tides of January had apparently so changed the foreshores there by forcing the sand so far inland that the cudweed and the associated horned poppy [*Glaucium luteum* Scop.] had been covered or destroyed. There was some compensation however in finding a sea-louse of a kind Banks had not seen before and they returned to Sheerness in good appetite. The following day, 1 March, after studying the construction and operation of a fire-ship in some detail during the day, Banks in the evening was shown the collection of fossils which his friend Allchurch had made. From him Banks bought several crab specimens, a nautilus and some coralines of which one in particular had come from the bottom of a ship just after its return from the West Indies and which Banks considered to be of special interest. Later that evening, supping with a Mr and Mrs Purves, he saw what he was told was 'the real Snake Stone so famous for extracting Poison' but which, said Banks, had he picked up such a thing himself he would not have hesitated to pronounce it as being 'a Petrified bone or at Least a Fragment of one'.

At half-past-eleven next morning Banks and Sir Thomas Adams sailed for Chatham again in the teeth of a west-south-westerly gale and high seas, a voyage of two and-a-half hours in which both were very sick indeed. On 3 March next day, as a contrast to this beach-combing and sea-faring, Banks attended a court-martial on board HMS *Yarmouth*. He found himself greatly impressed with 'the Equity of such Courts' as a code of justice under the Articles of War and as a trial conducted in public. On 4 March he set out in the morning for London and on the way stopped to walk up Gad's Hill hoping to find 'the radical Leaves of the Toadflax [*Linaria* sp.?] that is Peculiar to that Place'. In this he was disappointed, nor was he more successful in getting echini or other fossils from the two or three flint-knappers of whom he enquired. But he made a bargain with a girl on Strood Hill to save for him all the echini she could get 'for one Penny apeice great & small', which she readily promised to do.

Next day he exhibited a jewel to the Society of Antiquaries 'supposd to be of some antiquity'; it was apparently a women's ornament used as a solitaire or stomacher which Banks described in detail.

But neither as the field naturalist on his 'peregrinations', as he called them, nor as the antiquarian of St James's could he escape the yoke of his estate responsibilities, with which Benjamin Stephenson pursued him with diligence and to whom he had replied from Chatham. Now back at his lodgings in Conduit Street there were more decisions on fen drainage and navigation awaiting his consent and signature, a chore partly brightened by the brace and-a-half of woodcock which was all the keeper could send from Revesby Abbey. It was perhaps more pleasant to retreat to the Reading Room of the British Museum. There was also botanical correspondence from the Revd John Walker of Moffatt, Dumfriesshire, and a parcel of plants from him to be shared with James Lee of The Vineyard, sent as a bait to Banks in the hope of receiving duplicates from the Newfoundland plants. Thomas Pennant was also pestering him on matters of ornithology, the feather trade and drawings for enlarging and correcting his own *British Ornithology*. A more difficult problem which Banks was trying to resolve was the defective copy of Pennant's *British Zoology* which Duhamel complained that he had received from the author. Through William Perrin in Paris he sent letters to both Duhamel and Buffon exonerating Pennant but laying the blame on the Cymrodorion Society as the publisher. To Pennant himself on 5 May he wrote at last explaining that he had been busy furnishing his house in New Burlington Street with little time for anything else. Much of the furnishing seems to have involved various commissions to Stanfield Parkinson as an upholsterer and whose brother, Sydney Parkinson, was even now settling into Banks's service to illustrate selected specimens particularly from the recent gatherings in Newfoundland. But Banks was under the goad of Pennant in other ways, for his aid had already been sought for the illustration of the *Arctic Zoology* to supervise the work of Peter Mazell in London and about which at this stage he was reasonably complaisant. Irksome though these commissions may have been, he was perhaps rewarded by being introduced to the Revd Gilbert White through Pennant at a distance. Banks had in fact met White probably on 5 May at New Burlington Street as one of his earliest visitors, bringing specimens of *Motacilla* spp. on Pennant's behalf. At this first encounter another meeting was arranged with Banks returning the call by a visit to White at his brother's printery, 'Horace's Head', to hold further 'Ornithological Converse' there. A week later, in his first letter addressed from New Burlington Street, on 14 May, Banks thanked Pennant for introducing White and making it clear that on matters of ornithology at least they had achieved a warm rapport. He recorded also the recent arrival, as a near neighbour, of Governor John Gideon Loten, from whom they hoped to gain much in the drawings brought by him from Ceylon which Sydney Parkinson was soon to start copying. However there was to be a lull in this activity as Banks announced that he was 'on the wing' for Dorsetshire and the West Country going thereafter to Lincolnshire – whence Banks promised he would try to bring for Pennant a natterjack toad.

II

Next day, 15 May, Banks travelled swiftly by post-chaise the 100 miles from London to Eastbury in Dorset, arriving the same night at Tarent Gunville after a journey too fast for many observations – though he noted *Myrica Gale* growing plentifully in a bog near the 21-mile stone on Bagshot Heath. His immediate plan was a visit of about a week to the aunt who stood high in his affections, Mrs Henry Grenville, the beautiful Peggy Banks of the former reign and the toast of London society. Here he would also see his young cousin Louisa, the future Countess Stanhope.

Heavy rain on the morning of 16 May confined Banks to an exploration of Vanbrugh's massive stone pile which he found more elegant and convenient than the exterior gave him hope of finding. The afternoon was clear enough however for him to search for a long barrow which the Bishop of Carlisle had told him was in the neighbourhood. This he found in the northern corner of the park in which some of it lay but the greater part was in neighbouring land for sale by a London owner and therefore beyond Banks's hope of excavation. During the next two days he enquired about and found two more long barrows, but time pressed and Banks again found himself thwarted as an excavating archaeologist.

On 19 May he visited Kingston Lacy, occupied by an elderly namesake but no relative, an excellent building in Banks's judgement but architecturally lacking in improvement as there was not a single sash window to be found. It was however full of fine furniture with an uncatalogued picture collection of which its owner was quite ignorant. In it Banks noted works by Sir Peter Lely, Murillo, possibly a Rembrandt, perhaps a Berghem landscape and four Guidos. On his return, he saw, near Blandford racecourse, two large birds strange to him with a white spot on each wing, and a shrill whistle. Larger than a grey plover they seemed to belong, he thought, to the genus *Charadrius* nonetheless. Also from Kingston Lacy he had noted a distant earthworks with three embankments, the Badbury Rings, not unlike the famous ones he knew near Dorchester. Then on 20 May he visited a Mr Sturt at Horton who took him to Crichel House two miles away to see one of the finest stretches of artificial lake 'perhaps in England', some 280 acres beautifully set between hills covered with oak woodland and heavily stocked with carp. This lake was drawn with nets every third year and all fish above a certain size sold in London. At the last netting some 16000 pounds weight of fish had been sold at 6d. per pound or £400 in all – an example of fish farming to be stored for his future guidance. He was regaled with the engineering details of the problems in creating this lake. These were formidable and arose from the nature of the underlying solid blue clay in which were found impressions of fish very like trout, of several kinds, but mostly, in his view, whiting and dories of which the skeletons were clearly to be distinguished. However any specimens recovered were evanescent, disintegrating within twelve hours on exposure to the air. Returning to the house at Horton, Banks was particularly impressed with a very fine Lincolnshire bull, four years old, which Sturt used as a working draft animal in single harness and able to draw as much as two or three horses.

Banks was again out on the Downs on 21 May to study another long barrow between the house of Tarent Gunville and the turnpike road on the way to Blandford, possibly Pimperne Long Barrow. This was the third he had found within a circle of two miles diameter without any chance of excavation and he was reduced to vague conjecture as to their purpose and the hope that one day he could return to resolve the problem. But in the course of these rapid field inspections he had noted some specimens of field senecio, *Othonna integrifolia*, as a rare species in that neighbourhood.

He set out for Bristol at night on 22 May travelling through Shaftesbury, Warminster and Bath, and about midday on Saturday the 23rd crossed by the Aust ferry to Chepstow. Here he found the castle and its situation high on the cliff above the Wye as fine and as strong as any such ancient fortification that he knew. After dinner he went to Piercefield, the house of Valentine Morris set in its semicircle of rocks with its wooded slopes down to the Wye. Here he botanized awhile before returning to Chepstow again to be intrigued by its situation as a declining port and yet with a greater tidal range than any other in England. Set as it was by the junction of the Wye and the Severn there were few ports, Banks thought, with such an extensive access to inland navigation. Yet it failed by comparison with Bristol, where ships of 300 tons were forced to unload as far down the Avon as King's Road and to depend on lighterage to carry their cargoes to the city. On 24 May after dinner he went by water up the Wye to Tintern Abbey, admiring as he went the romantic setting of Piercefield from below. For him the Abbey was a noble ruin 'by far the Lightest Peice of Gothick' he had ever seen and with the grass there kept constantly rolled and mowed. Next day, the 25th, he dined again with Valentine Morris, luxuriating in the outlook over

> ... the Richest cultivated Land in the world coverd with Corn and Pasture ... I am more and more convinced that it is far the most beautiful place I ever saw ...

That evening at Piercefield he was shown a collection of coins, once owned by a Dr Davis of The Devizes, in which he reckoned the Greek items very good, especially the Consular series, though he suspected one brass Otto among them to have been counterfeit.

The next morning he re-crossed the Severn by the old Aust passage and rode through 'sweet country' and the towns of Henbury and Westbury to the Hot Wells by the Avon at Bristol. Then with Richard Kaye he spent the evening and much of the next day botanizing on St Vincent's Rocks high above the river in the Avon Gorge and on the meadows below Jackson's or Cook's Tower. Then on 29 May Banks and Kaye drove to Wells where they admired the west front and the Lady Chapel. This was followed by a brief visit to 'Okey' [Wookey] Hole' which they rated as far superior to Pool's Hole near Buxton. On 30 May they rode out to see the Cheddar Gorge, travelling from Easton up through Westbury on to the Mendip moors where they gained a fine view south-west over the Somerset levels 800 feet below. Collecting on the rocks above the Cheddar Gorge they found what may have been a Cheddar pink, *Dianthus glaucus*, a poppy *Papaver cambricum*, the cut-leaved saxifrage *Saxifraga hyphoides* and one of a species they called *Marchantia*, all of which grew there in great plenty. Next day, after morning service in Wells Cathedral, they rode to Glastonbury to search for a sort of vetch, *Lathyrus luteus* on the steep sides of the Tor below the tower of St Michael; visited the Bloody Well held in great repute for the cure of asthma, scurvy and dropsy; then across the town to the site of the Glastonbury Thorn, dead for some years and beyond local memory. Next, in the Abbey ruins Banks noted its covering with the most venerable ivy he had ever seen and whose foliage was used there as winter sheep feed. Before leaving the precincts, however, he collected, by digging beneath the rotting root of a tree within the Abbey, a great number of the beetle *Scarabaeus paralelopipidus* with larvae of all sizes.

He explored the peat levels of Sedgemoor between Glastonbury and Bridgewater on 1 June, the best of which he likened to his own fens in Lincolnshire and the worst to the peat mosses of Lancashire. All of them he found as rife with gnats and ague as anywhere in his own county. Indeed at Glastonbury he had been badly bitten the day before and now the combined effects of rain and insect attacks curtailed his plant hunting on the moors and drove him through Bridgwater to Taunton. From here, after a cursory view of some antiquities, he visited Hestercombe, the seat of Coplestone Bamfylde,the landscape painter, whom he found not so successful in his gardening as he was at his drawing. Returning to Bristol, Banks and Kaye visited Burton Pynsent overlooking Sedgemoor which William Pitt, the 1st Earl of Chatham, had acquired some two years previously and was still extensively altering, showing, said Banks,

. . . that his Buildings in Brick are not more durable than in administration . . .

At Bristol on 4 June Banks and Kaye botanized by the Avon and on the 5th they visited Mr Champion's brass works where they also saw the making of spelter, a zinc alloy like pewter, by a secret process. In this factory the many wheels were turned by water-power of which there was only a small natural flow. To augment this, the water, after use, was pumped again into a reservoir by what Banks said were 'two of the Largest fire engines in England'. Each of these Newcomen steam engines had cylinders 6 feet 2 inches in diameter. One worked four pumps, each of 30 inches

View of the Severn from Clifton Downs, 1786, showing St Vincent's Rock, Jackson's or Cook's Tower and the pastures by the River Avon where Banks collected in June 1767. Aquatint by Nicholas Pococke.

diameter. One worked only one pump, but this was 60 inches in diameter which Banks was able to measure to his own satisfaction as it was not working at the time.

On 17 June Banks rode out to Clevedon on a visit to Sir Abraham Elton, Master of the Merchant Venturers and a close friend of his uncle Robert. From Clevedon Court he visited Walton Lodge above the town and enjoyed the wide view across the estuary to Wales. He studied the curious lines on the steep hill behind the Court itself and on his way back to Bristol along Tickenham Hill passed by Cadbury Camp with its double vallum which he himself thought was Roman.

Next day, again haunting the very brink of the cliffs of St Vincent's Rock, he found a great quantity of bulbs which he thought might be the autumn squill, *Scilla autumnalis*, and a profusion also of *Ophrys apifera*, the orchid-like bee ophrys, in full bloom. That afternoon he spent some two hours with the Revd Alexander Catcot, vicar of the Temple Church in Bristol, inspecting his small but instructive collection of fossils. Among them the most noteworthy, he thought, were the elephant bones found embedded in ochre on the Mendip hills and the skeleton of another species, possibly *Lemur macauco*, some early form of primate almost complete and found in the same place. He was also shown a very good specimen of fungus puff-ball, *Lycoperdon fornicatum*, but which Banks himself was more inclined to diagnose as another of the same genus, *L. stellatum*, with its volva still adhering, which was unusual. Then, spurred by the Revd Catcot's information, he rose early next morning and again searched the ledges of St Vincent's Rock for specimens of *Veronica hybrida*, a particular kind of veronica which he found eventually growing rather sparsely there. Later, after breakfast, he went to Redland Court to see John Innys's garden, of which he had heard great things, but where he saw nothing of note, though the place was well stocked with thistles, nettles and docks. Whereupon he set off for London through Keynsham to Bath to reach New Burlington Street on 20 June, having looked closely, as he crossed the Marlborough Downs, at the stones called the Grey Wethers. These at one point near Silbury were being broken for road-mending and house-building. They reminded him of similar material which he had seen gathered for a bridge at General Conway's home near Henley and which he was then told had come from the Downs in the stratum overlying the chalk.

Waiting for him in town were two letters from Pennant. The first, dated 10 June, asked for the loan of drawings and bird specimens from Newfoundland. It also wished Banks well for his proposed journey to Sweden and his visit to Linnaeus whom Pennant professed not to admire, thinking him a poor zoologist and superficial in everything except botany. He also hoped that the natterjack toad, which Banks had promised him from Lincolnshire, would be described for him by Solander.

The second letter, dated 19 June, brought Pennant's hopes for a visit by Banks and Solander, and the loan of more drawings to be sent to him by the Chester coach. He also said that John Loten had agreed to the publication of plates from his Ceylon drawings.

In reply to these, Banks, near the end of June, pleaded pressure of business as a reason for not visiting Pennant combined with his current intention of visiting 'our Master Linnaeus' and

. . . Profiting by his Lectures before he dies who is now so old that he cannot long last . . .

a gloomy judgement of Linnaeus in his sixtieth year. He told Pennant that Loten had already given him the Ceylon drawings and that Sydney Parkinson was doing nothing else then but copying them as fast as he could. He excused his brevity on the grounds of his imminent departure for Lincolnshire where he promised to learn as much about natterjacks and dottrels as he could for Pennant's benefit. But, unaware of all this as yet, Pennant on 27 June again pressed Banks about the Loten drawings, urging him to allow Parkinson 'as a good copyist' to make drawings from them before Loten (who was just 57) died – 'Loten is old his wife is young' epitomized his fears.

Banks had been pursued from another quarter also. 'Ubicumque es in Terrarum locis?', wrote his uncle Robert from Edwinsford, fearing that his restless nephew might even then be in Sweden – or even in St Petersburg – for all he knew. He was quickly reassured by Banks who, in effect, at the same time, as a matter of duty sought the approval of his uncle for his Swedish plans – as far as they had gone – before setting out for Revesby Abbey in the last week of June. This affectionate concern touched Robert Banks-Hodgkinson to the point that, on 2 July, he replied with his warm appreciation, adding:

> . . . far be it from me to throw the least impediment in a Scheme that I daresay will be satisfactory hereafter & will forward the pursuit of natural History in which Vinyard you now place your principal Labour & which I hope will produce fruits of honor & happiness both to yourself [and] all your Friends amongst which you know I hope and believe I wish always to be with the first . . .

Here is an unequivocal recognition that Banks had by now formulated the broad plan of his professional future.

About ten days later, after his return from Revesby Abbey, Banks sent another letter responding to his uncle's approval of his scheme for foreign travel and his scientific intentions for the future but also announcing his intention to visit Edwinsford before wandering elsewhere. Back came an invitation dated 15 July, thanking him for his

> . . . kind friendly and truly affectionate letter which gave me very great pleasure and not less to Mrs Hodgkinson who heard you was got back to Town safe and determin'd to visit the Land of Cymri before any foreign soil. You certainly will never be more welcome anywhere than here or meet with two Persons yt. more sincerely esteem you . . . you may bring as many Horses as you please, we have hay and oats enough . . .

Banks-Hodgkinson fully approved his nephew's passing of the accounts at Revesby and the settlement of all outstanding debts during his recent visit to the estate but there was a tinge of rebuke, mild but resigned, in his comment

> . . . that you do not give them so strict an examination as you might do [as] if you was resident . . .

On the other hand he was

47

... extremely glad to find the drainage is likely to answer so well. I was always convinced if well executed the Plan could not fail for [in] this Age of improvement 'tis not impossible yt. the Fen may become the Finest richest Country in great Britain with Trees and Houses upon it – . . .

in which lies a glimpse of the vision he certainly shared with the heir himself. But as an absentee master of a fenland estate Banks was well served by the assiduous Benjamin Stephenson, the conscientious steward and unrelenting correspondent.

After his June visit Banks was pursued by Stephenson for the rest of July and into early August on many counts. There was the matter of fines on the unbranded horses of John Linton of Freiston impounded from Banks's fens in Holland; the fining (in a different sense) and racking off of the wine in the Revesby Abbey cellars; and the killing of a fat buck from the deer herd in the park with the carcass to be sent through Sleaford for collection at the *Spread Eagle* in Gracechurch Street.

From Oxford there was the business of Lord Tyrconnel's dues to Banks for thirds on his room in Peckwater Quadrangle. However these were small matters beside the persistent begging of Thomas Pennant; seeking the loan of drawings; the graphic services of Sydney Parkinson and Peter Mazell; the taxonomic diagnoses from both Banks and Solander; commissions for Banks to execute for him in Sweden with the Society at Uppsala and the purchase of zoological books there; demands for access to the housekeeper at No. 14 New Burlington Street and a fire for his comfort in the library during Banks's absence abroad. As some return for these great expectations Pennant was prepared to divulge a little of his own low cunning. Pleased to hear that Banks was proposing to take Sydney Parkinson to Sweden with him, Pennant advised that on their return any drawings should be concealed in the covers and bindings of books to deceive

... the Custom House officers who will demand a guinea each . . .

From all this Banks escaped on 13 August 1767 when he set out for the West Country and Wales on his visit to the honest warmth of Edwinsford society.

III

With Gibson's 1695 edition of William Camden's *Brittania* as the antiquarian reference for his travels he began with firm botanical intentions by spending the whole day of 13 August with the Revd John Lightfoot at Uxbridge. There he slept for the first night, receiving from Lightfoot a number of scarce plants gathered by the clergyman from many parts of Great Britain. Next day, on his way to Oxford, Banks visited the ochre pits on the top of Shotover Hill and the freestone quarry at its base. Then in Oxford he called on his old professor, Dr Humphrey Sibthorp, to search the library for a specimen of *Bufonia tenui-folia* probably a sort of toad rush. He found there in Sherard's collection, a specimen of *Cerastium* spp. a cerast or form of chick-weed, such as he himself had recently got from Norfolk, though both the Oxford specimens had been sent from Montpellier.

Next morning, 15 August, he travelled through Witney, Northleach and Frogmill to Gloucester. At Witney, near the turnpike on a bank, he was intrigued by a species of brome grass that he could not immediately place, suspected it might be *Bromus giganteus*, the tall brome, but prudently set down his own Latin taxonomic notes for later verification. From Gloucester during the next two days he travelled through the forest of Dean and Monmouth, Abergavenny and Brecon, Trecastle and Llandovery, to reach Edwinsford by Tally on the river Cothy on 17 August.

For the next three months he stayed at Edwinsford using it as a base from which to range alone or with his uncle, combing the neighbourhood for plants and exploring the ten thousand acres of mountain and valley in the Edwinsford demesne. He exercised his gun against the grouse on the hills and among the partridges, which were scarce that year, in the fields on the low ground near the house in some of the worst and wettest weather ever known during August and early September. During this delayed harvest he was interested to observe in some detail the use of the Welsh cradle scythe, or Hainault scythe, and the smooth efficiency of its operation; the method of binding and stooking the sheaves into waterproof stacks; and the use of hay-rakes six feet broad, so effective 'that scarce enough will be left for pigs and geese'.

After some grouse shooting on Mathlaine mountain on 26 August Banks and his uncle dined with a Mr Jones of Dol y Cothy and from there they inspected the 'Caves of Gogotha', a mystery then to the neighbourhood and to Banks, though he suspected them (rightly) to be Roman workings for an unknown metal. These were in fact the gold-mines of Ogafu near Pumpsaint on the line of Sarn Helen, though on these points William Camden did not give much help.

Then with most of the harvest at least in stooks, Banks and his uncle, on 15 September, set out for 'a little excursion' on horseback through Llanwrtyd Wells, Llandrindod, Trecastle, Brecon and Trevicca, ending their five-days ride together with an ascent of the Brecon Beacons. From the summit Banks took compass bearings and later deduced on a map that he had seen the Bristol Channel from Swansea to King's Road, and also Plinlimmon, the Wrekin and the Malvern Hills. On 20 September the party returned to Edwinsford with plans for an expedition into Pembrokeshire.

With the barometer standing at 32½ inches, higher than Banks-Hodgkinson could ever recall seeing, there was every prospect of fine weather ahead. Banks agreed, with his own assessment derived from the manner in which the early morning ground mists dissipated by slowly rising up the hills. So, on 25 September, the two men set out again. From Edwinsford to Llandeilo was an easy first stage to Carmarthen. They noted Newton or Dynevor Park as they passed, with its castle set high on a hill as 'one of the Prettyest things in South Wales' certainly, but in Banks's own view bearing no comparison with Piercefield. Nearby Banks stopped to observe:

> . . . in a slate quarry are found figurd fossils remarkable as I believe they are found nowhere Else. they are something like the Dudleigh fossils & seem then to be a species of Aphrodita but the sides or possibly the Tentacula of these are much Extended & wider they are always found flat & seem more to resemble a Butterfly than anything I can compare them to . . .

From Carmarthen their route lay through St Clear's, on 26 September, to Tenby and Caldy Island on the 26–28th, Pembroke and Milford Haven 29–30th, Haverford West on 1 October, through Trefgarn on the 3rd, Carmarthen again on the 4th and so home to Edwinsford on 5 October with Banks, as he said, 'well pleasd with my excursion into Pembrokeshire'. For all its flatness and rough uncultivated commons full of coal-pits he found the country much redeemed by the Ridgeway with its command of the sea along the coast of South Wales between Tenby and Pembroke. In point of detail also it was enhanced by his unexpected close view of Carew Castle, 'a most noble ruin', with its strange combination of Norman defensive and Elizabethan domestic architecture, the latter reminding him strongly of Burghley House – altogether an impression stored for an artistic record to be made some five years later.

All through these ramblings he had been noting antiquities in many different forms but none with such a curiosity as the various kinds of 'barrow' about which so little then was known. Thwarted in his urge to excavate the 'long barrows' near his aunt Margaret at Eastbury, he found himself at last able to indulge his ambition on the 'round barrow' so temptingly placed about 1100 feet up on Llansaddern. This lay about 40 yards from some heaped stones or karnea within 300 yards of a small monument, Croos Vair or Mary's Cross, on the parish boundary of Tally. Perhaps by today's standard of archaeological method it was rough but it was systematic and, for its date, reasonably well recorded in its detail, a written account with which modern antiquarians can play to make their own assessment of this early burial site, as Banks intended they should. His reputation as a student of antiquities yielded other fruits in the Roman coins from various sites among the Welsh hills and valleys, more or less supported by site data.

On 16 November he set out again with his own horses to fulfil his promised visit to Thomas Pennant. He travelled slowly, taking nearly five days on the way and arrived at Downing on 21 November. Here he spent more than a week with Pennant

 . . . intirely at home reviewing a collection of English Shells and Crabbs . . .

an intellectual experience and academic confinement which left him unusually bereft of words.

With evident relief, on 30 November, he was able to explore the Vale of Clydd on horseback and to ride along the sands of the Dee estuary fascinated by the herring fishery and the innumerable fishing boats along the shore. Then, on 3 December, delighted with the beauty of the road by the sea to Holiwell he turned north for his estates in Staffordshire.

Here was a turning point on his journey, a crossing of the common ground between science and industry. Much of the day he spent observing the manufacture of white lead from the raw metal mined in Halkin mountain – 'like derbyshire in its appearance & like it full of lead'. Passing through Nantwych, Middlewych and Northwych, he noted the process of salt recovery and its economics. Near Stone he observed the size of the dairy herds and the production and value of cheese per cow. Then, on 5 December, he reached Cheadle and for several days inspected his Staffordshire estate in a countryside which he found unattractive and with intolerable roads. On 9 December he visited the Duke of Devonshire's rich copper mine at Ecton by the river Manifold, noting the lines of the strata on the exposed hillside and within the great chambers of the mine itself their more complex arrangement as he descended over 900 feet into its depths below the hilltop. Here at the bottom he found two different species of fungus growing in profusion on any timberwork present. In one of the drift passages at this depth he was also able to point out a small deposit of bitumen, a substance the miners themselves had not noticed before, and also traces of a whitish ore which he thought might be antimony.

Above ground again he continued his walks through the parish of Cheadle, taking note from a farmer, among other things, of some essential points in the life history of the mole. Then on 18 December with John Gilbert, his own agent at Cheadle and Kingsley as well as estate manager to the Duke of Bridgewater, he set off for Worsley to study the Duke's new canal works. Their road lay through Burslem where Banks found time to examine the potteries with their new engine lathes just introduced by Josiah Wedgwood. Staying that night at Knutsford, they saw the beginning of the canal passage through the hill called Hare Castle, well arched for about 100 yards but with a mortar so soft that Banks feared for its safety. Next morning they reached the canal at Dunham where it was being carried over a deep valley. As they rode along Banks noted the engineering details of its construction in its course to Worsley where they saw a mortar mill at work. Travelling on to Wigan on 21 December they watched the bubbling of fire damp gas (methane) from a coal-pit through water and its burning off above the surface. Returning next day through Ashley they saw the Duke's quarry from which he got the quick-setting Sutton lime and where Banks carefully noted the depth, thickness and direction of slope of the strata and their character. From Ashley he visited the 6000 acre extent of Chatmoss which the Duke had been trying to drain for some six to seven years. Here Banks dismounted to walk over its surface studying the structure and vegetation with the loving attention of a fen-man for whom bogs and bog plants remained a favourite hobby. By now, though, winter had settled down hard.

On Christmas Day the two men set out for Rochdale to see an alum works, and on the following day they visited a weaver to see 'the Famous Shuttle at work'. This was one of Kay's flying shuttles producing broadcloth at a small fraction of what it once cost per piece. The alum works were three miles beyond Blackburn, from which they walked. Here Banks had his first view of the process of crystallization which he would follow again elsewhere. They returned to Worsley on 27 December over bad roads and through weather as cold as any that Banks had felt before. Two days later he spent some seven hours in the Duke of Bridgewater's coal-mine studying the stall or bay method of working and the nature of the strata within which the seams lay. Pausing for a quick visit to Manchester, its public library and museum, he approved the streets themselves but found the architecture of the public buildings not at all to his taste – particularly the Exchange and the new church:

> . . . the first seems heavy to a degree, the second is a mixture of Gothick & grecian architecture which may please some tastes but mine I confess it does not . . .

On 31 December he returned to finish his underground exploration of the Duke's coal-mine, the mechanics of its water drainage system, and to write his considered assessment of the canal itself. This had been planned for 34 miles, including the branch to Manchester, and of this 21 miles had been finished when Banks saw it. He was particularly struck with the ingenuity of the engineering for the common tasks as well as for the new problems that had emerged, all of them inventions thought of and executed by Brindley, the designer-engineer of most of the canal. Banks described James Brindley as

... a man of no Education but of Extreemly strong natural parts ...

who had been recommended to the Duke by John Gilbert. Gilbert had found Brindley in Staffordshire

... where he was only famous for being the best Millwright in the Countrey ...

Banks and Gilbert left Worsley on 2 January 1768 to study the salt works at Nantwych again and in some detail before returning to Cheadle through Newcastle-under-Lyme where Banks recorded an immense flight of larks in the neighbourhood. There was also another flight which flew from south to north over Ashbourne in Derbyshire

... such as had never been seen in the memory of man being three hours in Passing over the town ...

Then on 6 January, his last day in Cheadle, he studied a new spinning invention introduced by George Godwin to the town from a friend in Yorkshire. This he found easier to sketch than to describe.

Turning aside now from industry to the arts and architecture, Banks left Cheadle and John Gilbert on 7 January to meet his friend John Sneyd of Bishton near Wolseley Bridge on the river Trent. Together they visited the great Anson mansion of Shugborough four miles away to enjoy its design and the decorating Greek marbles. A large company was present and the social demands of the dining room deprived Banks of an immediate view of what he had come to see. But after dinner he managed to slip away, with a candle, to view his host's principal marble – an Adonis – the fruit of the family's patronage of James 'Athenian' Stuart. Discovered near the statue at last by its owner, Banks was treated to a lecture on its graces by comparison with which the Venus de Milo was rated but a clumsy work.

The next day Banks and Sneyd returned at Anson's invitation to spend all day at Shugborough and to stay overnight. They were now able to explore at leisure and to admire the house and grounds with the statuary marbles, the Anson Arch and the Lantern of Demosthenes designed by James Stuart and just then under construction. But Stuart's Temple of the Winds was rated by Banks as his least successful work

... scarce more beautiful than a common Octogan Pidgeon House ...

Of living things he saw here for the first time a white long-haired Persian cat, the last survivor of a breed which Anson once had until it was destroyed by a distemper that had been especially virulent in Staffordshire. But Banks was especially interested in what he was shown as the Corsican deer or goat. Though it was new to him, he correctly diagnosed it as the moufflon or musimon of Strabo quoting his Latin source, otherwise the *Capra Ammon* of Linnaeus or *Ovis musimon* Pallas of today. He then set down in English his clear and succinct diagnosis from which there is no doubt that his recognition was correct.

Returning to Bishton on 9 January he set out through Stafford for Lillieshall near Newport to meet John Gilbert again and Gilbert's brother. Then on 10 January the three of them visited Lord Gower's lime-kiln and the canal he had made for the transport of both lime and coal from his mine at Donington Wood which they visited the next day. Between the coal-beds at Donington Banks saw the ironstone, much of good quality, which was one of the sources of supply for the Darby works at Coalbrookdale, and he studied this at close quarters within the mine in its natural strata. On 12 January he set out for a protracted visit to the Quaker works beside the Severn at Ketley, Horsehay and at Coalbrookdale itself. Here for three days he observed the whole process of smelting and casting iron. On 15 January he ventured into two of the safer iron pits to study the raw material *in situ* and to draw up a section of the strata mainly from the information of the miners themselves. On 16 January he returned to stay with John Sneyd at Bishton again.

Banks and Sneyd now made another visit to Shugborough to see, among other things, a Carthaginian head of Juno and a *bas relief* by Scheemaker derived from Poussin's 'Arcadia' and which Banks rated as superior to all others of the kind in the collection. He also saw a dead specimen of the great spotted loon, *Colymbus arcticus*, killed on a nearby pool in September 1767.

On his way to Stafford on 19 January he diverted to the garden of Sir William Wolseley, Wolseley Hall, near Bishton, to see the heated grape wall and one of the first cedars of Lebanon brought to England and now a tree with a girth of 10 feet 2 inches. In Stafford he saw two collections – a bad one of shells and fossils belonging to a Mr Green; and another belonging to a Mr Newton, the nabob returned from the East Indies with a vast fortune but his collection a confused mass of broken shells, drawers full of Indian artefacts and closets full of china. Among this confusion Banks found one species of *Echinus*, the sea-urchin, entirely new to him but, as a punishment, had to admire all the other miscellanea willy-nilly. He eventually escaped and set off for Birmingham.

There, on 21 January, he went to Soho armed with a letter to meet Matthew Boulton for the first time and with whom he evidently stayed. For several days he immersed himself in the manufacturing virtuosity of Birmingham – the making of buttons in steel, copper and tortoiseshell, watch chains and keys, saws, gun-barrels and locks, and the cottage industry of enamelling. He also glimpsed a vision of the future in a 'fire engine' which went with a wheel instead of a beam, on which he remarked:

> . . . trifling as this alteration is it seemd to me a great improvement as the Engine went Perfectly steadily without those Jerks and catches so frequently observd in them . . .

At Wednesborough he examined the coal-seam which was said then to be the thickest in Britain, 30 feet in the pit he entered but said to be 35 to 40 feet at times elsewhere, and one of the best for smelting. Again he closely followed in the shafts themselves the method of working the seams and the configuration of the various strata. Then on 23 January he went to Dudley to see the method of quarrying limestone and burning it, as well as to note the arrangement of the strata finding, as he had supposed, that everywhere the coal lay above the limestone. Moreoever he was able to assure himself that in the upper stratum of the limestone, but more often in the loose rubble just above, were found those species called Dudley fossils. These were said to be, by the contemporary terminology a sort of sea-louse, *Pediculus marinus*, in the *Philosophical Transactions*, but he was sure they were another species of the same genus as those he had seen in the slate quarry near Llandeilo at Dynevor Park.

Then, returning to Birmingham, he bade farewell to his new friends of the Lunar Circle yet to come, Matthew Boulton, Captain James Keir, and Dr William Small, and departed for Coventry the same day. Here he noted its ribbon manufactures, its impressive parish church and, of course, the Godiva legend. On 24 January he saw both Kenilworth and Warwick Castles, viewing them both with his antiquarian eye but, as a naturalist, not ignoring the two large pairs of horns in the great hall of the latter – one recently from America believed to be elk; the other a 'fossil', moose-like and much the larger by Banks's measurements. Next day on 25 January he paid his literary respects to Shakespeare at Stratford-on-Avon.

He now travelled on to Oxford through Long Compton with a detour on 26 January to see the Roll Right or Kingstones, and continuing through Woodstock he came at last by that approach to

> . . . a place which I always see with pleasure as there I spent those years of Education which probably are the happyest that Life affords . . .

For a day or two he sought out the few friends who were still in residence finding them mostly in Christ Church. Here he was delighted to see a large collection of pictures put up in the Old Library among which he especially remarked on some excellent works of the Caraccis. This had been the bequest of General John Guise, an old alumnus of the college and, in Banks's opinion, at last something had been done to redeem the reputation of the university which, in the matter of art, 'was before this despicable enough' with not 'a single picture worth a farthing'. But there was also another development of great significance associated with his old college friend and senior, John Parsons, returned from Edinburgh, established as the first Lee Professor of Anatomy at £200 a year, and now supervising the building of the first, the old, anatomy school itself.

He then set off for London on 28 January to review, as he said, his old fossil haunts on Shotover Hill associated with the geology of the calcareous Oxford stone and the strata above the freestone bed. Here in the ten feet or so above the blue stone layer were found, he said, the large bones and vertebrae of various animals. Beneath the stratum

> . . . are plenty of shells particularly oysters, tree oysters & Cornu ammonis but much the greatest Quantity of the first of which there is one bed Called the main bed 4 inches in thickness which runs all over this Part of the Countrey here are also Selenites & pyrites in abundance . . .

The Oxford freestone itself he noted as lying some 26 feet beneath the surface in a stratum about 22 feet thick perfectly level or with only a very slight dip

> . . . a congeries of Shells of many Kinds but mostly melted away . . .

From the quarry he went to the yellow ochre pits at the top of the hill, worked by open-cast method at depths seldom more than 17 or 18 feet and reckoned to be the best in the world. No one was working the pits when he came by and so he went on to sleep that night at Henley. Returning to the hill next morning he rated the ochre mine 'a Most noble work' should it ever be finished but that its present operation was ill-managed. With this last opinion formed he set out for London to reach New Burlington Street by dinner time on 29 January 1768.

IV

The plans for a Swedish journey, so much spread about since his return from Newfoundland and deferred for his visit to Wales, had ebbed further during the autumn. When he reached Chester on 20 November 1767 he had paused to write to William Perrin, then in Paris, that he was pleased to have put off his own journey as he would thus have time to study Perrin's *hortus siccus* when it arrived. He was definite also about two other points: his firm resolve never to be tempted into Parliament and never to consider marriage as an experiment with his own happiness until driven to it by the extent of his own misery. However, he assured Perrin that he would emulate his long letters 'when I have a country to see and describe', leaving a hint that this might still be Sweden but with a growing vagueness, as though other ideas were maturing.

On 19 November 1767 the Committee of the Royal Society had recommended that the Government be petitioned to send a ship with observers to follow the transit of Venus from islands in the South Sea. It is possible that Banks already had some inkling of this in letters received from London or in his meeting with Thomas Falconer, Recorder of Chester and kinsman of Thomas Pennant. Royal Society gossip ran free and fast among the Fellows and their friends in those days. For Banks a seed had been planted before June 1767 when he had got for William Perrin two copies of the illicit *Voyage round the World in His Majesty's Ship* The Dolphin ... By an Officer on Board the said Ship. Soon after seeing this account with its vista of a new world of adventure in the South Sea, Banks decided 'to visit the Land of Cymri before any other foreign soil'. Between the middle of July and mid-November when he left Edwinsford, Banks and his uncle had seen much of each other as they rambled through Wales together, cultivating and discussing that 'Vinyard' of natural history in which they were clearly agreed it was fitting that Banks should place his 'principal Labours'. Banks evidently avoided any overt mention of the South Sea as the immediate vineyard of his hopes until his return to London. He left the notion of a Swedish journey alive with Pennant, Falconer and Gilbert until the Royal Society's petition to the King was concluded with the royal approval at the end of February 1768. From this date there is a fast widening circle of those who knew that Banks had dropped his Swedish plans and was now committed, at least in his own intentions, to the Royal Society voyage to the South Sea. Perrin in Montpellier seems to have heard of this by letters he received in April at about the same time as Banks replied to a letter from Thomas Falconer, dated 15 February from Chester:

> ... but to say Truth my Intended Expedition (which I find our Freind Pennant has mentiond to you) has so intirely filled up my time Lately that my Correspondents in General find too much Reason for Complaint ...

Banks was already at work on the literature of southern discovery, and Falconer replied, on 16 April, acknowledging that Banks's plans were more extensive than he had supposed, saying that he regarded Banks as well qualified to investigate the natural history of new lands and to add to the stock of new knowledge from that quarter. Even earlier than this, Thomas Pennant wrote from Oxford on 10 April, well enough informed to recommend to Banks a young midshipman for the expedition coupled with some practical advice about umbrellas for tropical climates. Even more revealing was the current gossip which, on 11 April, Dru Drury was eager to pass on to Peter Pallas in St Petersburg:

> ... You know ye Transit of Venus will happen in June 1769 & as an accurate & nice observation of it in different parts of ye World will be of great utility & consequence to Astronomy Some Gentlemen in that Science are to go out this year from hence to ye South Seas in order to make those observations. Mr. Banks a Gentleman of considerable fortune is extreamly desirous of availing himself of this opportunity & going with them in ye same ship in order to make discoveries in Natural History & to this end is actually making preparations for that purpose. His being a strong Naturalist possessed of a Large Fortune & being determined to spare no expence are circumstances that give all well wishers to that study ye highest expectations of his Success.
>
> The Rout is intended first to Madeira Islands, from thence they are to go by easy Voyages along ye Coast of Brazil, thro' ye streights of Magellan & to refresh at some of ye Spanish Towns on ye Western Coast of South America having already a Passport or Permission from ye King of Spain to do so. After they have made ye observation wch. is to be done on some Island as much to ye Southward as possible they propose to return to Europe by ye way of ye East Indies. The whole will in all probability not take them less than 2 years & a half. Hence you perceive we have Gentlemen in England whose desires for ye improvement of Nat: Hist: are equal to those of any Person in ye World. But I must inform you of one circumstance & that is that Mr. Banks has judgement enough to prevent him engaging in Affairs of State & consequently detaching himself from all Parties has more leisure to pursue his darling Study. I wish for my Soul we had many more of his Stamp in this Kingdom but while avarice Luxury & Ambition hold ye Reigns we must not expect alterations for ye better ...

So from Perrin at Montpellier to Pallas at St Petersburgh by the middle of April the news had spread abroad that Banks had engaged himself to the voyage into the South Seas that was preparing as Great Britain's most ambitious part in the international 'geophysical' year of 1769. The Admiralty, it is true, may have thought fit to be mysterious and Banks, in his turn, may have chosen to be vague with Thomas Falconer but there is no doubt that the essential plan of the expedition was becoming clear at least to a small coterie of naturalists in and about London.

In the counties too the word had spread, so that before 20 April John Gilbert at Worsley, Banks's late travelling companion, knew that his travelling plans had changed. And from Gilbert White at Selborne there came a letter dated 21 April with his understanding, from a letter of Thomas Pennant written from Chester some days earlier, that Banks was soon 'to leave the Kingdom again in pursuit of natural knowledge', regretting that neither he nor Pennant could visit in what was a good district both for botany and zoology lamenting that

> . . . I must plod on by myself with few books and no soul to communicate my doubts and discoveries to . . .

but wishing Banks

> . . . all health and a great deal of success and satisfaction in your laudable pursuits, a prosperous voyage and a safe return . . .

From this correspondence alone it is clear that from the middle of February 1768 at least, it was becoming widely known that Mr Joseph Banks had explicitly committed himself to the Royal Society voyage to the South Sea even before its full purpose was understood, the ship selected or its commander appointed. Much had obviously happened in the few weeks since Banks had returned to New Burlington Street on 29 January 1768 – almost exactly the anniversary of his return from the voyage to Newfoundland, South Labrador and Lisbon. The interweaving of these events into the pattern of the *Endeavour* voyage to the South Pacific and the circumstances of its mounting is an element either distorted or missing in the usual accounts.

CHAPTER 4

THE 'GREAT PACIFIC OCEAN'
1768–1771

On 15 November 1767 James Cook as master of HMS *Grenville* anchored at Deptford after his Newfoundland survey. At the same time Joseph Banks was preparing to leave Edwinsford for his journey into the industrial Midlands. While Cook at Mile End was setting his Newfoundland charts and journals in order for the Admiralty, Banks was studying the art and engineering of canal navigation, the extraction of coal, copper and iron, the smelting of metal ores and the metal manufactures of Birmingham.

Within the same month a sub-committee of the Royal Society Council was deliberating

> ... the places proper to observe the ensuing Transit of Venus, and the method, the persons fit, and other particulars relative to the same ...

to produce on 19 November 1767 its report for the Society. In it Mr Alexander Dalrymple was recommended as:

> ... a proper person to send to the South Seas, having a particular turn for discoveries, and being an able navigator, and well skilled in Observations ...

with the implication that he would be a satisfactory commander of the expedition.

Dalrymple had already impressed the Council with his industry and apparent 'turn for discoveries' by his recent presentation of the case for resolving the problem of 'the Southern Continent', which was such a dilemma in the Admiralty mind. In October 1767 he had printed his summarizing chart of the South Pacific between South America and New Holland, marking thereon what was known or could be deduced from the literature of explorers' routes and discoveries to the year 1764. With this he had printed the first few copies of an octavo pamphlet of some 103 pages supplementing the graphic evidence of the chart. The astronomical intentions of the Royal Society, however, were centred on the deliberations and the calculations relating to the transit of Venus.

In this field the Revd Nevil Maskelyne, FRS, the Astronomer Royal, had already had experience with his attempts at observing the transit on St Helena in 1761. From this had emerged his work on the determination of longitude by lunar distances and its incorporation in his *The British Mariner's Guide* of 1763. With his appointment as Astronomer Royal in 1765 came the establishment of the *Nautical Almanac* and in 1766 his *Tables requisite to be used with the Nautical Ephemeris* for the general convenience of seaman. With these aids to rather more precise navigation across the challenging blanks and uncertainties of Dalrymple's South Pacific chart, Maskelyne had included with the *Nautical Almanac* for 1769 his 'Instructions relative to the Observation of the ensuing Transit of Venus'. From these sources the sub-committee of the Royal Society Council was prepared to define the arbitrary geographic limits in the South Sea within which acceptable positions for observing the transit could be fixed. As points of preference they decided

... the islands of Mendoza, Rotterdam or Amsterdam would be very proper for the purpose or any laying between them ...

a view supported by Maskelyne in his letter to the Council of 3 December 1767.

Within the first week after his return from his western travels Banks entered these affairs in person on Thursday 4 February 1768 when he took his seat as a guest of the Royal Society dining club then meeting in Middle Temple Hall. How far he was aware of the extent and maturity of the Society's plans is not clear, but there can be little doubt that thereafter he was certain of the opportunity it presented and that he quickly determined to exploit it. The previous week on Thursday 28 January, Maskelyne had presented to the Royal Society Council his paper on the instruments needed for the observation on the transit, and framing of the 'Memorial' to the King for the operating expenses. Banks's early and close interest in the proposed expedition is attested by the sequence of his appearances as a guest at the dining club of the Society in this vital month of February 1768. Not only did he attend on the 4th but also on the 11th, 15th and 25th – the very period within which the 'Memorial' was presented to the King and the royal grant of £4000 bestowed to meet the cost of the transit observations.

Lord Shelburne, as Principal Secretary of State, opened the matter with the Admiralty for the first time on Monday 29 February 1768, conveying the King's orders that a suitable vessel for the Royal Society expedition to the South Sea be found and manned by the Royal Navy. However, it was not until Thursday 24 March that the President, Lord Morton, formally told the Council of the Royal Society that the King had ordered £4000, clear of all fees, to be paid to the Society for the expenses. It is probable that Banks knew of this from conversation at the dinner of 25 February. Thereafter events moved swiftly. On 29 March the *Earl of Pembroke*, a cat-built Whitby collier of some 368 tons, had been selected by the Navy Board, possibly in association with Alexander Dalrymple, and bought for £2800. On 1 April this information had been given to the Royal Society by Philip Stephens (Secretary of the Admiralty), and on 2 April Lord Morton waited on Sir Edward Hawke (1st Lord of the Admiralty), to discuss 'the number and quality' of the party which the Society proposed to embark on the expedition. In expounding the scientific plans for the voyage Lord Morton nominated Alexander Dalrymple as the Society's choice for its principal observer and as commander for the voyage. This was vetoed by Sir Edward as wholly unacceptable to Admiralty practice with ships of the Royal Navy, a decision conveyed by Lord Morton to his Council on 3 April. Dalrymple was duly told and he withdrew from the expedition, adhering to the conditions he had set out for the Council in his letter of 18 December 1767; namely the full command and management of the voyage for himself without which he would take no part at all. So for a while the question of a commander hung in abeyance.

For Banks there were no such conditions, only negotiations, with all the persuasive skill he could muster, with the Council of the Society and the Lords of the

Admiralty. Astronomy and geographical discovery were the recognized and accepted bases of the Royal Society plan for the voyage. Natural history in any special form was not. Banks himself now ensured that it would be so to a degree that had not distinguished former British expeditions. Moreover it would also exceed that of the French expedition on the *Boussole* with Bougainville, Philibert Commerson and Pierre Veron, which was to precede the *Endeavour* by a few months into the South Pacific. There are few documents to tell us how he managed it. This is not remarkable for, as Banks was to note about other expeditions, with everyone in London discussions at personal meetings left only faint traces for posterity. That he had been preoccupied with his 'Intended Expedition' during February and March, in a manner and to a degree that almost obliterated correspondence, he confessed to Thomas Falconer in so many words at the end of March or early in April. By then it is probable that all essential decisions had been made, all resistance to his place on the voyage overcome.

As the amiable Fellow dining with the Council of the Royal Society in February, Banks may have had little difficulty in gaining the Society's acceptance of him as a supernumerary in natural history on the voyage. Such an extension of the plan in pursuit of natural knowledge lay well within the intellectual sympathies of his influential friends both on and off the Council – however novel or unnecessary it may have seemed to the astronomers or mathematicians. More decisive in his favour, perhaps, was his expressed intention of financing the cost of such an addition to the expedition, and his ability to do so. His voyage to Newfoundland and south Labrador had already proved his mettle as a traveller on a vessel under Royal Naval command in distant waters and his abilities as a naturalist working alone under hazardous field conditions. The range of his qualities as a man of courage and of harmony in his daily relations among seamen was well attested. To his immediate friends in the Royal Navy he was an acceptable companion under the rough conditions of their trade. To the Lords of the Admiralty much less was apparent. They had easily disposed of the notion of a civilian commander, an idea 'so totaly repugnant to the rules of the Navy'. Now they were faced with another civilian scientist to increase the personnel and to strain the accommodation which the *Endeavour* could provide. The critical occasion for Banks was probably on or soon after 2 April 1768 when Lord Morton was so firmly rebuffed over Dalrymple as commander. There was apparently a bluff acceptance of Banks alone as a supernumerary on his own merits by Sir Edward Hawke – but only alone and only an acceptance in principle.

Here was a test of Banks's resilience in meeting opposition and of his skill in negotiating difficulties. Rebuffed but not cast down he drew no doubt on the advantage of membership of the select circle in the Reading Room of the British Museum. Knowing how Whitehall bureaucracy worked, Banks now outflanked the First Lord and, by his own account, resolved his problems through the office of the First Secretary. Sir Edward Hawke had approved the passage of Banks alone; five months later a civilian party of nine led by Banks sailed on board the *Endeavour* from Plymouth.

II

The paths of Joseph Banks and James Cook were now rapidly converging again. The occasion was the matter of the Esquimo canoe, procured for Banks by Captain A.

Wilkinson of HMS *Niger* in the season of 1767 and consigned home in the care of Cook on board HMS *Grenville*. But the *Grenville* had unfortunately grounded in the Thames estuary in November on its way to Deptford and the canoe had been washed overboard and swept ashore somewhere alone the Essex coast. Wilkinson had told Banks, by a letter dated 18 December 1767, how Cook could be found at Mile End or, better, by enquiry at Deptford to see how the canoe could be recovered, perhaps by advertising. Nothing could be done, however, until Banks returned to London at the end of January.

On 4 March 1768 James Cook reported to the Admiralty with his journals and charts from the previous year's work in Newfoundland and to prepare the *Grenville* for the season's surveying ahead. On 5 March Philip Stephens sent the King's command to the Navy Board to find a proper vessel for the South Pacific voyage. Thus during March it is probable that Cook and Banks met at the old Admiralty in Whitehall, however briefly, even before the *Endeavour* command was settled. A month later, after the rejection of Alexander Dalrymple, the way was clear for the appointment of Cook, at some date after 6 April but probably before 12 April 1768.

On Thursday 14 April Banks dined with the Royal Society club for the last time until his return from the voyage in 1771. For the next four months he was preoccupied with his preparations for the expedition of which he was by now an important part.

From Worsley on 20 April John Gilbert wrote to Banks, having heard that his travelling plans were changed and that his attention now was

. . . upon Nobler things if possible than to Examining the Bowels of the Earth . . .

From Selbourne on 21 April the Revd Gilbert White also wrote to say that he had received a letter from Thomas Pennant with the news that Banks was going

. . . to leave the kingdom again in pursuit of natural knowledge . . .

This was a morsel that may have reached Pennant from Thomas Falconer to whom Banks had been reasonably explicit some two weeks earlier

. . . Our destination You seem desirous to Know & have been kind enough through Mr. Pennant to give me hopes that I may be Favour with some hints from you for which I can assure you that I should be particularly obligd.

The Admiralty have thought fit to be Mysterious about us so that I myself can not Positively say where we are going and when I tell you that it is my opinion we are for the South Seas I must beg the favour of you not to mention it again for those parts however we are pretty certainly design'd and if we proceed to make discoveries on the Terra Australis Incognita I shall probably have a finer opportunity for the Exercise of my Poor abilities than Ever man before had as there Seems to be a strong Probability From the Scarce Intelligible accounts of Travelers That almost Every Production of Nature is here very different from what we see at this End of the Globe . . .

This information in Banks's undated letter almost certainly belongs to a point no later than the first week in April 1768. But there is evidence from another correspondent that the possible association of Banks with the Royal Society plans relating to the transit of Venus observations was already gossip during March.

At Montpellier William Perrin had gleaned these rumours certainly by the end of March, coupled with word of the death of Laurence Sterne on 18 March in Bond Street, London. At this time Banks was an occasional visitor to the Perrin house in Bloomsbury Square as William sent home batches of his *hortus siccus* with other commissions for his sister. It may well have been through one of her letters to Montpellier that Perrin heard of Banks's new plans but in a slightly garbled form suggesting 'some Part of Asia' as the goal to observe the transit. William Perrin conveyed his blessing on this idea to Banks in a letter dated from Aix on 15 April 1768 but which had been written at intervals on the journey from Montpellier and therefore begun possibly some two weeks earlier. He had intended to write from Montpellier immediately to enquire about Banks's own part in the undertaking but was thwarted by his leave-taking from so many people there. Rather than lose more time he decided to write as opportunity offered on the way north. His thoughts, compounded in this letter during the tedious coach stages over the roads of central France, cast a revealing light on the background of past discussions with Banks and the small circle of which they were both part. Here is a plain expression of the international scientific rivalry both in ideas and in published achievement supported by a battery of arguments favouring this new English adventure in natural history, Perrin said:

> ... I shall be very glad to see the Royal Society execute such a Project & to see you bear a Part in it, the very Scheme is for the Honour of the Nation & if compleated in all its Branches as well as it will be in yours I have no Doubt but the Execution will be so too: It appears to me too that we are called upon to do something of this Kind for both in Botany & Mathematicks (which perhaps I have not named in their proper order) I think Engd: has hardly made suficient Advances of late years to support her ancient Character. In regard to Botany From this Time last Century till at least the Death of Ray Engd: had certainly the lead in Europe & she preserved too this Superiority perhaps until 1724 the Time of the Publication of the 3rd Edition of Ray's Synopsis which Linnaeus perfers to every Book of its Kind in the World, but for this Superiority she was in a great Degree indebted to Dillenius, a Stranger, tho' a naturalised one, on which I cannot help observing en passant that from the earliest accounts we have even to the present Time & at no Time more than at present Foreigners of Merit in all Arts, Sciences & Professions have in no Country of Europe met with so much Encouragement as in Engd: & those too even of this Nation [France], notwithstanding our Rivalry ...

Developing this theme, Perrin considered that from about the death of Dillenius (in 1747) English botany had declined to the point when

> ... about that Time Linnaeus & his Followers transferred the Palm from us to Sweden ...

Moreover he thought perhaps the same might be said for mathematics for though he held high the reputation of English mathematicians yet he thought:

... they have perhaps published nothing so likely to do Honour to their Nation as the Relations of the Voyages of Condamine &c to Measure a Degree under the Line & of Maupertuis [&] his Companions for the same Purpose at the Arctic Circel ... I am in hopes that the several objects which will be or ought to be at least attended to in such an Expedition as that in which you are to bear a Part will furnish such Discoveries as may do Honour both to the Projectors & Executors of the Scheme ...

All this high minded scientific nationalism bespoke a common bond of ideas and arguments between these two young Oxford alumni extending back to their College years together but polished and refined by their more recent exchanges in the small coterie at the British Museum. There was also that other catalyst of thought closer to the hub of the present excitement in that small volume of which, in May 1767, Banks had sent two copies to Perrin in Paris at the start of his French excursion – *A Voyage round the World in His Majesty's Ship The Dolphin, Commanded by the Honourable Commodore Byron ... a faithful Account of the Several Places, People, Plants, Animals, &c. seen on the Voyage ... a minute and exact Description of the Streights of Magellan, and of the Gigantic People called Patagonians ... An accurate Account of Seven Islands lately discovered in the South Seas*. By an Officer on Board the said Ship.

Unauthorized and highly coloured, as it was, this most recent account of a circumnavigation in the southern hemisphere, apart from some details – and, of course the controversial Patagonian Giants – carried sufficient truth to capture a wide European interest and was accurate in all its essentials, as time has proved. Translations followed in quick succession: into French in 1767; Italian in 1768; Spanish and German in 1769. Its publication was perhaps the critical event which directed Banks's attention from the northern to the southern hemisphere as veritable *terra incognita* for the naturalist as well as for the geographer and the navigator. But in June 1767 he was still sacrificing

... every Consideration to an opportunity of Paying a visit to our Master Linnaeus & Profiting by his Lectures before he dies who is now so old that he cannot Long Last ...

as he framed his excuse for deferring a visit to Thomas Pennant. Such plans, however, had weakened by 15 July when his uncle Robert was pleased to hear that he had returned from his visit to Revesby Abbey

... determin'd to Visit the Land of Cymri before any other foreign soil ...

It is clear that the idea of a voyage to the south had been maturing for more than six months when Banks returned to London at the end of January 1768. By the time that William Perrin's letter reached him in New Burlington Street he was already immersed in the details of his preparations for the voyage in which his part was now certain.

III

For James Cook also the future was now determined. He had been introduced to the Council of the Royal Society on Thursday 5 May 1768 to receive and accept the offer of service as an observer of the transit in company with Charles Green, assistant to the Astronomer Royal. For each the reward was to be 100 guineas a year with a victualling allowance of £120.

On that same day the manning of the *Endeavour* began, with Cook not yet formally appointed to the command. On that same day also the yards at Deptford erupted in disorder as a body of merchant seamen rose in demand for higher wages. In Stepney Fields another 5000–6000 were gathered in a mass meeting on the same issue. More were demonstrating in front of the Queen's House and yet more were gathering in St George's Fields south of the river and organized to march on the palace in St James's with a petition to the King. By 9 May the Navy Office reported that all ships in the Thames, without exception, had been disabled from sailing. On 10 May a number of sailors, variously estimated from 5000 to 15000 marched to Palace Yard to present a petition to Parliament, to give three cheers and then – to disperse. But on that day just across the river, with John Wilkes lodged in the King's Bench prison, a more violent scene was played out in the 'massacre' of St George's Fields.

A week later, Captain Samuel Wallis, from his anchorage in the Downs, brought HMS *Dolphin* along the Thames on his return from the South Pacific with details of his new discovery of King George III's Island or Tahiti. His arrival was providential, offering at once a specific site for the transit observations and a stiffening of experienced young men for the proposed circumnavigation. The commission for James Cook (2nd) to be 1st Lt *Endeavour* Bark was dated 25 May, and on Friday 27 May 1768 he hoisted the pennant. For the next two months Cook prepared the ship for sea 'with all despatch' against a tide of industrial unrest.

During the worst of this public disorder in London, Banks was at Revesby Abbey resolving the problems of estate management with Benjamin Stephenson that would arise in his absence and extending his hospitality to Thomas Pennant whose visit redeemed an old promise. With Stephenson he found time to plant Scotch firs in the ling lawns at Tumby where they struck well. With Pennant he clarified at least some of the fen mysteries of Lincolnshire to that literary entrepreneur of natural history whose claims would ever pursue Banks.

On this May visit Banks no doubt gathered in the 16-year old James Roberts of Mareham-le-Fen to join the 26-year old Peter Briscoe, the faithful attendant of his Oxford years, his London studies, the Newfoundland voyage and his county travels since.

By 9 June the Council of the Royal Society was ready to direct its Secretary to write to the Admiralty making formal its request for Banks and his small party, eight persons in all, to be received as supernumeraries on board HMS *Endeavour* – Banks, Sydney Parkinson, Alexander Buchan, Herman Spöring, Peter Briscoe, James Roberts, George Dorlton and Thomas Richmond – but not Solander as yet.

After spending some hours at No. 14 New Burlington Street on 10 June Gilbert White spoke gratefully of the time that Banks had afforded him,

> . . . notwithstanding he was so soon to leave the kingdom and undertake his immense voyage . . .

but, although Solander was also there, White did not then include him as one of the *Endeavour* group. Just when Solander, according to report, sprang to his feet at Lady Anne Monson's dinner table and volunteered as Banks's companion for the voyage we cannot be sure. It is a matter of certain record, however, that on 28 June the Trustees of the British Museum, under the signatures of the Archbishop of Canterbury and the Lord Chancellor at a General Meeting in Montagu House, formally released Solander from his official duties as Assistant Keeper, arranging for John Obadiah Justamond to serve in his absence on the *Endeavour* voyage. So the civilian party under the aegis of the Royal Society was complete when, on 22 July 1768, the Admiralty wrote to Cook with instructions

> . . . to receive on board the said Bark the said Mr. Charles Green & his Servant & Baggage, as also the said Joseph Banks Esq. and his Suite consisting of eight Persons with their Baggage, bearing them as Supernumeries for Victuals only, and Victualling them as the Barks Company during their Continuance on board . . .

A week later, on 30 July, Cook had taken the *Endeavour* from Deptford to Galleon's Reach near Rotherhithe to receive from the Admiralty his instructions for the voyage before sailing on the first leg down river to rendezvous with Banks and Solander rather more than two weeks later at Plymouth.

IV

As Cook sailed out of the Thames it was just four months since the Whitby cat the *Earl of Pembroke* had been acquired by the Navy Board and converted into HMS *Endeavour* Bark. It was somewhat less than six months since Joseph Banks had committed himself to the idea of the voyage as a desirable exercise for his scientific energies. Within these six months there had been a variety of impediments to be overcome rather less formidable than the first Lord's obduracy but collectively diverting him from the tasks of preparing for so perilous a voyage.

There was always Pennant, not so much asking as demanding his attention and claiming in effect the freedom of New Burlington Street should he want it, with a list of books, drawings and specimens for his use in Banks's absence, a fire in the library and the services of the housekeeper. There was also the request of John Sneyd for the loan of his herbarium, an easy favour to grant – probably as an insurance against possible raids by Pennant – though Penelope Sneyd's request for textiles from China and Japan was pressing optimism too far.

Then there was the nagging problem of George, the current black sheep of the family, at odds with his stepbrother Robert Banks-Hodgkinson, drinking himself to death 'merely to get rid of his troubles' at the *Castle* in Richmond – or so reported the distant cousin that other Joseph Banks to that other uncle Dr James Hawley. This family problem was duly passed to Joseph IV for action to set the alcoholic captain on his way to a country cure at Edwinsford, which he reached on 12 July 'well warmed within' after a 'blooding' at Llandovery.

There had been election matters too, calling for help with cash and voting interest for Constantine Phipps toward a seat in the House of Commons as a member for Lincoln at the election of 19 March. There was a steady trickle of estate worries sent by Benjamin Stephenson, such as the riots of the Holland fen men in Boston resisting

Sir Edward Hawke, later 1st Baron Hawke, First Lord of the Admiralty 1766–71.
Painting by Francis Cotes.

the enclosures. In Staffordshire there were the estate rents to be finalized with John Gilbert and some coal-mining problems at Cheadle. There was also the family at Edwinsford to be mollified, but as time pressed despairing pleas from his uncle for news of the *Endeavour* and its company went unanswered. Banks was cutting his social ties thread by thread immersing himself in technicalities, business matters and the company of those from whom a separation raised no strong emotions.

His impact among the women on these fleeting occasions left more shock waves in their hearts than in his. From Lisbon he had been pursued with touching stories of Miss Molloy

... who is ready to attend you whenever you send a frigate of war for her ...

and of the little Italian 'Condesshina' whose affections Banks had evidently touched. But now, as he prepared to leave London there was the problem of Miss Harriet, the second daughter of Mr and Mrs Blosset of Chancery Lane, friends of Daniel Solander and James Lee. They were devotees of the British Museum and its garden walks as guests of Solander rather than as special protegés of Banks himself. But Harriet Blosset sighed with a romantic melancholy designating Banks as the target and supposed willing victim of her amorous darts. Banks, however, while exuding charm as a bachelor of means, seems to have kept himself aloof from real entanglement. His attitude in this matter of female snares and the mirage of wedded bliss he had quite recently made known to William Perrin. It was simply to remain unmarried *sine die* – even as Harriet Blosset sighed and supposed she might die when he sailed for the South Sea.

On Monday 15 August Banks and Solander attended the opera *La Buona Figliola* with the Blosset family and M. and Mme de Saussure from Geneva. After the performance they supped with the Blossets in Chancery Lane when Saussure gleaned a good impression of the plans for the voyage from Banks. He also saw evidence of Miss Harriet's affections for Banks expressed, he thought, somewhat as the prudent coquette. The Swiss noted enigmatically that Banks drank freely to hide his feelings but were they thwarted love and hope deferred? Embarrassment more likely, if Fanny Burney's insights some years later have any value. Nevertheless Saussure gathered the impression that he had met a remarkable man.

It was the same man who next day received Cook's summons to join the ship at Plymouth and could reply soberly to William Perrin's letter from Aix. Banks's valediction from New Burlington Street on Tuesday 16 August 1768 epitomizes the past six months:

I am now on the Brink of Sailing on the Expedition you hinted at in your Last I shall therefore send as ample an account of the Expedition as I dare trust to paper hoping it will be some satisfaction to you to guess at the Station of a freind from whoom or of whoom you will not hear any more for three years at least.

In march last the Government at the Instance of the Royal society resolvd to send out a ship to any part of the world which should be found most Convenient for an observation on the transit of Venus which the latter was to supply with Proper instruments & observers the Place was soon fix'd upon somewhere in the South Sea over a large part of which the Limits Convenient for such an observation are Extended.

Philip Stephens, FRS, later 1st Baronet, secretary of the Admiralty 1763–95.

Upon considering the plan of this Scheme it immediately occurd to me that it would be a most desirable one for me to Engage in the Whole tract of the South Seas & I may say all South America is Intirely unknown to a Naturalist the South Sea at least has never been visited by any man of Science in any Branch of Literature

Upon looking at the Plan of the voyage it might easily be seen that this would not be the Extent of it a Ship in the midst of the South Seas would never attempt to return against the S E Trade she must therefore go forwards & visit the Ladrones some parts of the East Indies & the Cape of Good Hope all places much worth the attention of a Naturalist, this the Least of the plan she may do much more as if you look upon a Chart you may see

I was much Encouragd in this Scheme by our Freind Solander who so heartily agreed in the excellence of it that he promis'd to make application to the trustees of the Museum & if Possible get Leave to accompany me which has has [sic] done & got the necessary leave of absence signd & is now going with me I take also besides ourselves two men to draw & four men to Collect in the different branches of Nat. Hist. & such a Collection of Bottles Boxes Baskets bags nets &c. &c. &c. : as almost frighten me who have prepard them

England you say is behind hand with the rest of Europe in Undertakings of this Kind you will not wonder at it when I tell you that on application to the first Lord of the Admiralty when I stated the Case & told him what I meant to do his answer was you sire are very welcome to go & it will be my care that you have every convenience which I can Procure for you but we cannot find room for people skilld in Botany & drawers of Plants this at first hurt me much & I had almost given over my Plan but upon Application to the Secretary of the Admiralty he undertook to do it all without any more trouble to me So I have not been near Sir E: H: Since but made Every application to the Secretary who has done Everything we wanted with as much alacrity & spirit as could be wishd

adieu I thought to have made this much Longer but am sent for by Express to Join the Ship will write again from Madera [sic] till then believe me Sincerely Yours . . .

There was indeed another letter, not from Madeira but from Rio de Janeiro before all touch with known waters was lost. But with Harriet Blosset in London there was a lingering memory, two days after Banks and Solander had gone, in her visit to New Burlington Street, escorted by M. de Saussure to view the Banksian insects:

. . . a superb collection beautifully arranged, insects pinned with the name underneath each, English and foreign, in drawers covered with glass and framed in cedarwood . . .

This arrangement doubtless owed much to the summer collaboration between Banks and Johann Fabricius who, at their first meeting, had also been so helpful in preparing and stowing the expedition equipment on board the *Endeavour* at Deptford. The next day, Friday 19 August 1768, another colleague, John Ellis set down his impressions for Linnaeus. With his *Essay toward a natural history of the Corallines* of 1755 behind him, his continuing work on the zoophytes and its offspring in his modified 'aquatic' microscope made by Peter Dollond, Ellis had already made his own contributions to the voyage; not only with the book in its reference library and with the instrument amongst its equipment but with four years of a working association with Banks. Few men were better placed to give Linnaeus a clear picture of the expedition to the South Seas and of Banks's preparations for it.

V

Of the scientific equipment assembled by Banks on the *Endeavour* very little is known. The young traveller had at that time no system of records matching that of the Navy Board; the bound volumes and the neat Solander cases were yet to come. There are, however, enough hints from the scraps that survive. John Ellis to Linnaeus is a useful opening:

> ... No people ever went to sea better fitted out for the purpose of Natural History, nor more elegantly. They have got a fine Library of Natural History; they have all sorts of machines for catching and preserving insects; all kinds of nets, trawls, drags and hooks for coral fishing; they have even a curious contrivance of a telescope by which, put into the water, you can see the bottom to a great depth,

Left English compound microscope similar to that given to Joseph Banks by the Duchess of Portland for the *Endeavour* voyage.

Right Ellis aquatic microscope similar to the four such instruments taken by Banks on the *Endeavour* voyage.

70

where it is clear. They have many cases of bottles with ground stoppers of several sizes to preserve animals in spirits. They have the several sorts of salts to surround the seeds; and wax, both bees-wax and that of the *Myrica*; besides there are many people whose sole business it is to attend them for this very purpose . . .

In 'many people' there is the hint of that exaggeration which ever since has inflated the image of what Banks was supposed to have prepared for the voyage. As field assistants there were only four – Briscoe, Roberts, Dorlton and Richmond. Of these only Peter Briscoe had any former experience; the boy Roberts had everything to learn, and so perhaps had the two Negro servants, Dorlton and Richmond. Apart from the artists, Parkinson and Buchan, who had their technical part to play, there was, of course, Spöring as the invaluable secretary/artist with a medical education and knowledgeable at least with zoological specimens. Everything else rested on the knowledge and expertise of the two scientists of the party – Banks himself and Solander. For the rest John Ellis confirms what Banks had said in his farewell screed to Perrin, that his own concern with marine biology and that of Johann Fabricius with entomology at least had been well provided for.

For a more general view of the stowage problems presented by the Banksian equipment much may be deduced from John Codd's account of 17 June 1768. As a carpenter he had been engaged with repairs and fittings at No. 14 New Burlington Street but his work was extended to making the principal containers for the equipment and for the collections. No dimensions are given but experience and a few surviving items give an indication: a wainscot box with brass hinges and clasp; 20 strong chests with hinged lids and locks; eight strong tin cases with hinged lids and locks; six strong cases with hinged lids and locks internally partitioned for the glass 'rounds' or specimen bottles with ground glass stoppers, noted by Ellis; five small boxes of which four had locks fitted to accommodate documents, plate and various small items; finally one large case for the book cases. With an ample supply of brass screws and nails and many thousands of iron nails of various sizes with other sundries this part of the account amounted to £70.

In addition, several casks and kegs for bulk spirit and the preservation of the animal specimens larger than those which the glass-stoppered bottles would hold were gathered from other sources. There may have been 200 or more of these bottles.

For the collection of botanical specimens the portfolios, vasculums, presses, drying and storage paper would not have differed much from the items used in a modern expedition. These would have been stowed in the 20 large wooden chests. For the artists the paper and pigments and other supplies may also have found a place in the tin boxes, while the wainscot drawing tables would probably form part of their cabin furniture as far as space allowed. At other times they might be found in the great cabin, with the writing bureau of Banks, but ashore, as at Tahiti, in the central large bell-tent intended for this work. At sea, this bell-tent, with the great bulk of the equipment not wanted on the voyage, was probably stored in the after-peak deep below the officers' cabins. For instant use Banks's small boat – or lighterman's dinghy as Cook described it – somewhere on deck.

For Banks and Solander, and occasionally Parkinson, there was a battery of hand lenses, watch glasses, forceps, razors and small knives, compounds for mounting, spirits and chemicals for fixing and preserving, enough for most contingencies, with supplies of medicaments for the ills and accidents inseparable from such a voyage.

The most important instruments were the optical items: the three-foot achromatic telescopes for the study of passing coastlines and inaccessible places; the four Ellis 'aquatic' microscopes; the compound microscope of the Culpepper design by an unknown maker, said to have been a gift to Banks from the Dowager Duchess of Portland. Of these perhaps the most important were the 'aquatic' microscopes in their fish-skin cases, adaptable in practice both for observations in marine biology (as originally intended by Ellis) and as early forms of the dissecting microscope for entomology and botany.

For personal protection, as well as for the collection of birds and the larger mammals, there was a small armoury of pistols and guns; some in individual fabric covers; some clipped into a partitioned, baize-lined wainscot case, double-locked. Among those which at the end of the voyage were serviced and repaired by Messrs Griffin and Tow there were: eight brass-mounted guns, six of them fitted with bayonets; one termed a Brummett gun; two wall-pieces; eight pieces termed rifle bullet guns, two of which were German; one air-gun; and only one other specifically termed a shot-gun. With these Banks supplied the accessories: 200 or 300 pounds of gunpowder and shot; hundreds of flints for guns and pistols; ram-rods and gun-slings; shot-pouches and powder-flasks; bullet-moulds; and small tools such as turnscrews, wrenches and punches. Banks was a skilful performer with such weapons, as with the array of fishing gear and, under his hand, apart from their use for the collection of bird species and fish specimens, they added to the diet of the ship's company.

Then there was that large case for books, the 'fine Library of Natural History'. As with the equipment no list apparently survives, though some individual volumes are known. Such a one is the *Systema Naturae Regnum Animale* of Linnaeus the twelfth edition, 1766–7, interleaved and annotated in the hand of Herman Spöring, the 'writer', and now in the British Museum (Natural History), London. So also is the interleaved and annotated *Species Plantarum* of Linnaeus, the second edition, 1762–63, both volumes of which rest at the same museum. Other titles with more or less solid claims to have been with Banks and Solander on board are lodged with the remnants of the Soho Square library in the British Library. Some bear traces still of a hard life at sea; others are re-bound and 'conserved' with such traces cleaned away by nineteenth-century librarians. Altogether by direct and indirect evidence between 60 and 70 titles can be identified comprising over 100 volumes in all. In size they range from small octavo to fairly large folio, but mostly octavo and quarto. In subject they cover the classic publications of more than a century before the voyage of relevant travels by land and by sea – Thevenot, Narborough Tasman, Dampier, Sloane, Shelvocke, Frezier, Anson, to the collections of Harrison and de Brosses – and of natural history – Piso and Marcgrave, Sloane, Ray, Plukenett, Weinmann, Burmann, Edwards, Buffon, Rumphius, Linnaeus, Brisson, Pallas, Pennant and others. If there had been no more than these, the voyage would have been well served with significant items against the background in terms of the current knowledge about the southern hemisphere and the near void in both in the geography and natural history of the South Pacific Ocean, in particular – but there was something more.

There were two octavo volumes of recent vintage and a chart – small items but significant beyond their first appearance in their influence on the thoughts and decisions of Cook and Banks on the voyage. Even if the author of the anonymous *A Voyage Round the World in H.M.S. Dolphin . . .* of 1767 were not himself on board the

Endeavour, there were certainly two officers from that voyage now serving under Cook. Of those who sailed in the *Dolphin* under Byron, there were, in the present Ship's company, 3rd Lt John Gore, twice a circumnavigator and master's mate Charles Clerke. Moreover, of those who had sailed in the second *Dolphin* voyage under Wallis, apart from John Gore, there were also the *Endeavour*'s master, Robert Molyneux, and master's mate Richard Pickersgill. These officers formed a solid core of experienced seamen with some knowledge of the Pacific on whom Cook could depend and who had a background of intelligent observation on which Banks could draw.

Then, for all its wishful thinking, there was Alexander Dalrymple's printed but unpublished small volume, also of 1767, *An Account of the Discoveries made in the South Pacifick Ocean Previous to 1764*, summarizing rather more systematically and advancing in time the field covered by Charles de Brosses in his *Histoire des navigations aux terres australes* of 1756, with its excellent Vaugondy maps. But with Dalrymple's 103-page volume there was also his *Chart of the South Pacifick Ocean, pointing out the Discoveries made therein Previous to 1764*; both had been entrusted to Banks by the author before the voyage.

Here was the chart 'Publish'd according to Act of Parliament Octr. 1767', albeit without the newly-found King George III's Island. It showed clearly how much could be done after observing the transit of Venus apart from setting a course for the Ladrones in the tracks of Byron and Wallis. This was what Banks was hinting at in the letter he had sent to William Perrin within hours of leaving London to join Cook at Plymouth. The challenge lay in that vast expanse of unsurveyed ocean south of the Tropic of Capricorn between the west coast of South America and the enigma marked as Staat's Land with the blank east coast of New Holland, and whether or not there was any substance to the notion of a 'Southern Continent' somewhere between.

VI

The voyage of the *Endeavour* had already begun for Cook when he weighed anchor from Galleon's Reach on Saturday 30 July 1768. He had come to an anchorage in Plymouth Sound on Sunday 14 August and had immediately summoned Banks and Solander to join the ship. Their servants and artistic staff were on board already with perhaps some 20 tons of baggage and equipment. From 18 August the two naturalists lodged ashore, while the last fittings in their cabins were made by the dockyard shipwrights, an exercise platform laid over the tiller on the quarter-deck, and until the strong westerly winds abated. Some of this tense waiting time for Banks and Solander was relieved, as before the *Niger* voyage over two years previously, by the hospitality of William Cookworthy. Then in the early afternoon of Thursday 25 August 1768, with the milder winds veering more northerly, a signal jack at the fore topmast brought Banks and Solander on board at last. At two p.m. in the words of Cook, the *Endeavour*

> ... set sail and put to sea having on board 94 persons including Officers Seamen Gentlemen and their servants, near 18 months provisions, 10 Carriage guns 12 Swivels with good store of Ammunition and stores of all kinds ...

73

So also for Banks now the voyage had begun which, more than any other perhaps for nearly two centuries, has been mulled over and romanticized but only from sources, in a literary and historical sense, incomplete or more or less corrupt. It was not indeed until the publication of Cook's journal of the voyage in 1955 and of its necessary complement in that of Banks in 1962, both edited exhaustively by J. C. Beaglehole, that the means for a reasonable appraisal of its true character and achievement was made accessible. The enterprise has thus been relieved of the mystifications which sprang from the first anonymous account illicitly published by Becket in 1771, the official Hawkesworth version and the troubled Parkinson journal of 1773, with the sequence of other contemporary editions, foreign translations, abstracts and adaptations, which have bedevilled the literature ever since. In the bibliography of the voyage so much is now embedded under the key word of 'Cook', arising from the mass of literary, historical and scientific scholarship since, that it is a difficult, not to say a delicate, task to approach the theme from any other angle. And yet for the *Endeavour* voyage, if not for the two later Pacific voyages of Cook, the historical perspective merits another glance.

In all essential points the enterprise which had now begun must be considered a Royal Society expedition initiated 'for the Promotion of Natural Knowledge' in the fields of astronomy, geography and natural history; authorized and in part financed by George III, supplemented by the private funds of Joseph Banks; and serviced, as to the ship and crew, by the Royal Navy at the King's specific command, responding to the 'Memorial' of the Royal Society.

In its conception therefore it differed from the two former Pacific voyages of HMS *Dolphin*, which had been organized with political and naval objectives against a background of international and, particularly, Anglo-French rivalries emerging in the southern hemisphere. In its management, however, a conflict of interest was bound to arise with the Admiralty apart from its repugnance to the Royal Society's proposal of Dalrymple as commander of the voyage. Whatever the 'philosophic' aims of the expedition it was never likely that the Admiralty would concede control once a naval ship had been requisitioned for a purpose so closely allied to its own policies and intentions. Nor was the Royal Society, as an impecunious and suppliant civilian body able or likely to contest the issue of command so long as its prime objectives were met. In effect there was no contest for, in one central issue, the Admiralty and the Royal Society were at one – 'the Discovery of the Southern Continent so often Mentioned' and designated in the 'Additional Instructions' to Cook as 'the Object which you are alway to have in View'. This was an extension of the Admiralty instructions to Byron and Wallis and it absorbed Dalrymple's obsessive geographical enthusiasms which the Royal Society, for its part, had been prepared to graft on to its initial purpose of astronomical observation of the transit of Venus. This much had been implicit in its recommendations of Dalrymple as a man 'with a turn for discoveries'. Equally implicit was the Society's acceptance of the young Joseph Banks as one of its Fellows 'well versed in Natural History' and of 'great Personal Merit'. Here was an important auxiliary 'for the Promotion of Natural Knowledge' especially as a builder on the existing geographic foundations. Banks also had the notable virtue of being 'a Gentleman of Large Fortune' able and ready to sustain the considerable cost of his part in the voyage, a private entrepreneur of science in the national interest.

The course and details of the voyage need not be laboured here. They are now well established in the journals of its two principal figures published at last under their own authorship, annotated and free, on the whole, from the literary incrustation and confusions of the Hawkesworth synthesis. The Royal Society expedition of HMS *Endeavour* 1768–71 emerges as a striking partnership between two remarkable men unique perhaps for the relative harmony of the working association between them and the stimulus of their examples. It remains also unique among British voyages of exploration, for no other was conceived or conducted on such a pattern – a collaboration of civilian science under royal patronage with royal finance, joined with private enterprise funded from a county rent roll and executed under Admiralty management. That these elements were compounded without undue heat of fusion into a three-year circumnavigation successful in its main intentions is a testimony to the character and abilities of Banks, the young landsman from Lincolnshire, and Cook, the older Yorkshire seaman.

VII

After the inevitable bouts of seasickness in the first week at sea Banks wasted no time in settling his party into their respective routines and himself to his journal during the 18 days' run to Madeira. Marine zoology proved more fruitful than he had at first thought with specimens of salps and medusae captured with the small casting net, until Thomas Richmond in his eagerness let it slip into the sea. This yielded material for Solander's first taxonomic descriptions and Sydney Parkinson's first drawings. So rich and so large a field of natural history it seemed to Banks, 'almost unthought of when we embarkd in the undertaking', that, slow as the *Endeavour* sailed, he would have been content 'with a much slower pace'.

At Madeira, from 12 to 18 September, horses and guides were provided by the British Consul, Mr Cheap, for Banks and Solander to explore the island. However, even with these aids, they wisely chose to confine their collecting to an intensive survey of an area with a radius no more than three miles from the town of Funchal. With the generous help of Dr Thomas Heberden, principal physician on Madeira, some 329 species of plants and over 200 specimens of arthropods were gathered in this first land foray, a fine harvest to exercise Banks and Solander in their diagnoses and descriptions on the long slow leg of the voyage south, and for Parkinson, Buchan, and even Spöring with their pencils and their paints. For nearly two months, across the tropics of the North and into those of the South Atlantic, these Madeira specimens set a pattern of operation in the work at sea which was closely followed for most of the voyage until the distractions and disaster of the last year.

For each specimen, whether plant or animal, the sequence was clear – description and diagnosis by Banks and Solander first; then a selection for drawing by Parkinson or one of the other two, Buchan or Spöring; and finally a check-list of the Linnaean names with a local common name if it could be determined and, less regularly, a note of the place of collection within the region. For Banks this regime was diversified when, in the tropic calms off the west coast of Africa, south of the Cape Verde Islands, he launched out, alone or with a servant, away from the ship in his small boat, collecting marine specimens with his landing net and shooting birds. After seven such boating excursions just north of the equator his enthusiasm was temporarily checked by a sharp fall in his cabin, sustained in the course of some exercises he had devised for himself with a rope. This left him ill for several days with concussion and unwilling to venture out from the ship again until it was well to the south of the equator near the Tropic of Capricorn off the coast of Brazil. Here on 8 November Banks and Solander boarded a fishing boat and bought the greater part of its catch for 19s. 6d. with an attractive haul of new species for description.

Then came a period of acute unhappiness in the harbour of Rio de Janeiro. There, for some 24 days, in sight of the open field of South American natural history, one of the most attractive plums in the voyage was all but wholly denied to the aspiring young 'man of Science' in that 'branch of Literature'. From 13 November until 7 December 1768 the *Endeavour* lay under the armed surveillance of the Portuguese who remained totally unconvinced of the peaceful intentions of the voyage. Banks and Solander were consistently denied permission to land in pursuit of their collection. Only Cook and the ship's officers had that right and then only for the limited purposes of supply and replenishment. Together Cook and Banks drafted and re-drafted with care their memorials of protest to the Viceroy, Rolim Antonio de Moura, Conde d'Agambuja in a dignified exchange for some ten days to no avail. Old-fashioned courtesies concealed the frustration which Banks with difficulty contained. But it seeped through in his letter, echoed in that of Solander, to Lord Morton, President of the Royal Society, sent by the Spanish brig on its return from Buenos Aires to Cadiz, dated 1 December, and burst into full literary view in Banks's letter to William Perrin by the same mail:

> ... Before you receive this you will have traveld over alps & appenines & seen the customs of many nations & people but never I will venture to say met with so illiterate unhumanizd I may say Barbarous a set of people as I am now in the Possession of three weeks have I been laying at an anchor in this river the banks of which are crowded with plants animals &c. such as I have never seen before all this time I have not been permitted to set my foot upon land because forsooth the Gentry here think it impossible that the King of England could be such a fool as to fitt out a ship merely to observe the transit of Venus from hence they Conclude that we are Come upon some other Errand which they think to disappoint
>
> O perrin you have heard of Tantalus in hell you have heard of the French man laying swaddled in linnen between two of his Mistresses both naked using every possible means to excite desire but you have never heard of a tantalized wretch who has born his situation with less patience than i have done mine I have cursd swore ravd stampd & wrote memorials to no purpose in the world they only laugh at me & exult in their own penetrations to have defeated so deep laid a scheme as they suppose ours to have been ...

Balked but not defeated entirely Banks contrived to glean something of Brazilian natural history. At dawn on 22 November he managed to get Peter Briscoe and James Roberts ashore until, long after dark, they returned with a good harvest of plants and insects. They repeated a foray two days later. Then on 25 November Solander visited the town in the guise of the ship's surgeon. On the following day Banks himself managed a day on land from before dawn until late at night, meeting many people from whom he bought stores for the ship as well as collecting whatever came to hand, as he summarized for Perrin:

... You know that I am a man of adventure & as I scapd hanging in England have now taken it for granted that I am born for a different [end] in pursuance of this opinion I have venturd ashore once evading a boatload of soldiers who look after us & found such things as well repaid my risk tho the next morn the Viceroy had intelligence that such a thing had been done so I dare not venture any more ...

The confinement on the ship in the heat and humidity of the Tropic of Capricorn, aggravated by the discomfort of remaining on board even while the ship was heeled down for cleaning, was not entirely without benefit to the collections and the observations. The *Endeavour* lay within a quarter of a mile of the shore and much could be seen by telescope. An occasional bird could be shot and a fish caught while, with Monkhouse, the surgeon ashore almost every day, many plant species could be brought aboard in the fodder for the sheep and goats. Seafood bought at the shore market also augmented the marine species caught from the ship. At departure one last hot day on shore in passing Ilha Raza was spent strenuously gathering plants and insects 'in tolerable plenty' to enrich the Brazilian collections, a final relief as they at last broke free from 'these troublesome people' and their guard-boat on 7 December. Altogether some 315 plant species were listed by Banks from the vicinity of Rio de Janeiro and Ilha Raza, of which some 38 were nominated for drawing by Parkinson, with one bird 'Loxia Brasiliensis', apparently *Ramphocoelus brasilius* Linn.

Two weeks later, in latitude 36–37°, on 22 December, Banks let pass a large school of the southern pilot whale as specimens too large for his small harpoons but soon after, with Solander, put out in his dinghy while the new sails were bent on the *Endeavour* ready for the Cape Horn passage. On this day and the next, while the calm lasted, he shot from the little boat a range of petrel species (*Macronectes* sp., *Pterodroma* sp., *Pelogroma* sp., *Fregetta* sp.), netted some holothurians and medusae, harpooned a loggerhead turtle, probably *Lepidochelys kempi* (Garman); and shot his first specimen of the wandering albatross (*Diomedea exulans* Linn.), a bird in its second-year plumage with a wing span of nine feet. These were immediately described by Solander and recorded by Parkinson, one hopes, before the celebration of Christmas when, as Banks wrote

... all good Christians that is to say all hands get abominably drunk so that at night there was scarce a sober man in the ship, wind thank god very moderate ...

With the ship brought to under a mainsail Banks found the night a bad one with his bureau overturned, his books careering over the cabin floor battered by gales from the Antarctic.

VIII

Through intermittent gales and calms Cook gradually brought the *Endeavour* round the coast of Tierra del Fuego. As he worked the ship through the Strait le Maire along 'Staten Land' pitching violently in a gale from the south-west, Banks and Solander ventured ashore during the late afternoon on 14 January 1769. Here, in what is now Thetis Bay, they gathered, in slightly more than four hours, about 100 plant species of which, said Banks,

... every one was new and intirely different from what either of us had before seen ...

but of which Cook said,

... at 9 [p.m.] they return'd on board bringing with them several Plants Flowers &ca most of them unknown in Europe and in that alone consisted their whole Value ...

a bleak comment on an efficient exercise in field botany.

The next day the ship anchored in the Bay of Good Success and that afternoon Banks and Solander made their first contact with the Ona Indians of Tierra del Fuego. Then, on 16 January, while Cook surveyed the Bay and Gore supervised the wooding and watering, Banks led a party to botanize and penetrate as far inland as they could. They started early on a day that began

... vastly fine much like a sun-shiny day in May ...

With Banks there were Solander, Green, Monkhouse, Buchan, Peter Briscoe, James Roberts, George Dorlton, Thomas Richmond, Stephen Forwood the gunner, two other seaman, and Banks's greyhound.

In the euphoria of release from the cramped five months on board and seduced by the botanical expectations raised by his first collections in Thetis Bay, Banks, with a head full of thoughts on homoclimes and adaptations, had begun the day in search of alpines on the distant hill. Then, in the early afternoon, Buchan had an epileptic fit as a gale from the south-west brought flurries of snow and rain and the most penetrating cold that Banks confessed he had ever felt. The first to succumb to this sudden chill was Solander, about eight in the evening after Banks had abandoned any thought of a return to the ship that day. Then George Dorlton and Thomas Richmond gave up and could not be moved. With Buchan now recovered, Banks sent him forward with some of the others to prepare a fire under shelter while he and Peter Briscoe, with two of the seaman, stayed with his Negro servants and Solander. At last he got Solander to the fire but, returning for Dorlton and Richmond, found them beyond movement and the former insensible. Together they had drunk the whole of the party's rum supply and thereby hastened their own deaths. The state of the weather precluded making a fire and all that could be done was to improvise for them a rough bed and covering of branches. After an hour and a half of this work with Banks it was Peter Briscoe who now began to fail and who reached the fire only with difficulty. By six in the morning both Richmond and Dorlton were dead. By eight the sun had appeared and after a breakfast on grilled 'vulture', shot the previous day and carefully apportioned as their only food, the ten survivors set out for the ship which they reached in the early afternoon. Here they were all 'refresh'd' and put into warm beds – except Banks, who took a boat out into the bay hauling the seine net although without success.

For the next two days the strong south wind prevented any more landings but on 20 January Banks and Solander augmented their collection of molluscs and plants along the shore and ventured two miles inland to a village of the Ona Indians, in spite of the cold wind and scudding rain. Such were the last few hours of this best early recorded contact with the Onas of Tierra del Fuego and the subjects of Alexander Buchan's understandably few drawings at the time. Banks's keeping boxes were full of new botanical specimens, some 147 species by the manuscript list of which 78 were selected for Parkinson's attention. By now, as Banks remarked, the draughtsmen were so far inured to the vagaries of the ship's motion that it took more than the foul wind as they sailed from the Bay of Good Success on 21 January to deflect them from their work. The course was now set past Cape Horn to the *Endeavour*'s furthest south at 60°4′ S. and 74°10′ W. on 30 January 1769 – one year almost to the day since Banks had returned from his Midlands journey to become involved in the voyage now so far on its way.

From here, about the northern limits of the drift ice, the ship veered to a course broadly north-west into the Pacific. During the first week of February Banks took advantage of the brief calms, in spite of a bilious attack, to launch out from the ship and shoot more specimens of the albatross and petrel species, primarily for science but also as welcome items for the cook's galley. On 5 February Banks was so far recovered that he could join the ship's company in their preference for the albatrosses he had shot and which, now garnished with a savoury sauce, were served above the fresh pork on the table at the same time.

For two months the *Endeavour* held this general north-west course into the tropics but with calms enough only for Banks to make four excursions from the ship in his dinghy, netting his marine specimens and sampling the oceanic bird life with his gun, capped by his boatful of 69 dead birds on 3 March.

The tropical rain squalls of the late summer in the Pacific with hot damp air driving from the north through the window crevices of his cabin on the starboard quarter, directed his thoughts properly enough to the chart from Dalrymple and the speculations on the 'Southern Continent'. He found some pleasure in noting that over the long diagonal sweep from Cape Horn to latitude 25° S. and longitude 129° W. no land had been seen and that so far 'the opinions of Theoretical writers' had been disproved by the

> ... the number of square degrees of their land which we have already chang'd into water ...

which had no great help to the counterpoise theory either. Banks was intrigued by the great blanks in the charts of the South Pacific Ocean and, as he had written to Perrin on 16 August 1768, the challenge to 'discovery' that they posed. But he was no blind convert to the notion of a 'Southern Continent' beyond the fact that it was a useful hypothesis to be tested by direct exploration and survey. As he saw it on 20 March 1769 much of the ground for that hypothesis had been whittled away. However on the next day, 21 March, as he made his last small boat excursion from the ship for some time to come, he noted the steady flight of birds to the NNW, towards where Dalrymple had noted on his chart that Quiros had placed his islands of San Juan Batista La Encarnacion. The eastern Tuomotus were very near and the central phase of the expedition was about to begin.

At about ten on the morning of 4 April land was sighted by Peter Briscoe, a small island which, from the mast-head, was seen to be almost circular, with water in the middle and so named by Cook Lagoon Island. This was Vahitahi and for some days Banks spent hours high at the mast-head with his telescope studying the shore of the sequence of islands that lay across their course and what he could see of the human life ashore and afloat in their canoes as the ship tacked its way through the Tuomotus. His few days of incipient scurvy at the end of March had been swiftly countered by Dr Hulme's lemon juice and he was in good health for the landing on Tahiti now so near. He had been diligent with the sauerkraut (the salted cabbage), and the Admiralty's wort as an anti-scorbutic, but neither had impeded the development of symptoms. However six ounces a day of his own concentrated 'Lemon juice No 3', which Hulme had given him, had restored him in a week.

Rumours of high land to the west, on 10 April, had sent Banks to the mast-head but at sunset doubt remained. The next day this was removed and on 13 April at seven a.m. the *Endeavour* was anchored in Port Royal Bay 'King George the thirds Island' surrounded by canoes whose occupants

> . . . traded very quietly and civily, for beads cheifly, in exchange for which they gave Cocoa nuts Bread fruit both roasted and raw some small fish and apples . . .

Banks and the Maohi people of the Society Islands had met at last. During the next three months the process of change in the South Pacific, which Wallis in the *Dolphin* and Bougainville in the *Boudeuse* within the previous 18 months had set afoot, was now by the visitation of Cook and Banks in the *Endeavour* to be irrevocably determined. The primeval millenium of human occupation among these islands was at an end. The era of white European penetration of the South Sea had truly begun with Banks as one of the most powerful reagents in this new synthesis of cultures.

The encampment on Point Venus at Matavai Bay, Tahiti 15 April–13 July 1769. From a lost drawing by Sydney Parkinson, engraved by S. Middiman, 1773.

IX

The quiet civility of the first hours at the anchorage in Matavai Bay soon gave way to an uneasy groping for a working relationship that would allow the main purposes of the visit to succeed, and, hardly less, the gathering of knowledge on the island complex, its peoples and natural productions. From the beginning it is clear that Banks was the central agent in establishing a dialogue, first, by signs and miming, then by more direct communication within a week or so from his own acquired insights into the spoken language of the Maohi.

After two days of exploratory social contacts on shore, the first accommodation of the expedition on Point Venus, erected on 15 April, was one of Banks's small marquee tents. It was the butt of Banks's musket which drew the symbolic line of defence while it was being put up and while Cook marked out the plan of the small fort within which it would be contained. Soon after it was Banks who, with a single shot, killed three ducks, to the astonishment of the islanders and the satisfaction of Cook as a warning of the power behind the civilities. But it was from the marine guard on Banks's tent that same day that the first and only human casualty among the native population was inflicted by the *Endeavour*'s company, a hasty shot in the tensions of these first contacts. Then Banks on 17 April suffered the loss of Alexander Buchan (from epilepsy), to his own distress and the further depletion of his team. By 18 April his three tents were in position on the sands of Fort Venus – the large bell tent, 15 feet in diameter, flanked on each side by a marquee 20 feet long and 15 feet wide – and that night Banks and Solander slept ashore for the first time. On 1 May, the fort area, some 55 yards long by 30 yards wide, was complete with its defences and defending party of 45 men, and the observatory with its instruments for the transit observations had been set up.

What was perhaps the first resident European settlement in the south Pacific had now been established, however brief its tenure. Defensively armed as it was by custom and prudence, it was by intent a peaceful outpost of scientific enquiry and trade. Banks was the symbol of both facets. Daily, he sat at the seaward gate of the fort trading with the native Maohi for supplies, increasing his command of their tongue and his understanding of their society as well as the natural productions of their island. So it was that in all the episodes of Tahitian pilfering, European maladroitness or abuse of island hospitality, it was Banks's gifts of diplomacy and plain human sympathy that were continually invoked. His tasks ranged from the recovery of Solander's spy glass and Monkhouse's snuff box on the second day ashore, to the return of Bird's quadrant after its theft from the fort some time later, not to mention the smart first aid applied to the chief Tubourai threatened with acute nicotine poisoning after his first encounter with European plug tobacco. However there was more than genial diplomacy in the success of Banks in his relations with the people of Tahiti; there was an ultimate fearless authority and force of personality beyond his years.

In the three months ashore much was accomplished apart from the astronomical work of Charles Green, James Cook and Daniel Solander, in the transit observations from Fort Venus and the supplementary readings by John Gore and William Monkhouse, with Banks and Herman Spöring, on the motu or islet of Irioa, inside the reef at the north-west point of Moorea, on that important Saturday 3 June 1769.

In the time from the first Latin nicknames bestowed on a few of his early contacts,

Banks had acquired a vocabulary of rather more than 750 ordinary words and phrases with the Maohi names of over 100 persons. To them he had become 'Topano', and others of his party, with Cook and some of his officers, had acquired Maohi names in so far as he, Solander, Parkinson and the surgeon Monkhouse, could transliterate them. In addition to his social vocabulary there was also the extensive range of the Maohi terms for the plants and animals collected or seen among so many competing diversions – feasts of scientific novelties set beside the enticements of Polynesian society.

At the scientific level, the disciplined working scene in the great cabin of the *Endeavour* gave way at Tahiti to a similar dedication within Banks's large bell tent in the relative safety of Fort Venus. But here the 'Promotion of Natural Knowledge' was a continual battle with flies and other insects although Parkinson at least seems to have been partly defended from them by a large mosquito net within the tent, shared no doubt at times by Solander, Banks and Spöring. But the academic calm of the bell tent was at times shattered by other invaders, social interruptions especially from the exuberant folk of Pare and Papare to the east. At such times the great cabin of the ship was a welcome place of refuge. And yet somehow, either ashore or afloat, Sydney Parkinson managed to complete in colour some 113 out of the 128 plant species as well as the topographical and ethnographical sketches in pen and wash that his dead colleague Alexander Buchan might otherwise have done. In addition there were the descriptions and diagnoses of some 308 recorded plant species gathered by Banks and Solander, assisted by Briscoe, Roberts and Spöring. For the Society Islands there were some 160 species of fishes described and numbered in series. There was also an indeterminate range of birds and various invertebrates, molluscs and arthropods, including doubtless some of the troublesome species in the bell tent.

At the social level there was a counter-attraction to scientific solemnity in the varied attractions presented by the Maohi themselves, as pleasant companions or in the oddities of their customs and amusements. Banks was at some pains to record matters of ethnography and to participate wherever possible in the practices of the islanders. Solander remained the translator of names of people, places, plants and phases of the moon but also became the social gossip, memorizing incidents with which later to regale London tea-tables and clubs. Through him some of the relationships formed can be identified. There are Mrs Boba, Mrs Toaro, Mrs Eteree, Mrs Tate and Mrs Patini as the women in the lives of Robert Molyneux, John Gore, Charles Green, Charles Clerke and Sydney Parkinson – yes, even 'Shyboots Parkinson', as Solander recalled to Charles Blagden some ten years later. The artist was noted to be often out of the bell tent and one day, by chance, 'Mr Banks roving in the wood' with another girl, found Patini in bed with Piari, a 30-year old woman and elder sister of Banks's companion of the moment. And, of course, for Banks himself the satirists in London had their field days for many years to come, their sources hard to identify but surely to be found in the joviality of club conversations from Solander's evident hobby of polite pornography. The attenuated versions of Tahitian sociology that seeped into the Hawkesworth account of the voyage in 1773 were often enough for the ribald Georgian imagination.

When the transit observations were done, the remaining five weeks or more before the *Endeavour* sailed were full enough for Banks in his explorations of the island as well as the customs of its people. With Cook, between 26 and 30 June, he made a circuit of the island from which a good harvest of ethnographic detail was acquired. With John Gore he was active with his gun among the bird life, especially hunting the common duck of the South Sea for fresh food. With William Monkhouse he penetrated high into the centre of the island up the course of the Vaipopo river through the Tuauru valley, an important transect through the Tahiti vegetation and such food resources as bread-fruit and plaintain, but studying also the rock forms and concluding correctly that the land was of volcanic origin. Then, alone on 4 July, he set about planting in both directions along the coast from Fort Venus, in as many different kinds of soil as he could recognize, the seeds of water-melons, oranges, lemons, limes and other cultivars brought from Rio de Janeiro. Of these the melons had struck well in the hands of the natives to whom Banks had already distributed large quantities. Other seeds, even the melons, planted by Cook had failed to germinate, which Banks attributed to the manner in which they had been sealed up for transport.

From 6 July the process of dismantling the shore station at Fort Venus began and for this last week before the day of sailing the relations between the Europeans and the Polynesians became increasingly tense for many reasons, some material as attemped thefts increased, others social and psychological as friendships, physical and spiritual, came under stress. These pressures laid a heavy burden on Banks and his undeniable authority among the Maohi was tested to the full. In the delicate exchanges over the two marine deserters on 8 July, with the detention of Oborea ashore and of Tubourai and others of his good friends on the ship on 10 July, Banks spent an uncomfortable last night on land. Quite defenceless he stayed to face a partly-armed and threatening crowd outside his tents in the morning, adopting the tactics he had always used in what he termed their previous 'quarrels':

> . . . I made the best I could of it by going out among them. They we[re] very civil and shewd much fear as they have done of me upon all occasions, probably because I never shewd the least of them but have upon all our quarrels gone immediately into the thickest of them . . .

The danger passed and for the rest of the morning, while his tents were struck and stowed on board the *Endeavour*, he walked along the beach with Oborea and Tutaha firmly refusing their gifts of appeasement. By the time the anchor was raised on the morning of 13 July a 'perfect reconciliation' had been made, and as the ship set its course westerly from 'Otaheite' Banks, at the 'topmast head' with Tupaia beside him, waved a long farewell to his quietly weeping friends as their canoes disappeared astern.

For the next month the *Endeavour* wove a course through and round the other Society Islands – Huahine, Raiatea, Tahaa, and Borabora – with Banks and Solander making frequent landings and Cook taking possession of all he could see 'for the use of his Brittanick majesty' but narrowly missing disaster once or twice among the reefs. Then, on 14 August, with one final but fruitless attempt by Gore, Banks and Tupaia to land on Rurutu, Cook set the course firmly to the southward, obedient now to the terms of his 'Additional Instructions' that

> . . . Whereas there is reason to imagine that a Continent of Land of great extent, may be found to the Southward of the Tract lately made by Captn Wallis in His Majesty's Ship the Dolphin . . . so soon as the Observation of the Transit of the

Planet Venus shall be finished . . . You are to proceed to the southward in order to make discovery of the Continent above-mentioned until you arrive in the Latitude of 40°, unless you sooner fall in with it . . .

And Banks, obedient to his own self-discipline and the more general terms of the 'Additional Instructions', set about his account of the 'Manners & customs of S. Sea Islands' as they passed out of the southern tropics towards the unknowns of latitude 40°.

X

In the long sweep up from below Cape Horn to the Tuamotu Islands Banks had already noted how much the idea of a 'Southern Continent' in square degrees had been taken from the 'Theoretical writers' and changed to water. Now, as the *Endeavour* dropped south again to the 40th parallel, another stretch of imagined land had been liquefied, but as Cook retreated prudently from the rough forties, north-west and later west, the shadow was turning to the substance of Tasman's Staat's Land and the resolution of the puzzle of its place in the continental theory. The voyage had now passed out of the area of the South Sea delimited by the Royal Society as convenient for the transit observations. The astronomical purposes had in the main been served and the science of the stars was now to be invoked in the precise fixing of latitudes and longitudes in the hunt for unknown lands and questionable coasts as the ship probed westward. As Banks had forecast to Perrin 'this the Least of the plan' had been accomplished. The 'Ship in the midst of the South Seas' was now about to fulfil Banks's cryptic promise to his friend that 'she may do much more as if you look upon a Chart you may see'. And what chart more explicit in its blankness than Dalrymple's 'Chart of the South Pacifick Ocean, Pointing out the Discoveries made therein Previous to 1764'. For seven weeks below the Tropic the great blankness remained, an ocean void emphasized by the long Pacific swell from the south and south-west denying, as Banks could only note, the hint of any nearby continent.

As the ship returned to warmer and quieter latitudes Banks, after a few days of gastric unease, was fit enough to launch his small boat again on 19 September into a calm sea with his guns and his dipping net some 1200 miles south-west of Tahiti. About the same time Solander also became vaguely unwell and, on Monkhouse's prescription, Banks again had recourse for him to Hulme's 'Essence of Lemon Juice' with good effect. This was supplemented by an excellent pie made from the North American apples which Dr John Fothergill had given Banks for the voyage and which had somehow kept well for more than a year of ocean travel. Then, some further 600 miles on the same course to the south-west, on 1 October a seal was seen and then some driftwood among floating seaweed, all of them signs, Banks hoped, of the nearness of the 'Land of Promise'. On the next two days, 2 and 3 October, there were enough calms for Banks to be out in his boat shooting and dipping from which his harvest injected new life into the workers in the great cabin as he reflected:

. . . Now do I wish that our freinds in England could by the assistance of some magical spying glass take a peep at our situation: Dr Solander setts at the Cabbin table describing, myself at my Bureau Journalizing, between us hangs a large bunch of sea weed, upon the table lays the wood and barnacles; they would see that notwithstanding our different occupations our lips move very often and without being conjurors might guess that we were talking about what we should see upon the land which there is now no doubt we shall see very soon . . .

But there were still some 500 miles of sailing before, at sunset on Friday 6 October, he could from the mast-head assure himself that it was indeed land which early that afternoon Nicholas Young had sighted from the same high perch. By the following morning the land was plainly seen from the deck and in the afternoon calm Banks was again at work in his small boat gathering specimens which he now knew would have to wait before they could be properly examined as

. . . all hands seem to agree that this is certainly the Continent we are in search of . . .

It was certainly land but was it the answer to the long search? Another day of patience was required until the ship anchored late in the afternoon within the heads of a wide bay about two miles offshore. That evening Banks went ashore with the first landing party of marines seeking fresh water, and a partial answer to the great question came with a sharp suddenness. The natives threatened, shots were fired, and one man, apparently the chief, fell dead. In all important features of dress and physiognomy he was 'exactly as represented in Mr Dalrymple's book p.63', ominously enough in the engraving 'View of Murderers Bay in New Zealand'.

Next day, 9 October 1769, came those troubled scenes on shore and in the boats at Poverty Bay, when four natives were killed by musket shots which haunted Banks as he recorded that night:

. . . Thus ended the most disagreeable day My life has yet seen, black be the mark for it and heaven send that such may never return to embitter future reflection . . .

In this remorse Cook also shared but he justified the action as a measure of self-defence. It was abundantly plain from these first two days that the people of the 'Continent', as the new land for the time being remained, were more vigorously combative than the Maohi of the Society Islands with whom, from Tupaia's ability to understand the drift of what they said, there seemed to be at least some linguistic affinity. Thereafter caution was the keynote of all further relations with the Maori of New Zealand as Cook's masterly circumnavigation stripped the 'Continent' of its pretensions and converted Tasman's Staat's Land into the two islands that we know.

As the *Endeavour* withdrew from this first encounter to set about the geographic task, on 11 October, the bay had indeed been poor – for Cook in the poverty of supplies and fresh water; for Banks in the poverty of specimens collected, a mere 40 for the plant boxes but rich enough, one would think, given the hazards of their gathering. As Cook's running survey moved steadily north with landings at Araura Bay [Tegadu], Tolago Bay and through the Bay of Plenty, the moment came to observe the transit of Mercury. For this Charles Green and Cook landed with instruments on Thursday 9 November in a bay where the ship had previously been anchored for several days and Banks and Solander had peacefully botanized ashore. About midday one of the ship's guns was fired, a warning to those on land and a

85

deterrent round shot over two large Maori canoes in one of which Lt Gore had shot one man dead for cheating over a deal.

This infliction of sudden death on the native population hung as a bad memory far into the future, as did the deaths in Poverty Bay. Both Cook and Banks adjudged the punishment over-severe for a crime where wounding rather than fatal small-shot might have served, but the Maoris thought it just. Moreover, as it proved and all recognized, it secured the safe return of the astronomical observers and the botanists to the ship on that tense afternoon. The event was to be revived ten years later in a wider context at Soho Square as Charles Blagden jotted down the breakfast gossip of Daniel Solander and his occasional reflections on the voyage:

> Gore is the best practical Seaman now in the Navy; Cooke was jealous of him, conscious of not having that thorough stile in naval affairs, nor that determined courage. Gore had a sort of separate command in the vessel being appointed Master Hunter, which gave him superintendance over all the transactions with the Indians. He made use of this sometimes to disobey Cooke; & therefore they hate each other. Gore always blamed severity to the Indians, & yet by a sudden emotion shot the man who cheated, but told of it himself with the most terrible anxiety & did not recover for 12 days of the shock it gave him

The same incident also survived in the memory of a small Maori boy who, in his old age as the ancient chief Te-Horeta-Taniwha, recounted the circumstances of the *Endeavour*'s troubled ten days in Mercury Bay, and identified 'one supreme man in that ship' as the undoubted leader whom some discern to be Cook and at least one other to be Banks, a tantalizing morsel of folk-memory.

From mid-November, the difficult circumnavigation of the north island continued for two months as Banks made botanically profitable landings on its shores – in the Hauraki Gulf and up the Waihou or Thames river among the great forests of Kahikatea and Matai, the white pines, *Podocarpus* spp., and in the Bay of Islands. It was botany between skirmishes on the beaches with the ever-challenging Maoris, defiant chanting from their canoes, punitive or defensive bursts of small-shot from the intruding Europeans; science under the ultimate sanction of rounds from the ship's guns.

By mid-December the North Cape had been named and passed against the resistance of foul winds, and on Christmas Eve 1769, with Tasman's Island of the Three Kings coming into view from the mast-head, the weather fell calm and Banks fell to with his guns shooting once again from his small boat. His chief targets were New Zealand gannets or solan geese (*Sula bassana serrator* Gray) of which he shot enough to fall in with 'the humour of the ship to make a Goose pye' for the next day. As the old year turned into the new so also the weather turned foul, with south-westerly gales of a kind stronger and more prolonged than Cook had ever faced before. A week later, on 6 and 7 January, it was calm enough for Banks to spend two days shooting for science rather than the pot, some 50 to 60 miles off the Ninety-Mile Beach in the dinghy. Another week of uncomplicated sailing brought the *Endeavour* past the brief glimpse of Mount Egmont into the wide opening marked by Dalrymple as Tasman Road, or in some charts as 'Murderers' Bay', to a snug anchorage at Ship Cove in Queen Charlotte Sound on Monday 15 January 1770.

For three weeks Banks and Solander were able to pursue natural history in relative peace and with profit to the collections. But their ethnological probings, under the usual conditions of armed truce with the Maoris, revealed a darker side than they had yet encountered – with evidence of cannibalism in the tribe nearby indulged on the bodies of a defeated raiding party. Further evidence of such unnatural history occurred a few days later when six or seven preserved heads were brought to Banks for his inspection. He secured one by trading 'a pair of old Drawers of very white linen', an item accepted only under the threat of a musket presented at the owner. In general the area round Ship and Cannibal Coves was rich in plants and fish species for the scientists. For Cook the navigator it was also rich in discovery, as from a high hill he glimpsed a passage into 'the Eastern Sea', the strait between the North and South Islands which Banks, it seems, proposed should have the captain's name. Proof came as the *Endeavour* passed through on 8 February and turned north briefly for its confirmation at Cape Turnagain. From then on the final deposition of the 'Continent mongers', with whom for the sake of argument Banks grouped himself, remained to be concluded in the five weeks that lay ahead.

As the ship worked its way south again along the west coast of the 'Continent', there were three days calm enough for Banks to launch his small boat before the *Endeavour* rounded the peninsula which Cook named Banks Island in the haste of the running survey. Three weeks later, as the South Cape was passed and the ship turned on to more northerly bearings Banks lightly marked the change as

. . . the total demolition of our aerial fabrick calld continent . . .

Three weeks later still, in the anchorage at Admiralty Bay, he could write composedly of the two islands as New Zealand and as a discovery of great credit to Abel Tasman. Under that name he drafted his 'Account' during the five days before the ship set sail on its course toward Van Diemen's Land. Interrupted by two days of a gastric illness and violent headaches, Banks managed two botanizing days ashore with Solander before that decisive 'conference of officers' as Cook defined it, on 30 March, when the eastward route to Cape Horn was rejected and the westward course determined. There can be no doubt that Banks had certainly been a potent voice in that decision as he analysed the reasons for it. The prudent path to the East Indies which the state of the ship and the problem of supplies dictated was also that which would be to the obvious benefit of further important discovery. On Dalrymple's 'Chart of the South Pacifick Ocean', that blank, 'the East Coast of New Holland', remained as a last challenge which could not be ignored.

For Banks, however, the 'Southern Continent' remained also as the seed from which a second voyage could emerge, not in pursuit of Dalrymple's hopes for a large inhabited land-mass ripe for the benefits of trade, but as a more remote entity in high latitudes for which

. . . a Voyage, as a Voyage of Mere Curiosity, should be promoted by the Royal Society to whom I doubt not but his majesty would upon a proper application grant a ship, as the subject of such a voyage seems at least as interesting to Science in general and the increase of knowledge as the Observation which gave rise to the Present one . . .

He had long since discarded the pole-balancing theory of Dalrymple and others as 'a most childish argument' but, since the *Endeavour* had briefly crossed the Antarctic Circle, his reading and his observations had drawn him toward a 'Southern Continent' as a proper goal for polar geographic enquiry.

XI

For ten days on gentle winds veering from south-east to north-west, the *Endeavour* held its westward course for the most part between 37° and 39° S., and on 11, 12 and 13 April it was calm enough for Banks to sample the marine fauna of the Tasman Sea from his small boat. With his gun more sea birds came under his scrutiny – several species of albatross (*Diomedea* spp.) and petrel (*Pterodroma* spp.) in particular – enabling him to record in some detail the stinging mechanism of the Portuguese man-of-war (*Physalia* spp.) and the apparent immunity to its effects of the wandering albatross, whose prey it often was. Then the warm humid weather changed to a stiff Tasman gale from the west with a heavy sea causing Cook to shorten sail and steer to the north-west with caution, heaving to and sounding at night, as the gales veered wildly. Then at six a.m. on Thursday 19 April 1770 land was sighted by the 1st Lt Hicks, extending from the north-east to the west, with no sign of Van Diemen's Land to the south. The long running survey of 'the East Coast of New Holland' was about to begin and Banks's first impression of the new land was not unpleasing on 20 April:

> . . . The country this morn rose in gently sloping hills which had the appearance of the highest fertility, every hill seemd to be cloth'd with trees of no mean size . . .

On 23 April as he took advantage of the calm off Bateman's Bay to launch his small boat, the land was too far off to be appraised. When next it came in to reasonable view his imagination conjured up a likeness to 'the back of a lean Cow', more barren than it had first appeared. Then, with a more inviting prospect ashore, in the afternoon of 27 April, Cook, Banks, and Solander with four seamen in the yawl were tempted to try a landing.

This brought them within about two furlongs of the shore, close enough with the unaided eye to see four men carrying a canoe along Woonona beach near Collin's rock and to note the scattered 'cabbage trees' (*Livistona australis* R. Br.) hinting at future fertility on this northern tip of the Illawarra coastal plain. The slopes and steep 1200-foot escarpment a mile or so beyond with its glimpses of red soil and brush rain forest were seen with a three-foot Dollond telescope. But the long swell and the pounding surf was a barrier no yawl could pass. Another day and 25 miles further north, with a shore-line which 'appeard Cliffy and barren without wood', an opening that promised shelter was discerned. After the pinnace had verified the entrance, the *Endeavour* sailed between Cape Banks on the north, and Point Solander on the south head to a quiet anchorage a mile within the bay whose name has ever since immortalized the plant gatherings of the following week.

The six days round the shores of Botany Bay though rich in new plant species were less fruitful in relations with the local aborigines and poor in any but the most fleeting speculations about the nature of the elusive fauna. A scouting range of perhaps no more than five miles in any direction from the bay shores set limits to the knowledge won, denying sight of the great harbour ready for its place in history to

88

The *Endeavour* careened at the Endeavour River, North Queensland, 19 June–20 July 1770. Hawkesworth, J. 1773.

the north. Compromise, however, was necessary on several counts; the state of the ship and the drive to return home; the pursuit of natural knowledge in its broad sense; the technical demands imposed by a hydrographic survey of an unknown coast with all the risks involved. Time pressed and prudence set limits, but in the progress north, from 33° S. to the tropics about 15° S., Banks managed some seven days in various landings and some three occasions afloat in his dinghy. Not many collecting excursions perhaps along some 1500 miles of an enigmatic coast but they were enough to saturate the descriptive and artistic resources at his command. The strains of the long voyage were becoming more evident among seamen and scientists alike and it was no doubt a misjudgement born of stress that, on the night of 11 June 1770, brought the *Endeavour* abruptly to rest on the corals of the Barrier Reef. Suddenly all was at risk, but a week of heroic effort brought the ship at last into the river that now bears her name where, by a steep beach on the south bank, she was warped ashore by the head for repair.

For some seven weeks Banks and his party explored and collected with a thoroughness that had not been possible at Botany Bay. Indeed the Endeavour River neighbourhood yielded a greater harvest of new species in plants from both the north and the south shores than was achieved at the first landing. For the zoologist however there was more material than Botany Bay had been able to show of the evanescent marsupial fauna – though not much more. On the north shore on 22 June 'an animal as large as a greyhound of a mouse coulour and very swift' had been seen, and again the next day, but it was not until 25 June that Banks himself sighted it. On 29 June James Matra saw what was evidently a dingo (*Canis dingo*) and next day John Gore saw two more. Then on 6 July Banks, with Tupaia and Gore, the 'Master Hunter', set out inland by boat up the river past the mangroves to the open grasslands and further to the interior than any European had been. A dingo was again seen, some large 'Batts' or flying foxes (*Pteropus* spp.), and after some miles over the plains at last some four of 'the animals'. These were 'fairly chas'd' by Banks's greyhound who was defeated in the hunt by the long grass and the 'vast bounds' of the odd creature with its two powerful hind legs. Back on the river they travelled upstream to its tidal limit and freshwater origin and there camped on a sandbank for their second night. Next day, 8 July, they returned to the ship noting an estuarine crocodile (*Crocodilus* spp.) among the mangroves. Then on 14 July Gore shot a specimen of 'the animal' which Banks noted, in his 180-word 'Vocabulary of New Holland', as 'Kangooroo' or 'Kanguru'. At a dead weight of 38 pounds or 24 pounds clean, the two to three-year old male led Solander to the manuscript name 'Kanguru saliens', under which head also was compounded the description of Gore's second trophy on 27 July, 'a very large one', a male of 84 pounds dead weight, and finally the small female of some 8 pounds, caught by Banks's greyhound on 29 July. From Solander's manuscript, Parkinson's simple outline drawings and a lost skull from John Hunter's museum, the classification of what is amusingly still called 'Captain Cook's kangaroo' remains a matter of debate. The best that can be said at present is that, whatever the species, *Macropus* spp. will serve as the genus, and 'Kanguru' as its first introduction to the English language by Banks from the Guugu Yimidhirr language of the east coast of north Queensland.

Another taxonomic tangle developed on 26 July when Banks paused in his plant hunting to capture 'an animal of the Opossum (Didelphis) tribe', a female with two pouch young. This feat of dexterity brought the type specimen of the Queensland grey ring-tail opossum into the literature by way of Pennant (not surprisingly) who first described it from the slightly damaged skin in his *History of Quadrupeds*, Vol. II, 25, 1783 – with an attribution to Cook as the collector. It is a prime example of the vagaries in nomenclature that have beset the *Endeavour* collections, plant and animal, ever since. Specific respectability came with Boddaert, based on Pennant, as *Didelphis peregrinus* in the *Elenchus Animalium*, 1785, p. 78. Thereafter it is a riot of Latin convolutions: *Didelphis caudivolvula* Kerr, 1793; *Didelphis novaehollandiae* Bechstein, 1800; *Balantia banksii* Oken, 1816; *Phalangista cookii* Schinz, 1821; *Phalangista banksii* Gray, 1838. Finally with the generic name as *Pseudocheirus* Ogilby, 1837 it has found taxonomic peace as *Pseudocheirus peregrinus* Boddaert, 1785. So, in practice, are buried most of the *Endeavour* specimens under the inexorable codes of international nomenclature. But as to the original collectors – for the plants read Banks and Solander, not Parkinson or Cook; for the animals and birds for the most part read Banks and, for the kangaroos, at least read Gore and Banks – certainly not Cook.

Here there is perhaps room also for another still small thought. The world at large first saw 'Captain Cook's Kangaroo' as Plate XX in Volume III of Hawkesworth's *An Account of the Voyages ...*, 1773 by an anonymous engraver, the mirror image of a painting by George Stubbs, 1771 or 1772, on which it was based. Entitled 'An animal found on the coast of New Holland called Kangaroo' in Hawkesworth the strange beast was further immortalized in the prose of Oliver Goldsmith in one of his last works, *An History of the Earth and Animated Nature*, volume 4, pp. 351–353 as a form of 'The Gerbua'. His account begins

... The kangaroo of New Holland, where it is only to be found, is often known to weigh above sixty pounds, and must consequently be as large as a sheep. Although the skin of that which was stuffed and brought home by Mr. Banks, was not much above the size of a hare, yet it was greatly superior to any of the gerbua kind that have been hitherto known, and very different in many particulars ...

This circumstantial evidence strongly points to the young female caught by Banks's greyhound on 29 July 1770 as the material on which the Stubbs's painting, [23½ ×

Joseph Banks's Kangaroo
Left The painting by George Stubbs, 1771–2 [23½×27½ inches] of a young kangaroo.
Right The engraving derived from Stubbs's painting in Hawkesworth, J., 1773, *Account of the Voyages* . . ., Volume III, Plate 20.
This is on every count Joseph Banks's Kangaroo, *not* Captain Cook's. Whatever doubts there may be about its ultimate taxonomy it could with historic justice, for the time being, carry the name *Macropus Banksii*.

27½ inches] was based and supplemented, of course, by Parkinson's pencil sketches in consultation with Banks who was the original collector of the stuffed specimen. If this be so then much is explained, apart from its place as an element of the assistance in illustration which Banks undertook for Hawkesworth. However at the time when this controversial specimen was taken near the Endeavour River Banks himself was impatient to be sailing with signs that he had joined the increasing number of those who longed for home. The diligence of the seamen and the scientists was failing; human endurance in mind and body seemed to have a two-year term and this limit was now close at hand. The second anniversary of the voyage passed unnoticed in the general relief of escape from the confinement and hazards of the Barrier Reef and the much debated passage 'between New Holland and New Guinea' into the Arafura Sea on 25 August 1770. Instead of celebration Banks could now, with some returning peace of mind, study under his microscope the alga, *Trichodesmium* spp., that muddied the sea as the *Endeavour* probed its way westward after the 2000 miles of intricate coastal survey. However, as an assurance that the Dalrymple chart had been a faithful friend and that the ship was truly clear of the South Sea, a course was now set 'Northward in order to make the coast of New Guinea'. Then, on 3 September 1770, near De Jong's Point in present-day West Irian, a last, almost ceremonial, landing was made on a strange shore by Cook, Banks, Solander, Briscoe, Roberts and all but two of the boat's crew, in all '12 men well armd'. With the prints of naked feet on the mud below high water mark and the tree line scarcely more than 100 yards from the water, botanizing was marginal and field anthropology limited to minor hostilities in exchanges between small shot and some 'ill made darts of Bamboo'. When the pinnace returned to the ship and the course was once more directed westward away

91

from the land, both Cook and Banks agreed it was to the 'No small satisfaction' of most of the ship's company as 'the sick became well and the melancholy lookd gay'. Nostalgia reigned; the *Endeavour*'s explorations were at an end. The course was set for home, a journey's end that rather less than half would ever see.

XII

With 'Some Account of that part of New Holland now called New South Wales', written by Banks after the Endeavour Straits were passed, the days of his two-year role as Cook's Oxford tutor were effectively over. So too, very soon, would end Charles Green's long course of instruction to Cook and his officers in the intricacies and tedium of navigation with and without the aid of Maskelyne's *Nautical Almanac* and *Astronomical Ephemeris*. Since the end of 1769 off Cape Maria van Diemen on the North Island of New Zealand, the framework of Cook's inshore running survey had depended wholly on the precision of Green's astronomical observations, conscientiously followed over the whole 2000-mile survey of the east coast of 'New Holland' to the last occasion south of Timor in the Arafura Sea. Of his debt to Green there had been ample acknowledgement by Cook in his journal for 23 August 1770 after his symbolic declaration the previous day of British possession of the whole eastern coast by the name of 'New South Wales'. In the range of the other observations belonging to the 'Additional Instructions' which he was ordered carefully to note

> ... the Nature of the Soil, and the Products thereof; the Beasts and Fowls that inhabit or frequent it, the fishes that are to be found in the Rivers or upon the Coast and in what Plenty ... etc

there is not the same recognition of what was owing to Banks, not only in what was recorded but in the matter and manner of the writing. There is no doubt that Banks made Cook free to inspect his journal and use it for his own purposes in the record of the captain's log. There is no doubt also that the working relations between the two men, whether as fellow scribes in the great cabin of the *Endeavour* or in the crises at sea or the confrontations ashore, were close and informed with a mutual confidence and respect that easily bridged the gap of 15 years in age and experience.

Near the point of Green's last astronomical fix, Banks, on 9 September 1770, made his last onslaught on the tropical bird population from his small boat, with a bag of some three dozen assorted boobies, including some of the red-footed species, *Sula piscator*, for some of Solander's last descriptions on the voyage. The reunion with European outposts in the East Indies was now at hand as the island of Savu came in sight on 17 September. For the next five days the material needs of the *Endeavour* were met by the local rajah and his European adviser Johan Lange, the Dutch East India Company's man in residence. It was an intricate process which required the sacrifice of the last English sheep on board and Banks's greyhound as placatory gifts to the rajah. The negotiations, however, were nearly ruined by what Banks termed 'the imprudence of Mr. Parkinson' who inquired too pointedly about the local spices, the nub of the Dutch East India Company's interest in Savu and its surrounding islands. Somehow, with his imperfect German, Solander was able to resolve the issue with Lange and in the same way and by his own observation Banks was able to write a full appreciation of this outpost of Dutch influence and trade. Ten days later on 2 October the *Endeavour* came to anchor briefly off Anger Point close by two Dutch East Indiamen. Communication with western Europe and Great Britain was re-established – a Europe quivering under the Russian imperialism of Catherine the Great and England in a state of civil unrest, exacerbated now by signs of revolt in the American colonies. About one week later the ship was anchored in Batavia Road by Onrust Island and ten weeks of agonized life in the East Indies began as the ship was repaired at Kuiper Island and its inmates wasted away under the insidious array of tropical diseases.

Of those for whom Banks was responsible, Tupaia and Tayeto the Tahitians died in the tents ashore, and until the ship sailed on 25 December, Banks, Solander, Spöring, Briscoe and Roberts suffered from tertian malaria, relieved only in part by the nursing of two Malay women slaves in the country house rented by Banks some two miles from the town. Solander was the most serious case. It was at sea on the long leg to the Cape, among the 22 deaths, that the civilian party was almost destroyed. Between 20 January and 1 February first Spöring, then Parkinson died, probably from the combined effects of dysentery and malaria. Banks defended himself against the latter with his usual recourse to the 'bark' but suffered 'the pains of the Damnd almost' in the throes of what may have been typhoid fever rather than amoebic or bacillary dysentery. As he recovered, Charles Green, the astronomer and several others died, as Banks said,

> . . . all of the very same complaint as I labourd under, no very encouraging circumstance . . .

Then, from 17 February at the Cape anchorage, Solander was bedridden for two weeks with a violent and emaciating combination of the prevailing infections, to the acute alarm of Banks more than once during its course.

So it was that when at last the *Endeavour* anchored in the Downs at three o'clock on Friday 12 July 1770 only 41 of the original ship's company of 94 survived of those who had set out nearly three years before, a mortality of 56 per cent. Of the party which Banks had enlisted, only four had survived of the nine who had embarked – himself, Solander, Peter Briscoe and James Roberts.

Within the last year of the voyage, however, in spite of its dangers and tragic human loss, Banks managed to record useful accounts of the places where landings had been made – Batavia, Prince's Island, Cape Town and St Helena – and in a greater measure than Cook had either time or inclination to report. These formed the last pages of a journal that exceeded 200000 words of original observation for the most part serving the intentions of the voyage other than those of astronomical, hydrographic or geographical significance. It was both a complement to Cook's record and a source on which he drew heavily for his official report to the Admiralty. It was the background also to that other record for posterity condensed in the diligent notes of Solander and the specimens of natural history to which they refer. Solander kept no journal. The 'Slip Catalogue' is his memorial of the voyage. On this and perhaps, in a measure, the journal notes of Banks himself, was founded the fragmentary record in Parkinson's 'journal' as he illustrated the material to which they referred. In addition there is the assemblage of 'vocabularies' from the Society Islands, New Zealand, New Holland, Savu, Batavia, Prince's Island, compiled by

Banks himself and under his direction by Solander, Monkhouse and Parkinson as his main auxiliaries apart from Tupaia. His ability in the speech of the South Pacific languages was said by Cook to be greater than that of any one else on the *Endeavour*, while the written record of the word and phrase lists that survive exceed those which were put into or printed in the journals.

Home life at No. 14 New Burlington Street began again as Banks, on Saturday 13 July, wrote to Thomas Pennant announcing his return:

> ... a few short lines must suffice to acquaint you with the arrival of Dr Solander & myself in good health this day. Mr Buchan Mr Parkinson and Mr Sporing are all dead as is our astronomer seven officers & about a third part of the ships crew of diseases contracted in the East Indies not in the South Seas where health seems to have her cheif residence
>
> Our Collections will I hope satisfy you, very few quadripeds, one mouse however (Gerbua) weighing 80 lb weight. I long for nothing so much as to see you but must delay that pleasure some time My relations are dispersd almost to the extremities of the Kingdom & I must see them before I begin to arrange or meddle with anything winter however will soon come & doubtless bring us together ... in a few days I shall be able to write more understandibly now I am Mad Mad Mad My poor brain whirls round with innumerable [things] which the return to my native countrey have excited as soon as I enjoy a lucid interval I will write again ...

But not until some time after 18 July, when the *Endeavour* anchored at Galleon's Reach in the Thames, could the collections be taken to New Burlington Street.

Whatever the broad intentions of this Royal Society expedition when it began in August 1768, there is no doubt that the limits of time, circumstance, and the techniques of collection and preservation available on the voyage dictated that botany should be the dominant preoccupation. The pursuit of zoology often required a more active and complicated process than what Dr Johnson defined as the 'culling of simples'. Specimens of the animal kingdom called for skills with rod and line, with nets and netting, with gun and harpoon and, not least, the management of a small boat on the open sea. The plant world was *in situ* and for the most part evident. All the zoological specimens posed problems of conservation both in fixation and storage against the hazards of putrefaction and decay or other forms of destruction. Plant gathering has its own problems in ensuring the survival of collections, often time consuming and tedious as, for example, in the care and attention to drying and pressing. For the major part of the voyage decisions on the division of labour and skills in the field rested on Banks and Solander as botanical and zoological collectors and systematists, classifying and describing; Spöring as writer/secretary and occasional artist; Parkinson as recording artist; Peter Briscoe and James Roberts as field assistants and collectors in both botany and zoology. Banks was obviously the prime collector of marine fauna with his plankton net, and of sea and land birds with his gun, while in shooting and fishing he had Gore, 'the Master Hunter' as his frequent companion. Over all these activities Banks was the directing hand which had gathered the means for their execution – for all his youth. How, at this late date, can the results of this energy be summarized?

Perhaps for no expedition of discovery at any time is the story ever fully told or the collections worked through or displayed; and the *Endeavour* voyage even though the most successful pioneer of scientific exploration of its time, was to have criticism levelled at it on this count. However chequered or imperfect the history of the collections that came to New Burlington Street in August 1771, their conservation with the attendant manuscripts through the years at Soho Square and in the British Museum still enable us to make a reasonable guess at their order of magnitude. What was displayed in the three public rooms at No. 14 were the contents of some 24 wooden chests, some kegs and smaller cases. Out of these by degrees emerged a moderately coherent display of the natural history, art and artefacts of the new lands in the South Sea. Of the art and artefacts it is no longer possible to speak with any assurance, for they were dispersed to other *curiosi* though most perhaps now lie, more or less identified, in the British Museum. Only the harvest of natural history items can now be roughly assessed.

For the plant kingdom it is now estimated that more than 30000 specimens were gathered over all, yielding some 3600-odd described species, of which it is probable that the plant species new to science may exceed 1400. Measured against the contents of some 6000-odd species in the *Species Plantarum* of Linnaeus as the base of reference during the voyage, this was a formidable accession.

For the animal kingdom it would seem that rather more than 1000 species were collected: mammals, 'a few' as Banks said, 5; birds, 107+; fishes, 248+; arthropods, 370+; molluscs, 206+; echinoderms, 6; salps, 9; medusae, 30; and some others. Of

Cigadas collected by Joseph Banks in New Zealand, 1769, on the *Endeavour* voyage: *Tettigonia cingulata* Fabricius, syntypes in the Banks Collection, British Museum (Natural History). (a), (b) Syntype No. 2 = *Amphipsalta zelandica* (Boisduval), male; (c), (d), Syntype No. 1, Lectotype = *Amphipsalta cingulata* (Fabr.), male.

these, few actual specimens survive in any modern collection except the arthropods, mainly in the British Museum (Natural History) and some of the molluscs. Of the many bird species shot by Banks it remains a mystery why so few specimens seem to have survived.

For both kingdoms the graphic record in the 21 volumes now conserved in the British Museum (Natural History) attests mainly to the industry and diligence of Sydney Parkinson. For the plants there are 18 volumes with 269 finished drawings and 673 unfinished drawings by him. For the animals there are 3 volumes with 268 drawings by Parkinson; 21 by Alexander Buchan; 9 by Spöring; 298 in all.

XIII

When the *Endeavour* voyage was being mounted it was to serve a Royal Society purpose and Banks was, from an early stage, prominent in its preparation and in the gossip of London society as an enterprising Fellow participating in it at his own expense. It was natural on his return that he should again figure, at the end of a successful expedition, as a subject of gossip and social interest. Apart from his family, he was quick to pay his respects to the Royal Society and on Thursday 25 July 1771 attended the General Meeting of the Royal Society Dining Club to which he had been elected a year earlier while he was hunting kangaroos by the Endeavour River. A week later on 2 August he was presented by Lord Beauchamp to the King at the Court of St James's, apparently their first meeting, followed by his attendance with Solander at Kew on Saturday 10 August when they were presented to the King and Queen formally by Sir John Pringle, President of the Royal Society (1772–8). Here probably for the first time the question of plant introductions from the lands of the South Sea for the Royal Gardens was discussed as, during the next two weeks at Kew, the King was able to study the full range of plant, animal and topographic drawings. Before the month was out, talk was already rife that for Banks and Solander a second voyage to the South Pacific was likely in the spring of 1772.

Other rumours were also afoot among the tea-tables about the unrequited love of Miss Harriet Blosset, and on 11 August Valentine Morris had been 'excessively drole according to custom', at Lady Mary Coke's, about a supposed breach of promise of marriage by Banks that had been much put about. Morris hoped that Banks would at least requite the young lady for the many embroidered waistcoats she had worked for him as he circumnavigated the world. But this is a story with only a circumstantial beginning and an uncorroborated end.

On Sunday 18 August Banks and Solander dined with Sir John Pringle and their distinguished Fellow in the Royal Society, Dr Benjamin Franklin, who sought information on the peoples of the Pacific from the two men who could tell him more than anyone else. It was a Royal Society quartet of unique distinction and, on Monday 19 August, the essence of their conversation was sent to Dr Jonathan Shipley, Bishop of St Asaph, then in Portsmouth and a friend of Franklin as an avowed supporter of the American colonists. This rapid communication from Franklin, while the exchanges were fresh in his mind, fits well with what we know from Banks's journal and other prime sources but were perhaps altered a little to meet the temper of his episcopal friend. Three salient points of comparison appeared

... The People of Otahitee (George's Island) are civilised in a great degree ...
The Inhabitants of New Zealand were found to be a brave & sensible people, and
seem'd to have a fine Country, The Inhabitants of New Holland seem'd to our
People a stupid Race, for they would accept none of our Presents ...

Then came, in Franklin's words, the echo of what Banks and Cook had both recorded
somewhat differently in their journals as they left New Holland just one year before:

... We [call] this Stupidity But if we were dispos'd to compliment them, we might
say, Behold a Nation of Philosophers! such as him whom we celebrate for saying
as he went thro' a Fair, *How many things there are in the World that I dont want!* ...

For Banks the Australian aboriginal had much to teach:

... Thus live these I had almost said happy people, content with little nay almost
nothing. From them appear how small are the real wants of human nature, which
we Europeans have increased to an excess ...

and Cook had paraphrased the theme, to the distress of J. C. Beaglehole, his latest
biographer:

... they may appear to some to be the most wretched people upon Earth, but in
reality they are far more happier than we Europeans being wholly unacquainted
not only with the superfluous but the necessary Conveniences so much sought
after in Europe ...

The eighteenth-century world had suddenly been extended by the voyage and the
four Fellows of the Royal Society at dinner in Pall Mall were exploring the rich mine
of ideas it had exposed. One of them was soon to become a founding father of the
world's most materialist society.

The plan for a second voyage rapidly matured and on 25 September the Admiralty
ordered the Navy Board to purchase two vessels for service in remote parts. More
than one vessel had been envisaged by Banks in the plans he had formulated in his
journal in April 1770 and which Cook had also more briefly suggested in a postscript
to his own. The idea had been widely and openly discussed within the first month
after the *Endeavour*'s return and William Perrin from Lymington, also on 25
September had his own advice to give Banks. He thought it would be madness to
venture a second voyage with a single ship only. Indeed with a single ship its loss on
such an expedition could only be considered 'Felo de se'. But before Banks and Perrin
met in January 1771 the two ships *Resolution* and *Adventure* had been bought and
registered.

If any incentive beyond exploration were needed it had certainly come to Banks
and Cook at Batavia and again at the Cape as they returned in the *Endeavour*. The
French had preceded them in the Pacific at Tahiti and now in October the results
were published in Paris with Bougainville's *Voyage autour du monde*. The notion of a
Royal Society 'voyage of mere curiosity' paled under the pressures of nationalist
rivalry. But in the mean time the academic world at home recognized the triumphant
and profitable accessions to 'Natural Knowledge' that had accrued from the *Endeavour*

voyage and it was appropriate therefore that Mr Joseph Banks and Dr Daniel Solander should have been summoned to Oxford on Thursday 21 November 1771, each to receive the honorary Doctorate of Civil Law.

Deputizing for the Regius Professor of Civil Law, Dr Samuel Forster pronounced the Latin oration. But in common English the orator presented for the honour

> ... this most distinguished man, Joseph Banks Esquire of Revesby Abbey in the County of Lincolnshire, and not long since a gentleman commoner of Christ Church College ...

and with him also

> ... this most renowned and brilliant scholar, Daniel Charles Solander, of Sweden, Doctor of Medecine at the University of Uppsala ...

Banks was welcomed as a native son returning to his *alma mater* who

> ... indeed glories in having given birth to many children who have nourished the cause of literature and striven with the utmost energy to advance the frontiers of Science but of these, she confesses, very few can equal the man we see before us ...

He praised the voyage for its peaceful pursuit of knowledge but though he exceeded reality in attributing to Banks and Solander alone achievements in astronomy and navigation, the orator was at least not far astray when he said

> ... to both men natural history owes the fact that more than a thousand new species of plants and shrubs, and more than five hundred new species of animals, insects and shells, have been added to those already discovered ...

This scene in the Sheldonian Theatre was enacted two days after Dr John Hawkesworth had acknowledged receiving the first volume of Banks's journal in his letter of 19 November to Lord Sandwich, whose 'powerful influence' he recognized had been so effective in having it made free for his use. By this time however Banks was already well advanced in his preparations for the new venture and becoming the inevitable target of hopeful applications from aspiring 'voluntiers' and of unsolicited advice from helpful friends, which in time came to form part of what is probably his first bound volume of correspondence.

Between September 1771 and July 1772 he assembled some 42 letters and documents relating to the second voyage. Of these some 15 were academic or scholarly papers; some 18 were approaches from naval men already known to him from the *Niger* or the *Endeavour* voyages, clerks, artists, or surgeons. One application was on behalf of young George Shaw of Magdalen College, Oxford, from his father Timothy Shaw backed by Francis Dashwood, Lord Le Dispenser writing to Lord Sandwich; but the future Keeper of Natural History was not to be a traveller in this way. Nor was that seasoned literary seaman Commander Edward Thompson, RN, 'Poet Thompson' to his naval colleagues. He wrote to Banks from Kew on 27 November 1771 withdrawing in these few words:

... After I left you I had the pleasure of seeing Capt. Cook. I find that Explorers of an equal zeal cannot bear one another any more than rival Beauties. I beg leave Sir to relinquish all my pretensions to attend you: but tho' deprived of so agreable a voyage, you shall not go without my most ardent & pious wishes for every pleasure that can come to a sensible mind, & every success in so arduous an undertaking ...

But out of these applications came at least one man who would leave his mark in a most literal sense – Sigismund Bacstrom who from March 1772 became the neat amanuensis of many Banksian documents.

Christmas and the New Year were passed at Revesby Abbey settling estate affairs and with time enough also to receive the freedom of the town of Boston. Before this Banks had somehow managed to sit, or rather stand to Benjamin West for the first indisputable portrait of him that we know. Last seen by the public in 1866 when it was sold from its Derbyshire home it has been known until recently only from the excellent mezzotint by John Raphael Smith published in April 1773. Now, within the past year, the impressive original has re-appeared to find an Australian owner through a London sale again. Its original provenance is still unclear but it seems very likely that West was commissioned by Robert Banks Hodgkinson, the fond uncle of Overton Hall where its last years in the family were probably spent. It is Banks in his twenty-ninth year with the native artefacts of his Pacific voyage about him and at his feet, less clear, in an open folio the drawing of his *planta utilissima*, the New Zealand flax plant, *Phormium tenax* Forster as it was to be. Then, on his return from Revesby, he sat more fashionably arrayed on 15 January to Sir Joshua Reynolds for the first time and still possibly under family pressures, for a portrait that would not be finished until 4 March 1773, months after his withdrawal from a second Pacific voyage.

He outlined the pressures on his time to Thomas Falconer in a letter from Brampton in Lincolnshire on 7 January: collecting supplies for another long voyage and finding artists prepared to go; the demands of a social circle grown preposterously since his return; the added burden of overseeing engravings for the publication on which Hawkesworth was engaged for the Admiralty; and attending to the care and conservation of the collections themselves to ensure their safety in his absence

... in short the Steps necessary to be taken in order to render the observations made in the last Voyage usefull to the world even in Case we should perish in this ...

He proclaimed the general intentions of the next voyage to Falconer:

... our next is to reverse our last track Keeping to the Eastward from the Cape by Van Diemens Land & new Holland: we are to Sail from thence towards the South Pole in order to [See if the] immence portion of our Globe in that [Quarter is Land] or Water: if Land tis the new Con[tinent that] has so long been the desideratum of discover[ers]: [if] water why may we not penetrate to the [Pole] as Ice has been Observd no where in Large [quantity] ...

99

This great blank in geographic knowledge was well and truly shown in the frontispiece map in Volume I of Dalrymple's *An Historical Collection of the Several Voyages and Discoveries in the South Pacific Ocean* published in 1770 during the course of

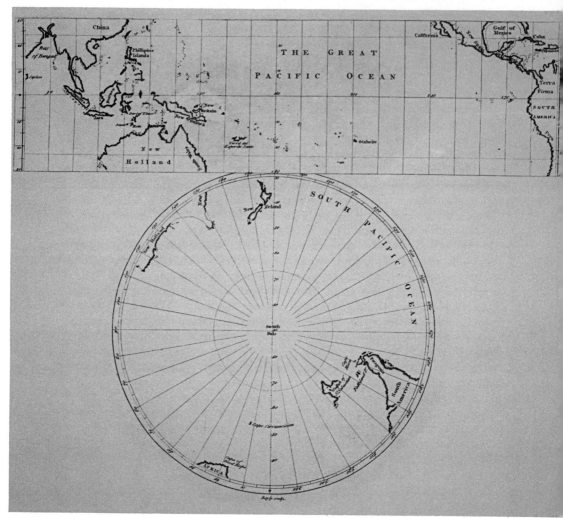

The 'great pacific ocean' engraved in Feb./March 1772 by John Bayley to the order of Joseph Banks for which the account rendered, dated 26 March 1772, is in the Mitchell Library, Safe 1/11. The copper plate, from which this is the first modern print made, was found by H. B. Carter on 7 January 1975 among the Banks plates in the Department of Botany, British Museum (Natural History). Though not published it is the first *printed* map in any form of the discoveries made on the *Endeavour* voyage. A similar polar projection was used by Cook in his memorandum of 6 February 1772 to Lord Sandwich, in the Mitchell Library, Safe 1/11. It appears also as a chart of the southern hemisphere showing the track and discoveries of the *Resolution* c. 1775 in the Public Record Office at MPI.94.

the voyage of the *Endeavour* on board which was his preliminary account. Of this new version Banks now received a copy inscribed to him by the author and, in an adaptation of the frontispiece he derived a map split in two parts: the upper rectangular portion on a cylindrical projection shows the equatorial region from 30° N. to 30° S.; the lower circular portion shows the southern hemisphere on a polar stereographic projection from 30° S. to the South Pole, a compact and convenient blank on which to trace the ships' tracks and any of the discoveries made. Banks had this engraved by John Bayly in February/March 1772, the same man who had already engraved Cook's chart of New Zealand. From it he ordered 50 prints on French super royal and 50 on thin post under the title of 'The great pacific ocean'. This engraving shows the discoveries of the *Endeavour* voyage – New Zealand and the east coast of Australia with the name 'New South Wales' – of which it is the earliest printed map. But all these preparations however were to be pointless as trouble brewed in the Admiralty dockyards over the fitting of the *Resolution*.

The mortality on the *Endeavour* voyage had told heavily on Banks and held a lesson for future planning. So for the new venture he organized a party of 16 – himself and Solander, four artists, of whom one was John Zoffany, two secretaries, eight servants and assistants. With a clear view from the past three years' experience of how much there was to be done and recorded and now with two ships on the service, this number was not excessive. For a three-year voyage, for salaries and wages alone, something more than £3000 would be required. For the Admiralty dockyard, however it posed a problem in supplying working space for two scientific enthusiasts. This was no longer a Royal Society voyage, the Admiralty was in the ascendant now and Admiralty decisions prevailed. The story of the dispute between Banks and the Navy Board over the alterations aboard the *Resolution* and the impairment of her sailing qualities has been documented well enough in the letters which, in their day, remained hidden from the public eye. But by the end of May it had become publicly apparent through the columns of the *Gentleman's Magazine* and others of the press that Mr Banks, Dr Solander and Mr Zoffany were not likely to embark on the new voyage. By June the inflated expectations of 'the Literati of Europe' which, it was said, had been raised to the highest pitch were abruptly deflated. Mr Banks and his party were certainly not going – on this voyage at least – and this had been made plain by Banks, with his reasons, to Lord Sandwich on 30 May. Early in June his uncle Robert Banks-Hodgkinson was in no doubt either that the south Pacific voyage was off and that Banks had in mind a plan for a northern expedition.

That there had been no rift between Cook and Banks in all this unpleasantness is clear from the correspondence between them. Cook on 5 June in a letter from Will's Coffee House acknowledged Banks's kindness in telling him of Lord Sandwich's intention of promoting him in the service. Moreover he said how much he felt he owed Banks in attaining the reputation he had acquired. It was an easy and friendly letter without any evidence of hard feelings. However, for Banks there were hard feelings to be overcome for into the vacuum created by his withdrawal from the *Resolution*, Johann Reinhold Forster had moved.

Working in the ambit of the Royal Society during the winter the elder Forster had caught the scent late in May of Banks's possible withdrawal. The hint had come from Charles Irving who was at work with Cook on problems of seawater distillation. With the Hon. Daines Barrington as his supporter Johann Reinhold gained the ear of

Phillip Stephens at the Admiralty and so the final authority of Lord Sandwich to embark on the voyage. Banks meanwhile, with the Parliamentary support of Constantine Phipps and Edmund Burke, had been unable to stay the processes of Admiralty and conceded his case as lost. He was grateful to Burke, however, in making it clear that he had a part to play in such voyages more useful than 'only in catching butterflies'. Both he and Solander clearly found it hard to exert themselves for the two Forsters beyond answering the questions that were put to them. To make them free of the collections and the drawings was more than Banks in the black mood of his disappointment could then bring himself to do.

As the Forsters left London to join the ship on 26 June, Banks turned to the question of his northern voyage. On 2 July he had procured from the Danish envoy a passport for himself and all those who would otherwise have sailed with him on the *Resolution* and the *Adventure* – except Zoffany. On 4 July he chartered the *Sir Lawrence*, a brig of 190 tons, Captain James Hunter, December and, almost to the day as Cook set sail from Plymouth, Banks with his civilian party moved down the Thames from Gravesend with Iceland as his subarctic goal.

XIV

The illicit account of the *Endeavour* voyage, Thomas Becket's anonymous edition of September 1771, had appeared with great speed after the expedition's return, to the irritation of all those most intimately concerned – the leading participants themselves, the Royal Society and, of course, the Admiralty. It was but a small foretaste of the sour elements in the literature to come.

For Banks the bitter aftermath was concentrated in the tangled vindictiveness of the publication of Sydney Parkinson's fragmentary journal. This was perhaps more dilute and less astringent in the official account prepared by John Hawkesworth at the behest of the Admiralty. In both cases Banks was a central figure and a victim of urgent pressures: from Stanfield Parkinson, a tradesman in furnishings whom he had once employed, claiming properties of putative family concern as the unstable but named executor of a dead brother's will; from Hawkesworth and the Admiralty for the substance of his own extensive journal on which they had no valid claim but in which lay the meat of the voyage apart from the navigational and cartographic particulars – certainly the account with the widest public appeal in a literary sense.

To both pressures Banks had submitted for different reasons in different circumstances. In both cases the outcome was to leave a sad and confused mess for posterity to brood and argue over. The manuscript relics of Sydney Parkinson, in the judgement of Dr John Fothergill as an arbitrator, were printed with reasonable accuracy from what were still only fragments pieced together by a venal and uncommitted editor; some parts were derived from other sources and all without benefit of revision and correction by an authoritative pen. The official account of the voyage, compounded by Hawkesworth from the disparate journals of Cook and Banks, was a synthesis by an editor of worthy intentions charged with a task of doubtful good sense, hard pressed for results, but bereft of any real working relation with either of the journalists themselves.

For nearly two centuries this unrefined distillate has intoxicated and bemused the literary world. Only within the last 25 years or so has it been possible to separate and assay the mixed elements in the Hawkesworth account or to judge Sydney

Parkinson's published fragments in their proper context as part of the surviving Banksian records of the enterprise. For this historical confusion Banks himself must bear a measure of responsibility, a sort of guilt by default, in which his failing was a lack of ambition as a populist writer in the manner of a Thomas Pennant urgent for public acclaim as a man of letters. Had he been adamant for such recognition it is certain that neither Stanfield Parkinson nor John Hawkesworth would have been able to prey in their different ways on the papers which Banks, in both cases but equally against his better judgement, generously released from his own legitimate possession as the resposible mentor.

If there had been kept for Admiralty and Royal Society purposes a clear separation between the account of Cook as the ship's commander, navigator and astronomical observer, and that of Banks as the representative FRS on the geographical, ethnographical and biological outcome of the voyage, then history, science and literature would have been properly served. To fuse them under the single guise of a naval commander's narrative through the pen of a third person who was an utter layman to the fields he described could please no one and only stand as a mockery of the historical record, blurring the truth and confusing the issues.

Here too the Royal Society as a scientific body is culpable. As the prime instigator of the voyage for all three of its intentions – astronomy, geographical discovery and natural history – it succumbed to Admiralty dominance and failed to insist on a published account commensurate with its true character as a Royal Society expedition. But there was no one in the Society with a personality or an understanding equal to the task of sustaining this view – save Banks himself perhaps and, possibly, Benjamin Franklin. However Banks was still the youthful man of adventure intent on another voyage, and Franklin was still a colonial emissary with other troubles on his mind. Again the case went by default as Banks pursued a distant vision of his own and Cook returned to the Pacific as the servant of the Admiralty, free from Royal Society complications certainly but not from supernumerary problems as the two Forsters formed a part of his command.

CHAPTER 5

THE 'MAN OF ADVENTURE' NO MORE
1772–1776

The withdrawal of Banks and his party of 16 from the second Pacific voyage left Banks with considerable equipment and a vacuum of action somehow to be filled. The group was to him 'a considerable expence', but also constituted a body of talent which he was anxious should be employed 'to the advancement of Science' on a voyage of some kind. Seeking (as he had done before the *Endeavour* voyage) some *terra incognita* for the natural scientist, a northern journey such as he had discussed earlier with Thomas Falconer at Chester in November 1767 was now to prove fruitful. To fix on Iceland as a country . . . 'visited but seldom or never at all by any good naturalist' . . . with . . . 'the whole face of the country new to the Botanist & Zoologist' . . . was an echo of the same challenge that he had discerned in South America and the South Sea nearly five years before.

With plans swiftly recast to take advantage of what remained of the short northern summer, he applied for a passport from the Danish envoy in London, Baron Diede von Furstenstein. Armed with this, on 2 July 1772 he chartered the 190-ton brig *Sir Lawrence*, Captain James Hunter, and a crew of 12 men for five months from 4 July to 4 December at £100 per month. All of the party intended for the *Resolution and Adventure* now embarked for Iceland, except for John Zoffany, whom the King had now commissioned to copy pictures in Florence and augmented by three others. They were Lt John Gore, weary perhaps from three successive circumnavigations and not wholly in accord with Cook; Uno von Troil from Sweden to pursue his studies of the Icelandic language; and young Mr John Riddell from Roxburghshire 'intended for the sea' but now on his first such adventure with Banks. For Banks too it was a first occasion – his first and only expedition as indisputable leader.

The brig sailed down the river from Gravesend on 12 July at 11 at night – on the same day that Cook with the *Resolution* and *Adventure* drew out of Plymouth Sound to begin the second voyage. Next day, at noon, the *Sir Lawrence* was off Deal. Here Banks landed his friend and passenger the Comte de Lauraguais, and also a bird, *Columba coronata* Linn., to go by another hand to France as a gift to the Comte de Buffon. A contrary west wind kept the ship at anchor in the Downs and Banks botanized on shore near Sandown Castle until after dinner on 15 July when he set sail on a deceptive east wind, to be checked again off Beachy Head by a western head wind. Four days of seasickness ensued before the brig was anchored at Cowes late at night on 19 July. For the next ten days it was a matter of slow working along the south coast round the Lizard and into the Irish Sea.

At last on 1 August the *Sir Lawrence* came to anchor in Lochindale off the town of Bomore on the west coast of Islay. Here, with no shore lodgings to be had or even a public room in which to eat, the tents were pitched and the party 'amused' themselves with a Highland meal of legs of mutton and various puddings. They were

Portable equatorial instrument of 1772–4 made by Jesse Ramsden similar to that made for Joseph Banks by Ramsden for £63 according to an account rendered on 29 June 1772 and paid the same day.

joined by some of the gentlemen of the island and later by some of the ladies. Next day was the sabbath and the excessive rain was the chief circumstance, as Banks observed, to which they owed 'the preservation of their Characters'. Had they done any form of work on a day so sacred, even botanized in the course of a sabbath stroll, 'the black seal would have been irreversibly set' on them, so rigid was the Calvinist observance. Then on Monday 3 August, free from all moral restraints but still rained upon, they walked towards Killara. Banks was struck by the miserable architecture of the houses but much impressed by the style and address of their occupants, cheerful and content,

> ... with that becoming ease and total absence of mauvaise honte that the whole scotch nation are blessed with in a degree so superior to the English to which cheifly I am much inclind to attribute the great success that their adventurers meet with in our capital ...

The artists, the two Millers and Cleveley, were set to work on these lowly structures and some of the tomb stones while Banks studied the strata of Mr Campbell's lead mine, leased to Mr Fairbairn. He found the lead lying in limestone with shale above it as in the familiar seams at Overton.

Sending the brig round the island to Freeport, Banks led his party on horseback across to meet it on the evening of 5 August. The morning of 6 August was fine and Banks, with Lind, took advantage of the day to estimate, by barometric observations, the height of the northernmost of the Paps of Jura. As they climbed they searched for alpines on the way and compared the plant communities they found with those on the mountains of Carmarthenshire and Snowdonia. Their barometric observations, done, they raised a seven foot cairn of stones on the mountain top but the descending mists blocked any further work on the other Pap. Back at the Fairbairn house by seven p.m. their calculations from the barometric differences with the usual corrections gave an estimated height of 2359 feet, somewhat lower than today's reckoning of 2571, assuming the same points of observation. Next morning Lind brought ashore the equatorial instrument which Banks had bought from Ramsden for the *Resolution* voyage. With this he fixed the latitude of Freeport at 55°52′32″N.

From Islay, Banks ordered the ship to Scarba where from a rough and remote spot chosen to avoid scandal, 'it being Sunday', he studied the mystery of the much vaunted whirlpool of the Corryvrechan. On close inspection, this proved to be but a tame phenomenon 'much sunk in the opinion of everyone'. Then, with a pilot, on 10 August they passed by Mull to Lough Don where Banks learned a new fishing method, the trolling with a small white feather for grey fish, *Cadus carbonamus* Linn., the coal fish of the Yorkshire coast. Next day he shot gulls 'as all our gentlemen think them excellent meat', among them an Arctic gull, *Larus parasiticus* Linn., considered rare in those parts. Later that day, 11 August, with Mull on the left and Morven on the right near Castle Duart, he rhapsodized secretly to himself about

> ... the Land of Heroes once the seat of the Exploits of Fingal and the mother of the romantick Scenery of Ossian ...

lamenting that he dared not risk the censure of his companions by coming to an anchor where

...to have read the pages of Ossian under the shades of these woods would have been Luxury above the reach of Kings...

Banks brought the ship to anchor on the Morven side of the Sound of Mull on 12 August near Drimnin, the house of a Mr McLean who invited him ashore. Here a Mr Leach told Banks of an island nine leagues away to the west ... 'on which were pillars like those of the Giant's Causeway ...' which he believed no one had examined. As it also lay in the direction of y Columb Kil or Iona, which Banks had intended to see, he set off in the yawl at one o'clock with his little tent, two days' provisions and a party of 11 – himself, Leach, McLean's son, Solander, Lind, Gore, von Troil, the two Millers, Cleveley and James Roberts. After eight hours of tedious sailing in an almost calm sea they landed on Staffa at about nine p.m., raised the tent in which Banks and five others slept, while Solander with four volunteers braved the parasitic uncertainties of the only cottage on the island.

At first light on 13 August Banks brought his party to the south-west corner of Staffa where lay the great range of pillars and

...the Cave of Fiuhn ... Fiuhn Mac Coul whoom the translator of Ossians works has calld Fingal ...

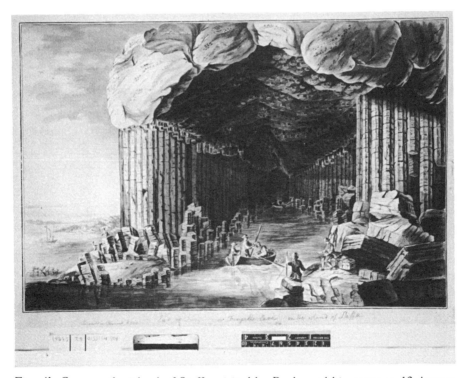

Fingal's Cave on the island of Staffa, visited by Banks and his party on 13 August 1772, measured and described by him for the first time. The original drawing by John Frederick Miller from which the engraving was made for Thomas Pennant, 1776, *A Tour in Scotland* ... II, 263.

and on which Banks mused

> . . . how fortunate that in this cave we should meet with the remembrance of that
> cheif whose existence as well as that of the whole Epick poem is almost doubted in
> England . . .

Then, returning to what was beyond doubt, he said brusquely

> . . . Enough for the beauties of Staffa I shall now proceed to describe it & its
> productions more Philosophically . . .

and he began the systematic study and measurement of the cave, some 12 hours of
concentrated activity.

When the party returned to the tent to prepare for the voyage to Iona there was
some slight peevishness between Solander's companions and the woman of the
cottage in which they had slept – a question on the source of some acquired lice. The
husband answered in Erse 'with a great deal of Sang Froid' that there were none on
the island until Banks and his people had come, a riposte accepted by the visitors
with good humour, whereupon

> . . . pleasd at his presence of mind we took leave having satisfied him for the
> Potatoes fish & milk which notwithstanding his poverty he has supplied us with
> during our stay with the utmost hospitality & which with two wild Pigeons &
> shags we shot had supplyd us with the greatest part of our diet . . .

At five o'clock they set sail for Iona where they landed at eight to be greeted by a
great crowd of people offering all manner of accommodation and help – at a price.

The overnight rain had moderated enough early next morning, 14 August, at five
a.m. to allow a visit to the ruins of a nunnery where there was little to be seen but the
recent traces of Mr Thomas Pennant, no less. He had excavated the gravestone slab
of a prioress with some fortitude 'from under above 3 feet of cow dung' in the chapel
which had been turned into a byre. By noon their guided tour of the Iona antiquities
was over and they returned on a calm sea to find the brig now moored by Banks's
orders in the fine harbour of Tobermory.

Next day, invited by the McLeans to a roebuck hunt on the island of Oronsay, not
all the beaters' noises even augmented by Banks's two French horns could raise a
deer. Returning in the cutter, Banks, although with safety precautions in mind,
carelessly lost his gun when he discharged it over the side of the boat holding it only
in one hand when the recoil jerked it from his grasp. After supping with the McLeans
at Drimnin they returned by moonlight to the *Sir Lawrence* and early next morning on
16 August sailed for St Kilda as the weather seemed moderate enough. At sunset the
Paps of Jura were still in sight 24 leagues to the south by the chart and 8° above the
horizon, enough for Lind to calculate the distance as 54 nautical miles – but which
was right Banks did not venture to judge. Sailing west between Skye and the
Hebrides on 17 August something like 'the Basking Shark of Pennant' was sighted,
though Banks, who had a poor view, could not be sure. Off the Butt of Lewis on 18
August the weather turned foul and the course for St Kilda was abandoned. Veering
north for Iceland everyone, even those who had been most at sea, suffered two days

of seasickness, which Banks attributed to the small size of the brig. Then, on 20 August, about latitude 59°44′ N. 10°10′ W. it fell calm enough for Banks to launch a boat in pursuit of ocean zoology. Some 90 miles south of the Faroes, he gathered three large specimens of *Phyllodoce velella*, or by-the-wind-sailors, *Velella velella* Linn. 1758 as it is today, a solitary floating hydroid which Banks judged from his experience never to have seen north of Mediterranean latitudes. Among the birds he shot a specimen of the 'least Auk' which he classified as *Alca lica* Linn. and thought it to be a young one, differing from the descriptions of Linnaeus and Pennant chiefly in having no white bar across the wings – and thus a possible confusion by Banks with the young of another species.

Then, with a brisk east wind and intermittent bouts of seasickness, land was sighted on the afternoon of 25 August. Next morning the ship was three leagues from the most westerly rocks called Gur-Jugl-Skir, the Penguin Rocks. That evening the snowy peaks of the western Jokulls were seen some 75 miles away. For the next two days, against an offshore wind, they sailed east along the coast with Lind sketching the coastal profile on the way. Near land on the morning of 28 August they found themselves surrounded by Icelandic fishing boats whose occupants were shy and evasive. Pursuit by Captain Hunter and Dr Solander in the ship's boat eventually brought three apprehensive Icelanders, fishy, rank, and 'Lousy to admiration' on board where Solander found he could converse with them readily enough from his knowledge of Norwegian. One of them, Stephen Tordenson, was induced to remain as a pilot and on Saturday 29 August at eight a.m. the *Sir Lawrence* was anchored about three miles south of Bessasted near the house of the Stifshamptman or Governor-General, the Norwegian Lauritz Thodal. Solander landed with the pilot to call on Thodal for further directions, returned about noon, and by dinner time the brig was anchored at Hafnarfiord. At four p.m. Banks and his party landed

... upon a country rougher & more rugged than imagination can easily conceive ...

and one, moreover, whose people were at first apprehensive about their real intentions.

Banks then set out on a formal visit to Thodal with Solander, Lind and von Troil, but also followed by two servants, probably Peter Briscoe and James Roberts, in full livery

... which is a Blue Coat turn'd up with Scarlet and Laced with Silver, a Scarlet and Silver Shoulderknot, a Scarlet waistcoat lac'd with Silver, Scarlet Breeches with broad Silver kneebands and a hat with broad Silver lace ...

Small wonder, then, with this colourful distinction in dress judged by the Icelandic custom of servants preceding their masters, that there was some confusion in the first introductions. However, when Banks was eventually identified as the master and leader of the party, he met, with Thodal, his deputy and amptman Olafur Stephensen with whom he established a lifelong friendship. Banks was assured that the building usually occupied by the Danish merchants on their trading visits was the only accommodation suitable for the party but that this could not possibly be opened before Monday. Again the barrier of strict sabbath day observance tested the patience of the English visitors but, with good grace and in their best apparel, Banks and his party attended the Sunday service in the small chapel, behaving considerately 'with all moderation and decency'. After the service the gentlemen dined with Thodal 'very genteely after the Danish manner' and were then shown his garden within its high sod walls.

On Monday 31 August there was a further delay in opening the Danish houses and Banks exercised his patience by trout fishing with great success. At last the sysselman handed over the two keys that gave access to the buildings. Banks was careful to make an inventory of their contents, with a copy for his hosts, though the furniture was sparse and 'scarce worth twenty shillings'. The party now had four rooms in the three houses – a dining room in which some were to sleep, a drawing room for the draftsmen to work and sleep in, a kitchen and a loft for the servants with some more space for the storage of baggage and equipment. On Tuesday 1 September everything needed from the ship was stowed on shore in a congestion not much less than on the brig. Apart from direct purchases, Banks was careful to set up a system of trade with ribbons and tobacco as articles of barter, and was delighted with the pleasant civility of the Icelanders in all their dealings.

With botanizing and seine-netting the days passed near Hafnarfiord with Banks making gifts of hams, porter and persico to his Icelander friends until 6 September when he invited Thodal, Stephensen and their families to Sunday dinner. The Icelanders admired the English mode of separate courses presented as they were on the Wedgwood Queen's ware dinner service which Banks had bought a few days before sailing from London. They were impressed with the variety of wines but what surprised them most was the music, especially the melody of the French horns. Banks was at some pains to assure them this was acceptable to English custom as 'a laudable pastime even on a sunday'.

The next week was disturbed by the arrival unexpectedly of the Danish snow *Christiana* to unload stores, an event which always made the Icelanders uneasy because of the arrogance of the Danes's behaviour. Banks was a good-humoured buffer as he entertained the Danish captain to breakfast on 8 September, before continuing his own explorations of recent lava flows and of 'some hot Springs at a place called Reikavik' on the 14th. The two Millers and John Cleveley were also kept busy this week with their drawings of the houses of the Icelanders, particularly those of the amptman and the sysselman. Then, on 18 September, with horses and guides arranged by Thodal and Stephensen, Banks set off on a journey to Mount Hekla somewhat more than 100 miles of circuitous travel inland to the east.

With him travelled Solander, Lind, von Troil, John Cleveley and James Roberts, and two of Thodal's servants as guides. Including their own mounts, several pack animals and spare horses there were 19 of the hardy Iceland ponies in the train. Apart from food and liquor in the packs there was Banks's small bell tent but no more than two blankets apiece. The first stage of the route lay past Thingvalla, over the river Broaran and past the hot springs of Laugarvatn on to the Great Geyser at Haukadal. The nature and frequency of its eruptions were noted and their height was measured by Lind with the quadrant. Here also, in the boiling water, on 21 September, a ptarmigan, which Banks had shot a short while before, was cooked in seven minutes, overcooked in fact, for only a few tasty morsels remained on the legs when the bird was withdrawn. On 22 September they were the guests of Bishop Finnur Jonsson near his wooden cathedral at Skalholt and with Bjarni Jonsson, headmaster of the cathedral school for 28 boys. There were regaled with dinners of roast mutton, cold

The Danish storehouses at Hafnarfiord with Dr James Lind (in left middle distance) making an observation with the portable equatorial instrument on a wooden stand. The original drawing by John Cleveley jun.

cheese, burned butter and fruit with currant sauce and that night they slept on good, if rather short, beds, with eiderdown mattresses. As a climax the visit was celebrated in laudatory odes in Latin and Icelandic by Bjarni Jonsson addressed to Banks and Solander, while 'Troilus' or von Troil bought cheaply some old manuscripts and a dictionary.

Next day, on 23 September, the party was ferried across the river Huitaae, with the horses swimming behind, and at Thiorsaarholt they all enjoyed the luxury of the turf-covered steam baths at temperatures of 93°–125° F. Then they crossed the river Thiorsa over the worst and longest ford that Banks had ever met, a rough and stony passage of more than one English mile. That night they slept behind the altar in the Skaro church, very cold, with the temperature at 43° F. In the morning they made the last stage toward Mount Hekla over a stretch of hraun 'with ashes flying like the deserts of Arabia' to reach Naefurholt where most other parties had usually lodged but without ever reaching the top. Banks therefore decided to sleep that night of 24 September in the small tent somewhat nearer the mountain. As the evening was fine he and his small party for the ascent rode for an hour to reach the last patch of finely grassed turf. Here the small bell tent was pitched and into this six people crowded for the night – Banks, Solander, Lind, von Troil, James Roberts and an Iceland guide – drawing lots for position, as it was coldest near the sides. James Roberts, who had drawn a place next to Banks recorded

. . . This Anecdote is mentioned to prove how Amicable our little Society was, and that no distinction was made in regard to Superiority in point of Fortune. here was

111

no Master and Slave but a willingness to assist each other put us all upon an equality, except in point of Learning and Philosophical knowledge . . .

Then, on 25 September at one a.m. they awoke, breakfasted, and at four a.m. rode to the hraun, where they left the horses, and began the final ascent of north Hekla in the teeth of a strong wind. Covered with ice and 'Cloaths like Buckram', the party reached what was thought to be the summit where 'all hands [drank] a hearty draught of Brandy' – unwisely one would think. The barometer stood at 24.838 inches and the thermometer at 24° F, their water was frozen and Lind's wind machine out of action in spite of filling it with warm water. But there was a peak even higher and they hurried towards it, leaving Solander exhausted in a warm cleft under the care of the Icelander. At the very top there was a spot three yards wide with steam emerging and much too hot for sitting on. The air itself was now intensely cold and the barometer reading down to 24.722 inches. Assuming that this was the summit, Banks now led the party down the mountain very fast to pass the snow-line safely, although they were almost frozen in the wind chill. At two p.m. they reached the tent where the barometer read 29.392 and the thermometer 42° F. One thermometer had been broken in the swift descent and all were greatly fatigued. They determined to reach Skaro as soon as possible, where they slept that night in good beds and between clean sheets. On 26 September the weather cleared and they could see a wisp of smoke on the highest peak of Mount Hekla as they travelled back over the bad ford and the rough country to reach the church at Hraun Garda where they slept. Next day rain and high winds from the south-east in the morning delayed a start but later in the day they were able to reach the church at Rycomba where they slept comfortably in deep hay. Passing the hot springs and the geysers again on 28 September they rejoined their old road and at five in the evening returned at last to Hafnarsfiord.

The following day, Olafur Stephensen visited Banks with gifts of Icelandic books and specimens of the local stone. Then, on Friday 2 October, the preparations for leaving began, with the ship's cow first to be hoisted on board again. On Saturday Banks visited Thodal and Stephensen with presents and dined again with Thodal on Sunday 4 October. On Tuesday 6 October Olafur Stephensen paid the English party a last visit and again there was an exchange of presents among which Banks was given an Icelandic musical instrument of an undefined species. On the following day the last items were loaded from the shore in drizzling rain and that night, after entertaining the officers of an English vessel to dinner on the ship, the whole party slept on board. At four a.m. on Thursday 8 October the anchor was raised and, to a parting salute from three guns on the Danish snow *Christiana*, a course was set for the Orkneys. By seven in the evening Iceland was out of sight. For a week the *Sir Lawrence* drove south-east in gales, rain, low clouds and poor visibility until on Thursday 15 October land was sighted. The next afternoon the brig anchored in Hoy Sound off the town of Stromness on the main Orkney island of Pomona.

Sleeping on the brig but dining for the most part at the inn ashore, Banks explored not only the old lead and copper workings but more particularly the antiquities along the sandy coast to the north on the Links of Skail, close by the lochs of Stenness and Harray. Here he set the artists to work recording the stones of Stenness; John Miller on the 'Ring of Loda' and Cleveley on the semicircle to the south-west, while Frederick Walden prepared a very competent survey of the whole area. While this work was afoot Banks and Solander roamed the Sound to the island of Hoy where, among much else, he was greatly struck with the resemblance of an old fort to the Maori hippah he had seen and recorded in New Zealand nearly three years before in the Bay of Islands. On 18 October he was again among the standing stones and the buried tombs of what we know as Skara Brae discussing antiquities with Dr Robert Ramsay and Dr George Low with whom he had consulted from his first day at Stromness and had planned his archaeological study of the site.

On Tuesday 20 October he visited Kirkwall, some fifteen miles away, with Solander, von Troil and Gore to receive from the Council the freedom of the town.

With a final burst of energy next day Banks, with the help of George Low, excavated two of the burial tumuli at 'a place call'd Sandwick' employing an organized working party of about 30. James Roberts noted in his small journal what came to light that day:

> . . . in each of them was found the Bones of a man, and woman, the form of their
> Interment was somewhat Singular. they were laid in a very coarse mat which was
> entirely rotten. the Bones of the woman were laid at the man's feet. the Tomb was
> form'd of Flagstones, one on each side, one at each end, and one on the top. the
> other was the same with the addition of one at the Bottom. I measured one of the
> Tombs. it was four feet Eight Inches long, two feet Eight Inches broad, and two
> feet four inches in depth. the other was nearly the same . . . the Draughtsmen made
> Drawings of both the Tombs . . .

But the full description and the drawings Banks evidently relinquished to George Low as the resident antiquary of the island, though the account of these proceedings

The return of Banks and his party after the ascent of Mount Hekla on 25 September 1772. The original drawing by John Cleveley jun.

lay in limbo for another 100 years. The day itself ended at Stromness with music from the two French horns played by John Asquith and Peter Sidserf accompanied on the violin by Sanders, the Eurasian recruit from Batavia.

Thereafter Banks fell idle, apparently struck by a mood of unusual depression, confessing to a tiredness as he had never done before. With this blackness on him next day, his notes for his journal ended abruptly with his 'resolve to go away fair or foul'. However it was another four days before the *Sir Lawrence* cleared the Orkneys on 26 October with a fresh breeze at north-east, to cast anchor at Leith Roads in the Forth in the early evening of 28 October.

Next morning Banks, Solander, Lind, von Troil and James Roberts walked the two miles up to the city of Edinburgh where, from 1 November to 18 November, Banks took lodgings with Mrs Thompson in Rider's Court off the High Street. As they approached the old city he took special note of the 'houses of many storys property in the air' rising against the morning sky. After two days dining and talking with the professors from the Old College of the University and visiting the Physic Garden, he found the society of Edinburgh 'so Learned and unpedantick' that he resolved to stay for some time. He debated with Lord Monboddo in that Law Lord's quest for evidence of men with tails, unable to satisfy him with examples of such appendages in the South Seas. He dined with James Boswell whose receptive ear must surely have heard in Banks's conversation opinions so favourable to the Scots and gleaned arguments enough from the encounter to lay a foundation for the tour in the following year with Samuel Johnson to the Hebrides and West Highlands.

For Banks at length the erudite company of the Edinburgh scholars gave place to the attractions of Hopeton House and its gardens where he stayed for several days with John Hope, the 2nd Earl of Hopeton. Botany and horticulture gave way to industrial technology as he moved to Kinneil House in the company of Dr John Roebuck with whom he studied the Carron ironworks for several days, saw the coal-mines and salt-works at Bo'ness, and almost certainly heard much about the Roebuck-James Watt partnership and their new steam engine. At Carron Hall he dined with Henry Dundas, probably a first meeting, and he found much to occupy him in the engineering of the Forth and Clyde canal with its locks and drawbridges.

Returning to Edinburgh, he explored both the old city and the new, but especially the old from the castle and its wide prospect of views to Holyrood House, taking in the Law Courts and Parliament with the Advocates' Library on the way. Nor did he neglect the Adamsian precincts of the Old College Library with its shelves well filled with volumes much to his taste. From this intellectual honeypot he drew himself at last on 18 November to travel south by road and to sleep for the first night at Ballencrief near Haddington with Patrick Murray, the erudite 5th Baron Elibank. Then on to Dunbar, where he was attracted by the basaltic pillars for which he assigned a possible volcanic origin. That night he slept at the house of a Sir John Hall and on 20 November set out for Alnwick. Here he spent a whole day exploring the castle and its fortifications, with the mock defenders on the walls, and also its domestic interior with

> ... its rooms beautiful but furnishd with Paper & stucco instead of Tapistreys pictures & Hangings ...

And so on to London through Morpeth and Newcastle, almost certainly by way of

Revesby Abbey, to discharge his charter of the *Sir Lawrence* due to end on 4 December 1722. He had now to gather his specimens and his artists back into the fold at New Burlington Street and for himself to pick up the threads of a sedentary metropolitan life.

II

The New Year of 1773 began with all the unsettling elements that marked it to the end. The herbarium of British, Newfoundland and South Labrador species was returned by John Sneyd to join the *Endeavour* collection and the latest from the Hebrides, Iceland and the Orkneys in New Burlington Street. Banks condensed his northern voyage into a long letter on 12 January, the first of two on the subject, to Thomas Falconer. This conveyed his firm intention to go on another Pacific voyage when the time should prove ripe; meanwhile two other plans were evolving. The first was his own idea of an immediate journey to Holland with Charles Greville, with whom his friendship had blossomed during the home leave from Naples in 1771-2 of Greville's uncle Sir William Hamilton. The other was the notion of an Arctic voyage by Constantine Phipps, intended to penetrate the polar ice to the highest latitude possible. This was an adventure from which Banks did not wholly exclude himself and he threw himself warmly into its planning. His proposed visit to Holland had its own relation to the Arctic plan in the information Banks hoped to glean directly from the Dutch whalers in Greenland waters during the winter off-season in their homeland. Apart from this weighty reason for his Continental journey there was also his rapidly clearing vision of the florilegium so heartily promulgated more than a year before.

Banks now had three young artists at his command, the two Millers and John Cleveley jun., proved on the Iceland voyage to be competent draftsmen. They could now set to work under his own eye and, in his absence, that of Solander in bringing the unfinished Parkinson drawings to completion, coloured and ready for the engraver. On the textual side there was competent secretarial and clerical aid in the presence of Sigismund Bacstrom, and perhaps briefly also of Frederick Walden. But there still remained the problem of engraving for reproduction and engravers to be found – another good reason for a search on the Continent to widen the field of choice and the standards of comparison. Banks could leave London for a few weeks reasonably confident that productive work on the drawings and the taxonomy of the collections could proceed. Before this however there was a detail to be settled with Sir Joshua Reynolds about the portrait begun a year ago and still unfinished. In a brief letter to his sister Sarah Sophia, probably on 11 February 1773, he enlightened her about the print on which his left hand rests in the painting. The motto, he said, were the words of Aeneas in Virgil's *Aeneid*

> . . . nunc vino pelliti curas
> cras ingens iterabimus equor

in English

> now drive away your cares with wine
> tomorrow we will again cross the immense ocean

the last part only you see I have chosen Adieu . . .

115

The 'last part' certainly defined his immediate plan but it also marked his hopes deferred for another Pacific voyage.

Then, late in the afternoon on Friday 12 February, Banks and Charles Greville left London for Harwich with Captain John Bentinck and Bentinck's young son William on the first stage through Ingatestone and Colchester, with Peter Briscoe and James Roberts almost certainly as servants. Waiting at Harwich on 13 February for wind and tide Banks and Greville explored the strata visible on the cliffs nearby before sailing on the postal packet. They landed on the quay at Helvoetsluys, and after another nine hours of varied travel on foot, by cart and by boat through ice-burdened canals they reached The Hague about six in the evening to be greeted by the elderly Count William Bentinck who had arranged their lodgings. At 11 that night Banks wrote to his sister 'quite tird' and sleepy to report his safe arrival and his first impression of the country as far as his eyes had been able to pierce the fog:

> . . . no two countries were ever so much alike as this & Lincolnshire especially that part between Spalding and Peterborough we have traveld all day Either over Banks like Crowland Bank or through rows of willow Trees with rich crops of Rape & Engines on each side of us . . .

Here was another reason for his concern with seeing the Low Countries. As the master of Revesby Abbey and the Holland estates south of the Wash, fenland agriculture and the problems of drainage were never far from his thoughts.

On 16 February he paid his courtesy call on Sir James Yorke, the British ambassador at The Hague, dining with Count Bentinck. Next day, being Sunday, Banks found himself again thwarted by a strict sabbatarianism augmented in its rigour by its proclamation as a fast day. Pierre Lyonet refused to show him his cabinets on the sabbath. So, with Greville, he ranged morosely through the garden of Count Bentinck's estate of Sorghted among the sand-hills by the shore. At last, interspersing social occasions at the Court of the Prince of Orange, Banks finally managed to see and study Lyonet's cabinet of shells and especially to admire Lyonet's own fine engravings for his *Anatomy of a Caterpillar* and those he had done for Trembley's *Polyps*. Here was what he had come to see by which to set a standard of copper engraving for his own botanical plates.

At the Bentinck's he met Jean Nicolas Allamand, Professor of Natural History at Leyden, and together they viewed the well-arranged cabinet of the Prince of Orange under the management of its curator Vermaes. They found it an excessively cold experience with no more than a single peat fire for its heating. Next day, in Count Bentinck's coach, Banks visited the Prince's menagerie at Loo and found it well-managed, especially in the tropical hot-rooms. Then, also by the Count's arrangement, Banks and Greville travelled to Leyden on 22 February in the luxury of the States's official yacht. Here Allamand showed them the university's zoological collection, and David van Royen the herbarium, the botanical garden, especially the greenhouse, and finally a Dutch commercial plant nursery. In the afternoon they went to Haarlem in a track schuit along the canal and Banks spent that evening with Enskeda, the antiquarian bookseller and printer. Next day he took Greville to see some of Enskeda's picture collection to pronounce judgement on them as an avowed 'amateur' of art. Later Banks indulged his love of music by paying handsomely to hear the Haarlem church organ, 'the Largest in the world by many degrees', produce

116

'the most noisy harmony and the most harmonious noise' but, as music, a good reward for all that he had paid.

From Haarlem, on 24 February, they went to Amsterdam a distance of eight miles or a two-hour journey in a track schuit. This was a convenient and cheap way to travel, for they were accommodated in a cabin with a table, good seats, a tallow candle, a warm stove with room for eight people, as Banks said, more comfortably than a coach would hold four. This relaxation clinched his decision to follow his sister's pressing advice to keep a journal. So he wrote to her from Amsterdam the same day, adding his admiration for the great sluices of Harlemer mere

... ten times larger & more magnificent than our Grand Sluice in Lincolnshire & yet the dutch think little of it ...

On Saturday 27 February in the State House on the dam in the Burghers's Hall he saw the pavement where once were laid out in brass the northern and southern hemispheres in polar projection. At his visit only the northern projection remained so that he could only speculate on the map of New Zealand which was said to have formed a prominent feature of the southern. This had been intended not only as a memorial to Abel Tasman's discovery but a reminder to the Dutch themselves that, in the South Sea, there was a political refuge if ever the state of Europe drove them out. Later that day he had dinner with a Mr Cross and was set next to a Mr Bourse, advocate to the Dutch East India Company, who quizzed him about what he had learned of the Dutch East India settlements during the *Endeavour* voyage. In this contest of wits Banks rated himself the winner in the knowledge he had gained for which he had given none in return.

On Sunday 28 February Banks and Greville were the guests of Admiral Reynst in the Admiralty yacht on an excursion to Sardam. On their passage they passed the point of land where the bodies of executed criminals were publicly exposed. Some were still sitting in the wheels on which they had been broken; others were on gibbets hanging either by their necks or their heels. But, said Banks

... upon the whole the quantity seemd very small for the offenders in so large a society ...

all of which was a great contrast to the orderly neatness and prim church-going that sabbath day at Sardam.

Banks spent some time next day with Nicolaus Burmann, Professor of Botany at the University of Amsterdam and there saw for himself the herbarium of Paul Hermann in good condition, the collection which, 20 years later, he would buy and add to his own. Piso's collection he rated as ill-chosen and puny but Oldenland's plants from the Cape of Good Hope impressed him favourably. Burmann's own collection of dried plants was large and the attendant library also good. The drawings however, though numerous, Banks thought indifferent, barring some large ones by a daughter of Sybella Merian which were tolerably well-designed.

On 3 March, again in a hired track schuit, they left Amsterdam for Utrecht where they were welcomed by John Loten, arriving with the storks, they were told. Here Banks met Pieter Boddaert 'a more liberal man than most I have found in this country', who was later to fix the specific name *peregrinus* to the Queensland grey ring-tail possum which Banks had caught near the Endeavour River on 26 July 1770. In this company Banks saw the botanic garden of the university which he noted as average though the stove facilities in it seemed to be good. From the steeple of the university tower he viewed again the flat Dutch landscape confirming the impression he had already sent to Sarah Sophia – its close resemblance to the countryside of his own Holland estates:

> ... Such a similitude of countrey inclines me [to] suppose that that very district of Lincolnshire was calld from its neighbour Holland & not as Cambden supposes from its fertility in the article of Hay Holiand ...

Two days later they travelled by canal and wagon to Rotterdam to lodge at the *Marshall Garbonne* where on 6 March they met an Armenian clergyman, Mr Noseman, to whom Banks had a letter of introduction. With only Latin as a common language they argued all that morning over the classification of a sponge, inconclusively as it proved, for Banks admitted that he was not fluent in spoken Latin. Equally unresolved, but on taxonomic grounds, was his argument with Frédéric Rainville the same day over the reality of the supposed 500 species of grass that he was shown and which were said to have been collected from five of the seven Dutch provinces.

Conversation took a different turn later after dinner that day when Banks and Greville were guests of the Rotterdam 'Society of Literature' and the discussion was confined to hydrostatics. To his embarrassment Banks was called upon to speak on the use of fire (steam) engines for draining marshes and the number of tons of water that could be lifted six feet by cylinders of specific dimensions. Although the subject was not strange to him he protested in vain that he could not carry such figures in his head. He said he could give a much better account in these terms for the drainage of mines. He was after all familiar with the old Newcomen engine installed and working at Overton in the Gregory Mine from 1768. But on the whole he felt he was dismissed by the Dutch as an 'incorrigible blockhead'. On 9 March he examined the botanic garden at The Hague with Professor Swenkins and then, on 10 March, he

> ... had a Levee of Greenland Captains who had been sent from Rotterdam to give me such information as they might be able which might forward Captn. Phipps Plan of Sailing towards the pole ...

From this meeting Banks gathered a useful body of information about the ice between Spitzbergen and Greenland as far north as 81°, the sea currents and the winds, the soundings and the variations of the compass, for the guidance of the expedition being mounted already.

The next four days, from 11 to 15 March, were spent with art and music, court and country, in and about The Hague interposed with cabinets and collections of insects, shells and birds, until the time came to set out on 16 March for Helvoetsluys on the homeward journey. Embarking at nine in the morning on 18 March in the 'stinking pacquet' again, they reached Harwich at noon on 20 March after another nauseous and exhausting passage leaving Banks more inclined to rest than to travel. Next day they set out 'very slow' for Colchester where they dined, fittingly enough, upon oysters, and afterwards inspected the castle and the meeting room of its gentlemen's

HM Ships *Racehorse* and *Carcass* commanded by Captain the Hon. Constantine Phipps breaking free from the ice about latitude 80°N off Spitzbergen, 10 August 1773. An engraving by Pierre Canot from a drawing composed by John Cleveley jun., 4 May 1774.

club with its 'tolerable library of old books'. That night they slept at Manningtree and at noon on 22 March arrived in London

> ... after as lazy a Journey as indolence itself could devise ever since we landed on English ground to make some amends for our Fatigues in the Land of Frogs & mud ...

III

Four days after his return Banks gave his penultimate sitting to Reynolds and, on 2 April, rounded off his remarks on Iceland in his letter to Thomas Falconer. In this second letter on his northern voyage he emphasized his active engagement with Phipps in preparing for the Arctic expedition as a further distraction from publishing an account of his recent travels. Banks was certainly no Pennant but Pennant was already at work plundering Banks's manuscript Iceland journal for his *Tour of Scotland*. So Banks's original description of Staffa and Fingal's Cave, with engravings derived from the drawings of John Frederick Miller and John Cleveley jun., recording that frantically busy 12 hours on the island became part of Pennant's *Tour ...*, 1776.

119

This brought Fingal's Cave to the notice of European romantics and the critical appraisal of Horace Walpole as the only passages worth reading in the entire book.

Meanwhile Banks was preparing his guiding notes for Phipps on the subject of natural history while the two bomb ketches, HM Ships *Racehorse* and *Carcass*, were fitting out ... 'as the strongest species of Ships therefore best to Cope with the Ice' ... in his words to Falconer on the subject. He did not expect a great yield of specimens in so short a voyage into so frigid a zone as the Arctic north in the high latitudes it was hoped to attain. He hoped for a live young white bear as an animal he suspected was generically different from the brown and black species, but he listed seals and whales as other mammalian species for particular observation. Birds, fishes, crustacea, molluscs and insects he also hoped for in addition to the flowering and other forms of plant life. He provided the means of collection and preservation under the care of Dr Charles Irving for the zoology, and of Mr Israel Lyons, astronomer and also his old tutor, for the botany. But he ventured further with some suggestions for observing sea currents and the density of sea water. As Banks forecast, the yield from this preparation was not large. When the ships returned on 25 September 1773 they had penetrated as far north as 80–81° until blocked by the ice-fields with no sign of a north-west passage through, and only a modest harvest in natural history. There were some 51 animal species and 28 of plants, mostly from near Spitzbergen, giving work enough for Banks and Solander in their classification and description for Phipp's official account, *A voyage towards the North Pole, undertaken by His Majesty's Command, 1773*, published in the summer of 1774. There was a little work also for Banks in directing Barnes, the draftsman on the figures, a man whom John Ellis had used for his corals, and in supervising the engraving by James Caldwell who had been engaged on some of the figures in Hawkesworth's *Voyages* ... so much under excited discussion since the spring of 1773.

The Hawkesworth *Account of a Voyage round the World ... by Lieutenant James Cook Commander of His Majesty's Bark the Endeavour* had burst upon an expectant public in June 1773 as Volumes II and III of the *Account of the Voyages undertaken by order of His present Majesty for making Discoveries in the Southern Hemisphere ...*, with a dedication to the King dated 1 May from Bromley, Kent. On 11 June, about the time of its appearance, Horace Walpole dined at The Grove, Muswell Hill, the charming white mansion of Topham Beauclerk and his Lady Diana. His fellow guests were the 'florists and natural historians, Banks and Solander'. It is tempting to wonder how much the Hawkesworth volumes and the voyage itself were subjects of discussion on that day. A month later Walpole was writing to Mason, after all his expectations about 'Mr Banks' voyage earlier in May:

> ... I have almost waded through Dr. Hawkesworth's three volumes of the *Voyages to the South Sea*. The entertaining matter would not fill half a volume; and at best is but an account of the fishermen on the coasts of forty islands ...

This and some other sour reactions to the official account was in no way sweetened by the publication in July of Sydney Parkinsons imperfect *Journal of a Voyage to the South Seas* ... under the crazed obsession of his brother Stanfield. But however unpleasant the literary atmosphere had become, Banks had other reasons for preparing a journey into Wales that summer. His stepuncle George Banks had died during the spring and there was the settlement of his affairs to be discussed at

Edwinsford. Banks had planned a visit to Wales on this account but had built round it some hopes for a 'philosophic' party to go with him – Jesse Ramsden, André de Luc, Charles Blagden, John Lightfoot, Charles Greville, William Curtis and Paul Sandby – but in the event it was reduced to a pleasant mix of topographic art and botany. Charles Greville was deflected by the death of his father, the Earl of Warwick; Ramsden by the confusion of his business affairs; de Luc and Blagden by other private calls.

The residue of the party set out in the last week of June broadly along the routes that Banks had followed during the spring and summer of 1767. So, while Phipps drove his bomb-ketches towards the Arctic ice of Spitzbergen, Banks botanized with Lightfoot through Wales and Staffordshire and Paul Sandby sketched those scenes from which he would select a modest few for the pioneering aquatints to come. With Edwinsford as a base for Banksian hospitality, the party ranged from Chepstow and Tintern Abbey on the Wye down the Bristol Channel and along the Glamorgan, Carmarthen and Pembroke coast and hinterland to St David's and Ramsay Island on the west. Then, travelling north through Hereford and Shropshire to recruit John Lloyd in Denbigh, they moved through Conway and Bangor to Llanberis, Dolbaden Castle and the very summit of Snowdon. Back across the Menai Strait and round the Isle of Anglesey, they finally turned east skirting the Carnarvon coast and the banks of the Dee to Chester, and so homeward to London with a brief pause at Shugborough. In this seven weeks of botanical field work, the last extensive journey of the kind in which he would engage, Banks left no written record of which we know. For him perhaps the plant presses with a harvest of some 220 species gathered were memorial enough to the passing of his thirtieth summer. He was content to let John Lightfoot set down the few notes for Sigismund Bacstrom to transcribe when they returned to New Burlington Street. He had written a journal of his Holland tour with some reluctance and only under the urging of Sarah Sophia. Since then had come the publication of the uneasy synthesis by Hawkesworth of his own with Cook's *Endeavour* journals followed in print by the distasteful fragmentation of whatever record Sydney Parkinson had kept. These episodes were too recent and too galling in their different ways as examples of literary pitfalls to lend much encouragement to his pen for the time being. In any case he was now more concerned less with the written word than the problems and perplexities of botanical illustration and the engraved plate.

IV

As 1773 approached its close various northern travellers had also reached their journeys ends. In September Phipps had returned from Spitzbergen and the Arctic ice-barrier with enough of his *Ursus maritimus* to prove Banks right in his supposition

> . . . that the white Bear is an animal differing even generically from the Brown or Black bear . . .

to stamp its identity in future taxonomy as *Thalarctos maritimus* Phipps 1774. By November Banks was already at work assisting Phipps in the appendix and illustrations for the formal account of the voyage.

At the same time James Boswell had brought his own great bear *Ursus major* to a

Paul Sandby sketching, *c.* 1776, by William Parry.

safe haven in Edinburgh on 9 November as he and Dr Johnson returned 'after an absence of eighty-three days' on their journey through Scotland to the Hebrides or Western Islands. Writing to Mrs Thrale on 12 November Johnson himself could not forbear to note that his Scottish friends in Edinburgh

. . . congratulate our return as if we had been with Phipps or Banks . . .

from what was, in fact, a feat of bear-leading by James Boswell than which, as Lord Elibank said at their first meeting, '. . . hardly any thing seemd to him more improbable . . .'

For Banks himself in London, another sort of journey was nearly done. In his thirty-first year, the days of distant travel were over and the 'man of adventure' had metamorphosed into the serious savant when, on 3 December, he joined the Council of the Royal Society for the first time, and with him both Phipps and Solander.

Then early in 1774, that last year of peace before the seven years of war with the American colonists began, John Zoffany returned from Florence bearing a letter for Banks from James Bruce weaving a leisurely course back from Abyssinia and the confusions of the Nile head-waters. Zoffany had perhaps been the chief sufferer from Banks's withdrawal from the *Resolution* voyage but the disturbance to his career as a working artist had been redressed by Banks with a gift of £300 (one year's salary for the voyage) and by the Royal commissions for paintings to be done in Florence for the royal collection. Zoffany now brought the request by Bruce that Banks should ease the passage of his 40 bound volumes of African and Mediterranean drawings through the customs by asking Lord North to waive the duty. At the same time Bruce

The house at Edwinsford on the River Cothy. An engraving by W. Watts from a drawing by Paul Sandby during the visit of July 1775.

123

drew Banks's attention to the seeds, mostly from Abyssinia, that he had sent already to William Aiton at Kew, from which, a year later, Solander would identify new species of *Ajuga* and *Coreopsis*. Above all Bruce was anxious to meet Banks and to hear about the *Endeavour* voyage. Later in the summer when James Bruce had at last reached Scotland, James Boswell met him for the first time in Edinburgh finding this 'tall stout bluff man in green and gold' apparently the 'very reverse of Banks – impatient, harsh, and uncommunicative'. He underlined the social view of these two men:

> . . . All extraordinary travellers are a kind of shows; a kind of wild beasts. Banks and Bruce however were animals very different one from another. Banks was an elephant, quite placid and gentle, allowing you to get upon his back or play with his proboscis; Bruce, a tiger that growled whenever you approached him . . .

But in their own territory these two animals were never less than friendly and free in their exchanges with each other.

There was however another traveller within the past two years whose tracks had interlaced with those of Banks, Boswell and Johnson in Scotland and the Western Isles, where the relation between the parties was more uncertain though, in 1774, all seemed to be sweetness and light. The dedication by Thomas Pennant on 1 March 1774 of his *A Tour in Scotland and Voyage to the Hebrides* no doubt had its own balm for Banks but it was no less than justice to the generous contribution he had made. For once also it is no less than just to Pennant to say that he handsomely acknowledged this in his dedication. None of this however saved him from the critical shafts of discriminating readers when the book was published in May. Horace Walpole was dismissive of it as whole but noted

> . . . The most amusing part was communicated to him by Mr. Banks, who found whole islands that bear nothing but columns as other places do grass and barley . . .

To this his correspondent the Revd William Cole replied on 18 July:

> . . . I have read very lately (last week) Mr. Pennant's *Tour* in two volumes quarto, and fully subscribe to your opinion concerning the book, which I think as trumpery an one as I have read, and wonder at myself how my former reading of his first volume could have so much deceived me. Mr. Banks's account of the Isle of Staffa is very different from the rest of the book . . .

But Pennant had his defender in Dr Johnson who, though he rated him a Whig and 'a sad dog', still reckoned him the best traveller he had ever read and a keener observer than any other writer of his kind. Conversely Boswell thought this praise too high for a writer who travelled so fast over such an extent of country that he could only put together 'curt frittered fragments of his own', borrowed from other sources too extensively, and treating his subjects too superficially. Such was the literary debate on the book into which the work by Banks on the Isle of Staffa had been grafted, and through which its geological curiosities and monumental beauties were put before the public. Quite otherwise were the labours of Phipps and Banks as they strove to present the same quirky public with the account of *A voyage toward the North Pole* . . . Phipps laid one copy of it before the King on Friday 5 August and reserved another with a set of prints for Banks but, alas, forgot his duty to the Queen. It is a sign of the growing intimacy between Banks and the Royal Family that somehow he found a way of redressing this lapse by Phipps and so easing him 'out of a scrape' with Queen Charlotte. This delicate task had been done as he grappled with his latest social problem – the care and protection of 'Omai the South Sea Islander'.

V

While James Cook in HMS *Resolution* at the end of his second summer on the voyage had reached his farthest south, farther than any man before him, and was retreating to the warmer tropics, Joseph Banks and his fellows on the Council of the Royal Society had been pondering the lessons arising from the penetration farthest north by Constantine Phipps in HMS *Racehorse* at the end of the last northern summer. Now on 10 February 1774 their thoughts had crysallized in a form which was to determine the course of Cook's third and last Pacific voyage. This was expressed in the three motions formulated by Daines Barrington on 17 February and passed by the Council from which a letter, dated 18 February, was sent to the Admiralty proposing a voyage of discovery up the north-western coast of North America seeking 'a passage into the European Seas'. The implication was that where Phipps had failed from the Atlantic someone else might succeed from the Pacific. The Admiralty saw no means of mounting such an expedition that year but Lord Sandwich in a private conversation with Barrington, gave the Council an assurance

> . . . that it will be undertaken after the return of Capt Cook in 1775; when a similar expedition will be fitted out, which will in general follow the outline proposed by the Council of the Royal Society to the Board of Admiralty . . .

Through all these deliberations Banks was assiduous in his attendance at the Council meetings until the summer break. He had also been busy taking stock of his own affairs; gathering into his own hands from Benjamin Stephenson the many deeds associated with his Lincolnshire estates and the marriage settlements related thereto; seriously considering the disposal of his Cheadle and Kingsley estates in Staffordshire; and apparently planning a botanical excursion into Wales in the late summer.

Quite suddenly there had been the unspectacular and premature return of Captain Tobias Furneaux with HMS *Adventure* after his separation from Cook in New Zealand waters to complete his circumnavigation in some haste through high southern latitudes with a battered ship, and a wasting crew diminished by the loss of ten good men killed and part eaten by the Maoris of Queen Charlotte Sound. The ship had anchored at Spithead on Thursday 14 July and Furneaux posted to London the same day bearing with him the former able seaman Tetuby Homy, otherwise Omai 'the Otaheitan', and his sympathetic shipmate 2nd Lt James Burney. At last a human specimen from Otaheite had been delivered on English soil and presented at the Admiralty on 15 July. It was inevitable that Banks should have been summoned as the most able exponent of the language and customs of the Maohi. Omai was taken immediately to New Burlington Street on Sunday 17 July by Banks and Solander to be presented to the King and Queen in the White House at Kew.

It was but a week since Horace Walpole had written to Sir Horace Mann on 10 July about the rival attractions in London society:

> ... Africa is, indeed coming into fashion. There is just returned a Mr. Bruce, who has lived three years in the court of Abyssinia, and breakfasted every morning with the Maids of Honour on live oxen. Otaheite and Mr. Banks are quite forgotten ...

Now the tables were turned and the distant improbabilities of Abyssinian Bruce were well-matched in the immediate presence of Otaheitan Omai and the wealth of taradiddles that ensued. Between the two there was at least one brief encounter when Omai, with Banks and Solander, met Bruce at dinner with the Duke of Gloucester on Thursday 21 July. On Saturday 23 July, Omai was spirited out of London by Banks and Solander to face the ordeal of Baron Dimsdale's process of inoculation against smallpox in Hertfordshire. The immediate steps taken by Banks to protect Omai against smallpox were stimulated by what the disease had done to the Esquimo families from Labrador brought over by his friend George Cartwright in December 1772. Of the five only the young woman Caubvick was alive in June to return to her homeland with Cartwright. Omai made no objections and during August the treatment was pursued to a successful though uncomfortable end at Hertford with Banks and Solander occasionally in attendance but with the ship's surgeon Andrews and Banks's servant James Roberts continuously at hand. By mid-August it was plain that Omai had passed the worst hazards of the course and by 24 August he was back in London with Banks; well enough to dine at Sir John Pringle's in Pall Mall with the Earl of Sandwich and others that day and with Banks and Solander in the Royal Society dining club at the *Mitre* on Thursday 25 August. On 27 August he was taken by Lord Sandwich, Banks and Solander to Hinchingbrooke, the Earl's seat near Huntingdon. He then made a brief visit with Banks to the University of Cambridge early in October where they mingled with the 'Doctors and Professors' in the Senate House when the election results were announced. After a few days with Banks in London at the end of the month tasting the amusements of the theatre at Sadler's Wells and Drury Lane, Omai returned to spend most of November at Hinchingbrooke.

By this time the first proofs of Francesco Bartolozzi's engraving from the drawing of Omai by Nathaniel Dance had come to New Burlington Street, accurate enough as to the details of dress and the items in his hands but less faithful in the likeness of the head. Banks had commissioned Dance and Bartolozzi for this as he had the previous year arranged with Dance for the pastel drawings of the two Esquimos, Attuiock and Caubvick in their native costumes.

By the end of the year Banks had discharged his immediate responsibilities for Omai. He had introduced him to British society and set him on the road to social independence, reasonably protected against smallpox, and reasonably well versed in the habits of the English at home. By a plan long agreed with Lord Sandwich he was now to be lodged independently under the care of Mr Andrews, former surgeon of the *Adventure*, but under the general surveillance of Banks. At an annual charge of £160 to HM Government the two men were installed in lodgings kept by Mr de Vignolles in Warwick Street just across Swallow Street from New Burlington Street.

This new regime did not start until after Omai's return from a Christmas spent with Lord Sandwich and Martha Ray at Hinchingbrooke.

With the opening of the Royal Society year in November Banks was now returning to academic affairs after his re-election to the Council with Phipps and Solander for their second term. Moreover, he joined the President, Sir John Pringle, Henry Cavendish, William Roy and Constantine Phipps, as one of the official Visitors to the Royal Observatory on 14 December – the first such occasion in what was to be a lifelong association. But the botanical work at No. 14 New Burlington Street was not neglected. In the late autumn Gerhard Sibelius, had joined the team to begin that splendid contribution to the botanical series of engravings from the *Endeavour* collection. The herbarium itself had also been enriched by Banks's purchase of Phillip Miller's collection early in December with the additional treasure within it of William Houstoun's earlier gatherings in central America. For two weeks Banks and Solander had been busy moving it from Chelsea to St James's and setting it in order in the elegant Chippendale 'cubes', inlaid with their ebony and boxwood stars, which founded the great herbarium to come. The year ended for Banks with Constantine Phipps, staying at Felbrigg near Cromer in Norfolk with their friend William Windham - a trio with a strong mutual interest in the voyage toward the North Pole of the summer of 1773. It had been a voyage on which Windham had started in hopeful emulation of his friends as men of adventure but from which he had withdrawn off the north coast of Norway defeated, it was said, by obstinate seasickness.

VI

From the extreme cold of the New Year in Norfolk, Banks and Phipps returned to London to face the extreme heat of the experimental chamber devised by Dr George Fordyce, physician of St Thomas's hospital, in pursuit of his studies of the temperature of the human body. The bodies in question on 23 January 1775 were those of Banks, Phipps, Solander and Blagden with Fordyce presiding. Fully clothed they first entered the small room about two p.m. as the cast iron round or cockle stove in the centre raised the temperature from 150° F to over 160° F during their 20-minutes exposure, indicated by several mercury thermometers in different parts on the Fahrenheit scale. The third entry was between five and six p.m., heroically, after dinner when all but one thermometer had broke from the warping of their ivory frames at a temperature of about 200° F which as a group they sustained for some ten minutes. Thereafter, with the stove glowing red-hot, they entered the room one at a time to meet air temperatures of about 210° F, a scorching dry heat which Banks was able to bear for seven minutes, somewhat longer than the others, but in which he was the only one to sweat profusely. These details and the subjective, rather than the measured, body responses of the group were recorded by Charles Blagden and read before the Royal Society on Thursday 16 February, an early study in climate physiology demonstrating the ability of the human body to maintain a stable body temperature in an extreme environment. This feat of endurance caught the attention of Richard Pulteney, FRS who, on 26 February from Blandford, Dorset, wanted to hear more from Banks about 'this audacious experiment' which so denied the assertion of Herman Boerhaave that any heat above 130° F was fatal to animal life.

On the same day as this ordeal Dr Nevil Maskelyne had written to Dr James Lind at Edinburgh acknowledging papers received for reading to the Royal Society but also sounding Lind out as a possible recruit for the voyage which had been proposed by the Society to the Admiralty 'for making discoveries on the N.W. side of America beyond California'. In no way disheartened by his personal disappointment and material loss over the *Resolution* voyage in 1772, though he pronounced himself unwilling to go 'to oblige Government after the ungracious treatment' he had received on that occasion, Lind said he would consider the next voyage 'provided my friend Mr. Banks goes',

> ... to serve and attend on Mr. Banks, on whatever Expedition he shall undertake, I shall esteem my Duty, as well as my greatest Pleasure for the real regard I have for so noble and excellent a man ...

That the Royal Society evidently hoped Banks would lead a party on the next voyage Maskelyne had made clear to Lind who, a month later on 2 March, repeated to Banks himself his acceptance in principle should the expedition take place. But from Banks, whatever his hopes, there came no word about his intentions nor was there by 2 June, as William Roy noted in his letter to Lind, a single word from Banks that he might voyage to some distant part of the world. He had instead set sail that very morning with Lord Sandwich to inspect the naval dockyards along the south coast and would be away for some five or six weeks. Since January much had changed in the nation's affairs.

The first Continental Congress of the 13 American colonies had gathered in September the previous year and by December the non-importation of British goods had come into force across the Atlantic. In February Earl Chatham had presented a plan of conciliation toward the colonists which Parliament had rejected; North had tried again and failed. On 19 April the first shots had been fired at Lexington and Concord and by May the home Government was in no doubt that a war had begun in which the Navy and the mercantile marine would be needed. In these circumstances an inspection of the great naval dockyards at Deptford, Woolwich, Sheerness, Chatham, Portsmouth and Plymouth was an urgent task for the First Lord of the Admiralty, John Montagu, 4th Earl of Sandwich. It is a measure of the cordiality restored between Sandwich and Banks, after the brief summer storm over the *Resolution* three years before, that he should have been invited to sail with him on this official Admiralty inspection in HM Yacht *Augusta*, captained by Sir Richard Bickerton. The inspecting party was a small one – Sandwich, his secretary Joah Bates, and Mr Palmer, an Admiralty official. The supernumeraries were three also – Banks, his dilettante friend, Kenneth Mackenzie, Earl of Seaforth and chief of the clan Mackenzie, and Omai.

After a breakfast at the Admiralty on Friday 2 June the party embarked at the Tower, with Dr Charles Burney as guest for the day, to be joined in the afternoon at Greenwich by Miss Martha Ray and a few others for the voyage down river to Erith. Here the visitors were set ashore in the late evening and next morning the voyage began in earnest with the run to Sheerness. From this point Banks, while pursuing his own diversions in natural history and social visits ashore, was an intelligent observer of the naval scene. From the *Victory* under repair at Chatham to the building of the *Royal Sovereign* at the smaller yards at Plymouth Banks, in the course of five weeks, had a view of his country's naval resources, both ashore and afloat, which few civilians in his time probably ever achieved. Although his 'Journal of a Voyage made in the Yatch [sic] Augusta . . .' was written with the light-hearted erudition, of a Dilettante at sea with two fellow-members of the Society it was primed with the evidence of a technical understanding no less befitting his future as a founding Vice-President of the Society of Naval Architecture in 1791. His inspection of Great Britain's maritime resources and technology in the summer of 1775 added a final ripening to his own sea-faring experiences of the previous nine years.

Throughout this voyage it is apparent that Lord Sandwich was engaged closely in his official work and only rarely diverted by the social courtesies of his Admirals on the ships at anchor or those of the Admiralty Commissioners ashore. Apart from the inspection of dockyard installations, forts and guardships, the First Lord had also to grapple with the official despatches from Whitehall. Twice the progress of the voyage was impeded while he coped with his correspondence and once, from 14 to 16 June, he was called back to London. However, while Banks was his constant companion in the preliminary inspections, there were long periods when formal musters and detailed dockyard business were in hand and reports being written. At such times the First Lord was incommunicado and Banks was free for his own pleasures. Only once was he, by his own confession, 'botanicaly inclind', and that on 20 June when he searched for a rare species of grass mentioned in John Ray's *Synopsis stirpium Britannicarum* near Drayton about five miles from Portsmouth, and found it in the marshes under Portsdown Hill. For the rest he indulged in explorations by small rowing or sailing boat away from the *Augusta*, trawling for fish or shooting birds along the marshes of the Medway or the cliffs of the Isle of Wight; along Southampton Water or up the recesses of the Tamar. Once in the Commissioner's longboat at Plymouth, on 29 and 30 June, he stood off the Eddystone Lighthouse in an attempt to visit it by rowing himself over to the rock in a small boat. The sea was too high, even at low water, and he withdrew. But early on 1 July, provisioned for two days' fishing, he tried again and with a calm sea he succeeded in spending a quarter of an hour on Smeaton's famous edifice with its two residents, the third man being absent on shore. His insatiable curiosity for the moment satisfied, he returned to his offshore fishing 'by hooking & trawling', recording some 23 different species, including crabs, squid and cuttlefish, but dominated by whiting, sole, dab, sand-ray and haddock.

While Banks was thus engaged Lord Sandwich was writing on board the yacht in Plymouth harbour and, as yet unknown to either of them, Cook in the *Resolution* was closing on the Azores from the south-west within a month of a home anchorage at Spithead. Here, on that famous stretch of water, Banks on 22 June had witnessed the Royal Navy in formal display as the massed squadrons fired the birthday salute. This sight he viewed with Lord Seaforth from the masthead of the flagship HMS *Barfleur* which

> . . . it being fine weather provd a most beautifull sight the smoaks of the squadron massd together in a thousand beautifull forms like Clouds & mists rolling below a vast mountain such a sight as well repayd the trouble of our ascent the Russians also saluted in honour of the birthday which added much to our spectacle . . .

Then after dinner with the Admiral, back on board HMS *Augusta*, he was entranced by the experience of sailing down the line of guard-ships with Sir Peter Parker's squadron of four ships of the line and one frigate to the east, and to anchor in Yarmouth Roads that night.

The previous day, with Lord Sandwich on a courtesy call, Banks had visited the three Russian men-of-war anchored on the Motherbank of which the flagship, though not larger than 50 guns, had a crew of some 650 men, 'some very large built monstrous men' but all healthy, well dressed and clean. He had been equally impressed with the appearance of the British seamen on the guardships as they dressed ship when the *Augusta* had first come to Spithead with

... the man all in a uniform Blue Jackets & white waistcoats & trousers ...

After a last day-long entertainment by the Commissioner on the Isle of Wight lasting into the small hours of 9 July, the *Augusta* weighed anchor in the early afternoon and sailed for home through a rough sea into the Thames, casting anchor at Woolwich on Saturday 11 July and at Deptford the next day. On Monday 13 July Banks left for London after a voyage which he reckoned to have been one of 'uninterrupted pleasure' beyond almost anything the capital could furnish.

VII

While Banks was enjoying himself on *Augusta* Solander was keeping a watchful eye on the art work in progress at New Burlington Street and the affairs of the herbarium. Banks had word from him that the return of Cook in the *Resolution* was near although Solander assumed that he had also heard of this from Sandwich by the official despatches sent down from the Admiralty. No approximate date for the ship's arrival had yet been estimated. Banks apparently had already worked out his plans for the rest of the summer with Constantine Phipps before the exigencies of the American war were to claim his friend for active naval service once more. He was to meet Phipps at York about the time of the races there and Banks was to spend some time with him at Mulgrave Hall. While Banks was away from London he had arranged for Solander to keep watch at New Burlington Street and to meet Cook as soon as the express arrived with word of his arrival, a point made by Solander to John Ellis on 21 July.

So, about a week after his return from the *Augusta*, Banks set off on the long road to Mulgrave, some 250 miles north. For some days he paused at Hinchingbrooke with Lord Sandwich, but not at Revesby Abbey or Lincoln races before meeting Phipps at York about mid-August. Omai was still his charge, a more experienced and independent Omai with a limited English vocabulary but sufficient for ordinary communication. The other members of this odd party of travellers were the elder George Colman, not long retired from the management of Covent Garden Theatre, his son, the 12-year old George on holiday from Westminster school, and Augustus Phipps, a schoolboy of the same age and the young brother of Constantine. Their lumbering vehicle was not only crowded but burdened also with more than its ordinary tally of travellers' luggage for botany was now to be a major subject for serious study. Banks had brought a reference sample of his *hortus siccus*, each specimen in its fold of 'whitey-brown' paper and an array of his wooden plant boxes for fresh collections. There were also one or two other novelties added for trial – a new form of safety drag-chain for additional braking on steep slopes and some form of early odometer for the coach, neither of which seem to have been effective. At York this impedimenta was added to by cases of nautical books, charts and instruments which Constantine Phipps loaded for the last stages to Mulgrave Hall. George Colman in later life recorded his vivid memory of Banks as the field botanist in action by day and the inspiring tutor by candle-light. As they travelled, he recalled

> ... we never saw a tree with an unusual branch, or a strange weed, or anything singular in the vegetable world, but a halt was immediately order'd:- out jump'd Sir Joseph; out jump'd the two boys (Augustus and myself) after him; and out jump'd Omai after us all. – Many articles "all a growing, and a growing", which seem'd to me no better than thistles, and which would not have sold for a farthing in Covent Garden market, were pull'd up by the roots, and stow'd carefully in the coach ...

Then at the journey's end, under the stimulus of Phipps and Banks, for the two boys 'active enquiry was their ruling passion' and the 'spirit of research' in botany and field archaeology dominated their amusements. In the first of these Banks was an able master who found a way to defeat the drudgery and 'turn'd science into a Sport', sending them out early each morning to gather plants in the Mulgrave Woods below the Castle:

> ... We were prepared overnight for these morning excursions by Sir Joseph who could speak like Solomon ... He explain'd to us the rudiments of the Linnaean system in a series of nightly lectures, which were very short, clear, and familiar; – the first of which he illustrated by cutting up a cauliflower, whereby he entertain'd the adults (Omai excepted) as much as he delighted the younkers. I soon got a Botany mania which lasted, after I returned to London not quite so long as a voyage to Botany Bay. It cost my father, however sundry reams of whitey-brown paper, which were sewed into books, and which I stock'd ... I can still distinguish a moss-rose from a Jerusalem artichoke; and I never see a boil'd cauliflower without recollecting the raw specimen, and the dissecting knife, in the hands of Sir Joseph; and thinking on fructification, sexual system, pericarpium, calyx, corolla, petals &c. &c. &c. . . . .

However, before these delights were opened to them, the boys had to exercise their patience while Banks studied the valuable alum mines on the Mulgrave estate at Sandsend and Kettleness. This was on the day after the party arrived, probably 20 August, and Banks condensed his observations on the strata in the vertical quarry faces, the incineration of the slatey stone, and the subsequent extraction of the crystals in the alum-house into a 1300-word paper of valuable detail. Thereafter botany seems to have been in the ascendant until 29–30 August, when archaeology at last concentrated the attentions of both Banks and Phipps on a tumulus 'about a furlong to the Westward of Goldsborough (a village in the parish of Lythe)', a round barrow or, as Banks noted, locally called a hoe. [Grid reference: NZ 836155] With a team of ten workers, including two energetic schoolboys the day was long, so provisions were carried to the site, a tent was pitched and Banks made a very palatable stew 'in a tin machine, which he called by a hard name'. The two-day operation revealed a burial urn and in this it differed from the excavation Banks had

131

made just eight years before on 19 October 1767 high on Mynydd Llansaddern near Edwinsford [Grid reference: SN687350] where no such vessel was found.

Soon after the two Colmans left Mulgrave for appointments further north. For two days they travelled with their former companions, no more than 20 miles a day, to sleep at Skelton Castle with J. S. Hall and at Kirkleatham Hall with Sir Charles Turner in the neighbourhood of Gisborough. Before they parted company with Banks and Phipps it is evident from the record of George Colman the younger that, in the village of Kirkleatham itself, the party paid its respects to James Cook the elder, in his eightieth year, the well respected father of the great navigator who had just returned. Of this latest voyage Banks had up to date news from the letters received from Solander who had discharged his engagement to welcome Cook on his arrival. The father could have had no more fitting messenger. However, as Banks returned with Phipps and Omai to Mulgrave Hall, there were other matters to discuss with his host. Lord Sandwich was anxious that Phipps should represent Huntingdon in Parliament and he had briefed Banks at Hinchingbrooke and by subsequent letters. Phipps was at first too distracted with estate affairs to give it any thought, but on this excursion into the Cleveland hills there had been time for Banks to put forward the case. Phipps's response had been broadly as Sandwich had hoped, qualified only by the by need to consult his father who was lying ill at Bath and, unknown to them all, dying. Phipps asked for three weeks in which to reach a final decision, as Banks told Sandwich by a letter of 8 September. Five days later, Banks stayed one night at Hinchingbrooke and on 19 September in London saw Phipps briefly as he travelled to Bath to find his father already dead. Two years later he was also MP for Huntingdon with support from Banks who, at the same elections in the summer of 1777, had made his own final refusal to stand for the Boston seat in Lincolnshire or for any other parliamentary seat at any time elsewhere.

This politicking, however, was a distraction from which Banks was anxious to be free, as he implied to Sandwich, in his hurry to reach London again. Apart from the return of Cook and his other circumnavigating friends, Solander had already told him of the return of Francis Masson from the Cape with the exciting botanical range of his first gatherings there as well as the delivery of the Indian plant collection from the Moravian brethren at Tranquebar. There were above all the four casks and one box of specimens which Cook had left at the British Museum and the two Forsters with their own collections and drawings for display and disposal with the account of the voyage for the Admiralty. There was too the impending publication of the second edition of Sydney Parkinson's *Journal of a Voyage to the South Sea* and Fothergill, as a good fellow-Quaker with the Parkinsons, was anxious that truth and justice should prevail against the accusations in the 'Preface' of the first directed at himself and Banks. Banks was inclined to let the case lie especially as Stanfield Parkinson had died as a confined lunatic in Luke's Hospital. At a meeting on Monday 30 October, however, they discussed Fothergill's outline for 'Explanatory Remarks' to be appended to the new edition with emendations to the text of the first. Fothergill's view prevailed and his vindication of what he and Banks had done was published at last in 1784, four years after his own death and 11 after the original calumnies had been spread abroad.

Among such distractions Banks again visited Lord Sandwich at Hinchingbrooke during October and from there, about the middle of the month, wrote to his friend John Lloyd, FRS at the Temple in London asking his assistance, as he himself was out of town, in executing some commissions from Lord Mulgrave who was now at Portsmouth taking up his command of HMS *Ardent*. He urgently wanted the latest *Nautical Almanac*, the *Connoissance de Temps*, a micrometer telescope from Jesse Ramsden, and a Foxon's log, which should have come down by the last alum ship from Whitby but, if not, Banks was prepared to buy one from the maker in Fleet Street. All were to go by the first Portsmouth coach. The realities of the American war were slowly coming closer.

During the year Banks had been away from London and his own houses or estates for an unusually long time without being actually on any voyage of exploration, but this had been mainly during the vacation of the Royal Society. His second year on the Council was drawing to an end and since his return from Mulgrave Hall he had been regular in attending its meetings. However, on Thursday 23 November, he did not attend and at the anniversary meeting of 30 November he was not re-elected. It is not clear whether this was by his own design or not but there was a rift also in his relations, in that same week of 23 November, with the regular Royal Society dining club at the *Mitre* in Fleet Street, of which he had been a member since his election *in absentia* on the *Endeavour* voyage in July 1770. But on that last Thursday before the meeting of St Andrew's Day 1775 six Fellows, with two Danish visitors, Peter Edinger and Captain Hornemann from Copenhagen, dined apart from the regular club at the *Mitre* of which Banks was the only member and to which the other seven would all have been visitors. Some however would have been excluded under the rule 'that no stranger be admitted on two succeeding thursdays'. To this Banks took exception and under his leadership his seven friends resolved that night to form a dining club where no such rule applied, a coterie which Edward Poore, FRS that morning had already dubbed the 'rebellious' society. With Banks elected as 'perpetual Dictator' the inaugurating rebel Fellows were: Lord Mulgrave; the Earl of Seaforth; Colonel William Roy; John Lloyd; Dr Charles Blagden. The two Danish collaborators, Edinger the botanist and Hornemann the army man, soon returned to Copenhagen and were seen no more in the five years of the club's existence. Blagden within weeks was to sail in the Detached Hospital Ship HMS *Pigot* for service in the war zone off the American coast. Lord Mulgrave had his command in the Channel fleet. Lord Seaforth was destined soon to raise around his highland clan the 78th Regiment of Foot, later the 1st Seaforth Highlanders, and to be involved in the defence of Jersey against the French. Only Banks, Roy and Lloyd remained through the short life of the club as the core round whom gathered, on some 20 to 30 occasions each year until 1780, on Thursday evenings, a group notable for the absence of botanists and for the presence of those with engineering, surveying, mathematical, or chemical and physical interests and abilities. Into this small society the first and only stranger admitted as guest before the end of the year was 'Mr Omai' at the invitation of Mr Banks for the last meeting on 21 December 1775 before the Christmas holidays.

VIII

About mid-morning on Sunday 30 July 1775 HMS *Resolution* came to anchor at Spithead returned from what Charles Clerke, in a letter to Banks written early that morning, called 'our Continent hunting expedition'. It was a warm letter looking to an early reunion and it travelled immediately to London the same day with Cook,

Wales, Hodges and the two Forsters. It was passed on to Banks at Hinchingbrooke the next day, Monday 1 August, by Solander who received it from Cook at the Admiralty after his formal reporting in the boardroom to the Lords Commissioners. The 'good Doctor' had been prompt to greet Cook from whom he returned to Banks the Captain's most friendly compliments and his regrets that Banks had not been with him on the voyage. The two Forsters, however, were not to be seen at the Admiralty but Solander had a first view of William Hodges's drawings and of Cook's map of the voyage.

As Banks journeyed north, Solander kept him well informed particularly in his letter of 14 August when, with Sandwich, he embarked from the Tower on an inspection of Deptford and Woolwich yards and to pay the official visit to the *Resolution* which had anchored at Galleon's Reach on the 11th. With 'Miss Ray & Co' aboard also, the visit was more social than scientific with Lord Sandwich dining Cook and the ship's officers later at Woolwich. But next day Solander and John Hunter visited the ship which had come up to Deptford, for a more careful view of the cargo which Cook, Charles Clerke and others of the crew had destined for Banks for it is clear that he had been remembered by his former shipmates of the *Endeavour* with affection and respect. It was not until 5 September, however, that Solander had anything to report about the Forsters of whom the elder had recently called at New Burlington Street with his insect collection from which Solander was to select one specimen each for Banks and for the British Museum. Indeed Solander understood that the Forster collections in general were to be divided between the Museum, the Royal Society, Banks, Marmaduke Tunstall and Sir Ashton Lever. Moreover, it appeared also that Johann Reinhold Forster had been asked by Lord Sandwich to submit a sample account of the events at Dusky Bay which, if approved, could lead to him writing an account of the voyage and dividing the profits therefrom with Cook, with William Hodges employed by the Admiralty to finish the drawings.

In preparing the account of the second Pacific voyage by Cook, though there was to be no expensive literary ghost writing as for the *Endeavour* voyage, the Admiralty was nearly as clumsy. It attempted to mix incompatible authors in Cook and Forster, by the agreement of 13 April 1776 which defined the separate areas to be covered by each man in a joint work. By June, however, this nonsense had been resolved and Cook finished his work alone at Mile End with his manuscript edited for the press by Dr John Douglas, Canon of Windsor. In this production Banks had little or no part except toward the end when, as Cook was about to sail on his last voyage in July 1776, the Captain asked the publishers, Strahan and Stuart, to submit for Banks's approval those parts of his manuscript with botanical descriptions. As a close observer, however, of its trials and tribulations in production he was well prepared for his own more decisive part as midwife in the birth of the third voyage volumes in association with Dr Douglas and given a fairly free hand by Lord Sandwich.

In the year which separated the two voyages of HMS *Resolution* under Cook there was much to involve Banks on many different counts. There was, of course, the growing problem of the Forsters but most immediately the financial worries of the father, Johann Reinhold, which Banks temporarily relieved by buying young George's drawings for 400 guineas in August 1776. There was also the year-long harrying of Charles Clerke by his creditors with Banks a sturdy help throughout in evading their pursuit and at the end in his safe embarkation on HMS *Discovery* for a belated departure in the wake of Cook. There was John Gore, the inveterate hunter and circumnavigator, commending his young son and his mistress to the care of Banks in the event of his death and entrusting him with his will. Then, in the last weeks of June, there was Omai and his not unwilling return to the South Sea on board the *Resolution* with Cook.

For two years Banks, often to his inconvenience, had watched over Omai and his affairs for the Admiralty. In the course of this guardianship he had developed a more qualified attitude to the introduction of individuals from the aboriginal peoples of the South Sea into the hazards of life in western Europe than that which he held when bringing Tupaia and Tayeto from Tahiti on the *Endeavour* voyage. The fate of Ahutoru, whom Bougainville had brought from the same island to Paris, and the tragedy of the Esquimo family from Labrador were in themselves indicators of the medical dangers alone apart from cross-cultural stresses and sheer unhappiness. A blinkered philosophic curiosity could have a tragic end as the humanitarian in Banks knew. From his experiences with Omai to July 1776 he tended increasingly to deprecate rather than to encourage the repitition of such introductions into the crowded and unhealthy urban life in Europe. Instead he saw more point in the counterflow of European implements, plants and animals, southward to the Pacific peoples for trial on their own ground and in their own way. In this philosophy no one was to be more active than he. Omai's return to Huahine was the focal point of Banks's advice to the King and the Admiralty on what should go as royal presents with Cook and Clerke for this European benevolence, however innocently misconceived it may have been. Apart from gifts of livestock, plants and useful implements and tools, Banks finalized the account for Omai's expenses to the Crown for the year 1775 on 29 April 1776 at £317.11s.11½d. From January to June 1776, with presents and clothing to Omai for his homeward voyage, Banks reckoned all disbursements on his behalf as £395.8s.9d. as the last charge on this account. The last news of his Polynesian ward for some time to come returned in letters from Cook, Clerke, Gore and Anderson written in November at the Cape after which came the long silence of the third voyage.

IX

In the high enthusiasm of the first months after the return of the *Endeavour* the idea for a publication in 14 folio volumes of the natural history of the voyage had clearly germinated. This was to be distinct from the more general account with which Hawkesworth was charged as the literary accoucheur. The notion had certainly come to the private ear of Mrs Delany in conversation with the Dowager Duchess of Portland at No. 14 New Burlington Street in November 1771 and had been transmitted in confidence to her daughter, Mrs Port of Ilam. Even as she did so, however, it is probable that the plan was lapsing for on this same day, 19 November 1771, Hawkesworth was telling Lord Sandwich that he had received the first volume of Banks's manuscript journal for use in preparing the official account in conjunction with that of Cook. Hawkesworth had come to New Burlington Street the previous day at Banks's request as the most sensible place in which to discuss the problem of publication and the matter of illustrations, for it was only at No. 14 that the drawings and collections could all be seen. Moreover the Government had already determined on another voyage to the South Pacific and in the previous week had bought the two barks which were to sail eventually as HM Ships *Resolution* and *Discovery*, with the agreement that Banks and his party were to be of the expedition.

Here then was a potential conflict. If Banks and Solander were to return to the South Sea then any plan for a written still less an illustrated account of the first voyage was impractical. There was risk enough in relegating to another hand the task of condensing the journals of previous naval commanders into some general narrative; the risk was even greater in synthesizing the journals of Cook and Banks. Some early form of official printed record was clearly needed in the context of European rivalry for territories and trade. The competing ambitions of savants in the natural sciences were perhaps of less public consequence however important to some of them. Banks was not a conspicuous combatant at any time in this literary arena. Linnaeus from Uppsala certainly lamented the delay that a second expedition so soon after the first would impose on the release of new discoveries in natural history, but to Banks the issue was less imperative than that of consolidating his first insights into the southern hemisphere with more precise and comprehensive studies as soon as possible. After the surrender of his journal to Hawkesworth it was with some reluctance that he agreed to supervise the engravings from the originals of his own artists. This was diversion enough from his planning for the next voyage. Meanwhile his vision of 14 volumes in folio at his own expense for an estimate of some £10000 was no more than a dream as he prepared for another three-year voyage to begin, it was thought, in the spring of 1772. It would be enough to ensure the safe storage of the *Endeavour* collections with the associated manuscripts and drawings until his return in 1775 – or so it seemed at the turn of the year.

The failure of his plans for a second Pacific voyage and the withdrawal of his party brought the dream closer to some hope of a fulfilment but the voyage to Iceland and the Orkneys and the visit to Holland had to be worked through before Banks, as the retired 'man of adventure', could settle down among his collections and his books. It is unlikely then that any serious work on the drawings and engravings had been started at New Burlington Street much earlier than January 1773.

Although the grand design for some publication must have been framed during the *Endeavour* voyage it is probable that Banks had not evolved any settled plan before April 1773. His journey to Holland with Charles Greville at his side, for the sharpening of his critical powers on matters of art was probably a last polish to a scheme already well forward in his mind. With the Dutch connection so prominent in the last stages of the late voyage at Batavia and the Cape, there were good grounds for pursuing it to its roots and assessing the natural history collections and their forms of illustration before settling to the presentation of his own harvest from the South Seas.

He seems to have been reasonably confident of the capacity of his own artists to complete the Parkinson drawings and it is probable that during January 1773 a system had been devised for the two Millers and John Cleveley jun. to work under the supervising eye of Solander when Banks was absent. At the same time Sigismund Bacstrom would have been directed to set up the master list of the selected plant species of which the drawings were to be finished and engravings ultimately made with transcripts of the related botanical descriptions. However it was the engraving that was a problem for Banks in 1773.

Coincident with his own plans for illustrating in published form the exotic flora of the *Endeavour* voyage were two other extensive projects on botanical themes almost matching the ambition of his own scheme – and already well forward in production. First, there was that of John Sebastian Miller, the father of John Frederick and James who were already at work for Banks. The elder Miller, an engraver of great skill and Germanic diligence, was from 1771 to 1776 preparing his plates for the three folio volumes to appear in 1777 as his *Illustratio systematis sexualis Linnaei*, with 108 coloured and 104 uncoloured plates. Then, second, there was the work in progress on the *Flora Londinensis* for William Curtis, planned as three large fascicules each of 76, of which the first folio volume with 218 coloured engravings appeared in 1777.

These two botanical enterprises had largely pre-empted the time and energies of perhaps the most able and experienced engravers in that field who might otherwise have been available to meet the exacting criteria of Banks for his *Endeavour* florilegium. With Curtis as a friend and travelling companion in Wales in 1773, and the elder Miller as the parent of two of his own artistic ménage, Banks was clearly in close touch with men whose standards were a gauge by which to measure the performance of his own staff, though where was he to find engravers to match the skill and facility of J. S. Miller himself, and of Kilburn, Sansom and Sowerby? In the productions of both Curtis and Miller he was able to judge at first hand the process and the problems inherent in applying colour to the prints from copper engravings, an embellishment so carefully prepared for in the water-colour notes of Parkinson, but which Banks never applied to his own prints. It is against these two contemporary works – the *Flora Londinensis* and *Illustratio systematis sexualis Linnaei* – that the unpublished plates of the *Endeavour* florilegium are probably best judged as pictorial art and effective botanical illustration.

In the hunt for suitable engravers Banks cast his net wide. In July 1773 he had already received the first trial prints of engravings by a certain Kaltenhofer of the Akademie der Wissenschaften at Berlin. These had been prepared from specimen drawings which Banks has sent to him soon after his return from Holland, an arrangement made by George Ebell of Hanover who compared Kaltenhofer's work with that of Geister of Geneva who had engraved for Albrecht von Haller. Whatever the quality of these proofs Banks found Kaltenhofer's prices too high. Further negotiation, through Ebell, with Banks enticing the engraver with the idea of a life in England at New Burlington Street, left Kaltenhofer unimpressed. A year later the affair closed.

But another Continental artist of the copper plate had crossed Banks's path during his visit to Pierre Lyonet at The Hague in February 1773. This was Gerhard Sibelius who had worked for Lyonet of whose standards in engraving Banks had formed the highest opinion. Just when Sibelius joined the group in New Burlington Street is unclear but the late autumn of 1774 seems likely. Certainly in January 1775 Lyonet was pursuing Sibelius for an unpaid debt, 125 francs owing to the baker, and, in a letter to Banks, added a lurid account of the engraver's desertion of his wife and his prostitution of his daughter. Lyonet offered to accept South Pacific shells in lieu of currency as a means of discharging the debt if Banks agreed. In the 195 plates against his name he was one of the three most productive among the 18 engravers who in time saw service in the plan.

Apart from his spring distractions in helping his friend Phipps prepare for his summer voyage toward the North Pole, Banks had his own excursion through the west country into Wales with other friends among whom was Paul Sandby. This jaunt was not so much a diversion as might be supposed. In Sandby he had not only

Thespesia populnaea (Linnaeus) Solander ex Correa
Original drawing by Sydney Parkinson finished at Tahiti, 1769.

Thespesia populnæa (Linnacus) Solander ex Correa
Black ink proof from the copper engraving by Daniel Mackenzie finished in London,
c. 1774–7.

the master who had trained John Cleveley jun. but a pioneer in aquatint whose instructive voice on the subject of engraving and the application of colour to prints for reproduction had in Banks a receptive listener. Some glimpse of what Banks was seeking at this period comes clearly through in a letter from Benjamin Franklin on 3 November 1773 to an unknown engraver:

> ... Mr. Banks is at present engaged in preparing to publish the Botanical Discoveries of his voyage. He employs 10 engravers for the Plates, in which he is very curious so as not to be quite satisfied in some cases with the expression given by either the Graver, Etching or Metzotints, particularly where there is a wooliness or a multitude of small points on a leaf. I sent him the largest of the specimens you sent containing a number of sprigs. I have not seen him since to know whether your manner would not suit some of his Plants better than the more common Methods ...

So, by the end of 1773, Banks already had a large team of engravers at work exploring ways and means of presenting botanical subtleties in sheer line in the search for perfection in this art form. This was further shown in the approach to Banks by Peter Perez Burdett in a letter of the same date as that of Franklin's, though prompted independently from discussions with Thomas Pennant on the application of colour to illustrations of natural history. The case in point was his inspection of Pennant's copy of George Knorr's *Lapides diluvi universalis testes*, 1755, volume 4 with its 57 coloured plates, excellent in their way as coloured engravings but, in Burdett's view, something to be improved upon if artistic precision were the aim. He enclosed for Banks's inspection several rough examples of his own method which were, in effect, aquatints. But while it is clear from the evidence of later years that colour in published prints was much in his mind at all times Banks apparently felt unable to depart from attempting the best that engravers on copper could produce in black lines alone and unaided in the first instance. He may well have shared in some measure the strictures of Burdett on 'the Pretty but Tawdery effect' and the risk to the force and harmony of the illustration when colour was applied to the engraving after printing. So, in spite of the possibilities opened by the aquatint experiments of Paul Sandby and Peter Burdett, Banks kept his engravers steadily at work exploring the virtuosity of pure line as the prime means of capturing the nuances of shadow and surface texture in seeking an exact pictorial record of a plant's essential structure for the purposes of botanical taxonomy.

X

The taxonomic and artistic work on the plant collections at New Burlington Street continued for slightly more than four years – from the late winter of 1773 to the spring of 1777. During this time some 213 unfinished sketches of Sydney Parkinson were brought into a state of readiness for the engravers by John Frederick and James Miller, with John Cleveley jun., for the most part. Thomas Burgis added a mere three to this number. Thus, by the summer of 1777, with those already finished by Parkinson himself on board the *Endeavour*, a total of 483 coloured drawings had been made ready for engraving. Whatever peripheral uncertainties there may be about the grand plan for the florilegium as it seems to have been launched, verbally at least,

140

among London society in November 1771, there is a firm base established in the list set out by Bacstrom within this period. On those double foolscap sheets is the final selection of those species chosen by Banks and Solander for engraving and publication. These were drawn from among those they had already nominated for Sydney Parkinson's close attention in the course of the voyage, a total of some 942.

In this check-list the species are set out in their Linnaean taxa with their original manuscript names in a tabulation with spaces to note: the artist of the drawing; the engraver of the plate; and the region in which the specimen was collected. A series of symbols defined the state of the original drawing – coloured, pen or pencil, finished or unfinished – and of the engraving, whether finished and checked or not. From this record it is possible to say that all three of the most productive engravers – Daniel Mackenzie, Gerhard Sibelius and Gabriel Smith in that order – were all working in and about New Burlington Street before Bacstrom left Banks's employ about the end of 1775.

It is also possible to deduce from this manuscript list that the number of plates intended for the *Endeavour* florilegium by this, our only firm record of decisions made, was at most slightly more than 800 of which 753 were marked as having been finally engraved. This agrees well with what Banks told Edward Hasted in February 1782 as the final approximate total of what he intended to publish. This number also accords well with the idea of a work in about 14 volumes – or perhaps fascicules, under which term they could be compared with the three components of the first volume of Curtis's *Flora Londinensis*. In this work each fascicule contained 76 plates. Had it ever been published, the Banks *Endeavour* florilegium could have been composed quite comfortably of 14 fascicules each of about 55 plates by the manuscript plan to which the artists and engravers worked for ten years or more. As a finished work the arrangement of text and illustration – the Latin diagnoses and the engraved plates – would have closely matched the published elegance of Curtis's volume.

Between April and September 1777 the removal from New Burlington Street to No. 32 Soho Square imposed a check on all artistic activity related to the florilegium but it heralded a more settled future for work on the South Sea collections. The most important single mark of the new era was the arrival of Jonas Drysander in London in early July that year and his almost immediate attachment as an assistant to Banks. Among the artists however a new order had also evolved. With Banks's agreement, John Frederick Miller had been diverted in 1776 to make drawings for Dr Alexander Hunter's new edition of John Evelyn's *Sylva*. However he had also published, without permission, some of the plant drawings made for Banks who had, in November 1776, therefore severed all relations with him on this account. James Miller and John Cleveley jun. had also each gone his separate way. In their place, from an obscure back-ground but with a deft artistic touch, had come Frederick Polydore Nodder to carry alone for the next few years the burden of finishing the Parkinson sketches and to add his own modest quota to the copper engravings.

So from the autumn of 1777, across the courtyard behind the house in Soho Square in the back premises under the herbarium, the engravers room became the scene for the last stages in preparing the plates for the florilegium. Here Mackenzie, Sibelius and Smith in particular continued the main task of the engraving, with Nodder alone as their colleague of the pencil and the water-colour brush. For nearly five years this regime operated with Dryander increasingly important as curator of the herbarium and library and as a sort of supervising clerk of the artistic works. The

141

death of Solander in May 1782 almost set a period to its progress. The work did not entirely cease but the pace diminished. Indeed the chosen list of plants for engraving had almost been completed, although there was certainly enough unfinished to keep Nodder and Mackenzie in partnership until as late as 1784 at least. However by this time Nodder, attracted toward zoology, seems to have begun work with Dr George Shaw and the burgeoning of their *Naturalist's Miscellany* . . . of which the first volume, dedicated to Queen Charlotte in 1789, was quickly followed in the same year by the second which was inscribed to Banks

> . . . To whose unwearied labours, enlarged knowledge, and liberal patronage, the Science of Natural History is so highly indebted . . .

With Nodder now claimed in effect by the British Museum for the last two decades of his life, Mackenzie himself had also been diverted by Banks, not from botany but away from the South Pacific flora. In these new fields his first task was the engraving of plates from the drawings of Engelbert Kaempfer for Banks's second venture in private publishing, the *Icones selectae plantarum* . . . 1791 of species from Japan. In turn these were followed by his engravings for the *Delineations of Exotick Plants* . . ., from the drawings of Franz Bauer at Kew, and for the *Plants from the Coast of Coromandel*, from the drawings of Dr William Roxburgh's Indian artists. But for Daniel Mackenzie, working alone until 1800 in the engravers' room, some of the finest examples of his art would remain unpublished among the great collection stored in the nine presses at his back. The plates of the *Endeavour* florilegium, after the first black ink proofs had been taken, would remain a sort of buried treasure whose site was known but whose wealth was tapped only by the learned few – those who made the pilgrimage to Soho Square and those very few to whom selected proofs were sent.

XI

It remains an unresolved mystery why no published volumes of the *Endeavour* flora appeared to find its rightful place in botanical bibliography somewhere within a decade of the voyage from which it evolved. By 1782 whatever was unfinished in a pictorial sense, as Banks put it to Johann Alstroemer, was not impossible to complete. Nor, with the diligent Dryander now a part of the Soho Square ménage, was there any convincing reason why the manuscriptions appropriate for each plate could not have been set in order for the printer. Technicalities were no barrier. Nor was the death of Solander a real impediment.

For some nine years Solander had been back in his post as Assistant Keeper at the British Museum and the future of the herbarium and the library no longer rested, if it ever did, on the continuing presence of the genial Swede. The plant collection grew, the books accumulated, the engravers worked on, the manuscript descriptions were consulted, and the ripe years of the establishment as a resource in the growth of natural history were to come. Only the florilegium as a concept remained unfulfilled and absent from the shelves of the cognoscenti. The drawings and the engravings had been done, some 753 at least, and enough to begin the issue of well-documented fascicules in the mode of *Flora Londinensis*. So much was already paid for at a rate of about £6 per plate and drawing, a round sum of say £4500 dispensed over nine years, or a drain of £500 a year. Ahead still lay the problem of financing the printing and binding of say 15 fascicules of 50 plates each with appropriate letterpress which, by Banks's own estimates a few years later, could not be done for less than £500 per fascicule or another £7500 to bring the publication to an end – over all a grand total of £12000 or, by the values of today, some £750000.

How was such money to be found? The plates had been engraved almost entirely during the course of the American War of Independence at the charge of a Lincolnshire landowner whose income had been severely reduced by the attrition of the trade in long wool. Financial restrictions during the war had been a great obstacle to publication. The prospect of a long post-war recovery was unlikely to be propitious for the sales of an academic work of this kind. The economic situation now made recuperating the costs of the work as originally planned unlikely. Moreover Banks now had competing demands on his time, and publication, however cherished at the outset, receded in the scale of Banksian values. He had become heavily involved in the affairs of other men and in other plans since his election as President of the Royal Society and these commitments pushed his aspirations as a savant to one side. The death of Solander was a great loss 'in the paths of Science and of Friendship', as Banks phrased it to John Lloyd, but it happened at a time when other forces were affecting the fate of the florilegium and the pattern of life at Soho Square.

The decade which opened with the news of the death of Cook involved Banks almost immediately in the process of publishing the account of the last voyage itself. In this he was intimately engaged from October 1780 until April 1784. This alone was a major diversion from any hopes he may have had for the *Endeavour* florilegium. In 1780 there was also the movement of the Royal Society from its old home in Crane Court to the 'elegant & convenient apartments' in Somerset House, with the turbulent years of 1783 and 1784 in the management of the Society itself to be weathered. Then too his marriage in March 1779 had brought not only a change in his mode of life in London but also the occupation of Spring Grove and the refurbishmnt of Revesby Abbey, diverting funds from large plans for publication. The decade closed in fact with the sale of the estates of Cheadle and Kingsley in Staffordshire probably to liquidate a variety of financial problems. Marriage, with the increasing demands on his fortune that it entailed, put an end to the bachelor euphoria with which he had returned from the *Endeavour* voyage and the hopes of publishing his findings in so opulent a form.

In no sense was there any decline in Banks's interest in the florilegium as such. What had supervened was a practical recognition of the realities in ten years of experience, bought and paid for, and an awareness of the new order evolving with such speed around him. It is possible that, apart from any other factors, Banks might have been true to Benjamin Franklin's earlier assessment of November 1773. In the strictness of his critical attitude to the fine detail of botanical illustration he might have been his own executioner of the grand design. In particular, the published plates of Curtis's *Flora Londinensis* might have given Banks much food for thought. There was a delicacy and a sensitivity in the engraving not so uniformly apparent in the plates of his own prospective work. Moreover he was well aware of the rising art of stipple engraving as a step toward achieving the surface textures and expression of form which he had evidently sought from the beginning and had not found completely to his taste in the bolder hatchings of his own men.

143

That Banks had learned many things of importance to the future of practical botanical illustration for public instruction is perhaps most evident in his citation of the *Flora Londinensis* to the East India Company in 1788. For him it was a model to be emulated for its union of 'elegance with perspicuity' but trimmed by his own hard earned experience in matters of publishing economy. This came to fruition six years later when in 1794 Daniel Mackenzie set to work at Soho Square engraving with a simpler touch from the coloured drawings of the Indian artists for the smaller fascicules of the *Plants of the Coast of Coromandel*, under the direct supervision of Banks. This pioneer in the publications of Indian botany is a veritable offspring from the original ambitions for the *Endeavour* florilegium, re-shaped by 20 years of sobering experience. So too, in the same modified style, is that small volume of African flora to the credit of Francis Masson – the *Stapelia novae* . . ., 1796 – with its 16 plates also engraved by Daniel Mackenzie and similarly managed by Banks through the excellent press of William Bulmer of Cleveland Row, St James's.

CHAPTER 6

THE 'DILETTANTE' OF ST JAMES'S
1779–1778

In the autumn of 1773 Banks had been a Fellow of the Royal Society for more than seven years. In that period he had, for more than five years, been a constant traveller both at home and abroad. Now there were signs that the sailor and circumnavigator was coming home from the sea; that the scientific hunter was settling to the study of his collections in St James's. Of this change there was a clear declaration on St Andrew's Day 1773 in his election to the Council of the Royal Society for the first time. By his own strict code of duty this was an earnest of his intent to be at hand in London as a servant of the Society, at least for the ensuing year. In fact it was the true beginning of a lifetime of devotion to science at large through the councils of that institution – and, effectively, the passing of young Mr Joseph Banks the traveller in foreign parts. Within the next five years he became the established savant of New Burlington Street and the diligent FRS.

Under the Presidency of Sir John Pringle, the Royal Society Council of 1773–4 was a fair sample of the Fellowship as a whole and as it would be for the next half century. The peerage and baronetage were, in effect, represented by the Hon. Henry Cavendish, the Hon.Constantine John Phipps, the Hon. Daines Barrington, and by Sir John Pringle himself; the knights by Sir John Burrow, the clergy by the Secretary, the Revd Samuel Horseley, and the Revd Francis Wollaston; the medical profession not only by the President but also by Dr William Watson, Dr George Baker, Dr Richard Brocklesby with Dr Charles Morton and Dr Matthew Maty, both of the British Museum; the law and letters, variously, by the Hon. Daines Barrington, Sir James Burrow, Owen Salusbury Brereton, and the dissident pamphleteer, Israel Mauduit; John Walsh and Joseph Banks, as landed gentry of independent means and scientific bent; finally Dr Daniel Solander, as that rare species then, the salaried civil servant at the British Museum. In this galaxy, the two young Etonians, Banks and Phipps were the youngest by a clear decade, with Phipps the junior by a year, and representing that small but important group of Fellows in the Royal Navy. With these as his regular associates at Crane Court, for the next year Banks served his apprenticeship in the affairs of the Royal Society. In 1774 this included his association with the motion framed by Daines Barrington on 17 February:

> ... That a voyage to make discoveries on the Northern coasts of the Pacific Ocean would contribute to the Promotion of Science in general, & more particularly that of Geography ...

with the ensuing motion to recommend this to the notice of the Admiralty. Arising from the voyage of Phipps in the summer of 1773 'for making discoveries toward the North Pole', with the planning of which Banks had been so much involved, this motion was another nudge to the Admiralty from the Royal Society and the essence of the plan for what became Cook's third and last voyage. Then, as a member of the 'Committee of Attraction' later in 1774, he was involved with the observations by Dr Nevil Maskelyne on the mountain Schiehallion in Scotland on the deflection by its mass on a plumb-line as data for the calculations by Charles Hutton of the earth's density. His companions on the committee were, apart from the Astronomer Royal, Henry Cavendish and Daines Barrington, Benjamin Franklin, William Watson, Matthew Raper and, again as secretary, Samuel Horseley. Such were some of the names to be written across the record of Banks's first year as a truly active Fellow of the Royal Society.

Elected again as a member of Council in November 1774 with Henry Cavendish, Constantine Phipps and Solander still beside him Banks had new company to broaden the range of his immediate associates – particularly John Hunter, the surgeon, William Roy, the military engineer and Peter Woulfe, the chemist and mineralogist. This was a year, 1774–5, that was to be marked by the first Bakerian lecture of which Woulfe was the opening pioneer; by the return of Cook from his second voyage to the Pacific; and by Banks's own first inspection of the Royal Observatory as a Royal Society Visitor in company with Pringle, Roy and Phipps. It was also that year when, in November 1775, he gathered to himself the small 'rebellious' group of Fellows.

For the next two years he was off the Council, apparently by his own choice, but attending the meetings of the Society with great regularity and dining assiduously as the elected 'perpetual Dictator' of his own Thursday evening club with such like-minded Fellows as Colonel William Roy, Sir George Shuckburgh, General Robert Melville, Captain William Calderwood, Dr George Fordyce and Dr Charles Blagden – a young man sitting at the head of a table of his seniors.

Then, at the St Andrew's Day meeting of 1777, he was again elected to the Council soon after settling at his new address in Soho Square, a transition which had its own effect in diverting him from Royal Society affairs over the spring and summer. Within the past two years much had changed. Benjamin Franklin had returned to America to be seen no more in the councils of the Royal Society, being now a rebel and a signatory of the Declaration of Independence. Constantine Phipps, now Baron Mulgrave, was away on active service at sea commanding HMS *Ardent* in the war against the American colonists. James Cook, after a year at home, was gone on his last voyage as the most recent Copley medallist.

But, during the summer of 1778, Solander with his gossip's ear had gleaned hints among the Fellows that Banks might be an acceptable successor as President to Sir John Pringle though Pringle himself preferred Alexander Aubert. From about August, while Banks was preoccupied in his move, the tide of support in his favour rose steadily. In the last month before the anniversary meeting Banks himself canvassed by letter and by word of mouth. In the event he was elected that November evening in 1778 almost unanimously by a majority of some 220 votes. Later, as he waited to learn who would succeed Dr Samuel Horseley as Principal Secretary, he heard the name of the Revd Paul Maty declared by about a two to one majority, with Dr Charles Hutton remaining as Foreign Secretary. The seed of the future disturbances to the peace of the Society had been planted, although no sign of this appeared among the 127 Fellows who sat down that evening to the annual dinner at the *Crown and Anchor*. Delayed by the last formalities, the new president hurried down Fleet Street and along the Strand to his first formal engagement. According to the Revd Sir John Cullum, who sat opposite him that evening, Banks arrived 'quite out of breath' and as he sat down remarked

> ... with good humour but with rather too little dignity "I believe never did a President of the Royal Society run so fast before ...

Otherwise apparently his behaviour was 'very Proper'.

With Sir Isaac Newton as the first, Banks was the second Lincolnshire President of the Royal Society. He was also the third youngest ever to occupy that Chair and eventually the longest in its tenure. But his inaugural speech in that office encapsulated both his qualms and sense of insecurity for the future:

> ... Placd as I am in this Honorable Chair by the unanimous suffrages of the most Eminent Literary Society in Europe at a Period of my life Earlier than my most Sanguine wishes could have hop'd, it would ill become me to delay my thanks to you my Learned & Candid Electors
>
> I accept then with the deepest sence of Gratitude the important trust which you have reposd in me, but conscious of my utter inability of filling the Chair in which a Newton has sat with any comparative degree of Literary reputation I must fix my hopes of your future favor on a humbler basis Care of your honor & dignity, attention to your interests & welfare & an equal encouragement given to all branches of Science without undue preference to my Favorite Study must in me supply the place of more Brilliant Qualifications ...

Announcing himself 'hitherto free from the Shackles of Politicks', he promised implicitly to remain so. The next 42 years would show how truly he kept this promise and how faithfully he performed his office as 'a Servant of the Society'. It is a reflection of the times that he should have been presented formally to the King at the Court of St James's on Friday 4 December as the new PRS, not by the former President, but by the First Lord of the Admiralty, the Earl of Sandwich, an FRS certainly, but more conspicuous that month as a convivial fellow-member with Banks of the Society of Dilettanti.

Although today we may raise an eyebrow on hearing the Royal Society described as 'the most Eminent *Literary* Society' in Europe, there was then another smaller closed society in London eminent in a more obvious literary way. The Literary Club of Sir Joshua Reynolds and Dr Samuel Johnson was a small coterie of 26 in 1778, meeting at the *Turk's Head* in Gerrard Street and a group for whose company Banks had a subdued but evident affinity. When he moved to No.32 Soho Square he had become a close neighbour of one early member of The Club, George Colman sen., the dramatist and already a friend. During the same year Banks had also been sitting to Sir Joshua Reynolds for his portrait among the two groups of the Society of Dilettanti and early in 1778 had paid Reynolds £36.15s.0d. for his share in the painting. These two were channels by which his inclinations could be made, as is apparent from the letter of Samuel Johnson to Bennet Langton on 31 October 1778:

> ... The session of the Club is to commence with that of Parliament. Mr. Banks desires to be admitted, he will be a very honourable accession ...

The Society of Dilettanti (1) by Sir Joshua Reynolds, PRA, 1777–9. Left to right: Constantine John Phipps; 2nd Baron Mulgrave; Lord Dundas; Lord Seaforth; Hon. Charles Greville; John Charles Crowle; Lord Carmarthen; Joseph Banks (clinking glasses with Charles Greville).

Then, three weeks later, on 21 November, Johnson wrote to James Boswell:

. . . we talk of electing Banks the traveller; he will be a reputable member . . .

Finally, on 11 December, Sir Joshua was able to tell Banks that he had been elected to the select circle bringing the number to 30 in the company of three others – the bibliophile Lord Althorp, later the second Earl Spencer; Sir William Scott, later first Baron Stowell, the international lawyer; and William Windham MP.

The pejorative roars from the learned Dr Johnson on the intellectual poverty of travel in the South Sea and the improbability of broiling ptarmigan in Icelandic hot springs were now in the past. Election to the chair of the Royal Society and a status of leadership in science, matching that of Sir Joshua Reynolds at the Royal Academy in the world of art, had perhaps altered the Johnsonian perspectives enough to accept that there was more to Banks the traveller than a botanist and a culler of simples.

II

It had been harder for Banks to pass through the doors of the *Turk's Head* in Gerrard Street in December 1778 as a member of the Literary Club with its predominantly middle-class, academic conversation than to be elected as he was on 1 February 1774, sponsored by James 'Athenian' Stuart, to the Society of Dilettanti and the more exuberant conviviality at the *Star and Garter* in Pall Mall. Though the Club and the Society had some members in common, the Dilettanti were pre-eminently peers of the realm and landed gentry. Among them a high proportion were diplomats, courtiers, senior civil servants and members of Parliament, mostly gentlemen of educated taste, whose wealth and independence allowed them to indulge their interests as scholars, savants and collectors.

Into this company Banks, an old Etonian and gentleman commoner of Christ Church, fitted easily as a landed gentleman of independent means, though not in the highest ranks of wealth. In recent years he had enlarged his range with his patronage of the art of botanical illustration and copper engraving, and his commissions to portraitists such as Benjamin West, Sir Joshua Reynolds, Nathaniel Dance, William Parry and topographical artists such as Paul Sandby. He had become a close friend and correspondent of Sir William Hamilton and an enthusiastic exponent of the neo-classicism stemming from the Etruscan, Roman and Greek antiquities collected by the ambassador in Italy. He and Banks had met for the first time in 1772 during Hamilton's home leave, from which time dated Banks's friendship with his nephews – the Hons Charles Francis and Robert Fulke Greville, younger brothers of George Greville, 2nd Earl of Warwick, himself a Dilettante. Banks himself, of course, had something to offer in exchange for objects of classical antiquity; he had his own collections of art and antiquity from the South Pacific to fire the interest of such *curiosi* in matters of comparative ethnology.

Apart from these enlivening encounters so soon after the *Endeavor* voyage, Banks had in 1767 studied and enjoyed the treasures of the Anson house and estate of Shugborough with John Sneyd and again with John Lightfoot in 1773. Here perhaps was his real contact with the hopes and aims of the Dilettanti, embodied in Thomas Anson and his architect James Stuart. Through them emerged his membership of the

149

Society and his loyalty to the essence of one of its formal toasts: 'Grecian Taste and Roman Spirit'.

So, after four years among the arbiters of neo-classical theory and practice in the art and architecture of England, Banks was elected as Very High Steward of the Society of Dilettanti on 1 February 1778 in succession to Charles Crowle. In this guise he served as Secretary and Treasurer for 16 years until June 1794, and then as Secretary alone until 19 February 1797.

Within a week of his election as President of the Royal Society, and two days after his presentation to the King, we have a glimpse of the Dilettanti at play in the *Star and Garter* on 6 December, recorded no doubt on the authority of the Very High Steward himself:

> . . . Ld. Sandwich and Mr. Banks having called this respectable Society by the disrespectful name of Club were fined a bumper each which they drank with all proper humility. Lord Mulgrave do. do. Ld. Sandwich having again called the Society by the disrespectful name of Club was again fined a bumper and again respectfully submitted . . .

III

Among the Dilettenti, and indeed among the Club as James Boswell clearly showed, there was an active appreciation of beauties other than Graeco-Roman antiquities and the cadences of Johnsonian prose. The appearance of Hawksworth's *Voyages* . . . in June 1773 gave a certain background to the gossip of the clubs that Banks had an eye to beauty in more than its botanical forms on distant Otaheite, a theme of value to the satirists and not overlooked by the monthly periodical *Town and Country Magazine* with its concern for the peccadilloes, real or supposed, of public men. In the September number for 1773, 'Mr B–– The Circumnavigator' was fitted into the standard pattern which the magazine favoured, of noblemen or wealthy gentlemen who exercised their charity by taking as mistresses the daughters of impoverished but respectable middle-class merchants or professional men. The 'Memoirs of Miss B–––n' was just such a social case history. The circumnavigator, albeit with the most laudable and platonic first intentions, was said to have succumbed to her beauty 'on a jaunt to Hampton Court' and to have become the father of her child. How much fire there was behind this journalistic smoke we cannot say. There are however the felicitations from Johann Fabricius, who had been working on the Banks insect collection in New Burlington Street that summer, dated 10 November 1773 from Copenhagen:

> . . . My best compliments and wishes in Orchard Street. What has Shee brought You? Well it is all the same if a Boy he will be clever and strong like his father, if a girl, she will be pretty and genteel like her mother . . .

If indeed it was to Miss B–––n that Fabricius referred, and Banks had in fact become a father in the autumn of 1773, then the spontaneous passion at Hampton Court must have been truly a winter's tale, somehow enacted in passage between the cold winds of Iceland and the dank fogs of Holland.

There is much more substance in the evidence for another establishment – in

The Society of Dilettanti (2) by Sir Joshua Reynolds, PRA, 1777–9. Left to right: Sir William Watkins Wyn; Sir John Taylor; Stephen Payne Gallway; Sir William Hamilton; Richard Thompson; Walter Spencer-Stanhope; John Smyth.

Chapel Street, just across Horseferry Road from Orchard Street, in that twighlight zone south of St James's Park now swept away in the clearances for Victoria Street. There is no room for doubt about the existence of Sarah Wells in the last years of Banks as the wealthy bachelor of New Burlington Street though, like so many of her contemporaries in the demi-monde of London then, the rest of her life is a mystery. For several years Sarah seems to have been a pleasant and appreciated element in the social circle of Banks and his foreign visitors during those years of dalliance before he submitted to the check reins of matrimony.

Glimpses of this other side of a savant's life life appear here and there about this time as gossip and hearsay. In May 1776 David Hume wrote from Bath to William Strahan, the printer that Lord Sandwich, Lord Mulgrave and Banks, with 'two or three Ladies of pleasure' were spending several weeks trout fishing near Newbury from lodgings in the inn at Spine Hill. Later in the year the *Morning Post* hinted darkly on 22 August that the circumnavigator had been seen in the company of

... J---y Twitcher who is almost the only surviving member of that club (formerly called the Hell-Fire Club) ...

on a visit to Medmenham, even though the esoteric mysteries of that circle were past.

But it is in November 1776 that Charles Greville provides the first evidence of Sarah in his letter to Banks from Matlock Bath on the 3rd, reporting his introduction of Sir William Hamilton to '... the widowed Sarah who gave us a good account of you ... ' with his '... best Compts to Sol[ander] and Sal[ly Wells] ... ' Banks had been away from London in Lincolnshire from mid-September and it is evident from the context of Greville's letter that the relationship with Sarah was well established by the autumn of 1776 in an affair that may have had its beginnings in the spring.

For more than three years the house in Chapel Street seems to have been a sociable haven where Banks was able to entertain his friends with Sarah Wells as his acknowledged mistress and hostess. This is apparent in the visit of Johan Alstroemer during 1777. In October he wrote home to Sweden that he had been dining and supping from time to time '... at MMe Walls [=Wells], Mr. Banks's *maitresse* ... ' with Solander and Banks and at ease enough under Sarah's roof to compose his letters there. Charles Greville was also a welcome mutual friend in Chapel Street when his duties as Mayor of Warwick and in the House of Commons allowed.

Charles Greville was one of the three trustees, with Banks and Thomas Dundas, of the estate of Kenneth Mackenzie, chief of the Mackenzies and Earl of Seaforth, Lord Ardlive and Viscount Fortross. This was a troublesome burden for them all. The estates in Scotland, forfeited in 1715 and recently recovered by the family, were in poor financial shape and the careless life of Lord Seaforth was a heavy embarrassment to Banks and Greville, especially in 1777. For a week from 5 to 12 June that year Banks had disappeared from London helping Seaforth escape his creditors by crossing the Channel with him and Harriot Powell, Seaforth's mistress and a friend of Sarah Wells. Having seen them safely lodged at St Omer, this was in fact Banks's last foreign journey as the 'man of adventure', and an interruption in his move from New Burlington Street to Soho Square. For a year Seaforth remained at Nielle in France under the name of John Wilson and his letters regularly conveyed his love and that of Harriot Powell to Sally, occasionally to 'Mrs Wells'. Then in June 1778, Lord Seaforth left France by sea direct for Aberdeen, avoiding London and the few creditors that his trustees had not been able to satisfy. Harriot, who had been under the care of Banks and Sarah Wells for some little time, then joined her lover at Aberdeen. In 1779 Seaforth was brought under some pressure by his officers of the 78th Foot; the regimental sense of decorum prevailed, and Harriot Powell became Lady Seaforth.

For Banks too there had been tensions associated with the women in his life as in the summer of 1777, the turning point in his career, when he moved to No. 32 Soho Square. There are hints at this time of an estrangement from his mother and sister arising, probably, from the existence of his Chapel Street ménage, which shows through in Sarah Sophia's pleading to be allowed a share in making the purchase of No. 32 or, at least, to be allowed to throw her 'thousand mites' into the buying of the furniture. It is there in her complaint of her brother's selfishness and self-indulgence, and at the last in her despairing cry, '. . . pray do not be angry with your Sophy . . . ' Another view was put later in the year as Charles Greville, on 23 August 1777, takes Banks to task for his 'grumpyness' with Sally Wells during the summer but expressing pleasure at the change in her at his last visit to Chapel Street. Whatever the cause of the former trouble he said:

> . . . I was happy to leave the Family enjoying that comfort which its little menage gives to its Friends & may that comfort long continue . . .

But the ties of this quasi-matrimonial state were already unravelling as Banks returned to the Council of the Royal Society in December 1777 and the mantle of the savant fell more heavily on his shoulders. The adventurous youth metamorphosed rapidly now into the serious man of science.

IV

The house in New Burlington Street may have been large enough for a young traveller as a haven between voyages and for the safe custody of collections awaiting study and description; as a base for organizing young artists and engravers; and as a simple rendezvous for scientific friends. However it lay rather too far west for convenience in relation to the British Museum and the committments to the Royal Society in Crane Court, to say nothing of the City and Whitehall. From this viewpoint the virtues of 32 Soho Square as a strategic centre were clear. As a matter of capital investment there was the attraction of the accommodation it offered as a house with commodious back premises already designed for an academic purpose with its library and adjacent schoolrooms. There was also the simple but important matter of either rent or price as was admitted by Messrs Christie and Ansell in the words of John Lane on 26 December 1776:

> . . . as poor Soho is not a fashionable Residence, as fashion is so very rife, I should fancy it will have few admirers & therefore go at a less rent than is now demanded . . .

And, indeed, when Banks signed the memorandum of agreement with George Steuart the owner, on 29 March 1777, the original asking price for the leasehold premises had been reduced from £7000 to the final figure of £4000. But however

153

unfashionable the area when Banks moved there in the summer of 1777, his neighbours were mostly middle-class landowners like himself but, unlike him, with seats in Parliament. The ambassadors of Sweden and Venice were at Nos. 37 and 12; Sir George and Admiral Hugh Pigot were at Nos.25 and 26, in both of which Alexander Dalrymple had lodged for some years until 1775; George Colman sen. was within yards on the south side at No. 28; next door, No. 31, was re-building but its former occupants had been in succession Allan Ramsay and John Zoffany until 1772. Banks's neighbour on the other side of the party wall at No. 33 was Charles Penruddock, MP from Wiltshire. Across the square at No. 22 Dr George Armstrong had his Dispensary for Sick Children, but Carlisle House, the former Assembly Rooms of the notorious Mrs Cornelys, was empty and silent.

By August 1777 the move from New Burlington Street was sufficiently advanced for Sophy Banks to look for her brother at the new address. Her uncertainty of his whereabouts, even in London, at this period is a measure of Banks's separation from his immediate family, including his uncle Robert. Banks kept the much-extended link with Sarah Wells in Chapel Street until the autumn of 1778. Then, with the vision of Newton's chair approaching the semblance of reality, the scene changed with some speed.

In October 1778 Banks had been introduced by a relative of his aunt Bridget Banks-Hodgkinson, a Mr Francis Filmer, attorney of John Street, near Bedford Row, to his ward Miss Dorothea Hugessen. At the age of 20 she was a co-heiress with her sister Mary, aged 17, to the estate of the late William Hugessen of Provender, near Faversham in Kent. The two girls had been orphaned for several years and educated in John Street under the care of their bachelor uncle and maiden aunt, the Filmers. Dorothea was said to have inherited a fortune of some £14000 and Mary about £10000, and each to hold land and property to the value of about £1000. Within six months the courtship had ended in marriage at St Andrew's Church, Holborn, on 23 March 1779 with a marriage settlement between Banks and Dorothea Hugessen witnessed on 20 March by Dorothea's guardian uncle Francis Filmer and by Banks's Dilettante crony, Charles Greville.

The academic stillness of 32 Soho Square was now to be enlivened by the presence of the young Mrs Banks, who was said by Solander to be

. . . rather handsome, very agreeable, chatty & laughs a good deal . . .

and brightened further by the presence of her sister Mary. The foundation of a new social focus in London had been laid.

At this time breakfast was taken in the library overlooking Dean Street, with the young ladies both present, and a moment in the new regime was captured for us in a letter from Sir John Cullum, FRS to the Revd George Ashby on 22 May 1779:

. . . Yesterday morning I took breakfast with Mr. Banks, who told me he was always glad to see his friends at that meal. And when can one see him so well? For after breakfast he retires into his study with those that please to attend him; where those who are likely to visit him will meet with ample entertainment. His wife is a comely and modest young lady.

Solander was particularly cheerful and talkative . . .

Lady Banks (née Dorothea Hugessen) *aet.* 30. Pastel drawing by
John Russell, RA, 1788.

But this occasion was on a Friday, the day after a meeting of the Royal Society, when Banks stayed overnight in London.

For most of the week now Banks and his ladies, not yet including his sister Sarah Sophia, were in the country at the villa of Spring Grove by Smallbury Green in the parish of Heston, taken by Banks on a short lease of four years from Elisha Biscoe. This was to be the answer to a hope deferred from as far back as 1773 when he had been attracted by the botanical display of Dr John Fothergill's estate at Upton, a *hortus vivus* to complement the aridity of a *hortus siccus*. Now in his honeymoon house of Spring Grove, with its attendant acres, he had at last the space for the botanical garden he sought for himself and conveniently close to the Royal Garden at Kew, across the river, to which he was already committed as the effective curator. There was however another attraction which was probably the main determinant in his choice of Spring Grove. It was in the same parish and within two miles of the estate known as Heston House which Robert Banks-Hodgkinson had bought at auction in 1775. The last pieces had now fallen into place to define the pattern of the years ahead. In the process one other piece had been displaced.

Sarah Wells and the Chapel Street forms of hospitality were past. Solander condensed the end of the affair for John Lloyd, on 5 June 1779, into the few brisk words that stand as its epitaph:

> ... Banks and Mrs. Wells parted on very good terms – she had the sense enough to find that he acted right, and of course She behaved very well. All her old friends visit her as formerly ...

How much human heartache those few lines conceal it is impossible to say. Banks the Benedict of New Burlington Street (and Chapel Street) was now transformed into the married man of Soho Square and Spring Grove, appearing now at the Court of St James's with Mrs Banks, both of them 'very splendidly drest', and on Thursdays, in the President's chair at Crane Court, very properly decked in 'a Full dressed Velvet or Silk Coat'. This is a contrast to the sober garb of the Benjamin West (1771) and William Parry (1776) portraits of the work-a-day Banks in his bachelor years of travel and professional uncertainty. Now it is more the image of Banks in the first Reynolds portrait in 1773 briefly in the ascendant over the John Russell pastel of the sober husband in 1779 or even over the mildly convivial Dilettante of the Reynolds groups in 1777.

In the heady excitements of these London events it is evident that his affairs at Revesby Abbey had somewhat lapsed. Less than a week after the marriage Benjamin Stephenson, from Mareham-le-Fen, wrote a dutiful but acid letter of congratulation, patently hurt that the news had come to him from the newspapers. For the rest he took a quiet revenge for his master's oversight with a seemly but pointed display of the righteous steward observing his duty. The opening thrust

> ... Your House & Furniture at Revesby cuts a most dispicable appearance ...

set the tone for the rest, a solemn and depressing catalogue, room by room, of the state of the family establishment summed up in one comprehensive damnation

Sarah Sophia Banks *aet.* 44. Pastel drawing by John Russell, RA, 1788.

... as to the Furniture it was old when my late Master dyed and 'tis now 17 years since that happen'd ...

This indeed was a measure of the neglect which the mansion house had suffered since his widowed mother had left it soon after her husband's death and Banks, the young heir, had for the most part been elsewhere. Stephenson was promptly ordered to London for a full review of what was needed and for a first meeting with his young mistress on whose taste and decisions so much for the future at Revesby would depend.

The scene was being set for the first of the autumnal migrations to Lincolnshire and Stephenson hastened back to his cottage at Mareham-le-Fen with a list of tasks in painting and re-decoration, repairs and upholstery of the furniture, and all other things necessary for bed and board in the house of a country gentleman who, from this year, was clearly intending to attend more closely to his county responsibilities. There was also the matter of the horses needed in London for riding, at least, of which five could be comfortably stabled under the Library in the back premises accessible from Dean Street. Stephenson nominated from the Revesby stock in the park three geldings and a mare, the latter '. . . far from handsome, that is not fit for a Gentleman to ride ... ' but strong and suitable enough for a servant's mount. All were at grass and would need corn and exercise before setting out on the road to London. There was accommodation also for two vehicles, a chaise and a carriage, beside the stalls under the library by the Dean Street entrance and for these a coachman, postillion and four horses could be found in London at a contract hiring rate of about £240 a year. But before these arrangements in London and Lincolnshire could be finally shaped according to the taste of either the young mistress or her more nearly middle-aged husband there were other affairs to attend to.

In August and September there were things to be done in Kent; looking over the Hugessen properties near Provender and Faversham – an extension of the honeymoon for Banks and evidently the beginning of a romance for young Mary Hugessen with Edward Knatchbull of Mersham Hatch, just down from Oxford at 21 and heir to the baronetcy. Then came the first autumn visit to Revesby Abbey, from the end of September to early November, by Mr and Mrs Joseph Banks, possibly with Mary Hugessen but probably not with Sarah Sophia Banks, a Lincolnshire honeymoon to set the old mansion house in order for the new life.

For the two young heiresses from Kent the time of parting came in the following summer when, from Spring Grove on 27 July 1780, Mary Hugessen was married to Edward Knatchbull by licence in the parish church at Heston. The relationship of Banks with the Knatchbull family was now consolidated but there was also a spare room in his houses and a place from now on for his sister Sophy. From the autumn of 1780 Banks and his ladies – Dorothea and Sarah Sophia – became an almost inseparable trio at home and abroad on their travels and in the felicitations of letters from friends the world over.

V

When Banks moved from St James's into the parish of St Anne's, Soho, another event, the importance of which was not discernible at the time was the advent of Jonas Dryander, the serious Swede and sober bachelor who was to serve so diligently

Jonas Dryander *aet.* 46. A drawing by George Dance jun., 9 June 1796.

and well for so long in the back premises at 32 Soho Square. Dryander at 29, an alumnus of the University of Uppsala, had left Christiansund on 1 July 1777 to land in London at Southwark on 10 July with funds enough, apparently, from a scholarship to support himself as he sought a place in the academic community. With the Swedish connection already so strong it was inevitable that he should soon be entangled in the Banksian net and, on 18 August, Banks himself introduced him for the first time to the Royal Botanic Garden at Kew. Ten days later he made his first visit to James Lee at The Vineyard, Hammersmith, the nursery garden which would be a constant focus for his interest until he died.

Whatever else he found in Dryander, it is plain that Banks, from the beginning of that summer, employed his services as a field botanist to keep a constant eye on the flora of all the important cultivated gardens in and about London for the next 33 years. From Dryander's first months in England there is abundant evidence to support the later judgement of Richard Salisbury comparing him with Solander

> . . . Solander preferred dried specimens that he might not use characters liable to disappear in an herbarium; Dryander on the contrary never trusted to a dried plant if he could see it living . . .

He paid almost weekly visits to Lee for the next 22 years as the central part of a regular pattern which took him over a wide range within the Home Counties in all but the most severe winter months.

At what point exactly and under what conditions he became an established part of the academic household at Soho Square and the presiding spirit of its back premises is not at all clear. But certainly from early in the year 1778, either on funds from his own scholarship or as a paid assistant to Banks, his presence at No. 32 as a member of the household seems to have been accepted. His arrival in England just as the new regime was being organized may have been fortuitous but for Banks and the biological sciences in Great Britain it was a happy chance and a fruitful union.

PART TWO
1778–1797

THE SAVANT
SIR JOSEPH BANKS,
BT, KB, DCL, FRS, FSA

CHAPTER 7

THE PRS IN SOHO SQUARE
1778–1796

Almost nine years after Cook and Banks had first sighted the eastern coast of Australia a committee was sitting under the chairmanship of Sir Charles Bunbury by an order of the House of Commons, dated 16 December 1778, to consider and report on the state of the felon population 'in the City of London, and the Counties of Middlesex, Essex, Kent, Herts, Surrey, and Sussex'. During the course of its sittings Cook was killed at Kealakekua Bay, Hawaii, on 13 February 1779 and Banks was married at the church of St Andrew, Holborn, on 23 March. Within a few days of that event Banks had also given evidence before the committee as it examined 'how far Transportation [of Felons] might be practicable to other Parts of the World'. His opinion was sought

> . . . in Case it should be thought expedient to establish a Colony of convicted Felons in any distant part of the Globe, from whence their Escape might be difficult, and where, from the Fertility of the Soil, they might be enabled to maintain themselves, after the First Year, with little or no aid from the Mother Country.

The point and urgency in these questions stemmed from the critical state of the war with the American colonists and their French allies which, with the impending entry of Spain into the conflict, presented the British government with problems of wide significance in trade and security apart from the practical disposal of its felonry by transportation across the Atlantic. The resurgence of French power after the Seven Years War and its increasing evidence across the oceans of the world added a global dimension, always present in some degree, aggravating the devastating rupture of the trans-Atlantic trade with the colonies. The old orientation of international politics and commerce had been irreversibly changed by the Anglo-Saxon revolutionaries of the eastern American seaboard. Now, in the first months of 1779, with the shattered British economy near its lowest ebb some easement in the heavy burden of the prison population had an immediate high priority.

The terms of the act 16 Geo.III.c.43 authorizing the transportation of convicted felons to the colonies in North America had been ineffective since the Declaration of Independence in July 1776. The act 18 Geo.III.c.62, the so-called Hulks Act, of May 1778 had only partly bridged the problem and was due for renewal and reappraisal. It was against this background that the Bunbury Committee was now sitting to consider 'the Acts relative to Transportation, and the Practicability of recurring to that mode of Punishment'. In devising a plan for establishing distant colonies of young convicts in a healthy climate and a state of self-sufficiency, the Committee emphasized it as 'equally agreeable to the Dictates of Humanity and Sound Policy', and that it 'might prove in the Result advantageous both to Navigation and Commerce'.

Banks's response survives only in the skeletal form of the record condensed in the *Journal of the House of Commons* as Bunbury reported it on 1 April 1779. Though short, no more than 500 words, it was enough to ensure the foundation of a white European settlement in the South Pacific. The questions were specific and his answers equally so. His opinion as reported, was:

> '. . . That the Place which appeared to him best adapted for such a Purpose, was *Botany Bay*, on the Coast of *New Holland*, in the *Indian Ocean*, which was about Seven Months Voyage from England; that he apprehended there would be little Probability of any Opposition from the Natives, as during his stay there, in the year 1770, he saw very few, and did not think there were above Fifty in all in the Neighbourhood, and had Reason to believe the Country was very thinly peopled; those he saw were naked, treacherous, and armed with Lances, but extremely cowardly, and constantly retired from our People when they made the least Appearance of Resistance; . . . that the Climate, he apprehended was similar to that of *Toulouse* in the South of *France*, having found the Southern Hemisphere colder than the Northern, in such Proportion, that any given Climate in the Southern answered to one in the Northern about Ten Degrees nearer to the Pole; the Proportion of rich soil was small in proportion to the barren, but sufficient to support a very large Number of People; . . .

In what followed it is clear that his remarks were confined to the conditions close to Botany Bay itself. There is nothing in the printed record to suggest what the colonists might find either north, south or inland from the Bay in any detail although his collecting excursions from the *Endeavour* must have carried him well beyond the confines of Kurnell peninsula, perhaps anything up to five miles from the shoreline and far enough to see reasonable grounds for his general statements about the local soils, the water supply and the nature of the timber for building and for fuel. Did he also somehow convey what he had seen from the ship's yawl with Cook and Solander as they made their first landing attempt off Woonona beach near Collin's Rocks some 25 miles south of the entrance to Botany Bay on the afternoon of Saturday 28 April 1770? Here they came within a quarter of a mile of the shore, close enough to see the general character of the soil and vegetation and the persons of several aborigines with four small canoes on the beach. This was the northern verge of the fertile Illawarra coastal plain with its cabbage palms and scattered timber free from undergrowth set against the steep escarpment of the range behind rising to 1500 feet and more with its red soil and dark patches of rain forest vegetation – altogether a different and in many ways more promising vista than the terrain round Botany Bay itself. But on this his journal and the House of Commons record are both equally silent. He had seen enough, however, to recommend the sending of a large number of persons 'Two or Three hundred at least' equipped with enough implements and supplies for a year as the foundation of a colony. And then came the vital leading question:

> . . . Whether he conceived the Mother Country was likely to reap any Benefit from a Colony established at Botany Bay?

164

To which came the answer:

> ... If the People formed among themselves a Civil Government, they would necessarily increase, and find Occasion for many *European* Commodities; and it was not to be doubted that a Tract of Land such as *New Holland*, which was larger than the whole of *Europe*, would furnish Matter of advantageous Return.

From that day the young President of the Royal Society was committed to the prospect of a white settlement in the South Pacific as the one person on the *Endeavour* voyage who would live long enough and have sufficient persistence and influence to ensure its establishment and survival. The testimony of Banks, for all the difficulties and dangers implied, was a small white light of hope to the Committee after its study of the other plans proposed for places such as Senegal and the Gambia, even Gibraltar, all fraught with hazards to health or political dangers, or both. The Committee resolved

> ... That it might be of Public utility, if the Laws which now direct and authorise the Transportation of certain Convicts to His Majesties Colonies and Plantations in *North America* were made to authorise the same to any other Part of the Globe that may be found expedient.

From this grew the bill that became the act 19 Geo.III.c.74 with effect until June 1784, permitting transportation

> ... to any Parts beyond the Seas, whether the same is situated in *America* or elsewhere.

But there was a war to be lost and a peace to be made before any of this new philosophy of colonization could reach fruition under the shrewd management of the younger Pitt in his first administration. For Banks himself there was another management to be mastered and other conflicts to be resolved in the affairs of the Royal Society before the theory and practice of colonization in remote places returned to trouble his working day.

II

The first year of Banks as a married man and as President of the Royal Society was also a year of military distractions. The French attacked the island of Jersey in May 1779; on 16 June Spain declared war on Britain and the four-year siege of Gibraltar began; two days later the French captured the island of St Vincent. The war was much in their minds as Benjamin Stephenson and Banks corresponded over the financial and estate affairs arising from Banks's marriage. For the greater part of the year Banks was out of London: honeymooning at Spring Grove until early August; in Kent at Provender and at Mersham with the Knatchbulls until late September; then at Revesby Abbey for some five weeks until his return to Soho Square in the first week of November for the opening of the Royal Society year. During the summer there had also been some pressure on Banks to stand as a candidate for the Boston seat in the forthcoming elections. This form of public service he once again rejected and made his reasoning clear to Stephenson. From now on it was at last clear to the county that Banks was committed to science and the Royal Society and his own view of its place in the world rather than to the vagaries of a Parliamentary career.

On the place of the Royal Society, however, there were many opinions abroad. This was evident in the uneasy relations with the Society of Antiquaries over the sharing of the new apartments now almost ready in 1780 for occupation by the two societies in Somerset House. Since 1775 Sir William Chambers had been engaged in replacing the old building between the Strand and the Thames with a new one to accommodate, as in the old, government offices and the Royal Academy but now also to include the Royal Society. From this the Society of Antiquaries, although under the same royal patronage but with a more equivocal status, was excluded. The Antiquaries, smarting under this implied inferiority, framed a petition to the King in protest, supplemented by some judicious elections to the Fellowship of the Society – the Prime Minister Lord North, a Lord of the Treasury in the 2nd Visc. Palmerston, and Sir William Chambers himself. So, early in 1776, the Society of Antiquaries were also included in the accommodation plans.

The Royal Society, well prepared for the move under its young President, held its first meeting at Somerset House as the anniversary occasion on 30 November 1780. The Society of Antiquaries, less ready for its move from Chancery Lane under the easy-going President Dr Jeremiah Milles, met for the first time in its new rooms on 11 January 1781. The Royal Society felt aggrieved at sharing a staircase with the Antiquaries but, worse still, at having a common anteroom and hall on the first or principal floor from which the meeting room was entered. It complained also about the limited space for a library and the lack of provision for a museum, but Chambers stood firm. Both societies had perforce to compromise over the cost of heating, lighting and furnishing the hall and anteroom. The Royal Society gained a sort of victory by taking (and retaining) possession of the lodge for the benefit of its clerk or Assistant Secretary, John Robinson and, as a triumph of territorial marking, by its placement of the bust of Sir Isaac Newton over the main front door in the entrance from the Strand, where it remains to this day.

In this academic imbroglio the Antiquaries saw Banks as the culprit. Certainly there are signs that in the second year of his tenure he used the transfer from the houses in Crane Court as an occasion to enlarge his authority in both societies. That a new force had appeared was evident in one resolution of the Royal Society Council on 5 April 1781 – 'That Mr. Dryander be desired to inspect the removal and arrangement of the books (from Crane Court to Somerset House) & that the R: S: Librarian take his directions'. This resolution was a long step toward Dryander's later role as librarian of the Royal Society.

Chambers made the formal transfer of the new apartments to the two societies on 15 February 1781 when the plans and details of construction were duly signed. However, before this, each President had in his own style made acknowledgement to the royal munificence which had made it all possible. Both societies ordered these celebratory addresses to be printed. Couched in overblown eloquence, each address defined a little more clearly the academic divergence of the two societies. With so large a common membership there was not only the old confusion of status but also that of appropriate boundaries in the various fields of learning. However strong Banks's antiquarian interests, he spoke loud and clear as a Fellow of the Royal Society in his flamboyant recital of its scientific heroes:

The Emotions of Gratitude inspired by the very Place in which, by the Munificence of our Royal Patron, we are for the first Time assembled, render it impossible for me to neglect the Opportunity which this Season, when ye have been used to hear yourselves addressed from the Chair, affords me, of offering my small Tribute of Acknowledgement for a Benefit so eminently calculated to promote the Honour and Advancement of this Society.

Established originally by the Munificence of a Royal Founder; fostered and encouraged since that Time by every successive Monarch who has swayed the British Sceptre, ye have ever proved yourselves worthy the Favor of your Royal Protectors. a NEWTON, who pruned his infant Wing under your Auspices, when his maturer Flights soared to Worlds immeasurably distant, still thought a Place among you an honorable Distinction. A NEWTON'S immortal Labors, a BOYLE, a FLAMSTEAD, a HALLEY, a RAY, and many others, of whom I trust it is needless to remind you, have made ample Returns for the Patronage of former Monarchs . . .

And so on to a listing of the more recent achievements of the Society so richly fed with grants from the royal purse, including the voyage to which he owed – and had himself given – so much. With this address carefully attuned to the sympathies and interests of the Fellowship, Banks, from this date, had the management of the Royal Society firmly in his grasp. Only the recent displacement of Dr Samual Horsley from the Council and the continued presence there of Dr Paul Maty as Principal Secretary remained as a smouldering source of troubles yet to come.

III

The New Year of 1777 had brought Banks the last letter he was ever to receive from Cook. Written from Cape Town on 26 November 1776 it closed with a long and unusual valediction:

'. . . believe me to be with great regard and attachment Dear Sir [your] most affectionate faithfull and humble Servt James Cook'

Now, after three years of silence, the New Year of 1780 brought the news under the signature of Lord Sandwich on 10 January to Banks that Cook was dead. The despatches that shocked London, almost a year after the event in Hawaii, had been sent by Charles Clerke under cover of a letter to the Admiralty dated 8 June 1779 to travel overland from Kamchatka to St Petersburg. Two months later, on 10 August 1779, Clerke, a dying man, dictated to James King 'a final adieu' to Banks:

. . . may you enjoy many happy years in this world, & in the end attain that fame your indefatigable industry so richly deserves. These are most sincerely the warmest & sincerest wishes of your devoted affectionate & departing Servant Charles Clerke

Clearly these two men, so different in character and temperament, had found in Banks a friend for whom after ten years they had retained a more than ordinary regard. That this was reciprocated by Banks was never more clear than in his devotion to the publication of the narrative of the third and last Pacific voyage on which his friends had sailed. But it had been hallowed also before the voyage in the portrait which Banks had commissioned from Nathaniel Dance to whom Cook had sat in May 1776. The painting was now hung over the fireplace in the library at Soho Square. There it would remain for over 50 years until in 1828 it was removed to the Painted Hall at Greenwich. It is no coincidence that Dance also painted Charles Clerke about the same time, with the attendant young Maori flaunting a twisted hank of Banks's favourite plant fibre, New Zealand flax, the same *Phormium tenax* shown so prominently in the West portrait drawing of Banks in 1771. Now Banks was able to extend the Cook iconography when, as the last item of business at his first Council meeting on 20 January 1780 he ensured the passage of a resolution calling for some public act to commemorate the name and achievements of its own late distinguished Fellow. A week later, on 27 January, the Council proposed that a medal be struck in Cook's honour, the cost to be met by a voluntary subscription open to the Fellows. Eventually from 17 designs submitted, that by Lewis Pingo, Chief Engraver at the Royal Mint, was chosen in the first fortnight of June. For the next five years Banks added the minting and distribution of the Royal Society Cook medal as a personal task coincident with the publication of the narrative of the tragic third voyage.

The first pressures of this long process appeared in the surprising and unwelcome form of a short printed account of the voyage from George Forster with his letter from Cassel of 20 January 1780, laying an early claim, with the usual insensitive Forster gall, to a copy of the official account for foreign publication. Banks had helped him to secure texts for the translation of the second Cook voyage and was even then involved in providing financial aid to the elder Forster as he prepared to

Left Captain James Cook, RN, FRS. Painting by Sir Nathaniel Dance-Holland, May 1776, commissioned by Banks to hang in the library at 32 Soho Square.
Right Captain Charles Clerke, RN. Painting by Sir Nathaniel Dance-Holland, *c.* May 1776.

leave England at last for Halle. But nothing could be done about the account of the third voyage until James King arrived at the end of August with the charts and journals. Banks by then was on his way to spend the autumn at Revesby Abbey. It was not until 10 October 1780 that Lord Sandwich wrote to seek Banks's opinion about the mode of publication and the preservation of the 200 drawings from which illustrations were to be selected. Before the end of the month Banks had advised the Admiralty that James King be charged with preparing the account from after the death of Cook and so he informed King, who was honoured to accept. The publication of the account of the third Cook voyage would for the next four years be a major task for Banks as the principal adviser and co-ordinating authority. He was hampered by the sequence of Parliamentary changes resulting from the dissolution of the North administration in March 1782 until the advent of the second Pitt cabinet in July 1784. More directly relevant were the changes at the Admiralty during the last stages of the American war. What began with a decision of Lord Sandwich as First Lord in October 1780 had to survive the appointments of Admirals Keppel and Howe from March 1782 until the more favourable regime of the 2nd Earl Spencer in July 1784.

Banks, from Revesby Abbey, apparently offered Lord Sandwich the advice that the cost of engraving the illustrative charts and views should be at the public expense, but that the cost of the paper and the printing should be a charge against the sales of the work itself; that George Nicol, the King's bookseller, should be the publisher; and that the book should be sold at a price as though it were not illustrated. With agreement on these principles Lord Sandwich convened a meeting of an advisory committee: himself in the chair; Phillip Stephens as Secretary of the Admiralty; Dr John Douglas, Canon of St Paul's as the prospective editor; Captain James King, as the author of the third volume; Alexander Dalrymple, hydrographer of the East India Company, as adviser on the charts; John Webber, the artist of the voyage; James Stuart, publisher of the Greek antiquities, as art consultant and Mr Joseph Banks. After looking over Webber's drawings, the committee listed those it favoured for publication. These were then put under the care of Banks who undertook the supervision of the engravers with the aid of John Webber, whose salary was to be continued while the work was in hand. Alexander Dalrymple was charged with overseeing the engraving of the charts and the views of land.

Banks mobilized 25 engravers, of whom 12 had been used before, either for the Hawkesworth account of the first or for Cook's narrative of the second voyage. The first plate, a young woman of Otaheite bringing a present, was allotted to Bartolozzi in April 1781 but not finished until March 1784. This proved to be the favourite illustration. The most expensive was William Woollett's 'Human Sacrifice' at £157.10s.0d., finished last of all in April 1784. For both artists these plates were their only contributions. The most productive engraver was William Sharp of Kennington Lane with 12 plates, mostly in the cheaper range at £26.5s.0d. Peter Mazell contributed the three animal engravings – the opposum, the sea otter and the white bear – at a modest £10.10s.0d. each. In all 61 plates were engraved at a total cost of £2997.12s.0d., an average of about £49 per plate. As a group these 25 engravers were altogether separate from those other 18 who, over the years, were at work on the botanical plates of Banks's ambitious private venture working at the much lower cost of about £3 per engraved plate.

In all later references to the publication of the account of the third voyage, Banks was content, in the main, to ascribe its management to Lord Sandwich. Perhaps in principle this was proper; in practice however it is evident that Banks was the guiding and effective managerial authority to whom all turned as various problems of production emerged. Moreover his was also an opinion of weight in the negotiations over foreign translation and publishing rights and in establishing the equality of the final distribution of the profits from the sales.

From January 1781 George Forster renewed his first importunate demands for the rights to the German translation through Banks as a mediator. Banks deflected Forster, who was out of favour with Lord Sandwich, until he, Sandwich, was out of office advising that application be made through a reputable publisher and not under the Forster name. Three years later the sheets were given to Spener and Haude for George Forster to translate, though not without Forster trying to appropriate the copper plates which had been loaned for the illustrations and using them for his own purposes in the autumn of 1784. Thomas Pennant also attempted a similar predation in May 1783, seeking some of the drawings by Webber for his *Arctic Zoology*, emphasizing his status as 'a public man meriting the assistance of his friends'. This plea only elicited a stern reminder from Banks that Admiralty property was not his to lend for private publishing.

In providing the edited English text for the French to use, Banks cunningly wove into this negotiation one for a supply of paper from Paris on which to print the engravings. French paper had been used for the illustrations in the account of the second voyage and the same quality was recommended by Charles Pancoucke, the eminent Paris publisher, for those of Cook's third voyage. Peter Elmsley, the Strand publisher, was a useful go-between at first, although John Webber was anxious to visit Paris and choose the paper himself. Banks however wanted Webber in London where he was of more use watching and prodding the engravers. From Revesby Abbey in September 1782 Banks persuaded the Admiralty to underwrite his negotiations for the paper with Pancoucke in exchange for the right to publish a French translation by Jean Demeunier, at a suitable interval after the appearance of the English first edition. On this, and all matters concerning the publication, Admiral Keppel, successor to Sandwich as First Lord, agreed to accept Banks's advice. On 25 October 1782 Banks wrote to Pancoucke with a formal proposal that he and Demeunier should have the use of the sheets of text and the copper plates in return for the delivery of an estimated 130 reams of French colombier of the right quality as approved by Banks himself. There was a further delay until Lord Keppel had been replaced by Lord Howe at the Admiralty and Banks secured the approval of the new regime. Then on 28 March 1783 Banks was able to settle the matter, having that day got Admiralty agreement on the method of payment – by bills drawn on Banks after he had received and certified each package of paper, at one month's credit and the money to be remitted to Paris within three months of delivery. It was not however until October 1783 that Banks could tell Pancoucke that the first sheets of the text were ready to be sent in return for the eight cases of paper received in July. He wrote in French, thanking Pancoucke for his account of the Montgolfier balloon ascent from Versailles on 19 September 1783 and added:

> ... J'écris par la Post aujourdhui pour donner l'ordre que les Feuilles de voyage seront avance à votre adresse par M. Nicol Libraire au Roi qui est celui qui publie pour nous et Je n'ai point de doute de sa ponctualité.

The winter passed with Banks urging on Dr Douglas with his preparation of the manuscript for the printer and James King with his proof corrections, while settling disputes between Henry Roberts, King and Dalrymple over the polar and general charts. On 30 March 1784 he gave a final suggestion to Dr Douglas about directions for the bookbinder to be printed and inserted in the sheets, giving the order of insertion of the engravings and charts, and expressing the hope that the book would be published on 18 May, the day Parliament was due to assemble.

By the end of May the three large quarto volumes of the first edition with the 78 engraved illustrations and charts were ready, and Banks was now beset with claims and requests for the book, as well as for the Royal Society Cook medal of which the minting was now also in progress. Of the first 2000 copies printed, 1942 sold rapidly at £3.5s.0d. each and 47 were given as presents by the Admiralty, in addition to the customary 11 to the Stationers' Company. Some of the presentations were magnificently bound at the expense of the profits – those to the King, the Queen and the Prince of Wales and those to the King of France, the Empress of Russia, and to Benjamin Franklin. In relation to these last three, on Sunday 30 May 1784, Lord Howe called at Soho Square to consult Banks, at the King's behest. Banks however was at Spring Grove with William Roy but returned to London on Tuesday 1 June and at the Admiralty drafted the three letters to accompany those presentation copies.

In spite of the delay caused by an application to the Court of Chancery for an injunction against the sale of the pirated Kearsley abridgement in July 1784, which the Lord Chancellor refused, a clear profit of some £2715 was soon achieved by the original publication. In August, Banks was called to a meeting at Lord Sandwich's house to decide the division of the profits in principle, but the critical first stages of the baseline survey kept him at Spring Grove. He made his views clear by letter and on 9 September Lord Sandwich wrote that he, Lord Howe and Phillip Stephens were all agreed with what Banks had proposed as an equitable division of the profits from the first and second editions. In brief, these arrangements were: one-half to Captain Cook's family with the interest to Mrs Cook during her life; one-fourth to Captain James King; one-eighth to the legal representatives of Captain Charles Clerke; one-eighth to Mr William Bligh, master, for much of the surveying, from which £100 was to be deducted for the executors of William Anderson, surgeon, whose journal was used for the natural history. In this arrangement a belated recognition was given to Bligh's real contribution to the voyage obscured as it had been by Lt Henry Roberts's management of the engraving of the charts under Dalrymple's supervision. A final meeting on 28 July 1785 between Banks, Phillip Stephens, Sandwich and Howe confirmed the equity of this mode of dividing the profits from the three official editions which amounted to some £3863.

In his management of the Royal Society Cook medal, Banks had taken his first step in an association with the Royal Mint which would involve him in the intricacies of the coinage in later years. This would continue the links with Matthew Boulton who, in 1772, had already produced for him the medals to commemorate Cook's second voyage at his own expense.

IV

The new order of collecting abroad for the Royal Botanical Garden at Kew which Banks had been so prominent in persuading the King to approve and finance in 1772 had flourished for ten years in the labours of Francis Masson. Banks had in the intervening years become the scientific intermediary between the Garden and the King, more effectively perhaps after Masson's return from his three Cape journeys in 1772–5. The following year Banks successfully approached the King again through Sir John Pringle as President of the Royal Society asking him to support Masson in the botanical exploration of Madeira, the Canaries, the Azores and the West Indies. On 19 May 1776 Masson left England for an absence of six years until the exigencies of war brought him home again in April 1782. Banks now took up the management of Masson's affairs directly as PRS and in November 1782 secured royal approval for Masson to visit Lisbon. During the next three years he collected in southern Spain, North Africa and finally again in Madeira before returning in 1785. But while Masson was botanizing for the King among the Atlantic islands and elsewhere from 1776, another man under the management of Banks was collecting in the Pacific for the Banksian herbarium itself and solely at its owner's charge.

On 24 April 1776 James Lee made his second recommendation of a young man to the service of Banks. This was David Nelson who 'understands something of botany, but does not pretend to have much knowledge of it' though in character he was well suited 'for the purpose of a collector'. Nelson was accepted and on 26 April 1776 'Receivd of Master Joseph Banks Esq're the Sum of twelve pounds twelve Shillings on account of wages commencing this day' under the terms of an agreement of the same date. For the sum of £35 a year Nelson agreed:

> . . . that I will sail with Capt. Clerke on board his Majesties ship Discovery & that I will under Capt. Clerkes orders collect & preserve all such plants & Seeds of plants as I shall be able to find in all such places as the ship may touch at also that I will take & preserve as many insects as I shall be able & that I will send back or on my return give to Jos. Banks Esq're my employer all & every one of such plants seeds & insects as I shall collect not retaining to my self or disposing of to any other person any of the Same . . .

Here is an echo of that troublesome aftermath in the case of James Lee's other protegé, Sydney Parkinson, four years before in the resolution of his posthumous affairs and the publication of his journal. A signed agreement avoided much misunderstanding. Three months' tuition in botany and entomology at New Burlington Street however was the most that could have been arranged for Nelson before he left the Thames in the Discovery as a supernumerary with the status of AB. But Charles Clerke found him 'one of the quietest fellows in Nature' and 'very attentive' and Cook promised Banks that Nelson would have 'every assistance in my power to give him'. William Anderson was also pleased that Nelson would supplement in botany what he himself would cover for Banks in other ways. The full measure of this investment in such a modest and obscure young man cannot be known but his name ranks high in the records of the Hortus Kewensis as a contributor to the Garden and in the General Herbarium at South Kensington as a collector of new species after his return and discharge from the Discovery in the first week of October 1780.

While Nelson was extending the boundaries of botanical science in the Pacific much was happening at home. The near coincidence of the purchase of the leasehold in Soho Square and the appearance of Jonas Dryander three months later in 1777 was in itself important. Its back premises offered generous space to accommodate the expanding library, the herbarium and its increase of fitted 'cubes', with room enough beneath for the engravers to work on the copper plates of the *Endeavour* voyage plants. The British Museum with Solander in residence was within a comfortable strolling distance. A study on the ground floor of the main house behind the main staircase was well placed to receive visitors from the front hall or to conduct them by the long covered passage through to the books and collections at the rear. It was also a quiet cul-de-sac with a good light from the courtyard and the south in which to pursue botany or, increasingly, the ramifications of a correspondence that had now sprung into vigorous life amid what Banks was later to define as 'the unarranged regularity of my little den'.

One of the first accessions in the new premises was the herbarium of Nicolaus von Jacquin, which Banks bought for £238 in May 1777, laying the foundation of a rich correspondence from Vienna. From this followed an early visit by Jan Ingenhousz, FRS, the plant physiologist, to Soho Square in March 1778, perhaps the first of its foreign visitors. He was soon followed by Joseph Gaertner, FRS, the Wurtemburger whose classic work *De Fructibus et Seminibus Plantarum* ten years later would be dedicated to Banks. In the autumn came also Gaertner's inspection of the herbarium of J. F. Gronovius for Banks in Amsterdam and the purchase of some books for him at the sale. To close the year Dryander was able to welcome his fellow student Carl Thunberg, FRS on 14 December. Thunberg was immediately introduced to Banks and Solander and for most days in the ensuing six weeks he spent the mornings either in the herbarium or the library with free access to the plant collections of the *Endeavour* voyage, at that time kept separately in the attic rooms above the main herbarium. It was a distinct privilege that he was allowed to study every one of the species collected on that voyage in discussions with both Solander and Dryander who brought them to him. He was one of the first also to record his appreciation of the library and its convenience and completeness for his studies in natural history. With the daily visits of other scholars like himself to enrich his stay, Thunberg rated Soho Square 'as it were ... an Academy of Natural History'. For Banks this hospitality was to yield enough in specimens and inspiration from Thunberg's Japanese collections to lead him to his own private publication of Engelbert Kaempfer's drawings from the British Museum more than a decade later.

The following year his correspondence with India began its long course with William Roxburgh, surgeon of the HEI Company at Nagore, reacting to Banks's invitation to send plant specimens to London for identification and description. Finding their way slowly from Canton at the same time were João Loureiro's plants from Cochin-China and his manuscript 'Nova Genera Plantarum', later to be printed in Lisbon under Banks's editing as the *Flora Cochinchinensis*. Henry Smeathman returned in August 1779 with his West African collections for Dr John Fothergill, the Dowager Duchess of Portland, Dr William Pitcairn and Banks after four years of hazardous residence in Sierra Leone. But the shape of many things to come was evident in the letter from Antoine de Jussieu from Paris in the same month telling Banks that he had been entrusted with the description of Philibert Commerson's Pacific herbarium and generously declaring his wish not to encroach on Banks's intentions in the same region. He raised also the problem of captured plant collections and proposed the reciprocal use of his own and Banks's name as a form of protection when consignments fell into either French or English hands because of the wartime conditions. Implicit also in Jussieu's engagement with the Commerson collection was the publication ten years later of his *Genera plantarum secundum ordines naturales disposita*, that important departure from the Linnaean system of classification with which Banks was in time to declare himself in sympathy. During 1780 William Brass at the expense of Banks, Dr John Fothergill and James Lee, grappled clumsily against heavy odds of both transport and climate collecting seeds and plants on the Gold Coast and the edge of the Ashanti country.

In England too there was much activity with Dr Erasmus Darwin in Lichfield at work organizing the translation from the Latin into English of Linnaeus's *Genera . . .* and *Species Plantarum* during 1781. He constantly sought the advice of Banks on matters of terminology, translation and publication. He drew also on the library at Soho Square for titles such as John Murray's edition of the *Regnum vegetabile* and volumes of the *Amoenitates Academicae* not easily come by in the provinces. At length there appeared in 1783 under the editorship of Dr Darwin *A System of Vegetables* published by Strahan and Cadell at the expense of the Botanical Society of Lichfield and dedicated to Sir Joseph Banks.

In spite of the war with France there was a scientific welcome still at Soho Square for a young Frenchman with a turn for zoology. Pierre Broussonet arrived in December 1780, and for the next 18 months worked on the Banksian fish collection, to produce in 1782 his *Ichthyologia, sistens piscium descriptiones et icones. Decas I*, published by Peter Elmsley of the Strand. He was elected FRS on 14 February the same year. For much of this first visit to England, Broussonet had as his companions at Soho Square the younger Linnaeus, who in 1781 had edited the supplement to his father's *Genera plantarum . . .* with its publication of the genus *Banksia*, and Johann Fabricius, who had already published so many descriptions of the Banks insect collection. All three of these foreign visitors were at Soho Square during that harrowing week in early May 1782 when Dr Solander slowly died there from a massive celebral haemorrhage. For Banks this tragic loss carried as a sort of memorial the distribution of his own private printing of the catalogue and engravings of William Houstoun's Caribbean and central American plant collection in 1781. As the *Reliquiae Houstounianae . . .* Banks was sending this small quarto volume as gifts to selected botanists, with its 26 engravings by Houstoun himself and in its lists an indication of the specimens which Banks had acquired for his herbarium on the death of Phillip Miller of the Chelsea Physic Garden – to Pieter Bergius at Stockholm; to John Ryan in Curacao; to John Hope at Edinburgh, three copies by the hand of Broussonet; to J. R. Forster at Halle; to Pieter Boddaert at Utrecht; to Carlo Allioni at Turin; to Jean Hermann at Strasbourg; to Casimero Ortega at Madrid; to the Gesellschaft Naturforschender zu Berlin – and so on as a modest exercise in private publication in which he hoped still for greater things with his copper plates from the *Endeavour* voyage. But the obstacles against the fulfilment of this visionary plan were growing formidably in another quarter.

In the autumn of 1781 Banks had been inexorably drawn, as a large landholder, into the arguments of the Lincolnshire growers of a superior long wool against the wool manufacturers, especially those of Yorkshire, over the causes of the disastrous decline in the state of trade between them. With the transatlantic trade in coarse woollens disrupted, there had been a massive growth in stocks of unsold long wool on Lincolnshire farms. The price had fallen from about 8 pence per pound in 1776 to less than 4 pence in 1781 and it was still falling when Banks and George Chalmers joined forces to produce a pamphlet of 88 pages to be published in 1782 by Peter Elmsley anonymously under the title, *The Propriety of Allowing a Qualified Exportation of Wool Discussed Historically*. Commonly attributed to Banks as the sole author, it was in fact largely written by Chalmers with Banks contributing the tables of the appendix and the commercial information. Its keynote was struck by the preliminary quotation from the speech of Sir Edward Coke to the House of Commons in 1621:

> . . . Freedom of trade is the life of trade and all monopolies and restrictions of trade do overthrow trade . . .

In a few years Chalmers would become a clerk to the Privy Council for Trade and Plantations and so a lifelong associate of Banks. For Banks himself the long course of his engagement with the British wool industry and its fortunes had begun.

CHAPTER 8

THE BARONET AND OUTER SPACE
1781–1785

As physician-in-ordinary to Queen Charlotte Sir John Pringle, the youngest son of a Scottish baronet, had been created a baronet in 1766 in his own right. Banks, as Pringle's successor in the chair at the Royal Society for three successive years early in 1781 took discreet steps to correct this difference in status. He had by descent some claim to an entry on the Roll of Baronets, headed as it was by the name of Sir Francis Bacon, ancestor in spirit of the Royal Society itself. The arms of his grandfather, Joseph Banks II, had been approved if not officially registered at the College of Arms. He himself was a country gentleman of property with an income more than sufficient to support this qualification within the prevailing terms of the Order. He had moreover raised himself to distinction in a field of science where his merit had been recognized by his peers at home and increasingly by those abroad. His ancestry was clear as far back as his great-great-grandfather beyond which his claim to the family arms was tenuous and hallowed only by family usage. As plain Joseph Banks of Revesby Abbey in the County of Lincolnshire, esquire, he had continued the use of the Bank Newton shield of arms 'according to tradition' – quarterly, sable, a cross or between four fleurs-de-lys argent – and as such had it engraved for a bookplate with a heron for its crest. From Downing Street on 20 February 1781 John Robinson as a secretary of the Treasury wrote:

> Lord North having laid before His Majesty your Wishes to be created a Baronet of Great Britain, and His Majesty having been graciously pleased to grant your Request I am commanded by His Lordship to desire that you will acquaint me for His Information with the Description of your Place and Residence which you wish to be inserted in the Patent, in order that Lord North may take His Majesty's Pleasure for the necessary Warrants to be Prepared for this Purpose . . .

A week later on Wednesday 28 February Banks was waited on by a Mr Broughton of the Treasury with another letter from John Robinson to say that the warrants had been ordered for preparation and to receive Banks's further instructions in the matter of his claim 'for Exemption of the Fine of £1000' as a last formality. Then three weeks later came the final word and royal command on 22 March:

> . . . I am directed by Lord North to acquaint You that His Majesty has been graciously pleased to sign a Warrant for creating You a Baronet of Great Britain, and that You may kiss Hands at the Levee Tomorrow

So on Friday 23 March 1781 Banks attended at the Court of St James to emerge from the palace after the levee as Sir Joseph Banks, the first and only Baronet of Revesby Abbey in the County of Lincolnshire.

Three weeks later, on Friday 13 April, he set out on an unseasonal visit to Overton Hall by way of his estates near Cheadle and on his first visit to Derbyshire as a married man, Sir Joseph abroad with 'his Ladies' – his wife and his sister – to become a notable trio. This journey was occasioned by the need to consult with his uncle Banks-Hodgkinson on the site of the new engine to be installed by Boulton and Watt on the escarpment above the old engine at the Gregory Mine, a matter on which he had reached agreement with James Watt at last and signed the contract on 16 February. The party's progress was briefly recorded by Sarah Sophia in what was evidently her own first visit both to Cheadle and Ashover, and it gives a glimpse of the circumstances and rate of travel in the Banks's family coach. The whole journey was 284 miles, travelled in seven and-a-half days at an average of 39–40 miles per day with baiting distances of about ten miles or every two hours.

Within the first year of his baronetcy Banks was approached by Edward Hasted for some biographical details to be included in the second volume of *The History and Topographical Survey of the County of Kent*, merited by virtue of his marriage to the daughter of William Hugessen of Provender, perhaps also by his recent title. In his reply to Hasted, about 25 February 1782, there are otherwise rare traces of self-appraisal and recorded opinions. Banks directed attention to the details of his family history which he had lodged with the College of Heralds, evidently in March 1781. As to his achievements he declined to express a view beyond making this point:

> ... I may flatter myself that, being the first man of Scientifick education who undertook a voyage of discovery & that voyage of discovery being the first which turned out satisfactorily to this enlightened age I was in some measure the first who gave that turn to such voyages, or rather to their Commander Capt Cook ... but of this I shall leave others to judge – ...

Here is a revealing gleam in the thoughts of the man who was even then immersed in the consequence of these voyages; his hopes and feelings, some two months before the death of Daniel Solander were compressed into one short paragraph:

> ... Botany has been my favorite Science since my childhood; & the reason I have not publish'd the account of my travels is that the first, from want of time necessarily brought on by the many preparations to be made for my second voyage, was intrusted to the care of Dr. Hawkesworth; & since that I have been engag'd in a Botanical work which I hope soon to publish, as I have now near 700 solid plates prepar'd: it is to give an account of all the new plants discover'd in my voyage round the world, somewhat above 800 ...

At the end there was a curious down-beat in his flat statement:

> ... In my return from Iceland, I livd in no particular station till ... I was elected President of the Royal Society; in which post I still remain ...

Here, it would seem, is the confession of a man who had searched long for an identity and which now he hoped he had found. There is also the first hint of his private attitude to his place as President in the Royal Society, as perhaps less an honour to be enjoyed, more a 'post' to be filled with a function to be performed much as a man might head a department of state in a managerial way.

177

II

While the warrants were being prepared for the Banks baronetcy William Herschel at 19 King Street, Bath, was scanning the heavens with his seven-foot Newtonian telescope. On Tuesday 13 March 1781, between ten and eleven in the evening, he saw a body of 'uncommon magnitude' which at first he took to be a comet. As such he reported it to the Bath Philosophical Society in March and as such also to the Royal Society, where his paper 'Account of a Comet' was read by William Watson jun., FRS on 26 April 1781. By 4 April the Astronomer Royal was already suggesting that the new discovery might be a planet, but another year was to pass before the train of further observations, at home and abroad by other astronomers, was to confirm that this was indeed so. Herschel had added an eighth planet to the seven known to man and the course of his own life had been changed. On 12 November Banks told Herschel that he had been awarded the Copley Medal and that he would be speaking on the occasion commending the new discovery. Thomas Hornsby, Savilian Professor of Astronomy at Oxford, from early doubts, had moved to a conviction by his own calculations that the new star was indeed a planet. On 6 December 1781 Herschel was elected a Fellow of the Royal Society and Banks, in

Left Sir Joseph Banks *aet.* 45. Pastel drawing by John Russell, RA, 1788. In his left hand he holds a pastel drawing entitled 'Carte de la Lune par J. Russell', an early impression of the surface of the moon which Russell had begun to draw in 1785 using one of William Herschel's six-foot reflecting telescopes with a six-inch mirror for his details carefully measured and plotted by micrometer. Banks was the link between the astronomer and the artist in the development of Russell's apparatus, the 'Selenographia', 1797.

Right William Herschel, FRS *aet.* 47. Painting by Lemuel Abbott, 1785.

practical recognition of Herschel's poverty, arranged an exemption for him from the usual fees. He did more than this. At an early opportunity he drew the King's attention to the new discovery and by 24 February 1782 Herschel was aware that he was indebted to Banks for the royal invitation to bring his instruments to London. Herschel proposed that the name of the new star should somehow be linked with the King but in what way he was content to leave Banks to decide. On 25 May Herschel had an audience with the King in London and on 2 July showed the royal family his seven-foot telescope.

Meanwhile Banks and William Watson jun. were moving to have Herschel appointed to the place of Dr Stephen Demainbray, the King's old tutor and court astronomer at the Kew Observatory but without success. Instead, on Banks's advice, the King provided Herschel with a pension of £200 a year and a royal grant of £2000 for the enlargement and improvement of his telescopes. On 1 August 1782 Herschel and his sister Caroline moved into an old house at Datchet. From this point on Banks was the immediate supervisor of all Herschel's expenditure as year by year the size and power of his telescopes grew to the culminating triumph of the giant reflector and 40-foot telescope of 1795 with the aid of a further grant from the King of £2000 in 1787. Banks was a close and interested observer especially in the first years at Datchet. A week after his rejection of the offer of the Linnaean collections he spent a morning at Datchet with Herschel on 30 December 1783 in the depth of that vicious winter. Returning to Spring Grove he had a happy thought:

> Excuse me if I offer you as a new years Gift a pair of old Shoes I should not have venturd so whimsical & so unusual a present had it not occurrd to me in the short walk we had this morn that the Construction as well as the materials of them might be usefull
>
> I solvd also the problem of the different size of our Feet by the addition of the various stockings you will necessarily use when you wear them . . .

How apposite the gift was may be judged from Herschel's reply on New Year's day 1784 in gratitude to Banks for the thought and for the size of the shoes. With them he was able to wear seven pairs of stockings in his night vigil of the stars as some protection against the intense cold when the temperature fell to 7° F and threatened to crack the great speculum of his telescope.

With the Herschels at last settled as royal pensioners near Windsor the matter of naming the new star emerged again. Banks had suggested that the King's name might be celebrated appropriately in this way and Herschel enthusiastically consulted his friends in the Bath Philosophical Society on the point. From this, on the Galilean model, came the suggestion of *Georgium Sidus* and, on 7 November 1782, a letter to this effect from Herschel to Banks was read before the Royal Society. As such it entered the literature for a while, both scientific and poetic, until it submerged under the weight of German argument to rise again in Johann Bode's catalogue of stars, *Allgemeine Beschreibung und Nachweisung der Gestirne . . .*, 1801, as the planet Uranus we know today. But it was as the *Georgium Sidus* that it was commemorated by Josiah Wedgwood on a medallion of William Herschel in 1783, though by no means to the satisfaction of the scientific community. So Banks on 17 January 1784 was constrained to admonish Wedgwood at the behest of William Watson jun. in the name of Herschel's friends:

...You know that the wise ones here have criticised most plentifully on the symbol of a star and two circles which are put on the medallion of Herschel publishd by you & that it was generally Pronouncd as not sufficiently characterising him from the dificulty of showing any demonstration of the Star in Question being the Georgium Sidus deducd from the Circles which seem to have been put there for no purpose whatever if not to furnish such a demonstration.

it was therefore proposd a few days ago that if the star alone was left without any circle whatever the end would be answerd, and all agreed that the star may be arbitrarily Calld Herschel's Star provided no circles are with it to prove the contrary . . .

Othersise all were highly pleased with the bust as an admirable likeness. The representation of the *Georgium Sidus* medallion however remained troublesome and Banks on 24 January 1785 had cause to criticize a second version. Where the first had shown the star with radiations, the second showed it appropriately as a plain orb, in Banks's view merely an undistinguished 'white speck upon the Ground'. He suggested that it be placed on one of two orbits shown on the plaque in contrast with Saturn

. . . whose Ring may easily be modeld in such a manner as will prevent the most ignorant pretended to astronomer from mistaking him for any other of the Lamps of heaven

A fine idea in principle but in his haste Banks placed Uranus on the orbit nearer the Sun than Saturn instead of the more distant. Perhaps in this he was diverted by the excitement of receiving the letter from John Jeffries in Paris with the news that he and Blanchard had made the first crossing of the Channel by air in a balloon from Dover to Calais.

III

In the spring of 1780 Charles Blagden returned from active service on board HMS *Pigot* Hospital Ship off the east coast of America to garrison duty at Plymouth. As the American war dwindled to its close Blagden found increasing occasion to visit London where he was welcome as a breakfast visitor at Soho Square. For Daniel Solander also it was a regular custom to enjoy this form of hospitality from Banks and his new matrimonial menage after a short stroll from his quarters in Montagu House. From his first visit to Soho Square in May 1780 Blagden adopted the habit of keeping notes of what passed in conversation from time to time. As an avid scientific and social gossip he had much in common with Solander and during 1780 especially many odd snippets of this kind found a place in Blagden's notes with the *Endeavour* voyage and its personnel in particular as the subjects of his probing curiosity. During these last two years of Solander's life these breakfast occasions included Pierre Broussonet, Johann Fabricius and the younger Linnaeus. It was at one such breakfast about ten o'clock on the morning of 8 May 1782 that Blagden was listening at table to Solander describing the stresses and dangers of his experience with Banks and the shore party in the snowstorm on Tierra del Fuego that day in January 1769 when Thomas Dorlton and George Richmond died of exposure.

At one point in his narrative Solander stopped to complain that his left arm was in some way affected so that he could not control its movements in relation to the table as he wished. Earlier that morning he had also spoken of a pain in his right great toe attended by a slight redness not unlike gout though he had never before had a sign of that disease. He returned to his story and in a few minutes Blagden noted a change in Solander's facial symmetry affecting the movement of the left corner of his mouth as he spoke and then, soon after, an unnatural extension of his left leg. During these changes his speech remained clear and intelligible but the general signs of a left hemiplegia had already alarmed Blagden and he ordered Solander to lie on a couch. A messenger was immediately sent for John Hunter from Leicester Square while the younger Linnaeus went in search of the doctors William Heberden and William Pitcairn as senior physicians. All of them came quickly and the hopeless course of Solander's last slow agony began. He was in no condition to go back to his rooms in Montagu House and Lady Banks ordered one to be prepared for him in the house. Banks himself was on a visit at some distance from London, probably in Kent with Edward Knatchbull his brother-in-law at Mersham. At 2.30 p.m. Blagden sent off a letter to him with the news of Solander's 'paralytic stroke' and his own unhappy forebodings. With this to spur him Banks travelled through the night to join the mournful group at Soho Square.

Solander's condition fluctuated through the first night and all through 9 May, becoming feverish. By 10 May he was intermittently unconscious and though seemingly better on 11 May by the following day his pulse had dropped rapidly. Although he rallied a little, at 9.30 p.m. on 13 May, he died. It had been a hopeless case of a massive cerebral haemorrhage from the beginning as Blagden had clearly recognized and a distressing course of five and-a-half days to its inevitable end for all associated with this much-loved, good-natured man from Sweden. Next day 14 May 1782 the autopsy by John Hunter added its small quota of information setting the seal to Blagden's clinical record. Various points of debate among the physicians were clarified and in a measure settled in Hunter's short statement to Blagden: 'I found about two ounces of coagulated blood in the right ventricle of the Brain. Some of the thinner part had made its way into the left. The Intestines were only inflated. You will be so good as to explain this to Sir Jos: Banks'. Blagden, from a later conversation with Hunter, found that the posterior part of the right ventricle was damaged in its texture and that the septum between the ventricles was also broken through to admit the blood-stained serum. A ruptured aneurysm of the posterior cerebral artery may well have been the cause of death.

Solander was buried next to the body of his famous compatriot Emmanuel Swedenborg in the Swedish Protestant Church on Sunday 19 May in the presence of a large group of his English and Swedish friends. Banks himself, who had been able to do little more than wait beside his dying friend, was his only English pallbearer to the grave. As he wrote to Edward Knatchbull on 14 May immediately after Solander had died: 'I have had little hopes of him from the first the Loss of an old Friend you may conceive is not a little distressing to us all', an understatement one would think, but of a piece with the restrained stoicism with which Banks always faced calamity and death. The veil over his inmost feelings parted a little further a month later as he exposed them to John Lloyd:

181

... to write about the Loss of poor Solander would be to renew both our feelings for little purpose Suffice it to say then that few men howsoever Exalted their pursuits were ever more feelingly miss'd either in the paths of Science or of Friendship.

Eighteen months later, in his long letter to Johan Alstroemer of 16 November 1784, Banks still could not bring himself to do more than relate the facts of those last grim days, begging to be excused any further revelation of his own deep feelings beyond a full and clear recognition of his friend's ample merits and professional diligence.

Within the month Banks and his wife succumbed to 'a curious disease', influenza as it was being called and about which people were beginning to talk. This ailment, apart from any other pressures, interrupted his concern with the affairs of his late friend until mid-June, though he had evidently asked Charles Lindgren soon after Solander's death to act for him in some degree in finalizing the arrangements. On 20 June however Lindgren asked to be relieved of this responsibility on the grounds of his own acute ill-health, suggesting Dryander and Aron Mathesius, the Swedish clergyman, as the most eligible of the Swedish community in London to take his place. Some steps had already been taken to have Solander's furniture at Montagu House valued for sale and Lindgren's friend Ingham Forster had reckoned that the collection of shells and fossils would sell well if the sale were deferred until the autumn or early the following spring. He sent Banks a ring of keys to open a bureau of Solander's kept at 32 Soho Square and the problem of the packing and cataloguing which remained, he hoped, could be finished with Dryander's help.

IV

From those February days in 1768 when the Council of the Royal Society was framing the 'Memorial' to the King for the *Endeavour* voyage, particularly that last critical dinner of the dining club in Middle Temple Hall, Banks and Benjamin Franklin had been friends. Franklin had been one of the first to hear at length from Banks and Solander on their return about the course of the voyage and in August 1771, as they dined together at Sir John Pringle's, his vision had been enlarged further about the character of the Pacific peoples. The War of American Independence had separated them and they never met again after 1775 though they remained occasional correspondents during its course. Franklin, in Paris, as Envoy from the Congress of the United States after the Declaration of Independence in 1776, procured the French alliance in 1778. Thereafter he persuaded the French Government to exempt the ships of Captain Cook from attack by the French Navy, and hoped by his general passport issued from Passy on 10 March 1779 to all American armed vessels to ensure the safety of the English 'discovery' vessels from hostility in that quarter. This precaution was never put to the test for Cook was already dead and the long voyage almost over, but a year later Banks expressed his personal appreciation of Franklin's act, linking it with the feelings of some, though not all, of the Fellows of the Royal Society. A more public appreciation, he said, would have been conveyed 'were they not sensible that such an act might be wilfully misunderstood'. For himself, on 29 March 1780, he put it thus:

I perusd this paper with the Greatest pleasure for having never doubted that the liberal & enlarged sentiments I had always admird in your mind remaind there in full lustre, I could not but rejoice at the triumph which such an indisputable proof afforded me over those who warp'd by politicks or party wish'd to entertain a different opinion of your character . . .

He told Franklin of the memorial medal for Cook already being prepared with his hope that if he could learn that Congress itself had really followed the French example he would in time be able to prevail on the Royal Society to present one to America as they were proposing to do for the King of France. Then the voice of old friendship spoke again as he ended:

. . . Adieu my Dear Sir beleive my Mind incapable of being Led astray by the influence of political opinions I respect you as a Philosopher & sollicit the continuance of your Freindship in full persuasion that all your actions are conformable to your most conscientious Ideas of rectitude whatever my wishes may be as a native & inhabitant of a country with which you are at war

The war however did not bar further exchanges between them as both yearned for more peaceful times and the renewal of free scientific communication. Pierre Broussonet returned to Paris in the summer of 1782 after nearly two years in London carrying with him a letter of introduction from Banks to Franklin, who replied with his earnest longing

. . . for a Return of those peaceful Times, when I could sit down in sweet Society with my English philosophic friends, communicating to each other new Discoveries and proposing improvements of old ones . . .

He was glad also to hear from Broussonet of progress in the 'great Work' on the botanic illustrations of the *Endeavour* voyage which he had seen begun, saying

. . . I admire your Magnanimity in the Undertaking, and the Perseverance with which you have prosecuted it . . .

In January 1782 the war ended with the Treaty of Versailles, although it was not until March, under the new Fox/North coalition, that the treaties were ratified and unhampered travel across the Channel revived. An early visitor to France in these last years of the *ancien régime* was Charles Blagden in his new role as the Hermes of Anglo-French scientific exchange, more particularly as Banks's philosophic gossip abroad and carrying his personal introduction to Franklin whom he met in June. For two months he was busy in Paris observing the ferment of scientific activity as a zealous agent of the Royal Society restoring communication with the Académie des Sciences. He witnessed Lavoisier's repetition of Henry Cavendish's production of water by the combustion of oxygen and hydrogen and, at a meeting of the Académie in July, heard the first account of the Montgolfiers's first experimental hot-air balloon ascent at Annonay on 5 June 1783. Early in August he was home again in London with a letter from Franklin to Banks and first hand news of further advances in the new field of 'aerostatics', especially the scheme of the young Académician, Jacques

Alexandre César Charles, with the brothers Jean and Nicolas Robert for a balloon filled with hydrogen, funded by a public subscription opened by Faujas de St Fond.

The public interest had grown to such a pitch that the intended site for the ascent was removed from the Place des Victoires to the more open spaces of the Champ de Mars 'darkly at dead of night' to the relative safety of a fenced enclosure under armed guards. This was conveniently close to Passy just across the river and Franklin was well placed to witness this 'new aerostatic Experiment'. At five p.m. on Wednesday 27 August, on the firing of two cannons, the cord was cut and in 150 seconds, to Franklin's eyes 'scarce bigger than an orange', the balloon had disappeared in the clouds. Next day it was found 15 miles from Paris near the village of Gonesse where it had landed some 45 minutes ater its release, having burst under the rapid change of pressure, it was supposed, after attaining a height of over 3000 feet by some estimates.

All this and more Franklin set down in a letter to Banks on 30 August replete with speculations on what this new technical art could mean for the future of mankind. He gave Banks advance notice also of the 'great one of M. Montgolfier' preparing for an ascent from Versailles and the ambition of Pilâtre de Rozier to go up with it and from which he was dissuaded by the Académicians until more experience had been gained 'in the management of these Balls'. This was the first eye witness account of a balloon ascent received by Banks and it found him at the races in Lincoln from whence he replied on 13 September. Franklin had written under a sense of duty

> ... to send an Early Account of this Extraordinary Fact, to the Society which does me the honour to reckon me among its Members ...

Banks replied in much the same spirit and with gratitude

> ... For having it in my power to answer with precision the numerous questions which are askd me by all sorts of people concerning the Aerostatique experiment which such as they may be are suggested by every newspaper now printed here & considered as a part of my duty to answer! ...

He proposed to make it the first paper to be put before the Society after the vacation and indeed it was read at the meeting of the 6 November. He added:

> ... I have thought as soon as I return from my Present banishment of constructing one & sending it up for the purpose of an Electrical Kite a use to which it seems particularly adapted ...

The ascent from the Champ de Mars was soon eclipsed in the public excitement attending the Montgolfiers's plans for an ascent from Versailles with a balloon of a new shape with their secret 'gas' on 19 September before the King and Queen and the assembled Court. In the event it was a nearly spherical balloon 41 feet in diameter and 54 feet high with a capacity of 37500 cubic feet, resplendent in blue and gold cotton cloth backed by paper, carrying a wicker cage enclosing a sheep, a cock and a duck. It rose from the Minister's Court at the Palace of Versailles from over its furnace of straw and wool in the afternoon of the 19th to make a short flight of about two miles not above 1700 feet in altitude, far below the estimate of its creator, Joseph Montgolfier. All the livestock survived.

In spite of the obvious dangers, the way was now paved for the first manned balloon flight by the irrepressible Pilâtre de Rozier and the Marquis d'Arlandes from the Château la Muette in the Bois de Boulogne on 20 November 1783, a brief affair of some 25 minutes aloft at a moderate altitude of a few hundred feet over a course of 9000 yards to their landing on the Butte-aux-Cailles near the present Place d'Italie. Man's first flight in a hot-air balloon was also his first flight into atmospheric space.

The day of the hydrogen-filled balloon as a vehicle of flight, however, was close behind as Charles and the two Roberts designed and built the structure which would determine its shape for years to come. On Monday 1 December 1783 at 1.45 p.m. Charles and Ainé Robert rose swiftly from the gardens of the Tuileries before a vast crowd to about 1800 feet above the Seine drifting on a light breeze north-east beyond the Oise to land close to Nesles. This was a flight of more than two hours covering 27 miles and, by the skill and judgement of Charles, completing a perfect landing. In the euphoria of the moment, however, Charles impetuously and alone made a second short flight almost immediately in the sunset, rising with great speed to a height of nearly 10000 feet as he estimated by his instruments. He made a second perfect landing in a ploughed field near the wood of Tour du Lay, three miles from Nesles, after a flight of 35 minutes.

Earlier, in answering Franklin's letter of 30 August about the ascent of Charles's first hydrogen balloon from the Champ de Mars, Banks said:

... I consider the present day which has opend a road in the Air as an epoche from whence a rapid increase of the stock of real Knowledge with which the human species is furnishd must take its date & the more immediate effect it will have upon the Concerns of mankind greater than any thing since the invention of Shipping which opend our way upon the face of the waters from Land to Land ...

This optimism had been fueled now with a succession of first-hand accounts of the swift march of events in Paris. Immured at Revesby Abbey and suffering some recurrence of pain in his chest, badly bruised in the fall he had sustained in a boat in June, he was kept informed by Dryander and Blagden of 'aerostatic' news in the London papers. However these were amplified and corrected by direct news from France in Broussonet's account, dated 22 September, of the Montgolfier hot-air ascent of 19 September from Versailles. This in turn was supported by that of Charles Pancoucke about the same event as a by-product of the negotiations for French paper for the printing of Cook's last voyage. To Pancoucke his reply in French, dated 7 October, was written by Dorothea Banks to whom he had dictated it. Very soon after he received a copy of the official French report of the flight of Pilâtre de Rozier and the Marquis d'Arlandes on 20 November a document signed on 21 November by an array of Académicians including Benjamin Franklin, Faujas de St Fond, Delisle and Le Roi. Then to cap the year, Franklin had sent him a detailed written account of the final triumphant flight of Charles and Jean Robert on 1 December with a diagram of the hydrogen balloon itself and a picture of it in the air. To this Banks replied on 9 December thanking Franklin for so speedily sending him 'Accounts of the Progress of the new Art of Flying' and regretting that he had nothing to return in this field from England. The abiding sense of Anglo-French rivalry in science and 'discovery' emerged in his further reaction:

185

Left Dr Benjamin Franklin, FRS *aet.* 76. Painting after J. S. Duplessis, 1785.
Right Dr John Jeffries. Pastel by John Russell, RA, 1785.

... Charles's Experiment seems decisive & must be performed here in its full extent I have hitherto been of Opinion that it is unwise to struggle for the honor of an invention which is about to be Effected. Practical Flying we much allow to our rivals. Theoretical Flying we claim ourselves. Bishop Wilkins in his Mechanical magic has as I am informd (for I have not yet got the book) a proposal for flying by means of a vessel filled with rare Air & Mr Cavendish when he blew soap bubbles of his Inflammable air Evidently performd the experiment which carried Charles on the memorable flight of the 1st. instant ...

He hinted at further rivalries in the penetration of outer space and the application of theory to what was being found 'in the Armories of heaven' through the telescopes of Herschel and the speculations of John Michell on the probable influence of gravity on the light from distant stars. Finally, as he closed the letter, he could thank Franklin for the arrival at that moment of the long-promised account by Faujas de St Fond of the balloon experiments in Paris. Then, on 15 December, Franklin sent to Soho Square the account of the classic flight by Charles himself with the hope that he might yet be able to send Banks a letter by air to London when the first fair wind appeared.

For the rest of England the subject was divided between scoffing and extravagant speculation as the art of making balloons on a small scale for sheer amusement spread rapidly. As early as 23 August Blagden had reported to Banks the arrival of a M. Guyot in London with reports about the balloon craze in Paris. This may have been the man from the Faubourg St Martin who had already established a market with a published price list for models ranging from small ones of goldbeaters' skin to some as large as 12 feet in diameter of silk for the more ambitious. Whatever influence Guyot might have had on the flying of balloons in England, credit for the first unmanned flight must be given to two Italians – Count Francesco Zambeccari and a Cheapside artificial flower maker, Michael Biaggini. Their first balloon, five feet in diameter flew quietly from Highgate to Waltham Abbey. Their second, twice the size and of gilded oiled silk, released from the Artillery Ground at Moorfields, on 25 November 1783, was carried by a northerly wind to land at Graffham near Petworth in Sussex, a flight of some 45 miles. The next day, 26 November, another foreigner, Aimé Argand, with Matthew Boulton demonstrated a small hydrogen balloon to the King and his family at Windsor.

Then, almost coincident with the crisis in the febrile 'dissensions' at the Royal Society, came a letter from Paris, dated 11 February 1784, written surprisingly by Henry Smeathman with a vision of the future far removed from west African botany and the life of the white ant. An ardent witness of the Parisian balloon ascents in 1783 and immediately critical of their wayward flights, he now sent Banks his own plans for a radical change from the globular to an elongated horizontal form with wings, 'a dirigible aerostatic machine' able to alight with ease on both land and water. Such a plan, he said, had met the approval of the 3rd Duke of Dorset as British ambassador, of Franklin and of Broussonet, while Faujas de St Fond, as a far-sighted Frenchman, was only too anxious to undertake its construction. Such offers from the French Smeathman had refused until he had word of Banks's approval and of practical encouragement from the British government for a machine which he viewed as of national importance for the transport of mail in particular. There seems to have been no answering cry of joy from Banks. Though Smeathman's call to shape a future in the air was eminently to his taste, as Banks had made clear to Franklin six months before, this chance was apparently lost under the weight of competing cares. In the end that year it was the French who published Jean Meusnier's visionary design for an airship.

In the current orthodoxy, however, the first British aeronaut undoubtedly was the luckless Scot, James Tytler, with his relatively crude and dangerous hot-air 'Montgolfiere' and his two short flights from Comely Gardens, Edinburgh, on 25 August and 1 September 1784 as the first successes in a chapter of accidents. But it was an Italian, Vincent Lunardi, on the staff of the Neapolitan Legation in London, who succeeded in a more effective way as an aeronaut with a hydrogen balloon built with finance from a public subscription headed by Sir Joseph Banks and slowly gathered over the summer from July 1784. Preparations were sufficiently advanced by mid-August for Banks to comment on the prospect of a flight when he wrote to Franklin on 13 August officially presenting the Royal Society gold medal in memory of Cook, another honour to supplement the King's gift earlier in the year of the recently published account of the third voyage.

The balloon had a diameter of 33 feet and a capacity of 18000 cubic feet, made in red and white alternating strips from 520 yards of oiled silk. It was larger than that of Charles the year before, with which it compared well being inferior mainly in lacking a release valve for the gas at its north pole. There were considerable improvements however in the net which now covered two-thirds of the envelope with 45 cords supporting a wooden ring or hoop from which a plain strong basket was suspended. At first intended to rise from the grounds of Chelsea Hospital it was, after much difficulty, arranged to ascend from the Artillery Ground at Moorfields on 15

September. The problem of filling the balloon was assigned to Dr George Fordyce, FRS, physician of St Thomas's Hospital and Essex Street, Strand, an old crony of Banks in the 'rebellious' dining club and a talented chemist who had designed an 'improved' hydrogen generator. Excellent theory was not quite matched in practice and, amid scenes approaching riot, the balloon was only partly filled by two o'clock on the day. Alarmed by the impatience of a sceptical English crowd of perhaps 150000, and before a privileged audience of the Prince of Wales and a number of members of Parliament, Lunardi hurriedly ascended at about two p.m. alone but for a cat, a dog, and a caged pigeon. A south breeze carried him north into Hertfordshire where, two hours later after a flight of more than 20 miles, he landed in the parish of Standon near Ware. The art and practice but not the science of balloon flying had begun in England.

The advent of entrepreneurs from abroad continued with the appearance in London of Jean Pierre Blanchard, as unattractive in person and personality as Vincent Lunardi was attractive in both, but equally courageous. He came in August 1784 equipped already with the balloon he had used with some success in France but obscured by the more resounding exploits of the Montgolfiers, Charles, the Roberts and Pilâtre de Rozier. England was almost a virgin field for the egotist aeronaut among the growing cluster of hopeful and enthusiastic amateurs. Among these Dr John Sheldon, FRS and Dr John Jeffries were the most serious and probably most scientific.

These two men financed Blanchard's first ascents in London. The first, with Sheldon, was from Lochee's Military Academy, Chelsea, on 16 October across Hammersmith, Chiswick and Twickenham to land at Sunbury where the doctor disembarked. Lunardi then went on as a solo eventually to descend at Romsey after a total flight of some 73 miles. His second ascent, now with Jeffries, was from Mackenzie's Rhedarium between Park Lane and Park Street, Mayfair, in the presence of the Prince of Wales on Tuesday 30 November. The flight lasted two hours and finished at Stone Marsh near Ingress in Kent, 20 miles to the east at the end of Long Reach close to Greenhithe. Sheldon never flew again but Jeffries, the wealthy American from Boston, was inspired to plan and finance the balloonist's dream – crossing the Channel by air. For both these flights the system for hydrogen generation, planned and operated by Aimé Argand, proved more effective than that of Fordyce for Lunardi. This was now a mere matter of two hours at half the expense according to Argand himself.

This progress in ballooning during the summer and autumn of 1784 was a distraction which Banks could support and encourage but not witness. His engagement with William Roy on Hounslow Heath in the measurement of the baseline followed by his usual migration to Lincolnshire drew him away from both the Lunardi and the first Blanchard ascent. His letter to Benjamin Franklin of 19 November expressed his view fairly clearly:

> ... The Whole of the middle Class of people here have been inconceivably amusd by the ascention of Lunardi and Blanchard & some of superior rank have attended for my own part I had not any option being away from town but I shall not miss the next which ascends no more than I would miss any other spectacle which was likely to amuse & not likely to be after exhibited.

From this we do not know, but may reasonably assume, that he was among those in

Mayfair who assembled on St Andrew's Day to watch Blanchard start his second flight with John Jeffries aboard equipped as he was with a range of instruments for at least some small degree of scientific observation. On this score Banks continued:

> ... we Lament in the R[oyal] S[ociety] that so little addition of Science has accrued from a discovery which certainly opend a new Field of enquiry & feel hurt that men who in the outset attempted to make us beleive he had got the dominion by this means over another element has constantly hitherto been the abject Slave of that element whenever he venturd to intrude himself into it

In Jeffries however he evidently sensed there might be a man both able and willing to advance the cause of science in exploring the problems of the new element. Jeffries was made welcome at Soho Square that December as he prepared, with Blanchard, to attempt the Channel crossing at his own expense, a sum which in the end exceeded £700. The balloon and its hydrogen generator was taken to Dover Castle where Blanchard, capable and courageous though he was, behaved like an affronted *prima donna* striving by a variety of stratagems to keep his patron Jeffries at the last moment from joining him in the flight. The American was unruffled and by genial diplomacy preserved his good relations with the Frenchman.

Eventually on Friday 7 January 1785 at one p.m. on a fine clear winter day the balloon was launched from the edge of Dover cliff. It was lumbered, as had been Lunardi's, with much useless gear such as wings and rudder and, particularly dear to Blanchard, the *moulinet* or propeller. For Jeffries the mercury barometer and thermometer were the more significant essentials. After two hours of wild variations in altitude from sea level to several thousand feet, the French coast was crossed between Cap Blanez and Calais at a great height. The wind changed and they were swung round to land south of Calais in the forest near Guisnes where Jeffries caught the top of a tree and held it while Blanchard opened the valve and deflated the balloon, a matter of some 28 minutes. Man's first sea crossing by air had been made and his first air mail carried but at a slight cost to his dignity, for not only was the balloon stripped bare but so nearly were its occupants.

Within the week, on Thursday 13 January, Jeffries wrote to Banks from Paris what must have been the first direct account of the flight, in short staccato phrases that have all the appearance of a transcript of notes made during its course. He acknowledges a letter received from Banks at Dover with its valedictory encouragement 'when surrounded with different difficultys of opposition of various kinds', as he tactfully covered Blanchard's intransigence at the point of departure. He ended with an apology for troubling Banks with his letter 'but thought it my duty to do this in return for the notice you were pleased to shew me in Soho Square'. Jeffries was full of praise for his reception in France, unannounced as he had been, and clear in his account of Blanchard's triumphant homecoming which he had made possible. For the little Frenchman there was the freedom of the city of Calais presented to him in a gold box; for them both an ecstatic reception in Paris by the Académicians, and at Versailles by Louis XVI and his Court, with a pension for Blanchard and the Order of the Black Ribbon; nothing for Jeffries. The authorities at Calais were swift in laying claim to the balloon and its car and in proposing a marble monument on the site of their landing near Guisnes.

The air mail, wrapped in a bladder, consisted of letters to Louis XVI and Benjamin

Franklin with one from William Franklin to his son Temple. Only the last survives as a record of this episode which, whatever its curious and amusing details, certainly marked a forward step in man's appreciation of the world he inhabits. To Horace Walpole these 'aerostatic' antics appeared in a different light, as he wrote to Sir Horace Mann on 2 December 1783, the day after Charles's epic ascent from the Champ de Mars:

> When the arts are brought to such perfection in Europe, who would go, like Sir Joseph Banks, in search of islands in the Atlantic [sic] where the natives have in six thousand years not improved the science of carving fishing hooks out of bones or flints! Well! I hope these new mechanic meteors will prove only playthings for the learned and idle, and not be converted into new engines of destruction to the human race as is so often the case of refinements or discoveries in science. The wicked wit of man always studies to apply the results of talents to enslaving, destroying, or cheating his fellow creatures. Could we reach the moon, we should think of reducing it to a province of some European kingdom.

V

The year 1783 was pregnant with a full litter of embryonic ideas. The Preliminary Treaty of 30 November 1782 between Britain and the 13 rebellious colonies had been converted into the Definitive Treaty with the young United States of America on 3 September 1783. The central figure among the American negotiators, Benjamin Franklin, was in frequent correspondence with his old friend now Sir Joseph Banks about the balloon ascents in Paris. Interlaced with this theme Banks in London during the summer had been exploring the possibilities of creating a white settlement in the South Pacific as an indirect by-product of the loss of the American colonies. James Matra, a victim of that loss, had embodied the essence of Banks's thoughts in 'A Proposal for Establishing a Settlement in New South Wales', dated 23 August 1783, while Banks himself was preoccupied in publishing the account of Cook's last voyage at the behest of the Admiralty. The preliminaries of peace had restored communication with France. Charles Blagden, in an early role as Banks's personal envoy abroad, had reported on 25 June that Antoine Lavoisier had repeated the experiment of Henry Cavendish in producing water by the combustion of hydrogen and oxygen. Banks had passed this challenging information to Cavendish whose paper, now preparing as 'Experiments on Air', was to be read before the Royal Society on 15 January 1784 in the white heat of the 'dissensions'. In this paroxysm of London scientific society both Cavendish and Blagden would be the staunch but not uncritical supporters of Banks against the clerical onslaught of Horsley and Maty at Somerset House. But before this crisis burst into public view Banks was already engaged with another facet of the new peace with France, accepting as a task for the Royal Society the proposals in the Cassini memorial for a survey to determine trigonometrically the relative positions of the Paris and the Greenwich observatories. Lt-Col. William Roy was already alert and poised for this work as Banks retired in December to Spring Grove, a Christmas haven from the Royal Society turbulence. As this storm gathered over the head of Banks in Middlesex the old problem of what to do with the collections, manuscripts and library of Linnaeus revived again.

At Uppsala in Sweden the young Linnaeus had suddenly died on 1 November

1783. During the previous year Banks had been looked to as a possible recipient but his offer, apparently of 1000 guineas, seems to have struck the devoted son as 'cruel' and the matter had lapsed. Now it had become urgent again as the university house had to be vacated for the younger Carl's successor, C. P. Thunberg. Fru Linnaea, the old man's widow, sought advice from the Professor of Medicine at Uppsala, Dr Johann Acrel. On her behalf he offered the whole collection again to Banks through a Dr Engelhart who was then in Britain. The figure of 1000 guineas that had formerly been rejected was again suggested. Engelhart's letter with this offer reached Banks at Spring Grove on Tuesday 23 December to find him very near the trough of his anxieties in the Royal Society upheaval. Among those who braved the cold journey to Spring Grove from time to time that hard winter was young Dr James Edward Smith, at 24 fresh from his botanical studies under Professor John Hope in Edinburgh, with an introduction to Banks whom he had met for the first time possibly in September. By chance he was at Spring Grove on the very day that Engelhart's letter arrived with the offer of the Linnaean collections and library. But for Banks times had changed and he evidently had no difficulty that morning in refusing the Swedish windfall. His main reason was doubtless financial pressure, for the seven years of the American war had severely pinched his income, his rent roll directly affected by the unsold piles of long wool on the farms of his tenants. It is ironic then that he should hand the letter from Engelhart to the son of a wealthy Norwich wool merchant with the suggestion that he, not Banks, should make the purchase. It is clear that Banks knew well that there was money enough in the Smith family and intelligence enough in its only son to support his judgement in passing on the Linnaean offer.

Dr Engelhart was already well known to Smith from their meeting in Edinburgh and on the afternoon of 23 December they met again in London. That same day both of them wrote to Sweden; Engelhart to recommend his young friend to Dr Acrel; Smith to ask from him a full catalogue of the collections. Next day Smith wrote to his father at Norwich putting the facts before him and citing the strong recommendation by Banks that the purchase be made:

> ... There is no time to be lost, for the affair is now talkd of in all companies, and a number of people wish to be purchasers. The Empress of Russia is said to have thoughts of it.

Among the others there were, of course, right-thinking Swedes like Johan Alstroemer, Professor Carl Thunberg and the clamorous voices of the Uppsala students in support. For England Dr John Sibthorp, botanizing at Montpellier with Broussonet, raised a distant cry. And there was also a hint of purchase from King Gustav of Sweden, himself absent in Italy almost beyond reach of appeal. But, in spite of the patriotic uproar, Smith had received his catalogue on Tuesday 6 April 1784 and, against some last minute complications raised by Baron Alstroemer in his claim for what was called the 'small herbarium' (which Smith conceded), the bargain was struck at 900 guineas for the 'great herbarium' and everything else. By 18 June Smith had received the confirmatory letter from the executors in Sweden that declared him to be the unequivocal owner. On 17 September 1784 everything was shipped for England in the brig *Appearance*, Captain Axel Sweder – some 3000 books in 6 cases; 5 cases of plants; 4 cases of minerals; 3 cases of shells, fish and corals; and

2 cases of insects; at a gross cost of £1088.5s.od. including freight and the Captain's fees. The net cost to J. E. Smith was £998.15s.od.

In pleading with his father early in January 1784 for the funds he needed, Smith had already gained a good impression from Dryander of the state of the Linnaean collections, though not of the library which Dryander had not seen. From this source he gathered that the herbarium of the elder Linnaeus contained about 8000 plants and that of the younger about the same number. The latter contained plants from the son's European travels, especially in France, with many received also from the Banks herbarium. The impression which Dryander conveyed was well supported by the inventory received in June. From this Smith expected to receive some 19000 dried plant specimens, including many duplicates; of insect species, 3198; shells, 1564 with another 200 unclassified; geological specimens, 2424; birds, 35. Of books there were some 1600 titles in the library amounting to between 2 and 3000 volumes, apart from the manuscripts, the greater part in Latin, but many in French, English and Italian and some in Swedish. A few were rare works and Smith cited particularly a small book on insects with coloured illustrations for which Banks had exchanged books to the value of £30.

Such in broad terms was the consignment in 26 chests to reach London in late October 1784. For its reception Smith tried to secure space in the British Museum but in the end leased apartments in Paradise Row, Chelsea, not far from the house of Mrs Banks. Such were the Linnaean collections and library which, during the ensuing winter and the spring of 1785 were unpacked and rearranged by Smith with the help of Banks and Dryander. From this cross-breeding of the Lincolnshire landed interest and Norfolk merchant wealth the gestation of a new scientific society had begun.

VI

In 1782 Thomas Percy, Vicar of Easton-Maudit, Northamptonshire, was translated from his comfortable studies on ancient English poetry to a remote bishopric at Dromore in County Tyrone. Here in 1783 he turned archaeologist and delved in a marl-pit under the peat-moss at Quilly to uncover the fossil remains of a giant deer. In London on Tuesday 11 November 1783 this news was read by Banks in the papers of that day. Turning aside without delay from the fascination of balloon flights, he wrote immediately to the Bishop of Dromore:

> ... I could not refrain from taking the Liberty of acquainting your Lordship as a natural historian that altho we have in England seen several times the Horns of that wonderful animal we have not to my knowledge been yet in possession of any other part except a portion of the Cranium without teeth or under jaw
>
> Now if the paragraph is true & your Lordship is realy in posession of many bones of this hitherto unexamind animal I only beg leave to State a Claim for their being Lodgd in the British Museum if your Lordship does not intend to reserve them for yourself
>
> in that noble Collection they will be inspected by naturalists who will be able to ascertain whether the species of animal they have belongd to Still continues to be represented in the Known parts of the world a disquisition of no small Curiosity as the real abolition of a species once created & in course necessary to the harmony

of the works of Creation is a matter which I hesitate most considerably to beleive but concerning which I am curious in no inconsiderable degree . . .

Banks concluded in the hope that they should meet again as they had formerly on Tuesdays at The Literary Club.

The Bishop rose to this tempting bait on 28 November with details of the discovery and the geological stratum in which it lay, the weights and measurements of the bones and skull with the magnificent antlers, affirming his intention to keep the collection, but promising it to the British Museum should he ever part with it. Banks replied on 30 December 1783:

> . . . if your Lordship Should at any time part with what I consider as a most interesting discovery it might be deposited in some permanent Establishment for the benefit of Learning where Naturalists of the succeeding as well as the present generation might have an opportunity of Comparing the bones with those of known animals & Examining by the test of discoveries yet to be made that problem of natural history which asserts that animals once Existed on this Planet that are now annihilated. I confess that I never could bring myself to Credit the Idea of a Species being Extinguishd . . .

This made his scientific intentions plain enough in support of which he had earlier sent the Bishop a copy of George Stubbs's skeleton of a horse, as a separate sheet from *The Anatomy of the Horse*, 1766, as being the nearest structure available to that of the fossil animal in question. But, perhaps as a sop to theology and the character of his correspondent, he interpolated some unconvincing 'reveries' concerning his view of the divine plan and again voiced the protest of his heart rather than of his head. '. . . how can I admit the Loss of a Species into my Creed . . .'. Such agonizing, muted as it was, disappeared from his letter of 7 February 1784 as he acknowledged the arrival of the drawing of the horns of the giant elk and proceeded to discuss the structures of those other species from America and Europe then living when compared with the specimen from a remote past, in particular the presence or absence of brow antlers and the proportional sizes of the beams. He concluded that the Irish animal was a species 'hitherto unknown to our Naturalists' and emphasized how desirable it was to see the Dromore skeleton mounted. In his pursuit of the Bishop and his excavated material Banks was undoubtedly hunting up wind on the scent of an argument that would flourish within the next half-century as William Buckland and the 'diluvialists' came to grips with the consequences of alternate 'theories of the Earth' expressed by John Fleming and George Poulett Scrope. The day of the giant Irish 'elk' had yet to come.

CHAPTER 9

DISSENSIONS AND DELINEATIONS
1783–1784

Politically the year 1783 had been one of troubled uncertainty and change as the sequence of short administrations – Rockingham, Shelburne, and the Fox–North coalition – finally ended with the formation of Pitt's first cabinet on Friday 19 December. For the Royal Society the simmering dissent with what some regarded as 'the Cabinet in Soho Square' and the man at its head as 'incurably sick with the lust of domination', reached boiling point at the meeting on Thursday 18 December. What had been cooking for the past two years now spilled over. It was a mixed confection of reasonable complaint over-seasoned with academic rivalry, a touch of purblind religiosity and social envy, and more than a little personal malice. In essence it had the character of a sort of palace revolt centred in the bureaucracy of the Royal Society with its secretaries turning against Council decisions taken under the influence of a young President whose brand of leadership denied the secretarial office a large measure of its self-assumed authority.

For ten years the daily business of the Society had operated under two Cantabrians in holy orders: Dr Samuel Horsley, FRS and Paul Henry Maty, FRS with Joseph Planta, FRS as their altogether more sober and polished academic co-worker in the office of secretary. It was however the two Cambridge prelates who formed the centre of the disputes labelled, almost with affection by historians, as the 'dissensions'. It is possible that the seeds of the dispute had been germinating since the election in 1778 of Paul Maty in succession to Dr Horsley as Principal Secretary coinciding with that of Banks as President – men of comparable age but of notably different origins, personal style and academic experience, one from Cambridge and the other from Oxford. Maty was the brother-in-law of Captain Charles Clerke, RN, the likeable and ill-fated successor to Cook in command of the third voyage, and the admiring friend and fellow-voyager of Banks himself. Maty had moreover acted for three years, 1772–4, as Assistant Secretary without a place on the Council coping with the Society's foreign correspondence. It was this function which served as a spark igniting the dispute when Banks proposed, at the Council meeting of 24 January 1782, that the duty of translating foreign papers and making extracts of foreign books should cease and that the office should be re-defined, which was done by a committee under the President. The new duties were accepted by its incumbent Dr Charles Hutton, FRS at a Council meeting of 25 April 1782. However on 20 November, Council resolved that the work should be done by a person resident in London – unlike Hutton who was domiciled nine miles away at Shooter's Hill near Woolwich Common and the Royal Miliary Academy at which he held the chair of mathematics. Dr Nevil Maskelyne and Paul Maty dissented and the first overt move in the dissensions had been taken. On the following Thursday, 27 November, Hutton, not unreasonably taking umbrage at what seemed to be implied by this

194

resolution, resigned the office of Foreign Secretary. The annual elections took place on Monday 1 December and for the time being this office was taken by Joseph Planta who had held it previously from 1775–9. On Thursday 11 December Edward Poore, seconded by Paul Maty, moved a vote of thanks to Dr Hutton for the services he had rendered. To this Banks, from the chair, objected, on the grounds that only the Council and not the Society as a whole could judge how far such thanks were merited. On this he was defeated by 33 votes to 28, and the motion thanking Hutton was carried by 30 votes to 25.

Banks summoned a meeting of Council on Wednesday 17 December to which Hutton submitted a written defence of his former position. The Council however reaffirmed its decision of 20 November, an action challenged as invalid by the opposition on the grounds that a proper quorum had not been present under the terms of the statutes of 1776, page 34. At the meeting next day Dr Horsley, seconded by Paul Maty, moved that Hutton's written defence be read. This was done, supported by Dr Maskelyne. The business closed with a motion by Governor Thomas Pownall, seconded by Lt J. Glenie, that in the opinion of the Society, Dr Hutton had justified himself against the suggestion that he had neglected his former duties. This was carried by a majority of 49 votes against 15.

The year 1783 drew to its close with the affairs of the nation now firmly in the hands of the younger Pitt but the affairs of the Royal Society less firmly than had been supposed in the hands of Banks. A real threat to his continued Presidency had emerged on grounds on which he was vulnerable though probably not more so than some of his predecessors. The difference lay in the element of ambition and personality which embittered the otherwise formal exchanges at Somerset House, and the pamphleteering which was soon to appear and make an otherwise not uncommon disagreement about a society's management into a public spectacle. The meeting of 18 December had made very clear where the trouble was centred. The driving force was primarily a clearly rebellious secretary in Paul Maty and an ambitious Dr Samuel Horsley coveting the president's chair, hunting as a couple. The baying of other voices followed them for a variety of personal reasons.

By contrast Joseph Planta remained quiescent and soothing. Earlier in the year he had had his brush with the President and Council over the publication of papers read before the Society. In April he had proposed releasing the substance of such papers in full or in abstract to appear elsewhere in advance of their formal printing in the *Philosophical Transactions*, citing in support the House of Commons practice and that of the Academy of Sciences at Berlin. Banks however had been adamant in defending the Council's opposition to any such practice as a necessary step in tightening the management of the Society's affairs as a scientific body. Planta continued to assert that he could see no harm in the advance publication at least of the abstracts of papers delivered at Somerset House, but Banks closed the argument saying that Council's decisions about publications were absolute. Nevertheless, another unauthorized publication had occurred before the end of the year. The letter from Sir William Hamilton, FRS to Banks, describing the Calabrian earthquakes of February to May 1783 and read before the Society on 3 July, had appeared in the *St James's Chronicle* in advance of its publication in the *Philosophical Transactions*, volume 73. This had been leaked, as Banks noted, after it had been lent in good faith to Sir William Fraser, FRS before and after its formal reading to the Society. When Banks heard this from Blagden at Revesby Abbey in September he reiterated his belief that in order to stop such practices no author should receive printed copies of his own papers before their publication in the *Transactions* and that the Council should make this a rule. Planta seems to have accepted this presidential ruling with equanimity as a well-argued case not as a piece of heavy-handed dictatorship. Through the dispute which had now come into the open he remained a cool rather than a partisan contributor.

After the meeting of 18 December the lines of cleavage in the Society had become pretty clear, and Banks retired to Spring Grove to ponder his problems. During the weekend Blagden was busy on his behalf and Banks was visited at Spring Grove by Dr William Heberden. Heberden himself had consulted Henry Cavendish before visiting him and although they both supported him as President they were unable to approve any vote of censure against Horsley whom they recognized as the main focus of the opposition as well as its most vigorous exponent. Cavendish, on Monday 22 December, spent some time with Blagden at his house in the King's Road from which emerged his qualified support and shrewd advice on future strategy. He was still prepared to give Horsley the benefit of the doubt on the grounds that there had been no proof that he acted other than for the good of the Society. He thought the best way to prevent untimely debates in the ordinary meetings was by choosing a Council that would remove any abuses and he framed a possible resolution to that effect. Cavendish was sure that such a resolution would be carried by a large enough majority to deter Horsley and his allies from bringing forward endless matters for debate. He also said that on the whole at the St Andrew's Day elections he would certainly support the House List for the office-bearers unless it were exceptionable. He held Banks a little to blame for the present trouble but he forgave him. He allowed that Banks's method of determining the Council House List was fair and the best he had known in the Society. Sir John Pringle as President had acted just like Banks, he said, and was open to the same criticism; James West had acted like King Log, though Lord Morton had been different and more acceptable. He implied also that if Horsley did not heed the warning in his resolution then a vote of censure might be needed. Blagden summed up the attitude of Cavendish thus:

> . . . The sum is that like his namesakes elsewhere, he is so far loyal as to prefer you to any other King but chooses to load the Crown with such shackles that it shall scarcely be worth a gentleman's wearing . . .

The next day Blagden called on Dr Heberden, after a visit to Lord Mulgrave whose bluff seaman's support of Banks was scarcely in doubt. With Heberden he had more difficulty though the old man was open and forthright. He had in fact himself paid a call on one of the opposition leaders – not Maty he was quick to say – and had found that the Hutton affair was but a small matter compared with long-standing grudges which he refused to discuss with the gentleman in question. He emphasized the need for peace at the ordinary meetings and the reservation of debates for St Andrew's Day. On this point he apparently made no impression. Heberden was warm in his praise of Banks and the sacrifices he was making in the cause of science and emphatic that there was no one in the Society fitter for the office of President. On the other hand Heberden was averse to Blagden's suggestion of bringing forward a 'Vote of Approbation' on the grounds that it would only serve to 'irritate passions'. In the end though he accepted the idea and was also wholly with Cavendish in the resolution for choosing a proper Council to correct abuses without endless debate. However he admitted to Blagden that he did not think that or any other method would curb Dr Horsley.

Later in the day Blagden briefly met William Roy at the War Office and found that he was entirely in favour of the 'Vote of Approbation' and advised its framing in moderate terms. On the whole, Blagden told Banks, the general feeling was against any vote of censure on Horsley.

So passed Tuesday 23 December with Blagden feeling ill and out of sorts as he pursued his self-imposed diplomacy. Banks himself had spent the morning with young James Edward Smith whom he had told about the offer he had just received of the Linnaean collections. He would have liked Cavendish to visit him for direct consultation but this Cavendish could not or would not do, pleading a prior call on his time. However Cavendish did call on the ailing Blagden on Wednesday 24 December to explain his attitude. He made it clear that he wished to live on good terms with Banks, that he respected his many good qualities and wished to be as intimate with him as would be consistent with holding different opinions from time to time without an open quarrel. Moreover Cavendish apologized for not attending the meeting of 18 December, felt he ought to have done so and would certainly be present at the next. It appeared from this conversation that it really was Horsley whom Heberden had seen, and Cavendish took the view that however violent the views expressed by Horsley and his friends, they should be met with moderation. He therefore proposed a vote of approbation provided the words used were without offence but, on the other hand, he seemed not to be against the idea of Horsley's expulsion from the Society if, in spite of moderation on Banks's part, the ordinary business of the meetings were to be constantly interrupted.

All this was no doubt mulled over again on Christmas Day at Spring Grove to which Blagden had walked in the morning after breakfast and where he probably spent the night. He was back in London the following day and sufficiently active to send Banks on Saturday 27 December a general appreciation of the state of opinion and the alignment of forces – Paradise, Jodrell, Price and Kirwan in support; Maseres, Wilson, Partridge, Barrington, Harper, very much against, suggesting that Lord Mahon be proposed as President. Blagden was afraid that the only resolution on which Banks could reasonably depend among his friends would be a vote approving him as President. Indeed several had expressed the view that he neglected the business too much by remaining at Spring Grove while his opponents were so actively stirring in town, and, said Blagden:

> ... These give out that it is a struggle of the men of Science against the Macaroni's of the Society, signifying your friends by the latter title ...

This produced an immediate and peremptory reply which condensed as clear a statement as Banks ever made about his attitude to the Royal Society. Struck off with obvious feeling and with much speed its punctuated version bears recording:

> I cannot consider it as a real matter of Complaint against me that I have put Gentlemen into the Council nor do I wonder at all when I hear the names of any one of the Gentlemen who oppose me. They have every one of them had their papers repuls'd & probably wish to print them in the R[oyal] S[ociety] Transactions.

For the Charge of remaining in the Countrey I never intend to Canvas for approbation of my Conduct. I stand or fall according to the Estimation in which it is held. I have meant well & [I] believe done well for the Society & so many of my *Macaroni* friends are convincd. We shall see how many think so.

To hold the Presidency under any tenure of being the moderator in any Shape whatever of a debating Club I shall always reject. The Statute explaining the business of the ordinary meetings is in my opinion sufficiently explicit. Under that I accepted & by that only will I hold my seat.

It is a matter of Glory to me to be President of the Royal Society but I am too independent even for a Salary to accept the place of Chairman among debaters.

In Short if I am supported I shall do well & if I have deservd support I shall be supported. If I have not I shall resign without a repentent thought for, as I have always done what I thought for the good of the Society, I shall always continue the same conduct if I remain & upon that Conduct I must be judgd as I cannot honestly adopt any other.

Cool headed people will consider the real advantage of the Society. If it is judged for the advantage of it that I remain I shall. If not I shall retire to my plough without a sigh.

Blagden replied on Sunday 28 December reporting further progress. He noted that one of the complaints against Banks was that Henry Clarke, the mathematician had been rejected, allegedly by his influence on the grounds that he was a schoolmaster, but he was sure that such personal charges would carry few votes against him. More cunning, he said, was the pretext that freedom of debate ought not to be impeded and 'that the Society, like all literary bodies, is & should be a republic'. This language had many partisans in the Society and would divide even those friends of Banks who wished him to remain as President, so that Blagden was not sure which way the majority would go.

Then, on Monday 29 December, in spite of these doubts, Blagden sent Banks the form of the resolution which, he said, Cavendish had just approved:

Resolved, That this Society approve of Sir Jos: Banks as their President, and mean to support him in that office.

To this he added a postscript that Joseph Planta had just been with him:

He thinks that one part of your paper is not quite defensible as I do too; it will be easily modified.

This clearly refers to the statement being prepared for the meeting on 12 February 1784 (which was read by Dr William Watson, one of the vice-presidents) as a defence of the proceedings in Council. Planta and Blagden met again on Wednesday 31 December to complete its revision.

Meanwhile Banks had visited William Herschel at Datchet on Tuesday 30 December when, on that very cold morning, they had taken the short walk together which had inspired Banks with his practical thoughts about astronomy and how to keep feet warm while star-gazing in winter. Jonas Dryander had evidently also been at Spring Grove for the next day he wrote to John Lloyd in Denbighshire:

... It is very cold here. The thermometer stood this morning [31 December] at Spring Grove at 8 o'clock at 13½ degrees [Fahrenheit]

Then he closed the year with a pertinent paragraph:

... The Royal Society is all in a ferment just at present. Dr. Horsley Dr. Maskelyne & Dr. Hutton have declared open war against Sir Joseph, but the history is too long for a letter, nor could I give you the full information of it as I don't know myself all that has passed. You will soon come to town, and then you will hear all about it.

The New Year was opened by Banks with the circulation of a card to all Fellows requesting their attendance at the next ordinary meeting on 8 January

... as it is probable that questions will be agitated on which the opinion of the Society at large ought to be taken ...

About 170 Fellows attended and no strangers were admitted. The resolution framed by Cavendish and Blagden on 29 December was now put to the meeting by Thomas Anguish, the Accountant-General, and seconded by Henry Cavendish. This formal motion of confidence in the President released a storm of opposition in which Edward Poore led the attack, followed by Francis Maseres, Dr Horsley, Dr Maskelyne, and Paul Maty, Lt James Glenie and John Watson. Horsley, in an excess of rhetorical fantasy, expressed the essence of his belief:

... But, Sir, I am united with a respectable and numerous band embracing, I believe, a majority of the scientific part of this Society of those who do its scientific business. Sir, we shall have one remedy in our power when all others fail. If other remedies should fail, we can at last SECEDE. Sir, when the hour of secession comes, the President will be left, with his train of feeble *Amateurs* and that Toy [the Mace] upon the table, the Ghost of that Society in which Philosophy once reigned and Newton presided as her minister ...

But, when the motion was put, it was evident that this ultimate deterrent had not availed, for the 'Vote of Approbation' was carried by 119 in favour and 42 against. As Heberden and Cavendish had foreboded this was not enough to dissuade Horsley and his party from further action, and the Council was constrained to add a new section VI to Chapter XI of the Statutes of 1776 before the ordinary meeting of 29 January. This required that notice of a motion signed by at least six Fellows be given two meetings in advance. Some hint of this must have emerged, for the Horsley party was already armed with a motion

... that the resolution of Council requiring the Foreign Secretary to reside in London be rescinded; and to request Dr. Hutton to resume the office.

This was flourished by Francis Maseres ready for signature after the new section had been formally read to the ordinary meeting. Twelve signatures were in fact attached that evening: Francis Maseres, Nevil Maskelyne, Samuel Horsley, Edward Poore,

199

William Brown, James Horsfall, Sir George Shuckburgh, Isaac Gosset, John Hyacinth de Magellan, William James, John Wilson, Thomas Brand Hollis.

Again Banks circulated a card calling for a full attendance of the Fellows on Thursday 12 February when the motion became the occasion for another stormy debate. In the end the motion was defeated by a majority of 38; with 47 for and 85 against. The contest was carried forward at the same meeting with a notice of two further resolutions intended to restrain the President from exerting undue influence in the selection of Fellows. At the ensuing debate on 26 February the first motion was defeated by a majority of 88 with only 27 for and 115 against. The second motion, after amendment without dissent, was also defeated by a majority of 79 with 23 for and 102 against. After this the fires of the dissension seemed to have been damped but the embers were still glowing in the heated brain of Paul Maty.

After the preliminary business at the ordinary meeting of Thursday 25 March a pamphlet was produced by Maty which, according to the Royal Society Journal Book, he offered to the Society as a present from the anonymous editors. This printed tract was entitled *An Authentic Narrative of the Dissensions and Debates in the Royal Society*, a somewhat partisan but not wholly unfair account of what had transpired so far. It acknowledged that Maty's speech at the meeting on 12 February had been cast 'into a stronger form than he originally gave it'. The editors hoped that this 'not unusual liberty' would 'not be thought improper by the public'. Whatever the public may have thought Banks from the Chair made his own view clear. According to the minutes, he told the meeting that the pamphlet contained much misrepresentation and many passages reflecting on the honour of the Society. He refused to propose the usual thanks to the donor unless called upon to do so by a large majority of the meeting. Whereupon Dr Horsley rose to the challenge and moved accordingly, seconded by Dr Hutton and supported by Paul Maty in an unusual act of secreterial defiance to the Chair. Several Fellows called for the withdrawal of the motion and the question was not put. The dissensions had now reached a climax. Maty refused to go on with the regular business of the meeting until Horsley's motion had been properly voted on. Banks ordered him to proceed with the reading of the papers, which were the main business of the evening and, after a brief acquiescence, Maty declared his resignation from the post of Secretary.

This unhappy occasion, with strangers present to witness the Society's embarrassing dilemma, was in fact the end of the more acute disturbances. So it appeared to Banks as he wrote to Josiah Wedgwood on 6 April:

> ... We have had a series of disputes in the Royal Society which have employed me fully from Christmass to Easter. now however the disaffected, at least the active ones, who were at first 47 are reduced to two. I think we have a fair prospect of Peace returning which too is likely to be permanent ...

There seems little doubt that the ultimate 'disaffected' two were in Banks's view Dr Samuel Horsley and Paul Maty. There seems to be no reason to differ from the conclusion that these two men were the central activists, however well-intentioned their motives. There is strong evidence that Horsley's ambition was to displace Banks from 'Newton's chair' and that, by the time of Maty's resignation, this had become clear to the Fellows of the Society. At all events the change in mood must have been clear to Banks for, during the next week, he circulated among the Fellows a card, dated 29 March declaring that Blagden had 'at his desire' declared himself a candidate for the office of Secretary. Then on Wednesday 5 May at the usual time of 11.30 a.m., with Sir Joseph in the chair, the voting for the office began. There were only two candidates – Blagden and Hutton – each representing differing viewpoints in the Society. Blagden was elected by a large majority of 139 to Hutton's 39. The authority of the President and the Council had prevailed and the ordinary meetings returned to their habitual calm and orderly procedure.

The public however was further regaled with the evidence that the issue was far from settled among those who had raised the storm. In midsummer 'Some Members of the Minority' launched a parting broadside as *An History of the Instances of Exclusion from the Royal Society which were not suffered to be argued in the course of the late Debates, with Strictures on the formation of the Council, and other Instances of the Despotism of Sir Joseph Banks the present President, and of his Incapacity for his High Office.* This was echoed about the same time by 'A Friend of Dr. Hutton' as *An Appeal to the Fellows of the Royal Society concerning the Measures taken by Sir Joseph Banks their President to Compel Dr. Hutton To resign the Office of Secretary to the Society for their Foreign Correspondence.*

By this time Banks himself was fully occupied with William Roy in the baseline survey and, in any case, was not perturbed since he knew that the field was won. However the non-conformist divine Dr Andrew Kippis took time off from Volume III of his *Biographia Britannica* to raise a lance against the militant prelates of the established church. By 6 August he announced to Dr Matthew Garthshore that he was about to write an account to be entitled 'Observations on the Late Contests in the Royal Society' which he would have ready when he returned to London in October and that he would ask Banks for any additional remarks he might care to make. By 14 October Blagden had seen a copy of the pamphlet and urged Banks to ensure that Kippis put his name to it instead of leaving it anonymous. Banks authorized Blagden to see that this was done and in November the pamphlet appeared in time for the opening of the Royal Society year.

On 19 November, Banks, in his correspondence about balloons with Franklin, sent him a short summary which stands as an epitaph for the 'dissensions' viewed from the President's chair:

> . . . I am in great hopes that the dissensions of the Royal Society are at an end, at least that the opposition will at last give way to the decided & continual majorities which have appeared against them. Convincd I do not expect any more to be whose whole arguments have been founded & supported in misrepresentation. in truth Hutton did not like to Lose twenty pounds a year which he usd to receive without any trouble whatever. Horseley would have been glad to make himself President which I am convincd he thought easy & considerd as a good step towards a Bishoprick. Matys disappointments in Life tho all of his own seeking and arising from a perfect beleif that he is a man of very superior talents have renderd him so waspish that his cheif pleasure is in stinging about with a feeble Pen which can scarce Penetrate the hide even of Bashfullness & the rest seemd to have espousd the matter as a party affair which they were afraid to desert . . .

He finished with a brief comment on the pamphlet by Kippis:

> . . . I have enclosed you a Pamphlet written by Dr. Kippis who you may remember living in great intimacy with the late Sir John Pringle. it is fair & very well temperd

but so very mealy mouthd that it will possibly be right to publish something else as no foreinger [sic] can conceive a man right who is not praisd . . .

About ten days later, at the Royal Society meeting on St Andrew's Day 1784, Banks took the opportunity which seemed to offer in the award of the Copley Medal to apply balm to the Society's self-inflicted wounds. This was made clear in his address covering the award of the Medal to Dr Edward Waring, Lucasian Professor of Mathematics at Cambridge for his paper that year on the summation of series. The general tenor of his speech was a personal disclaimer of any mathematical insight and a statement that the boundaries of science were indeed so wide that the limited bounds of his own talents, as he put it, directed to other fields since his youth would not allow him to attempt it. But he felt no humiliation in saying so; he thought it fortunate that the Society could bear testimony to the merits of a mathematical paper delivered at the time it had been accused of neglect and deficiency in that particular field. He thought that from the appearance of that anniversary meeting the 'dissentions' [sic] in the Society were at an end and that those with whom he had had the misfortune to differ in opinion would agree with him

> . . . in a Determination to throw a veil of Oblivion over all past animosities and unite once more in sincere Efforts towards the advancement of the Society . . .

Certainly the fury of the debates of the past year had disappeared and on the surface there was a calm which covered less generous attitudes than those which Banks on the whole displayed and which his Fellows generally recognized. The text of his speech was ordered to be entered in the Journal of the Society but on the following day someone made a detailed copy of the autograph manuscript which Banks had used that evening – 'Exactly copied, both as to Orthography, Punctuation, &c.' as it was announced in a revival of these old schisms less than two months after his death, continuing the sequence of anonymous attacks begun in 1784 beyond the grave. The 'veil of Oblivion' was never completely drawn over these 'past animosities', which linger to this day as haunting shadows often enlarged beyond their proper scale in the affairs of the Royal Society and in the life of the President at whom the invective was directed.

II

It had been a severe winter and Banks had gloomily noted its devastations in his garden at Spring Grove from a 'duration & Excess of Cold' beyond his experience. The prevailing east wind however had changed to the west bringing squalls of snow and, on 13 April 1784, a rime frost. Then, on Friday 16 April, he recorded

> . . . The weather yesterday was somewhat warmer. Today it looks like spring . . .

– a bright augury for the beginning of an enterprise of some importance to the nation.

All that day Banks had been walking over a five-mile stretch of Hounslow Heath from near the Hampton Poorhouse north-west to the King's Arbour near the Bath

Road west of Harlington. His companions had been Lt-Col. William Roy, Henry Cavendish and Charles Blagden. Their purpose had been the inspection of a suitable tract on which to survey the baseline from which would develop the triangulations whose expansion would lead in time to the Ordnance survey of the United Kingdom, though this was not the immediate aim. When the party returned to Spring Grove that evening Banks recorded that

> . . . a Large flock of Swallows were seen crossing Houndslow Heath flying near the ground. soon after the Jynx [wryneck, *Jynx torquilla*] was heard to sing. about 4 in the afternoon the cuccow . . .

From this excursion William Roy was able to recommend officially to the Royal Society that the course they had traversed was suitable for the establishment of the baseline

> . . . as being very conveniently situated for . . . any future operations His Majesty may please to order to be extended . . . to more remote parts of the Island . . .

For Banks, as President of the Society to which this report was made, the baseline was now to become a prime call on his time and an activity which kept him in residence longer at Spring Grove and much less at Soho Square than was his custom.

It had all begun in the autumn of 1783 with the 'Mémoire' from France *Sur la jonction de Douvres à Londres. Par M. Cassini de Thury, Directeur de l'Observatoire Royal; de la Société Royale de Londres etc.* transmitted by the French Ambassador, Comte d'Adhemar, to Charles James Fox, the Foreign Secretary on 7 October. Within the next week Fox, by the King's command, had sent this document to Banks at Revesby Abbey. On 13 October Banks had passed the essence of the 'Mémoire' to Blagden with his opinion that the task of connecting the triangulations of England and France would do honour to British science with great benefit to astronomy and that there were enough people in the Royal Society to meet the challenge. He was sure that with the advice of the Society's Council he would be able to advise the King accordingly on a suitable plan. Blagden however was not so sure of the virtues of Cassini's memorial as he told Banks on 18 October. All this was temporarily obscured by the flush of excitement over the Montgolfier and Charles balloon ascents conveyed in the letters to Banks from Franklin and Broussonet with Blagden passing on to Revesby Abbey everything that came to hand in London about the new 'aerostatic machines', especially the gas-filled as distinct from the hot-air balloons.

However, about the middle of November, Banks had already taken some action on the Cassini memorial by sounding the feelings of the man most obviously prepared for such a task – William Roy, who for so many years had been his regular dining companion in the days of the 'rebellious' Royal Society club. Indeed Banks, as the 'Dictator' of that small coterie, with Roy and Sir George Shuckburgh was even then charged with the responsibility of investing the residual balance of the club's assets in the Funds as its last dying breath. The inauguration of the London–Dover triangulation which was now to emerge may justly be claimed as a final dividend of the club and a lasting memorial to the association from 1776 to 1784 of the four men – Banks, Roy, Shuckburgh, and Calderwood – who did so much to set the survey in motion with such excellent criteria of accuracy in practice.

203

The appointment of William Roy to the direction of the survey was soon approved and Banks, as PRS, was entrusted with the disbursement of the £3000 which the King made available from the Privy Purse for the instruments and equipment. It was the first operation of its kind on any extensive scale to be undertaken in Great Britain and its opening stage lay in the choice and establishment of a baseline with the highest order of accuracy possible from which the pattern of triangles could flower. Hounslow Heath had always appealed to Roy as one of the most eligible areas because of its extended area of level ground so free from large obstructions. Its proximity to both the capital of London and the Royal Observatory at Greenwich rendered it peculiarly convenient also as a base from which to extend future surveys in other directions.

On 26 May, an army party of the 12th Regiment of Foot – a sergeant, a corporal and ten men – were ordered from Windsor to encamp on the Heath by the Summer House at Hanworth Park. They were to begin clearing the furze bushes and ant hills from a narrow tract, about three yards wide along the projected line sighted roughly with a telescope by aligning tall bell-tents with the spire of Banstead parish church some 11 or 12 miles south-east. The spring and summer of that year were extraordinarily wet and this clearance was not finished before the first week in July.

Meanwhile the instruments needed for the measurements were being made by Jesse Ramsden under the strict eyes of William Roy and Banks. One of the first was a steel chain of 100 feet in length of a more accurate design than had been used before. This weighed about 18 pounds and folded easily into a deal box 14 inches long, 8 inches wide and 8 deep, and survives in the Science Museum, South Kensington, to this day. It was intended only to yield a first approximation of the baseline length, a determination which was made between 16 and 22 June in conjunction with Ramsden's portable transit instrument and his loan of an excellent telescopic spirit level for assessing the relative heights of the different sections. For this preliminary operation the volunteer assistants were Captain Calderwood, FRS of HM Horse Guards, Lt-Col. Pringle of the Corps of Engineers and John Lloyd. All this was done during more or less continuous wet weather.

For the final measurement of the baseline, wooden deal rods were first chosen, on the basis of general precedents elsewhere, their lengths being checked against some metal standard. These were to be made by Jesse Ramsden from well-seasoned pine of sufficient length and free from knots. As timber of this quality and kind was hard to find, Banks applied to the Admiralty for access to its stocks in the yard at Deptford. An old mast of New England white pine was the first choice. It was eventually discarded as too knotty and decayed to yield a sufficient number of rods even though less liable to warp or be affected by moisture than the Riga red wood which was finally chosen. This was a remarkably fine specimen, smooth and with a very straight grain. Each rod was 20 feet 3 inches long, the exact length of 20 feet required being marked by fine black lines on inset strips of ivory. In use these were set on special stands after the accuracy of their length had been checked against Roy's own standard brass 42-inch scale with Vernier divisions at each end and made by John Bird under the trade name of Jonathan Sisson. This in turn was checked against the similar Bird scale at the Royal Society by Roy and Ramsden together after two days' equilibration at a temperature of 65° F. The two lengths of the standard yard were found to agree perfectly as measured by Ramsden's beam compasses.

The making of the deal rods on which Ramsden bestowed such admirable care 'in order to render them the best that had ever been made' was a six-weeks' trial of everyone's patience. Finished at last on 15 July, they were brought by Ramsden himself to the army camp now set beside the Wolsey [=Longford] River. Next day they were taken to the south-east terminal of the projected baseline near Hampton Poorhouse with the other instruments. The fine details of this process need not be followed here except to note that by the first method applied with the deal rods, five tedious hours were spent in measuring the first 300 feet. The party that had gathered to inaugurate this survey and to assist in the actual mensuration were Roy, of course, and Banks as the two principals in its organization with John Smeaton, Henry Cavendish, John Lloyd and Charles Blagden. Blagden and Lloyd were working assistants during the first few days of difficult trial and error until a smooth procedure was established, but in the end the deal rods proved too unstable in length under the changeable wet weather that dogged the engineers in the first month of the operation.

The visit of the King and Queen to the site on Monday 19 July to observe the process was thwarted by heavy rain. Apart from one day, the 24th, work was suspended on account of the rain until August. During these two otherwise unprofitable weeks Calderwood, whose proposal it was, was deputed to develop glass tubes as a more stable substitute for the deal rods which had been Ramsden's pride. Calderwood was successful at the glass house in achieving long and very straight tubes of an inch diamater, one as long as 26 feet. Three of these were converted into standard 20-foot units with all the skill that an unwilling Ramsden could apply. Then, on 2 August, the weather allowed the work to resume with the deal rods and on 3 August the north-west terminal had been reached. The observed length of the baseline by the deal rods was recorded as 27404.31 feet, a very close agreement with the distance as first measured by the steel chain which was exceeded by only 2.9 inches.

By the middle of August the new glass rods were ready after two days' equilibration against the standard length at 68° F. Each unit, complete with brass fittings, weighed 61 pounds compared with the 24 pounds of each deal rod and, like these, three were used. On 18 August the reverse measurement from the north-west to the south-east terminal began as a double operation, using both the glass rods and the steel chain, the latter moving in advance precisely along the same line. This was done by using twice the number of coffer stands for the support of the two kinds of unit.

On Saturday 21 August the King visited the baseline about noon for some two hours, just after a critical comparison had been made of the two systems for accuracy over 1000 feet. He himself watched the details of the operation, for which he was paying, as it progressed from the 39th to the 35th stations.

On Tuesday 31 August 1784 the field work was done – with Sir William Hamilton, Charles Greville, John Lloyd, Captain Bisset and Dr Usher, Professor of Astronomy at Dublin, as observers on the last day. By the evening the working party had been discharged and all the apparatus removed to Spring Grove for temporary storage in the barn there.

Here a final test of the vagaries of the deal rods was made by comparing their dry or contracted length with that after exposure overnight to the absorption of atmospheric moisture as dew or fog. After resting dry in the barn for several days, the three deal rods were taken out on 4 September, a fine bright day with the temperature about 68° F, to be measured over a distance of 300 feet or 15 coincident rods. For this purpose 17 stands were precisely aligned down the long walk which extended north from the Pleasure Ground and divided Cold Bath from Park Field. When this was done the rods lay overnight on the smooth grass, exposed to the falling dew, and then from sunrise to about eight a.m. to a thick fog. In the re-measurement that followed an expansion of 0.493 inches in 300 feet was observed to have occurred in the 14 hours of overnight exposure, enough it was reckoned to have added 45.484 inches to the length of the whole baseline had it been sustained. This extreme sensitivity to moisture variations, confirmed by this final and most accurate comparison with the standard, was the great objection to the use of deal rods in the measurement of long bases where variation of thermal changes alone were troublesome enough.

Banks was now free to set out north for Revesby Abbey, somewhat later than was to be his custom in future years. He had taken part in an historic operation which could fairly be said to have met his own criteria, set out eight years before in 1776, to Andrew Armstrong criticizing his early surveys of Lincolnshire:

> ... But supposing the Execution to be amended, it would be very necessary, that the mode of Surveying be explained, and the Instruments shewn to me, before I could venture to take an active part in recommending the Survey; as I should not chuse to encourage any Survey which is not grounded upon several large Triangles which can only be accurately measured by Instruments of the best Construction ...

In Roy's survey of the baseline on Hounslow Heath, Banks had seen and helped to apply 'Instruments of the best Construction' in preparation for those 'several large Triangles' measured to a precision with which he could have no quarrel and which he could in every way encourage.

The nature and practical extent of this encouragement was gracefully acknowledged by William Roy as a potent benefit to the whole operation from start to finish. From Spring Grove Banks had been a frequent visitor and helper during the preparatory phase after the main line of the base had been determined, but from mid-July until the end of August he had been in attendance, as Roy put it 'from morning to night during the whole progress of the work'. As the engineers moved over the ten-mile course involved, from the south-east terminal to the north-west with the deal rods and back again to the south-east with the glass tubes and the steel chain in the second measurement, Banks had ordered his own tents always to be pitched near at hand. Here he gathered his scientific guests and the numerous other visitors drawn by curiosity to the spot and plied them

> ... with the most hospitable supply of every necessary and even elegant refreshment ...

on which Roy was clear

> ... how greatly this tended to expedite the work, and how much more comfortable and pleasant it rendered the labour of all who obligingly took part in it ...

206

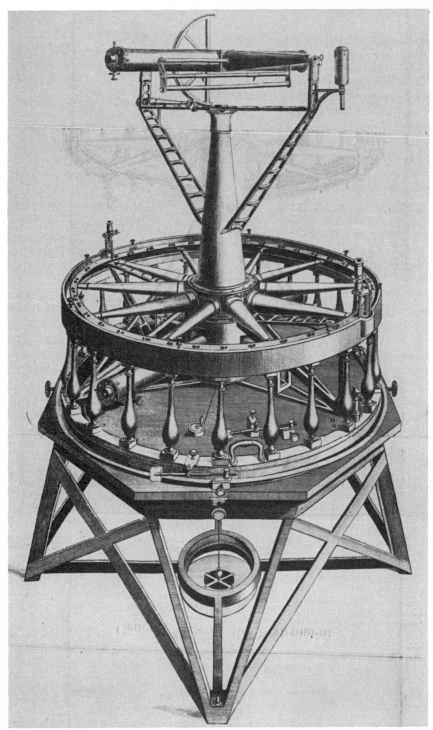

'The great circular instrument' made by Jesse Ramsden for the triangulations of 1787 from the Hounslow base-line to Dover and Calais. Known as the '3-foot theodolite R.S.' it served the Ordnance Survey until 1853. It was destroyed in the 1941 blitz on Southampton.

The details of this first stage in the London–Dover survey were presented by William Roy in his paper to the Royal Society read at successive meetings from 21 April to 16 June 1785 and duly published in the *Transactions*. The next stage was already in preparation in the discussions during August 1784 between Roy, Banks, Maskelyne and Ramsden. These ended in the ordering of 'the great circular instrument' which has come to be regarded as the 'father' of accurate theodolites, capable of azimuthal readings to two seconds of arc at 70 miles. The order for this classic instrument, placed in the summer of 1784 with Jesse Ramsden, was not fulfilled for three years. By some this was said to be due to the procrastination of the master himself but was surely due also to his exacting technical standards and competing demands on his skills. In the end an instrument came from his workshop which served the Ordnance Survey until 1853 as 'the great theodolite' or the '3-foot theodolite R.S.' made at the expense of HM King George III and presented by him to the care of the Royal Society.

In the hands of William Roy and his assistants, 35 months after it was first ordered, 'the great circular instrument' began its work on 31 July 1787 at the south-east terminal of the baseline. From there the difficult triangulation was pushed south-east some 80 miles as far as Wrotham Hill to complete a chain of ten stations before 20 September when arrangements had been made to meet the French representatives from the Académie des Sciences – Cassini de Thury (the fourth), Pierre Méchain and Adrien Legendre. The last details of the cross-Channel observations from Dover to Calais were amicably settled with them on 23 September. The Anglo-French trigonometrical connection was made successfully on 17 October 1787 with the help of 'white lights' fitted for long distance sightings. In this last stage Charles Blagden was at the centre of the negotiations with the French and from 25 September to 20

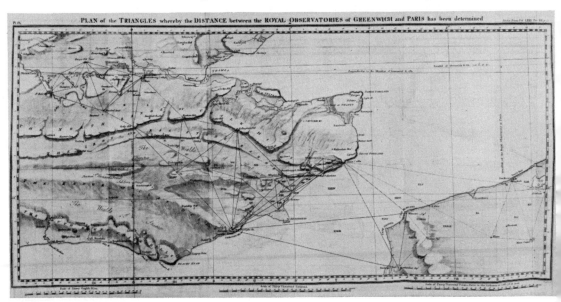

The plan of the triangles developed from the Hounslow base-line (Triangle I, top left) for determining the distances between the Royal Observatories of Greenwich and Paris, July–October 1787.

October was at Calais recording the last details of the survey. From the French side he assisted in the display of 'white lights' from the tower of the church of Notre Dame in Calais to match those lit from Dover Castle. Throughout these last months he had kept Banks briefed on the progress of events albeit disturbed by the rumours of impending war and pondering his own plans for resignation as Secretary of the Society.

'The great circular instrument' had moved cumbrously from station to station, a mass of 200 pounds, travelling in a four-wheeled spring van. Of all the angles measured by Roy with it, and with such splendid accuracy, none have been used in the triangulation on which the modern survey is now based. This in no way detracts from the praise due to him for his pioneer work in providing the first truly reliable basis for map-making with an accuracy of a remarkably fine order. When the Hounslow Heath baseline was re-measured for the definitive triangulation in the nineteenth century, its error was assessed at 1 in 158000, or two inches in five miles, and the mean triangular error of the 16 fully observed triangles which sprang from this base, independent of sign, at just over one second. With the same original baseline to compute from there was a striking agreement between the English and French values for the cross-Channel distance from the station at Dover Castle to the spire of Notre Dame at Calais:

The English value = 137449 feet
The French value = 137442 feet

With such standards established, the formal beginning of the Ordnance Survey of the United Kingdom soon followed. The work which had begun that early spring day has a respectable place in the history of modern cartography.

III

Two weeks after Banks had drawn what he hoped was a 'veil of Oblivion' over the rankling dissensions in the Royal Society another figure quitted the scene of many debating duels of a more literary kind. On Monday 13 December 1784 Dr Samuel Johnson died at 8 Bolt Court. A week later his body was carried to its grave in Poet's Corner, Westminster Abbey, by six pallbearers from among his friends of The Literary Club – Bennet Langton, Esq., George Colman, Esq., Sir Charles Bunbury, MP, William Windham, MP, Edmund Burke, MP and Sir Joseph Banks, PRS. Surrounded by other members of The Club and of the Reverend Chapter of Westminster the burial service was conducted by Johnson's old schoolfellow the Revd Dr John Taylor, LLD.

Soon the task of gathering a fund for a monument to his memory was set in motion by The Club and Dr Edmund Malone, one of the latest members admitted to the small circle, was charged with this work. A committee was formed to consider the problem but in the usual way found that agreement was hard to achieve. Some years passed until the Dean and Chapter of St Paul's enlivened the issue by a new plan for admitting mouments within its precincts.

Banks had always been a party to the general discussion but by 1790 had been drawn closer to the committee work involved as Malone tried to bring the affair to an end. At a public meeting on 5 January 1790 a special committee was elected: Sir Joshua Reynolds, Edmund Malone, James Boswell, Sir Joseph Banks, Phillip Metcalfe, William Windham and Sir William Scott. The bubbling mixture of views about the kind of monument now separated into a sharp divergence between those who were for placing it in St Paul's and those who were faithful to an admittedly overcrowded Westminster Abbey. Another year passed and The Club was still divided when Phillip Metcalfe forced some action about 16 March 1791 by suggesting to Reynolds that the committee meet in his house to consider the hint from the Dean of St Paul's that a niche for the statue might be had there at half price. Reynolds demurred in favour of a meeting in a tavern and on 17 March Banks drafted a circular to all members of the committee calling them to a meeting at Baxter's in Dover Street at two o'clock on Saturday 26 March.

He protested against divorcing the monument from the burial site because he was sure that Johnson had expressed his clear wish for Westminster Abbey and because his executors had already engaged with the Dean and Chapter of the Abbey to have it erected there. Such an engagement, he believed, had also been confirmed by the subscribers to the memorial fund who had given their money on the understanding that the statue would be erected in the Abbey. Moreover, he said, the committee had not been invested by the general meeting with any power to alter the monument site nor given any power beyond that of procuring funds for the purpose. The next day he sought the views of Edmund Malone who had not been present at Baxter's. The lines of division were clear as Banks drew them:

> Sr. Joshua [Reynolds] who preferrs St. Pauls says that the honor as well as the interest of the arts are materialy at Stake in the business & will receive a material advantage if we set the example of erecting a monument in a Church which has hitherto Lain Fallow from the harvest of the Chisel, that Westminster is already so stuffed with statuary it would be a deadly sin against taste to increase the squeeze of Tombs there & that St Pauls is the most honorable station for the monument of a Great Man.
>
> [Edmund] Burke says waggishly this is borrowing from Peter to give to Paul but he supports Sr Joshua Fully & Firmly

At the same time Banks asked Robert Mylne, FRS, as surveyor of St Paul's Cathedral, for an estimate of the cost bearing in mind the fairly modest funds available:

> at what expense do you think it will be possible under the strictest Ideas of Economy to Erect such a monument in St Pauls church as in order to suit with the dignity & grandeur of the building is likely to be requird if every part of it is to be on a colossal Scale & one human figure at Least required as I understand is intended.

Mylne's answer is unknown but Malone was clear that if a monument were erected anywhere but in Westminster Abbey the committee could be charged with receiving the subscription money under false pretences and that he personally objected to cenotaphs away from the place of burial. William Windham, who had also been absent from the meeting in Dover Street, on the other hand was prepared to follow the majority.

Another meeting was called for Friday 15 April at which nine people were present. This was a general rather than a committee meeting and a vote was taken which showed six for and three against the site in St Paul's. Sir Joshua led the majority party. His opponents were James Boswell, Phillip Metcalfe and Sir Joseph Banks. Thereafter both Banks and Boswell withdrew from the committee after Banks had again expressed his strong dissent, pleading that whereas Westminster was established as 'the Repository of the illustrious dead' St Paul's was not and that a future Dean and Chapter might change their minds about the erection of future monuments. The clear difference between the two presidents – Sir Joshua of the Royal Academy of Arts and Sir Joseph of the Royal Society – was not Art against Science, rather was it on a point of principle and the ambitions of art against ancient practice. Another five years passed before Dr Samuel Johnson appeared in St Paul's chiselled by John Bacon, clad in his toga as the *ultimus Romanorum*, at a cost to his friends of The Club and his other admirers of some £1100.

211

CHAPTER 10

THE BAY, THE *BOUNTY* AND THE BOOK
1783–1787

The war which had set the background to the evidence given by Banks to the Bunbury Committee in March 1779 had been lost and the Preliminary Articles of Peace had been signed with America, France and Spain by the end of January 1783, though not yet with Holland. At home the political furore over the peace negotiations had brought the fall of the Shelburne ministry and the emergence of the Fox–North coalition under the Duke of Portland in April. The image of a new and potentially dangerous world was re-shaping round India and the Indian Ocean in the rivalries of Britain, France and Holland. Beyond their eastern footholds lay the South Pacific, as yet *mare nullius*, whose hour had now come as the account of Cook's third and last voyage approached the point of publication.

There was a certain historical logic perhaps in the reappearance at this moment of confusion in British affairs of the young American loyalist, James Mario Matra, formerly J. Magra, AB on the voyage of HMS *Endeavour*. Never far from the protective sympathy of Banks, he now wrote a hopeful letter to him at Spring Grove on Monday 28 July 1783, of which the first three paragraphs condensed the speculation and debate current in Westminster and the City:

Although for many months past, I have been obliged to lead the life of a Solitary fugitive, I have heard a rumour of two plans for a settlement in the South Seas; one of them, for [New] South-Wales, to be immediately under Your direction, and in which Lords Sandwich [and] Mulgrave, Mr. Colman, & several others are to be concerned. The other a distinct plan, in which Sir George Young, & Mr. Jackson, formerly of the Admiralty, are the Principals.

I have met these Stories in several romantick Shapes; but secluded as I was from Society, have not been able to get any intelligence to be depended on, except immediately from Sir George Young, who avowed it to an acquaintance of mine, tho' in such cautious, equivocal terms, as barely served to authenticate the fact, without clearing away any of the obscurity it is involved in.

If there be any truth in either of the reports particularly the first, I shall be extremely obliged to You for some information which I assure You shall never be communicated by me to any one. I have frequently revolved similar plans in my mind & would prefer embarking in such a scheme to anything much better, than what I am likely to get in this Hemisphere . . .

This letter found Banks at Spring Grove relaxing at the end of an ominously difficult Royal Society year and more or less recovered from his fall in a boat at the end of July.

Before the week was out it is probable that Matra found himself fully in the confidence of Banks and Lord Mulgrave at Soho Square on the subject of South Sea settlements. Of those whom Matra had named in his letter as parties in the Banks's plan three were close neighbours in Soho Square – George Colman sen. at No. 28 on the corner of Bateman's Buildings; Mulgrave at No. 30 on the corner of Frith Street and Banks himself at No. 32. Moreover both Banks and Mulgrave were in close contact with Lord Sandwich at this time – Banks over publishing the account of Cook's third voyage and Mulgrave, also at the Admiralty, as the sitting MP for Huntingdon in the Sandwich interest. In these circumstances and with James Matra's promise never to divulge any details he might receive, the preparation within three weeks and the more or less open circulation of 'A Proposal for Establishing a Settlement in New South Wales' becomes less a matter for wonder. During the first three weeks of August Matra, from a state of self-confessed ignorance, produced a reasonably argued case for a settlement on the coast of New South Wales, not specifically at Botany Bay.

The area was viewed primarily as a favourable homoclime for the settlement of white Europeans. It was to rest broadly on the exploitation of natural resources such as the flax plant and timbers of New Zealand with their potential for the Navy; the development of a tropical and sub-tropical agriculture devoted to spices, sugar-cane, tea, coffee and tobacco as articles of maritime trade in competition with the Dutch; the exploration of trade with China and Japan in furs from the north-west coast of America and woollen goods from England; the establishment of a colony of displaced American loyalists; and finally, its development as a strategic base from which to launch naval forays against the Dutch and Spanish if necessary. These proposals for colonization were set against the assumption that the aboriginal inhabitants were few and unlikely to resist effectively; that useful Chinese settlers could be attracted as they had been by the Dutch in their East Indies settlements; and that any imbalance in the sexes could be redressed by bringing women from Tahiti or the Friendly Islands – all points specifically attributed to Banks himself. For the development of a European, as distinct from a tropical, agriculture, the livestock and appropriate seed supplies from the Cape of Good Hope or the Moluccas would augment those that could not survive the long voyage from the home country.

The 'Proposal' as signed by Matra on 23 August 1783 made no reference to New South Wales as a 'very proper region for the reception of criminals condemned to transportation'. This recommendation appeared later as an addendum after Matra, in his own words, 'had conversed with Lord Sydney on this subject', presumably after 23 December 1783 in Pitt's new administration. Until then the idea had been for a colony of free settlers growing from a foundation of

> ... those unfortunate American loyalists to whom Great Britain is bound by every tie of honour and gratitude to protect and support, where they may repair their broken fortunes, and again enjoy their former domestic felicity ...

In this form, as Matra emphasized more than once, the 'Proposal' was approved by Sir Joseph Banks, who was ready to present his opinion to His Majesty's Ministers whenever they should require it. In fact, of course, what Matra proposed was in substance an adaptation to peace-time conditions of the evidence Banks had given to the Bunbury Committee four years earlier with a convict settlement specifically in mind. Now it included information arising from Cook's third voyage relating to

China and the fur trade, supplemented with ideas about extending the British wool trade to the Far East as a by-product of Banks's recent engagement with the wool industry. The preamble contained a hymn to the virtues of that *Planta utilissima* of the *Endeavour* voyage, now the *Phormium tenax* Forster, the New Zealand hemp or flax plant, whose industrial potential Banks had visualized from his first sight of it at Poverty Bay in 1769. The 'Proposal' also contained Mulgrave's thoughts on naval strategy later to be found in his Admiralty papers.

It would seem that in James Matra the two old friends had found a convenient disseminator of their own thoughts on New South Wales until their mutual friend William Pitt could bring them to a practical conclusion. It was only in Soho Square then that Matra could have found and crystallized these ideas in so short a period and to such effect. It was however to take another four years before the First Fleet was on its passage to their fulfilment and then as a convict colony, not as a settlement of free American loyalists.

In the country's straitened economic condition the expense and complications of a colony as distant as New South Wales was daunting. In spite of the hazards to a white man's health, for many reasons the western African coast had more appeal. Before the year was out an exploratory voyage to west Africa was evidently mooted and Banks found it convenient to engage David Nelson (at his customary salary of £35 per annum) on 1 November 1783 to sail as botanist on board HMS Swift, Captain Laudsay. The ship sailed from the Thames on 23 December for Plymouth here it remained until ordered back to the river in March 1784 as Pitt reviewed the position, leaving Nelson unemployed until at least June 1784.

Meanwhile others had been building on the substance of the ideas formulated in Matra's 'Proposal', which Banks and Mulgrave had been content to see in circulation. John Call, home from India and recently elected to Parliament, developed the notion in his own way as in extended paraphrase during 1784. Sir George Young of the Royal Navy produced another version of the 'Proposal' as his 'Plan' for settling New South Wales which Lord Sydney, as Home Secretary, received in January 1785. Meanwhile the Transportation Act had been renewed as 23 Geo.III c.56 and, by Orders in Council, Africa was chosen with the island of Le Main, some 500 miles up the Gambia, as the first experiment in this ill-favoured region. But this plan was aborted after deliberations by the Committee on Transportation under the 1st Earl Beauchamp. Re-convened in April 1785 it presented its report in May.

Among the witnesses called, Matra and Banks appeared on 9 and 10 May 1785. The testimony of Banks, as recorded, echoed his evidence to the Bunbury Committee but now there was a new urgency in the questions. They were framed against the background of

> ... it being in the contemplation of this Committee to suggest such place as may be most proper to send the whole or part of the Convicts now under sentence of Transport ...

In answer to the first question on where Banks thought such a place might be, he said

> I have no doubt that the soil of many parts of the Eastern coast of New South Wales between the latitudes of 30 and 40 is sufficiently fertile to support a considerable number of Europeans who would cultivate it in the ordinary modes used in England

Pressed on which part of the coast would be best suited, he answered

> Botany Bay is the only part of that Country which I have actually visited and I
> am confident that it is in every respect adapted to the purpose

Thereafter his testimony covered details about the people, the country and the nature
of its resources but there was a finality in his last answer. On being asked if he knew
of any place as preferable 'for the purpose of sending convicts to it', he said

> From the fertility of the soil the timid disposition of the inhabitants and the
> climate being so analogous to that of Europe I give this place the preference to all
> that I have seen

There was however another obstacle to be surmounted before a final decision could
be made.

Commodore Edward 'Poet' Thompson had long fostered the notion that
somewhere along the southern stretches of the western coast of Africa a suitable
region might be found and this he had reinforced by a reconnaissance in 1784 as
Commodore in command of that station. In the end the Beauchamp Committee
plumped for Thompson's Das Voltas Bay scheme, and on 22 August 1785 Lord
Sydney asked the Admiralty to delegate the Commodore for a survey of the region.
The Navy Board responded with some speed and HMS *Nautilus*, Captain T. B.
Thompson was added to the small African squadron for that purpose.

On 29 August 1785 Banks wrote to William Aiton from Revesby Abbey

> . . . I am applied to by Government to Provide a man for them to visit a part of the
> Coast of Africa (which is unknown to us in the article of natural history) with
> Commodore Thomson [sic]

He expected the appointment to last a year, with a salary of about £60 and the mess
bill paid at the rate of master's mate. He defined the man he sought as 'a gardener
active and healthy able to write a good hand' and with qualifications similar to those
of David Nelson, to operate under his own written instructions. John Graeffer, of the
nursery firm of Thompson and Gordon at Mile End, had hinted that his brother
might go but in the end he recommended a young Pole Anton Au, who later called
himself Hove. Blagden interviewed him and Banks found him acceptable though
Evan Nepean, under-Secretary at the Home Office, at first objected to the
engagement of a foreigner. With Hove on board HMS *Nautilus*, the squadron sailed
from Portsmouth at the end of September 1785 and returned on 23 July 1786.

Das Voltas Bay turned out to be only a barren and rocky shore, treeless and
waterless, with no vestige of a suitable harbour. The case for an African colony
lapsed and that for Botany Bay as a possible site revived. On 18 August 1786 Pitt
accepted the dismissal of the Das Voltas Bay scheme by the Home Office, and on
Saturday 19 August the Cabinet approved the 'Heads of a Plan' prepared by Evan
Nepean and presented by Lord Sydney that day. Thereafter the plan to colonize the
east coast of New South Wales at or near Botany Bay, with a nucleus of about 750
convicts, moved steadily forward under the meticulous management of Evan

Nepean. On 21 August he approached the Treasury for the necessary funds and by 31 August the Admiralty had been formally requested to prepare a warship and tender 'fitted for Sea with all possible expedition' and a force of officers, sailors and marines for a service 'entirely unconnected with Maritime Affairs' to be under the immediate direction of the Home Secretary. By this date also Captain Arthur Phillip had been selected, largely on the judgement of Evan Nepean, to command the expedition despite reservations by the First Lord, Howe.

The details of preparing the extraordinary array of 11 vessels commonly known as the 'First Fleet' – HM Ships *Sirius* and *Supply* with three storeships and six convict transports – belong elsewhere and are to be found scattered through the public records in the files of the Home Office, Admiralty, Treasury and Colonial Office in particular. What is less apparent is the part enacted by Banks at this stage in the history of the colony of New South Wales. This is not surprising. Banks was a private citizen with no established place in the hierarchy either of the Civil Service or Parliamentary government. His only overt influence might perhaps seem to stem from his Presidency of the Royal Society, and then only as a fount of wisdom in a scientific sense. But clearly he was something more. He was a point of general reference and relevance as the sole surviving figure of intellectual weight from the first Cook voyage and a continuing link with all subsequent expeditions to the Pacific. He had become important also as an independent line of communication with the outside world, notable for his honesty and sturdy sense of public duty. Few traces of this however would enter the public files except when Banks was away from London, mainly in Lincolnshire during September and October at this period or at Spring Grove on certain days of the week in the spring and summer. For the rest his opinion or advice was conveyed in person by direct consultation in and about Whitehall and the City or during visits made to him at Soho Square. Such verbal exchanges would then be absorbed into the more or less official papers under other signatures without much more than a minuted aside as a desultory hint of its origins. The 'Proposal for a Settlement in New South Wales' has already been cited as essentially a contribution from 32 Soho Square, its real birthplace. It remained through all the political and departmental shifts of the ensuing three years as a powerful influence in the administrative process from which the convict fleet and the convict colony emerged at length as a viable enterprise.

Banks was at Revesby Abbey for the first two of the seven and-a-half months of preparation, from the appointment of Captain Arthur Phillip to his sailing from Spithead on 13 May 1787. But even at this distance he attended to the preparation of a list of seeds necessary for the colony in October/November 1786 and it is apparent from his later correspondence with Phillip that the two men must have met more than once thereafter as the equipment of the ships advanced, and the official instructions were framed. At the same time the working relations between Banks and Evan Nepean were growing stronger and closer as the industrious under-secretary translated thoughts and ideas into official documents and effective action.

II

The virtues of the bread-fruit tree as a source of food had long been known and Banks had added his own praise of the Uru (*Artiocarpus* spp.) of Tahiti from his first encounter with it in 1769. Soon after the return of the *Endeavour*, his friend Valentine

Vice-admiral Arthur Phillip, RN, first governor of New South Wales, 1788–92.
Painting by Francis Wheatley, RA.

Morris who owned property and many slaves near Kingstown on St Vincent, wrote from Berkeley Street on 17 April 1772 in search of further information. He wished to know from Banks

> ... whether there was no possibility of procuring the bread tree either in seed or plant so as to introduce that most valuable tree into our American Islands in which having considerable property, and thinking e'er long to visit I cannot but feel myself much interested and would if possible procure to its habitants what must if once it could be made succeed be one of the greatest blessings they could possess. As my motive for giving you this trouble is a humane benevolent desire of benefitting so considerable a body of people, I know I need not use many apologys to a gentleman who like yourself has manifested in so exemplary a manner similar feeling ...

The idea however was a plant of slow growth. The Standing Committee of West Indian Planters and Merchants offered financial inducements in 1775 for any enterprising trader to the East Indies who would bring the bread-fruit tree from the South Seas but without practical effect. The Society of Arts, Manufactures and Commerce in 1777 took up the theme with the offer of a premium and a gold medal but also to no avail. Thereafter the state of war stifled any further hope of such a plant introduction, but the approach of peace which coincided with a succession of devastating hurricanes in 1780–1 and again in the years 1784–6 brought a revival of the idea. With the rising interest in the South Pacific pointing to a more permanent European presence there the time was ripe in 1786 for reconsideration of the bread-fruit. Hinton East, Receiver-General of Jamaica and planter of Liguanea, had in July 1784 raised with Banks the possible value of the bread-fruit tree as a more stable source of food than the plantains which were so vulnerable to high winds. Again now, at just the right moment, in August 1786 East visited Banks at Spring Grove to press the case for introducing bread-fruit on the very day that Pitt and the Cabinet decided to settle a convict colony at or near Botany Bay. The two themes of bread-fruit and Botany Bay were now entwined with Banks at their centre.

During the autumn Banks had been in touch with Charles Jenkinson, 1st Baron Hawkesbury, as Chancellor of the Duchy of Lancaster in whose patronage lay the living of Miningsby, to secure it for the parish of Revesby. Thus began an enduring partnership with Lord Hawkesbury as the long-serving President of the revised Board of Trade. During the winter in London he then secured Hawkesbury's interest in bread-fruit and through him, by January 1787, the support of Pitt on the need for it in the West Indies. In addition Banks and the Cabinet were well aware that the French were moving useful plants from the East to the West Indies. On 13 February 1787, Pitt conveyed the decision to mount an expedition to the Pacific to collect the bread-fruit tree in a letter to Samuel Long, Treasurer of the West India Committee and at about the same time Banks prepared a plan of the voyage for Pitt. This was on the premise that Governor Arthur Phillip would detach a vessel from the fleet at Botany Bay to gather growing plants of New Zealand flax at Queen Charlotte Sound, bread-fruit trees at Otaheite, mangosteens and other fruits at Princes Island, and spice plants at the Isle de France by exchanges with the French. The eventual plant cargo was to be divided equally between St Vincent for the Windward Islands, and Jamaica.

218

Artiocarpus altilis (Parkinson) Fosberg (the breadfruit). Original drawing by Sydney Parkinson finished at Tahiti 1769.

During March however a closer study of the problems involved, both economic and practical, changed the plan from that of a subsidiary operation of the Botany Bay fleet to that of a separate expedition sent direct from home waters. Banks prepared a revised paper copies of which, on 30 March 1787, he sent to Lord Hawkesbury at the Board of Trade, to Lord Mulgrave at the Admiralty, and to Lord Sydney at the Home Office. It was they who, on this basis, finally framed the instructions on 5 May which set the expedition afoot. From the beginning, as Evan Nepean made clear, the whole enterprise was 'under the Direction of Sir Joseph Banks' and this the Navy Board was content to accept – a measure of the respect which Banks had gained, and was to keep, in Admiralty circles.

He had appointed David Nelson as the responsible gardener for the voyage with effect from 1 March and William Brown as his assistant. Then between 16 and 23

May Banks and David Nelson, with the assistant surveyor of the Navy Board at Wapping, selected the *Bethia*, of about 215 tons, to be purchased from Wellbank, Sharp and Brown for £1950 as a suitable vessel. On 23 May the Navy Board directed the officers of the yard at Deptford to fit and equip the ship according to Banks's instructions. So HMS *Bounty* was born and by 14 August had left the dock in readiness for manning.

Banks had already decided that William Bligh should be appointed to command the expedition, news which greeted Bligh on his return from Jamaica on Sunday 5 August. Since 1783 Bligh had been on half-pay but occupied in the service of his wife's uncle, the merchant and shipping contractor Duncan Campbell, known to the Pitt administration and to Banks as an authority on the costs of convict transportation. Bligh had been Campbell's agent in Jamaica and in command of the merchant ship *Britannia* when the first hints of new employment in the Navy had reached him in May by a letter from Duncan Campbell. Now it was confirmed when Bligh met Banks, probably at Soho Square, on Thursday 9 August and was officially sealed in his commission of 16 August from the Admiralty. Apart from his four years' experience in Jamaica and the West Indies, the choice of Bligh made good sense for he had been master of the *Resolution* on Cook's last Voyage. Moreover Banks already knew him well as someone for whom he had secured a belated justice in the division of profits from the published account of the third voyage, a tribute to Bligh's masterly surveys on which so many of the finished charts were based.

Competing naval demands for seamen elsewhere delayed the sailing of HMS *Bounty* until late in the year although she had been nominally ready at Spithead since 4 November. Bligh's sailing orders were dated 20 November but adverse winds during December compounded the delay and rendered a passage round Cape Horn according to the original sailing plan doubtful. At Bligh's request Banks extracted from the Admiralty modified orders allowing a change of course if necessary and on 23 December 1787 the vessel finally sailed. For Bligh his lifelong association with Banks had begun.

III

Since the publication in June 1784 of *A Voyage to the Pacific Ocean . . . for making discoveries in the northern hemisphere*, the tempo and range of Banks's committments had rapidly increased. The volume of his correspondence had grown and his handwriting gradually changed to the hard-pressed scrawl from which it never recovered. The account of that third voyage to the north Pacific had had implications which were not lost on the merchant venturers of Britain and France. After the Definitive Treaty at Paris in September 1783 a succession of voyages was planned by both countries and some mounted to enter this virgin trading territory. Some of the British entrepreneurs were responding to the formulations in James Matra's 'A Proposal for Establishing a Settlement in New South Wales', focusing on the opportunities which the furs from America offered in expanding and developing a favourable trade with China and Japan. In the voyages which followed during the next three years, it is not surprising to find Banks as a nodal point in the communications relating to them. His involvement was strengthened by his friendship with Lord Mulgrave who was a member of the Board of Control of the East India Company and of the Privy Council Committee for Trade and Plantations since 18 May 1784.

220

French plans for an extended Pacific voyage were known about in London early in 1785 and two groups of British merchants reacted swiftly once the government had approved further expeditions in March. Soon thereafter James Strange, of the Madras Civil Service, sailed for Bombay after a long period of sick leave. There he told David Scott about his ideas for a voyage to the American north-west coast. Scott, a free merchant, then submitted a plan to the President and Council of Bombay, which was received with cautious approval. This led to an expedition consisting of two vessels, Indian-built but European manned, the *Captain Cook* and the *Experiment* with James Strange in command. His instructions dated 7 December 1785 stated

> The Principal Purposes for which we mean this Expedition are in the first Instance Exploring for the benefit of Navigation, and secondly with a view to Establish a new Channel of Commerce with the North-West Coast of America

The voyage, from 15 January to 15 November 1786, had no value as exploration and probably resulted in a trading loss for David Scott and Company although 604 sea-otter skins to the value of about £5100 were obtained. From the correspondence between Scott and Strange with Banks over the mounting of the expedition it seems probable that the plan itself had been hatched in Soho Square at or about the same time that a second different venture was being planned in London independently from the same central stimulus.

During April 1785 a syndicate of London merchants was formed under the lead of Richard Cadman Etches of Fenchurch Street. It included Nathaniel Portlock and George Dixon as sea captains and veterans of Cook's last voyage as master's mate and armourer respectively on HMS *Discovery*. Established as the King George's Sound Company it sought a charter from the government to trade along the whole of the north-west coast of America from latitude 43°6′ N. to Behring Strait. Mention was made of searching for a sea passage into the Atlantic but despite government support no charter was forthcoming.

The East India Company which resented all intrusions by independent merchants within its sphere of operations was not in favour of it. However on 6 May the Company's Committee of Correspondence recommended that the Court of Directors might 'by way of experiment', as it was thought to be in the national interest, license two ships for one voyage with restrictions on the mode of selling the fur cargo. It was to be offered 'at a fair price' to the supercargoes at Canton who could then impose further restrictions on the return freight to London. The conditions in the license and the deed of covenant were considered by the Board of Control and passed to Lord Sydney on 27 May for ministerial approval, which was granted with some easing of the more severe terms later.

It was not until 8 July however that the two ships acquired were moored at Deptford ready to be commissioned. At a small ceremony during that month the ships were inspected by Sir Joseph Banks and Lord Mulgrave with Sir John Dick and George Rose, the Secretary of the Treasury. The larger vessel, a ship of 320 tons, was named by the Secretary the *King George* to be under the command of Nathaniel Portlock, leader of the expedition. The smaller, a snow of 200 tons with George Dixon as her captain, was named the *Queen Charlotte* by Banks. The expedition left the Thames on 31 August 1785 on a voyage that would last almost exactly three years. In the course of it, unlike the expedition from Bombay under James Strange, valuable contributions to the cartography of the American coastline would be made with many new features named. Among these, inside the Dixon Entrance to Hecate Sound, George Dixon in 1787 called one of the larger islands after Banks. But as a trading venture the Portlock–Dixon voyage was hardly more profitable to its promoters than that of Strange from Bombay. In November 1787 the two ships reached Canton with a cargo of 2552 sea-otter skins which was sold to the supercargoes for some 50000 dollars or less than 20 dollars a skin. This represented an inadequate profit for which Richard Etches blamed the two captains, though in fact as in the venture by David Scott and Company, the fault lay in the stringent terms imposed by the East India Company licence.

Before the depressing outcome of the Portlock–Dixon voyage was sheeted home to the firm of Richard Cadman Etches and Company it had already mounted another during 1786. This consisted of the *Prince of Wales* under James Colnett and the *Princess of Wales* under Charles Duncan – with a licence from the East India Company even less favourable to mercantile notions of gain. The ships left the Thames in September 1786 carrying as surgeon on the *Prince of Wales*, the 32-year old Archibald Menzies on his first voyage into the Pacific and visit to the American west coast. For more than two years Menzies had been corresponding with Banks at the behest of his old Edinburgh professor, Dr John Hope. Since the peace he had served as surgeon on HMS *Assistance* on the Halifax station where he had botanized along the coast and in the West Indies when the ship was ordered there. From these places he had sent seeds and dried plants to Banks from time to time. In August 1786 the *Assistance* returned to Chatham where she was paid off. Menzies had brought Banks a box of living plants as he had promised and he sent them up to London on 21 August saying he would follow in a few days. His first meeting with Banks must have been during this week, for on 28 August Sir Joseph set out for Lincolnshire. The occasion was fruitful, however brief the encounter, for within the next month and from a distance, Banks had arranged with Richard Etches that Menzies should sail as surgeon on the *Prince of Wales*. On 27 September Menzies paid a farewell visit to Soho Square leaving specimens of *Cypripedium bulbosum* among some others from Halifax as a parting token wth Dryander before setting out to join the ship at Portsmouth. Etches, in a letter to Banks of 29 September, confirmed his agreement that Menzies should have every reasonable facility to pursue his scientific bent on the voyage, which was to be of three years by way of Cape Horn to the north Pacific and home via China and the Cape of Good Hope. This was to be a troubled voyage, as Colnett discovered at Nootka Sound, but it brought Banks a good harvest of specimens from far-flung sites in the Pacific through Menzies's assiduity.

Banks was not only the common factor linking these three British voyages, but was also involved in one being prepared by the French. Translation of Cook's third voyage, which he had made so speedily possible, acted as a challenge to emulation by the French in the Pacific. By April 1785 Banks had heard from Broussonet rumours that an expedition was being mounted under the command of La Pérouse. This was confirmed on 5 May. It is pleasing to record that when La Pérouse sailed from Brest on 1 August 1785 he carried not only two dipping needles used by Cook which Banks had sent with his own present of a pair of pistols but also with a long list of various items which he had, at the French request, gathered in London for the naturalists Martinère, Dufresne and D'Antic.

As La Pérouse passed south to Cape Horn and the Pacific, Commodore

Thompson's squadron with Anton Hove on board HMS *Nautilus* was poised to investigate the mysteries of Das Voltas Bay. At the same time another African visitor was the subject of arrangements developing between Banks and Evan Nepean. Francis Masson, back home from Madeira and his two years on the Iberian Peninsula and in North Africa earlier in 1785, was now ready for his second stint at the Cape of Good Hope if, in the still delicate relations with the Dutch, this could be arranged.

Masson was to sail with Sir Archibald Campbell, who was about to take up his new appointment as Governor and Commander-in-Chief at Madras. A passage had been arranged for the Kew collector on board HC Ship *Earl Talbot* for the Cape, if the Dutch would accept him, to India if not. Nepean was struggling to extract a favourable letter of introduction for Masson from De Lynden, the Dutch Ambassador in London, for presentation to the governor at the Cape to support those from Sir Archibald and William Devaynes, the Chairman at the East India Company. Masson had still not received the Ambassador's letter when he made his parting visit to Soho Square to receive from Dryander a final note from Banks at Revesby Abbey, just before setting out on 19 September to join the *Earl Talbot* at Portsmouth. The Ambassador's letter in the end reached him at Portsmouth and on 10 January 1786 he presented it to the Dutch governor at the Cape, who, though his Council was reluctant, granted him permission to stay as a collector for Kew. His most productive nine years at the Cape had begun.

IV

In the flurry of renewed Anglo-French relations after the signing of the peace preliminaries on 30 November 1782 Banks was well served – by Charles Blagden and by Pierre Broussonet, both in Paris. Each in his different way played a part in the episode of Charles L'Héritier de Brutelle, the Dombey collection and the publication of the *Sertum Anglicum*. In 1783 soon after his first visit to England Broussonet introduced L'Héritier to Banks as a correspondent and on 2 February 1783 this long cross-fertilization in matters of botanical publication began between Soho Square and Paris. The intricacies of what followed have since been a hunting ground for bibliographers but the visit of L'Héritier to Soho Square has much to reveal in other ways. For three years Banks had given aid and comfort with botanical diagnoses, plant specimens and plates, to L'Héritier in his work of publication, and the first parts of the *Stirpes Novae* appeared at great expense during 1785 and early 1786. Blagden had met L'Héritier in July 1783 in Paris and Broussonet had made two further visits to London one in August 1784 with Bertier de Sauvigny, Flandrin, and Faujas de St Fond, and the second in March 1786, with Banks always a point of focus in their arrangements. Francis Masson too, as collector in the field of so many of the species whose beauties L'Héritier was seeking to perpetuate, was a significant though silent party in these publications.

Early in 1785 Joseph Dombey returned to France after ten years of travel in Peru and Chile as *médecin-botaniste* seconded to the Spanish expedition under Hipólito Ruiz and José Pavon. Bound by an agreement with the Spanish Government Dombey was unable to publish anything botanical in his own right and despondently gave the surviving dried plants that he could claim for France to the Jardin du Roi in return for a modest pension and a grant to cover his debts. Meanwhile L'Héritier, possibly with the connivance of André Thouin, had offered to publish at his own expense

Dombey's new plant species so suitable for his *Stirpes novae*. Attracted by this notion Buffon, director of the Jardin du Roi, passed the Dombey herbarium to L'Héritier to the manifest discontent of Antoine de Jussieu and contrary to Dombey's promise to the Spaniards. Jussieu managed to abstract some of the specimens while the Spanish Government made a firm protest to the French, who ordered Buffon to regain the herbarium from L'Héritier. By chance this order was issued at Versailles when L'Héritier was there and, warned of what was to come, he returned with speed to Paris and packed the collection that night with the help of Broussonet and his own favoured artist Pierre-Joseph Redouté. The next day, 9 September 1786, he set out by coach for Boulogne leaving a false trail to his estate at Brutelle in Picardy. He carried with him a letter of introduction to Jonas Dryander from James Edward Smith who was in Paris at the time. Landing at Dover L'Héritier reached London on 19 September, leaving the packed herbarium, consigned to Sir Joseph Banks, with the customs at the port.

Banks was in Lincolnshire after a London summer which had been filled with pleasant social activities: boating parties with Lady Banks and her friends on the Thames; a day spent with Horace Walpole at Strawberry Hill near Twickenham and dinner with the Duke of Northumberland at Sion House, Isleworth, on the Thames opposite the Royal Garden at Kew. He had left London on 28 August in the family coach with his ladies, dallying for two days as guests of the Duke of Ancaster at Grimsthorpe. For the first week of September the family stayed with Sir Richard Kaye, Dean of Lincoln, at his home near the cathedral while Lady and Miss Banks indulged their sporting fancies at the Lincoln Races and their other social inclinations in two dances at the Assembly Rooms and one at the City Room. Banks himself sought some relief by ranging off on his own to visit Henry Willoughby, 5th Baron Middleton, at his seat of Wollaton Park near Nottingham for two days, some 50 miles from Revesby Abbey to which he returned in time for the Witham fishing on 15 and 16 September. On this occasion, as on all the other such parties on the Witham, the Banks trio were guests of Thomas Fydell, MP at Fydell House in Boston. For the next month the house at Revesby was filled with guests enjoying the Banksian hospitality. There now burst the news of L'Héritier's sudden appearance at Soho Square, in a letter from Dryander dated 21 September. Broussonet had written to Banks on 11 September announcing L'Héritier's departure with the Dombey herbarium and James Edward Smith had capped this on 13 September from Paris with an account of the escapade. On 24 September Banks replied to Dryander:

> L'Heritier's business is in truth a veritable French one; he means, as Smith informs me, to publish a Prodromus Florae Peruvianae at London, thinking that after such a manoeuvre the Spaniards will consider the game as up & make no further requisition. This however is a secret. L'Heritier must certainly have every assistance that the Herbarium or library can give him. As he stays three months I shall be up at least half the time he is here. I write to him by this to offer him all civilities & regret my absence.

The same day Blagden, just returned from several weeks exploring the northern counties and visiting Lord Mulgrave, sent Banks his own comment on the situation while on the following day Dryander was helping L'Héritier rescue the herbarium from the Customs House. To complicate things at Soho Square, young Olof Swartz

224

had arrived from Jamaica with his collection of West Indian species intending to stay in London until the following spring. And then from Revesby Abbey came Banks's protest.

> I have a letter from L'Heritier which alarms me a good deal I have from it conceived that of all the impudent Frenchmen in the whole world he is the most impertinent and dangerous. He begins with telling me that he has used my name in importing Dombey's herbarium & tried at least to do the same in passing it through the Custom House. He next asks my leave to publish a monograph of my Gerania & ends by telling me that the gift of the Genera which were intended for him is a *charité bien placée*. I have written him a cool answer & desired him to return the Genera which be so good as to send down to me here taking notice before you send them whether he has faithfully returned the whole he received, if a man does one thing not quite in the square of sight we have a right to suspect the rest of his conduct; if I am wrong in doing so you will be so good as to set me right . . .

Banks was rightly irritated but unusually severe, hoping that he was wrong to suspect so much. He wrote also to Blagden whom he wished to confer with Dryander and advise him accordingly. He enclosed a letter of strong reproof to L'Héritier protesting, rightly, at the use made of his name at the Customs House but still offering him the use of the library and herbarium at Soho Square, as 'without such assistance your intended publication would run the risk of many imperfections'. However he explicitly reserved the right to dissect his own herbarium specimens for his own descriptions and publication, though he was prepared to do this to help verify L'Héritier's diagnoses when he returned to London. Dryander replied on 3 October that he and Blagden had discussed Banks's letter:

> . . . Dr. Blagden thinks Mr. L'Heritier, from what he has conversed with him, a strange fellow and I have in my two visits with him to Kew seen several instances of his having in a pretty high degree the french impudence or want of consideration in asking for what we may not like to grant. We therefore perfectly agree with you in the necessity of keeping him at a good distance . . .

But they thought it unwise to ask him to return the plants from Geneva, which were in any case destined for him, as risking the charge of ill treatment, so they agreed not to deliver Banks's letter to him until Banks told them otherwise. They agreed also that Swartz ought not to open his West Indian herbarium which he had not yet proposed to do. Dryander promised close supervision in the herbarium itself with the door to the room above with the *Endeavour* collection kept locked. He also expressed a qualified view of L'Héritier's ability to recognize a new genus if he saw one but 'it is not my business to teach him botany'. Then on 12 October Dryander reported that he had delivered to L'Héritier a second more moderate letter from Banks, after which all seems to have been well though Blagden retained a sour opinion of L'Héritier's behaviour.

L'Héritier's intended three months' stay became 15, with Dombey's herbarium and the idea of a 'Prodromus Florae Peruvianae' gradually sinking into the background. L'Héritier fell victim to the temptations of the Royal Botanic Garden at Kew and the Banksian herbarium spread before him, as Banks's instinctive generosity and good humour opened one new species after another to his gaze. From the ashes of the Peruvian 'Prodromus . . .' with all its prickly ethical defences there rose the *Sertum Anglicum* . . . or, in its English translation, 'An English Wreath or Rare Plants which are cultivated in the Gardens around London especially in the Royal Gardens at Kew observed from the Year 1786 to the Year 1787'. It was published in Paris and printed by Didot and L'Héritier's dedication, dated 20 April 1788, was a charming acknowledgement of the celebrity of English gardens and English botanists in general, to whom the work was offered as a small gift of new genera described. There was not a word to link the hospitality and help at Soho Square specifically with what was done. In all some 127 species were noted in the text and arranged according to the Linnaean system. With some a brief description was given but these were inadequate in any botanical sense. For most the collector and the region of origin of the species was also given, and of these some 53 were attributed to Francis Masson, mostly at the Cape of Good Hope but with some from Madeira, the Azores and the Canary Islands. Banks and Solander were credited with 3 and David Nelson with 2 species. For Joseph Dombey, whose collection was the prime cause of L'Héritier's visit to England, 5 species were recorded in the series. In all 34 plates were engraved, of which 21 were from the drawings of Pierre Redouté and 10 from those of James

Eucalyptus obliqua L'Heritier. *Left* The holotype specimen of the species; collected by David Nelson at Adventure Bay, Tasmania, 27–30 January 1777, now in the General Herbarium, British Museum (Natural History). *Right* The engraving by Fr Hubert from the drawing made by P. J. Redouté at 32 Soho Square of the central stem in the original plant specimen of which it is a mirror image. Plate 20, *Sertum Anglicum*, 1788.

Sowerby. Of these drawings 15 were of species attributed to Masson as the collector, 2 to Banks and Solander, 1 to David Nelson – but this last, the drawing by Redouté of the species collected in Tasmania at Adventure Bay, named by L'Héritier as *Eucalyptus obliqua* was to survive as the holotype of the genus and species to this day.

It is commonly said that L'Héritier was the first to use James Sowerby as a draughtsman for botanical subjects, but it is clear from Banks's letter to Dryander of 30 September 1786 that Sowerby was already drawing for William Curtis, and that he had orders to draw for Banks when not doing so. Indeed in Curtis's *Flora Londinensis*, 1775–87, there is ample evidence of the hand of Sowerby.

As for the *Sertum Anglicum* . . . as a whole, whatever the cloud over L'Héritier's elopement with the Dombey collection and whatever the first antipathies expressed by Banks, the final result could not have been achieved without the long months of generous scientific hospitality opened to the Frenchman and his artists. This obviously included the South Sea plants from the attics upstairs and, no doubt, also the examples of the engravings in the room below where Daniel Mackenzie (and possibly also Frederick Nodder) was still engaged in the service of Banks as a master of the botanical copperplate. When the Preface of the *Sertum Anglicum* . . . was dated on 20 April 1788 Governor Arthur Phillip with his convict charges had landed at Sydney Cove from the First Fleet. In the South Atlantic Lt William Bligh on the first bread-fruit voyage was in retreat from the rigours of Cape Horn to rest and replenish at Table Bay. All three enterprises – Botany Bay, the *Bounty* and the book – had a common denominator in the savant of Soho Square during the crowded 18 months, from August 1786, as they came to historic life.

V

The apprenticeship of Banks in the service of the British sheep breeder in the growing of wool had begun with his engagement on behalf of the farmers of Lincolnshire in the autumn of 1781. It had advanced in his enlistment of the Swede, Charles Hellstedt, whom he sent at his own expense to the Low Countries in January and February 1782 on a mission of mercantile espionage in the market in long wool on the Continent. He also kept up a correspondence with 'all the merchants of Europe where the woollen manufactury is at all Flourishing'. In the course of these enquiries he gained an appreciation of the intricacies of the wool trade, its manufactures and sources of raw material, but which raised a series of challenging questions touching the natural history and agricultural economics of the sheep, with few answers in any convenient form. He began as an ignorant amateur diligently seeking enlightenment wherever he could. Once again Pierre Broussonet proved to be of assistance.

Two important facts soon emerged from these investigations. English long wool, of which the Lincolnshire graziers were so proud and the Yorkshire merchants so jealously possessive, was less highly regarded on the Continent than they supposed, for the Low Countries in particular possessed local pockets of as good and possibly superior material. But the other fact to be reckoned with was that the clothiers of Europe were more concerned with the fine wool of Spain and the disruption in its supply caused by the war than by any disturbance in the long wool supplies from England. Early in 1782 Banks received from Hanover a first general clue to new opportunities when his attention was directed to the success of the fine wool grown in Saxony by cross-breeding from the Spanish fine-wooled breed sent as a gift to the elector from the Bourbon Court of Spain in 1765 and 1778. During the whole of this year in Banks's studies on the wool supplies of Europe and Great Britain Broussonet at Soho Square could not fail to be aware of his host's preoccupation with the sheep and its fleece covering. Soon after his return to France he spent some time with John Sibthorp botanizing in the Pyrenees until the late summer of 1783 before returning to Paris. In January 1784 he was appointed an assistant professor, under Louis Jean-Marie Daubenton during his brief but important tenure of the Chair of Rural Economy at the new École Vétérinaire Royale at Alfort. Banks by this time knew about Daubenton as an experimental breeder of sheep under government patronage at Montbard in Burgundy from his memoir to the Académie des Sciences 'Sur l'amelioration des bêtes à laine' in 1777 and above all from the recent summarizing volume *Instructions pour les Bergers et pour les Propriétaires de Troupeaux* of 1782. Now, in Broussonet, he had, as it were, a direct line to one of Europe's pioneers in the infant science of animal breeding for improved production – in this case the quality of the fleece for the manufacture of fine wool clothing. Then, for Banks, came the final challenge in Daubenton's most recent memoir to the Académie – 'Sur le premier drap de laine superfine du cru de la France', 1784. Before this appeared, Broussonet, on 15 April 1784, had already offered Banks rams of Daubenton's Spanish fine-woolled breed though his request for English long wool sheep for the École Royale Vétérinaire had foundered on the embargo laws then prevailing. Banks however was able to serve the new French school in other ways – especially with English turnip, enough eventually to sow some 6500 acres, and Chinese hemp seeds. Arrangements evidently progressed during the visit of Bertier de Sauvigny and Broussonet during the summer in London but it was not until 10 March 1785 that Broussonet could tell Banks that he had at last secured for him a ram and a ewe of the true Spanish fine-woolled breed from Montbard. At last in mid-June the two sheep, each with an iron collar stamped with Banks's address, were sent from Paris, by way of Rouen and Le Havre, to reach Spring Grove early in July 1785 – a gift from the École Royale Vétérinaire. They were the first sight for Banks and his fellow-Englishmen of the small animal which as the Australian Merino and its Botany wool in the next century was to have such an influence on the national economy.

For seven years the Spring Grove flock of Sir Joseph Banks was the centre from which spread a network of activities and ideas built round these two strange sheep from Burgundy. In gathering ewes to be mated in the autumn to 'Monsieur Ram', as Broussonet dubbed him, Banks attracted the attention of two men whose proselytizing energies would have other effects on agricultural economy. Two ewes of the rough-fleeced Scottish breed came from Caithness near Thurso Castle, the home of Mr Sinclair, a recent widower seeking another course in his life. The sheep came south in September to Spring Grove and before Christmas Sinclair was in Paris, with an introduction from Banks to Broussonet and the envigorating circle of young men clustered at Alfort round the elder Daubenton. When he returned early in the New Year from what had been in effect a short course in rural economy centred on the growth of fine wool Mr Sinclair had become the baronet Sir John. He had also found his new vocation as the self-anointed apostle of agricultural improvement. Armed with a large sheaf of introductory letters from Banks he set out on 29 May 1786 on that hard-driving journey of 7500 miles through Western Europe and deep into Russia at the rate of 33 miles a day in pursuit of political and economic wisdom. He returned on 16 January 1787 replete with information and

> ... full of ardour ... to make this island, the centre of various improvements, of which political society was capable, more especially those of an agricultural nature, to which a person of landed property is naturally partial.

In Sinclair, Banks had acquired a recruit whose obsessive energies would accomplish much but at a terrible cost to the patience of his friends.

The seven smooth-fleeced ewes of the Sussex breed which followed in October came from Sheffield Park where John Baker Holroyd, the 1st Baron Sheffield, had already embarked on his hobby as a political pamphleteer with a bent towards agriculture and international commerce. His contribution to the Spring Grove flock marked the beginning of a long and, in its way, fruitful friendship between the Holroyd and the Banks families with Edward Gibbon the historian as a link between them.

The four fine-fleeced Herefordshire ewes which came to Spring Grove late in September were from the flock gathered by Robert Bakewell, the tenant farmer of Dishley by the Soar in Derbyshire. In him Banks had the assistance briefly of the man who, with his new Leicester breed capturing the attention of British farmers, presented a rising threat to the fat Lincolnshire long wools themselves and implicitly the defeat of any hope for Spanish fine wool growing in the British Isles.

The two long-fleeced Lincolnshire ewes were brought from the flock of Mr Fowler of Ketsby on the wolds just north of Revesby Abbey, and two Wiltshire ewes with their Roman noses and bare bellies were extracted from the flocks grazing on Hounslow Heath nearby.

These few sheep laboriously collected round a small Middlesex villa were the mere shadow of the larger enterprise in Burgundy. Among them however were all the important variants of the contemporary British sheep population – the fine and the coarse, the long and the short and the tall, the rough and the smooth – in fleece, in form and aptitude to fatten. And, as a sire for their cross-bred progeny, just one small Spanish fine-woolled ram. A tenuous beginning indeed but for Banks it was a practical way of checking what he had read in the French memoirs. And even as the matings at Spring Grove began there was a further French challenge as Daubenton, on 16 November 1785, read before the Académie his 'Observations sur la comparaison de la nouvelle laine superfine de France, avec le plus belle laine d'Espagne, dans la fabrication de drap'. It was to be another two years before Banks was able to make his own first small trial in the same manufacture.

From the first lambing in the spring of 1786 came one pure Spanish ram which Banks sent in 1787 to Lord Sheffield to mate with his Southdown or Sussex ewes eventually to produce a small flock of half- and three-quarter bred Spanish × Southdown sheep with a notable advance in fleece weight combined with fineness and value per pound – to the surprise of the woolstapler Thomas Bell and Sheffield alike. A second pure Spanish ram born at Spring Grove in 1787 went north to Revesby Abbey where he mated with a draft of Nottinghamshire forest ewes in the Park, and also with two black-faced Norfolk ewes sent from Holkham by Thomas William Coke. Again there was the surprising gain in weight and fleece quality in the first cross. A third Spanish tup born in 1788 went to Major John Cartwright at

Marnham in Nottinghamshire to be mated in 1789 with twenty Notts ewes and from the two-year first cross fleeces valued in 1792 by John Buxton of Bermondsey to show once again the double advance in fleece weight and fibre fineness. Then in 1791 Banks sent the original Spanish ram from Daubenton to mate with 11 Southdown ewes at Woodmansterne near Banstead in Surrey, the flock of Mr Lambert, brother-in-law to John Hunter. As a final touch Banks presented the ram at the age of eight to Hunter as a specimen for his museum. In its place he received that year a ram from His Majesty's flock at Windsor Castle but the following year, after seven years' pioneering, he disposed of all the pure Spanish and Spanish cross-bred stock at Spring Grove confident that in the royal enterprise across the Thames the future of the fine-woolled breed in British hands was now secure. The pure Spanish stock, some seven head in all, he gave to Arthur Young of Bradfield Hall near Bury St Edmunds in Suffolk, editor of the *Annals of Agriculture* and Banks's active colleague in the wool growers' cause.

Before the ending of fine wool growing at Spring Grove Banks had in miniature run the gamut of procedures through which the imported pure Spanish pile had supposedly passed before conversion in the hands of the West Country clothiers into their fine broadcloth. In the autumn of 1786 he had sent ten ounces of 'Monsieur Ram's' fleece in its natural state to Charles Blagden's brother, Richard Blagden, clothier of Uley in Gloucestershire, for a test of its behaviour in spinning. This was encouraging enough and Banks, with the aid of John Maitland, of the wool merchants Fludyer and Company in Basinghall Street, prepared to go further. Maitland had come into his life at the end of 1786 by an introduction from Maxwell Garthshore, FRS. On Maitland's advice the 1786 fleeces of the ram and ewe were washed on the sheep's backs before shearing in the English manner; in 1787 the next two fleeces were washed after shearing in the Spanish manner, first in warm and then in cold water. The fleece of the first ram lamb, now a shearling, was treated in this way also and all five fleeces then sent to Thomas Bell for valuation where they were accounted far below that of Daubenton's wool in his memoir two years before. The four adult fleeces were now sent to Matthew Humphreys, clothier of Chippenham, Gloucestershire, for a full report and manufacture into cloth. By mid-November 1787 this produced 5¼ yards of fine blue broadcloth in all from a total of 11.3 pounds of clean wool entirely grown on Spring Grove pastures. At 2.16 pounds of wool per yard this was a close comparison with Daubenton's figure of 2.08 pounds per yard which he had reported two years before. The cloth from the sheep of the École Royale Vétérinaire was presented to His Most Christian Majesty Louis XVI of France; that from the French sheep at Spring Grove made two blue coats to adorn the back of the President of the Royal Society as the first of its kind to be made in England.

The story of the Spring Grove fine wool as a practical guide to sheep breeding and wool manufacture was not yet done. The stimulus of Banks in search of fine wool had already been felt in Lincolnshire with his inauguration of an annual Stuff Ball, the first of which had been held on 12 October 1786 in Lincoln 'for the encouragement of the Woollen Manufacture'. Now on 7 March 1787 Matthew Ives, corn merchant of Spalding, drew Sir Joseph Banks's attention to the cloth woven in Norwich from the fine yarn 'spun on the Distaff with the Spindle' from pure Lincolnshire wool by his second daughter Ann. At 'near 60 Skeins to the Pound' of clean wool, where 70 to the pound was reckoned superfine spinning for the worsted manufacture, this was remarkable. If this could be done with the relatively coarse long wool from the fens, what might not be possible in the hands of this young woman with finer wool? Banks sensed in her an instrument of great value to show what fine wool of English growth could be in cloth.

The raw material for such a test was at hand in the first fleece of the young cross-bred ram shorn that summer at Revesby Abbey after a wintering on the Revd Edward Wall's marsh nearby. Sired by Daubenton's Spanish ram out of Mr Fowler's Lincolnshire ewe, this young sheep foreshadowed a whole new future for the British wool trade in the century to come and the deft hands of Ann Ives clearly pointed the way ahead. From its fleece by November 1787 she had produced a thread so fine that, in Norwich skeins of 560 yards, it was rated at 186 to the pound of clean wool, a threefold advance on her spinning of the Lincolnshire wool and far beyond the limit of 150 skeins per pound reached by Mary Powley of East Dereham, Norfolk, recorded in the minutes of the Royal Society for 30 May 1754. Excited by this dramatic demonstration, Banks sent Ann Ives, in early December, one pound three ounces of scoured wool from the fleece of the first pure young Spanish ram born at Spring Grove. On 14 January 1788 Ann Ives sent Banks the first clear proof of the spining performance possible with English-grown fine wool from the pure Spanish breed – a thread which ran at the rate of 256 Norfolk skeins to the pound of clean wool. Whatever the errors and approximations involved these were small compared with the scale of the advance now shown to be possible in the combing and spinning of the fine-wool fibre for the worsted system.

Apart from these practical demonstrations Banks had made his own direct evaluation of the fineness of the Spanish wool grown at Spring Grove within the previous two years. When Matthew Humphreys, on Wednesday 21 November 1787, delivered to Banks at Soho Square the web of blue broadcloth from the fleeces of Daubenton's ram and ewe, it was with the grudging admission that they were sufficiently superfine for the market. But he had been sent a staple of fine wool from Spain to show that the Spring Grove wool was not so fine. Under this pressure Banks studied both under the microscope and found that his own wool was finer than the specimen from Spain – clearly a lesson learned from Daubenton's early use of micrometry recorded in his paper 'Sur un Moyen de Connoître la Finesse des Laines' of 1799.

CHAPTER 11

So much begun
1787–1789

While Banks was grappling with the doubts of the British wool trade on fine-wool growing in England and laying foundations for the British sheep breeder as he unravelled the mysteries of the Spanish Merino fleece at Spring Grove, Governor Arthur Phillip was on his passage to colonize that country where the ultimate industrial future of that animal resource would be determined. Banks had sent Phillip a farewell letter as the convict fleet waited at the Motherbank and which Phillip first read at sea, with no chance to reply before his arrival at Santa Cruz in the Canaries. From here he sent a brief reply dated 5 June 1787 with his gratitude for all that Banks had done before he sailed.

During the three weeks at Rio de Janeiro in August, among all the problems of refreshment for the fleet, Phillip was assiduous in attending to the advice of Banks in the collection of useful plants for the colony-to-be, gathering the seeds of indigo, cacao, coffee, cotton, tobacco, vines, oranges, lemons and limes, jalap and, with some optimism, the cochineal insect. In particular he investigated the different kinds of Brazilian ipecacuanha (*Uragoa* spp.) of which he sent four to Banks by the hand of Mr Morton, late master of the *Sirius*, invalided home and bearing also two letters dated 31 August and 2 September 1787. These were the Governor's last letters to Banks before his first from the colony nine months later, except for a brief note from the Cape in November.

This long interval however was bridged with news from Cape Town through Francis Masson, to whom Phillip carried a letter from Banks dated 11 April. The fleet anchored in Table Bay on Saturday 13 October and for the next month was engaged in taking on board stores, livestock and more plants. Masson wrote to Banks on 13 November, in a covering letter, for seeds and bulbs he was sending in a Danish ship in the care of Captain Cox, an East India Company officer. Written on behalf of Phillip, it gives a glimpse of the fleet in transit:

> ... We had for some months ago the news of this extraordinary expedition to the Antarctic regions, but I always doubted the truth of it. The Fleet left us yesterday all in good health; Besids [sic] cattle & stock of all sorts they have taken trees, plants, & seeds of every sorts which the season would admit. Indeed G[overnor) Phillips Cabbin was like a Small Green House with Plants from Brassil, among which was some rare Plants viz *Ipecacuana, Jalapa*, & *Cactus Tuna* with *Cocus Cochinilifera* breeding on it. There was also Coccoa, and Coffee trees. G: Philip desired me to mention in my letter that it was not within his power to visit the Salt petre mountain of which he had some account of ...

This letter did not reach Banks until 13 May 1788.

A view of Cape Town, 1772. Painting by William Hodges, RA.

As he had promised Banks in his letter from Santa Cruz Phillip wrote by the returning transports under the command of Lt John Shortland, naval agent of the convict fleet, on board the *Alexander* transport. His last letter had been a short one from the Cape dated 9 November 1787 briefly supplementing what Masson wrote on the 13th. The next letters, dated 2 and 10 July 1788, travelled with Phillip's first official despatches to Lord Sydney, Evan Nepean and the Admiralty, and with La Pérouse's last despatch from Botany Bay. Returning by way of Batavia on more than one ship, they did not reach Banks until 13 and 31 May 1789 and had been preceded by Phillip's much later letter of 26 September 1788. This had been sent on board HMS *Sirius*, sailing fast by Cape Horn to the Cape of Good Hope and from thence by another ship home to Soho Square on 22 April 1789. This was the first of a long series of vice-regal letters to Banks from Sydney Cove but evidently not the first news he had received from the colony. As early as 9 April 1789 John Linton was replying to a letter from Banks that had evidently given him first-hand news from the new colony:

> . . . I think myself much obliged by your Account of what is hitherto known of the Success of the Expedition to Botany Bay & Cumberland County; an inconsiderable removal from the precise Situation where the Embarkation was intended to be made alters not the general Nature of the Plan, & whatever may eventually happen as arising from our Settlement on the Coast of new Holland is undoubtedly to be attributed to the original Promoters of the Scheme On this

233

Account I truly acknowledge I was more anxious to hear Tidings from that part of the Globe, than from any other Consideration. – In search of our new Rome fewer disastrous Events have attended the Emigrants from this Country, than befel the followers of Aeneas in the Flight from Troy to the founding of their City . . .

So by April 1789 it was known that the settlement was not at Botany Bay but at Port Jackson and that a large area of the hinterland was now named County Cumberland – as indeed it had been since 4 June 1788 after dinner in Phillip's tent at the first celebration of the King's birthday in New South Wales.

By the end of May 1789, two years since the fleet had sailed from England, Banks had received ten letters from Phillip. They supplemented the official despatches which Phillip assumed Banks would see and about which he would exchange views and information, particularly with Lord Sydney and Evan Nepean. How closely Banks was involved with the affairs of the new colony appears in a tantalizing slip of paper in his own script and dated February 1789:

I could not take office and do my duty to the colony. My successor would naturally oppose my wishes. I prefer therefore to be friendly with both sides.

What office he refers to is not clear although the political overtones are. William Pitt was casting round for able men in his new administration and Lord Sydney was under some pressure to resign as Home Secretary. For several years Banks had been showing his abilities as a man of energy, tact and judgement at the service of the Cabinet and not least with the Home Department. It is possible that Pitt had tried to enlist Banks with this Cabinet place as a bait, though he must have known that acceptance was unlikely. Banks continued on his independent way and probably served the colony no less as governors came and went and the home administrations rose and fell. Meanwhile Banks stood solid as the centre about whom gathered the new knowledge of a strange antipodean environment.

The letters from Captain Arthur Phillip undoubtedly brought the first information. Their tenor suggests that before sailing he had seen more than a little of the Banks family and that he was on a pleasant social footing with the man to whom he directed the first consignment of plants, seeds and gum, a stuffed kangaroo in a wooden case, a young kangaroo and the first flying fox or 'fox bat', *Pteropus* spp., shot on 27 June 1788, both in a keg of spirits. They were sent under the care of Lt John Shortland of the *Alexander*, and came to hand on 13 May 1789. They had been preceded by his letter of 26 September 1788 sent with Captain John Hunter on the circumnavigating voyage to the Cape for stores and so on to England by a Dutch ship. In November, by the *Fishburne* transport, Mr Browne master, Phillip sent among other things a case of the white clay used by the aboriginals in marking their bodies and a small vial of the oil extracted by distillation from the leaves of a gum tree by the surgeon-general John White, as well as a keg with more young kangaroos and a kangaroo-rat in spirits. At the same time, by the *Golden Grove*, William Shairp master, he sent four tubs of flowering plants. By the same ship David Considen, one of the assistant surgeons well known to Banks through a friend in common (Captain Charles Hamilton), sent an array of stuffed parakeets and a stuffed 'flying Squirrel stuffed kangaroo skins, two live parakeets and two live opossums, and specimens of two kinds of gum. One of the live parakeets Considen nominated as a present for

The first Government House at Sydney Cove, 1790, drawn by Midshipman George Raper of HMS *Sirius*.

'your daughter' in his letter of 18 November 1788 and so laying the trail of another mystery which we cannot here pursue.

In his letter of 16 November 1788 Governor Phillip struck a moderately cheerful note. Apart from the occasional heavy rain storm, the winter had been pleasant. His oranges, figs, apples and vines, from Brazil were thriving. In his garden, vegetables of all kinds were plentiful and his strawberries from the Cape, with cauliflowers and French beans, had been available for some weeks. There was little to say about the native flax, and as to the Norfolk pines, the returning store ships each carried a lower yard and a top gallant mast by which the people at the Deptford yard could judge its value against the fact that trees of 130 feet in height had been felled which were perfectly sound. Within a month of receiving these letters from Phillip, Lord Sydney, with his viscountcy and his pension, had retired and been replaced by Pitt's first cousin, William Wyndham Grenville, first cousin also to Banks's own first cousin Louisa Grenville. Banks had now to indoctrinate a new regime in which kinship with the new Home Secretary in no way eased the problem.

II

As economic stability returned after the peace treaties of 1783, industry in Great Britain began that steady climb, measured by the volume of its exports, which was to be the envy of Europe for the next 20 years. All forms of woollen goods ranked high in this recovery as profitable exports and the Yorkshire wool growers fell silent after

235

having successfully quashed even a qualified sale of long wool abroad. They now turned their attention to closing the loopholes by which they were smuggled along the south and east coasts. Although no one was sure of its scale it offered the protectionist merchants and wool manufacturers an excellent pretext for new restrictive legislation. The cudgels in this fresh battle with the wool growers were taken up by the West Country clothiers, headed by John Anstie of Devizes in Wiltshire. Under his chairmanship a Committee of Manufacturers was appointed in April 1786 and the first form of what was to become the Wool Bill of 1788 was drafted. Its aim was to repeal the confusing list of existing laws and produce one more precise and effective act. This action from the broadcloth interests was not without its impact on the northern worsted trade with implications for the long-wool growers.

The Lincolnshire Wool Committee had remained in being after its earlier defeat by the Yorkshire manufacturers. On its behalf Charles Chaplin of Blankney wrote to Banks on 31 May 1786 appreciating his warning about the new Bill, accepting it as a general attack on all wool growers and calling for a general meeting to plan resistance. This took place at the Peacock Inn on 14 June in Boston under Robert Vyner, the Member for Lincoln and culminated in a plenary meeting at Lincoln in the County Hall on 19 October under the chairmanship of the Lord-Lieutenant, the Duke of Ancaster. A petition was signed and a general subscription opened. An executive committee of seven was appointed, for which Daniel Douglas as High Sheriff and Banks were named, with powers to select the other five. Before the end of the year 272 Lincolnshire wool growers had signed and subscribed £1383 for the expenses of the tussle ahead.

It was five years since Banks had been drawn into this wrangling with the wool trade and again he was called upon to assume a leading part in a political gamble which was against all his inclinations and which he clearly knew was lost from the beginning. In spite of doubts he worked loyally on behalf of the county, contesting the Bill through all its stages over the next 18 months. With Arthur Young as the voluble publicist, especially for the wool growers of Suffolk, Banks strove to elicit the relevant facts to shed light on what he regarded as dubious statements from the Committee of Manufacturers. They could find no evidence to support the notion that the French could not make good export cloth without an admixture of what was fondly supposed to be the superior English staple. In particular they could not swallow Anstie's extraordinary estimate that some 10000 packs of mainly combing wool was lost annually by the home manufacturers in smuggling operations to France. This was an amount which would have equalled the entire import of Spanish fine wool into England. They found it strange also that Anstie, a clothier in fine wools, should presume to speak for the worsted users of combing wool with such authority. Their suspicions of Anstie's competence to represent the wool trade was shared by the men of the West Riding. Under such an onslaught Anstie's first Bill did not survive a second reading. But a new Bill rose, no less inimical to the interests of the wool growers, and pushed its way to the House of Lords, modified only slightly by Banks and Young, with the aid of Lord Hawkesbury and Lord Sheffield.

The second form of the Bill was framed by the West Riding Committee of Merchants, Manufacturers and Dealers in Wool under the formidable chairmanship of Pemberton Milnes in the early months of 1787. Under this challenge Banks was stimulated to compose a paper of some 10000 words, reviewing the history of the

English wool trade over the centuries, and so framed that it concluded as a strong plea against the terms of the new Wool Bill on behalf of the wool growers. As 'my pamphlet' he submitted it in May to Lord Sheffield intending it

> ... as a broadside against the manufacturers when they make their attempt next autumn or as Feu de Joie on their ceasing their absurd attempts What however I should best like if I could bring it about would be that you would accept it as a basket of Raw wool which you would card spin & weave &c, & by that means render it a piece of your own superfine ...

but though it returned from Sheffield Park on 8 June 1787 richly annotated it seems never to have fulfilled its first intentions. It lay dormant for a year while Arthur Young set out on his first visit to France in the meanwhile to gather, among other things, relevant information from Broussonet and Bertier de Sauvigny, now Controller-General of Finance in Paris. Then in April 1788 Banks revised his draft pamphlet including more recent information into 5000 words as 'Instruction given to the Council against the Wool Bill', which Arthur Young published in Volume 9 of his *Annals of Agriculture*. In the same month Young and Banks on successive days stood before the Bar of the House of Commons as principal spokesmen for the wool growers. In early June they again appeared before the Bar of the House of Lords. But by this time the passage of the Bill was certain, and the most that Banks could achieve was some modification in section 14, which he dubbed with affection 'my clause', whereby the fleeces shorn from sheep destined for the market between 1 March and 1 July each year escaped certification until after the general shearing. This, achieved with the aid of Lord Hawkesbury, was the last of many small details which he had been able to modify. On 18 June 1788 the Bill passed its Third Reading by a majority of 24 votes to 9 to enter the statutes as Act 28 Geo. III, c.38 thereby firmly confining the sheep, the wool clip and the woollen manufactures of Great Britain behind a protectionist barrier for the next 36 years. This was due to the illusion that English wool enjoyed a superiority that condemned foreign cloth manufacturers to a lower status if the English staple were denied to them. Only the fine short wool of Spain was seen as the exception necessary to the commercial well-being of the West Country broadcloth trade. But Spain had, for more than 400 years, kept a similar guard on this prized resource, only permitting its export as washed fleeces, subject to duty, but maintaining a strict embargo on the export of the small mysterious sheep that grew it. The long controversy from 1781 to 1788 over English wool and English sheep had raised attractive issues to the man who was now beginning to think clearly as a scientific biologist in his view of agriculture and its natural products. His small adventure in animal breeding at Spring Grove was opening new vistas to him in the matter of improved wool production. His researches associated with the Wool Bill of 1788 had broadened the base of his technical and economic understanding of the wool industries of Europe at large. His apprenticeship was over and, even as the Bill passed into legislation, he was already engaged in an enterprise that would extend the boundaries of his influence in this field from a county to a national scale.

III

Although Banks and the King were in frequent conversation about affairs in the

Botanic Garden at Kew it is certain that the subject of sheep and, more particularly now, of wool was also discussed. It is not at all unlikely therefore that about mid-January 1787 the subject should occur as the King and Colonel Robert Fulke Greville, his equerry, strolled through Richmond Gardens to inspect the Wiltshire flock at the King's Marsh Gate Farm. Robert Greville, the younger brother of Charles, was already in the Banksian circle and a friendly link between it and the Court. Banks had recently been made more fully aware of the success of the Spanish fine-woolled sheep in the flocks of the Elector of Saxony in the account by Georg Stumpf in his *Versuch einer pragmatischen der Schaferereien in Spanien, und der Spanischen in Sachsen* of 1785, a topic then active in Banks's correspondence with Lord Sheffield. According to Greville the story of the Spanish fine wool grown so well in Saxony was new to the King. It was a new twist also in Banks's wool investigations abroad but he was hotly following the trail. According to Greville, the King was impressed with his account

> ... & having paused upon it a little in fixed consideration, His Majesty asked Me if some Spanish Sheep might not be procured & brought into this Country. I readily replied that I thought that they might but that I was not prepared at once to decide by what means ... His Majesty then commanded me to give further consideration on the means most advisable & to report the result to Him, the next time He took his Ride ...

A few days later Greville told the King of his consultation with Banks who had immediately offered his services 'could they be thought at all useful'. In Greville's words

> ... The King instantly replied 'Sir Joseph Banks is just the Man. Tell Him from Me that I thank Him, & that his assistance will be most welcome'.

Banks was immediately called to an interview with the King on the subject '. . . & the speculation was instantly and carefully begun'. So by the last week of January 1787, the process of gathering His Majesty's flock of Spanish Merinos commenced but in as much secrecy as possible, under the name of Sir Joseph Banks not that of the King.

With practical directness Banks opened this business with two enquiries through diplomatic channels. His first was to Mr Robert Walpole, British Ambassador at Lisbon, sent in the official pouch by Evan Nepean. He enquired whether sheep might be got during the winter while the Spanish *cabanas* of 'the Famous Merino breed' were in Estramadura. If so Banks was prepared to send a shepherd at his own expense to bring them home and if necessary to go with the buyer to ensure 'that the Finest only are procurd'. His second, on 12 March 1787, was directed to Morton Eden, the British envoy to the Elector of Saxony at Dresden. With seven leading questions the sting was in the last:

> 7. Are the Spanish sheep so defended that it would be impossible to procure any or could a score be procurd for a handsome price & driven to a Place from whence they might be sent here.

Banks gave the 'long & very sensible answer' to this to the King who did not return it. So the Saxony gambit yielded nothing. The Lisbon approach however, after a silence of a year, suddenly yielded three sheep bluntly announced in the letter of a sea captain, Michael Firth of the *Betsy* off Dover on 4 March 1788:

> I have got for you 2 Yews & one Ram of the best Spanesh Breed & if you Like them you May Have More of the same sorte the next season as the Spanish Contrabandays Can get me any quantity I want . . .

These were the first Spanish fine-woolled sheep to enter England direct from Spain. On 4 April the King and Banks viewed them together at Kew, a date that Banks later marked as the true beginning of the Merino in England and the birthday of His Majesty's Spanish flock. He rated the ram and one ewe as very fine and altogether excellent, the other ewe slightly inferior. The King was delighted and ordered Banks to pay Michael Firth a gratuity of 20 guineas. From this 'the Lisbon Plan' grew over the next five years to yield a total of 10 rams and 66 ewes, gathered 'by gradual means' through the agency of Thomas March and Company of Lisbon.

'The Bilbao Plan', attempted through Evan Nepean's correspondence with British merchants at Bilbao and Oporto, when the Spanish sheep were on their northern summer pastures in Old Castile yielded almost nothing – 4 rams and 7 ewes in the two years of its operation to the end of 1789. The first to arrive, a ram lamb on 28 June 1787, was a hairy travesty of the breed whose appearance, combined with the discouraging reports sent from Spain by Nepean's merchant collaborators, cast a gloom over that summer's meetings at Kew between the King and Banks. But the French connection, in the person of Broussonet, was more optimistic.

On 2 April 1787 Broussonet told Banks that he could have eight or ten sheep as fine as his Spring Grove pair but six weeks later the number available was uncertain. Daubenton, from whom these sheep were to come, seems to have vacillated on the subject until the autumn. Then early in December, soon after Arthur Young's return from France, Banks heard that a small flock under the care of the French shepherd Villard was approaching Calais. On 18 December he wrote to Louis Mouron, merchant of Calais and owner of Channel packet boats, about arrangements for their transit through the port. At the same time he alerted John Walcot, agent for HM Packet Boats at Dover, to prepare for their reception. On 30 December Mouron reported to Banks the arrival of 43 sheep at Calais, that Villard was willing to cross to England with them, but that a rest of a few days for the foot-weary little flock was necessary. On 4 January 1788 Mouron shipped on board the *Union* packet, Captain Sutton 42 ewes and 4 lambs newly born, which reached Dover at nine p.m. on 5 January. After resting for another four days they set out for London under the care of Villard, joined now by a Romney Marsh drover, Thomas Winstone, with a tilted cart on hand to assist if necessary as the roads were bad and many of the ewes were heavy in lamb.

On 15 January the flock arrived at Kew Green to be dubbed by Banks as 'Dr. Broussonet's Flock' though he later identified it as 'Daubenton's Flock'. Its story had been a long one and its composition was mixed. Villard had started his journey in Provence with 2 rams and 12 ewes from the presumptive Spanish flock of the Baron de la Tour d'Aigue north of Aix. Travelling along the Rhône valley he added 3 rams and 22 more ewes from Daubenton's flock at Montbard. Finally he took up 5 ewes from the École Vétérinaire Royale at Alfort to make up a flock of 5 rams and 39 ewes.

Only two ewes died on the way, a small loss in a journey of 700 miles by road and sea. With 6 lambs added en route the flock to reach Kew Green was 48. The total cost was £73.13s.9d. for the sheep themselves and the travelling expenses of Villard, all paid for the time being by Banks. However only the 3 rams and 12 ewes from Daubenton's flock could be rated as 'real Spanish'. The others were *métis*, that is, cross-bred or grade Spanish fine-wools. Such was the genesis of the royal flock at Kew and Richmond which was to be the abiding care of Banks for another 25 years.

IV

Early in 1785 James Edward Smith had unpacked the collections and library of the elder Linnaeus at No. 14 Paradise Row, Chelsea, with the help of Sir Joseph Banks and Jonas Dryander. In March the Revd Dr Samuel Goodenough had been elected to membership of the Society for Promoting Natural History at a meeting when Smith was in the chair. Goodenough, the older man, had been a contemporary of Banks's at Christ Church and shared his abiding interest in botany. It is not surprising that the notion of a new society should evolve within the next 18 months among these men as they studied and discussed the relics of the sage Linnaeus now deposited among them in Chelsea. Something was evidently wanted to replace the constipated proceedings of the Society for Promoting Natural History and before Smith set out on his Continental tour in June 1786 both he and Goodenough had discussed the idea of a 'Linnaean Society' with Banks. The idea was kept simmering in Smith's letters to Soho Square as he travelled through Holland, France and Italy. Goodenough added his own warming enthusiasm in letters to Smith and in conversation with Banks who, while in support of the plan, could not promise to be an active member. It was perhaps enough to invoke his duties to the Royal Society but he was aware that other competing and, to his academic friends unknown, pressures were rising to limit his time. He seems to have had faith in the abilities of Smith and Goodenough, and content to see Jonas Dryander working with them.

Smith returned to London in the first week of November 1787 and in February 1788 moved from Paradise Row to No. 12 Great Marlborough Street. On 26 February 1788, at the Marlborough Coffee House nearby, the inaugural 'Fellows Meeting' of the 'Linnaean Society' was held with its original seven – Smith, Goodenough, Thomas Marsham, Jonas Dryander, James Dickson, John Beckwith, and John Swainson. At this meeting Smith was appointed President, Goodenough, Treasurer and Marsham, Secretary, with Dryander as Honorary Librarian, and these four are the only original Fellows named in the Charter of 26 March 1802 creating 'The Linnean Society of London' as it is known (and spelled) now. When Smith deserted the Society and left London for Norwich with the Linnaean collections in 1796 he had suggested that Dryander succeed him as President but the quiet Swede refused, agreeing only to remain as a 'perpetual' Vice-President. As such he usually presided until his death in 1810 during Smith's frequent absences.

Banks, however, remained an honorary member from the beginning through all the changing circumstances of the Society, always supportive but never an executive member, feeding the library with donations from his own through Dryander. In the Linnean Society there emerged the first scientific society during Banks's Presidency of the Royal Society whose activities impinged on the fields covered in the *Philosophical Transactions* which had always been a vehicle for contributions under the broad heading of 'natural history'. Now a new society, with a constitution, office-bearers, and, implicitly, a new scientific journal to express the interests of its members, had been launched. Far from obstructing its rise Banks steadily supported it and was at all times a friend and colleague of James Edward Smith and Samuel Goodenough, even though at times their special interests may have conflicted with his own.

V

Natural history in all its forms lay at the root of Banks's first direct association with maritime discovery. The wide Pacific stimulated his geographic curiosity; Asia and the Far East became areas of attention as he interested himself in the activities of the East India Company; Africa on whose southern tip he had so briefly touched in 1771, bore for him the same intellectual challenge as those he had found in the antipodes under the names of New Holland and New South Wales; Chelsea had witnessed the conception of the Linnean Society; Pall Mall in the same year was to be the base for a more esoteric group devoted to geographic enquiry. There was logic in the association of Banks with both.

A month of convalescence at the Cape on the return of the *Endeavour* was all that Banks had seen of Africa, but he had pursued his interest in that mysterious land mass during his visit to Holland in 1773 and kept it alive in his Dutch correspondence. He had gained further insight through his relations with Francis Masson on both his visits. His knowledge had been enlarged through his engagement, with others, of Henry Smeathman for several years on the tropical West Coast and William Brass as botanical collectors. His concern with the voyage of HMS *Nautilus* and the collections of Anton Hove in 1785 only served to emphasize the great void in European knowledge of the 'dark Continent'. A new turn had now been taken with the same HMS *Nautilus* on the ill-judged mission to Sierra Leone, a site proposed by Henry Smeathman, in a tragic first attempt at colonization with liberated slaves by the London Committee 'for relieving the black poor' in 1787. Banks was in touch with this expedition both as a botanist and a philanthropist as his sympathies lay with the rising tide of public concern for the abolition of slavery. Banks had by now become a centre about whom revolved a group of men not unlike himself that was to be found in that characteristic eighteenth-century social coterie, the Saturday's Club, which dined from time to time at St Alban's Tavern off Pall Mall. Of the 12 members who belonged, nine were present when it was resolved on Monday 9 June at an adjourned meeting

> That as no species of information is more ardently desired, or more generally useful, than that which improves the science of Geography, and as the vast continent of Africa, notwithstanding the efforts of the ancients, and the wishes of the moderns, is still in a great measure unexplored, the members of this Club do form themselves into an Association for promoting the discovery of the inland parts of that quarter of the world: . . .

From this Banks emerged as one of a committee of five chosen by ballot – Henry Beaufoy, MP, FRS as Secretary; Banks as Treasurer; Lord Rawdon, FRS, the Bishop

241

of Llandaff, FRS, and Andrew Stuart, MP as assisting members. The committee was entrusted with the preparation of the rules of the new institution, the selection of the persons to be sent on expeditions of discovery to the interior of Africa, the conduct of the correspondence and the management of the funds. But the committee was enjoined not to disclose, except to members of the Association, 'such intelligence as they shall, from time to time, receive from the persons who shall be sent out on the business of discovery'. Moreover the committee was only to communicate to the members 'such parts of the said intelligence, as in the opinion of the committee, may, without endangering the object of the Association, be made public . . .' This was in fact a recognition not only of the international rivalries but also of the dangers implicit from the indigenous Muslims. So charged, the committee set about its work and from Pall Mall the centre of executive action moved to 32 Soho Square where it remained for the next 25 years.

On Friday 13 June 1788 the committee which met consisted of Banks and Beaufoy, Lord Rawdon and Andrew Stuart. Banks was appointed to approach Lord Sydney, the Home Secretary, to solicit the services of Simon Lucas, then an oriental interpreter at the Court of St James's, 'for the purposes of exploring the Interior parts of Africa' from Tripoli into the Fezzan. On Tuesday 17 June Banks reported to the same committee that he had seen Lord Sydney who had promised to submit their request 'to his Majesty's pleasure'. Meanwhile the committee approved in principle a sum not to exceed £250 for the use of Lucas on the journey should the King release him. This fund was to be found by an advance of 50 guineas from each member of the committee, exclusive of his subscription of five guineas, to be paid into the hands of the Treasurer. Proposals were also received from John Ledyard, the marine corporal of Cook's last voyage, 'for traversing the Continent of Africa'. Ledyard, with money supplied by Banks, had set off in 1785 to cross northern Europe and Siberia to Kamschatka with the intention of crossing what is now Canada overland from the west coast. Destitute in St Petersburg he drew 20 guineas in a bill on Banks and set off with a party carrying stores to the expedition that Joseph Billings, another Cook veteran, was leading to north-east Russia in the service of the Empress. He met Billings at Yakutz but was arrested by the Russians and transported back to the border of Poland from where he found his way to Konigsberg. Here he drew another bill on Banks's name for five guineas and so returned to England where he immediately waited on his benefactor. Banks passed him on as a recruit to African exploration to the care of Beaufoy who advanced him 30 guineas on behalf of the Association.

On Saturday 21 June seven members of the African Association met at St Alban's Tavern to approve two rules 'for the good government of the Institution' and to admit 15 new members. Then on Thursday 26 June Banks and Beaufoy as an executive duo resolved that Ledyard should

> . . . proceed with all possible despatch, by the way of Marseilles and Cairo to Mecca; that from thence (unless insuperable difficulties shall occur) he shall cross the Red Sea, and taking the rout of Nubia, shall traverse the Continent of Africa, as nearly as possible in the direction of the Niger, and with the Towns and Countries on its borders, he shall endeavour to make himself acquainted – and that he shall return to Britain by the way of any of the European Settlements on the Western Coast . . .

This committee of two further required the Treasurer to pay Ledyard 70 guineas in addition to the 30 already advanced. The Secretary was instructed to write to Mr Baldwin, the British Consul at Cairo, asking him to furnish Ledyard with another 50 pounds and more if necessary up to 80, being

> ... persuaded, that in such an Undertaking Poverty is a better protection than Wealth, and that Mr. Ledyard's address will be much more effectual than money, to open to him a passage to the Interior of Africa ...

Four days later, on Monday 30 June 1788, John Ledyard set out from London reaching Cairo on 19 August. By the end of November he was dead, either from dysentery or an excessive dose of tartar emetic or from a combination of both, and 'decently interred' in the neighbourhood of Cairo. The Association's first mission had failed but a pattern had been set and an objective defined which it would pursue for another 30 years with persistence and a steady mortality among its young 'missionaries'.

Almost as abortive but less disastrous was the mission of Simon Lucas whose departure was more leisurely and who did not reach Tripoli until 25 October 1788. At first appearance Lucas would seem to have been a more likely agent of the Association, for from his early youth he had been a slave among the Moroccans and later spent 16 years as a vice-consul at Tripoli. He knew Arabic and the local customs. But the country south of Tripoli was disturbed with Arab tribesmen in revolt and it was not until 1 February 1789 that Lucas could make a tentative foray in a caravan with two sherifs from Tripoli. But a short way from the coast they were stopped by the Governor because he judged the desert crossing to be unsafe. Lucas returned to England on 26 July 1789 his mission unfulfilled though he had gleaned at second-hand useful intelligence for future years which he plotted on a map of the Fezzan with more accuracy than had been available before.

Such were the opening moves in the affairs of the Association for promoting the discovery of the interior regions of Africa. Under the impetus primarily of Banks it was sustained on the pattern of his management mainly from the meetings in his house for the first 20 years of its eminently economical operation as an instrument of geographical exploration.

VI

As the last phase of the Wool Bill campaign was ending, a new and more exotic problem was thrust on Banks's attention by the Foreign Secretary, the Marquis of Carmarthen, in a letter of 29 May 1788 prompted by one just received from Mr P. Bond, British Consul at Philadelphia. The Foreign Secretary asked Banks

> ... how far He may consider the Importation of Grain from that part of North America liable to the Introduction of the destructive Insect of which that Grain is supposed to contain the Eggs.

Bond's letter of 22 April was a warning of impending shipments of American grain from the middle states where great damage had been wrought for several years among the crops 'by an insect called the Hessian fly'. This question found Banks, as he later confessed, 'utterly ignorant what insect it was that the americans meant by the Hessian fly' but thought it his duty to investigate a subject 'so pregnant with danger to his Country'. Thrust back on the resources of his library and the advice of entomologists like Thomas Marsham, the Secretary of the new Linnean Society, Banks worked with speed and delivered his reply on 4 June, believing that to be the day when the monthly despatches were sent to America. In his haste to meet this deadline he had – as he soon confessed – followed a false trail. From all the Americans of whom he had made enquiry he had conceived the insect to be the 'flying weevil' described by Colonel Landon Carter in the first volume of the *Transactions of the American Philosophical Society* in 1771. False trail or no, he pronounced the danger of such an introduction to be great and the general level of ignorance about such insects in England high. Caution dictated a prohibition on the entry of American wheat pending an investigation of the problem. But during the ensuing month some cargoes had reached Liverpool where they were impounded under an order-in-council. Petitioned for their release, the Privy Council sat on 4 July to hear the merchants' case and to consider the arguments concerning the validity of samples as against direct inspection of the cargo in the hold to determine the presence of insects. The meeting was adjourned to the following day and a letter sent to Banks requesting his attendance. So after a month of intense activity, bringing the African Association into the world and sending John Ledyard on his way, Banks was brought roughly back to the world of natural history – with a difference.

At one o'clock on Saturday 5 July in the Council Chamber at Whitehall he faced an impressive array of the Lords of His Majesty's most Honourable Privy Council: the Prime Minister, Pitt; the Lord Chancellor, Lord Thurlow; the Foreign Secretary, the Marquis of Carmarthen; the Home Secretary, Thomas Townshend, not yet Lord Sydney; the Lord Privy Seal, the Duke of Rutland; the Master-General of the Ordnance, the Duke of Richmond; Henry Dundas as a member of the Committee for Trade and Foreign Plantations; and the Master of the Rolls. Here it was agreed that Banks should prepare his opinion of a method of inspection by the Commissioners of His Majesty's Customs suitable for application at the ports to the cargoes of grain from America. At this meeting Banks corrected his earlier misjudgement of the insect and reported that he had that very morning inspected two samples of grain from the impounded cargoes at Liverpool, in one of which the suspected fly was present. Then, on Sunday 6 July, he prepared his proposal for the testing of the grain cargoes by a process of sampling. To this on Tuesday 8 July he added a further statement on the Hessian fly with an assessment of the written accounts from America. On 12 July William Smith and William Lintott, as customs commissioners at Southampton, supervised an examination by Banks's method of the cargoes of wheat on board the Ships *Mary* and *Jenny* from New York. The specimens obtained were sent by Stephen Cottrell, Clerk of the Privy Council, at Pitt's request on 15 July to Banks for an opinion. This he gave on 17 July, pronouncing the cargoes free of suspicion and recommending their release from quarantine. At this point Banks thought it appropriate to summarize his views and on 24 July he presented them as a paper of some 3500 words to the Privy Council. He set out the important features of the life history both of the 'flying weevil' and the Hessian fly as insects 'capable of considerably diminishing the quantity of bread corn produced' whose introduction 'should be considered as a calamity of much more extensive and fatal consequences than the admission of the plague or the murrain'. He concluded

... that in a matter of such serious consequences to the prosperity of Great Britain, a positive proof of danger is not requisite on the contrary, a positive proof that no danger whatever exists should be exacted ...

In the light of this, the Privy Council, on 5 August, made an order 'not to permit the Entry of any Wheat, which, upon Inspection, shall have been found to have been infected, but that it might be expedient for Government to purchase such Cargoes'. The next day, as it happened, the Customs officers at Bristol sampled the cargo of the *Coalition*, John Atkinson, master, from Virginia. On 8 August the samples were examined by Banks at Soho Square, found to be infested with numbers of the 'flying weevil', and duly denied entry.

The problem of American wheat importations pursued Banks to Revesby Abbey through the autumn and all through the winter in London. On 31 August Banks summed up the situation to John Lloyd:

The business of American Wheat which you enquire after has no immediate connexion with the dearness or cheapness of that article or with the good or bad conduct of the Liverpool merchants it is only that two species of Insects infest the wheat of America & are unknown here consequently if Either or both should be imported we shall be dreadfull sufferers The business was referred to me by the Sec[retary] of State & since by the Privy Council & I have reported that as long as Wheat is allowed to be imported from parts of the united States where this insect is Found there will be danger of its being brought here with it in Consequence of this report no wheat which is suspected of having been infected with either insect is admitted to Entry & there is now a very large Quantity 3/4th. at least of what they have imported under that predicament at Liverpool.

On 3 September Dryander sent Banks a letter with a box containing three insects for identification but on 22 October he replied to William Fawkener at the Privy Council Office pleading that he did not have the proper reference books at Revesby Abbey to confirm his diagnosis. These were insects sent by the customs officers at Exeter which greatly resembled the Hessian fly though he could not be finally sure. However he counselled precautionary kiln-drying of the wheat and fumigation with brimstone of all the granaries where any of it had been stored. He sent this opinion south by express as urgent action seemed to be required.

Meanwhile a wide-ranging correspondence had been instituted through various channels, diplomatic, commercial and academic, in Europe and the United States, gathered in largely by the Foreign Office and placed in Banks's hands for assessment. On 2 March 1789 he presented these findings in the form of a report to Lord Carmarthen, supplementing it with a short appendix on 27 April. This was his last report to the Privy Council and, as he noted, 'in consequence of which the business was removed to Parliament'. But the correspondence, particularly from American sources, extended over the summer of 1789 with the subject still alive in 1792. Altogether the cargoes of some 34 vessels came under Banks's scrutiny during the year of his active investigations, most of them at Liverpool. In the process a great deal of information was gathered about the history of wheat cultivation in America and the trade with Britain from as early as 1697, when records began. There remained the true identity, life history and nature of the depredations of the Hessian fly to be investigated. It had set alight a flare of interest in economic entomology and concentrated the attention of British natural historians on the need for greater precision in the systematics and diagnoses presented. The *Transactions of the Linnean Society* soon carried the evidence of this but earlier Arthur Young in his *Annals of Agriculture*, volume 11 for 1789, had presented the 'Proceedings of His Majesty's Most Honourable Privy Council, and Information Received, Respecting an Insect Supposed to Infest the Wheat of the Territories of the United States of America'. Young noted in the same volume how much

> ... has been owing to the indefatigable exertions of Sir Joseph Banks, P.R.S. to whom his country (should we escape the contagion) will be obliged for its security.

VII

In November 1787 Banks had been struck with his first short sharp fit of the gout at the end of a year of rising pressures. Now in October 1788, harried by the Privy Council, even at Revesby Abbey, on the insect infestations of American wheat cargoes and by the East India Company and Lord Hawkesbury on matters relating to tea culture, cochineal and cotton, Banks suffered his second and more protracted gouty episode which clung to him for more than two months. It was in this painful and uncertain state that Banks returned to London in the first week of November to receive news of the serious change in the King's health that had occurred on Wednesday 5 November. For several days Banks was out of London, visiting his property in Sussex, and Dorothea Banks wrote to him on 9 and 10 November on the fluctuating reports from Windsor on the King's condition received from George Nicol and James Lind. Back in London for the first meeting of the new Council of the Royal Society on Thursday 13 November, he received a sheaf of papers from Thomas Morton, Secretary of the East India Company, calling for an opinion on a botanic garden for Calcutta and a proposal for a publication on the natural history of India by Patrick Russell. At the same time he was being pressed by William Pitt to take his tenure as High Sheriff of Lincolnshire. In despair he appealed to Lord Hawkesbury on 18 November to see Pitt and obtain for him exemption from this office for the time being pleading, with good cause, the sustained pressure of scientific business confining him to London. There seems to have been little difficulty about this as such a detail paled in the political confusion arising from the King's illness and his removal from Windsor Castle to the White House at Kew on 29 November. Here, during December, the King passed through the most distressful and violent phase of his mysterious disorder with Robert Fulke Greville as the sole equerry in attendance while Banks at Soho Square continued in the agonies of gout.

Eventually, on 27 December, as Banks delivered to William Devaynes his report on the possibilities for tea culture in India, Greville from Kew sent him in a message from the senior Dr Willis himself the first news of a real improvement in the royal patient, adding however – 'Outward & Visible signs to us ignorant Spectators do not flatter much'. Banks himself had earlier formed a depressing view of the King's general state. To Sir William Hamilton at Naples he had written on 28 November

George III in Windsor uniform on one of the Castle terraces, 1807. Painting by Peter Stroehling.

... his Physicians appear to have given over all hopes of his being re established and the two parties who have for this Fortnight Past been reporting in absolute contradiction to each other on the probability of recovery are more acrimonious than I ever remember them to have been ...
Sheridan who has of late enjoyd more of the Prince's Favor & Fox who in consequence of Mrs. Fitzherbert has less of it Feel awkward. Fox came from Turin

247

in 9 days & has of course been out of the way at the Commencement of these bad
Times

... [The] R[oyal] Soc[iety] however goes on well & will stand unmovd amid the
Shock of Contending Politicians but when she will get so good a Patron as the
Last I confess I do not Ever hope ...

But now the long winter gloom seemed to be lifting. Relieved of his gout, Banks, on
Saturday 17 January, had gone to Kew to inspect the new flock of Spanish Merinos
grazing there. Robert Greville had met him on his arrival and given him a full account
of the King's condition. However on his walk through the flock Banks met the senior
Doctor Willis who cheerfully stated 'He is charmingly, & is now as Mild as Milk',
adding that one of the King's pages that morning had reported finding His Majesty
more 'sensible' than he had ever seen him. Banks now swung to a premature
optimism, earning a reproof from Greville who deplored the indiscretion of
spreading such news. And yet Greville was prepared to concede that the King had
been morely nearly normal that day than at any time since the disorder had begun.

At last on 6 February the King had so far recovered that, on his second walk
abroad he went to the Botanic Garden and saw William Aiton with whom 'He
conversed & talked of Sir Joseph Banks who He wished much to see'. This was
arranged to happen on the following day, as if by accident, at the King's Marsh Gate
Farm. From then on Banks played a useful part in the King's slow convalescence as
one of the few people whom the physicians would allow him to see. In one such walk
together on 21 February the King and his devoted commoner strolled for three hours
from the Exotic Garden – soon to receive the botanical first-fruits from the settlement
at Sydney Cove – through the grazing grounds of the Spanish fine-wool flock and
across the London road to the Marsh Gate farm buildings. From this long period
together, Banks formed the impression that the King 'was very near right' which
pleasantly surprised Greville, who again warned Banks about the political risks in too
much gossip on the subject. Banks was well aware of this though two days later on
23 February he conveyed his optimism to Dr James Lind at Windsor, on whose
discretion he could trust:

> ... I was sent for on Saturday [21 February] as usual and attended in the Gardens
> and Farm for three hours, during all which time he gave his orders as usual, and
> talked to me on a variety of subjects without once uttering a weak or foolish
> sentence.
>
> In bodily health he is certainly improved – he is lighter by about 15 lb. than he
> was – he is more agile, and walks as firm as ever he did. We did not walk less than
> four miles in the garden and adjoining country.
>
> I have no doubt that he is able at this moment to resume the reins of
> Government, but he will not do it for some time, lest too much exertion of mind
> might endanger a relapse.

Master and subject were both in a fair way toward recovering their former active
health after a bad autumn and winter. Almost daily now they walked together by the
river and through the gardens and farm, and by early March it was apparent that the
King was almost a whole man again. A prayer of thanksgiving was read in all the
churches on 1 March proclaiming the King's recovery and on 4 March Robert

Greville was relieved by Colonel Robert Manners from his long and exhausting
service in the White House at Kew. Normality seemed to have returned as the King,
on 14 March, with a large company of gentlemen, rode back to Windsor Castle and
London responded with the ecstatic explosion of 40 guineas' worth of fireworks.

VIII

When the first fascicule of L'Héritier's *Sertum Anglicum* . . . appeared in January 1789,
the first ships from the settlement ostensibly established at Botany Bay were on their
passage home. In Tahiti the *Bounty* was already laden with its bread-fruit and ready
to sail. But at 32 Soho Square, the intellectual centre from which so much in all three

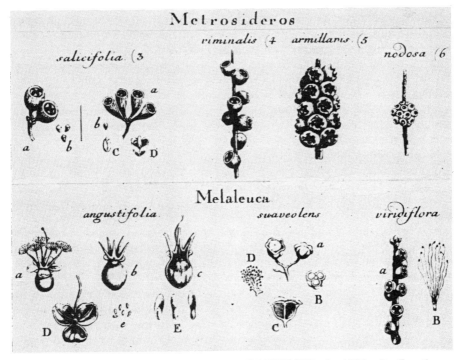

Figures from Plates XXIV and XXV in GAERTNER, J., 1788, *De Fructibus et
Seminibus Plantarum*. The specimens are 'ex herbario Banksiano' among many others
given by Banks during Gaertner's visit in 1787.
From left to right above:
Metrosideros salicifolia = *Eucalyptus crebra* F. Mueller (Bay of Inlets); M. viminalis =
Callistemon viminalis (Solander ex Gaertner) G. Don, holotype, (Endeavour River); M.
armillaris = *Melaleuca armillaris* Smith (Botany Bay); M. nodosa = *Melaleuca nodosa*
(Solander ex Gaertner) Smith (Botany Bay).
From left to right below:
Melaleuca angustifolia = *Melaleuca angustifolia* Gaertner (Endeavour River); M.
suaveolens = *Tristania suaveolens* (Solander ex Gaertner) Smith (Endeavour River);
M. viridiflora = *Melaleuca viridiflora* Solander ex Gaertner, holotype, (Endeavour
River).

249

enterprises had sprung, there was a pause as the King's illness and the political uncertainties brought the shadow of a Regency nearer. In this 'melancholy situation of affairs', as Banks described it, work was not wholly at a standstill. In the engravers' room Daniel Mackenzie had been quietly engaged in preparing the copper plates of Kaempfer's Japanese drawings, prints from which Banks hoped soon to be able to send to Antoine de Jussieu. In the herbarium and in the library Dryander was spending much time on the forthcoming 'Hortus Kewensis', the first proof sheets of which he had sent to L'Héritier in July 1788. Drawings for 10 of the 13 plates to appear in that work, at the expense of Banks, had already been engraved by Mackenzie – from Ehret 5; Sowerby 3; J. F. Miller 2 – in particular the *Strelitzia reginae* Ait. and *Phaius tancarvilliae* (L'Hérit.) Blume as they are today. There was a steady cross-fertilization between the *Sertum* . . . and the *Hortus* . . . as Dryander and L'Héritier communicated over details and Banks organized arrangements with James Sowerby, settled accounts on L'Héritier's behalf with the draftsman, and engaged the attention of English reviewers with the new French work. In return the Banksian library benefited greatly by L'Héritier's enthusiasm as an agent in Paris seeking and sending catalogues and desiderata. The threatening undertones of 1788 had already diverted many of Banks's French correspondents and friends into political activities which set botanical interests to one side. A copy of Jussieu's *Genera Plantarum* was brought to Soho Square by L'Héritier in September 1789 where it joined Johann Gaertner's *De Fructibus et Seminibus Plantarum* as the two most important and stimulating acquisitions of that year.

In the mounting confusion of French affairs Pierre Broussonet remained for Banks a steady source of information. On 1 January 1789 he told Banks that among the savants in France science was now subordinate to politics. By the spring he had nothing of interest to report from the Académie such was the decline in active science but he reminded Banks of his promise to send a kangaroo should one become available from New Holland and asked for news of La Pérouse. On 23 April he pressed Banks further on both subjects and on 1 May Banks replied, confirming his promise about the kangaroo of which live specimens were evidently on the way. Then, by whatever ship it came, Banks in June sent the first living kangaroo to France. On 1 July Broussonet reported its arrival at Dieppe and on 29 July its arrival in Paris. In this letter of grateful acknowledgement Broussonet introduced its bearer, Floret, a German who, he said, could give Banks an account of what had occurred since Louis XVI on 11 July had dismissed Jacques Necker.

The Bastille had fallen on 14 July and on 18 July Bertier de Sauvigny was arrested. On 22 July Broussonet, an elected member of the National Assembly, was called to the Hôtel de Ville. There he saw Bertier struck down and his mutilated body dragged through the streets of Paris. Thereafter Broussonet himself was in frequent peril even as a member of the Assembly and one charged with the provisioning of Paris. Only three years remained before he would leave France as a refugee from the Terror and as an exile. Meanwhile he continued as a channel of valuable information and introduced to Banks various French emigrés who found a safe haven and in some cases a new life opened for them through Soho Square.

In November 1789 the first edition of *Hortus Kewensis*, in its three volumes, was published under the name of William Aiton, gardener to His Majesty in the Royal Botanic Garden at Kew. This was much more than a compendium of the species cultivated at Kew and much more than William Aiton, honest Scot and excellent gardener though he was, could have put together and seen through the press. In all its essentials it was a product of the organization centred at Soho Square. Of this Jonas Dryander was the important instrument. He had enjoyed over four years of direct working association with Daniel Solander in the Banks herbarium and was the custodian of the library. It is also clear that from 18 August 1777, when Banks first introduced him to the Royal Botanic Garden at Kew, Dryander was his field worker among all the important gardens of the Home counties as well as the commercial nurseries, observing, collecting and classifying, especially in the months of flowering. This form of outside activity was especially notable in the years up to and during 1789. By then he had covered, apparently, every major garden in the metropolis and many in the neighbouring counties, including also the Botanic Garden at Oxford under John Sibthorp and R. A. Salisbury's at Chapel Allerton near Leeds. Undoubtedly his most frequent visits were to James Lee at The Vineyard, to the Royal Botanic Garden at Kew and to Spring Grove and Chelsea. It is not surprising therefore that the specimens on which the *Hortus Kewensis* was founded are still to be seen in the Banksian herbarium now incorporated with the General Herbarium in the British Museum (Natural History). This gathering process clearly began with Banks and Solander, as the evidence of the surviving 'Day Book' shows, but the accumulated annotations on the mounting sheets of the specimens and the draft and proofs of the *Hortus* . . . in Dryander's neat script underline the long continuity of his association with the publication. There is one explicit comment by Banks in his letter to Olof Swartz of 30 September 1788:

> . . . Dryander works always at Aitons Hortus Kewensis & makes good Progress I hope it will be out in the spring with some plates & two volumes 8vo . . .

Whatever the origins of the first edition of *Hortus Kewensis* in the lifetime of Solander on whose manuscript diagnoses so much at first depended, the notion of a formal publication almost certainly developed later. This was probably accelerated by the advent of L'Héritier as a correspondent when, in February 1783, he sought the advice of Banks after Broussonet's introduction to him. His presence at Soho Square for so long with Pierre Redouté and James Sowerby as his artists during the Dombey affair in 1786-7 and after the first fascicules of his *Stirpes novae* had appeared in 1785, seems to have provided the final stimulus needed to establish a record of the garden species under cultivation in Britain. This seems clear from the text of Banks's letter to L'Héritier on 29 April 1788:

> . . . We have a project here which I fancy will be speedily put into execution, to publish the Plants as they flower at Kew in Numbers, which mode we prefer to any other; as, by that means, the publication will go on as long as it succeeds, and consequently an opportunity remains of inserting new things very soon after their first appearance. As I wish every possible success to your Fasciculi, I mean to conduct it with every attention to you; and as you in your stay here last summer took drawings of most of our best Plants, to interfere as little as is in my power with your publication of them. As the work is intended to be ultimately compleat, we shall be obliged probably some time or other to publish many of those you have got; but we may as we mean as seldom as possible to delay our figure of a plant till a considerable time after you have published yours; provided you do not

delay too long, that is for several years, your publication of them. To enable me to manage this I must request you to put me in possession of a list of your drawings made in the English Gardens, that I may not inadvertently interfere with you . . .

There is a certain affinity in the idea propounded here with the intentions of William Curtis and *The Botanical Magazine* of which the first part had been published in February 1787. L'Héritier would have seen the first plates and the enthusiasm with which they were received during his English visit when James Sowerby was the artistic bridge between himself and that publication. Was Banks now more than hinting at another project of the same kind – or was he also rising in defence of Curtis as a vigorous newcomer to botanical illustration? Be that as it may, Banks received the following month the list from L'Héritier and in due time Dryander was given the Frenchman's diagnoses, some at least of which were inserted verbatim in the published *Hortus Kewensis*. That such a work was in contemplation seems to have become generally known in 1787. James Edward Smith wrote from Naples on 5 October 1787 to Banks with the remark

> . . . I am very glad to hear of the publication of Hortus Kewensis that England may put in some claim to her own property . . .

and L'Héritier himself was certainly well aware of what was in hand at 32 Soho Square. But the letter to L'Héritier from Banks, though it referred to a supplementary plan of which the only example achieved was Franz Bauer's *Delineation of Exotic Plants* . . . in 1796, had certainly a wider purpose and a greater urgency than had previously been apparent at Soho Square. Indeed Banks had elsewhere expressed his intentions about the publications as arising from his sense of what was due to the generosity of the King and the dedication of his servant William Aiton in developing the Royal Botanic Garden at Kew.

CHAPTER 12

DISCOVERY SHIPS AND SPANISH SHEEP
1785–1791

Almost two years had passed since Governor Phillip and his motley fleet had left home waters. Now in April 1789 the first despatches to the Home Department and the first private letters to Banks had arrived reporting a successful landing but a less than cheerful outlook for the settlement itself. Indeed Banks had put his impression grimly to Broussonet on 1 May:

> ... The accounts we have of Botany Bay are so little Favorable as to fertility or comfortable Colonisation that some have actually refusd their Pardons on the Condition of going there. I suppose when it comes nearer the Ceremony of hanging that they will repent at Present they remain unmovd & prefer death to banishment there ...

This element of realism however had not deterred him from making an early proposal to Evan Nepean on 27 April that HMS *Guardian*, already being commissioned for service in the South Seas, should be fitted in a manner similar to the *Bounty* for the transport of plants home to the Royal Botanic Garden at Kew. But from letters to him and his study of the official reports from Phillip to Lord Sydney and Evan Nepean he knew that there was more to be done than pursuing botanical curiosities.

William Wyndham Grenville succeeded Lord Sydney at the Home Department on Friday 5 June 1789. On Sunday 7 June Banks developed his proposal for the *Guardian*, in a letter which drew attention to the background of discussions he had already pursued, not only with Grenville but with others in various Government departments. In essence the plan was

> ... to send to the colony in New South Wales such trees and plants as are useful in food or physic, and cannot conveniently be propagated by seed in potts of earth ...

Banks had visited the *Guardian* only two days before and had found it a crowded ship with the cabin space bespoke. Accordingly he had proposed a new plan in the form of a special plant 'coach' or greenhouse on the quarterdeck. This he chalked out on the deck with the agreement of the Woolwich Navy Yard master-builder and the master of the *Guardian*. He had evidently done this in response to a suggestion from the commander, Lt Edward Riou, who had on 3 June invited Banks to Woolwich to consider the problem. This was in advance of official directions from the Admiralty, for it was not until Monday 8 June that Grenville wrote to the Lords Commissioners stating that Banks's letter had been laid before the King and that it was now His

Majesty's pleasure that the small coach for trees and plants should be erected – unless there were material objections. But there were none, for Riou, who had missed Banks on the Friday, wrote on 6 June with his approval and confidence that there would be no effect on the handling of the ship. By the middle of July the 'garden-house' had been built, filled with plants, and two gardeners from Kew charged with its care on the voyage. They were James Smith and George Austin; the former was brother to John Smith who was gardener to Banks at Spring Grove and much approved by Riou as a conscientious and capable man. This was evidently the reason that Banks had prepared and addressed to him in the first place the instructions for the care of the plants as well as the directions on the pattern of behaviour to be observed on the voyage and ultimately in the settlement. These orders were an adaptation of those he had framed for David Nelson on the *Bounty* and were admirably clear and to the point.

As the *Guardian* left the Thames for Spithead, Riou reported to Banks on the excellent state of the plants, promising to write frequently. At the same time he asked Banks to help him obtain a chronometer in which he had been so far unsuccessful. On 24 August he wrote again from Spithead in some concern over the accident in which Banks had been flung from his phaeton, commending the diligence of James Smith but still unable to give a sailing date. The plants which had been put on board on 5 July were in good order but one camomile plant had died. The *Guardian* was heavily laden with stores, more or less according to the needs which Phillip had defined, and, apart from Smith and Austin, carried eight others rated as superintendants of convicts and paid at the same rate of £40 a year. These included experienced farmers and 25 convicts selected as artificers and farm hands under their supervision.

On 29 September Riou reported from Tenerife the plants all well but that George Austin was 'a Lazy Dog' plagued with 'rheumatic gout'. The convicts, he said, were in Paradise compared with what they had been used to elsewhere. He complained also of naval parsimony in sending him only six spare panes of glass in case of accident to the greenhouse when he had in fact ordered a large quantity. On 10 December from the Cape he wrote a parting letter to Banks expecting to sail the next day for Port Jackson. He gave an account of the plants and of the livestock he had brought but no news of the transport *Lady Juliana*, his intended consort, which had left Portsmouth two weeks before him. He noted also the presence of American and French vessels at the Cape anxious to develop trade with New South Wales.

Two weeks later, on 24 December, the *Guardian* was wrecked on an iceberg some 1200 miles south-east of the Cape in latitude 44°S. Riou stayed with the vessel after sending off about 70 of the crew in the ship's boats. With the remainder of the crew and the convicts Riou succeeded in keeping the ship afloat and bringing it to False Bay for repair, arriving there on 21 February 1790. Except for nine survivors, those in the ship's boats were never seen again, and the *Guardian* itself, after the skill and heroism of its commander, was finally wrecked when it was driven ashore in one of the violent storms of that season. Of the 'garden-house' and its custodians, James Smith and George Austin no more is heard. Of the others, five superintendants and 20 convicts survived to be sent on to New South Wales in the *Lady Juliana* and succeeding transport. On Riou's recommendation the convicts were pardoned and given their freedom for the sterling service they had rendered in helping to bring the *Guardian* into False Bay.

Thus the colony at Sydney Cove was denied its vital supplies and Banks's second attempt to transport useful plants from one hemisphere to the other had failed. As the *Guardian* foundered on the shore at False Bay, William Bligh was on his passage home from Cape Town with his story of how the first expedition had been lost among the amatory reefs of Otaheite.

II

Bligh had written as assiduously to Banks as he had to the Admiralty from the *Bounty* at Tenerife, at sea in the tropics, and from the Cape of Good Hope in June 1788. The last of these letters had found Banks at Revesby Abbey and from there he sent the latest news on bread-fruit to Olof Swartz in Stockholm on 30 October 1788:

> ... The French have at an expence of £2000 Sterling in Freight brought a large Cargo of Spices & East India plants to their West Indies the bread fruit is among them but whether of a good or a bad sort I Know not I suspect it is from the East Indies where the good sort is not found.
>
> our Bread fruit ship has been beat back in attempting to pass Cape Horn but arrived at the Cape of Good hope in good Condition & proceeded from thence on her voyage we look for her return next summer ...

But the ensuing year was to bring no news of the *Bounty*; nothing from the East Indies, the Cape or St Helena, to which Banks had sent additional instructions for Bligh, and certainly nothing from the West Indies to announce the success of the voyage. As with La Pérouse, so also Bligh had disappeared into the silence of the South Pacific. Then early in 1790 came the despatches to the Admiralty and to Banks from Batavia as Bligh recounted the traumatic events of 1789. They recorded the failure of this latest voyage for 'the advancement of science, and the increase of knowledge' which, as he recorded later, had been 'the object of all the former voyages to the South Seas, undertaken by the command of his present majesty'. In those intervening 18 months the bread-fruit in plenty had been successfully gathered by Nelson and Brown at Tahiti, a sight that Bligh had 'looked at with delight' every day until the mutiny on 28 April 1789 had abruptly deprived him of this pleasure. Then had come the six weeks' ordeal of the open boat voyage north-west across the Pacific, the physical torture and brave command with brilliant navigation to reach Timor on 15 June. After two months of recuperation under Dutch hospitality at Koepang he sailed with a hired schooner on 20 August for Batavia which he reached on 1 October. From here, on 13 October, he sent Banks an extended account of the *Bounty* voyage, the mutiny and subsequent events before sailing for the Cape on the *Vlydte* packet three days later. On 16 December he arrived in Table Bay to learn that the *Guardian* had sailed for Port Jackson just one week before. Still aboard the *Vlydte*, with its friendly captain, Peter Couvret, Blight left the Cape on 2 January 1790 to reach Portsmouth on 14 March with John Samwell his faithful clerk and John Smith, a seaman. Of the other 16 who had been forced on to the ship's launch by the mutineers, only nine would survive to return home from the East Indies. Among those who died was David Nelson on 20 July 1789 at Koepang 'of an inflammatory fever'. For him Bligh was genuinely grief-stricken, lamenting his loss as that of an honest man who had served on the *Bounty* with care and diligence and not less so in

255

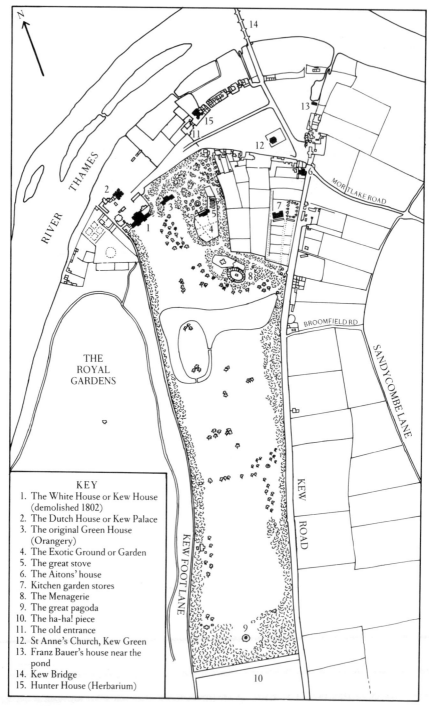

KEY

1. The White House or Kew House
   (demolished 1802)
2. The Dutch House or Kew Palace
3. The original Green House
   (Orangery)
4. The Exotic Ground or Garden
5. The great stove
6. The Aitons' house
7. Kitchen garden stores
8. The Menagerie
9. The great pagoda
10. The ha-ha! piece
11. The old entrance
12. St Anne's Church, Kew Green
13. Franz Bauer's house near the
    pond
14. Kew Bridge
15. Hunter House (Herbarium)

A map of Kew Gardens as they were during the period of Banks's unofficial direction, 1773–1820. Derived from the survey of 1771 by T. Richardson.

the hazardous voyage of the launch where his patience and fortitude were noteworthy. So Nelson, the first of the Banksian, as distinct from the Kew, collectors, lies buried somewhere behind the chapel in Koepang.

In the summer of 1790 by degrees the other nine survivors from the open boat voyage returned to England and Bligh had to endure a court-martial on board HMS *Royal William* at Spithead on 22 October. On 24 October Bligh wrote telling Banks at Revesby Abbey that he had been honourably acquitted in the matter of the loss of the *Bounty*. Before the end of the year, with support from Banks in a letter of 10 December to Earl Chatham, he had been promoted first to Commander and then Post-Captain by a waiving of three years in the conditions of service. In addition he had been presented to the King and for a while from 8 January 1791 he continued a sort of convalescence on half pay.

Meanwhile the substance of the *Bounty* voyage, the mutiny and its aftermath had been printed as an 88-page quarto slender volume under the title: *A Narrative of the Mutiny on Board His Majesty's Ship Bounty and the subsequent voyage of part of the crew in the ship's boat from Tofoa, one of the Friendly Islands, To Timor, a Dutch settlement in the East Indies.* Put together by Bligh while waiting for the court-martial it was the first public revelation of what had passed and the first spark to the explosion of legends that followed.

A year later the subject was expanded under the editorial hand of James Burney and the collaborative guidance of Banks, a process begun with the agreement of Bligh in the months before he sailed on 3 August 1791 with HMS *Providence* and HMS *Assistant* on the second less dramatic but wholly successful bread-fruit voyage. Printed again for George Nicol of Pall Mall, it is another important example of the long partnership in publication between the 'bookseller to His Majesty' and the savant of Soho Square. For James Burney it was a forward step in his literary apprenticeship and devotion to 'the history of discovery in the South Sea or Pacific Ocean', his *magnum opus* of later years. Burney's close working association with Banks is revealed in his correspondence as the first proofs emerged from the printer from the first week of September to the end of October 1791, all submitted to the man to whom the management of the voyage had been entrusted from the beginning. There is little overt acknowledgement in the book itself of this background beyond the single statement on the first page that the fixtures and other preparations of the vessel for the voyage

> ... were completed according to a plan of my much honoured friend, Sir Joseph Banks, which, in the event, proved the most advantageous that could have been adopted for the purpose.

Thereafter the name of Banks appears only twice more: on page 3 concerning the appointment of David Nelson and William Brown as the gardeners and on page 61 as a matter of enquiry by the natives of Tahiti.

The integration of the first narrative of the mutiny into one comprehensive account of his voyage as a whole was a change from Bligh's first idea of two separate accounts. His bare statement in the 'Advertisement' of the later volume – 'This method I have since been induced to alter' – probably covers a wealth of discussion and advice at Soho Square. The sparseness of any direct allusion to the role of Banks in this case is consistent with his cryptic part in other ventures of which perhaps the

257

culminating example is the concealment of his true relation to the origin and management of Matthew Flinders's voyage in HMS *Investigator* and the publication of *A Voyage to Terra Australis* nearly 25 years later.

The close association of Soho Square with the publication of the 1792 account of the *Bounty* voyage and its sequel is also evident in other ways. The plate of the sections of the bread-fruit was engraved by Daniel Mackenzie as a special illustration, differing from that done by John Miller for the Hawkesworth account of the *Voyages* ... in 1773 and also from that originally submitted to Lord Sydney with Banks's first proposals for the *Bounty* voyage. The printed extracts relating to the bread-fruit are themselves from among those gathered and printed by Banks for the information of the Home Department in 1787. Mackenzie also engraved the plate of the drawings from which the famous launch of the *Bounty* was made and possibly also that of the plan and section of the ship's quarters aft where the system of stowage for the bread-fruit pots was shown. Eventually, some three years after publication, Bligh accorded his own recognition to Banks as he finished his official charts for printing by Aaron Arrowsmith in 1795. Here he named the most northerly group of islands in the New Hebrides as Banks Islands at the point where he turned his course in the launch west toward the coast of Australia, about latitude 13°S. and 167°W., less than two degrees south of the island of Vanikoro on which the ships of La Pérouse, as yet unknown to the world, lay wrecked.

III

In the summer of 1789 amid the flurry of preparing HMS *Guardian* and its plant house for the voyage to Port Jackson, Banks received a letter from Archibald Menzies dated 14 July from the *Prince of Wales*, anchored off the Isle of Wight after nearly three years fur trading on the north-west coast of America. Announcing his return, he told Banks of a brass weapon he had seen in the hands of a native near the islands to which he had given Banks's name to commemorate this discovery. This was one of the replica Maori *patu onewas* engraved with his name and the date 1772 of which Banks had 40 cast by Mrs Eleanor Gyles of Shoe Lane in March that year. Here was a survival from those that Charles Clerke evidently had traded here and there when he was on that coast in HMS *Discovery* during Cook's last voyage in the summer of 1778. The return of the *Prince of Wales* was almost coincident with the publication of the two volumes – one by Nathaniel Portlock, the other by George Dixon – entitled *A Voyage round the World, but more particularly to the North-West Coast of America: performed in 1785, 1786, 1787, and 1788, in the King George and Queen Charlotte, Captains Portlock and Dixon*. That by Portlock was dedicated to His Majesty; that by Dixon to Sir Joseph Banks, after whom Dixon had in fact named Banks Island in Hecate Strait at approximately 53°N. and 130°W.

On 21 July Menzies sent Banks from Deptford a box containing all the dried plants he had collected on his voyage. Their discussions at Soho Square must have been fruitful for on 27 August Banks sent Menzies to Whitehall bearing a letter to Evan Nepean as

> ... the person I mean to recommend to attend the Voyage now in Contemplation, I will answer for his abilities industry and discretion the terms you know we agreed upon when last we met the only thing necessary is that they should

commence immediately as he has at present no engagement & is not in circumstances to wait for one.

Not until 8 October could Menzies tell Banks that the King had finally approved his appointment on the basis of his recommendations. By this time a new ship of 340 tons had been bought by the Admiralty to be commissioned as a sloop of war and, with some nostalgia, named *Discovery*. A small brig of 135 tons built at Dover was selected as her tender and named *Chatham* after the First Lord. Fitted as a survey ship HMS *Discovery* was to be commanded by Captain Henry Roberts, formerly master's mate on the *Resolution* and draftsman of the charts for engraving in the publication of *A Voyage to the Pacific Ocean . . . to determine the position and extent of the west side of north America*, under the authorship of Cook and King and the supervision of Banks in 1784. George Vancouver, formerly midshipman on the old *Discovery* under Charles Clerke, was appointed as 1st Lieutenant. Thus as early as the summer of 1789 this new expedition to complete the charting of the west coast of America was broadly planned and preparing with Banks at the centre of developments.

But into this 'work of peace' there broke the disruption of the incident at Nootka Sound as the Spanish, alarmed by the spreading British presence in the Pacific, sent their warships under Don Esteban Jose Martinez to challenge the settlement on the island. By January 1790 the news of the arrest of British ships at Nootka Sound by the Spanish had filtered to London and the *Discovery* was absorbed into a hasty plan by the Pitt administration which cast Botany Bay as a base for the protection of a small trading post on the north-west coast of America. This required the *Discovery* to sail for Port Jackson in company with HMS *Gorgon* and from there, under orders from Governor Phillip with reinforcements from the slender garrison in New South Wales, to sail for Hawaii to wait for a frigate from the East Indies squadron. By the end of April 1790 the *Discovery* was almost ready for sea when a fresh and highly-coloured account of the happenings at Nootka Sound induced the Cabinet to cancel the first plan and instead to send an ultimatum to Madrid, backed by the mobilization of a large fleet. Thereafter, for more than a year, 'the Nootka Sound controversy' ebbed and flowed in a spate of diplomatic exchanges varied by more or less overt naval threats.

In this period of crisis the Spanish Ambassador at the Court of St James's was the Marquis del Campo di Alange, owner of the Negretti *cabana* of fine Merinos. At its onset the British *chargé d'affaires* in Madrid was Anthony Merry until Alleyne Fitzherbert arrived as Ambassador. All were to be figures in another diplomatic round involving Banks more directly when the business at Nootka Sound had been resolved by the Anglo-Spanish Convention signed at Madrid on 28 October 1790. Its terms required that a British officer be sent out to receive from the Spanish the formal surrender of the site at Nootka Sound. This was an important stimulus in reviving the expedition originally planned for the *Discovery* and the *Chatham*. In April 1790 Henry Roberts had been replaced by George Vancouver in command of the *Discovery* but who during the fleet mobilization was assigned for service in HMS *Courageux*. He rejoined the *Discovery* in December but the *Chatham*, under William Broughton, was not ready until January 1791.

Meanwhile Banks had prepared in detail a draft of the instructions for Menzies which he passed to Evan Nepean on 15 December 1790 and by 22 December he had learned that Lord Grenville had agreed to 'the whole proposition'. Set out in 13

Archibald Menzies, FLS. Portrait by Eden Upton Ellis.

paragraphs, this draft was a precise but rather more comprehensive presentation of what had been part of the 'Additional Instructions' to Cook on the *Endeavour* voyage, brought up to date and adapted to the special aims of this new voyage. In their final form of ten paragraphs, Banks dated the document 22 February 1791 and sent them to Nepean who replied on 24 February to the effect that Lord Grenville had passed it on to the Admiralty. However Grenville thought it should carry Banks's signature rather than his own, and that the allusion to 'the abominable custom of eating human flesh' should be matter for a private letter to Menzies rather than part of the official paper. So a charming circumlocution was found and Menzies was formally instructed in observing the natives:

> . . . if any part of their conduct, civil or religious should appear to you so unreasonable as not to be likely to meet with credit when related in Europe, you are, if you can do it with safety and propriety, to make yourself an Eyewitness of it, in order that the fact of it's existence may be established on as firm a basis as the nature of the enquiry will permit . . .

Meanwhile Banks had been at work preparing advice for Lord Grenville on the technical, as distinct from the political, purpose of the expedition – the survey of the western American coast from 30° to 60° N. lat. These he embodied as 'instructions for surveyors' under cover of his letter to him of 19 February coupled with a set of 'opinions'

... concerning the mode of carrying on the survey of the N W coast of A[merica] in the most speedy and effectual manner consistent with the degree of accuracy required in an undertaking intended of a general nature.

In submitting his advice in this form, Banks admitted the assistance 'of one of my friends in the matters relating to that business', namely, the practical details of surveying. Whether this was Bligh or Major James Rennell is uncertain – probably the former as Banks was in close touch with him over the bread-fruit voyages during these same weeks. But it is clear that Rennell was also a source of advice as was Alexander Dalrymple: all three, Bligh, Rennell and Dalrymple, were certainly visitors at Soho Square during that winter as Grenville's term at the Home Office drew to an end.

When Menzies joined the *Discovery* at Portsmouth and acknowledged the instructions from Banks, as well as his patronage and kindness, on 1 March, there were many unresolved questions about his future relations with Captain George Vancouver. Most of these had been foreseen by Banks but when the ships left Falmouth on 1 April 1791 Banks had still not been able to secure from the Admiralty a copy of the directions to Vancouver which would regulate his relations with Menzies. These related to the management of the plant hatch, storage space, use of the ship's boats and help from the crew, salary, servant's wages and mess arrangements. From the beginning of the voyage the personal relations between Vancouver and Menzies were strained and unhappy. As late as 10 August, when the expedition was at the Cape, Banks could only write to Menzies deploring that he could still not send him a copy of the instructions given to Vancouver 'to regulate his conduct towards you'. In part this could be attributed, he thought, to the political changes as Grenville moved from the Home to the Foreign Office. Although he did not say so, there was another possible factor in Nepean's bout of poor health and recourse to the waters at Bath. There was also the possibility of subtle obstruction at the Admiralty and there certainly was a persistent disinclination to be helpful on Vancouver's part as the events during the voyage showed. In spite of strong pressure by Banks the matter was never properly resolved. Nepean had not answered his letter dated 11 July and on 10 November Banks wrote again with unconcealed anger and an accumulated list of complaints touching the *Guardian* and the *Providence* as well as the *Discovery*. He emphasized that he had not been given copies of Vancouver's orders relating to his conduct toward Menzies during the voyage

... tho' you promised I should have them, which will be essentially usefull to me if the difference which existed between these gentlemen before they went to sea should continue during their voyage.

But those differences continued to the end and it is a tribute to the pertinacity and patience of Menzies that he was so successful in pursuing both the spirit as well as the letter of the instructions which Banks had framed. The survey and the main purposes of the four and-a-half-year voyage were brilliantly achieved by Vancouver but the tension between him and Menzies did not lessen and indeed for the last three months of the voyage he placed him under arrest. The living plants for Kew were the chief victims but Menzies was able to deliver safe the dried plants and his journal to Soho Square and the other 'Curiosities and Natural Productions' to the British Museum through Banks.

IV

As early as March 1787 Banks had enlisted the help of his old friend William Eden in his search for enlightenment on the subject of fine wool. This had followed the successful negotiation by Eden in September 1786 of the Anglo-French commercial treaty which Banks had hailed as an augury for 'the blessings of a mutual commerce between two nations who have been enemies these thousand years'. While Eden was still in Paris, Banks asked him to procure if possible Daubenton's pamphlet *Observations sur la comparaison de la nouvelle Laine superfine de France avec la belle Laine d'Espagne* of March 1786 – and on 11 May he acknowledged its arrival. The subject had a close but occult relevance to the fleet which sailed from the Motherbank two days later for Botany Bay and the future of the settlement it was to establish on the coast of New South Wales in January 1788. By the time Eden had reached Madrid as British Ambassador in May of that year, Banks had drawn him deeply into the hunt for the secret of Spanish fine wool and charged him with the task of getting authentic samples for his inspection, and even to explore the remote prospect of securing some of the sheep themselves. But a year passed without success until in May 1789 Eden was again called to Paris to defend against the National Assembly the commercial treaty he had negotiated and signed on 31 August 1787. Meanwhile Anthony Merry the acting *chargé d'affaires* reported to him on 16 July that samples of the true Spanish fine wool had been obtained. In September Eden returned to England (to be raised to the Irish peerage as the first Baron Auckland) and about mid-November he and Banks met in the quiet of Lambeth Palace. Here Banks was shown for the first time specimens of true Spanish fine wool in its natural state as grown in Spain and before it had been washed. On 25 November Banks reported to the King that Lord Auckland had shown him samples of the finest wool he had ever seen and had said that procuring the Spanish sheep that grew it was a matter of little difficulty 'if His Majesty would lay Commands on his Lordship or honor Sr. Jos: with directions to confer with him on the subject'. If such were done, Banks was sure that what had now become 'his Majesties patriotic Plan' would be materially accelerated. Early in the new year of 1790 Banks received the royal command to see what could be done and from this point began what, for convenience and due secrecy, was dubbed 'Lord Auckland's undertaking'.

In March 1790 Auckland went as ambassador to The Hague but almost immediately wrote to Anthony Merry 'respecting the cargo of Rams & Sheep to be procured . . . for the purpose of *ornamenting* His Majesty's Farms'. These instructions were encoded and sent by more than one route to Madrid, a standard of secrecy that both Banks and Auckland hoped would be kept by Merry whose reputation for discretion was high. But the Nootka Sound controversy again intervened to thwart Banks. In September Auckland wrote to explain that his letters to Spain had 'arrived in the inauspicious period of the Paper War and Naval Preparations' and that Merry could not in the circumstances find the right moment to raise the matter either with the Spanish King or his chief minister Floridablanca. By the time that the political temperature had dropped at the end of October the flocks were out of reach for the winter. Banks however was anxious about progress and wrote to Auckland on 17 December to enquire 'how all Foreign correspondence goes on'. Early in the New Year he received Auckland's reply with the season's greetings and a patriotic shout:

... We certainly are at the Height of foreign Pre-eminence & of internal
Prosperity: – to introduce the Bread fruit of the South Sea Islands into the West
Indies: – The Moment is equally suitable to the examination of the Soil,
Production, & Manners of the Inhabitants of the Regions Yclipd Nootka Sound. –
'These are imperial words & worthy of our Sovereign' I most sincerely wish
success to them.

But though he had encouraged Anthony Merry on the subject of Spanish sheep, he
greatly doubted whether in the Spanish Court 'the returning cordiality & good
Humour are yet such as to ensure all the Compliance that we wish'. Thereafter there
was a silence for a year in the matter of 'Lord Auckland's undertaking'.

Then quite suddenly at Revesby Abbey on 22 October 1791 for Banks came a
letter late that night from a merchant captain, John Burnell, written a week before
from Southampton:

I here acquaint you that I have on board forty-one sheep shipt. at Santander by
order of Anthony Merry Esqr. consigned to you . . .

This was tempered with the news that the flock had been confiscated by the Collector
of Customs 'according to Law' in spite of Burnell's protest that he thought 'the sheep
belongd to a power that would not permit any such thing'. But by 26 October Banks,
with smooth efficiency, had secured a clearance from His Majesty's Commissioners
of Customs in London on the general ground that 'these sheep are imported solely
with a view to the improvement of the Quality of British Wool'. There was no hint in
this application that they were indeed destined for the royal flock though the bill of
lading was clear in their consignment to 'Sir Joseph Banks, President of the Royal
Society or His Brittanic Majesty'. On 27 October Captain John Burnell and his ship,
the schooner *King George*, were released. At sea two days later on his return to Spain
the captain addressed his account to Banks for freight and other charges of £34.5s.0d.
Meanwhile the sheep rested comfortably in William Rogers's coach house and stable
until, on Monday 14 November, they set out on the 60-mile journey on foot to
Windsor. Travelling in stages of 12 miles a day, the droving route passed by
Winchester, Basingstoke and Bagshot Heath to end at the Queen's Lodge in the
Little Park where they were delivered to John Robinson. For the small flock it was
the end of a journey that had begun near Cervera in Old Castile in September when
they had been droved more than 100 miles over the Cantabrian mountains to
Santander. They had been in the care of a shepherd at the expense of the young
Countess del Campo di Alange, wife of the former Spanish Ambassador now back in
his native land. The original number of 4 rams and 36 ewes with a tame wether or
manso to lead them had in fact been drawn from one of the most famous of the
Spanish *cabanas*, the Negretti, though it was some time before their provenance was
made clear. Shipped on board the *King George* on 7 October they sustained a rough
sea passage of seven days. All the ewes were in lamb and two died shortly after
landing. Otherwise, when they reached Windsor on Friday 18 November, after some
two months of varied travel from their home pastures, these 38 Negretti sheep and
one nondescript wether were in good order when Banks viewed them for the first
time next day to leave orders for their proper care and management with Ramsay
Robinson, superintendent of the royal farms and gardens.

263

This was the nucleus of the flock that was to be Banks's constant care and preoccupation for the next 15 years and from which would come, 13 years later, those eight sheep to sail from Portsmouth on 29 November 1804 for the small colony on the coast of New South Wales. These were no 'contraband lot' like those of 'the Bilbao plan' under Evan Nepean or 'the Lisbon plan' managed by Thomas March and Company. Nor were they sheep of cloudy and mixed origins at one remove from Spain as in 'Daubenton's Flock'. These of 'Lord Auckland's undertaking' were an open gift from a former Spanish ambassador and his wife as a gesture of sincere appreciation, in spite of recent international tensions, of their years in England. But this was unknown to Banks as, with some anger, he reviewed the case in his notes on Sunday 20 November.

As it seemed to him then, Anthony Merry 'by his impudent and unauthorisd application to the Court of Spain' had put a final stop to what he had originally intended – a supply of not less than 50 or 100 rams and the services of an expert Spanish shepherd who might have been induced by a £50 annuity for life to stay for six or seven years 'during which time the whole of his knowledge would be easily got from him'. Instead the situation was getting out of hand, for Lord Auckland had now revealed to him the letter from Anthony Merry authenticating the source of the sheep on which he had himself waxed lyrical:

> ... The Transaction on the Part of the Alange's Family is certainly handsome in the extreme; & I think it possible that our Flock may prove a Treasure of infinite value to His Majesty's good old Island of Great Britain.

Merry was embarrassed at the Spanish refusal of payment and entreated Lord Auckland to explain the case to Banks and somehow to get the transaction 'compleated in a becoming handsom manner' – in other words to arrange a diplomatic *quid pro quo*. For Banks there lay the irritating rub. By his own calculations, based now on firm knowledge, he reckoned the sheep to be worth, at Spanish rates, no more than £25.12s.0d. But it had brilliantly occurred to Merry that 'a proper and acceptable return', more acceptable indeed than anything else as a present from the King, would be a set of English carriage horses – 'the Countess being very sick & overstock'd with diamonds'. This clearly outraged Banks and his sense of proper business values relating to the flock. He warmly disputed the matter with Merry and assembled much evidence to validate his own private estimate but in the end he conceded the case to the diplomats as perhaps something beyond the cold logic of farm economics. So on Wednesday 22 August 1792 as some return of kindness to the fair Spaniard 'eight fine bay carriage horses' of uncommon beauty were shipped from near the Tower in the Pool of London for Bilbao as a gift from the King. Before this however, on 11 August, Banks had written his 'Statement relative to the Sheep received from Madrid in consequence of Lord Auckland's undertaking' in which he concluded

> ... and it is no more than Justice to Mr Merry to state from a Letter of his, dated May [1 17]92 that he had no idea, even when the sheep were embarked, but that he would have been allowed to pay for them.

He had by this time also assured himself of the real value of the Negretti stock by his consultations especially with John Maitland of Basinghall Street. He found the Negretti wool was rated as the second best to be imported into England. The first, in the estimation of the merchants, was that from the Perales *cabana*, which he had seen in the samples shown to him by Lord Auckland at Lambeth Palace nearly two years before. But he found that the best judges scarcely made a distinction between the two and he was satisfied that in the Negretti flock the King had a most valuable acquisition. His innate caution held him back from Lord Auckland's use of superlatives.

CHAPTER 13

COROMANDEL, AFRICA AND KEW
1779–1795

There is a certain logical progression in the engagement of Banks with the botany of India and his concern with the affairs of the East India Company and the economy of the sub-continent. Perhaps the earliest explicit sign appears in the letter from Solander of 22 August 1775 to Banks as he rambled with Constantine Phipps, Omai and young George Colman near Mulgrave in east Yorkshire:

> ... Mr. Hurlock has sent to your house the plants I mentioned in my last Letter; they are collected near Tranquebar by the Bretern [sic] of the Moravians, and as good specimens as any I have seen. If things come in, in this manner, you will soon want another dozen of cubes. Mr. Koenig's plants are now pasted and I thought they made a fine figure, but these surpass them by 100 per cent. I dont intend to touch them before you come to town as they must be counted and I suppose paid for – They seem to be about 3 or 400 –––...

The association of Banks with the Moravians or United Brethren was already of ten years' standing from before his Newfoundland voyage. They were part of the Chelsea scene – the propinquity of his mother's house at Paradise Row, the Apothecaries' Physic Garden almost opposite, and the Moravian headquarters at Lindsey House not far to the west in Cheyne Walk.

Now it would seem that another fortuitous propinquity was to extend the botanical chain from the Moravian mission at Tranquebar to the Danish pupil of Linnaeus, Johan Gerhard Koenig, then in the service of the Nabob of Arcot in the Carnatic. From Koenig the next link was forged with Dr William Roxburgh when they met in Madras in 1776 as the young Scot took service with the East India Company there. They botanized together for ten years – the elder leading the younger student of John Hope and the Edinburgh school into a correspondence with Banks. For Roxburgh this grew steadily from March 1779 when he replied to an appreciative letter from Banks to whom, from 1777 in Nagore, he had sent the first of a stream of Indian plants.

The partnership of Koenig and Roxburgh as field botanists drew the Dane into the service of the Company at Madras in 1780 after a probationary expedition in 1779 into Siam and the islands of the Molucca Straits. On his return Koenig sent to Banks, on the East Indiaman *General Baker*, a large collection of plants and other specimens and manuscript papers. The ship was wrecked off the Dutch coast in March 1781 and, through the good offices of Jan Deutz at Amsterdam, in May Banks received the remains of some hundreds of dried plants, apparently all that was salvaged. After five years as a botanist to the East India Company Koenig died of dysentery on 25 June 1785 with Roxburgh in attendance. He bequeathed to Banks all his specimens and manuscripts and Roxburgh passed these to the Company at Madras to be sent to Soho Square.

Early in 1787 Banks was asked how useful he thought the post that Koenig had occupied was and on 22 February he gave the Court of Directors a warm appreciation of the man himself and a recommendation that a young graduate of one of the northern universities well versed in natural history – 'not Botany only but Zoology Mineralogy & Chemistry also' – be appointed in his place. This gave support to the choice of another man already there, the Midlothian Scot, Dr Patrick Russell, as Natural Historian in the Presidency of Madras, an appointment confirmed in London on 16 February 1787. Thus the Court of Directors accepted Russell's plan 'for rendering the Botanical improvements of the late Dr. Konig more immediately subservient to the Uses of Life' but laid down that his pay would depend on him communicating his 'discoveries and improvements' to the Royal Society in London, in other words to Banks. Failure to do this would result in the cessation of his allowance.

Russell was already known to Banks who, with Solander, had revised and extended the catalogue of plants in readiness for the second edition of the elder brother Alexander's *The Natural History of Aleppo and parts adjacent*, 1794. Moreover Russell since his arrival in India had been a steady correspondent with his younger brother Claud, the administrator of Vizagapatam in 1782. He was also in the confidence of Koenig and Roxburgh and he had been nominated as a successor to Koenig as early as November 1785. He had been an untiring collector of plants and animals with a particular interest in reptiles, especially the snakes of the Coromandel coast. In 1784 he had proposed the publication of 'curious and useful plants' by the East India Company and during 1788 Banks was asked for advice and estimates on the cost of printing it.

Banks strongly upheld the idea in a report to the Court of Directors dated 25 November 1788. He suggested that the *Flora Londinensis* of William Curtis be taken as a model to be followed with fascicles of 20 plants each, at an estimated cost of £23 per plant engraved, or £460 per fascicle of which 500 copies should be printed. He put the sale price per fascicle at £1.5s.od. 'if elegance is adopted', or £1.1s.od. 'if ordinary Workmanship' only was required. Russell would be expected to send home coloured drawings and dried plants as complete botanically as possible. With these at hand Banks offered 'to provide a proper Person to conduct the Work', to overlook its management himself, and to supplement it with such notes and descriptions of plants as were in his own possession, in Koenig's papers, or elsewhere. Slow communication between London and Madras prevented any final decision before Russell resigned in January 1789, nominating William Roxburgh as his successor before returning to England. The plan however was accepted but it was late in 1790 before Roxburgh, on whom the task now fell, had official confirmation from the Board at Madras. The first drawings and dried plants were sent to Banks from Roxburgh's station at Samul Cattah in the Northern Circars in December 1790, passing through the hands of Patrick Russell in London.

During the next four years Roxburgh sent home drawings, descriptions and dried plants of more than 500 species. From these Banks selected some 300 for engraving and publication in fascicles of 25, of which the first appeared in May 1795 and the second in November. The engravings were made by Daniel Mackenzie, from the coloured drawings by unnamed Indian artists who worked from the fresh material.

Left Dr William Roxburgh, MD, FLS, superintendent of the Botanic Garden, Calcutta, 1793–1813. From an engraving by C. Warren.
Right Col Robert Kyd, founder and honorary superintendent of the Botanic Garden, Calcutta, 1786–93.

under Roxburgh's eye, and at his personal expense, each man producing about 12 drawings per month for about 35 rupees in all. The text was printed by William Bulmer, under the editorial scrutiny and management of Banks, with an introduction by Patrick Russell, the whole appearing as published by George Nicol for the Court of Directors of the East India Company. This procedure had emerged from a final plan by Banks of 4 July 1794 and acceptable to both Russell and Roxburgh. Banks estimated the cost of each engraving at £3. Had the original drawings been made by English artists he reckoned each would have cost 2 guineas, a contrast to the approximate 3 rupees per drawing which Roxburgh had paid his Indians. Daniel Mackenzie in the last five years of his life produced 250 of the 300 illustrations finally published, about 50 every year. They had a simpler line and less elaborate textures than those he had been directed by Banks to employ for the *Endeavour* plants. This in part reflected the more naïve Indian originals but it was also probably a sign of the compromise Banks was aiming at between his first high flights of botanical art and the sober economics of practical publication. Roxburgh died before the third volume appeared in 1815 and Banks lived just long enough to see the last completed about March 1820. A solid foundation for the *Flora Indica* had been laid in the protracted publication of *The Plants of the Coast of Coromandel*.

If the origins of systematic botany in India belong to the province of Madras, the beginnings of the horticulture of modern India perhaps emerged in Bengal. During Warren Hastings's last years as Governor-General, Lt-Col. Robert Kyd, secretary to the military inspectorate at Calcutta, had been having ideas. Early in 1786 these had crystallized in the notion of a botanic garden for the introduction and propagation of plants important as food, as medicinal sources, or as industrial species of trading significance, not for scientific purposes, as Kyd was careful to emphasize for tactical reasons at the time. He presented the case in a memorial to the acting Governor-General, Sir John Macpherson, dated 15 April 1786. This was recommended to the Court of Directors in London soon after the arrival of the new governor-general, the 2nd Earl Cornwallis, in a general public letter of 21 August that year. The Government in Calcutta was so impressed with Kyd's proposal that land for the garden was selected in anticipation of the approval sent from London dated 31 July 1787. This was only after the papers had been submitted to Banks for his opinion by Henry Dundas from the Board of Control and by Sir George Yonge, Secretary for War, who was concerned also with the garden at St Vincent and anxious to form a working relation with the proposed establishment at Calcutta, now that the *Bounty* voyage to the South Pacific was in a forward state of planning. It is clear that Banks had seen the papers early in May for he had written a long appreciation of their contents to Yonge on 15 May 1787. His formal opinion however was not framed until 15 June 1787 when he wrote to Dundas on the subject, with a copy sent to Yonge.

From the outset Banks was in harmony with the ideas expressed by Kyd, the cultivated Scot from Forfarshire. There was a compelling eloquence in his case for the garden as a step toward defending the Indian population from

> . . . the greatest of all Calamities, that of desolation by famine, and subsequent pestilence . . .

proposing the introduction of the sago palm from Malaya and the date palm from Basra as its first priority in the development of a stable food supply. Banks applauded the humanity of Kyd's intentions

> . . . by whose means blessings of such infinite importance will speedily be conferrd on a populous nation in a manner which will secure their continuance to the latest Posterity who will wonder how their ancestors were able to exist without them & revere the names of their British conquerors to whom they will be indebted for the Abolition of Famine the most severe Scourge with which nature had afflicted the countrey . . .

But this high-flown endorsement, however practical and wise, lay close to the common denominator of enlightened self-interest on which he knew the policy of the East India Company was based, as he continued

> . . . Ample as the testimony drawn from first principles of humanity in Favor of this Plan must be deemd, I am happy to Say that those of sound policy give as decisive a one in Favor of the second that is the Establishment of a Botanic garden at Calcutta Principaly for the purpose of Cultivating Plants likely to become usefull to commerce & distributing them to such as may chuse to undertake their culture on the scale of real utility . . .

Thus, on these twin themes of compassion and plain business common sense, Banks advised the Company to support Kyd's proposal and supplied his own schedule of species that could with benefit be considered as importations to India from Ceylon, Cochinchina, Sumatra, the Red Sea and Java, with a list of drugs whose places of

269

origin had yet to be found. He reminded the Company also of the list of fruits from the Dutch East Indies to be found in Hawkesworth's account of the *Endeavour* voyage and especially emphasized the competitive advantage which the French had already gained in the spice trade with the cultivation of nutmegs and cloves, for example, on Isle de France (Mauritius).

Before news of this support could reach Calcutta, Robert Kyd had, on 30 August 1786, already nominated two possible sites for the garden on the western bank of the Hooghly and of these the area once occupied by the old fort of Muggah Tannah was finally chosen. On 18 May 1787, Kyd accepted the title of superintendant of the Botanic Garden.

The process of clearing and ditching the ground, somewhat over 300 acres near the village of Sibpore and Kyd's house of Shalimar, had already begun, limited by the care in removing the inhabitants from the site and the conscientious mode of estimating compensation. The sums were paid by the end of the year, while requests for a variety of plants and seeds had been despatched to China, the Prince of Wales Island, Madras and Bombay, Butan and the borders of Burma.

For six years Robert Kyd supervised the growth of the Botanic Garden until his death on 26 May 1793. William Roxburgh was then appointed his successor and took up his duties on 29 November 1793, combining the elements of systematic botany with that of the enlightened experimentalist in horticulture. In this new post he was immediately aided by Banks's recommendation of Christopher Smith as botanical gardener, a step which had been taken before the news of Kyd's death had reached London or the *Providence* had anchored in the Thames. For 20 years, with periods of convalescence at the Cape in 1798–9 and in Britain in 1805–7 Roxburgh developed Indian botany with the unwavering support and collaboration of Banks, to whom he directed a steady flow of specimens and through whom the Royal Botanic Garden at Kew received a rich harvest of new species.

Left Charles Jenkinson, 1st Earl of Liverpool and 1st Baron Hawkesbury. Portrait by George Romney, *c.* 1786.
Right John Baker Holroyd, 1st Earl of Sheffield, 1798. Drawing by Henry Edridge.

II

Early in November 1788 Banks, during his second attack of gout and soon after his return from Revesby Abbey, received from the East India Company two large bundles of papers, the accumulated correspondence relating to the Botanic Garden at Calcutta under Colonel Kyd's direction. From these he distilled an abstract of events for his own benefit and a report for the Company, dated 19 November 1788, directed to William Ramsay its secretary. In the latter, two points were made clear. First, Banks clearly viewed the 50 acres already prepared as more than ample for the purpose, emphasizing that two acres only sufficed for the King at Kew, and defining the function as one of the establishment and preservation of new species rather than of propagation. Second, he advised the directors on Kyd's request for more fruit trees from England. He attributed the success of those previously sent out to the skill and care with which they had been prepared and packed by the supplier, James Dickson, nurseryman of Covent Garden. He proposed that Dickson should again be commissioned to provide what was wanted. He could not forbear to add a few words on tea, about which Kyd had been despondent and critical, grumbling over the dilatory mismanagement of the supercargoes at Canton. A few days later the Deputy-Chairman of the Court of Directors, Francis Baring invited Banks to enlarge his views on the possibilities of the tea trade for India. These found expression in a paper of 27 December 1788, but before this he had explored the literature in his own library and the verbal testimony of as many merchants or travellers as he could find in London with first-hand experience either of the trade or of the growing of the tea plant. The subject was not new to him for early in the year he had been asked by the President of the Board of Trade Lord Hawkesbury

> Will it not be possible by proper Premiums and wise Instructions to encourage the Growth of the Tea Plant, and the Manufacture of it's Leaves in some Part of the British Dominions in the East and West Indies, so as to be supplied from thence with a Part of the Tea consumed in this Country, and not with the whole as at present from China?

This question from the President of the Board of Trade was another important example of Banks's attention to the supplies of raw materials in the expansion of British commerce. Lord Hawkesbury's '... wishes to receive Sir Joseph Banks's Sentiments' was of a piece with similar requests from other quarters – the East India Company and the Board of Control. Now with Pitt's Commutation Act of 1784 in full force, the China trade, with tea at its centre and silver bullion as its principal ransom, raised problems in the struggle to meet the rising British thirst. That India might ease the stranglehold of China on the tea supplies of western Europe and especially England, was an appealing idea. But the mysteries of tea culture remained. Francis Baring, with his double interest as private trader and company director, and Hawkesbury, with Dundas holding a sort of balance, drove Banks hard.

In replying to Hawkesbury, about May 1788, Banks drew attention to the existence since about 1770 of the tea plant, *Camellia sinensis*, in English gardens where from the degree of its adaption to cold, there was reason to believe that in China the growth and manufacture of the leaf belonged to the temperate rather than the sub-tropical regions. No one in England had yet succeeded in producing anything but a most disagreeable infusion from the leaves grown in English gardens. He therefore inferred that much of the flavour in tea depended on its preparation as a leaf, and that perhaps the Chinese had many varieties of the plant. It was known that preparing the leaves was labour intensive; for example, in the tedious and careful rolling by hand of the green tea said to be for the European market only. He recalled the attempt by the French Government to cultivate tea in Corsica in 1785 when he himself had procured some 100 plants for £50 and sent them to Pierre Broussonet that year for the trial of which he had yet to hear the result. Finally he noted the embassy to China then on its way under Lt-Col. the Hon. Charles Cathcart mounted at the instance of Henry Dundas. Were that to succeed, Banks thought it might be possible 'to Furnish ourselves with the mode of Culture the Art of Manufacture & the right Plants'. He thought

> ... the Country which seems fittest for the experiment is that which lies between Bengal and Boutan where in a Few days journey you get from the Tropical heats & consequently Tropical Productions to a climate similar to that of Europe

In other words he defined the area known as Assam from which the first Indian tea export would not in fact emerge for another half-century. Nor did Cathcart's embassy succeed for he died on 10 June near the East Indies and the mission was aborted, though news of it did not reach London until the autumn. By this time the thoughts of Banks on tea had extended as he addressed himself to its culture and possible interest to the East India Company in his paper of some 2000 words on 27 December 1788 to Francis Baring.

His engagement with the subject of tea displays something of the nature and range of his scholarship, one example among so many. From his own library came a dozen or more titles ranging back for over a century beginning with John Ogilby's English editions of the early embassies to China in *Atlas Chinensis* . . ., 1671, by Arnoldus Montanus, and *An embassy from the East India Company of the United Provinces* . . ., 1673, by Johannes Nieuhoff. They included Louis le Comte's *Nouveau mémoires sur l'état présent de la Chine*, 1697, James Cunningham's paper on tea in the *Philosophical Transactions* for 1702–3, Engelbert Kaempfer's *Amoenitatum exoticum* . . ., 1712, Georg Meister's *Der Orientalisch-indianische kunst-und lust-gartner* . . ., 1730, Jean Baptiste du Halde's *Description de l'empire de la Chine et de la Tartarie Chinoise*, 1735, and Richard's *Histoire naturelle, civile et politique, du Tonquin*, 1778. From these and others emerged pages in his own hand of abstracts and notes in English distilled from the four languages involved. To these were added table after table of his own characteristically neat and sensible arrangements of statistics derived not only from William Richardson's accounts for the East India Company but from many other sources with Lord Sheffield prominent among them. Nor did he neglect to acquire information from the merchants engaged in the trade or from returning Company staff. One of the most clear-cut is his written interpretation of 24 Chinese drawings brought home by the returning British resident at Canton, Mr Bradshaw, showing the processes of tea culture.

Explicit references to his sources in his paper are confined to James Cunningham on the single identity of the tea plant species and to Duhalde for his authoritative summary of the regions of China where tea was grown. From this he inferred that all the merchantable teas were produced between the 26th and 35th degrees of latitude;

the area most favourable for the culture of the Black teas (Bohea, Congou, Souchong, in ascending order of quality from 26 to 30 degrees; that for the Green teas (Singlo, and above all, Hyson) between 30 and 34. In seeking a homoclime for possible Indian tea culture he now drew the attention of the Company to the same region that he had broadly sketched to Lord Hawkesbury. Arguing that 'all undertakings of new manufacture should commence with articles of inferior quality', he mooted the northern parts of Bihar as appropriate for the growing of good Black teas in a climate similar to their native region in China as the starting point. From here he said

> The mountains of Boutan afford in a short distance all the climates that are found in the cooler parts of the Empire of China, & consequently every variety necessary for the production of the Green Teas; if then the culture of the Black Teas is once established in the neighbouring provinces of Bahar, & the inhabitants of Boutan are invited by proper inducements, they will certainly undertake that of the Green; & thus, by a gradual change, the whole of the Tea trade will be transferred into that quarter

So much for the climatic strategy. What of the practical tactics?

Assuming the specific identity of the tea plant, he argued that the apparently inferior product of the island of Hainan could be exploited, in default of the obviously inaccessible mainland interior, on the theory that transplantation to a more favourable environment would raise the quality. Enough Chinese from Canton itself were ready to man the East Indiamen as it was. He concluded that liberal terms would easily tempt the men of Hainan to migrate with their tea shrubs and tools to Calcutta, where 20 acres of the Botanic Garden might be prepared to receive them. Under Colonel Kyd the native Indians could then be taught the culture and manufacture of tea and the industry eventually established in the region he had indicated. To do this however the initiative should come from the Court of Directors in London. To entrust the management of such a plan to the supercargoes at Canton would be unwise, for they would have an interest in its failure, an attitude which Kyd had already experienced.

Urging secrecy in its execution if the directors approved the plan, Banks placed himself at the disposal of the Company, convinced that the objective was also of real importance to the country at large. Beginning with tea as an article of the greatest national significance, he focused the Company's attention on indigo as another product ripe for Indian development – to which he added coffee, chocolate, vanilla, cochineal and cotton, 'even Sugar itself' although he recognized this as the staple commodity of the West Indies. He expressed himself ready to submit his thoughts on cochineal 'provided however that the necessary secrecy be granted' without which failure was almost inevitable, and that the Court of Directors would finance the matter fairly in proportion to its likely value to the Company if success were attained. His Indian philosophy at this stage was simple and clear as a centre point to his paper

> A Colony like this, blessed with advantages of Soil, Climate, & Population so eminently above its mother Country, seems by nature intended for the purpose of supplying her fabrics with raw materials: & it must be allowed that a Colony yielding that kind of tribute binds itself to the Mother Country by the strongest & most indissoluble of human ties, that of common interest & mutual advantage.

273

III

As the attention of Banks focused more sharply on the broadcloth industry of the west of England in the controversies of the Wool Bills he had become aware not only of the real place of Spanish fine wool but also of another related industrial necessity, the scarlet dye called cochineal. Old Spain held a monopoly of the wool-producing sheep. New Spain, it appeared, had as firm a hold on the curious industry from which the brilliant pigment emerged hedged about with as much mystery as the fine-woolled flocks themselves. Again Banks found in the textile industry of France the clues that seemed to offer hope of a release for British industry from the shackles of a foreign monopoly in a vital raw material.

In the Gobelin tapestries, France displayed spectacular evidence of what the original 'Dutch scarlet' could produce in textile effects. As Daubenton had done with the fine-woolled sheep, so another French naturalist, Thierry de Menonville, now sought the means of escape from another Spanish monopoly. In 1777 he succeeded, with official French Admiralty support, in transferring the two varieties of cochineal insect and their obligatory host plant from Oaxaca in Mexico to Port au Prince in San Domingo. From this plain exercise in commercial espionage emerged his book *Traité de la culture du Nopal, et de l'éducation de la Cochinelle* ... 1787, of which a copy soon appeared in the library at Soho Square. From the original French Banks made an admirable technical digest in English and from it and other sources compounded a clear account of the two forms of cochineal known to the English trade – the grana fina, granilla or fine cochineal and the grana sylvestra or sylvester cochineal. The former, otherwise known as refined or mestica cochineal, produced the richer dye from an insect twice the size of the latter or wild variety, the wood cochineal. By January 1788 he had obtained samples of each kind from John Maitland, with the current prices of 5 shillings per pound for the granilla and 3 shillings for the sylvestra; lower than the figure of 18–19 shillings per pound he had elsewhere determined as general.

Meanwhile, since February 1787, he had been in correspondence with Dr James Anderson, later Physician-General of the East India Company at Madras, about a form of the insect apparently native to India. The substance of Anderson's ideas was printed in the *Madras Courier* and later published in quarto as *Letters to Sir Joseph Banks on the subject of cochineal insects discovered at Madras*, 1788. The problem had now become a fascinating ecological issue as well as an industrial challenge. From what insect species came the two forms of the so-called 'grain' and of what plant species were the obligatory host plants? To what environments were they limited and of what species were the competing insect forms that hampered their population growth? Anderson at Madras had managed to acquire specimens of the Chinese *Opuntia* spp. and also what he believed to be the true nopal of Mexico by way of Manila as examples of the reputed host plant. Of the latter he had planted a small colony near Madras. Of the Chinese species he had sent several to Colonel Robert Kyd for the Botanical Garden at Calcutta. Kyd was confident that as soon as they were able to get the true Mexican nopal with the right insect that the culture of cochineal would be possible and he had already ordered ground to be prepared. But there was less optimism and more caution at Soho Square on the identity of the right plant hosts, and various directors at India House were yet to be convinced of its economic validity.

Before any official proposal was made to the East India Company Secret Committee, Banks had already arranged for Governor Arthur Phillip to collect specimens of the nopal of Brazil with its attendant insects at Rio de Janeiro for transport to Botany Bay. Phillip had collected these from the *nopaleria* near the town and had succeeded in keeping both the host plant and the insect alive over the winter of 1788 in New South Wales. But in Leadenhall Street the subject tended to languish in spite of the memorial by Banks to the Court of Directors in January 1788 proposing it as an 'object of national importance deserving the attention of the Company'; in spite also of the enthusiasm of Anderson and Kyd, each of whom had established a plantation of the nopal species presumed to be the host plant of the insect they expected to receive. Banks confessed in a private note to himself in August 1792 that he no longer felt that 'warmth of inclination toward promoting it' that he had in 1788. However he eventually responded to pressure from Francis Baring and set about reviving his original plan.

This was to induce his correspondent in Honduras, James Bartlet, for a suitable reward, to smuggle out sufficient living nopals with insects attached 'of the real Grana fina or true Cochineal' to reach London in a viable state. Banks intended to prepare a hothouse planted with nopals which could then serve as a reservoir for their culture while sample specimens were transported to India. This was the essence of a proposal he had set out on 11 March 1790 to William Devaynes, in which he had recommended £1000 as a reward. Now, more than two years later, on 16 August 1792, the Secret Committee told Banks that not one but two thousand pounds were still available for 'procuring the true Cochineal from Spanish America' and asking him to proceed with the business at the Company's expense. On 21 August, writing from Holkham, he accepted the task but rejected any form of emolument for himself. However he did not write again to James Bartlet until 14 January 1793, stalling to assure himself of the Company's firmness of purpose.

In the meanwhile he took advantage of the sailing of the Macartney Embassy to China on 1 October 1792 to charge Dr Hugh Gillan on board HMS *Lion* with the task of procuring at Rio de Janeiro 'the Cactus Opuntia Cochinillifera and the Insects that produce Cochineal', knowing that this would be the sylvester not the grana fina cochineal. On 12 December 1792 Gillan shipped three healthy Brazilian nopal plants covered with thousands of the cochineal insect (*Dactylopius* spp.) on board Messrs Enderby's whaler *Hero*, Captain Folger. These were packed and managed on the winter voyage north according to instructions prepared several years earlier by Banks for just this purpose. With them also were several drawings of the Brazilian nopal by William Alexander. The cargo reached the Thames in excellent condition on 25 February 1793, 'a sharp frosty day', and was taken by Banks himself to Spring Grove immediately where space had been cleared for the plants in the hothouse among the pineapples. Beside them he had placed two specimens of the cochineal fig, *Cactus cochinelifer*, introduced by John Sherard in 1732, and one other plant more nearly resembling the Brazilian species, all of them from Kew. By the end of April Banks reported almost complete failure to Gillan suspecting that the fault may have been in the heating system of his hothouse, where fermenting oak bark was used, rather than in unsuitable host plants of the *Opuntia* spp. One small comfort lay in the successful sea passage of both plant and insects from South America. There was no comfort to be had from James Bartlet, however, and the plan for a clandestine operation in Central America. Banks had no reply to the two letters he had sent, not altogether surprising considering the state of war prevailing. But before the whole subject died of financial starvation by the Company there was a glint of hope from India.

Before the *Providence* returned, Banks had in May 1793 recommended Christopher Smith as gardener to the Botanical Garden at Calcutta. Early in September 1794 Smith, with Peter Good from Kew as his assistant, sailed on board the *Royal Admiral*, Captain Bond with a large consignment of useful plants from the Royal Botanic Garden for Calcutta. These were landed on 27 February 1795 and on 4 March Smith and Peter Good began to gather the plants for the return voyage to Kew. As the *Royal Admiral* sailed home with Peter Good, there arrived at Calcutta on 5 May 1795 'the meritorious Capt. Nelson of the 74 regiment' with two small nopal plants from Rio de Janeiro 'with abundance of that kind of Cochineal Insect upon them called Sylvester'. Placed under Christopher Smith's charge, he tried to foster the egg-laying insects on the putative host species in the Calcutta garden which had at various times been introduced for just this purpose from China, Manila, Mauritius, and Kew. On all of these the insects died. Then he transferred the eight or nine insects surviving on the Brazilian host, as a last resort, to the 'Species of Nopal which grows in the Jungle, and is common all over Bengal', a plant with a large yellow flower. By mid-August he had succeeded in obtaining three broods from the insects on plants kept within a conservatory where he had 600 pots protected against the seasonal rains. However he had also found that a few which he had put on plants in the open had thrived and grown much larger than those indoors. A month later he sent Banks two samples of the dried adult insects, a practice he continued for some time. Other samples were tested by Dr James Dinwiddie, who had left the Macartney Embassy at Canton in September 1794 to bring a range of specimens (tea, varnish, plants, silkworm eggs) to William Roxburgh at Calcutta. His report to the Supreme Council of the Company on the extracted dye rated it at least equal to the sylvester cochineal of South America.

After another year Banks reported this success to Sir Hugh Inglis on 18 August 1796, satisfied that the cochineal insect could be reared in India more satisfactorily than in Brazil and that a lucrative trade could now grow to remove the monopoly from New Spain. Contemporary letters from other sources had noted that many thousands of begas (1 bega = *c.* 1600 square yards or one-third of an acre) had been planted to the native nopal species with the insects thriving well. But at this point Banks had reached the limit of his patience, after more than eight years of what he described as alternate encouragement and neglect from successive chairmen of the Court of Directors. This he was prepared to excuse in part as

> ... a laudable disinclination to give implicit credit to the Statements of a man [i.e. himself] who uniformly declard that his Assertions were founded on a general knowledge of the subject only, for no experiment had been made to verify his opinions ...

There had also been a damaging breach of confidence when the instructions he had prepared as a secret document on the care of the insects had been opened at Madras by the Council and the contents published abroad by Dr James Anderson and even sent by him to a botanist of the Spanish Government at Manila. This disclosure, as well as the war, seemed to destroy any hope of acquiring the true cochineal or grana fina from New Spain. He was sure now that two-thirds of the original difficulty had been surmounted – that of transporting the insect by sea and establishing it successfully in India. One-third only remained – that of securing the better form of the species from New Spain. Then, with strong feelings, he declared that this was

> ... a difficulty possibly more likely to be removed by artifice & Cunning, than by Prudence & discretion, as the undertaking has certainly no dependance for success on the Knowledge of Theory or the formation of Speculative opinions ...

He was, though unwilling, still prepared to continue the task if he could be allowed time to devise a new plan that would guard against 'the danger of official disclosure' and allow him sufficient Company funds for the purpose. He closed the memorial, and his own further part in the project with a splendid postscript:

> ... nothing can give more Convincing proof of the ignorance of all Natural historians on the Subject of Cochineal, at the time I first moved the Question of Procuring it to the Court of directors, than the Fact of the Insects now in India having Refusd to Feed on the Nopal sent by me from Kew ... Linnaeus Calls it Cactus Cochinelifer & it was upon his Authority that I Sent it out; I never however Faild in any Proposal for Procuring the Insect to State, that unless the Nopal upon which it Feeds in Mexico was deliverd with the Insect the Premium could not be securd.

IV

The idea of a second voyage to obtain the bread-fruit for the West Indies was germinating as early as 5 March 1790 as that alert receptor of Pacific gossip, John Linton sought the influence of Banks in favour of William Trollope for a place in the new expedition. Banks however had no need for such outside pressure and in April he had gained the King's approval for a second venture. But, as with the Vancouver expedition, the contretemps over the Nootka Sound settlement delayed further progress until December.

In the West Indies the idea had never languished and the loss of the *Bounty* was deplored by the planters of Jamaica. Their appreciation even of the failure of the first mission found a practical expression at the suggestion of Banks. On 26 January 1791 Bryan Edwards told him that the House of Assembly in Kingston had voted the sum of 500 guineas to Bligh for his attempt. In February Banks replied that by this generous act the Assembly had 'made a good man happy, and a poor man comparatively rich', taking the opportunity to set the record straight:

> ... I take some credit to myself for having successfully urged Government to forward the equipment of another bread fruit ship during the present turbulent times. Good fortune was my friend, as the application which settled the vote was not many days before the Cabinet resolved to fit out a squadron of ships: and had it come later, the business of the bread fruit would inevitably have been post-poned, and perhaps have been totally neglected.
>
> Captain Bligh is to have the command. His principal ship is four hundred tons, and we hope they will give him a tender besides. I do not, therefore, entertain a

doubt that Jamaica will possess some hundreds of bread-fruit trees within a year and a half of the present time.

Then on 23 February Bligh now back in London, told Banks that the *Providence* had been purchased at Blackwall, that a smaller vessel to serve as a tender had been reported on, and that he was about to direct the fitting out of the ship. Of this Chatham, the First Lord, seemed blissfully unaware when, on 9 March, he wrote to Banks agreeing with all his proposals. But he intended to expedite matters by issuing the necessary directions and had sent for Bligh to decide on what he little knew was already a *fait accompli*.

The health of Bligh and his fitness for the long voyage was a matter of concern not only to himself but also to Banks and the Admiralty. So too was the health of Nathaniel Portlock, who was to command the *Assistant* tender. Banks had, in December 1790, offered Portlock the command of the brig *Chatham* which was to accompany Vancouver as a tender on the voyage to the north-west coast of America in the survey of a region that Portlock had already reported on so ably in the recently published volume of his circumnavigation in 1785–8. On 26 December 1790 Portlock wrote to Banks, declining the command primarily on the grounds of his own poor health which, he said, had been impaired during his service in the *King George* but adding that he had hoped for 12 months' leave to recuperate as well as to settle his private affairs in America. Somehow in the ensuing months these barriers were charmed away and, whatever the state of their health, Bligh and Portlock sailed in company from Spithead on 3 August 1791, a talented pair of naval officers whose experience and abilities were complementary. Together, and for the most part harmoniously, they efficiently completed what had so tragically failed on the *Bounty* voyage. This time the *Providence* and *Assistant* had a detachment of marines to underpin the authority of the commander of the expedition, and the atmosphere on board both ships was one of reasonable calm among the officers and with the men.

As with the *Bounty* two gardeners were sent out as custodians and curators of the plants for the accommodation of which the arrangements were much as before. The senior man was James Wiles, formerly gardener to R. A. Salisbury through whom the recommendation came to Banks. His name was substituted for that of Nelson in the original instructions as re-drafted by Banks on 25 June 1791. The assistant gardener in place of Brown was now Christopher Smith from Kew. Of these two, Wiles was to be given the opportunity of staying on at Jamaica in the garden being developed near Kingston. Smith on the other hand was directed to return to Kew with the plants intended for the Garden. In general the instructions which Bligh handed to Wiles on the *Providence* at Portsmouth on 22 July were similar to those that David Nelson had received from Banks almost four years earlier. In all other respects the second bread-fruit voyage pursued the original course intended for the *Bounty* after the collection of the plants at Tahiti – north-west through the straits between Australia and New Guinea to Timor, then direct to St Helena avoiding the Cape, and so to Jamaica via St Vincent for the main discharge of the bread-fruit trees and the uptake of West Indian plants for Kew. This was done with Bligh executing several important surveys on the way – the charting of the Friendly Isles or Tonga group, Bligh's Islands or the Fiji group, Banks's Islands to the north of the New Hebrides, and the difficult course through the Torres Strait. Apart from the primary purpose of the voyage, which precluded any other living plants 'to be received on board except those intended for his majesties use', Banks allowed Wiles and Smith to collect on their own account 'Birds shells & insect specimens &c' if it did not conflict with their principal duties. He also proposed that they should provide him with dried specimens of all the plants they encountered. For this he would repay them on their return and he gave them each £10.10s.0d. in advance 'for service done on his account during the voyage in collecting & Preserving Specimens of Plants &c'.

As the ships approached St Helena in December 1792 Bligh wrote to Banks with relief and elation:

> ... I give you joy of the success of your Plants. I am happily arrived with a beautiful collection ...

This was his first report on the progress since Tahiti. In spite of the diligence of the gardeners, the losses among the plants had been considerable and the details of the sea-borne collections since Cape Town on the outward voyage were given in the joint letter to Banks by Wiles and Smith of 17 December. When the ships left Tahiti on 18 July Wiles reckoned there were 1996 useful plants in some 1174 containers (pots, tubs and boxes) of which 1156 were occupied by 1686 bread-fruit plants. Approaching St Helena this had been reduced to 658 containers with 826 healthy bread-fruit. At St Vincent, on 26 January, only 678 bread-fruit were alive, to be divided between that island and Jamaica.

At St Helena the expedition was hospitably received by the Governor, Lt-Col. Robert Brooke, prepared for this visit from the correspondence with Banks relating to the *Bounty* voyage. Henry Porteous, the East India Company's gardener, responding to advice from Banks, had prepared excellent sites for the reception of the plants he had been told to expect. Among these were 11 healthy bread-fruit plants, one very large, and 12 others not otherwise expected to survive the voyage to St Vincent. These were transplanted from the pots into a fine loamy soil and a situation highly approved by Wiles. In return Porteous had prepared a range of some 48 species, a few only native to the island, for transfer to the West Indies and Kew. From the Governor and Council of St Helena Bligh duly received a letter of gratitude.

A fast passage of 27 days brought the ships to an anchorage at Kingstown, St Vincent, on 22 January 1793, where again their reception had been prepared through correspondence between Banks and Dr Alexander Anderson, the long-serving and diligent superintendent of that pioneer among colonial gardens. Here now the first major part of the voyage was fulfilled. From Tahiti 439 plants of 8 species were landed, of which 331 were bread-fruit; from Timor 104 plants of 16 species; from St Helena 10 plants of three species. From Dr Anderson 465 pots and 2 tubs of plants were ready for immediate loading. For Bligh again there was a resolution of gratitude from the Council and Assembly of the island, supplemented with a piece of plate valued at 100 guineas. For the officers there was a public dinner; for the ships' companies two bullocks.

On 5 February the ships moored in Port Royal Harbour, Jamaica, the ultimate destination for the bread-fruit, to public acclaim and the manifest delight of the Negro population. The remaining 346 bread-fruit plants were distributed to the Government Botanic Garden at Bath, 66; Hinton East's Spring Garden in Liguanea, 30; Surrey County, 83; Middlesex County, 84; Cornwall County, 83. The plants of 32 other useful species were concentrated mostly in the Government Garden at Bath and of these the mango (*Mangifera indica* L.) was in time the most appreciated.

The Jamaican House of Assembly voted Bligh a grant of 1000 guineas 'in consideration of the very essential benefit this country hath acquired by the importation of the bread fruit and other useful plants and from the constant, tedious, and painful care exerted by him for their preservation during a long and dangerous voyage'. To Lt Nathaniel Portlock they voted 500 guineas 'for his important service in guiding the ship *Providence* through a very difficult and intricate navigation, whereby that ship was enabled to fulfil the end of her voyage' – a citation carpingly disputed by Bligh, though it was no less than justice to Portlock and his part among the islands of Fiji and the shoals and shallows of the Torres Strait.

For James Wiles on whom the botanical responsibility, with the able assistance of Christopher Smith, had fallen, there was the option of employment in Jamaica. On the voyage his salary had been £70 per year. Now the House of Assembly offered him the place of Superintendent of the Government Botanic Garden at Bath for £200 per year with board, lodging and laundry and on 5 March he told Banks of his decision to stay. He wrote with obvious satisfaction in a duty he had well performed, confirming his devotion to the collection of plants for His Majesty's Botanic Garden at Kew and asking Banks to send him '500 or more Pots of the large Bread-fruit size as soon as possible'. His next letter came by the hand of young midshipman Matthew Flinders asking Banks to pay him the remaining salary due to him for delivery to Wiles's father. The friendship between Flinders and Wiles had grown close on the voyage and remained lifelong. It was this also that brought Banks and Flinders together in the special relationship from which so much was to grow, as during the next year together, they resolved the problem of extracting payment for Wiles from the Treasury. The first contact was to be consolidated when Flinders visited Banks at Revesby Abbey in October 1793 to receive reimbursement of the 30 pounds he had lent James Wiles on the voyage.

For Christopher Smith there remained the last task of bringing home in good order the plant collection for Kew. To what was already in hand from the South Seas, St Helena, and St Vincent, the House of Assembly at Jamaica at its own expense added more. It deputed the two physicians, Dr Thomas Dancer and Dr Arthur Broughton to collect the plants and voted a preliminary sum of £250. Dancer's collections, which tended to be of economic interest, were in Wiles's view likely to sustain heavy loss before reaching England as 'they were neither dug up or planted with judgement'. Broughton's, on the other hand, had a greater proportion of native wild species with at least two of each rooted in each pot. Moreover each of his plants was identified by its Latin binomials whereas Dancer's list was without precision. The plant cargo, according to Bligh's reckoning, consisted of 1283 plants in all: from Jamaica, 876; from St Vincent, 338; from St Helena, 7; from Timor, 27; from Possession Island, New Guinea, 1; from Tahiti, 32; from Van Diemen's Land, 2. Under Smith's care most of them reached Kew alive in spite of the delay in sailing as the news of the outbreak of war with France arrived in March. For some weeks the two ships were involved in the local defence under naval orders. On 10 June Bligh was released to sail with the convoy from Honduras which he did not find. Eventually with some six other vessels, Bligh and Portlock crossed the Atlantic to sail up the Channel with a Windward Islands convoy and to anchor at Deptford on 7 August 1793. That day they were visited by Banks and Dryander in the same reach of the Thames where, two years and two months before on 11 June 1791 they had been wished farewell by them. For Banks it was the end of more than five years' patient planning and political endurance. For him, the gratitude of the House of Assembly was conveyed in a short but somewhat tardy letter from its Speaker on 20 December 1793.

> The House of Assembly have unanimously voted You their thanks for the great attention You have allways manifested for the welfare of this Island and the West Indies by promoting the introduction of the bread fruit and other valuable plants, now happily accomplish'd: in obedience to the commands of the House of Assembly and with very sincere pleasure to myself, I do therefore give You, their thanks.

Meanwhile Banks, on 1 September from Revesby Abbey, had paid his own tribute to the ships' commanders in a letter to Earl Chatham commending Bligh for outstanding abilities as an officer and recommending Portlock for promotion. But Bligh was to remain in limbo on half-pay for another 18 months as the shadow of the *Bounty* mutiny extended in the charges brought by Fletcher's brother, Edward Christian, Professor of Law at the East India Company College at Haileybury. In this 'paper war' Banks was firm in Bligh's support and practical in his assistance over the printing of Bligh's *Answers to Certain Assertions* during 1794 until his re-instatement on active service commanding HMS *Calcutta* with Admiral Duncan in the North Sea.

For Portlock the immediate future was brighter. On 4 November 1793 he was promoted to commander, and by April 1794 was captain of HMS *Reliance* as Banks sought approval from the Home Secretary, Henry Dundas, for the fitting of a plant cabin as on the *Guardian* for the voyage to New South Wales. But in July he was superseded by Commander Henry Waterhouse who took post as Second Captain at the specific request of Phillip's nominated successor as Governor at Port Jackson, Captain John Hunter. Perhaps this was a relief to Portlock, for his health, like that of Bligh had been sacrificed in that form of naval service.

There was another sacrifice, almost unnoticed, to the relentless probing of European curiosity. The island paradise, if such it ever were, which had yielded its bread-fruit to be the food of slaves was now changed beyond recall. The visits of the earlier European ships to 'Otaheite', ostensibly benign, bore the seeds of cultural damage to the ancient Maohi way of life. The appearance of the *Providence* and *Assistant* was a visitation which sealed its doom.

V

Whatever the results of the second bread-fruit voyage on the Pacific peoples it heralded a notable advance in the affairs of the Royal Botanic Garden at Kew. This resounding title referred specifically to an area of barely more than two acres in which were cultivated more than 50000 trees and other plants. It lay within the larger walled space of between nine and ten acres with the Temple of the Sun as its approximate centre – the Old Botanic Garden. To the north of the Temple was the Arboretum. To the south lay the Great Stove marking the northern margin of that small area which Banks evidently regarded as the true botanic garden. This was the

'Exotic Ground' which since 1773 had become the cynosure of interest for the King and himself. It lay east of the Pleasure Ground in front of the White House and the Orangery stretching as far as the lake, beyond which was the park land between Love Lane and Kew Road with the Pagoda at its southern end. This had all been the care of William Aiton the elder since 1783 as a result of his original association with the Old Botanic Garden under the Dowager Princess of Wales from 1759. For some 20 years Banks and the assiduous Scotsman had worked together in an amicable relationship. Banks had developed the same flexible free-lance liaison over the same period with the Cabinet and civil service at Westminster and Whitehall. At Kew his authority derived directly from the King as a personal friend and trusted adviser, a role he performed with integrity and good judgement for nearly 50 years during which he was in the main respected by the royal staff there.

As the bread-fruit ships at Jamaica were assembling what was to be the richest single accession of botanical prizes for the exotic plots and greenhouses, William Aiton died. When David Dundas, apothecary to the King, gave Banks this news on Friday 1 February 1793 he included a plea on behalf of the Aiton family, seeking Banks's approval for the appointment of William Townsend Aiton, the eldest son, to his father's post. He was under pressure too from other quarters for, on 2 February, Sir Francis Henry Drake from the Court of St James's was advising the son that a recommendation from Banks was 'the best assurance of your being equal to the situation'. Banks, Jonas Dryander, John Zoffany and Dr Samuel Goodenough were among the pall-bearers at the burial of the father in the churchyard of St Anne's, Kew Green. Soon after this the new order began with the appointment of W. T. Aiton to continue the working association with Banks on the same pattern as that in which his father had evolved as royal gardener.

Among the accessions to the Royal Botanic Garden, recorded up to 1789 in the first edition of the *Hortus Kewensis*, no more than 47 species are attributed to Banks directly as introductions and none is dated later than 1781. The majority of these were derivatives of the *Endeavour* voyage from New Zealand, Australia, the East Indies and St Helena, with several from Newfoundland and Iceland, the earliest dated 1767. It is probable that Banks first met the elder Aiton at Kew in 1764 about the time of his first encounter with Solander and as a natural extension from his early association with James Lee's nursery at Hammersmith and Phillip Miller at the Chelsea Physic Garden. Indeed the Exotic Garden at Kew was designed and laid out on the same Linnaean plan as that at Chelsea, of which it may be regarded as the scion, when William Aiton, the former pupil and assistant of Phillip Miller, became the first royal gardener to the young King George III. It was not until the second decade of the garden that Banks began his role as unofficial director of its botanical future in a scientific way. Its horticultural foundation undoubtedly stands to the credit of William Aiton but it was Banks who brought the desultory imports of exotic plants into a steady stream, backed by an organized herbarium and a comprehensive reference library. The Royal Botanic Garden in the grounds of Kew House and William Aiton were the King's to command and a charge on the Privy Purse. The herbarium and library and the services of Jonas Dryander at Soho Square were a charge on the income of Sir Joseph Banks. The combination, based on an unusual but strong friendship between the King and his subject, was recorded in botanical literature under the putative authorship of the Aitons, father and son, as the two editions of the *Hortus Kewensis* and the listing of the 11 000 odd plant species with which, for all practical purposes, this partnership ended soon after the publication of the *Epitome* in 1814, dedicated to Banks by W. T. Aiton

> ... with a deep sense of his cordial friendship, and in gratitude for his innumerable donations of the most rare exotics to the Royal Collection of Kew

'Innumerable' seems to be the right word, not for the magnitude of the donations but for the gaps in the record. Banks kept no separate note of the seeds, bulbs, corms, cuttings and growing plants that survived the exigencies of sea travel to reach home ground. For him the files of his correspondence, with so many lists, contained the evidence at least of what was originally sent, and often of what actually arrived. But at Kew during the lifetime of the first Aiton little or nothing remains to mark what actually entered there and in what state apart from the first edition of *Hortus Kewensis*. With the appointment of the younger Aiton Banks had a new disciple on whom he could impose more order. As in the management of the royal flock and the royal farm staff so too with the royal plant collection and the royal gardeners his position was delicate, and with no formal position at Court he had to tread warily. But at least from 1793 a more or less formal register was kept for the various accessions and donations. The listing of the species gradually became more complete and formal as botanical knowledge and expertise developed among the collectors and as the education of W. T. Aiton by Banks and Dryander matured. The first year of the new order at Kew was also the first of the new disorder in the war with France which added a further obstacle to transporting living plants by sea. But it was also one of the richest, potentially, in the accessions of new species to the Exotic Garden.

That year saw the arrival, on 7 June, of 82 boxes and tubs of plants brought by Governor Phillip in his return home on the *Atlantic*; on 8 June, 3 boxes of plants and 1 of seeds from Francis Masson, through Banks, with dried plant specimens for Banks packed with seed 'papers'; on 18 June, from Banks a box of seeds and roots collected in New Holland by Archibald Menzies, including new *Banksia* species; on the same date, also from Banks, 20 'papers' of seeds from Captain William Paterson at Norfolk Island and 80 such packets of seeds from Port Jackson brought by Phillip; with these was a letter from Dr Thomas Dancer at Jamaica enclosing a list of what was to be expected from Bligh on the *Providence*; also a letter from John Sibthorp with a list of plants as desiderata for the Botanic Garden at Oxford in response to the King's offer of a donation; on 26 June, a box containing a 'Camellia with white bark' brought in Banks's spring cart; on 28 June, from the same source, a parcel of seeds collected by Menzies on the NW coast of America with a list of the species contained; on 23 July, again through Banks, 3 boxes of plants from William Roxburgh at Calcutta; and, between 7 and 10 August the plant collection from HMS *Providence* – some 702 plants of 365 species. Of these, 17 were noted as from Tahiti; 3 from Van Diemen's Land; 1 (dead) from Possession Island, New Guinea; 12 from Timor; 6 from St Helena; 230 from St Vincent; and 96 from Jamaica. However, only 147 species remained extant to find a place in the second edition of *Hortus Kewensis*, 1810–13, as having been introduced in 1793 by Captain Bligh. Thus, in the record of these two months alone, we have a glimpse of the botanical returns arriving at Kew from three great voyages – the 'First Fleet' under Governor Phillip to Botany Bay; the Vancouver expedition to the NW coast of America; and the second bread-fruit voyage of Bligh to Tahiti – with Banks somewhere at the centre in the origin and management of them all.

283

The royal plant collection at Kew increased on this pattern for the next 30 years more or less according to Banks's plans emerging from his correspondence, until several years after his death when his absence was at last apparent. From about 1773 onwards both the Aitons found day-to-day guidance and inspiration in Banks, relying on his influence with the King and the Board of Green Cloth under the Lord Steward for the resolution of financial and managerial problems. Banks himself gave generously of his time and of his own money. There is little or no evidence that he was reimbursed for expenses relating to the garden as he was for the royal flock. The costs of transport for plants and such equipment as the glazed plant cabins to and from the ships in the Thames and other ports such as Deal, Portsmouth and Bristol were paid directly under the Aitons's accounts with the Lord Steward. Water carriage along the Thames from Kew as far as Greenhithe and Long Reach seems to have been conducted for many years by two women, Ann and Mary Layton, with items noted as 'from Sir J. Banks' month after month, in the form of cases, boxes, parcels, baskets and crates of plants and seeds – to and from India and China, America, New South Wales and the Cape of Good Hope. A letter from W. T. Aiton to Sir Henry Strachey at the Board of Green Cloth, dated 11 November 1807, asking for an increase of £100 per annum to cover the increased activity of the Garden is revealing. In the preceding five years he cited the extensive importations through the East India Company, the West Indies merchants, Francis Masson in Upper Canada, William Kerr at Canton and the Governor of New South Wales, but

> ... His Majesty's Collection is most especially indebted to Sir Joseph Banks, who has procured loads of seeds and plants from all Parts of the World at his own Expense.

As one measure of the growth Aiton cited from the evidence of the garden books from 1802–7 the receipt of 'upwards of Four Thousand Papers of Seeds and Roots ... many of which have vegetated', a general success in the Garden calling inevitably for more labour. However, it was not until Aiton's *Epitome of the second edition of Hortus Kewensus* that some overt recognition of Banks's role in the growth of the Royal Botanic Garden was made in the dedication. The 449 species recorded in 1814 against his name as viable introductions can only be a modest sample of the true figure.

CHAPTER 14

THE RED RIBBON AND WHITEHALL
1790–1797

Late in the afternoon of Saturday 20 March 1790 a man troubled with a tumour of one eye arrived at 32 Soho Square direct from Paris. It was the end of a journey which had begun in Hungary 1200 miles to the east before the death of the Emperor Joseph II on 20 February. The man was the Baron Vay de Vaja and his eye trouble was the pretext for his journey. The quest for medical advice had been the excuse given for his leave of absence from the Imperial Army. His real intention was a secret visit to London and Sir Joseph Banks was the man he sought for reasons that lay far from the natural sciences. It is a strange story with no clear beginning nor an obvious end. Banks, for once, was caught in circumstances beyond his knowledge or control and briefly enmeshed in William Pitt's manoeuvres within the Triple Alliance. It says much for Banks's reputation for political independence that he should have been chosen by a remote and, to him, unknown group of dissident Hungarians as a channel for their approach to the British Government.

The Baron lost no time in binding Banks to secrecy on those things 'relative to Hungary' about which he had come. At the Baron's urgent insistence, Banks immediately wrote to Pitt and saw him in person at half-past-eight in Downing Street that same night. The Baron insisted that word had been sent to Pitt from Vienna as early as the beginning of February with an identifying code of 12 figures. Of this Pitt denied any knowledge and asked for time to consider whether he should see the Baron. As the message was supposed to have been sent by Jacobi, the Prussian Minister at Berlin, the Baron was understandably cast down. He could only suppose, he said, that the Prussian Court did not deal openly with the British – in which there was much truth – or that he had been betrayed, but the Baron pressed Banks even more firmly for a meeting with Pitt. It was imperative, he said, that they should meet before the British Government made an official comment on the death of the Emperor. He stressed again that he was indeed the envoy of a large association of patriot Hungarians who were the soul and spirit of his country. They were, he assured Banks, a body of settled men as well as the most powerful families in the kingdom '. . . so that no danger of a democracy arising from a revolution was to be Feard'. He was in truth, he repeated, the chosen deputy of those men who were the real managers of Hungary and he could prove this by the extent and detail of his knowledge even without the secret numerical cypher. Enlarging somewhat, he said that he often met the Prussian Minister, Jacobi, in Vienna but always in the darker parts of the city at night and in the open air safe from eavesdroppers. Thus he was well informed on the secret proceedings of the Court at Berlin. The Hungarians, according to the Baron, wanted nothing new. They wished only to have their 300-year old constitution restored and they looked to England for help. In his own words: 'We look upon England as a sun which may warm us without scorching. Prussia is a

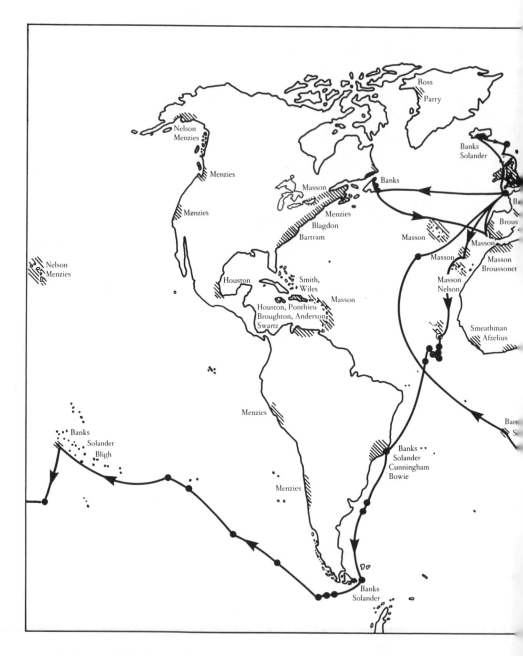

GEOGRAPHIC SOURCES OF BANKS COLLECTIONS

Plant specimens:
Collected by Banks: ▨▨▨
Collected by Others: /////////

Marine fauna
Collected by Banks: (at sea) ●

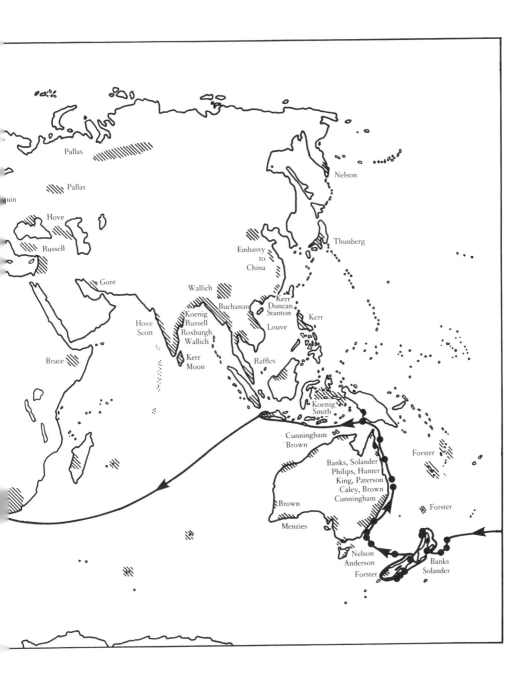

Pallas

Pallas

uin

Hove

Russell

Gore

Hove
Scott

Bruce

Wallich

Buchanan

Koenig
Russell
Roxburgh
Wallich

Kerr
Moon

Raffles

Nelson

Thunberg

Embassy
to
China

Kerr
Duncan
Stanton

Louve

Kerr

Koenig
Smith

Cunningham
Brown

Forster

Banks, Solander
Philips, Hunter
King, Paterson
Caley, Brown
Cunningham

Forster

Brown

Menzies

Nelson
Anderson
Forster

Banks
Solander

287

sun that may burn as well as warm'. The new King of Hungary, Leopold II, was judged to have the same arbitrary views as his brother the late Emperor in spite of his protestations of agreement to their just demands. They thought Leopold was merely more cunning than Joseph and in this they were close to the mark.

The Baron appeared at breakfast, in Soho Square, daily for a week or more with growing concern at the elusiveness of William Pitt and his own sense of being watched. At the opera on the very day of his arrival he had noted a man who studied him with particular attention whom he thought he recognized as one of Leopold's spies from Vienna. He was worried too about the state of his eye which, although he used it as a cover story, was still in a distressing state. Banks referred him to John Hunter who declared for the removal of the whole eye. This in itself did not distress the Baron but he agreed with Banks that excuses must be found to delay the operation until his negotiations with Pitt, from whom for seven days no word had come. Banks reminded him that the Prime Minister had much to ponder before he could reach a decision. Then on 29 March Banks received a letter from Pitt:

> Nothing but the multiplicity of business has prevented me writing to you sooner. I would now beg the favor of you to assure your Friend that I shall be very ready to see him as a private Man and to receive any Information He may wish to give me; but I am at the same Time desirous that it should be fully understood that the Circumstances under which He comes will make it impossible for me to enter any Ministerial Explanation on the Subject of his Communications . . . P.S. If it is not inconvenient to you, I believe the best mode of my Meeting you Friend would be to call at your House, which I shall be glad to do at Twelve Tomorrow.

Fearful still that he was being watched, the Baron and Banks played a furtive game. Pitt was to be met on the steps of the parish church of St Anne, Soho, precisely at 12 noon on Tuesday 30 March and taken by the back door in Dean Street into 32 Soho Square. On that day Banks waited for a quarter of an hour, only to be met by Pitt's private secretary pleading pressure of business for his master but fixing the appointment for the next day at the same place. On the Wednesday Pitt was punctual and swiftly escorted by Banks to meet the Baron in the privacy he sought. For an hour the Prime Minister and the Hungarian envoy conferred. From memory the Baron passed over the secret numbers which were to have been his passport to the full confidence of Pitt – 179009710971 – and later in the day left a copy of them with Banks in case his memory had failed him in the anxiety of the moment. Pitt then went back to the Treasury seemingly impressed with the Baron as someone well informed. Later that same day Banks sent him as full an account of the man as he could.

The Baron however had judged it wise to go only just so far with Pitt at this first meeting, emphasizing simply why it was proper for Great Britain to interfere in favour of Hungary: the House of Austria could never offer such advantages to England as Hungary with its nine and-a-half million souls, the market for English manufactures and the access it would give to the Turkish and Levant trade; the nature of Hungary's ancient constitution implied that it could never fall into a state of anarchy such as, presumably, in France; the characters of the Hungarians engaged in working for a revolution and a divorce from the Holy Roman Empire were moral and virtuous. They had no Mirabeau among them.

The Baron stressed that there was more to be said and Banks agreed that if nothing was heard from Pitt in four days he would write again. Ten days passed, however, and the Baron kept up his regular visits to Soho Square to preserve the cover of an ordinary social intercourse there. There was still no word from Pitt though Banks knew that however much the politics of Europe and the affair at Nootka Sound may have pressed, the Prime Minister was in fact away from London canvassing in his constituency at Cambridge and about his private affairs at Holwood House. Meanwhile the tensions of waiting had caused the Baron to open his heart more freely to Banks who was well aware that there was more to come. Finally on 23 April, although protesting that he too was under pressure from 'a variety of business', Banks agreed to write again to Pitt. He emphasized the importance of a Latin paper drafted by the Baron covering the points he wished the Cabinet to consider in their communications with Vienna. Three days later Banks again saw Pitt in person handing him the document as the Baron had insisted for reasons of security. The Prime Minister deferred a further meeting with the Baron for several days but suggested the same sort of clandestine appointment as they had used before.

Nothing further happened for more than a week until, again under pressure from his visitor, Banks saw Pitt on the morning of 6 May. The Baron was near the limit of his patience and clearly worried about his own position. He offered to meet Pitt at Holwood if necessary should there be no opportunity in London. At length the final meeting was arranged by Pitt at the East India House in Leadenhall Street on 9 May at nine o'clock in the evening when no one but the porter would be able to observe them. The Baron returned from this encounter to Soho Square disheartened, and the next day told Banks that it was all over. Pitt had still not received the secret numbers and he could do no more. It may have been that the arrival from Vienna at this point of the young chargé d'affaires George Hammond, with fresh advice that closed this clandestine episode. It was through Hammond in fact that the Baron had been authorized by his band of patriots to offer the throne of Hungary to the Duke of York as an expression of the strong Protestant affinities in the country. This had been during the illness of George III early in 1789 when the Prince of Wales had been to some extent involved but all notions of a British sovereign of Hungary rapidly faded on the King's recovery.

Some faint echo of this unsuccessful earlier episode may have prompted the Baron to turn again to Banks hoping that he could use his friendship with the King. Several times he asked Banks to arrange a meeting with the King but, true to his practice, Banks refused. At length the Baron conceded that it would be improper to expect it but as a last effort suggested the equerry General Budé as a pathway to the King, again without effect. In the course of these enquiries he asked Banks if the King could keep a secret. This brought the illuminating though unhelpful reply that His Majesty often spoke on subjects with Banks about which he, Banks, certainly thought the King should have been silent.

The incident, for us, came to its enigmatic end on 22 May wrapped in the mystery of a packet addressed to Freiherr Nicolaus von Jacquin in Vienna. Clandestine to the end, the Baron had found this means, through Banks, to send a letter to Count Harzberg enclosed with an official one from the Secretary of the Royal Society to another Count, Rohde, seeking a volume of his works. This in turn was covered by a short letter which Banks had written in French to Count Harzberg offering himself as a means of communication to the Baron. The final touch of undercover complexity was added by sending the cyphered message in the binding of one of the books in the package with another to Baron Padmanishki. He was to deliver it to 'Jos Vay by the Messenger from the foreign department to the care of Sr R M Keith', the redoubtable British Minister at Vienna.

The Baron seems to have stayed on in England until the end of the summer studying the industrial advances of the English manufacturers, in particular the engines of Boulton and Watt Ltd. He clearly found many reasons also for avoiding optical surgery for he returned to the Continent with his eye and his tumour intact. He still enjoyed the beneficent influence of Banks who had given him a letter of introduction to Johann Blumenbach at Göttingen. The Baron stayed with Blumenbach for a week during which he saw the oculist Richter. From him he was no doubt comforted to learn that his tumour, which had served the purpose of his abortive mission so well, was apparently benign and not carcinomatous; 15 years later the Baron's eye was still intact.

The secret mission seems to have ended in arousing Matthew Boulton's interest as an engineer in providing machines for the mines of Hungary rather than in a patriotic revolution there. But the Baron's contact with Pitt may have had some slight influence on his policy of detaching the Austrians under Leopold II from his ally Catherine II of Russia in her war against the Turks and in securing his alliance with Great Britain. There must have been some substance in the Baron's mission to deflect both Pitt and Banks from their courses and to occupy so much of their time in the troubled year of 1790.

II

As the incident of the Hungarian Baron was tucked away in the basement files of history a different exercise in international affairs was growing in the Home Office. At the elections of June 1790 Henry Dundas had been returned for the City of Edinburgh and became Home Secretary provisionally until he was confirmed in that office after the refusal of Cornwallis had been received from India. For ten years Dundas had been immersed in the affairs of the Far East and, since the passage of Pitt's East India Bill in 1784, he had been a member of the Board of Control of the Honourable East India Company. Though he did not become President of the Board until 1793 he was from the beginning almost alone in charge of Indian business. Both as a minister of the Cabinet and as a member of the Board of Control he was engaged, from as early as 1785, with Indian problems of mutual concern to himself and Banks. These extended to the East India Company's operations at the Canton factory in China, the troubles of its supercargoes with the merchants of the Co-hong and the more remote administration of Peking. Here too for more than ten years Banks had been exploring the mysteries of Chinese natural history. His helpers were John Duncan and later his brother Alexander as resident surgeons at the Company factory in Canton. The combination of Dundas and Banks in mounting an embassy to China followed from their regular association in the affairs of the Company and of the Privy Council Committee for Trade and Foreign Plantations. From Dundas, in harness with Pitt, came the political drive that set the Embassy in motion and framed its official instructions. From Banks came the advice which gathered men and information for the more technical purposes of this first real British adventure into the closed world beyond the precarious *entrepôt* of Canton.

In the late autumn of 1791 Lord Macartney was appointed to lead the Embassy as the man with the best diplomatic and administrative experience for such a mission. It followed almost as an axiom that Sir George Leonard Staunton should continue his long association with Macartney on foreign service and go as Secretary to the Embassy and as minister in case of the Ambassador's death. Staunton's friendship with Banks was long standing and serving him to some effect in the summer of 1791. Armed with a letter from Banks to Gaetano d'Ancora in Naples, he had made one visit to the city which would again claim his attention before his return home. It was to Banks that both Macartney and Staunton turned for non-diplomatic help. Banks wrote to Macartney in January 1792:

> I confess I Feel much interest in the Success of an undertaking from whence the usefull as well as the ornamental Sciences are likely to derive infinite benefit The Chinese appear to me to possess the Ruin of a State & Civilisation in which when in Perfection the human mind had carried all kinds of Knowledge to a much higher Pitch than the Europeans have hitherto done . . . What is there of the great inventions as we call them that are not known to these people . . . to Learn these arts alone [that is, the growing of tea and the making of porcelain] would be to give to Europe an invaluable blessing but how many of these wrecks of ancient wisdom China possesses we know not probably most of the manufactures stand upon the Same basis and a few Learned men admitted among their workmen might in a Few weeks acquire Knowledge for which the whole Revenue of the immense empire would not be thought a sufficient equivalent . . .

He lent Macartney immediately 78 volumes from what he had been in the habit of calling a Chinese encyclopaedia with 'Figures of all the Handicraft tools usd in the Empire' and the first volume of Benedict Herman's *Beytrage zur physik, oekonomie . . . und zur statistik besonders der Russischen und angranzenden lander*, 1786, 'which contains the short Statistical account of the Chinese Empire I mentioned when I last had the honor of seeing your Lordship'. This was the beginning of continuous help that would not cease until the final account of the Embassy was published in 1797.

His education of Staunton, who was eventually to bear the burden of writing and publishing the official account, began at the same time. On 26 January 1792 Staunton replied to a letter which he had received from Banks:

> . . . Nothing can be more advantageous or more gratifying to the Persons embarking in the Present undertaking than the favorable light in which you consider it. And I make no doubt that you will be able to induce administration and the Company to extend their views to every point of general Utility of which the Business may be made productive . . .

Failing to find Chinese interpreters in Paris, Staunton turned to his 'best and last resource at Naples', delayed by an accident crossing the Alps, bad roads, deep snow, lack of post horses and 'a variety of vexatious circumstances not a little felt by a hasty Traveller'. Supported by the letters from Banks to Sir William Hamilton and d'Ancora, Staunton was at last able to gain the services of Jacobus Li and Pablo Cho, two Chinese interpreters from the college of the Congregation De Propaganda Fide in Naples.

Meanwhile in London a sequence of short notes and unrecorded meetings passed

291

between Banks and Macartney. Through the winter and spring the search went on for skilled and knowledgeable men in a range of technical fields to man the Embassy as savants and servants. This posed a dilemma. The early cloak of secrecy which had been cast over the mission had successfully stifled public curiosity and denied Banks 'the thousand tongues at work who are the only good beaters up for voluntier recruits' as he made the point to Staunton in April. Moreover he did not find the Government and the Company sharing his views of how the business could be made productive 'in every point of general Utility' as Staunton had fondly hoped. Indeed it was so far from going well at this stage that, as Banks said:

> ... Everyone Complains that the arrangement is made without any regard to natural history which some think should have been the first thing attended to as it certainly is the foundation of the whole. The mechanic cannot seize the chance of discovering the ore of a new metal in Europe the dyer of getting the Plant from which a new dye is extracted nor a Potter the Clay of which China ware is made The naturalist alone can by considering these investigate their advantage to the Produce of /Europe/ the rest of the World & take advantage of the affinities or identities he may find to things already Known ...

Here are the clues to what was being sought in gathering the personnel of the Embassy. It involved Banks in long but fruitless negotiations with the luminaries of the Manchester Literary and Philosophical Society, Thomas Percival, FRS and Thomas Henry, FRS, for a chemist competent in the mysteries of bleaching, dyeing and printing fabrics. This foundered in the failure of the Government to meet the standards of remuneration of the Manchester trade.

The search involved Banks also with the shades of his own youthful past. For many reasons Dr James Lind, FRS, now a prosperous physician settled at Windsor, seemed admirably suited to the aims of the Embassy. With a period of residence in India and a voyage to China behind him he was also 'well acquainted with experimental Philosophy Chemistry and mechanics', a tolerable astronomer, an ardent performer of 'amusing experiments', an admirer of the Chinese with a smattering of the language and writing. Banks presented him to Macartney who was prepared to offer him £2500, of which £500 was out of Macartney's own pocket, for two years' absence. Banks was mortified to learn that Lind would not now consider less than £6000 in advance, because, he thought, of the parliamentary grant of £4000 intended for him had he gone with Cook on his second voyage. It was found that Lind had consulted Dundas who had given him little or no hope of the East India Company making much contribution to the expenses of the Embassy and had advised him against joining it. So Banks had to set his sights a little lower. In the end he recommended an Aberdonian graduate, Dr Hugh Gillan, who modestly accepted £200 a year.

Gillan was evidently lacking in experimental philosophy, mechanics and the performance of 'amusing experiments'. To remedy these deficiencies Macartney found Dr James Dinwiddie, another Scot and a graduate of Edinburgh. Banks and Macartney together interviewed him at his exhibition room in Clifford Street where he was appearing as a public lecturer in popular science, decorating his discourses with a show of 'philosophical fireworks'. Macartney had found him modest enough in appearance but professing a knowledge of almost everything. Bemused, he called for Banks to assess the man more closely; Banks pronounced him adequate for the Embassy's purpose, free to take with him his planetarium, his air balloon, his diving bell, and his equipment for experiments in electricty and mechanics and other branches of 'experimental philosophy'.

On the botanical side there was no one with matching expertise. Staunton himself was an ardent and well-meaning amateur, but he was to be supported by David Stronach, a young man from the commercial garden of A. Thomson of Mile End, who recommended him as 'strictly honest, sober, industrious & of an obliging disposition' with a 'considerable Knowledge in the management of plants in general'. He was a gardener and a valuable man but he was not a botanist. He was to be accompanied by another gardener, John Haxton. The Embassy therefore sailed without any naturalist or botanist of the calibre that Banks or, indeed, Macartney and Staunton, thought necessary.

Although both Gillan and Dinwiddie were to play useful parts on botanical matters their main interests and abilities, in the eyes of Banks and Macartney, lay elsewhere. For such botanical results as were to accrue the burden lay on Staunton assisted by Stronach and Haxton. Banks certainly had very qualified expectations of what they would achieve but hoped for some useful accretions of living plants or seeds for further cultivation. He sent the Embassy on its way with a paper of more than 3500 words entitled 'Hints on the Subject of Gardening suggested to the Gentlemen who attend the Embassy to China'. He supplemented this with a 'Note relative to the method of bringing to England seeds from China & Japan in a state of vegetation' and emphasized his wants with 'a list of curious plants, natives of China and Japan, wished to be obtained from thence'. Here he listed rather more than 20 species from Thunberg's *Flora Japonica*, Kaempfer's *Amoenitates exoticae* and some of those from his own recently published edition of selected species based on Kaempfer's drawings in the British Museum, the *Icones Kaempferianae*.

Although in these 'Hints . . .' matters of horticulture had precedence over those of a *hortus siccus*, Banks was careful to end with an explicit statement 'Relative to the Collecting Plants for the Purposes of Botany . . .' advising the same comprehensive approach to the flora that he and Solander had adopted on the *Endeavour* voyage and whose wisdom is still appreciated by the plant geographers of today:

> . . . To leave behind one scarce & curious plant under the mistaken Idea of its being a common one will be a source of vexation for ever afterwards if the circumstance happens to be discovered to bring home a hundred common ones will be no great matter either of Labor or inconvenience I should also advise that many individual specimens of each species be brought home in order that different Botanists may be consulted in case of any difficulty & presents of Specimens made to various professors of Botany on the Return of the Embassy for the honor & credit of those who have been concernd in it . . .

Written at Spring Grove early in August these 'Hints . . .' were sent to Staunton under cover of a letter in which Banks wished the Embassy farewell with every good wish to all his friends

> . . . the Endeavours they make for the Promotion of Science, the increase of Commerce between distant nations & the Real prosperity not only of their own Country but also of that they intend to visit . . .

As a parting gift he sent Staunton a copy of his *Icones Kaempferianae*; as a parting request he reminded him also of his promise relative to the Ipecacuanha plant, botanically still undetermined in spite of the specimens collected for him five years earlier by Governor Phillip at Rio de Janeiro. Although Phillip had apparently sent him specimens of two species these were imperfect being only leaves and roots. So he emphasized that other paramount axiom for plant collectors:

> ... you Know that without Flowers & Fruits the distinguishing Characters cannot be investigated Either Flowers or Fruits however would be a valuable addition to our medico-botanical knowledge ...

The Embassy set sail from Spithead on Wednesday 26 September 1792 with Macartney and his entourage on board HMS *Lion*, Captain Erasmus Gower. The guard and the greater part of the presents were on the *Hindostan* Indiaman, Captain William Macintosh and these two ships kept close company during the outward voyage to its furthest point at the mouth of the Peiho, near Tientsin. The third vessel the *Jackal* brig, tender, did not overtake them until March the following year in the Straits of Sunda.

The Embassy reached Chusan Roads, on 3 July 1793, from whence Chinese pilots conducted them somewhat uncertainly to a station deep in the Gulf of Chihli, about 20 miles from the mouth of the Peiho. Here they laboriously disembarked for the journey upstream in smaller vessels to Tientsin and Peking arriving on 26 August to prepare for the final stage to the Imperial Court at its summer home in Jehol beyond the Great Wall. Macartney and Staunton reached this distant goal on 8 September and on 14 September were presented to the Emperor Ch'ien Lung for the serious business of the mission. It had taken nearly a year. Having journeyed so far for so long, the Embassy from the 'Western Ocean' was allowed to spend rather less than two weeks at the summer court before returning to Peking to await the formal return of the Emperor.

Here, in a quaint ceremony, Macartney received the Latin translation of the 'edict' from Ch'ien Lung to George III. With this splendidly arrogant document the Embassy was dismissed from the 'Celestial Empire', perhaps no wiser but in some measure better informed about China and the Chinese. On 7 October it began its laborious journey of more than 1800 miles south by river, through the Grand Canal, and by land. More than two months later, on 19 December, it reached the neighbourhood of Canton. On 8 January Macartney embarked on HMS *Lion* and on the 12th anchored in Macao Roads. For another two months the gentlemen of the Embassy lodged for the most part at the English Factory in Macao or nearby, while Macartney himself was quartered in the upper part of the town in a house that was by tradition in Macao the home of Camoens and the birthplace of *The Lusiads*. Here in this old garden between January and March the plants therein were listed by David Stronach and perhaps a few specimens gathered for the official collection.

On 17 March 1794 the ships of the Embassy, in company with the East India Company ships of the season, set sail for home, dependent on the 64 guns of HMS *Lion* for their protection, for the war with France meant that the Eastern Seas were no longer safe. The convoy reached home waters without loss, on 6 September 1794, having taken almost two years as had been estimated. All it had achieved was a few days of a quasi-diplomatic negotiation with the Imperial Court of China and little advance in trade beyond the modest links already established through the English Factory at Canton and Macao. In this rebuff the Embassy had not differed from the six other European attempts during the previous century or more to penetrate the closed society of China and its philosophy. As a first attempt by the English however it was not unrewarding for the course of future commerce in the knowledge gained toward the growth of Oriental studies. Hurriedly mounted in the vortex of a great upheaval in European politics at the outset of a long and disastrous war it was, of its kind, a brave adventure into the unknown mysteries of the Far East.

Throughout the two years Banks was in touch with the Embassy by a steady correspondence which, though sparse, made use of every opportunity. By each available ship on the homeward course some sort of message was sent to the man in Soho Square who replied whenever a reasonable chance of reaching the Embassy occurred. From Madeira, from Oratava and Rio de Janeiro came letters from Macartney, Staunton and Gillan on matters of natural history and the progress of plans laid – the search for the Ipecacuanha plant and for the cochineal insect and its host cactus. From HMS *Lion* off the coasts of Sumatra and Java came letters from Staunton about his 'philosophical adventures' on the passage from South America, his search for the truth behind the legend of the Cayu upas, the 'poison tree' of Java, and for specimens of the nutmeg, the mangosteen and the litchi, lamenting that Adam Afzelius was not with him to guide his amateur hand. By the homing Indiamen *Royal Admiral* and *Sulivan* he sent live nutmeg and mangosteen plants, a nutmeg nut 'fit for germination', six volumes of the *Transactions* . . . of the pioneer scientific society in the tropics, the Bataviaasch Genootschap, and from one of these a Latin translation from the Dutch original of a paper refuting the horror stories associated with the 'Upas-tree'. In return and waiting for him at Canton, Staunton found a letter from Banks written ten months before acknowledging the receipt of letters from Madeira, Tenerife and Brazil up to December 1792. Banks wrote after the recent execution of Louis XVI and the declaration of war with France:

> . . . the French nation are certainly in a state of Canine madness very desirous of biting all mankind & by that means infecting them with the disease they themselves are vexd with I conceive them like a Pack of mad Foxhounds who cannot be confind to their Kennell & Feel sometimes a kind of horror lest they should infect too many of the Quiet animals who are Feeding around them . . .

Staunton replied with sombre agreement that the French conduct was a disgrace to human nature and that '. . . if freedom had at once been granted to the slaves of Jamaica or St. Domingo They could not act more shockingly' – a revealing note on the social perspectives of the times and a foreboding of what the next decade would bring. By now however the business of the Embassy was over. He had already sent Banks a letter from Hangchow, capital of the province of Chekiang and was lugubrious about the achievement of the Embassy and his own defeats 'in point of Curiosity':

> . . . I cannot say that I have as much enriched my mind by my present Tour as I expected, owing to the obstructions we met. My son has learnt a little Chinese, which may be useful . . .

Still, there were some useful accretions in the collections of plants made on the journey south from Peking, the two pairs of live Chinese cormorants, the eggs of the Chinese silkworm, some coins for Miss Banks – and a promise of some young tea plants.

Early in the New Year the last letters from Staunton to Banks were sent on their way, with pots of living plants and other specimens by the *Minerva*, Captain Smith. With these went also letters from Dr Alexander Duncan and from the French Consul at Macao, Chrétien de Guignes shedding light on the fortunes of the Embassy in various ways. Duncan could affirm that, despite the evident abilities of the gentlemen of the Embassy and their ardent pursuit of knowledge '. . . 'tis much to be regretted that many of the regions of Science in this delightful Empire remain still unexplored from the jealous nature of the Chinese' and that '. . . nothing as yet transpires in the smallest degree advantageous to the Honble Company'. Guignes was shocked at the outbreak of war between his own country and England but in spite of this he chose Banks as the safe hand through whom he could send his report from the French ship which had sought shelter in Macao from the guns of HMS *Lion*. This, with Alexander Duncan's letters, would go home on the *Bombay Castle*, Captain Burgess which these same English guns would now protect.

Before this news from China reached him Banks was deep in his committment as High Sheriff of Lincolnshire and although 'encumberd with a Load of new Business' could find time on 15 February 1794 to send at a hazard a last letter to Staunton. This recorded the arrival of all that had been sent to him from 15 April 1793 which indeed was all that had been sent. In fact as far as is known all the letters between Soho Square and the Embassy reached each other. The same could not be said however for the live plants.

When the ships of the Embassy anchored in the Thames Banks was still away in the country. Blagden however had met Sir George Staunton on 11 September and next day reported to Banks the particulars about the Embassy that had escaped the metropolitan press, with further gossipy details on 6 October. So when Banks returned to London in the first week of November he was well primed to scan the notes which Macartney had prepared for him to see in advance of the journal which was in the hands of Henry Dundas. Before the end of the year Staunton was charged with producing the official account of the Embassy in spite of his declining health. Because he wished to include as much as possible of the natural history of the journey he sought Banks's aid. Henry Dundas however had involved Banks more generally in the whole plan of the intended publication. A meeting was arranged at the East India House for 15 January 1795 and here, between Dundas, Banks and Staunton, the guide-lines were set on the basis of what had been adopted for the publication of Cook's last voyage ten years earlier. No one was more competent than Banks to explain how that was done nor to advise on this new publication.

The next day Banks prepared his statement and in his covering letter to Dundas said:

> . . . I am ready to undertake any part of the business you may chuse to commit to my charge. I think it my duty in all matters of literary import, which I consider my department, to give every assistance in my power to his Majesty's Ministers . . .

But he tactfully refused to take any detailed charge of the work provided George

Nicol, was employed. With Nicol he felt that he could act unobtrusively as watch-dog over the expenditure in the interests of the HEI Company and the Government but not deprive the editor, Staunton, of the credit for the work as a whole. Thus it was as a form of sheet-anchor that he gave support to Staunton struggling for the next six months to produce the official account and to regain his health at Bath. Banks himself was also in the grip of a severe attack of gout, but with the help of John Barrow, supervised the work of selecting from Alexander's drawings those to be engraved and in managing the engravers themselves. At the same time he contrived at least a preliminary study of the plant collections which had been put in his hands. He had this to say to Staunton on 2 May 1795:

> . . . Respecting your Plants the coldness of the Season soon after Christmas which always prevents the possibility of doing business in my Library that requires references to many Books & the subsequent fit of the Gout which rendered me incapable of much exertion for six weeks have put that business very backward which otherwise would have been nearly finished by this time . . .

Banks had seen enough of the collection of plant specimens to realise that his careful instructions on the gathering had not been well observed. Staunton had wished to include as much natural history as possible in his account but Banks, after his first scrutiny, was not encouraging. His comments were restrained and he tried to conceal his disappointment but by degrees he could no longer forbear to voice his criticism. Apart from the imperfections of the specimens in the *hortus siccus* he was emphatic about the failure of Dr Gillan who, he had understood, was to provide notes on the botanical structure at least of those plants which seemed to claim some particular notice. It soon appeared that no such notes had been made. Banks complained:

> . . . the dried specimens alone are our only Guide & Linnaeus's example holds for the Enlightened the danger that those incur who write from dried Specimens without some notes taken from these Plants when alive Strongly Enough to deter modern botanists from dabling too deeply in that dangerous undertaking . . .

In November 1795, after a strenuous year, with Staunton's account almost ready to go to press, Banks found it necessary to impose a note of reality on what botanical material could reasonably be included, he said:

> . . . I fear you have notwithstanding I have from time to time done my Endeavour to Prevent it Led yourself to Expect much more from me towards the intended publication than the Collections put into my hands will Enable me to do to have enterd into a Botanical discussion upon Every Plant Collected in the Voyage would have been a Task far more Tedious & possibly more laborious than to have Compiled the details of the Journal if dried specimens are very good it is Possible tho not without some risks to make usefull description of remarkable Plants but I am sorry to tell you that as far as I have looked over your Collections & Ld Macartneys the specimens have been very indifferently selected & as ill managd in Drying . . .

297

He pointed out that during this month the Royal Society took precedence over everything else. Natural history had no place until after the anniversary meeting. Then he settled down to finish the task. It was directed to making a simple catalogue with as many preliminary determinations as the state of the specimens would allow. This meant arranging them into their Linnaean classes and genera and, where possible, the species. In his opinion however none were in a sufficient state of completeness or of preservation '. . . either to be drawn or to be fully described'. He did indeed go so far as to suggest engravings of the Moutan (*Paeonia moutan* syn. *P. fruticosa*, the Chinese Tree Paeony) and the double Camellia (*Camellia sesanqua*). For the former he thought a Chinese painting would suffice as a model. For the second, which had already bloomed several times in England, a drawing was possible. He said, to make his point clear,

> . . . these are sure to interest all persons who are amusd by horticulture a class who have more pretensions upon you than scientific Botanists . . .

So the work went on with Banks, as he told Staunton, generally engaged with the plants '4 or 5 days in the 7', until on 7 March 1796 after finishing those from the Straits of Sunda he had to set the task aside. The great new accessions gathered by Archibald Menzies on the long Vancouver voyage through the Pacific and along the west coast of the Americas had come at last to Soho Square. Banks had done as much as he could at that time for the plants of the Embassy to China.

Although Banks was critical of the Embassy's material – the lack of proper written notes, the poor drying and preservation, so many specimens without either flowers or fruit – he had less to complain about on two other important points. His dictum on making the collection comprehensive as far as possible, even to the most common and well-known species, seems to have been well taken. So too was his injunction that as many duplicates as possible should be brought home to spread the burden of work widely among suitably capable botanists. From this procedure his own herbarium was enriched with others such as A. B. Lambert's and, ultimately perhaps the most important for this collection, that of Candolle. The work that Banks and Dryander performed intermittently over a period of 18 months was no more than a first view and it was to some extent reluctantly done. There was much pressure of other work – Dryander for one, was heavily committed to producing the first volume of the *Catalogus Bibliothecae Historico-naturalis Josephi Banks*. There was also Banks's awareness, as he emphasized, of just how much concentrated and detailed work was needed to make reasonable botanical diagnoses and proper descriptions, as he made clear in his letter of 6 May 1795 to Staunton:

> . . . What is going on here is an arrangement of all your Plants into Genera & species after which they are tied up docketed & put in their Places so that with the List which is kept of them the access to Ld. Macartneys Specimens to yours & to those you have been so good as to allow me to place in my herbarium will be as Easy as Possible if then at any time you find that any of your Freinds will under take to do more than I have venturd to attempt they will find a good deal done to their hands and all facilities of my Library &c &c shall be most heartily at their Service . . .

298

I have no doubt however that a sufficient Quantity of the more interesting objects may be brought before the Public in such a way as they will approve that is without the use of too many technical [terms] so that your work may have Quite as much Botany in it as the Public will in my opinion expect to Find or relish when it is Read

Of Staunton's plants there were certainly more than 400 species represented, gathered into six main parcels: those collected near Peking in the province of Chihli and about 'the Summer Palace', Yuan-ming Yuan, in Jehol; those collected on the return from Jehol to Peking; those taken on the first stages of the journey south through the Grand Canal and the provinces of Shantung, Kiangnan, and Chekiang; those gathered after crossing the Yang Tse River in the provinces of Kiangsi and Kwantung and after their arrival in the vicinities of Canton and Macao; those collected on the outward passage at Amsterdam Island and Pulo Condore and finally those from Java and Sumatra and about the Straits of Sunda.

Of all these specimens, it was only the contents of the first four parcels, some 398 species, which appeared in the lists published by Staunton, for they alone belonged to the Chinese mainland. Although credited to Staunton in the botanical literature it is evident that they were almost entirely gathered by John Haxton, whom he paid for this purpose out of his private resources. It is clear also that there was a second collection made by David Stronach, in the name of Lord Macartney. Stronach was an accredited servant of the Embassy paid from the public purse. There was also young George Thomas Staunton's collection. How many plants in all were gathered we do not know. From the two main collections the specimens have been dispersed through herbaria in Great Britain, France, Germany, Italy and Switzerland – as Banks in principle had recommended. Even today by no means all have been finally traced nor fully determined and described.

By the end of the nineteenth century some 222 species from 141 genera had achieved a formal taxonomic place in the botanical records, of which 194 were attributed to the Staunton collection alone, 17 to that of Macartney, while the remainder were assigned to both sources. Among these at that date only 27 species were recorded as being lodged in the Banks herbarium. The greater part, certainly those of Staunton's collection, seems to have finally graced the herbarium of Augustin de Candolle. He recorded the determinations of at least 31 species from this source in his two great works, the *Regni Vegetabilis Systema Naturale* and the later *Prodromus* . . ., which included in the former the new genus *Stauntonia*, a climbing shrub. Indeed botanical commemoration was more lavishly given to Staunton, the diplomatic-amateur of botany, than most men achieve in a lifetime of scientific devotion to the subject. Apart from the new genus, no less than ten species and one variety were named after him. For Macartney, who had his barony of course, there was but one species to mark his passing brush with field botany.

The true labourers in the field, John Haxton and David Stronach, found no such enduring memorial – apart from the linking of Haxton's name with Staunton's in the record of five plant introductions to the Royal Botanic Garden at Kew. It is only from the journal of John Haxton, of which Banks transcribed his own extracts, that we have a glimpse of how much he found 'Botany in bad repute' among the Chinese; for example, as the Embassy passed through the Grand Canal:

299

... having on the 14 Octr. 1793 Obtaind Leave to go on shore for the purpose of
Collecting I was surrounded by a Croud of People who when they saw my
Employment was Collecting Plants and Catching Insects began hooting &
Running after me & as the Soldier who protected me rather encouraged them they
began to pelt me till I Retreated to the boats, on Complaint being made Strict
orders were given for our future protection from this it appears probable that one
of the Reasons for Keeping so Strict a watch over us was, because the Lower
orders of Chinese are so prone to maltreat strangers ...

Banks saw this modest record about a year after the publication of Staunton's
official account. Here were some extenuating conditions explaining several
deficiencies in the plant specimens of which he had complained. Seen earlier it mght
have tempered his hard judgement. But his knowledge of these hazards could not
really help Staunton as he finally recognized the small botanical achievement of the
Embassy. His depression is apparent in his letter to Banks of January 1796:

... I have received the several parcels of Specimens about which you have had the
goodness to take so much trouble. and I regret exceedingly that there was not that
attention paid by the People of the Embassy in the collection of Them, which
might have made it worth while to examine them. If ever there should be another
expedition of the same sort, it is to be hoped that more careful and able Persons
may be found for the department of natural History, as well as that better
opportunities and more leisure will be allowed in the Country for finding out and
preserving every object worthy of curiosity.
    From the present imperfect heap of Specimens I fear nothing can be drawn for
the purpose of the intended publication, unless perhaps a mention may be made in
travelling thro the different Provinces, of some of the Plants which are found to
grow there; somewhat in the manner of Gough's Edition of Camden's
Britannia ...

So in the end Staunton's official account kept well within the unpretentious limits
on matters of natural history which Banks had advised, a counsel with two elements:
the imperfections of so many of the specimens and the time and care needed to
prepare descriptions, identifications and drawings to meet the rising standards of the
new systematists and the scientific world. There were additional problems in finding
the men with the abilities and the time to set aside for such work in the atmosphere of
a nation now struggling for its survival. The record of the Embassy to China was not
the only casualty.
    However one man's dilemma may be another man's mounting stone. For the
young John Barrow his engagement with the Embassy was a beginning. Now back in
London and tutor to the precocious young George Thomas Staunton, he mounted
the next and critical step. This was the working association with Sir Joseph Banks
whereby, on Staunton's orders, he was established as the go-between from 17
Devonshire Street to 32 Soho Square. Thus he played a part in managing the
practical problems of the engraved illustrations according to Staunton's agreement
with Banks in April 1795 – an apprenticeship in book production which this earnest,
energetic and ambitious young man turned to full account. As the industrious

penman he was to become on matters of travel, exploration and geography, Barrow's time with the Embassy and his contact with Banks were lucky strokes.

With Staunton fighting against ill-health to produce the official account and for nearly a year isolated at Bath, the long process of selecting the illustrations and of managing the team of 16 engravers was an obvious task for Banks. Behind him lay almost a quarter of a century of experience as he made clear to Staunton. As with the publication of Cook's third voyage, the burden of coping with the problem of the illustrations was shouldered by him, with Alexander and Barrow running to and from the engravers themselves. Banks's opinion was paramount in the final selection of what was engraved, bearing in mind the rise in the cost of engraving and what would present a balanced picture from the profusion of William Alexander's sketches and water-colours. For the technical supervision of the actual engraving Banks recommended Josiah Boydel who did so at a charge of 30 per cent for the small scenes and 25 per cent for the middling and the large. Illustration of the natural history had been reduced to the blooms of the moutan and the double camellia. For everything else there were the fat folios of Alexander for whom the Embassy was a long stride toward his future as Keeper of Prints and Drawings in the British Museum. His industry in line and colour-wash had produced a rich store from which to select challenges to the art of the engraver. Banks reduced these to 26 for engraving – 9 of the largest size, 9 of the middle size, and 8 of the smallest. These with the supplementary plans, charts and drawings of tools and utensils, according to a later estimate by Banks cost about £3500 – including Josiah Boydell's commission. The two quarto volumes of the first edition, with a guard case of separate plates, was priced at three guineas, very little if anything more, said Banks, than the books alone would have sold without the plates.

On 27 July 1797 Banks acknowledged receiving from Staunton his copy of *An authentic account of the Embassy . . . to the Emperor of China*. He regretted, he said, that he had not been more useful in its preparation.

III

The affair of the plant collection sent to Russia from Kew in 1795 has its own modest place as a footnote in history and a sidelight on Banks at work in the service of the King. To employ the language of flowers as an instrument of international diplomacy was a novel twist even for him.

Throughout the eighteenth century, by a series of commercial treaties, Great Britain had kept an uneasy but on the whole steady trade with Russia. For the most part this was conducted through the Russia Company in London and almost entirely in British vessels, with the fleets taking the Baltic passage in the limited season between spring and autumn. Politically Great Britain needed Russian support against the weight of France with her satellites Denmark and Sweden. Strategically she needed access to Russian naval stores – timber, pitch, tar, hemp, sailcloth, iron and steel. Commercially she needed the Russian market for her wool textiles as a defence against Silesian competition especially when woollen exports formed about a third of the whole British export trade. The advantages for Great Britain were clear enough even though the trade balance was in general about one-third against her. On the other hand Russia was almost entirely dependent on British merchants and British shipping for the greater part of her own export income and a steady inflow of finance.

301

On the whole the political balance was kept fairly even and survived the stresses of the Seven Years War and the American War of Independence as the balance of trade shifted even further against Great Britain.

With the accession of Catherine II in 1762 the Anglo-Russian relations improved and a new treaty was successfully negotiated in 1766 by Lord Macartney. For a while all was well until Catherine's expansionist ambitions led to the partition of Poland, threatened Turkey, and jeopardized British trading interests in the Black Sea. Then, in 1791 after the Russian capture of Ochakov from the Turks, war between Great Britain and Russia seemed likely but was averted when Catherine made peace with the Turks and signed the Treaty of Jassy in January 1792. Sir Charles Whitworth had been British Envoy-Extraordinary and Minister at Warsaw since 1785 and was at the centre of the negotiations. Although British influence on the Russo–Turkish peace was marginal it was in no small part due to Whitworth's skill in recovering Catherine's favour and for this he was created a Knight of the Order of the Bath in November 1793. A few days before his investiture Whitworth had presented a request from the Tsarina of All the Russias. She had asked for seeds and plants from His Majesty's Royal Botanic Garden at Kew. On 16 November 1793 George III wrote to Lord Grenville at the Foreign Office:

> ... I shall order the seeds wished for the Russian Empress's garden to be collected at Kew and such plants as the present early state of cultivation can be spared to be sent at the proper season to Petersburgh.

The Russian Empress was beguiling her last years with building the magnificent palaces of Tsarskoe Selo and Pavlovsk for herself and the Grand Duke Paul, her son. These fine specimens of neo-classicism designed by Charles Cameron were nearing their completion too. Set in one of the most elaborate park landscapes of the eighteenth century they were surrounded by the embodiment of Catherine's dream so fervently expressed to Voltaire more than 20 years before:

> ... I love to distraction these gardens in the English style – their curving lines, the gentle slopes, the ponds like lakes. My Anglomania predominates over my plantomania ...

Whitworth could have had little difficulty in fostering the notion with the old Empress that plants from the Royal Garden at Kew would be a final adornment and a fitting seal on the new goodwill if His Majesty would but agree.

The exigencies of war in 1794 tended to obscure the relevance of botanical *douceurs* between the crowned heads of nation states. It was not therefore until February 1795 that, during the initialling of a preliminary defensive treaty between Catherine and the Coalition Powers, the notion seemed to revive. The royal intention was at last put into operation after one of those frequent meetings between the King and Banks at Kew, probably on 4 April 1795. Thereafter Banks found himself burdened with another royal command.

Every detail of the plan depended on Banks's good sense – his skill as a communicator with crowned heads and government ministries; his practical expertise as a man to deal with kings' gardeners and ship's captains; his special knowledge as a botanist to select and approve the list of plants for the royal 'Present'; his astuteness as an accountant to estimate costs and to wring reimbursement from obscure contingency funds.

The King's command to Banks was quite specific: to select from the Royal Botanic Garden at Kew as complete a collection of exotic plants as could be spared; to have prepared by the clerk of works plans and elevations of the principal hothouses at Kew for the benefit of the Russian gardeners; to have one of the gardeners from Kew travel in charge of the collection and to instruct the Russians in the English mode of cultivation. This was made clear to James Bland Burges at the Foreign Office and the search for a suitable ship began. Banks at first, but perhaps not with much hope, tried to secure the services of Captain William Bligh and HMS *Calcutta* as a safe and appropriate vessel. The Admiralty, despite the implied compliment to one of its most able captains, valued his services for more active and urgent work elsewhere. In the end, by the aid of the merchants of the Russia Company Banks had to make do with the little *Venus*, Captain Marmaduke Vickerman as the only merchant ship likely to sail for St Petersburg within the narrow time limits imposed by the seasons. Too small at 70 tons to provide a great cabin large enough to hold the full collection, the ship's hold alone had space enough, and this Banks himself measured carefully on 15 June. He then devised a platform of two tiers to fit it, some 22 feet long and 16 feet wide, placed almost amidships. The collection of more than 300 pots of two sizes making a total weight of 3 tons 1 quarter and 22 pounds according to the weight taken by Banks at Kew, which had come down the river by lighter, was carefully stowed on 2 July. A few days later the *Venus* dropped down river from Adermann's chains at Rotherhithe to the Nore where after a further week she sailed in convoy under the 32 guns of 'a nice little frigate' HMS *Daedalus*.

In charge was George Noe, the foreman-gardener at Kew whom Banks thought himself fortunate to have for the operation. Noe was a Wurttemberger from Stuttgart who, Banks was assured, spoke German 'precisely the same as that of her Imperial Highness'. After a fairly rough passage of nearly four weeks, the 'Present' reached Kronstadt. In a procession of 15 four-horse coaches, the pots were carried to the gardens of Pavlovsk where they were lodged in the newest and best of the hothouses about midnight on 11 August. Before George Noe could arrange them in these excellent buildings, each some 350 feet long with ten pits in two divisions, he was surprised at six a.m. on the 12th by a visit from the Grand Duchess Maria Feodorovna. Later in the afternoon the same day Noe was ordered to the imperial drawing room in the palace to display and explain the coloured engravings and drawings of plants and hothouses which he had brought. After a busy month instructing the Russian gardeners at the palaces in the methods of plant culture practised at Kew Gardens, Noe left St Petersburg on 11 September and, with a month's delay at Elsinore, reached London on 27 December 1795. He reported to Banks at Soho Square before the year was out and on 4 February 1796 he received from him the balance of the wages and expenses due.

The plant collection was composed of 226 species of about 130 genera, dominated by those from the southern hemisphere, notably the Cape of Good Hope, Australia and New Zealand, as the rarities of greatest interest to the gardens of Europe. A high proportion was due to the industry of Francis Masson from both his first and second periods at the Cape (1772–4, 1786–95). Here the most numerous were those of the genus *Erica* supported by some recent coloured engravings of those drawn by Franz Bauer for the forthcoming volume *Delineations of Exotick Plants cultivated in the Royal*

Garden at Kew. For beauty the list was headed with Banks's favourite, the bird-of-paradise flower *Strelitzia reginae* Ait. a genus and species which he had himself named after Queen Charlotte when he had introduced it to Kew in 1773. For utility Banks had nominated his original *Clamidia tenacissima*, the New Zealand flax *Phormium tenax* Forst., illustrated with the engraving developed by F. P. Nodder from Sydney Parkinson's first drawing of the plant during the *Endeavour* voyage. Banks himself had established the species at Kew in 1789. For the Empress he had included in the box with the engraving 'a small bundle of this Flax manufactured by the Indians', a part of what he had himself procured in New Zealand in 1769–70. Beauty and utility were ever the twin guides in the pursuit of botany by Banks.

Banks had estimated the cost of the whole operation as likely to be about £188. When all was done he found in fact that £162 had been disbursed when he settled as a last item the claims of George Noe in February 1796. Again, as in so many other cases, he had advanced the whole of this sum from his own private resources. He found the Foreign Office dilatory in settling this debt – in spite of the 'shots' he had aimed across the desk of Bland Burges during January 1796 of which one had stung the under-secretary to a brief spasm of action:

> . . . I told my whole story to Ld Grenville the other day, he heard me Patiently but did not deign to give me even a Sentiment of approbation much less of Thanks. Give me then my dear Sir your advice for if I am to do all to write all to direct all & to pay all & no human being feel inclind to thank me I Shall I fear in due time feel as sulky as a measly Sow who has lost her scrubbing Post

This briefly galvanized Bland Burges who promised to pass the matter on to George Hammond his incoming successor as under-Secretary. There the matter rested for another three years when at last Banks noted on his draft of the account:

> I receivd the whole of the money Feb 11 1799 being exactly 3 years after I paid it & nobody has Thankd me

This was not wholly true. He had received a brief note from General-Major Sergius Plescheyeff conveying, at second hand, from Catherine her appreciation

> . . . of the Complacent part you took in forwarding to her the compleat and valuable Collection of Exotic plants which His Majesty was pleased to Send her as a present . . .

There was no other acknowledgement of his leading part in the affair from any other quarter. Bland Burges on the other hand received a fine diamond-encrusted snuff box valued at £400 for his evident friendship to Russia. George Noe, properly enough, had a gold watch and 100 ducats for his pains.

Little trace beyond these few documentary scraps remains today of this piece of diplomatic botany. The palaces of Tsarskoe Selo and of Pavlovsk and their surrounding parks and gardens were almost destroyed in the German siege of Leningrad during 1941–4 and although lovingly restored none of the plants which came from Kew in 1795 are at present known there. Perhaps one day some diligent Soviet botanist may find a stray survivor from the collection which Catherine herself did not live to see mature beyond its first Russian summer.

IV

As Banks turned 50 in the month of February 1793, and war with France turned the world upside down, he himself entered a quinquennium, 1793–8, which has a good claim to be the grand climacteric of his life.

As a phase in his long medical history it was assuredly so. In the summer of 1792 he had been laid low in bed for the first time with gout. He noted, in a letter to John Linton on 26 June, that it was the first real illness he had suffered for 22 years since his close call with death in the East Indies. Now from the winter of 1793 he was to suffer his longest gout attacks, bad enough to delay his return from Revesby to his Royal Society duties by a clear month.

As a phase in his long history of public service and rise to a place of national influence and honoured recognition it has the semblance of an apotheosis, albeit on a modest scale within the limits of his few pretensions. In 1788 he had successfully persuaded Pitt to defer his term as High Sheriff of Lincolnshire on the grounds of scientific and other business. Now the war with France and its attendant dangers weighed heavily with him. Among three named in 1794 as possible sheriffs, he was the one willing to accept. For Banks this year was marked by the death on 16 January of his friend and fellow-martyr to gout, Edward Gibbon. It entailed a loss of companionship at The Club and a challenge as a medical anomaly to be deferred until the spring for examination. Meanwhile the defence of the realm against the rising threat of a French invasion was a charge on his time and interest especially as the appointed High Sheriff of a large and vulnerable east coast county.

On 6 March Banks set out for Lincoln where, on 11 March at the Lent Assizes, he presented the five-point plan from the Home Department 'to provide more completely for the Security of the Country against any Attempts on the part of the Enemy'. This was a scheme to augment the militia by volunteer companies of foot and troops of fencible cavalry raised by 'Gentlemen of Weight and Property' to operate under the authority of appropriate Acts. Of these the first important measure was the 'volunteer' act 34 Geo.III. cap.16 of 28 March and the second 34 Geo.III. cap.31 of 17 April 1794. But while the legislation was being enacted at Westminster Banks had already opened the subscription among the gentlemen gathered at Lincoln Castle with his own £300 contribution to the total of £1728. The Grand Jury directed Banks to call another meeting of the principal landholders of Lincolnshire resident in London, which was held at the Thatched House Tavern in St James's Street on 20 March. The Duke of Ancaster, as Lord-Lieutenant, was in the chair and led the subscription list with £500 to achieve a total that day of £4129.2s. By the end of March, £5857 had been raised as a working sum and before the enabling Acts were on the statute book a formidable sum had been gathered from 54 of the Lincolnshire gentlemen which was almost enough to cover a full year of the volunteer service eventually achieved.

On 11 March Banks had penned his thoughts on both the practicalities of home defence and the resources of money, men and material that his county could provide. On 4 April these appeared as a pamphlet of some 3300 words, *Outlines of a Plan of Defence against a French Invasion*. It had been prepared with information from Evan Neapean, now under-Secretary at the War Office, from whom he had extracted it in his letter of 18 March:

... If you have any occasion for me at the Office I shall come immediately on being sent for the business now in hand has with me the Preference over all others, but I shall not unless sent for attend any more as my occupations will not any longer allow me to wait in the antichamber for whole mornings as I have formerly done.

This was the voice of the 'independent Landowner' and the voice of 'the man of adventure' anxious to be up and doing, the 'bird of peace' rising to defend its nest. His *Plan of Defence*, designed for the County of Lincoln, he presented as

... applicable to all other Counties whose Inhabitants are sensible of the Danger of the present Crisis, and willing to subscribe a small Part of their Incomes for the Security of the Remainder ...

His plan premised sufficient loyalty in the country for the gentlemen, yeomen, and substantial graziers to serve as commissioned officers without pay; for all others to volunteer for paid service in training or on active duty. From a county population which he assessed at appreciably above 243 540, it should be possible to raise 4 troops of horse and 20 companies of infantry – with officers, 232 cavalrymen and 1660 foot soldiers. The annual cost he assessed at £11 109, including contingencies at 10 per cent, a sum easily covered by a charge of about six pence in the pound on the county rate. However it was already clear that the cost of these volunteer supplemental militia would be met from the voluntary subscriptions, at least for the first year.

As to weapons for this body of volunteers he reckoned from the game certificates of the county of Lincoln, that there were more than 850 persons authorized within its limits each upon average with more than two fowling pieces. There were probably some 850 more weapons held by others who gained a partial living by shooting duck and other wild fowl. All these could be swiftly converted to fire ball cartridge for no more than five or six shillings apiece and plug bayonets fitted to the barrels. Thus, if necessary, sufficient arms to oppose an enemy could be provided for 2450 men. He did not flinch from contemplating

... the last resource of extremity, from which, may Heaven defend the happy isle we inhabit, to the utmost times of our latest posterity ...

– in other words, an invading enemy established on English soil and poised to attack the capital itself. Nothing less than such an emergency would, in his opinion, justify his proposal that the rich should arm the poor with pikes. He appended to it an engraving of a specimen dug up at Sir John Thorold's Syston Park 'proposd as a pattern having been an actual weapon of service'. He noted that two blacksmiths, with an unskilled bellows-blower, could forge 25 such pikes a day or 150 in a 6-day working week. Clearly this was not a paper for general distribution and in the first instance no more than 60 were dispensed.

These calculations concentrated the minds of the Lincoln nobility and gentry and advanced the raising of subscriptions and of volunteers. This was the English response to the *levée en masse* across the Channel. That Banks had been a successful inspiration in these first steps toward national mobilization had been recognized by the King and the Government and conveyed by Henry Dundas in a letter of 14 March and confirmed at a meeting between Banks and Dundas on Wednesday 2 April. It was enlarged now by the proposal that he be made a Knight of the Order of the Bath. Banks was expansive in his refusal as he replied on Saturday 5 April to the formal letter from the Home Secretary.

It was five years, he said, since the King had first offered him the Red Ribbon for the reputation he had created abroad by his foreign correspondence and the flourishing state of the Royal Society under his presidency. This must have been a confidence passed between master and subject during one of their walks together at Kew in February 1789. Banks had replied then with a full heart that this was a mark of royal approbation beyond his warmest hopes and one that he felt he could receive

> ... without suffering any diminution of my Pretensions to the Character of an
> independent Landowner ...

Since then, he now told Dundas, he had never mentioned this conversation knowing as the years passed that the King never forgot such things but that his time had evidently not yet come. Now, since his appointment as High Sheriff and his success in raising subscriptions for the militia, the case had changed. He felt himself politically engaged and any honour would bear that tinge among his friends, let alone his enemies, since none could know that the King's first intention had been to pay tribute to his 'Literary' services to the country. He must, he felt, decline

> ... a mark of Royal approbation which I have sought after with diligence for years
> & now have obtained only as Tantalus did his Banquet to have it snatched from
> my Lips untasted ...

Then he turned in pursuit of the case history of Edward Gibbon which, with the details of the autopsy, had been promised to him by the senior attendant physician, William Farquhar. With his own curiosity unsatisfied Banks was also being pressed by Gibbon's friends

> ... for regular information on the Subject of the disease of a man whose
> importance in the Literary world certainly raises a great Curiosity Concerning his
> disease which from its great size was an object which must have been Observd by
> every person who was in Company with him ...

By the end of April Banks had extracted a statement of the last months in the life of Edward Gibbon with an English version of the findings *post mortem* which Lord Sheffield printed only in its Latin form. A 'tumour' had become, after 30 years of steady growth, the large, awkward and embarrassing scrotal hydrocele which Gibbon in desperation agreed at last should be punctured and drained on 16 November 1793. He lived on for over three months in fluctuating agony until the end in St James's Street on 16 January 1794. Scarcely had Banks elicited the facts of Gibbon's last days than, a week later, another distinguished Fellow of the Royal Society succumbed to the sharp efficiency of the French knife. On 8 May Antoine Lavoisier was executed 'for conspiracy with the enemies of France against the people', among other factors a victim of his own correspondence with his Fellows in the Royal Society with Banks at their head. Neither this tragedy nor the escape of Pierre Broussonet from the same fate would be known to Banks for some time.

Meanwhile, before May was out, he could turn with some satisfaction to the survey of the Revesby estate with five sheet maps just finished for him by Thomas Stone – 3401 acres in all at 6 pence an acre, plus the cost of drawing paper, canvas and map cases, a gross sum of £88.5s.6d. But over all there still hung the burden of his duties as High Sheriff leading him during June to resign from his place in the chair of the St Anne's Association in the parish of his London home where it had been formed some 18 months before as a local barrier to the spread of Jacobin forms of 'democracy'.

The prevailing sense of insecurity in what Banks himself had termed 'times like ours teeming with the Monstrous Birth of Equality' emerged through the hints of his cousin, Henry Hawley, that a baronetcy might be his very soon. But he repeated to Banks

> ... As I told you before, it is very uncertain, whether the thing may take place or not, & God knows in the present situation of affairs how short a time either honors or property may be secure ...

He had the support of the Speaker of the House, of William Pitt and of Sir Edward Knatchbull but he had not sought the support of Banks knowing, as he said

> ... that your thoro' independence, & the line of Conduct You have always pursued might have render'd it disagreeable to You, to have made application for a favor to a Minister ...

Banks agreed that this was indeed so, making it clear that though he rejoiced in his cousin's pretensions he was relieved that his influence had not been invoked. On 14 May 1795 Henry Hawley became the first baronet of Leybourne Grange in Kent without benefit of his cousin's self-styled 'Feeble claims on the Fountains of honor'.

A few weeks later Sir Henry Hawley was congratulating Banks on receiving the Red Ribbon of the Order of the Bath, news he had gleaned only from the public press. On Tuesday 30 June Banks had been summoned quite suddenly to appear at the Court of St James to receive the Order the next day, Wednesday 1 July, with Sir Ralph Abercromby as his fellow Red Ribbon. In the event Sir Ralph, hero of the British rearguard in the disastrous Flanders campaign, found the notice too short and Banks alone knelt before the King to receive his first and last honour for civil, not military, services rendered. He explained his feelings to his cousin on 6 July:

> ... While I was kneeling on the Cushion before the King & the Sword which had [dubbed] me a Knight was Still hanging over my Shoulders the King Said to me in a Low voice Sir Jos: I have many years wishd to do this. a mark of distinction so flattering has made me pleasd with an honor which as it came without Sollicitation you may easily beleive not to have been any Object of my wishes, it had in the First instance been made palatable by coming in a direct Course from the pure Fountain of honor without any portion of Ministerial Contamination but this Latter instance of Gracious Condescention had made it inexpressibly valuable to my Feelings ...

The satisfaction it gave him was modified within the week of the investiture by the appearance of Gillray's cartoon transforming the image of the earnest and high-minded President of the Royal Society into that enduring phenomenon of unnatural history 'The great South Sea Caterpillar, transformed into a Bath Butterfly'. But his general good humour remained unruffled as the bright and literate elder daughter of Lord Sheffield, Maria Josepha Holroyd, noted on Sunday 2 August:

> ... The Red Ribbon has made no alteration to Sir Jo. in any other respect than that there is a red ribbon on his waistcoat. He sprawls upon the Grass kisses Toads and is just as good-humoured a nondescript of an Otaheitan as ever! ...

By the end of the month this nondescript Otaheitan was locked in correspondence with the 1st Baron Hawkesbury over the corn supplies of the kingdom, replying from Overton in an 1800-word letter on 30 August to a request for his opinions from the President of the Board of Trade. This 'very elaborate and satisfactory reply from Sr. Joseph Banks' on the state and prospects of the corn crops and the expediency of laying in stocks by the Government was submitted to Pitt and the Committee of the Privy Council by Hawkesbury on 2 September. Next day, it was sent by the Home Secretary to the King at Weymouth. His Majesty received the Duke's account of the state of the corn trade with 'infinite satisfaction' enhanced as it was by 'the sentiments of a person of such authority in matters of that sort' as Sir Joseph Banks. The King found that the opinions coincided entirely with his own. That autumn Banks had moved closer to the ranks of 'the great Council'.

V

The spring of 1796 was a relief to Banks after a hard winter of confinement in the herbarium at Soho Square. At least this was the substance of his excuse for neglecting the Board of Agriculture as he acknowledged the annual Address of its President Sir John Sinclair. Writing from Spring Grove on 30 May he confessed:

> ... I grieve I have not been able to attend oftener: but I have had a season more than usually full of employment, having this winter looked over, and put names to two vast collections of plants, the one brought from China, by Lord Macartney, the other from the north-west coast of America, by a botanist [Menzies] of your country, sent by Government for the sole purpose of improving natural history ...

He was more than usually worried also about the state of his Codlin apple trees at Spring Grove and the failure of their crop for two years in succession due to their infestation with the woolly aphid [*Eriosoma lanigerum* (Hausmann)] whose appearance in England he had been following closely since 1790. Now 'as a natural historian' on 28 June, he troubled Sir Henry Hawley to enquire among the apple orchards of Kent what the course of the insect's ravages may have been. Twenty years later his accumulated 'Notes relative to the First Appearance of the *Aphis Lani gera*, or the Apple-Tree Insect, in this Country' would appear in the *Transactions of the Horticultural Society*, illustrated by Franz Bauer. Further afield, on 1 July, he answered the enquiry from Giovanni Fabbroni in Florence seeking a good specimen of the kangaroo for his country. Banks knew of no such animal for sale in England but suggested that if the Grand Duke of Tuscany applied to the King then perhaps a live male and female of the species '*Macropus giganteus*' might be had from the royal menagerie at Kew where they were breeding fast. Indeed, in the *Philosophical Transactions* for 1795, a paper by Everard Home had already been published on the esoteric breeding habits of the kangaroo as observed at Kew and of which the peculiarities of its birth had been first observed by the King's apothecary, David Dundas, in December 1793. Such things, however, were for the most part submerged under the delicate task of restoring to the French Directory the captured and tantalizing collections of La Billardière, an operation whose success he reported at last to Antoine de Jussieu on 10 August, just before he set out for Derbyshire and fishing on the River Witham in September. But this autumn of activity was to prove unusually stressful and to hold him in Lincolnshire longer than usual.

On 5 September he reminded John Lloyd of the 'Equinoctial operations' he had planned, hoping he would join him not only for this but to brief him in the adjustments on a new level that Lloyd had arranged for him to receive from Edward Troughton in the Strand. But John Lloyd was too busy with local politics in Denbighshire to join Banks and the Portuguese Abbé Jose Correia de Serra in the expedition whose purpose Banks had defined:

> ... I have several times read of Forests under the Level of the Sea but I have never yet heard that any body has investigated the Reason of so unaccountable a Phaenomenon ...

The Abbé had come to Banks in the spring of 1795 on the recommendation of his noble patron the Duc de Lafoens FRS and since then, as a botanist, had enjoyed the scientific hospitality of 32 Soho Square. He had earned the special regard of Banks for the aid he had given to Pierre Broussonet during the first confused months of his asylum in Portugal after his escape from Paris in 1794. Elected as a Fellow of the Royal Society in March 1796, Correia de Serra was now to savour the hospitality of Revesby Abbey and to join Banks in a tricky excursion during the low ebbs of the neap tides in a study of the 'submarine forest' off the Lincolnshire coast near Sutton-in-the-Marsh. On 11 September Banks sounded a last clarion call to John Lloyd:

> ... The Moon who you know is Governess and Comandress in cheif of the Sea has ordaind that the 19–20–21 of this month are to be the Equinoctial Tides. Correa will be with me & I Shall set out for Sutton where we are to Find one of our birds at day Light on Monday the 19th. Pray Come if you Can ...

But Lloyd was still too preoccupied in North Wales, so Banks and the Abbé had their excursion in submarine palaeobotany to themselves.

The 'bird' at which Banks aimed in particular was the post-glacial submerged forest south of Sutton and apparently just opposite Huttoft bank, the 'moors' as he termed them, which appeared as small islands at the extreme ebb of the equinoctial tide. He had hired the services of Joshua Scarby of Sutton and his boy for three days with a boat brought down by road on a horse-drawn truck. About one p.m. the islands with their tree-stools appeared out of the ebbing tide and soon after Banks and Correia de Serra landed on the largest they could see at low tide, some 30 yards from east to west and about 25 yards wide. About three p.m. the rising tide forced them to retreat. Next day, with three labourers to excavate for them, they assessed the profile of the plant layer as shallow, not much more than 18 inches before a buttery clay was reached. An hour and-a-half was the limit of the working time that day but on 21 September the tidal vagaries reduced this to a half an hour. Less than four hours of total working time on the island 'moors' had been possible. In the hours between Banks gathered evidence from the Sutton villagers that the encroaching sea had reduced the parish from about 15 000 acres to its current limit of about 1 500, and that somewhere under the waters lay the remains of an earlier village with its church and graveyard. From Joshua Scarby he took down the details of the strata he had encountered in sinking his well at Sutton to a depth of some 93 feet and then, by hiring a wimble or auger with extension rods from a Mr Trow of Mablethorpe, he attempted a matching study of the strata in a pasture belonging to the Royal Society nearby. Banks found himself out of pocket to the extent of £2.19s.11d. for the hire and the feeding of his assistants, the use of the boat and the wimble and some blacksmithing repair to the rods.

His notes on the field observations extended to some 2500 words of first impressions and brief speculation. He noted the species identified as oak, pine and birch, some holly and traces of the common reed *Arundo phragmites* L. He postulated that this ancient forest was perhaps coextensive with other traces in points as far apart as Blankney, East Fen and Peterborough turned up in the excavations when banks were made. The thought occurred also that this may have been part of the lost Sylva Anderida of the Romans. In the end, however, the substance of this inshore probing was embodied in the paper, with Correia de Serra as the sole author, 'On a submarine forest, on the east coast of England', read on 28 February 1799, published in the *Philosophical Transactions* for that year and also in the *Annual Register*.

As the time approached for a return to London and the business of the Royal Society two barriers intervened. In the last week of October gout attacked Banks severely in the left knee, confining him to a chair in his bedroom swathed in flannels. In the first week of November while his neighbour Thomas Coltman, the fox-hunting magistrate of Hagnaby, was taking the waters at Bath, riots had begun in the nearby towns over the bungled issue of the new militia lists. As the signs of a growing civil disorder flared across the Parts of Lindsey, Banks was pressed by the magistracy to delay his return to London. The riotous assemblies consisted mainly of the servants of the larger farmers and the sons of the smaller. They were the young men most directly affected by what they wrongly thought was a general enlistment for the next five years, with compulsory service abroad. In fact only a few men were required to fill the usual vacancies under the usual terms. The issue however was badly scrambled in the precept circulated by the Clerk of the General Meetings of the Lieutenancy, identified by Banks as 'the Duke of Ancaster's drunken son in law', a gentleman whose 'sottishness' had been the cause of blunders in many other ways. To 'the execrable carelessness' of this man and the dilatory attitude of the Lord-Lieutenant, the Duke of Ancaster himself, Banks attributed the main cause of the riots. He made this clear to John King at the Home Office and through him to the Duke of Portland, supported by reports from Thomas Coltman. Horncastle, Spilsby, Louth and Alford were the towns most involved where, among other forms of persuasion, the young men relieved the chief constables of the militia lists by the simple expedient of 'lifting them up by the Ears', a local device for gaining the interest and attention of unwilling listeners. Supplemented by other forms of intimidation, the young men from the farms held the townsfolk to ransom for some two weeks until the vigorous actions of Banks and Thomas Coltman in particular, supported by troops of the Somerset Fencible Cavalry deployed from Lincoln to the affected towns. With the arrest of a few ringleaders who were lodged in the castle, the trouble subsided. For some ten days Banks and Coltman had moved swiftly from town to town, themselves unarmed but with cavalry in attendance. With his gouty leg Banks travelled in his carriage but Coltman rode his best hunter to the point where it foundered and nearly died. By 19 November all was quiet, and that day the Duke of Portland wrote to Banks thanking him for his part in quelling the disturbances and for his commendation of the part played by Thomas Coltman. On 21 November the new Clerk of the General Meetings of the Lieutenancy, B. Cheales, conveyed the formal thanks of the Lieutenancy to Lord Gwydir, Banks, Coltman and various others for

> ... their activity, zeal and judicious conduct in putting an end to the late unhappy disturbances in the vicinity of Horncastle and Alford ...

For Banks the direct outcome of the affair was that, with Lord Gwydir as Colonel, he volunteered his service as Lieutenant-Colonel of the Northern Battalion of the Supplemental Militia whose formation had been somewhat hastened by the events of the past month. But back in London Banks found progress in amending the Militia Bills less than admirable as he emphasized to John King after fruitlessly waiting his convenience at the Home Office on 3 December. He now found that arrears in his own business affairs weighed heavily and that he had no time 'to Practice the necessary waiting in antichambers' which attendance on 'his Majesties Servants' entailed. Moreover he deplored the neglect of the new MP for the county whom Pitt had supported, who was more concerned with attending a ball in Lincoln and running pony races than with the pressing affairs of the nation. He now proposed to be quiet and to mind his own business as he focused his aim again on where he felt the trouble lay:

> ... if I am peevish excuse me I do not think I am so but I feel more than I Chuse to express in seeing all the Spirit which I left in full vigor when I came from home ouzing out by imperceptible degrees through a Leak I cannot stop because our L[ord] L[ieutenant] is a Duke & a Fool ...

VI

While the business of the Supplemental Militia simmered on, Banks was becoming more tightly enmeshed in the toils of the 1st Baron Hawkesbury, mediating problems of the design for a new copper coinage with George Dance the younger and the process of its production with Matthew Boulton on his new presses at Soho, Birmingham. On 14 March he sent Lord Hawkesbury not only Dance's designs for the new halfpenny coin, with his own corrections for Britannia and the position of her trident, but also his deductions on the size and weight of the coin in relation to the value of copper and the cost of minting. The long years of back-room advice were now over and before the month was out he was officially translated to the place he had in truth occupied for so long.

On 29 March 1797 at the Court of St James's he was

> ... Sworn of His Majesty's Most Honourable Privy Council, and took his Place at the Board accordingly ...

Without further preamble he was absorbed into the working machinery of 'the great Council' in terms which codified the areas of service he had already rendered 'The King's Most Excellent Majesty' with the Council. First, that he

> ... be a Member of the Committee of Privy Council appointed for the Consideration of all Matters relating to Trade and Foreign Plantations ...

and be

> ... appointed to consider of the Measures necessary to be taken for procuring an immediate Supply of such Copper Coinage, as may be best adapted to the payment of the laborious Poor in the present Exigency ...

Of the duties implied by membership of these two committees it was those of the latter that now pressed, and by midsummer Boulton had coined both penny and twopenny pieces in great quantity. On 19 July Banks ordered a guinea's worth of each denomination to be sent to him and a week later told Boulton that the Committee was well pleased with the new coinage and that the King had accepted from him one for each member of the royal family and one for the Keeper of the King's Medals. He confirmed that the proclamation of the new coinage would receive the royal assent that day, 26 July, and that it would be printed on Saturday 29 July. Banks now proposed to visit Birmingham on his way to Overton on 21 August. His purpose, he said, was to see the coining press in full activity and to give the Coin Committee an eye-witness account of its excellence in operation. But he declined Boulton's invitation to stay at his house; he and his ladies would spend the day with the family as a mark of his 30 years' friendship but they would lodge at St Philip's Hotel.

Success with the new copper coinage, however, had stimulated an interest elsewhere. The Bank of England now pressed for the issue of a new silver coinage and Hawkesbury, on 21 August, pursued Banks with the subject when he arrived at Overton. The Coin Committee, he said, were prepared to consider it, although Pitt could spare no time to deal with it. Nor could anything further be attempted with the currency until the Mint itself had been reformed. Banks agreed with this in his reply from Overton on 3 September but, having now studied the operation of Boulton's machines, doubted whether the speed with which they minted copper coins could be sustained for silver. However he had found the Boulton mint efficient beyond his expectations and as the demand for pence was great he recommended that, when the present supply of 200 tons of copper was exhausted, the Committee should indent for more. Hawkesbury agreed to obtain Treasury authority for Boulton to buy more copper, but on all other matters touching the coinage he would do no more until Banks returned to London.

By contrast progress with the new Militia had been hard to win. During March 1797 Banks found himself as the centre of difficult personal negotiations in London between the Duke of Portland as the Secretary of State and the Lord-Lieutenant of his county, the sick and fumbling Duke of Ancaster. The crux of the problem lay in the stubborn disinclination of the ordinary folk of Lindsey to submit themselves for enrollment in the new Militia for reasons they had already made clear. Then they had said they would accept the ballot for service in the new battalion if their officers were drawn from among the noblemen and gentry whom they knew, but not if they were commanded otherwise. It was for this reason that Lord Gwydir and Banks, after the autumn riots had been quelled, had volunteered their services, a gesture that had still received no formal recognition. A precedent had already been established in the Supplemental Militia of the West Riding of Yorkshire for this departure from the Duke of York's plan, and at last Banks was able to induce the Duke of Ancaster to present the case for the Northern or Lindsey Battalion to be commanded in the same way. The Duke was constrained to say that he had been given the strongest reasons to understand that the difficulties of raising the Supplemental Militia in Lincolnshire would be insurmountable

> ... unless Government will give permission for the Noblemen & Gentlemen of Landed Property in the County to set them the example, by being appointed to Commissions to command them when embody'd or call'd into actual Service ...

This letter of 9 March to the Duke of Portland from the Lord-Lieutenant was the required instrument by which the commissions could be made formal but it was mislaid at the Home Office for some ten days. Thus it was not until 3 April that Banks was officially confirmed as Lieutenant-Colonel of the Northern Battalion conditional on other gentlemen of the Parts of Lindsey coming forward as subalterns to the number of two-thirds of those required – 10 captains, 10 lieutenants, and 10 ensigns, or 30 in all.

The path of patriotism and public service, however, did not run smooth for Banks. The claims of his Militia commission and of his Privy Council committee work were in obvious conflict. So it was not surprising that on 16 February 1798, the Duke of Portland should signify to the Duke of Ancaster that the attendance of Banks as Lieutenant-Colonel of the Supplemental Militia should give way to

> ... His Majesty's particular Service requiring Sir Joseph's daily presence in Town ...

But what began as a leave of absence to attend his Privy Council responsibilities acquired a different complexion before the end of the summer as Banks succumbed to his longest and most severe bout of bedridden incapacity, denying him his visit to Lincolnshire. So on 3 November he wrote to his commanding Colonel, Lord Gwydir

> ... after having been Compeled by disease To Spend the Two Months in bed that I had destind for my Military duty I am now upon Crutches & unable to mount a horse. There is not a joint in my body which has not an ache belonging to it which tells me plainly that I am unfit for Military duty & that I have little if any hopes at my age of ever becoming a Souldierlike man again
>
> Under these feeling which in reality are no other than a Continuation of what I have suffered for the Last Twelve months your Lordship will not be surprisd to Learn that I find myself very much disposd to Resign my Commission ...

By 24 November the formalities of his resignation were complete and Banks had resumed the full plumage of a 'bird of peace', distinctive now with its broad red slash across the breast. For the past four years his influence in rallying the volunteer forces of county and, indeed, of the kingdom had been forceful and generally effective but only briefly, if at all, had he worn the uniform of the Lincolnshire Supplemental Militia, royal or otherwise.

VII

Ever since 1786 when Banks had facilitated the whirlwind progress through Europe of Mr John Sinclair he, the farmer of Middlesex, had come increasingly under the harrow of the Scotch laird's obsessive enthusiasms. Scarcely had he adjusted to the appearance of the Society for the Improvement of British Wool at Edinburgh under the impulsive drive of Sir John Sinclair, now the 1st Baronet of Ulbster, than its more or less logical extension into a 'Plan for Establishing a Board of Agriculture and Internal Improvement' was thrust at him with a demand for his opinion. Sinclair's intrusion into the political life of William Pitt with useful but unsolicited ideas for easing the currency shortage and business chaos early in 1793 evoked a grudging reward from Pitt for services rendered in his support for the formation of such a board. Before this came to the floor of the House of Commons, Sinclair once again sought moral support from Banks who, on 23 April, found the draft of the plan on his desk covered by Sinclair's habitual curt form of demand for his thoughts. These were few and to the point and returned to Sinclair the same day. Banks gave the plan his qualified blessing as creating a body without any statutory powers and as one 'calculated merely to examine the progress and encourage the improvement of agricultural efforts', but considered it 'far better suited for a private than for a public establishment'. He corrected Sinclair's invocation of the Royal Society in its support, pointing out that it was not a landowner nor was it in receipt of any funds either from land or the public purse. Neither of these points evidently registered with Sinclair whose published text appeared unaltered. Banks also queried whether the President of the Royal Society ought *ex officio* to be an official member of the Board. He doubted whether any of his predecessors would have contributed much of value even though he considered that he might have some claims as a student of rural economy. However, above all, he queried the function of the proposed board as the collector of a statistical account of England. He thought that if the Government wished for such information there were other better ways of doing it than to expect a result from a board of 24 members 'independant of all Idea of Emolument'. He feared that in fact the expense would far exceed Sinclair's calculations.

None of this deflected Sinclair from his course. On 15 May he rose in the House to propose the establishment of a Board of Agriculture and after an adjournment to 17 May and appropriate debate, it was carried on a division by 101 votes to 26 against. In the end Sinclair had the public semblance of a Board with a tenuous link to the Treasury, but it remained an anomaly to the parliamentary lawyers – that 'heterogenious arrangement' which Banks had pronounced it – without executive authority and largely ignored by the Government on major agricultural issues. Whatever it was to achieve would have to come from its own private initiative. In practice, at the beginning under the presidency of its Scottish begetter, the fuel for its operation was derived mainly from that source. For five years it functioned indeed almost as a private enterprise with Arthur Young the Secretary, William Cragg as under-Secretary, and two clerks crowded into one room in Sinclair's London house, 5 Terrace, Palace Yard, Whitehall. The ambitious series of county surveys for England, extending those already proceeding in Scotland, were optimistically set in motion by Sinclair even before the Board came to official life on 4 September 1793. For five years Banks watched the Board approach the financial crisis which from the beginning he had seen coming, driven inexorably by Sinclair's passion for publication at any price. Throughout these years Banks served on the Board as an official member, named in the letters patent under which it was constituted on 23 August 1793 and so he continued through all its vicissitudes. He attended its meetings as far as he could and he received papers for review as a referee and for advice on publication in the *Communications* . . ., as well as for the county surveys, over which he always kept a sceptical and restraining voice.

The finances of the Board were bound to be precarious with the strains on the Treasury because of the war with France but they were compounded by the impetuous miscalculations of Sinclair. Signs of concern among the Board's members and by its secretary, Arthur Young, were evident as early as 1795. In September of that year Sinclair indeed admitted to Pitt that many of the Board thought he was pressing forward too rapidly. The printing of the *Surveys* in the first three years alone had drained £6000 away from the gross income of £9000 with little hope of a return from their sale. Then in 1797 the first volume of the *Communications* . . . appeared as a further charge, lavishly printed by William Bulmer and produced by George Nicol. In June 1796, while Sinclair was away in Edinburgh, nine members of the Board held an extraordinary meeting and cancelled all spending on the county surveys as a first step to meet the growing debts. There still remained however the costs of the printing already in hand. Young pointed to Sinclair's impatience with any 'deviation from his sole object of incessant printing' and there seems no doubt that this was the main cause of the overspending. What Banks had foreseen had now occurred, so it is no surprise to find that Sinclair was voted out of the chair at the annual general meeting in March 1798 by one vote that Banks cast in favour of the youthful Lord Somerville. Banks found Sinclair an uncomfortable burden and much as he may have approved the principle of gathering information about the state of the nation and its rural economy, he had his own ideas on how this should be done. Although, in his heart, he generally approved the 'statistical' ideals which Sinclair pursued, his was certainly a powerful voice in Sinclair's defeat as president.

Through the succeeding presidencies of Somerville, Carrington and Sheffield, the central thread of the Board's activities until 1805 was guarded largely by Young and Banks. This was expressly acknowledged by Lord Carrington in his retirement speech of March 1803, while with Lord Sheffield, his long and close association with Banks on agricultural matters was foundation enough. In 1805 Sheffield announced his intention to retire from the chair, though he seems to have had second thoughts. However before the general meeting of March 1806 Banks told Young that Sinclair was to be reinstated 'under promises of good behaviour' – presumably in a financial sense. On 25 March 1806 he was re-elected by 20 votes to Sheffield's 10. Sinclair *redivivus* was not quite the same incubus for Banks as the first President of the Board.

In the years that followed there was a subtle change of role. Banks became the gentle goad that ensured a more solid productivity in Sinclair's agricultural writings by focusing his attention on what Scotland had to offer the world. He flattered

Sinclair's vanity with a generous tribute to Scottish skill as a 'nation of gardeners', an opinion he honestly held. His letter to Sinclair of 3 September 1809 expressed his views in a way that could not be resisted. So in 1812 there appeared the *Account of the Systems of Husbandry adopted in the more improved Districts of Scotland* in two volumes, complete with Sinclair's mania for appendices. It was a valuable distillation of the essence of Scotch agriculture and its copious sales to an appreciative public attested to its worth.

However from the Board of Agriculture itself life was draining. Arthur Young, blind from 1809, was failing. The reprinting of the County Reports had been almost achieved. The founding generation were all ageing and the stresses of the long war were sapping such expressions of national vitality while financial constraints were a growing impediment. Sinclair spent less and less time in London and he did not even attend the annual general meeting in March 1814, when he formally retired from the chair. After 14 years in that office, his preoccupation with his own financial problems drove him to a monumental error of judgement which strained the credulity and goodwill of even the most patient of his friends. In January 1815, improperly using a back room in the Board's premises in Sackville Street, Sinclair set about opening a public subscription to himself. He circulated printed testimonial forms and invoked the endorsement of Banks and Lord Egremont to their joint outrage for the manner in which it had been done. Out of pity they subscribed but damned the whole scheme in terms that anyone but Sinclair would have read as a signal to retreat. He persisted but in the end a very lame regret was wrung from him and a long friendship seemed to have ended. Somehow it survived, and four years later this is evident in the cordial tone of Banks's reply to a note announcing Sinclair's visit to the south again:

> ... I rejoice to learn from your favor of the 9th that you have pitched your tents in my neighbourhood; that I shall sometimes see you in London, and oftener I trust while I am at Spring Grove, where I always reside during the best three months of the year ...

Nor could anything be more soothing than his short and final touch:

> ... I rejoice to hear that your Scottish Agriculture has met with so extensive a sale. The adoption of it in England will probably be the consequence, and a more beneficial one can scarce be conceivd. That a Scots farmer can get more crop from the earth than an English one seems a fact not to be disputed. To have been the cause of imparting to Englishmen the skill of Scots farmers is indeed a proud recollection.
>
> A Code of Agriculture from your hands will be an agreeable present to the public. No one has so much experience in the theory of husbandry as yourself. No one, therefore, is so able to lay down the most approved modes of practice.

If perhaps there was a hint of irony in the last paragraph Sinclair never saw it nor, indeed, did Banks intend it. The *Code* ... was finished in September 1817 in London and would see five editions and several foreign translations. Banks had already seen two editions and his praise for the work was sincere, for he never spared Sinclair the bite of his criticism nor his ridicule if he felt the need was there.

317

VIII

The commitment of Banks to service on the Board of Longitude was in pronounced contrast to his engagement with Sinclair's new Board of Agriculture. For this latter he could lay claim to a measure of fitness in his own knowledge and experience as a great landowner with an active and intelligent concern in estate management. For the work of the Board of Longitude his qualifications are not so readily discerned and his place as a Commissioner at first sight would appear to rest heavily on the *ex officio* element in his appointment as President of the Royal Society. Of his predecessors in the Chair his Lincolnshire fellow-countryman, Sir Isaac Newton had genuine claims for real competence as a Commissioner supported by his second *ex officio* place as Lucasian Professor of Mathematics at Cambridge. Only two other Presidents of the Royal Society after Newton and before Banks had any relevant qualifications or practical knowledge of use to the Board. They were George Parker, 4th Earl of Macclesfield, with his own finely equipped observatory at Shirburn Castle in Oxfordshire, and James Douglas, 14th Earl of Morton, who was so active in the astronomical preparations for observing the transit of Venus which was the prime aim of the *Endeavour* voyage. For Banks himself it was this voyage that gave him a solid appreciation, grounded in practical observation, of the aims and intentions of the Board. Whatever his limits as a mathematician there is no doubt that from the *Endeavour* years onward he developed and kept a lively interest in the problems with which the Board of Longitude was concerned and a sufficient competence in matters of theory and instrumentation to keep the respect of those contemporaries whose special fields they were. Moreover costly and innovative instruments of astronomical,

Left Sir John Sinclair, FRS, 1st Baron of Ulbster, *c.* 1815–20. Portrait by Sir Henry Raeburn, RA.

Right Dr Nevil Maskelyne, DD, FRS, Astronomer Royal 1765–1811. Painting by Van der Puyl.

318

navigational and geographic intent had formed a weighty part of his abortive preparations for the second Cook voyage. They had consisted of a very early equatorial instrument from Jesse Ramsden in 1772, a Gowin Knight's azimuth compass from Henry Gregory, an early pocket timekeeper, No. 5, from John Arnold, two 15-inch sextants, one from Jesse Ramsden, and another from P. & J. Dollond with a new form of adjustment, barometers from Edward Nairne – an expenditure of more than £400 on these items alone. With James Lind as a specialist in these areas of natural philosophy it is interesting to speculate what Banks and his party with this equipment might have found on the *Resolution* voyage to the far south with Cook.

In the seven years after the return of the *Endeavour* there evidently accrued enough proofs of Banks's practical and constructive interest in other fields of applied science to assure the Fellows of the Royal Society that in him they would have a President who was more than a botanist though less than a Newton. At all events from his election in 1778 and his accession *ex officio* as a commissioner of the Board of Longitude he was to be a dominant figure in all its activities. For 40 years he was more constant in his attendance than any other commissioner. In the meetings of the small committees where most of the work was done he was most frequently in the chair. For 30 years he was in harness with Nevil Maskelyne, the Astronomer Royal, a difficult and uncertain man, with whom he kept an enduring friendship in spite of their many disagreements. His diligence in coping with the human and technical problems of the Board is evident in the mass of memoranda, notes and drafts of correspondence in his own autograph which still survive. As in the management of the African Association, it is difficult to see how the business of the Board of Longitude could have been so well sustained without his devotion to it.

The origin of the Board in the last year of the reign of Anne lay in the encouragement of research into the best method of determining longitude, the testing of the merits of ideas and instruments, and the disbursement of rewards for successful inventions. Under the terms of the act *12 Anne c.15* of 1713, the Board offered a reward of £20000 for a timekeeper or chronometer which would determine longitude within 30 geographical miles. After many years of caution by the Board, an act of 14 June 1773 finally awarded the full sum to John Harrison for having achieved this order of accuracy, but only with the personal intervention of the King himself after tests in his own observatory at Richmond. This was followed in the same year by the offer of a reward of £10000 for an improved instrument which kept to within two minutes of time over a period of six months, with £5000 if it kept within four minutes for the same period. An instrument with a claim for this degree of precision was made by Thomas Mudge sen. in 1776, but the report of Maskelyne was adverse and Mudge was only granted £500 as an aid to further work on its improvement. He fought against this decision until, in June 1791, his eldest son succeeded in a petition to the House of Commons which presented his claims. These were referred to a Select Committee consisting of Pitt himself, Fox, Burke, Windham, Dudley Ryder and Sir Gilbert Elliott, leavened by one or two more technically qualified members such as Sir George Shuckburgh who, on 24 April 1792, warned Banks of what was afoot. '. . . What do you think of this? Is it much to be dreaded?' At this stage Banks supposed it to be nothing more than a display of parliamentary ignorance. He concluded that Pitt 'conceives a watch to be a thing composed of wheels within wheels like the Government of a Country and thence deduces that he may throw new light upon it'. He was however seriously concerned at the corrosive effect which the petition might have on the authority of the Board of Longitude in making its appeal to parliament on such a central feature of its responsibilities. He had studied the younger Thomas Mudge's defensive pamphlet *A Narrative of Facts relating to some Timekeepers constructed by Mr. T. Mudge* ... and the reply by Nevil Maskelyne, *An Answer to a Pamphlet entitled A Narrative of Facts* ... He had also read the son's concluding public shot in reply to the Astronomer Royal and, on 13 March 1793, had administered a strong reproof for the terms of its attack on Maskelyne. He did not himself feel much injury for his own attitude in defending the counterclaims of other watchmakers, John Arnold in particular. Banks was much more concerned at the presumption of the politicians in taking parliamentary measures in support of the petition instead of leaving the case within the judgement of the Board where it was properly vested. In this administrative fencing match William Windham was again, as so often, his active opponent.

The Mudge affair in the spring of 1793 had come after a winter of many distractions for Banks. On 1 February the declaration of war by revolutionary France so soon after its arbitrary act of regicide had shocked the whole country. On 2 February William Aiton the elder, the King's gardener at Kew, had died and Banks had been faced with the task of easing the son, William Townsend Aiton at 27, into the responsibilities of his father's place. On 9 February Banks had sought his 'quietus' from the Treasury for the ten years of his accountancy on the King's grant to William Roy in fixing the baseline on Hounslow Heath and the surveys which followed. This task in bookkeeping had merged with his duties as co-executor with his cousin Henry Hawley in disposing of the Heston villa and its land in the estate of his uncle Robert Banks-Hodgkinson and which was sold by auction at Garraway's on 22 March. At the same time he had been preparing one of his first reports to the King on the state of the Spanish Merino flock with the details of the cloth manufacture from its fleeces by George and John Hawker of Lightpill in Gloucestershire. This he had dated 18 March 1793, the day he had arranged with Robert Fulke Greville to meet the King and into whose hands he gave it with some technical papers from Count Rumford on fire arms and the boring of cannon as urgent matters touching the defence of the realm.

On 12 March Banks reproached Windham with his persistent advocacy of a flawed claim in the Mudge petition. On 14 March Windham denied any reflection on the Board of Longitude and hoped that his friendship with Banks would not suffer in the argument. Banks accepted the apology but kept to his view that the action of Parliament in awarding £500 to Mudge was an interference with the statutory operation of the Board and that the Mudge petition reflected on the merits of other instrument makers by its manifestly false statements. On 17 March Banks asked for time to collect his technical supporters before the vote on the Select Committee's report was taken in the House, but on 18 March he was content to rely on the strength of the paper which he had prepared for circulation to its members and which he sent to Windham. In this paper he argued against Mudge's claims on no other grounds than his own defence of the decisions of the Board of Longitude in the case and the valid claims of John Arnold and other watchmakers whose timekeepers were considered on test to be the better instruments. All through April and May Banks tried to convince Windham and, through him, the Select Committee that the Board was right in contesting Mudge's claim and in directing attention to others of greater operational merit. In the end however he thought defeat was unavoidable, when he considered that Mudge numbered Pitt, Fox, Windham and Burke among his political friends. This impending rebuff did not silence Banks and on 16 June he chose to measure a lance with William Pitt himself. He gathered to himself all the authority of his Presidency of the Royal Society and challenged the Prime Minister, even at that late hour to 'rescue Science from the discredit she must fall into if public rewards are given to those who have the greater [political] interest in preference of those who have the most merit'. He hoped, he said, to find in Pitt 'that fostering love of Science which Ministers are always believed to possess'. This was a sentiment which evidently ran thin in the veins of the Prime Minister for on this issue he gave no sign of resisting what Banks termed 'a claim upon the public Treasure wholly unfounded in fact'. The House voted on 17 June in support of the Committee's proposal and awarded Thomas Mudge the further sum of £2500 making the reward £3000 in all.

The long search for perfection in chronometers continued with Banks as steadfast in support of the Arnold instruments as he had been from the beginning of his interest in 1772. However although he and Maskelyne had been in harmony during the Mudge dispute they differed when, on 3 march 1803, Maskelyne reported in highly favourable terms on the going of Thomas Earnshaw's instrument for which he proposed the same reward as that given ten years earlier to Mudge. On this occasion he received the support of the Board of Longitude against the advocacy of Banks for the Arnold watches. Stung by the unusual disagreement with Maskelyne Banks set about his own tests with the aid of George Gilpin, Secretary of the Board and Assistant Secretary of the Royal Society, formerly assistant to William Wales on the second Cook voyage. These seemed to show the superiority of Arnold's instruments over those of Earnshaw. This practical objection was embodied as a printed paper entitled *Sir Joseph Banks's protest* . . . and was dated from Soho Square, 19 March 1804. A particular source of annoyance for Banks was that in a competitive test set up by the Board at the same time it had used John Arnold, Nos 82 and 176, two earlier and much travelled watches, both of which had been sent home in 1801 by Matthew Flinders to the Astronomer Royal for repair and checking. No. 176 had been specially made in 1791 for George Vancouver on the expedition to the north-west coast of America where it had worked effectively. These veteran instruments were certainly open to some doubt as being proper specimens for comparison with the latest versions under competitive tests. The argument simmered on for another five years with Thomas Earnshaw seeking to emulate Thomas Mudge by presenting a petition to the House of Commons but without effect. For Banks also the conclusion was a stalemate when the Board awarded equal sums of £3000 to John R. Arnold (the son) and to Thomas Earnshaw, a judgement which on 31 May 1809 a Select Committee of the House saw no reason to change. The relative claims of Mudge, Earnshaw and Arnold were in the end all equated in terms of the financial recognition accorded.

The service of Banks as a Commissioner of the Board ended with his last attendance in May 1819 about a year before his death. Before this however in 1818 he achieved a change in the Board which he had for many years hoped to gain. He had never been happy with the role of the professors and he proposed to Parliament that the Royal Society 'should be empowered to elect from among the Fellows, five of those persons most conversant in those sciences upon which the discovery of the Longitude at sea most immediately depends'. Parliament duly agreed to this change in the composition of the Board stimulated and directed no doubt by the rising concern with Arctic exploration and the active engagement of Banks and other

Fellows of the Royal Society, particularly Henry Kater, in the expeditions being mounted that year. The Board itself did not long survive Banks and was dissolved in 1828, a period almost coeval with the tenure of the Revesby Abbey estates from their purchase by Joseph Banks I in March 1714 to their partition between the Hawley and the Stanhope families after the death of Lady Banks on 28 June 1828.

CHAPTER 15

THE INDEPENDENT LANDOWNER
1790–1797

The first adventure of the Banks family into Lincolnshire was the purchase of the Holland estate, a transaction concluded in 1702 by Joseph Banks I. For the most part, it contained over 3000 acres of fen and farm land scattered to the east of Spalding from Moulton through Whaplode and Holbeach to Fleet and Gedney, including the manors of Hurn and Dame Amyas with Hurn Hall itself and the Chequer Inn at Holbeach, the whole at an outlay of some £9000. When this portion of the Lincolnshire estates came by the entailed inheritance to Joseph Banks IV there were some 60 tenant farmers in the parishes of Holbeach, Fleet and Whaplode, with 16 tenants of the manor of St John of Jerusalem in Moulton, yielding a gross rent in 1791 of £1772 which was reckoned to be £4186 in 1820. During his tour of the county in 1797 Arthur Young noted the enclosed acres in 1796 as 3122 from which the gross rental was £2058 and a net value of £1703 after deducting tithes at £251 and dykes-reeves rates of £112.

It was the marriage of Joseph Banks II in 1714 that fixed the family centre of gravity firmly in Lindsey on the edge of the wolds within the eastern drainage system of the River Witham south of Lincoln at and about the village of Revesby. The greater part of the Holland estate was settled by Joseph Banks I on the young couple as a marriage settlement to balance the Hodgkinson inheritance of Overton Hall and its environs in Derbyshire. It was the Jacobean mansion house of Revesby Abbey that he envisaged as the family seat in which to set up his only son as a true landed gentleman of Lincolnshire.

By what channel there came word that the Revesby estate was to be had from 'the representatives of Craven Howard' there is no clue. By 14 March 1714 the purchase was complete although it was not until 22 August 1715 that Joseph Banks I took formal possession. These lands were originally those of the Cistercian Abbey of Revesby, founded in 1142 by William de Romera, Earl of Lincoln. After the dissolution of the monasteries the abbey estate passed to Charles Brandon, first Duke of Suffolk in 1538. Thence through the female line in 1575 it passed from William Cecil, first Baron Burleigh by the marriage of his great-grand-daughter Elizabeth to Thomas Howard, 1st Earl of Berkshire. With the death of Henry Howard, 3rd Earl of Berkshire, in 1663 the estate came to his nephew the Honourable Craven Howard by whom the nucleus of the Revesby mansion house was built.

At this stage it is hard to say how much land this purchase included but it almost certainly added at least 3000 acres and a rent roll of about £900 per annum when it was acquired. By 1735 this income had been enhanced to £1270 per annum. In 1796 the enclosed area was said to be 3401 acres with 62 farms yielding a gross rental of £1397 that year.

These 6523 acres north and south of the Wash were not however the limits of acquisition by the founding patriarch of the Lincolnshire family fortune. In 1726, ill but undefeated and almost in his last year, he acquired at 22 years' purchase the manors of Fulstow and Marsh Chapel, the 'Marsh' estate just south of the Humber estuary. This added an area enclosed by 1796 of 1882 acres with 27 tenants and in that year an income of £1079. The manors of Mareham-le-Fen and the soke and town of Horncastle added another 978 acres and in 1796 an income of £1041. Thus in the 1790s the Lincolnshire estates amounted to some 9383 enclosed acres in Lindsey and Holland yielding a gross income of some £5500 derived from about 400 tenants in the towns and on the farms. This was the main substance of the wealth of Sir Joseph Banks.

It is perhaps well to remember that the mansion house at Revesby with its adjacent parkland and farm was set close to the edge of one of the last English frontiers in land use, not much more than 100 feet above mean sea level and about 60 feet above high-water mark in the West Fen a mile away. There were more elemental problems than parterres and terraces and upland lawns to whittle at the rent roll. There was, for example, still the matter of a pure water supply for the house and farm. William Banks in 1749 had excavated the Long Pond some half a mile north of the mansion and made an unfruitful search there for a source of spring water. This need was not supplied until in the summer of 1795 when Sir Joseph applied the theories learned the previous year from Joseph Elkington. From this piece of water engineering came a spring with a head of some 40 feet and a yield of 700 gallons or 14 hogsheads an hour as it was flowing when Arthur Young saw it in 1797.

The park was finally fenced in 1721 to enclose an area of about 340 acres and hence from about this date secure grazing for the deer herd as well as the working horses in saddle and harness, the milk cows and the small Derbyshire sheep. When all was done the house and precincts of Revesby Abbey remained for its relatively short span of days a modest example of its kind among the country seats of the period. However its sharp dismissal by John Byng after his fleeting and unrequited visit in July 1791 leaves us with a mild surmise on the standards implied in his judgement. Deserted it may have been by its masters for periods in the past but neglected it had never wholly been so long as Benjamin Stephenson retained his health and diligent writing hand.

The park itself ranked high in the household economy not only during the family residence in autumn but throughout the year in what it provided for the larders at Soho Square and Spring Grove and also for those of relatives and friends in the metropolis. The main item of produce was venison for which there was a list of warrants for those who were to receive it. How far the deer herd was part of the original Abbey stock, how many red deer were descended from the Burghley herd and how far they were the fallow species from elsewhere is not known. The evidence suggests that at least in the last decades of its Banksian years the fallow stock prevailed. Numbers varied but the policy set by Banks was to keep the herd at about 300 head in all. Under the park keeper George Bull and, after 1794 his successor Josiah Mills, this figure seems to have been well observed, with an annual slaughter of about 10 or 12 brace of bucks and 6 brace of does and haviours. Most of this would be sent as carcasses weekly during the season from May to August by the Boston coach to London, a meat supply valued by Banks in 1802 as worth about £250 or more for the year.

A small breeding herd of dairy cows, usually about five in milk yielding rather less

Revesby Abbey near Horncastle, Lincolnshire, c. 1800. Watercolour by John Claude Nattes in the Banks Collection, Central Library, Lincoln.

than two gallons a day, ran continuously with a bull and as many young heifers as there were milkers. For beef there were commonly six Scotch beasts, drawn no doubt from among the thousands that were droved from the north to graze in the nearby West and East Fens. The dairy herd was home-bred and for many years seems to have been a gay mixture of broken colours, red predominating and marked by a preference for a type called 'sheet', that is, an animal with a broad band of white round the body for which the term now is 'belted'. The bull most often used was described as a red sheet and the cows were variously red sheet, black sheet or white with blue roans and red brindles appearing among the offspring.

Between 20 and 30 head of horses shared the grazing all the year round, about equal numbers of bays and browns, rarely a grey or chestnut. These were mostly home-bred like the dairy herd and the parentage or provenance of each with its age was also noted in the annual livestock returns. Among these would be at least six saddle horses and as many heavy waggon horses, the remainder being lighter draught or carriage types. In the summer and autumn these numbers would be increased by six coach horses down from London with the family equipage and a varying number of visitors' horses during the period of the family's residence. One animal at this time is often noted as 'Sir Joseph's poney', which he undoubtedly used a great deal but it must have been a redoubtable little beast for its master in later years never weighed less than 15 stone.

Amongst this mass of the larger ungulates there seems always to have been a small flock of between 20 and 30 sheep mostly described as 'Derbyshire woodland [occasionally forest] sheep' of which fresh stock were droved from time to time from

Overton Hall. This practice began when Joseph Banks II first took possession of Revesby Abbey in 1715 and remained so under his grandson Joseph Banks IV. Lambs from these were fattened for the table on the edge of the fens nearby, a contrast to the massive mutton joints from the long-woolled Lincoln breed which dominated the county.

There were in time other strangers in the park from even further afield. From Spring Grove and its experimental flock came a young Spanish Merino ram in 1780 for a joint cross-breeding experiment with Major John Cartwright of Brothertoft using Nottingham Forest and large Northumberland ewes. Later, in the hey-day of the King's flock, Banks indulged his curiosity in the breeding of a pure black Spanish Merino flock at Revesby Abbey and, most noteworthy, during the winter of 1803–4 agisted the young Merinos rams from the royal flock at Kew as an experiment. Out of these emerged the six shearling rams bought by Captain John Macarthur at Kew in August 1804 and which in July 1805 were grazing at Elizabeth Farm near Parramatta in New South Wales, just one year after leaving Revesby Abbey.

Despite this number and variety of grazing stock on the 340 acres of what Banks regarded as 'moderate land', it was possible to set aside 100 acres fenced off with 'trags' [= hurdles] for grass hay making in the early summer. From this came part of the fodder for the coach horses and those of the numerous visitors, at a cost of some ten shillings per acre over all. In 1801–2 strangers' horses consumed 8 loads of hay each valued at 30 shillings or £12 in all. For agistment purposes 2 shillings a week was allowed per head for each horse or grown ox, from which may be deduced a rough notion of the hospitality thus dispensed.

The estate office, which so caught the attention of Arthur Young in 1797, symbolized the essential character and management of the whole. It consisted of two rooms specially built in local brick over the winter of 1793–4. These rooms had a frontage together of 33 feet, with windows facing south, under which benches broad enough to accommodate the estate and other maps and plans were fixed. The rooms, each 16 feet wide, were divided by a brick wall with an iron-plated door protecting the inner room containing the estate papers free from any risk of fire from the outer room where one was usually kept burning most of the time. This outer room, where all the practical activity took place was furnished with desks, tables, a bookcase, surveyors' rods and levels etc., and a large wooden case which when open formed a bookcase for 40 document boxes, folio size, most probably the well-known Solander cases so much used by Banks. Thus papers needed in London, Revesby Abbey or elsewhere were easily transportable. The inner room contained an impressive bank of 156 mahogany drawers made to Banks's exacting specifications by a Boston craftsman under James Roberts's critical eye. Each drawer had an inside measurement of 13 inches from front to rear by 10 inches broad and 5½ inches deep. The bookcase in the outer room was a handsome glass-fronted piece which occupied a span of wall 10 feet 8 inches long. However in the first winter after the installations Roberts found the drawers of the document cabinet swollen by the damp. This problem had doubtless been resolved by the time Arthur Young saw it, and Banks showed him its contents. There was a catalogue of names and subjects and a list of every paper in every drawer, according to Young, '... so that whether the enquiry concerned a man, or a drainage, or an enclosure, or a farm, or a wood, the request was scarcely named before a mass of information was in a moment before me'.

Here too was stored the evidence of how many noble woods and parks came to receive the trees which grace them now. During his last visit to Revesby Abbey in May 1768 before sailing in the *Endeavour* one of Banks's last acts was to plant Scotch firs in the ling lawns of Tumby Wood. The seeds from these firs probably in later years found their way as far west as Alderley in Gloucestershire to the Blagden estate in 1787, but certainly many other species found their way far afield from Tumby, especially the oak and birch. Another link with the *Endeavour* voyage will illustrate this process at work. James Roberts, the young servant who had survived that voyage with Banks and was now his steward at Revesby Abbey wrote on 9 December 1794 to his master from the new estate office. He reported the gathering of nine quarters of good acorns from the woods ready for Baron Yarborough to go to Brocklesby Park as one of many other contributions from Revesby Abbey to afforest that great estate. On 30 December he reported the safe despatch of 40000 young birch plants gathered from the same ling lawns in Tumby Wood. These were destined for the grounds at Willingham House the new mansion of Ayscoghe Boucherett, MP for Great Grimsby.

Arthur Young in 1797 denoted as the leading planter of forest trees in the county Lord Yarborough who had for the previous ten years planted 100 acres a year. It is clear from the estate correspondence of Revesby Abbey how much this extensive planting at Brocklesby park owed, at least for its oaks, to supplies from the 805 acres then of Tumby, Fulsby and Sherwood woodlands. These woods had been carefully husbanded since 1727 on a 23-year rotation, the full grown oaks being taken out on the best land to the extent of one-fourth of the stand. These trees were usually calculated to be four successive growth periods of 23 years, that is 92 years old at felling. Occasionally some were retained for five growths or 115 years, but very few. Of ash and elm a high proportion was cut with only a minority left for a second growth period. The so-called 'aquatics' such as the willows and the alder were cut clean every period and similarly with the hazel and other brush woods. John Parkinson sen. calculated in 1797 each acre per period of 23 years yielded an income of £45 from timber, bark, poles and brush or just under £2 per acre per annum. This was reckoned by Arthur Young to be about twice the general average for the kingdom as a whole and to reflect management of a high order. He did not however hesitate to level his critical eye at this use of capital assets and, with recondite calculations of is own, to reflect that the land could be made to yield much more. He coated the advisory pill in this way:

> There is not a clearer head in Great Britain than that of the Right Honourable Possessor of these woods; and whenever the immense extent of his respectable pursuits will permit attention to such questions of his private interest, he will doubtless reflect on the vast capital he has thus employed at an interest, to speak in the mildest terms, rather inadequate: 800 acres at 200£. are 160,000£.; at 100£. are 80,000£.; such sums are worth attending to.

The management of the Lincolnshire estates however always formed a regular and important component of the 'respectable pursuits' from day to day of their 'Right Honourable Possessor', absent though he was for ten out of the 12 months of the average year. For 33 years he was served with exemplary diligence by Benjamin Stephenson of Mareham-le-Fen as his estate steward, the man who had given the same quality of faithful service to his father from about 1741. When he died in the cottage at Mareham-le-Fen in 1795 Stephenson had given 54 years of his life to the family for about £80 salary plus £30 board wages, with a retirement annuity of £100 for the last three or four years of his life. He was succeeded from 1792–4 by James Roberts, the boy from Mareham-le-Fen who had been Banks's servant from the age of 16 in 1768, had sailed round the world with him in the *Endeavour* and to Iceland and the Orkneys with him in the *Sir Lawrence* and had remained ever since then as a trusted member of his household staff. For these three years Roberts enjoyed a salary of £130 and was assisted by John Steel at £100 after his transfer from Cheadle in Staffordshire when the manors were sold in November 1790. For some years George Bull was the park keeper at £40 a year until he retired to his own farm in May 1794 and was succeeded by Josiah Mills at the same figure. Within the same period Paul Slight was keeper at Fulsby wood for £12, Joseph Smith at Tumby for £6 and John Tomlinson at Sherwood for £2. In the house Martha Webster reigned for £21, assisted by Ann Scott for £12 with keep included. Robert Hewing as a rat catcher harassed all such vermin for £3.3s.0d. and Robert Alliwell for £10 a year taught the nearby children at Revesby village school as a charge on the estate.

Over the years this was the more or less settled establishment at Revesby Abbey, changing usually by death or illness rather than for dereliction of duty or some disharmony. After the death of Benjamin Stephenson in July 1795 and that of John Steel (who had never been well at Revesby) about the same time, the regime moved into the pattern it would retain until the death of the master himself in 1820. John Parkinson sen. of Asgarby, professional land agent and valuer, took over the reins of estate management and James Roberts became more closely associated with Banks as his right hand man at Soho Square and Spring Grove combining the function of house steward with that of estate manager for all the country properties. In time John Parkinson jun. became an assistant to his father who, in any case had other responsibilities, for example, as one of the three commissioners for the Fourth District in the Witham Commission for fen drainage. John Parkinson sen., under the terms of Banks's will, inherited his leasehold estates in Lincolnshire and together father and son laid out and developed as a result the small village of New Bolingbroke, two or three miles south of Revesby in the West Fen. This was a well merited reward for the long years of sterling service which Parkinson sen. had given Banks as his active partner in the field during the legal and enginering processes by which the drainage and subdivision was effected of the Wildmore, West and East Fens and all that stemmed from John Rennie's report of 1800. Parkinson was if anything an even more diligent correspondent than the assiduous Stephenson and it is possible that there are few more detailed and continuous records of the evolution of an estate in relation to developing land use in the surrounding district than the exchanges between these two men and Sir Joseph Banks from 1763 to 1820.

More could be said and there is certainly much more to be learned about the growth and operation of the Banks estates in the Parts of Lindsey and Holland in Lincolnshire. This is enough, however, to define the base of the family fortune which placed him firmly among the large but not the largest land-holders of the county gentlemen in his day.

II

Those '. . . other Lands in the County of Stafford . . .' which were the manors of

Cheadle and Kingsley were acquired in 1714 as an appendage of the Revesby Abbey estate bought from the Howard family. Of land held it was no more than about 478 acres, mostly a scattering of small crofts, with town houses in Cheadle and Kingsley, eight farms ranging from 26 to 133 acres, and a brass foundry. There were some woods and wastes with a few drift collieries as a hint of future wealth. All this lay compactly on the hills between the rivers Churnet and Tean, midway between Stoke-on-Trent and Ashbourne and mostly within a five-mile radius of Cheadle. Joseph Banks II reckoned it 'a good estate of £300' rental in 1735, about a tenth of the income from the Lincolnshire holdings then. More than at Revesby a system of tenure by leases seemed to have prevailed.

During the minority of Joseph Banks IV a general watch on the estate was kept from Lincolnshire by Benjamin Stephenson with Robert Banks-Hodgkinson, as trustee and guardian, some 30 miles away at Ashover. Banks himself did not see this corner of his possessions until December 1767 during his tour through Wales and the Midlands when he spent two weeks on its inspection. He was depressed by the general view – 'the road exceedingly Bad & the Countrey very ugly' – but found his possessions in better order than he expected although he deprecated his tenants' excessive lopping of the timber. He commented on the quality of the marl, which he tested on the spot with *aqua fortis* (nitric acid) for evidence of its lime content and was concerned with the character of the coal, noting in particular one seam of six feet with the slope and direction of its stratum which seemed to leave little on his own land. Other types of coal near Kingsley he rated as of low quality. He was impressed with the high quality of the 'raddle' or red ochre and interested in the possibilities of ironstone, faint though they were. One of the most important results of this visit to north Staffordshire was his meeting with John Gilbert, right-hand man of the Duke of Bridgewater. Banks travelled with Gilbert from Cheadle to study the Duke's canal at Worsley and his coal mine, both supervised by this man of 'most indefatigable industry' as Banks described him and who was to become a good friend. Though his visits to his Staffordshire manors were infrequent and brief, he made two soon after his marriage. On both he had the company of his wife and sister. The first in 1780 was made from Revesby

> ... Travelling slow through Cross Country roads in a mountainous countrey &
> Sleeping at miserable alehouses without ever any maid to assist their Toilets ...

This must have referred especially to the stages between Overton Hall and Cheadle for he had evidently travelled that way to consult with his uncle Robert – and possibly also James Watt and Matthew Boulton – on the installation of the new engine for the Gregory Mine over which there was at that time a delay in the delivery of parts from Soho, Birmingham. It was for the same reason that the family returned the following year in April 1781 to Overton to see the Boulton and Watt engine begin its work. A detour through Cheadle on the way north was a sensible diversion, for the extra 30 miles or so that it involved, giving the opportunity of three days' study of the local industries: the hemp spinning and ribbon weaving at Cheadle; the tape manufacture and bleaching at Tean; the wireworks on the Churnet at Alton; and finally the tin sheet manufacture at Oakmoor where also the copper sheathing for ships' bottoms was made. Ten years later it would seem, when it was clear that the industrial future of North Staffordshire was to be based on coal rather than on water power, Banks finally decided to sell the Cheadle and Kingsley manors. In the summer of 1790, when he was financially pressed to meet the £600 a year required by his mother's jointure, it made sense to realize his capital asset underground. The manors and other freehold estates were put up for sale in 90 lots. The possibility of further coal seams enhancing the value of both manors beyond the deposits already known and being worked was specifically noted and further trial boring advised before the sale.

The sale took place by auction over a period of four days, 9–11 November 1790 realizing a figure of at least £15 116. It is not clear if this figure represented the whole sale as the payments dragged on in some cases until 1793 but certainly it was the gross sum recorded up to May 1791. The total rental for both manors at the date of the sale was £343, not greatly in excess of what Joseph Banks II had reckoned it to be worth in 1735. With the steam age well advanced and proven coal seams underground (especially in Kingsley, the least remunerative of the two manors) and the rents fixed in terms of so many old leases, it is clear why Banks decided to sell. With a sum or more than £15 000 invested in the funds at the prevailing interest rates the jointure due to his mother from the estate was comfortably secured, and an outlying piece of real estate ceased to be a burden.

It left his agent, John Steel, however without full employment. So, with the declining health of old Benjamin Stephenson, Banks took Steel over to Lincolnshire to ease his burden.

III

After the patrimony in Lincolnshire and Staffordshire had been firmly established each succeeding head of the family coveted and in the end acquired a London residence. Joseph Banks I had the house in Boswell Court; Joseph Banks II had the house at 36 St James's Square; William Banks paid rates notably at 30 Argyll Street (west), the birthplace of Joseph Banks IV who, more than any of his three progenitors, became an established London man. All four heads of the Lincolnshire Banks family depended primarily on the estate income from that county to sustain their London footholds though none were wholly dependent on that source. Certainly Banks at his majority had a useful income from investment though not a large one.

The personal fortune which Banks had under the care of his guardian and trustee, Robert Banks-Hodgkinson, for some three and-a-half years after the death of his father, was in total £15 185 by the account signed on 19 April 1764 – an income of about £4400 per annum of which he received an allowance of £400 a year during his minority at Christ Church. Thereafter he was well-placed financially to settle on a London house but for some time enjoyed his freedom in rented rooms from time to time, apart from those he still retained in Peckwater Quadrangle, Christ Church. Not until a few weeks after his return from the *Niger* voyage did he acquire a house of his own at No. 14 New Burlington Street, probably during April 1767. From this date there are accumulating signs of his activity in modifying and furnishing his new premises for a professional future which he seems at last to have determined for himself. Sydney Parkinson was already at work for him on the Newfoundland collections and the Loten drawings and Stanfield Parkinson, the artist's brother, was providing the furnishings to Banks's orders.

No details survive of the exact size and interior arrangements at New Burlington Street but it seems to have been one of the two largest in the street with a frontage of 26 feet, a probable depth of 125 feet, and a rateable value of £150. Among the houses built at first there was a high degree of uniformity in the general façade under the stipulations of the Earl of Burlington and they were broadly similar to those in Savile Row where almost identical houses may still be seen. Originally they seem to have been built with a reddish-brown brick, three or, in the case of No. 14, possibly four windows wide with a basement, three storeys and a garret floor. The three public rooms in which the collections from the *Endeavour* voyage were first to be seen would have been on the ground and first floors. It was here also that the collections from Newfoundland and Labrador were gathered in the spring of 1767 and where Sydney Parkinson first began his work on this material. Here also was the base from which the scientific party for the *Endeavour* voyage was organized in the spring and summer of 1768 and to which its survivors returned with the South Pacific harvest in the summer of 1771.

Again it is not clear what prompted Banks to move to Soho Square. It was probably a slow process of searching in tune with a growing commitment to academic pursuits lying further east at Montagu House where Solander had his apartments and Council work at Crane Court where the Royal Society had its rooms. On Banks's return to London in the autumn of 1776 from Lincolnshire he asked John Lane of King Street, Covent Garden, to investigate the house of Sir George Colebrooke in Soho Square, of which the lease was with Christie and Ansell for sale. At Christmas he was told that it could be rented for £280, or the leasehold bought for the 'very extravagant price' of £7000 but that if it was not let by private contract it must come to auction. Lane thought

> ... as poor Soho is not a fashionable Residence, as fashion is so very rife, I should fancy it will have few admirers & therefore go at a less rent than now demanded ...

The owner proved to be George Steuart, painter, of St James's. It is possible that he was also the architect when the house had been re-built on the site several years before Sir George Colebrooke's brief occupation. It was Colebrooke's bankruptcy that had now put the house on the market and it certainly had features of practical value not present at 14 New Burlington Street, whatever the decline in the social milieu.

By the end of March 1777 a memorandum of agreement had been signed between George Steuart and Banks. Under this agreement Banks paid a deposit of £1000 for the lease of the residual 78 years promising the balance of £3000 on or before 29 April, free of all encumbrances except the ground rent of £22 per annum due to the Duke of Portland on whose estate King or Soho Square was situated. The sum of £4000 in all, for which the lease was acquired, fulfilled John Lane's forecast that something less than £7000 would be accepted. For this sum Banks had now gained possession of that 'elegant and Spacious Leasehold House with stabling for five horses and two Carriages' opening onto Dean Street. It was the 'extensive back premises' above this stable and coach accommodation that formed the real advantage of Soho Square over New Burlington Street. However this was a benefit not immediately obvious from the modest but elegant frontage of only 18 feet which 32

The south-west corner of Soho Square, 1812, with No. 32 facing at left. Drawing by
George Shepherd in the Dixson Galleries, Mitchell Library, Sydney.

Soho Square presented to the world outside, nor even from the interior, with its
'superb Embellishment *au dernier Gout*'. It was rather the 'Neatness and Utility' of the
arrangement of the various apartments that struck the decisive note.

Behind the narrow frontage to the west side of the Square the family dwelling
house itself was built of a reddish-brown brick in an L-shape of three storeys and a
garret floor over an extensive basement. It extended to a full width of 52 feet 6 inches
behind No. 31 and along the dividing wall with No. 33 to a depth of 56 feet 6 inches.
Along the same wall it was connected to a detached building, the so-called 'back
premises', by a covered passage of 26 feet 6 inches. In this way an L-shaped courtyard was enclosed in a site area with a depth of 115 feet from Soho Square to the
Dean Street frontage of 32 feet 6 inches. The main entrance from the Square was
through a large hall with the entrance to the great stairs of Portland stone on the left
and the door to the servants' stairs on the right. To the left was the main eating
parlour and behind the foot of the main stairs was the small library, the 'little den', off
which the so-called 'passage room' gave access to the covered way leading to the
back premises. On the first floor above the entrance hall was the front drawing room
and next to it, above the eating parlour, the 'great room' or south drawing room, 28
feet by 25 feet, the largest in the house.

The ground floor frontage on Dean Street was occupied by the stable facilities for
five horses and two coaches. Beneath this was the extensive vaulting which probably
joined at this level with the basement passage from the house, a subterranean storage
facility of much value. But the space of immediate concern to Banks in 1777 was
clearly on the upper floors, especially the library with its windows opening over
Dean Street and what was probably the schoolroom adjacent with its windows facing
east into the courtyard. Above these rooms again was an attic floor with three other

rooms designated the 'young gentlemen's bedrooms'; the chaplain's room with a chimney-piece of Portland stone, and a dressing room with a chimney-piece of veined marble with wood dressings.

The library itself as Banks first found it was already fitted with 11 bookcases in mahogany with brass wire panels. This was a room some 32 feet long and 20 feet broad. There was a chimney-piece of marble against the north partition wall with a fluted frieze and a tablet bearing a draped head and mouldings of plain veined marble with black marble covings. There was also a prominent enriched cornice and a screen of columns.

Such was the general state of the site at 32 Soho Square at the time of its purchase by Banks. Major structural alterations and occasional refurbishments mostly took place during the months of August to October when the family was away in the north with Jonas Dryander who was very often in effect clerk of works. Indeed it is possible that his services began with the effective occupation of the new house about August that year, though we have no direct evidence of when his regular salary began.

By September 1777 Banks had already written to Charles Blagden, who was then on active service at sea off the American coast, telling him of the change of address; and one of the earliest surviving letters from the new address is that dated 6 November 1777 to Sir William Hamilton in Naples.

It is impossible now to be sure of all the diversions of use in the two buildings and the details of the structural changes wrought on the site in Banks's lifetime. A few important ones however are fairly clear. The Colebrooke's eating parlour on the ground floor immediately beneath the south drawing-room seems to have continued as such but the small library entered from a door at the west side of the foot of the great staircase quickly became the study or 'little den' of Banks himself, a room of about 20 feet by 13 feet wide. Otherwise in No. 32 the use of the rooms on the first, second and garret floors above and the various domestic offices in the basement beneath would seem to have retained the original use for which they were designed.

The major changes were in the back premises, especially the library. This was greatly altered in 1791, probably under the advice and architectural supervision of George Dance junior. This work was carried out between July and November in that year with all the books taken across to the Soho Square side of the establishment. What was involved was no less than the making of a gallery round the library by encroaching on some of the garret floor which extended over the herbarium. This required the passage of strengthening iron bars from the external Dean Street wall through to the inner or courtyard wall to serve both as ties and supports. Above the centre of the library the flat roof was lifted to allow the insertion of a double-hipped lantern skylight some 20 feet by 8 feet. The gallery itself was fitted with open-fronted bookshelves and a decorative cross-barred iron railing. This was finished and ready for painting by mid-October except the loose shelves for the gallery bookcase. The paint was still drying in the gallery when the family returned about 9 November 1791, but the books had been replaced in all the cases of the main library below. By the end of the month the gallery cases were filled as well.

The herbarium itself is the one important workplace about which there is little information as yet. One glimpse we have from Robert Jamieson during his visit in August 1793 after George Dance's alterations had been made. He noted the library with its new gallery and the fine portrait by Nathaniel Dance of Captain Cook

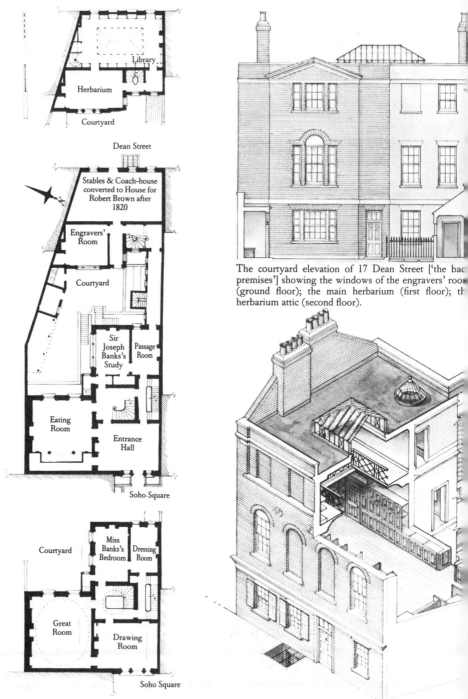

Library

Herbarium

Courtyard

Dean Street

Stables & Coach-house
converted to House for
Robert Brown after
1820

Engravers'
Room

Courtyard

Sir
Joseph
Banks's
Study

Passage
Room

Eating
Room

Entrance
Hall

Soho Square

Courtyard

Miss
Banks's
Bedroom

Dressing
Room

Great
Room

Drawing
Room

Soho Square

The courtyard elevation of 17 Dean Street ['the back
premises'] showing the windows of the engravers' room
(ground floor); the main herbarium (first floor); the
herbarium attic (second floor).

The back premises of 32 Soho Square or 17 Dean Street from the south-west,
showing the flat copper-covered roof, the top light over the library and a part of its
interior; with ground and first floor plans.

The main family house at 32 Soho Square from the south-west above the court-yard showing the windows of the great or south room on the first floor above the eating parlour; and the studio window of Banks's study on the left with the covered passage leading from it to the back premises.

Reconstructed from various plans, drawings, photographs and inventories by Harold B. Carter and John Sambrook, 1987.

The original Chippendale 'cubes' of the type made for Banks up to 1776 for the storage of plant and other specimens at 14 New Burlington Street.

hanging at one end. But his impression of the herbarium, though brief, is the clearest we have:

> ... After breakfast I observed the Hortus Siccus which occupies a large room from top to Bottom on 3 sides, a certain number of Genera are deposited in mahogany cases which are piled one above another, but are so uniform that they seem as if they were all one; these plants are kept in this manner in single cases that they may be the more easily removed in case of fire ...

Now these same cases form part of the storage accommodation in the General Herbarium in the Museum at South Kensington where the Banksian plant collection has finally come to rest.

Beneath the herbarium on the ground floor, and probably of a comparable size, was the engravers' room presumably fitted also with a studio window similar to the herbarium for the same good working reasons and facing east into the courtyard. This was fitted eventually with a range of eight presses with shelves and drawers, each press cable of storing 90 to 100 of the 18 inch by 11¾ inch copper plates of the botanical engravings. In this room Daniel Mackenzie and Francis Polydore Nodder more perhaps than any others worked for Banks, but all of them under the immediate eye of Jonas Dryander as the librarian and the curator. An external and separate door into the courtyard led by a path to area steps and so into the main house by way of the basement.

As a household for over 40 years it consisted of rather more than 20 persons in residence from year to year, including the master and two mistresses. It was maintained in the period 1785–90 for an annual sum of about £1400–1500 excluding food, much of which came from Revesby Abbey in the form of venison and game (worth about £300) but including liquor as wines and ales (about £120–130).

Heating by coal and wood cost about £120 and lighting by oil and candles another £30. The servants' wages amounted to about £300, including their clothes allowance, but rather more than this in later years as in 1795 when there were apparently 14 men and 7 maid servants accounted as on the household staff, and presumably in residence.

From basement to garret the house fronting Soho Square stood five storeys high on a base of about 2220 square feet or a total of about 11100 square feet of floor space. The back premises opening on to Dean Street from vaults to garrets was effectively four storeys high on a base of 1335 square feet or effectively with about 5000 square feet of floor space. This latter was the working and storage space within which the plant and animal specimens were kept and the books and papers associated with their study duly stacked. By any standards, then or now, it was a modest establishment to measure against the influence it exerted on the evolution of the natural sciences of western Europe at the turn of the eighteen and nineteenth centuries.

IV

With his academic base now established at Soho Square Banks continued exploring the rural margins of London for a house and land where botany and horticulture could flourish as field studies to offset the limitations of the herbarium and the library. The summer of 1777 had seen not only the move out of New Burlington Street but also the advent of Jonas Dryander and the beginnings of that long association with Banks which had as much to do with the search for fresh plant specimens from London gardens as with the care of dried plants at Soho Square. In his first months in England Dryander was soon introduced by Banks not only to the Royal Gardens at Kew but also to Dr William Pitcairn's five acres of a living plant collection at Islington and more important and more extensive, to the garden of Dr John Fothergill at Upton Park, Stratford. It was probably the paramount example of John Fothergill that drove Banks to a form of emulation but it was his uncle, Robert Banks-Hodgkinson, who was again influential in his choice of locations. In 1775 Banks-Hodgkinson had bought the villa and its surrounding 23 acres known as Heston House, which he enlarged and improved. In addition the Royal Botanic Garden was nearby on the south bank of the Thames. We have Solander's word that Banks first leased the estate of Spring Grove from Elisha Biscoe early in 1779 for four years because of its proximity to Heston House. The lease was by degrees extended to 1791 and in June that year Banks reminded Biscoe of a promise to establish a more permanent arrangement after the coming of age of Miss Biscoe on whom the final decision depended. At this date Banks apparently had the offer of Whitton Place, the Italianate villa of the aged Sir William Chambers, about two miles across the Heath near Twickenham, thickly sown with antique marbles and classical conceits but also a botanical sanctuary with many fine exotics well established. The temptation to move receded quickly as Miss Biscoe agreed through her father, to a long lease on Spring Grove with the ultimate possibility of buying the freehold. Under the terms of an indenture dated 30 July 1781 Elisha Biscoe demised to Banks

> ... all that capital Messuage or Tenement called *Spring Grove House* situate and being at *Smallbury Green*, in the county of *Middlesex*, with the Household Offices,

337

Barns, Stables, Outhouses, Yards, Gardens, Pleasure Grounds, and Appurtenances thereunto belonging; and also all those Four several Closes of Meadow or Pasture Land, called by the several Names following; (that is to say) *The Park Field*, containing by Estimation Fourteen Acres; *The Thirteen Acre Field*, containing by Estimation Thirteen Acres; *Pond Field*, containing by Estimation Ten Acres; and *The Cold Bath Field* (formerly called *Hangman's Close*) containing by Estimation Four Acres and an Half (more or less) situate, lying, and being adjacent to the said Messuage or Tenement . . . etc

It was agreed that Banks should now have a formal lease of 21 years at a yearly rent of £200, free of all taxes and outgoings, with the option of buying the fee simple for £6000 if this should occur within three years of the date of the indenture. The final purchase of the title however was not made until 1808, but from 1791 Banks was free to manage the land and to modify the house and its out-buildings as he wished – and could afford. He quickly set about these changes and Spring Grove with 32 Soho Square underwent an orgy of building construction and alteration during 1791. In the first week of August Lady Banks laid the first brick of the new garden wall that symbolized the new order.

The changes started with the rebuilding of the pine succession house and the greenhouse, the addition of a new peach house, a grape house and an ice house. The kitchen garden was enlarged to the east, walled round and divided by a cross wall. In its north-east corner, a melon ground was laid out isolated by a reed hedge. The gooseberry garden to the north of the house was extended a further 30 yards and enclosed with a seven-foot deal paling fence. The four acres of the Cold Bath field were added to the pleasure ground west of the house and encircled with a gravel walk planted with shrubs. The Park field to the north and east of the house and kitchen garden was also given a walk round its boundaries similar to that of the enlarged pleasure ground. The frontage to Smallbury Green south of the house was completed by the new garden wall and the gates of the new entrance between this and the kitchen garden on the east side. The turning of the Heston road off the London road across the Green was moved several chains to the west.

Within the house extensive changes were made to the kitchen and the adjacent servants' hall and a raised *porte-cochère* was planned for the east entrance 'with Pillars to drive under as at Mr. Pierponts'. A coach house for four carriages was joined to the south end of the barn in a matching clapboard construction. It is a tribute to the working organization involved that the main building was finished before the end of the year, probably under the supervision of James Roberts. The plan of the Spring Grove estate incorporating these changes was recorded in the survey of D. Todd of Hounslow in 1800, apart from the addition of new glass houses and the enclosure of about eight acres of Smallbury Green to advance the frontage to the London road about the time of the Enclosure awards in 1818. In 1800 the surveyed area was 49 acres 3 roods and 15 perches.

Spring Grove lay about ten miles from Soho Square along the old London road, a journey of perhaps two hours by carriage. To Heston House it was two and-a-half miles by the Lampton road; to the Royal Botanic Garden at Kew by way of Kew Bridge some three miles; and to Windsor Castle along the old Roman road by way of Staines some 14 miles or two to three hours travel by carriage. These distances and times give a fair idea of the ground covered by Banks as he moved in and out of London on the King's business and his own.

The day-to-day management of this small Middlesex estate was in the hands of someone whose function lay between that of farm bailiff and head gardener with a fairly constant staff of three gardeners and such *ad hoc* labourers as were required. Until 1803 John Smith held the senior position, at a wage which rose from 15 guineas a year in 1782 to £35.10s.0d. in 1791 and £50 in 1800–2, augmented by various perquisites including board and keep. He was succeeded by Thomas Fairbairn in 1803 at the same wage of £50 plus board and keep estimated at £21.10s.0d., who remained until December 1815 when he left to enter the service of the Prince of Saxe-Coburg in 1817. From the end of 1813 or early 1814 Isaac Oldacre was certainly employed at Spring Grove uncovering the mysteries of mushroom culture which he had learned in the service of the Tsar of Russia. From January 1816 he succeeded Fairbairn as head gardener and remained so until the death of Lady Banks in 1828.

The annual outgoings, including the rent, tithes and taxes, ranged until 1791 between £400 and £800 a year. This included a fairly regular outlay of about £150 for malt and hops in the annual brewing of small beer as at Revesby Abbey. In 1801 this cost about £2.2s.0d. a hogshead of 54 gallons or 1.2 pence a pint. The beer was brewed by Joseph Tiller who charged 8s.6d. for each brewing of about three hogsheads on 25 or 26 occasions during the year. During the 1780s and early 1790s the average annual Spring Grove brewing seems to have been 75 to 80 hogsheads, that is over 4000 gallons.

As Revesby Abbey yielded venison and game so Spring Grove produced fruit and an increasing variety of vegetables. There was also milk from a few dairy cows, later to become one of Lady Banks's hobbies, and augmented with importations from Jersey and Alderney; occasionally mutton rather than lamb from sheep of various breeds and crosses culled from the breeding experiments; and pork from some 16 or so pigs of the 'good old breed'. Banks diligently farmed the ponds for fish, in particular carp and tench for the table. These were netted and their numbers adjusted as seemed necessary. A 'stew pond' was kept for those for immediate eating and surplus stock given away for the ponds of friends. On at least one occasion, in 1785, Banks also experimented with the effect of castration in carp in the 'Round Pond on the Common' but with what result there is no record.

Almost from the beginning of his tenure Banks was active in developing the kitchen garden with cabbage, kale, Brussels sprouts, lettuce, peas and beans prominent among the greens and a wide range of potato varieties. Asparagus seems to have been an early and especial favourite with some 21000 roots in the first ten years at £3.15s.0d. per 1000, supplied by William Watts, Robert Walker and Ann Waller. Mushrooms were cultivated in 1786 with three bushels of spawn bought for 12s. Dwarf apricots appeared in 1784, pineapples in 1786 while cherry trees from Richard Wilmot in 1790 and Duke cherries from William Watkins in 1791 were early examples of the relationship that was to grow between Spring Grove and the nursery gardens of Isleworth. To the kitchen garden area east of the house there must be added the gooseberry garden of more than half an acre beside the Long Walk – a total of more than two and-a-half acres in all devoted to the fruits of the earth. These and the arable areas were fertilized with dung from the cow yard and the stables augmented by purchases from commercial sources elsewhere: for example in 1792 for the year's supply of dung 70 guineas was paid to S. Charlton. Banks noted the charges for the royal horse dung which Ramsay Robinson applied to His Majesty's gardens at Kew and elsewhere: from the King's stables at Windsor, 4d. per horse per week; from the Prince of Wales's stables in London, 3d per horse per week. Then taking the latter figure, one horse would produce 13 shillings worth of dung per year. Thus seventy guineas would represent the output of approximately 113 horses in a year.

The greenhouse and the glasshouse stoves were ranged on the south face of the kitchen wall on the north side of which lay the rickyard and over its western corner the cow yard and the dairy. To the east of the house lay the three and-a-half acres of the pleasure ground and gardens. They included a stretch of fine lawn which Fabricius assures us as early as 1782 had a bowling green in which the dominant grass was *Poa annua*. That Banks paid much attention to his lawns is attested by his regular purchases, annually, of 4–6000 turves, some 36000 between 1782 and 1791, enough perhaps for an acre more than the fine lawns Fabricius saw. On the western edge of the pleasure ground, dividing it from the Cold Bath field, was a row of elms whose great stumps were still visible in 1975, as were several of the cedars of Lebanon which once graced the southern edge of the main lawn.

Apart from its value as a source of food for Soho Square, there is no doubt that Spring Grove served a more clearly defined experimental purpose than any of Banks's other estates. Its farm produce were by-products of an establishment with other functions. While it could be seen as a rich man's hobby, a farm and garden from which to retreat from the metropolis it could also be regarded as an out-station to 32 Soho Square, an ally of the Royal Botanic Garden at Kew, an experiment station at times serving the national interest in matters of plant and animal breeding and at others stimulating the rising market garden and nurseries. Over the years, whatever the returns from various forms of farm or garden produce, Banks usually found himself 'out of pocket', as he rated it, by rather more than £500 every year for its upkeep and operation, which he regarded as a reasonable indulgence of his personal interests and hobbies. His close engagement with Spring Grove as something more than a haven of relaxation probably began with his extended periods of residence there in 1783 and 1784 during the establishment of William Roy's baseline across Hounslow Heath. It was at this time also that he was beginning to receive consignments of seeds and plants from Dr Johan Koenig and Dr William Roxburgh in India and from Dr John Duncan and William Pigou at Canton. Indeed before 1785 there is not much evidence that Spring Grove had much claim as a field station to Soho Square. But from 1786 we have the traces of a sequence of practical trials, taking advantage of every opportunity that came Banks's way to gain some insight beyond the written or the spoken word. He never made any claims for his activities there as 'experiments' in any scientific sense. He was content to accumulate experience and to pass on its fruits sometimes literally as garden produce but also in his conversation and correspondence with an occasional venture into the printed word in later years for such as the Linnean and the Horticultural Societies. One of the first examples of this shrewd empiricism was clearly his sheep breeding on the meadows and pastures of Spring Grove, 1785–92, breeding the Spanish Merino and its crosses with a variety of other breeds. At the same time there is a teasing glimpse of his attempt at a quantitative comparison of potato varieties over the summer of 1786 – Manley's Dwarf, Manley's Early, Round Dwarf, Early Kidney or Yellow Dwarf, versus Bell's Early and Dutch Early from Forsyth, and those of his own

Spring Grove, Smallbury Green, near Hounslow, Middlesex, *c.* 1800, from the Great Western Road. The fabric of the building is now incorporated in that of the present Hounslow Borough College, formerly the Isleworth polytechnic. Water colour by an artist unknown.

stock. In 1791 there is another tantalizing fragment of a manurial trial laid out in graduated strips across more than six acres of the Park field. This was a comparison of French versus English gypsum (hydrous calcium sulphate), or 'plaster' as he termed it, in two rates of application – approximately 384 and 576 pounds per acre – compared with the unmanured, each with a buffer strip of five yards between. The dry spring and summer brought the worst hay crop Banks had known in his 12 years at Spring Grove and even after the late summer downpour no discernible difference between the treatments of the pasture strips. What differences there may have been in weight of hay per treatment there are no surviving notes to say, though from the state of the season none were expected for that year or perhaps at all as Park field had been well manured with dung for many years past.

In contrast to field agriculture we have his abortive efforts to sustain and cultivate the cochineal insect (*Dactylopius* sp.) in a corner of his heated pine house at Spring Grove during the late winter of 1793. Another casualty in the long list of his attempts with exotic species at Spring Grove is noted the following year, 1794, in the failure of the 'New Zealand Cloth Plant', his old love (*Phormium tenax* Forst,), once again to be killed by frost after transplanting from the hothouse earlier in the year, as had the magnolia Yu Lan which John Duncan had sent him from China. On the other hand his *Costus banksii* from Dr Koenig was surviving; his turnips from Butan were still there after five years as were his wheat from Bihar and his rice planted in 1790 probably acquired for him by Captain Bligh in the East Indies after the mutiny on the *Bounty*.

Though the documentary evidence is sparse we know enough to confirm the importance of this small Middlesex estate as a significant element in the rise of modern British horticulture. Apart from its presence as a modest adjunct to the Royal Botanic Garden at Kew there is its relation with the nursery of Lee and Kennedy at Hammersmith. Over the last 25 years of Banks's life there is its importance to plant breeding and plant physiology as the background of his correspondence and association with Thomas Andrew Knight at Elton and Downton Castle in Herefordshire. There can be little doubt that the commercial market gardens of Isleworth, Heston and Brentford directly benefited from the new or improved varieties, especially in fruit trees and strawberries, with which Spring Grove was blessed from time to time.

V

The estate of Overton Hall near the village of Ashover in Derbyshire lies for the most part east of Matlock between the valleys of the Derwent and the Amber near the headwaters of the latter. It was acquired in 1556 by the Hodgkinsons of Northedge Hall whose fortunes during the seventeenth century rose with the development of lead-mining in the parish of Ashover and brought under the management of the Banks family of Revesby Abbey by Anne Hodgkinson's marriage in 1714 to Joseph II. The house itself is less than a mile almost due south of the village which today is hardly larger than when Banks last saw it in 1812. The hall as a building is the only one used by Banks which survives to the present day more or less in a state which he would recognize and in surroundings not greatly changed. Placed some 200 feet above the River Amber, almost in the shadow of the 1000-foot escarpment to the west, it was once the centre of some 103 acres of pleasure ground, woods, plantations and fields. It was by far the largest of the 203 houses in the parish in 1798–9 when Banks paid tax for 75 windows, more than three times as many as the next in size, the houses of John Nodder at Marsh Green and of William Milnes at Butts. The basement once accommodated a large servants' hall, two kitchens, two scullerys, a closet, butler's pantry, housekeeper's room and three good cellars. Two stone staircases gave access to the ground floor with entrances at both the front and the rear. At this level there was a back lobby and a long front hall, a lofty dining room, a large drawing-room communicating by folding doors with a smaller pannelled drawing-room; a library, two bedrooms and a water closet. On the first floor were five principal bedrooms and on the second floor seven more rooms. The ground sloped in such a way that under the dining room there was a stable outside which was a lumber room over which was a loft and pigeon cote. In the garden was a garden house with a room above.

At the rear of the house, on the southern side, a large paved yard was surrounded by a brew house with a laundry over, a larder, a joiner's shop, stabling for seven horses, a barn, a cow house and a cow yard, with kennels. Separated from the mansion house complex by a roadway was a building with a double coach house with two mens' rooms over, a coach house with a loft over, and stabling for six horses. To the north and west of the house were two walled kitchen gardens.

About 1783 the enclosed land of the estate was 1058 acres with some 63 rent-paying tenants. By 1817 these had increased to 93 occupiers from whom Banks derived £1678 supplemented by some £408 as income from wood sales and

Overton Hall, near Ashover, Derbyshire, *c.* 1869.

pasturage when the estate income was almost entirely from these sources. But when Banks first saw Overton Hall in the summer vacation of 1762 a richer return came from the Banks-Hodgkinson holdings in the lead-mines that tunnelled deep down along the western slope of the Amber valley and beneath the grounds of the house itself. These were particularly the Gregory, the Overton and the Cockwell mines in which Robert Banks-Hodgkinson and Banks together held the controlling shares.

The immediate vicinity of Ashover has been associated with lead-mining since the time of the Roman occupation; and by the end of the seventeenth century most of the important veins in the parish had been found and to some extent worked, with the Hodgkinson family closely involved as pioneers. Between 1734 and 1737 active mining of the ore was continued until the workings reached a point near Ravensnest House when it was abandoned as worthless. The syndicate then sought to develop a new mine to be known as the Overton which eventually joined the Gregory vein from the north-east. In 1758 attention was directed again to the Gregory vein and the old Nether Sough Company gave way to a new partnership, the Gregory Mine Company, in which the Banks-Hodgkinson family held 12 of the 44 shares and Isaac Wilkinson, lead smelter and merchant of Chesterfield another 11, with the remaining 21 shares divided among at least 9 others.

From 1770 to 1775 the Gregory mine reached its peak of profitability with the zenith in 1772. Between 1775 and 1778 a gross profit of over £40000 was made, though in the next two years losses of aout £700 appeared before returning to profit again in 1781. However from 1783 a decline set in, and by 1788 output had fallen and thereafter the Gregory Mine fast became a liability. After some £23000 had been spent during 13 years from 1790 in various attempts to restore profitable working the Gregory Mine was closed in October 1803 and lead-mining on a large scale in the parish of Ashover effectively ended. However, at Christmas 1803, a new company was formed to work what had been one of the richest parts at the junction of the Gregory and the Overton veins at a depth of about 200 feet some 500 yards west of the Hall itself. In 1807 at Christmas this forlorn attempt was abandoned and the two steam pumping engines finally removed to bolster the fortunes of the Westedge Mine where it had all begun so long ago. This in turn succumbed in 1808.

These 'fire engines', installed to solve the prevailing problem of water in the mines, were important early examples in the application of steam to industry, bridging the evolution from the Newcomen to the Boulton and Watt machines. The first or 'old engine' was of the Newcomen design and had been built in 1748 by Darby of Coalbrookdale. It had been purchased from the Mill Close Mine in Darley Dale. The second or 'new engine' was a Boulton and Watt patent designed under the terms of an order very largely negotiated by Banks in direct consultation with James Watt. Although many of the parts came from Smith's foundry in Chesterfield the rest were transported by a difficult route from the Soho Works in Birmingham. It started work in July 1781 having been finally inspected on the site by Banks in April during a special visit to Overton for that purpose. In operation it was a success from the beginning. In its first quarter at work it consumed 100 tons of fuel compared with 350 tons required by the old Newcomen engine using the same coal.

Then, between May 1790 and September 1795, about 264 yards further west from the new engine, another shaft was sunk to a depth of 912 feet through the gritstone, shale and limestone strata in a last attempt to restore profit. This was to be known as the Forefield Shaft and cost the Company £5000. It was a development which concerned Banks in the first years after his uncle's death in 1791. Over this shaft was erected a small 'fire engine' called a whimsy, developed out of discussions between Banks and Francis Thompson, the local engineer. Thompson agreed then to build an eight horse-power engine for £280. The components were made by various local firms. The whimsy began work in February 1796 to draw gear from the bridging floor and a small amount of water from the bottom of the shaft up some 90 feet into the water course leading to the pump worked by the Boulton and Watt engine.

According to John Milnes the clear profit to the proprietors from the Gregory Mine over the years 1758–1806 was £101 535. Of this Robert Banks-Hodgkinson and Banks would have derived about £27600, but against this must be set their losses from Lady Day 1790 to Christmas 1803 in the abortive development of the Forefield Shaft. The total loss was £23 398 of which the Banks-Hodgkinson/Banks share would have been £6400 over the 13 years. For ten of these the debit in the quarterly reckonings would have been set against Banks's name alone.

Until Robert Banks-Hodgkinson died in November 1792 Joseph had made few but important visits to Overton. Those in his vacations in 1762–3 introduced him to estate and financial management; those in 1778, 1781 and 1785 were as an active major shareholder in the Gregory Mine Company. He came to Overton in late August 1793 for the first time as the man in full possession under the terms of his grandfather Hodgkinson's will without the need to hyphenate his name. For almost 20 years Overton Hall was his working base in late August and early September for several weeks as a stage in the long coach drive to Revesby Abbey.

One of his first acts as the new incumbent of the estate was to order George Nuttall, surveyor of Matlock, to prepare a map of the parish of Ashover giving particular attention to his mine at Alton and the suspected coal-bearing land in its

Left Matthew Boulton, FRS. Portrait by an artist unknown.
Right James Watt, FRS, 1792. Portrait by C. F. von Breda.

neighbourhood, with a plan and levels for its extension. This map covering some 9000 acres, at a charge by Nuttall of two pence per acre or £75, was an important nucleus from which much was to grow in the surveys of John Farey 15 years later. In the ten effective days of his visit in 1793 he set a pattern of activity which he followed thereafter until his last visit in 1812.

He set the miners to work sinking the pit for coal at Alton and eight days later measured for himself the distance through the overlying strata to the coal which had just been uncovered. Some of this coal he took with his visitor, Matthew Boulton, to the Boulton and Watt engine on the moor above Overton Hall where he observed it to burn 'with much smoak and great heat' but also to be very bituminous and to cake a little. Then Boulton, with Lawson his chief manager, inspected the engine which had been working well enough since July 1781 but which they now agreed with Banks was out of order and in need of repair. For this Banks thought some abatement in the premiums paid was in order but Boulton demurred. He considered that the working efficiency of the engine at half-a-hundredweight of coal per hour at six strokes per minute was still a good performance. He promised however to put it into better repair.

Other matters of engineering concern were afoot at this time and Henry Cavendish was also a guest for a few days during Boulton's visit. The papers of the late John Smeaton were certainly under discussion that week as Banks prepared to finalize their purchase from Smeaton's son-in-law, John Brooke of Austhorpe, Leeds. There was also the beam engine at Westedge mine to be inspected with Boulton. Installed at a cost of £600, with many parts second-hand, it was larger than necessary but was rated as an economical unit. Banks was impressed with its great beam of American oak, compounded of two 14-inch timbers braced together with cast-iron heads and a harness similar to Smeaton's design. Banks approved the

345

economy of using American oak at 3s.6d. a yard instead of English oak at 5s.0d.

On Tuesday 27 August 1793 after breakfast he entered Overton Mine, where he was able to see for himself the yellow matter 'of a Clay like Consistence & very Buttery' spread over the stones that were under water and 'also a pale Jelly like substance which some of the miners beleive to be the origin of Spar or Spar in a state of formation' resembling grease in appearance and to the touch, and with no smell. Here we have Banks, at the age of 50 and between two periods of gout, making one of his last direct observations of the earth's strata. Thereafter his appraisals were limited to observation from the surface or on the specimens brought to him by the miners themselves or by surveyors like George Nuttall and later by John Farey. But there was enough from his own view of the strata below Overton Hall to prompt him on 21 August 1794 to write to Phillip Rashleigh of Menabilly, Cornwall, asking whether he had any specimens from Ashover and the Gregory Mine in his important collection. In particular he sought for any traces of petroleum, mineral pitch, or 'Calcareous Spar', while offering Rashleigh further specimens of mineralogical interest.

These underground activities were varied by a decent attention to the social niceties of the county. On 24 August 1793 he received as breakfast guests Phillip Gell of Hopton Hall, Wirksworth, with Sir Henry and Lady Hunloke from Wingerworth, the latter a sister of Banks's Norfolk friend, Thomas William Coke. Two days later Banks returned the Hunlokes's call and, being close to Chesterfield when the races were being held, he accepted the office of steward for the following year; and on 27 and 28 August 1794 Banks and Lord Titchfield acted together at an event that did not wholly please that ardent race-goer, Lady Banks. She found the course itself indifferent where, with no special stand for their comfort, the ladies were obliged to rest content in their carriages. However at the two assemblies she rated the rooms very pretty and the company pleasant.

At the first assembly the Duke of Devonshire usually gave a supper but, in his absence, he was represented by Lord John Cavendish, the newly elected MP for the county. Banks himself was also 'much hurried' that year as High Sheriff of Lincolnshire. As such he was called away to Lincoln on 25 August for the nomination of a new county member there on the 26th. However early on 27 August he had rejoined the party at the Hunlokes's in time to take up his stewardship at the races that day.

Thus, from August 1793, these visits to Overton Hall by Banks and his ladies continued as annual affairs except in 1798 and 1799 when because of gout he did not go. His last visit was in 1812.

Over the years there is no doubt that the mining of lead and other minerals dominated his thoughts and activities and even with the demise of the Gregory Mine Company in 1803, there was no slackening in his concern for what lay beneath his lands. The focus merely moved elsewhere and into the wider fields of structural geology. The Westedge mine inherited the two 'fire engines' from the Gregory for a few years, until 1808 when it too closed, in spite of the spectacular short boom in the price of lead as the Peninsula War sent values soaring from £23 in May to £35 per ton in September. By this time Banks had become wise in the technology and economics of the lead trade. This was well shown in his detailed calculations of smelting and transport charges for the various grades of ore recovered from Westedge, backed up by the analysis of samples he had gathered himself. These

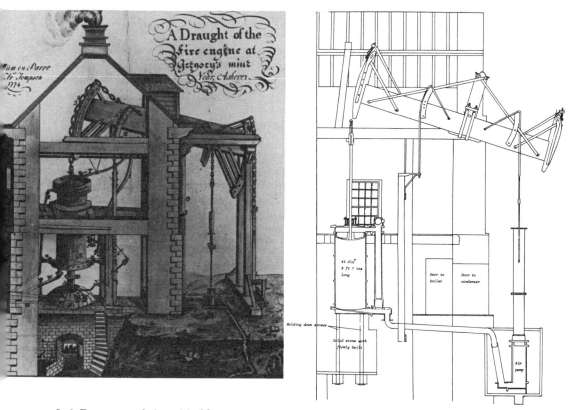

Left Drawing of the old (Newcomen) engine of the Gregory Mine by Francis
Tompson, engineer of Ashover, 1774.
Right Drawing of the new (Boulton and Watt) engine of the Gregory Mine, 1781,
based on the original in the Birmingham Reference Library, Birmingham.

analyses were first done by John Johnson, assayer of metals in Maiden Lane, London,
and then in somewhat more detail by W. H. Wollaston, FRS. In his table for
calculating the price of lead ore based on the price of a fodder of lead at Hull Banks
was helped by the arithmetic of John Farey. But his knowledge of the base metals of
industry such as lead and copper was matched closely by his understanding of the
precious metals, silver and gold, as his years with the Coin Committee of the Privy
Council so clearly showed.

VI

As a youth of 18, within a few weeks of his father's death, Banks had made his first
contribution as a responsible landowner to the evolving topography of Lincolnshire.
At the meeting in November 1761 at Sleaord he was one of the principal subscribers
to the fund that inaugurated the scheme for improving the drainage of the fens along
the River Witham and restoring it as a navigable stream between Lincoln and
Boston. With the act 2 Geo.III, c.32, 1761, the plan formulated by John Grundy,
Langley Edwards and John Smeaton was set in motion and the course of the Witham

was changed, its bed enlarged, its banks raised and the Grand Sluice opened in Boston on 15 October 1766. Less than 20 years later the transformed Witham had become the scene for an annual diversion that ruffled its sluggish waters and drew a rare mixture of Lincolnshire society to its banks in the 11 miles between Dog Dyke near Tattershall and the Grand Sluice itself. Here, each autumn from 1784 to 1796 for several days at the end of August and early September, Banks opened his county activities with a remarkably regular pattern of fishing parties.

These were no desultory affairs of rod and line but altogether more heroic and organized excursions in which the river was fished systematically up and down with a large seine net dragged between two horses, one on either bank. In later years the catch was augmented with trammel nets at strategic points. The seine net was some 70 yards long and 20 feet deep and so free from roots, weeds, and other obstructions was the new course of the river that it was seldom snagged or torn. Behind the net came the boats. From the smaller of the two, covered by a black canvas awning, the servants managed the hauling of the net and the landing of the catch which was carefully classified and weighed. In the first four years no detailed records were taken by Banks or noted by his sister Sarah Sophia beyond the bare dates, times and places, and the names of the participants. The larger vessel, of the type used in the Lincolnshire canals, accommodated Sir Joseph and his guests. As Banks described it to Lord Sheffield on 26 June 1793, it required a horse with a boy to tow it, one man to steer and another to manage the towing line, unless, he said

> . . . as in the case of my navigations occasionaly the gentlemen undertake the steerage which saves a man & keeps the party clear of the crew so that they need have no restraint on their conversation . . .

The first boat, used from 1784 to 1791, was 48 feet long and 10 feet 4 inches wide; the second, from 1792 to 1796, somewhat larger at 52 feet long and 11 feet wide. For some 24 feet amidships it was covered by an awning under which Banks reckoned he could comfortably dine about 30 people, on which Lady Banks had a qualified view. In bad weather an extra awning could be mounted but in the 13 years of these parties it was only needed on four occasions. Each year the boat hire cost Banks 11 guineas with 3 guineas for the fishing rent. Otherwise the event seems to have been essentially a friendly collaboration between the Banks and the Fydell families in its arrangements.

Apart from the first and third occasions (1784 and 1786), all the fishing parties on the Witham took place from Wednesday to Saturday in the week before the picnic races at Lincoln, four days each year from 1787 to 1796. From 1788 the results of the fishing were systematically tabulated, catch by catch and day by day. The numbers and weight of pike, perch and eels were separately listed but the 'white fish' (chub, bream etc.) which formed the main catch were bulked as one. For the first three years the fishing parties were on two or three days only with about 14 to 20 guests each day, but from 1787 onwards the pattern of four days' fishing became regular and the guests numbered above 20, sometimes as many as 36, sitting down to their fish dinner under the awning or ashore on the river bank. For the most part this feast was composed of the pike, perch and eels cooked on a portable iron stove in fish kettles by the servants on the river bank. Sometimes the diet was varied by some of the 'white fish' such as the chub and bream, and occasionally salmon and flounders. At

The fishing on the River Witham – lunching at Anton's Gout. Banks's boats near the bank, with Thomas Fydell's yacht *Union*, 1790. Drawing by William Brand, Custom officer at Boston.

this meal, taken mostly between five and six p.m., an average one or two pounds of fish were eaten by each person.

The social arrangements were much the same from year to year. At about half-past-ten or eleven on a Wednesday morning the Banks party would set off from Revesby Abbey for the seven-mile drive of an hour or more to the big boat waiting at Dog Dyke. The servants with the long seine net would already have begun the fishing when they had been overtaken, in about another hour a light lunch, occasionally an earlydinner, was eaten usually at Coppin Dyke. Depending on the weather, the net would be hauled about 10 or 12 times during the day, sometimes as many as 16, sometimes as few as five. An average of 300 to 400 pounds weight of fish seems to have been caught in a day with the largest catch of 843 pounds on 2 September 1785 and the smallest of 62 pounds on 1 September 1791, a day of high winds and heavy rain. Each evening the boats discharged their passengers at the Grand Sluice in Boston, mostly between nine and ten p.m. Banks and his ladies, with perhaps one or two other guests, would then sleep and breakfast at the charming early Georgian home of Thomas Fydell who was their host. On the fifth day, the family coach would roll north again to Revesby Abbey along the 12 miles through the West Fen.

The company varied over the years. Of the 143 identifiable individuals, only three were titled: the 1st Baron Yarborough was of the party on ten occasions but this was as Mr Charles Pelham of Brocklesby Park, the widowed husband of Banks's first cousin Sophia Aufrere. For the rest, the company was mainly the gentlemen of Boston and the Revesby neighbourhood with their wives, unmarried daughters and occasionally a young son. Thomas Fydell sen., merchant, and MP for Boston and twice mayor of the city, with his wife, eldest daughter and sons were the most diligent partners of the Banks's family. Scarcely less so were the Pacey family, the children of Henry Pacey, FRS, a former MP and recorder of Boston. No less ardent as a Witham fisherman was John Linton, landowner of the eastern fens and a colleague of Banks on problems of drainage and enclosure. Most notable perhaps was the Cartwright family led by the redoubtable political reformer, anti-slave trader and agriculturalist, Major John Cartwright, the eldest, with his brothers Charles, Phillip and Edmund and their wives and daughters. The Major was already active as a farmer and settled at Brothertoft about a mile south of Langrick Ferry, busy with his woad culture, his incipient woollen mill and the Spanish Merino crosses from Banks's Spring Grove sheep. His younger brother Edmund, had also now picked up the clues in Derbyshire from Richard Arkwright of Cromford that were to lead him to the power-loom design and the woollen factories for their installation. Edmund's youngest daughter, the future poetess Frances Dorothy, made her only appearance on the Witham as a small girl in 1789. Less prominent but faithful adherents of the parties were the Rogers and the Brackenbury families, the Kenricks, the Batts and the Stephensons, Thomas Coltman the magistrate from Hagnaby, the Reverend Edward Walls of Spilsby and his wife and daughter, the Doctors Laycock and Petrie and, shadowy but most frequent, Mr Calah. Then there were the recording artists of these expeditions – the Revds John Wheeler and Robert Chaplin, William Brand the customs and excise man from Boston, and the excellent Mr Batty with his party groups in action.

Among the hundred other friends invited a few merit a brief note. We cannot pass the appearance of Jonas Dryander, that inveterate metropolitan, on the first of his few excursions, spending four of his ten days in Lincolnshire more or less afloat on the Witham, 4–7 September 1793. But who was the Miss Lavoisier in the same party this year? Was she of the French scientist's family, an emigré in that fatal year? And who was the Miss Bligh? Was she also the Miss Blythe of the previous years, misspelled as Banks was apt to do in reference to the Captain of the *Bounty*? In these weeks so soon after the return of the *Providence* was she perhaps the future Mrs Putnam, stalwart daughter of the Governor-to-be? There is no vagueness however about the visit of John Lloyd in 1795, driving his own horses across from Wigfair in North Wales responding to a long-pressed invitation, nor about the three days lavished by the Honourable Charles Francis Greville on such a bucolic excursion in 1796 so far from Paddington Green and Warwick Castle.

PART THREE
1797–1820

HM MINISTER
OF
PHILOSOPHIC AFFAIRS
THE RT HON. SIR JOSEPH
BANKS, BT, PC, GCB, PRS

CHAPTER 16

DESERT SANDS AND CORAL COASTS
1791–1802

It is a long stride from the heather hills of the parishes of Traquair and Caddonfoot that lie between the River Tweed and Yarrow Water to the hard going on the desert steppes and the savannah scrub stretching from the Gambia and the Niger Rivers of West Africa. Such was the path traversed by a farmer's son from Foulshiels, near Selkirk, by way of Covent Garden and Bencoolen in Sumatra. Mungo Park's journey into history was mediated by his brother-in-law, James Dickson, who had sprung from similar social roots at Kirke House, near Peebles, and the estate of the Earl of Traquair. The migration of Dickson from the borders of Scotland to become the eminent nurseryman of Covent Garden, the botanical associate of Banks and a co-founder of the Horticultural Society, may have owed something to the 5th Baron Elibank whose castle and estate lay a few miles down the Tweed. It was at the Elibank house at Ballencreif, over the hills near Haddington, that Banks had stayed in November 1772 on his journey south from Edinburgh as he returned from Iceland and the Orkneys. Dickson's pursuit of cryptogams among the hills and valleys along the Tweed was perhaps enough to have him made known on the Elibank estate, a territory rich in the species. It is probable that it was both the Baron and botany that opened the Banksian herbarium and library so freely to Dickson in London. It is certain, however, that it was the botanizing jaunts with Dickson on the Scottish borders by Mungo Park, in his student days at the University of Edinburgh, which brought him freshly equipped with his surgical diploma to the notice of Banks about the end of 1791.

Mungo Park's first venture abroad quickly ensued under the management of Banks. He went, in February 1792, as an assistant surgeon on board the *Worcester* East Indiaman to Bencoolen in Sumatra, a year's apprenticeship in foreign travel with discriminating botanical collections and enough zoology for him to present a succinct paper on eight new species of Sumatran fish, read before the Linnean Society on 4 November 1794.

Between his return from the East Indies and this first venture into recorded literature he had so impressed Banks with his ability and diligence that, in May 1794, he was offered the chance of service under the Association for Promoting the Discovery of the Interior Parts of Africa. His formal appointment as a 'Geographical Missionary' to the task of exploring the course of the river Niger was confirmed on 23 July 1794 by the Committee consisting of Henry Beaufoy, the Secretary, and Sir Joseph Banks, the Treasurer.

This engagement was to begin on 1 August 1794 with an allowance of seven shillings and six pence a day until Park's departure from Gambia, a sum to be doubled thereafter until the day of his return to Europe or to some European settlement. Two hundred pounds was also allowed for the purchase of such goods and equipment as the Committee should think necessary for the African journey itself. These preparations, however, were enmeshed in the plan for establishing a British Consul to 'Senegambia', protected by a fort and garrison at the mouth of the river Gambia as a base for expanding commerce with the interior by some of the London merchant houses. This was a matter of politics and war strategy under the Government, with James Willis, as the Consul-Designate, incurring large expenses for an enterprise that came to nothing in the end. It served to delay Park until the spring of 1795 when, with the support of Banks and Andrew Stuart, he shook himself free from mercantile politics to receive at Soho Square, on 17 April, the further sum of 50 pounds to defray the expense of his outfit and his passage alone in the small brig *Endeavour* from Portsmouth. His instructions, dated 21 April 1795, were in all essentials the same as those drafted by Beaufoy for the Association and given to Major Daniel Houghton in September 1790. Before Park sailed on 22 May 1795, Beaufoy died and Banks took sole charge of affairs on behalf of the Association. As he put it to Mungo Park in September from Revesby Abbey:

> ...I have undertaken the Office of Secretary to the Association for a time but I shall soon give it up I have so many things to do that in truth I should not have done it now if it had not been that I had such expectations from you & was unwilling that your affairs should be conducted by any one else I will take care when I give it up to see every thing concerning you properly managd ...

Waiting at Pisania on the Gambia, with Dr John Laidley as his mentor on the spot, Mungo Park endured his first encounter with the rainy season of tropical Africa in a long and painful illness. Then, detaching himself again from fruitless waiting for the 'Consul to Senegambia', he set out with his small party westward to pursue the task for which Houghton had died four years before. One letter only came to the hands of the Committee of the African Association, dated 1 December 1795, from Pisania the day before his departure – thereafter silence until his return to Falmouth, by way of Antigua, on 22 December 1797.

He was the first young 'missionary' of the African Association to return alive with a stimulating tale to tell. Though he had not, in fact, succeeded in reaching 'Housa' or Timbuktu, he had indeed seen the Niger, or 'Joliba', and determined the direction of its course as far inland as Silla beyond Segu. He reached London to meet Banks early on Christmas morning in the gardens of the British Museum, two years and eight months from their last conference at 32 Soho Square. Soon he was settled under the tutelage of Banks and Bryan Edwards, now the Secretary of the Association, to produce the narrative of his journey, while Edwards with some speed had prepared an abstract to be printed and put before a General Meeting of the subscribers on Saturday 26 May 1798. Here, in a resolution proposed by Banks, the African Association recorded its approval and gave Park permission to publish his full account under its patronage but for his own emolument.

The first stages of its writing were pedestrian and stumbling but, by the end of the year, Edwards could report to Banks that 'Park goes on triumphantly' and now needed little guidance with the account of which some parts were 'equal to anything in the English language'. So Banks now had no cause to demur in arranging for its printing by William Bulmer and publication by George Nicol. The first edition in two volumes dated 5 April 1799, of 1500 copies priced at one and a half guineas, was sold

Mungo Park *aet.* 33, about the time of departure on his second journey, January 1805.
Drawing by Thomas Rowlandson.

355

within a week of its appearance. From this edition alone Mungo Park received the handsome sum of 1000 guineas. Two more editions followed in the same year and a fourth in 1800. This success owed much to the generosity of Banks as the moving spirit; from Bryan Edwards as literary tutor; from Major James Rennell, who vested in Park the property of his own incorporated memoir on the geography of Africa; and not least from George Nicol, who released Park from the usual charges of production. Banks put this and more in his address to the General Meeting at the *Star and Garter* on Saturday 25 May 1799, in the absence of the dying Bryan Edwards.

Before this endorsement of his achievement and material reward for his sufferings in its pursuit, Mungo Park had, in May 1798, offered himself as a volunteer to explore the interior of New Holland. He had responded to the prompting of Banks who had told John King at the Home Office of it, linking the idea with his plans for the employment of Matthew Flinders in charting the Australian coastline. At the General Meeting of 25 May 1798, the Committee of the African Association – Banks and Andrew Stuart – were empowered to recommend Park for this to the Government which the Home Office accepted. Banks had set out Park's qualifications to John King on 15 May 1798: a moral character unblemished; a temper mild and a patience inexhaustible; sufficiently versed in astronomy to make and calculate observations and to determine latitude and longitude; with geography enough to construct a map of his routes and the country traversed; able to draw a little with a competent knowledge of botany and zoology; educated 'in the medical line'. With expenses at 10 shillings a day and his rations, his own pay at 12 shillings a day, and about £100 for his outfit of instruments, arms and trade goods, his terms were moderate. He would require a decked vessel of about 30 tons with a lieutenant in command to receive his orders and advice in all matters of exploration. Banks was sure that Flinders, already in New South Wales, would enter the spirit of his orders and agree perfectly with Park.

But Banks did not allow for the light hand of love. The few summer weeks in June 1798 which Park spent in his native Selkirkshire were enough to unsettle his resolve as an explorer, for there he fell in love with Alison Anderson, the daughter of his former master Thomas Anderson, surgeon of Selkirk. He returned to London to write tentatively on 14 September to the sick man at Spring Grove, with more than a hint of his change of mind, though not giving the real reason for it.

A visit to Spring Grove and a bedside talk with Banks did nothing to clear the matter but only, said Park, to dampen his enthusiasm further. Banks found this degree of depression surprising for the small difference in the rate of pay expected and that offered. On 25 September Banks, tormented as he was by rheumatism and gout at this time, demanded a short answer and the real reason for Park's equivocations. Park's final letter of refusal on 26 September 1798 was indeed a short answer but gave no more enlightenment on the underlying cause. However James Dickson, a few days earlier, conveyed the view of his wife, who was Park's sister, that Park's refusal was in truth a matter of the heart and not of the rate of pay. There the affair ended. A year later Captain P. G. King, lieutenant-governor, sailed in the *Speedy* for New South Wales without Mungo Park as a passenger. Instead Park had retreated to Scotland, had married his Ailie, and settled down to a period of domestic happiness at Foulshiels.

356

II

While the African Association was adjusting its thoughts to the death of John Ledyard and the failure of Simon Lucas as the unprofitable pioneers of its exploratory hopes, a minor epic in the human colonization of remote and empty spaces was unfolding in the South Pacific. Its short course is recorded in the journal of Philip Gidley King, late 2nd Lt of HMS *Sirius*, superintendant and commandant of Norfolk Island from his landing there on 6 March 1788 to his departure on 24 March 1790. Within three weeks of the establishment of the parent colony in Sydney Cove on 26 January 1788, HMS *Supply* had been detached with a tiny group of 23 Europeans to form that most remote of white settlements on the small uninhabited island where Cook and the Forsters had landed in 1774. This speck of land, 1053 miles north-east of Sydney Cove, had been viewed as a possible source of native flax for cordage from *Phormium tenax* and of ship's spars if not masts from the distinctive pine *Araucaria excelsa*. This, and its notional value as a staging post for the China trade and the furs of North America combined with its place as a strategic outpost of some weight, had lent an urgency to its occupation. On 7 March 1788, within 24 hours of the landing, the first seeds of the new crops had been sown and thereafter, for more than 30 years, this isolated penal colony struggled and survived. Within two years of King's first period of command the population had grown to 498 when, a sick man, he left the island in March 1790 to find his way home from Sydney Cove bearing despatches from Governor Phillip and his own journal for perusal by the Admiralty and Sir Joseph Banks. Its appearance in print soon followed between the same covers as that of Captain John Hunter, under the editorial eye of George Chalmers. Commissioned as Lt-Governor of Norfolk Island, he joined HMS *Gorgon*, Captain Parker to sail with his wife post haste with supplies for the hard-pressed colony in New South Wales baulked of them by the loss of HMS *Guardian*. He sailed in March 1791 to reach Sydney Cove on 22 September. On 4 November 1791 he landed at Norfolk Island for his second term of command. He found the population swollen to about twice the number he had left, free civilians and convicts simmering to the boil under the hard rule of Major Robert Ross and his marines. With their departure, and for nearly five years, King managed to maintain a reasonable authority. Throughout this period he kept alive his correspondence with Banks. Then, worn down by the stresses of his arduous command, he was granted sick leave by Governor Hunter in August 1796. He reached England on 6 May 1797 bearing a box of Norfolk pines (*Araucaria excelsa*) and some young plants of the waratah (*Teleopea speciosissima*) for Banks. The pines at least would be a welcome addition to the lone survivor at Kew from previous consignments sent by King, as Banks recorded in a letter of 30 March 1797. Depressed by the state of the country and the course of the war, he told King that he was somewhat cheered by his appointment as a Privy Councillor for which he had taken the oath the day before. Thereby he hoped that he might be of more service to his 'favorite Colony', so much neglected by HM Ministers with their military distractions. For King at least this was an upturn in his fortunes. Although the Admiralty refused his promotion to Post-Captain, Banks had secured for him from the Home Office a dormant commission as Governor of New South Wales in the event of Hunter's absence or death.

The war, however, had lodged another problem with King and Banks in the person of Susanne Gordon, widow of the lamented Dutch commandant of the Cape garrison, returning to her native Switzerland with her young family and two boxes of the papers, drawings and maps of her husband's travels in the African hinterland. She had already disposed of his legacies in the small flock of Spanish sheep which were even then making their passage across the Indian Ocean to New South Wales. Here now for Banks's consideration and advice were some of the first important riches in the geography and natural history of southern Africa offered by the widow's own wish to the British crown rather than to the new Dutch republic. Banks eased their way through the Customs House and, in the care of Captain Edward Riou, they waited for the Treasury to decide to buy them. No such decision was forthcoming, and the widow Gordon had to wait almost another ten years before a financial appreciation of her gallant husband's lifework came her way.

Beyond the Cape a new phase was opening and Banks was already involved in its synthesis. George Caley, the son of a Yorkshire horse dealer had flung off 'the drudgery of the stable' to become another homespun botanist, graduating from Gibson's *Farriery* to Gerard's *Herbal* and Withering's *A Botanical Arrangement of all the Vegetables Naturally Growing in Great Britain*. Stimulated finally by Dr Erasmus Darwin's dedication to Banks of his translation of Linnaeus's *Systema vegetabilium* for the Lichfield Botanical Society, Caley wrote direct to Banks in March 1795 seeking a future as a roving collector. A chastening but not discouraging reply from Banks, with enlivening botanical exchanges on Caley's specimens of *Drosera longifolia*, eventually brought the young stableman to his first post in the Chelsea Physic Garden under William Curtis and the guidance of the savant in Soho Square. His patience was strained by two years of this horticultural discipline but then with hints of further exploration in New Holland rife, he approached Banks on 28 November 1797 offering to collect there, a volunteer responding to 'the thousand tongues at work' which Banks orchestrated as the 'only good beaters up' of his recruits. He met Banks and James Dickson at Soho Square and from then on his future was assured, although a further period of botanical apprenticeship was imposed on him, against his will, in the Royal Botanic Garden at Kew. Banks bore his impatient retreat home to Manchester with equanimity knowing that his fish was hooked and that he would in the end bring him ashore. James Dickson meanwhile served as the line of communication and when in September 1798 Mungo Park withdrew from the voyage of the *Porpoise* the way opened to New South Wales for Caley, not as a collector for Kew but gathering specimens for Banks personally. His acceptance on 18 November 1798 showed that he recognized his limitations as a botanist and enabled Banks to recommend him to the Home Office as a suitable addition to the population of the colony. Banks took it upon himself to pay Caley's salary of 15 shillings a week being, he said, 'unwilling to recommend to Government any person as a botanist who has not received a scientific education', though he had no doubt he would himself receive a competent return from the young man's 'abounding zeal'.

While Caley was coming to terms with his qualified place, a new vessel was being designed by the Admiralty and built under the Chief Surveyor Sir John Henslow at Sheerness for service in New South Wales. This was to be HM Armed Vessel *Porpoise* and it was an integral part of the planning for Lt-Gov. King's return to duty in the colony. When Colonel William Paterson returned home in the spring of 1797 Banks had been able to discuss in some detail the need for European plants and fruit trees in the colony and had got the Home Office to send a plant cabin on the *Porpoise*. It would be filled with a well-selected 'garden' of the right species, which he himself would provide, together with the necessary tools for the gardener who should go out in attendance. Banks believed he had found such a man in George Suttor 'an ingenious young man, educated as a kitchen-gardener, who wishes to marry and carry out his wife to settle at Sidney' and was prepared to care for the garden on board without pay, on condition that he should have the usual indulgences of a free settler and the chance to set up as a market gardener in the colony. In this he was a true son of his father William Suttor, market gardener of The Manor or Manor House, Chelsea, close by Gough House, the home of Banks's uncle George Aufrere, to whom the Suttor family was well-known and largely indebted for its modest success in the trade.

From the beginning the *Porpoise* however was a sorrowful ship. King disliked her lines from his first sight of her at Sheerness and would have lengthened her by 10 to 14 feet but in this he was over-ruled by Henslow, who said it was too late for such changes and was confident that she would be a good ship as she stood. Banks also had his doubts when he met Sir John Henslow at Deptford on 23 June 1798 to discuss the size and placement of the plant cabin which was intended to be much the same as that he had put on HMS *Discovery* in 1791 for the Vancouver voyage. With the *Porpoise*, Banks repeatedly asked if the size, 6 × 12 feet, would not be too large and too inconvenient for her safe working at sea. but Henslow insisted that all would be well. The weight of the 18 boxes, when filled with soil and plants, which were to occupy the cabin on the quarter deck and its expected effect on the angle of heel worried Banks but apparently did not trouble Henslow or the dockyard. In the end the worst fears of King and Banks were realized in the explosion of letters which followed the report of Lt William Scott on the behaviour of the *Porpoise* as he brought her round from Deptford to Portsmouth at the end of January 1799. She proved to be a 'crank' ship 'most certainly the worst calculated I ever saw for such a service', said King, as he reported to Banks the weight of the 'garden' which he had taken at 3 tons 3 cwt. and 3 quarters and which he agreed should be now placed amidships, though this in no way relieved his 'gloomy presage' of the voyage ahead. A long series of sickening delays in and out of dock at Portsmouth now followed until at last King and his party set sail under convoy with a great fleet of 500 merchantmen and 20 men-of-war under Admiral Sir Roger Curtis on 6 September 1799. A week later in the Bay of Biscay the *Porpoise* sustained critical damage to her rudder. After consulting Admiral Curtis, Lt Scott was ordered to return, and by the 17 September the ship was at Spithead again. King could report to Banks that whatever the state of the vessel, the garden was still in good order and that he had, he feared, expressed himself perhaps too freely about the ship in his letter to Sir Andrew Hammond, the Comptroller of the Navy. The Navy Board however could only agree and condemn the *Porpoise* as unfit, and by 5 October the Duke of Portland instructed the Admiralty to prepare another ship for the service. At King's suggestion this was the *Infanta Amelia*, a Spanish prize to HMS *Argo* which was lying in Portsmouth. Re-fitted and re-named as HMS *Porpoise* she received George Suttor and the garden to sail for Sydney on 17 May 1800. Meanwhile Lt-Gov. King and his lady, with George Caley, Ensign Francis Louis Barallier and Edward Wise, the weaver and his family transferred to the whaler *Speedy* Captain George Quested, owned by Enderby and Company. The party sailed on 12 November 1799 to reach Cape Town on 3 February 1800. After two weeks at the Cape the *Speedy* reached Port Jackson on 15 April 1800. King's well-earned sick leave had stretched far beyond its first intentions to more than three years of varied frustrations and worried domesticity.

Through the protracted tedium of the Navy Board's bungling with the first *Porpoise*, Banks was steadily engaged, despite his own ill-health, in equipping Caley and absorbing the overspill of the Yorkshireman's impatient boredom. At the same time he was coping with the problems of George Suttor in the gathering and sustenance of the 'garden' for Port Jackson. For George Caley there were the instruments from Jesse Ramsden with which Banks hoped he might be able to attain some of the navigational skill of Mungo Park under King, who found his student heavy handed at least with the sextant. From the herbarium at Soho Square came the Ellis aquatic microscope as a personal gift from Banks and a further stimulus toward converting the base metal of the young gardener into the more precious compound of the scientific botanist. Such a transmutation was always close to the hopes of Caley and much on his mind when he sought from Banks on 16 September 1798 'an *aquatic* microscope after much the same plans as Mr. Dickson's'.

For George Suttor the overriding dilemma was that of a practical gardener faced with the care of about 50 species and many varieties of useful plants somehow to be coaxed alive across 12000 miles of unfriendly salt seas. For his 18 boxes he had only the frail protection of small plant cabin on the exposed quarter-deck of a small and cranky sailing ship in which to face a voyage of five or six months from 51°28′ N. to 33°52′ S. For Banks there was the task, often from his sick bed, of selecting and organizing the supply of such species as his knowledge of horticulture and his assessment of homoclimes led him to expect might succeed in the hinterland of Sydney Cove.

Banks had received formal commands from the Treasury on 22 June 1798 'to provide such Fruit Trees, usefull Plants and Seeds' as he found on enquiry 'to be wanting in his Majesties Colony of New South Wales' but without any allocation of funds either for this or for the appointment of the gardener to care for them. Soon after, probably in July, his uncle George Aufrere introduced young George Suttor to him, and from 8 August the new recruit started planting the collection in the Royal Botanic Garden at Kew. For more than two months he gathered plants and seeds from the nurseries at a salary of 15 shillings a week in line with that of Caley. For most of this period Banks lay bedridden at Spring Grove and supervised from there. On 22 October 1798 Thomas Layton, the waterman at Kew, carried the whole collection in a large tilted boat down river to where the *Porpoise* lay anchored at Long Reach. The 18 boxes contained according to the groups defined by Banks: culinary plants; medicinal plants; vines for wine-making; vines for table grapes; vines and other fruits for drying; fruits for the table; apples for cider; mulberries for silkworms; hops for brewing; hedge plants; garden plants; plants for cattle fodder; trees for timber. Great emphasis was laid on the hops for brewing beer as a counter to the evils of rum and other spirits, the predominant currency and vice of the colony. Box No. 18 was a handsome array of well-rooted hop cuttings, provided by the Revd Peter Rashleigh from Northfleet, near Gravesend in Kent. All the exotic species came from the Royal Botanic Garden at Kew as gifts and among these were the carob bean tree (*Ceratonia siliqua*) and Dr Roxburgh's 'Spring Grass' (*Agrostis linearis?*) as cattle fodder; Dr Roxburgh's 'wormwood' (*Artemisia* sp.) and James Bruce's anti-dysenteric 'Wooginoos' of the Abyssinians (*Brucea antidysenterica*) an acid fruit of the East Indies (*Averrhoa* sp.) and with some optimism, two tea plants (*Thea sinensis*).

From October 1798 to May 1800 George Suttor grappled with the problems of keeping these varied species alive on board the first *Porpoise* until her final condemnation. The second *Porpoise*, on her voyage of more than seven months to Sydney Cove was no easier and when he arrived on 6 November 1800 he had a sorry report for Banks on the few survivors. On 28 December 1800 he could list only: 1 olive; 6 apples; 6 black mulberries; 6 white mulberries (for silkworms); 4 willows; 18 Chile strawberries; 2 walnuts; 2 Spanish chestnuts; 2 oaks; 4 pomegranites; 2 plaintains; some mint; and of the grapes, Tokay, White Frontiniac, Black Frontiniac, Constantia for wine making, and only the White Muscadine and Muscat of Alexandria for eating. All the hops had gone but John Burrow at the Cape had assured Suttor that a supply could be got from there. This was a poor return for the time and thought that had been expended during the past two and-a-half years although for Banks the cost had not been excessive. He had only advanced something less than £100 for the plant cabin and the purchase of plants and seeds to HM Treasury over this time.

The ultimate return, both to Banks and the colony, was the success of George Suttor as the first effective market gardener and viticulturalist with his 186-acre grant (No. 118 in the parish of Castle Hill), Suttor or Chelsea Farm, some 18 miles inland. Not only was he the first productive citrus orchardist of the colony but in his migration further west across the Blue Mountains he was also to become one of the patriarchs of the new pastoralism two decades later and of a family which has served the country with distinction to the present day. In choosing the stripling from Chelsea Banks had done well as a selection of human stock for securing the future of the colony as a free society. But he had not done this lightly. He had clearly set out, for George Aufrere as the young man's sponsor, the Government's terms for those it allowed to go to New South Wales 'in the character of honest men'. In a letter on 3 July 1798 he pointed out to his uncle the economic burden implied for a young man who could not himself raise £20 when something like £200 was needed over and above what the Government would provide.

> . . . As he is a very young man, and as I suspect that his motive for going is the love of a very young woman, I would still have him consider carefully what he does before he finally resolves to engage himself. I do not insist upon his offer now, but he must in a very few days let me know his determination . . .
> . . . Will you, my dear sir, be so good as to converse with him on the subject of his expectations. I am quite ready for him if he chuses to go, and the cabbin intended for him and his wife, which I have approved of, is by this time fixed up; but I would not by any means wish a young man for whose family you seem to have a regard to engage without sufficient warning of the difficulties, as well as full knowledge of the benefits, likely to accrue to him . . .

Against this background, then, young George Suttor hazarded his future to sail nearly two years later on the second HMS *Porpoise* supported, it must be supposed, by that vital £200 without which no grant would have been possible. The most likely source apart from the immediate family, would have been George Aufrere or Banks or more probably both. Just over 100 years later one visible result of this patronage would emerge in a grandson of young George as Sir Francis Bathurst Suttor (1839–1915) who, on 25 May 1905, became the first president of The Sir Joseph Banks

Memorial Fund of which J. H. Maiden FRS, the Government Botanist and Director of the National Herbarium at Sydney, was the Honorary Secretary.

II

On Monday 21 October 1793 a young midshipman visited Revesby Abbey. Matthew Flinders, at 20, had returned that summer from service in HMS *Providence*, Captain William Bligh, on the second bread-fruit voyage to the South Pacific Ocean. When James Wiles, one of the two gardeners, left the ship at Jamaica he was in debt to Flinders for £30 advanced during the voyage. It was for the reimbursement of this sum that the young man had travelled from his house at Donington the 25 miles north across the fens to meet Sir Joseph Banks through whom all such financial worries in the late voyage were solved. This is the earliest evidence of what became a long working friendship between two men where the difference of a generation was of no account. When Flinders returned to naval duty again, their correspondence later that year is of two men settling the financial problems of a distant friend in the West Indies. The impression remains that the meeting at Revesby Abbey in the autumn of 1793 was not their first. It will serve however, until we know more, as the effective beginning of the long association which yielded the mounting and fulfilment of the voyage of HMS *Investigator*.

In 1794, that year of disasters for the embattled British, there was but one relieving gleam. In the naval action off Brest on 1 June which national euphoria sanctified as 'the Glorious First', the circumnavigators from the South Seas were all engaged. Captain John Hunter, as a volunteer, saw action that day in the flagship HMS *Queen Charlotte*; Lt Henry Waterhouse served under Captain Thomas Pasley on board HMS *Bellerophon* and with him Midshipman Matthew Flinders.

On 26 July Hunter took command of HMS *Reliance* in the Thames with Waterhouse as his second commander and Flinders as master's mate. From April 1794 Banks had been at work on the affairs of the *Reliance* with his proposal for her plant cabin to succeed that of the *Guardian* with its failure, in 1789–90, under 'the gallant Riou' in the plan '. . . of providing usefull fruit-trees and esculent vegetables' for the new colony at Sydney Cove. With George Bass, brother-in-law to Henry Waterhouse, as surgeon on board the *Reliance*, the small group had come together which was finally to establish the geographic reality behind the vague names of New Holland and New South Wales.

The evolution of the voyage of HMS *Investigator* may reasonably be traced to early in 1791. One element lay in the Society for the Improvement of Naval Architecture, of which Banks was Vice-President, founded in that year and Captain John Schrank's development of the double keel from whence emerged the design of the *Lady Nelson* tender for coastwise exploration close inshore. Another lay in Banks's concern with the need for accuracy in the survey of the north-west coast of America in the planning of Vancouver's voyage in February 1791. There were also the fertilizing thoughts of Bligh in his second outward passage for the bread-fruit on the uncharted mysteries of New Holland and sent from Cape Town on 17 December 1791 to Banks at Soho Square. But despite extensive debate on these notions, it was not until after the *Reliance* reached Sydney in September 1795, and after Waterhouse's circumnavigation in her, with William Kent in the *Supply*, during 1796–7 to take supplies to the hard-pressed colony from the Cape, that there was time to indulge in geographic enquiry.

From the intermittent adventures of Bass and Flinders along the coast of New South Wales south of Sydney, whenever time allowed, one salient point emerged. Van Diemen's Land was an island separated by 'Bass's Strait' from the main continent. Bass had put this forward but it was at last clearly established in Flinders's charts from their voyage in the *Norfolk* published with his *Observations on the Coast of Van Diemen's Land* . . . and dedicated to Banks. However, before these confirmatory works came to Soho Square, Banks was aware of the geographic fact, for he had been continually in touch with Hunter on the subject of Australian exploration. Was there not also possibly a strait from north to south which divided the mass of New Holland from New South Wales? This was the last great puzzle of the Australian continental outline still to be solved and there were many good strategic reasons, in the state of the war with the French, why it should be.

Before Bass and Flinders had circumnavigated Van Diemen's Land at the end of 1798 Banks in May of that year had thought that Mungo Park might be the man to penetrate the unknown interior of New South Wales. Mungo Park's involvement became tangled with the fitting out of the first HMS *Porpoise* but Banks summarized his ideas to the Under-Secretary at the Home Office, John King on 15 May 1798:

> . . . We have now possessed the countrey of New South Wales more than ten years, and so much has the discovery of the interior been neglected that no one article has hitherto been discover'd by the importation of which the mother country can receive any degree of return for the cost of founding and hitherto maintaining the colony.
>
> It is impossible to conceive that such a body of land, as large as all Europe, does not produce vast rivers, capable of being navigated into the heart of the interior; or, if properly investigated, that such a country, situate in a most fruitful climate, should not produce some raw material of importance to a manufacturing country as England is . . .

After presenting Mungo Park's credentials for such a service he suggested a decked vessel of about 30 tons for the coastwise exploration under the command of a lieutenant. Such a man was he said:

> . . . Lieutenant Flinders – a countryman of mine – a man of activity and information, who is already there – will, I am sure, be happy if he is intrusted with the command, and will enter into the spirit of his orders, and agree perfectly with Park . . .

To this he added

> . . . I will readily undertaken to draw up instructions for all parties, and to correspond with them during the execution of their plans, under the superintendance of your office; such hopes have I of material discoveries being made, and such zeal do I really feel for the prosperity of a colony in the founding of which I bore a considerable share . . .

In the end nothing came of this plan for Mungo Park changed his mind. Captain King sailed for New South Wales to succeed Governor John Hunter well informed on Banks's views on Australian exploration but with gardeners, not explorers, at his side. The seed of an idea however had been planted at the Home Office and the name of Flinders associated with it as a man of competence and promise at the time that he was preparing to give further evidence of his qualities about the coast of Tasmania.

Park withdrew finally from the challenge of the southern hemisphere in September 1798 and it was common knowledge in October that another volunteer had come forward. From the library at Soho Square the Abbé Correia de Serra wrote to the convalescent Banks:

> ... I hope you will not take amiss, my interference in the subject of this note. Mr. Brown, a very good naturalist, who frequents your Library, where I have made acquaintance with him, hearing that Mungo Park does not intend to go any more to New Holland, offers to go in his place. Science is a gainer in this change of man; Mr. Brown being a professed naturalist. He is a Scotchman, fit to pursue an object with constance and cold mind ...

The two essential elements for the future *Investigator* voyage had now been brought together.

By the spring of 1799 a further step had been taken in the allocation of the *Lady Nelson* to the service of Australian exploration by sea. This little vessel of 60 tons, fitted as a brig, was the embodiment of the design that Captain Schrank had discussed with Banks in 1791 and whose sketch plans for such boats were stored at Soho Square. Now she was the first ocean-going vessel with a sliding keel. The Transport Boart, under pressure from Banks and Lt-Gov. King, had reluctantly let her go but it was not until January 1800 that her first commander, Lt James Grant, could write glowingly to Banks of her sailing performance and stability in wild weather at sea or at anchor. She seemed to have all the qualities needed for inshore navigation and Grant hoped he would be the man to use her in the proposed surveys. He was certainly the man to take her to the southern hemisphere but Banks and King had always intended that Flinders should command her as a survey vessel. Yet it was under Grant that she became the first ship to traverse Bass Strait from west to east and in doing so to mark the names of Schrank and Banks as capes on the new map near the point of her continental landfall.

In April 1799 Governor John Hunter in Sydney had received the Duke of Portland's despatches from the Home Office enclosing Banks's suggestions for further exploration. It was a subject close to Hunter's heart but he had no means of executing it. He had this to say:

> ... The idea suggested by Sir Joseph Banks, as appears from an extract of that gentleman's letter to Mr. [John] King, is in my judgement the only practicable means of gaining an early knowledge of this immense country – a country, my Lord, which there is much reason (as far as we have carried our discoverys) to believe may afford many usefull articles. A vessel such as Sir Joseph mentions cou'd be built here; and I wou'd recommend, if such an intention and means of exploring the country shou'd be determin'd on, that the necessary naval stores for fitting her be sent out

364

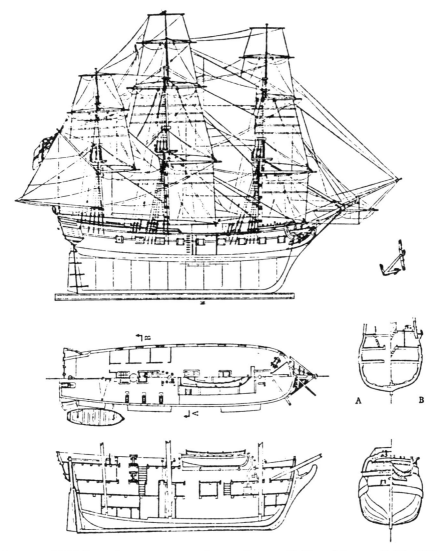

Details of HM Sloop *Investigator*, according to Geeson, N. T. and Sexton, R. T., 1970, *The Mariner's Mirror, 56*: 279, Fig. 1.

By the time this despatch reached the Home Office, the *Lady Nelson* was already fitting out and almost ready for her part under Grant's command and briefly that of Flinders, who found her a laggard sailer whatever her other virtues. The exchange of letters and despatches between the two hemispheres was this time too slow. When King reached Port Jackson in April 1800 to relieve Hunter as Governor, he was concerned to find that Flinders had already gone home in the *Reliance* but hoped he would be in time to bring out the *Lady Nelson*. However Grant was already at sea in his new experimental charge and, King had to amend the grand design. So, too, had Banks. King, in his despatch by HMS *Buffalo*, wrote of what was already common ground between himself and Banks:

> ... As you have seen Messrs. Bass and Flinders, any information on my part respecting the straits, &c., is unnecessary. As land has been seen to the westward since those gentlemen were there, I am anxiously looking out for the *Lady Nelson*, and her first trip will be to find out whether the western entrance of the straights is as good as the eastern and to run down the south-west coast from thence to ascertain whether there are any harbours in which the vessells can be sheltered, and to solve the doubt whether the mountains are separated from the other part of New Holland by a sea or strait running from the Gulf of Carpentaria into the Southern Ocean, which is a very favourite idea in this country, how far founded or not the *Lady Nelson*, I hope, will determine. Every calculation of mine respecting them is expired. Surely we shall not be left without a ship of some kind ...

Thus when Matthew Flinders wrote to Banks from HMS *Reliance* at Spithead on Saturday 6 September 1800 he was updating a subject which he knew had been discussed between Banks, Hunter and King. Banks who got the letter at Overton Hall on 10 September found in it a welcome confirmation that the man who for the past two years he had thought fit for the tasks in mind was indeed willing to meet the challenge. When he wrote his private letter from Spithead, dedicated his *Observations on the Coast of Van Diemen's Land* ..., and sent his other charts to Banks, Flinders knew that he was dealing with the man on whom everything turned, not as a figure of remote patronage, but as a working participant and sympathetic senior colleague. He could not have known, of course, how involved Banks was in matters relating to the colony and the mysteries of the continental land mass. But although not privy to the circulation of ideas between the Home Office, the governors and Sir Joseph Banks, he was aware of the general state of official thinking among the senior naval and viceregal authorities. Whatever he deduced from his official discussions and instructions it would have been augmented by the dinner table gossip in the relaxed conditions of an infant colony. Apart from his contacts with Banks more than five years before, Flinders was never far from the elbows of men who were the correspondents of that unswerving friend of distant navigators and adventurous young men.

Some measure of the state of readiness for mounting an expedition which Flinders met on his return to London may be found in the speed of events thereafter. Although Flinders did not meet Banks until mid-November within a week the Navy Board was directed to prepare the *Xenophon*, a three-masted vessel of 334 tons at Sheerness, by orders dated 21 November to be executed 'with all possible despatch'. Less than three weeks later, on 12 December, one meeting at the Admiralty of four

George John Spencer, 2nd Earl Spencer, First Lord of the Admiralty 1794–1801.
Portrait by J. S. Copley.

men set the official seal on the expedition. Earl Spencer as First Lord of the Admiralty approved the 'discovery ship' *Xenophon* proposed by Sir Andrew Snape Hamond, Comptroller of the Navy, as also her complement: a commander, two lieutenants, a master, a purser, gunner, carpenter, 60 seamen, a sergeant and 12 marines, with an armament of 12 six-pounders. Lt Matthew Flinders asked that the ship be fitted with a strong gripe and bilge keels; that he himself be equipped with an artificial horizon and surveying instruments, with stationery of all kinds, Cook's voyages and other books; and that the astronomer should have orders to communicate with him. Finally the President of the Royal Society proposed, and received, the First Lord's approval to add the civilian complement to the expedition: a naturalist, salary £400; a botanical painter, salary £300; a landscape and figure painter, salary £300; a gardener, salary £100; an astronomer to be lent by the Board of Longitude; four boys for servants to the gentlemen. The expedition was under way and orders that same day were sent to the yard at Sheerness for the fitting out of the ship. That same day Banks wrote to Robert Brown near Dublin offering him the post of naturalist to the expedition, followed by his offer on 14 December to Ferdinand Bauer of that of botanical artist.

Robert Brown had accepted Banks's offer before Christmas, shaken himself free from his regimental duties, and arrived at Soho Square on Christmas day. He was soon hard at work in the herbarium and library educating himself for the task ahead. On 19 January 1801 the *Xenophon* was registered on the list of the Royal Navy as HM Sloop *Investigator*. Before the end of January Banks had drafted and sent Lord Spencer his 'Hints respecting the Rout that may be pursued with advantages by the *Investigator* discovery ship' after a hasty visit to Lincolnshire immediately after Christmas. He had invited Flinders to travel with him but in the event he went alone. At the same time Banks presented to the First Lord the masterly 'memorandum of agreement' in its first draft form. Here the terms and conditions of employment of the civilian group, 'the Gentlemen' headed by Robert Brown, were defined with the general code governing their relations with the commanding officer. Prepared, no doubt, with the Vancouver-Menzies troubles in mind, this was the final distillate of all the lessons Banks had learned since the *Endeavour* voyage as a civilian scientist seeking a symbiosis with the Royal Navy. He set out a working code which wedded the broad fields of hydrography and survey with scientific natural history as for no other English voyage to that time.

In the ship and its manning, both naval and civilian, the new expedition was almost on the same scale as the old *Endeavour* enterprise, but different in the subtleties of its management, of which the 'memorandum of agreement' was a notable part. It can be said to reveal the nature and extent of Banks's own past frustrations and a clue to the management he might have adopted had he led such a voyage. In some degree it represented the unwritten code which he had set for himself and his party and observed in the *Endeavour* with Cook. It also clearly set out a course of scientific supervision for the voyage and the eventual publication of its results which became, as he knew it would, a burden of responsibility for himself.

The partnership of Flinders and Brown, young men of 27 and 28 respectively, in a voyage of this kind was a brilliant stroke by Banks and the fulfilment of a recurring dream. Its final urgency arose from the knowledge that a French expedition had been mounting for some time and had indeed already sailed for the Southern Ocean in October 1800. The very names of Nicolas Baudin's two vessels, *Géographe* and

Dr Robert Brown, FRS, FLS. Engraving from the portrait by H. W. Pickersgill, RA in the possession of the Linnean Society of London.

Naturaliste, were a flaunting challenge and a subtle irritant each in its own way. For Flinders there was the threat of pre-emption in discovery and survey around the Australian coastline. For Banks, through Brown, there was the spectre of new gains in natural history beyond his reach, of new species found for other herbaria than his own. There was over all the thrusting ambition of the First Consul and the imminence of French strategic penetration into the otherwise peaceful oceans of the southern world. Behind the overt scientific intentions of each voyage was the hidden imperial motive. The sciences were in fact as much at war as the battle fleets they sought to avoid.

Baudin carried with him in *Géographe* and *Naturaliste* 22 botanists, zoologists, mineralogists, painters, draughtsmen and gardeners for whom Banks had obtained a British passport. For the *Investigator* Banks had mustered before the end of January 1801 no more than five young men to be signatories, in his study at Soho Square on 29 April, of the 'memorandum of agreement' – 'In order to prevent all misunderstanding between the Lords Commissioners for Executing the office of Lord High Admiral of the United Kingdoms, and the Persons employed by their Lordships as Scientific Assistants on board His Majesty's Ship the Investigator, for the purpose of exploring the Country of New Holland'. Those who signed in the presence of Banks as the sole witness were: Robert Brown, William Westall, Ferdinand Bauer, Peter Good, and John Allen. John Crossley, the astronomer, appointed by the Board of Longitude, was not a signatory as his terms of reference belonged to the navigational side of the voyage and the work of Flinders himself. Crossley left the ship as a sick man at Cape Town on the outward passage and his affairs, including the instruments to be taken, were managed separately by Banks and Maskelyne, the Astronomer Royal.

The names of the civilian supernumeraries had been sent to Flinders on 1 March by the Lords of the Admiralty and all details concerning them had been managed by Banks with their support. All aspects of the voyage, from the concept to the fine detail, invoked the energies and judgement of Banks. Week by week wherever Flinders was – at Sheerness, at the Nore, at Spithead, or even at King Street – the letters passed to and fro and Banks mediated arrangements by his frequent attendance at the Admiralty. Every detail came under his scrutiny – problems of ship's boats; pay and table money; books for the library; instruments, charts and stationery; chests, tools and trade goods; the dismantled plant cabin and its stowage. So too, inevitably, did those larger and more tricky problems – the negotiation of the passport for the ship and its company, the drafting of the official 'Instructions for the Voyage . . .' into an acceptable compromise. Then there were also those personal scrapes from which Flinders had to be rescued which jeopardized Banks's good offices in securing his gazettal as Commander as well as leader of the expedition – the deception of his marriage to Anne Chappell and her presence on board the *Investigator*, the loss of a prisoner from the ship, the grounding at Hythe – all called for the utmost in Banks's skill as a defending counsel at the Admiralty and as a negotiator.

At last all was ready, and on 17 July Flinders, anchored at Spithead, received his sailing orders, instructions and passport. Before he cleared away down Channel, on 18 July 1801 in the morning, he wrote one letter to the man who had made all possible – but not without cocking a critical eye at certain points of difference between the final detail of his 'Instructions for the Voyage . . .', as they had come

Commander Matthew Flinders, RN. Miniature after an unknown artist.

from the Admiralty, and his own idea of the way to circumnavigate New Holland '. . . best suited to expedition and safety'. He concluded

> . . . I am happy at being able to proceed upon the voyage even at this late period, and to say that I am much pleased with my messmates, who, as far as I can at present judge, are very orderly, well-inclined men, and fitted for the situations which they fill.
>
> Most earnestly praying that you may see the examination of New Holland performed in the way that will be most gratifying to you . . .

With him he carried timekeepers from the Board of Longitude, both Arnold's (Nos 82 and 176) and Earnshaw's (Nos. 520 and 543) and a pocket version of the instrument as a personal gift from Banks, possibly his own Arnold No. 5, purchased nearly 30 years before in his high hopes before the second Cook voyage. The measurement of time was a central problem for the navigation ahead. Its relentless passage over the years was to be extended further than either Banks or Flinders would have wished to measure by any instrument, however refined and perfect in its running, before they met again.

IV

It is probable that the visit of Johann Blumenbach to London over the winter of 1791–2 and his first extended meeting with Banks, after so many years of correspondence from Göttingen, set in train ideas which led to the first deep penetration of Africa from the north by a modern European. Their common interest in ethnology founded on the specimens of human crania gathered by Banks from the South Seas had evolved into a lively concern with the antiquities of the Egyptians. Blumenbach had opened three Egyptian mummies during his 14 busy weeks in London in the presence of Banks and other savants and the English translation of his paper on the subject was read by Banks before the Royal Society on 10 April 1794. Thereafter the African Association had in Blumenbach a channel of academic gossip among the Germans and a stimulating evangelist on African themes which balanced that of Banks in London. In 1795 into their field of influence came Friedrich Conrad Hornemann, a student of theology at Göttingen, the son of a Lutheran pastor of Hildesheim in Saxony. The new light which had emerged from Major Houghton's ill-fated journey of 1791 seeking the probable course of the Niger and its further pursuit by Mungo Park had kindled a spark in Hornemann, whose self-generated interests had much in common with those of the young Scot.

In the summer of that year, through Blumenbach, he sought an introduction to Banks and the African Association but it was a year before his name appeared in its records. In the interim, with the aid of Blumenbach and several other professors of Göttingen, the 23-year-old Hornemann had prepared a plan for a journey across the north African deserts into the Fezzan. This formulated the notions already germinating in the Association and owed much to what lay behind the abortive effort of Simon Lucas, now English Consul at Tripoli. His proposals were accepted at a Committee meeting on 3 June at Soho Square and Blumenbach was provided with eight pounds sterling per month to cover Hornemann's expenses during six months' tuition at the University of Göttingen for the geographical and ethnological tasks ahead. On 7 December Hornemann made his first direct contact with Banks by letter. On 7 January 1796 Banks sent Blumenbach £30 for Hornemann's travelling expenses to London and by the middle of March the first German 'missionary' of the African Association had been welcomed at Soho Square. His London allowance was 12 shillings a week for lodgings, with further subsistence at a guinea and-a-half per week. His instruments were to be a small Hadley's sextant with an artificial horizon and a stand, a timekeeper, a three-foot achromatic telescope, two pocket compasses and appropriate stationery. Banks, as Treasurer of the Association, was empowered to offer Hornemann an annuity of £200 to commence from the date of his arrival at Cairo for an agreed term of five years. In the case of his death within this period, an annuity of £60 was to be paid to his mother at Hildesheim. These material arrangements were simple enough. However the menacing presence of the Revolutionary forces in the Mediterranean was a formidable obstacle to the Association's plans for Hornemann. Banks's successful pressure on the British Government in the previous year for the release to France of the collections of La Billardière had brought a generous reciprocity from the French. At the final committee meeting on 23 June 1797, when the instructions were read to Hornemann, Banks was able to provide the passport, effected through the French commissioner in London, Jean Charretié, which would ensure his travel through France to Marseilles and from thence to Alexandria. On 12 July Hornemann reported his safe passage by a neutral vessel from Dover to Calais and his welcome in Paris by Joseph Lalande and Pierre Broussonet through whom he was making important contacts for his African venture. In a difficult journey by way of Cyprus, he reached Alexandria on 13 September and Cairo on 4 October where he lodged in the Convent of the Propaganda. His letter of 18 October was not received in Soho Square until January 1798 when, in his prompt reply, Banks counselled Hornemann to stay quietly in Cairo until he had attained fluency in Arabic and a competent knowledge of the Muslim customs and the peoples through whose territories he was to pass. He also told him of the safe return of Mungo Park and his finding of the 'Joliba' [or Niger] River and referred to his hardships at the hands of the Arabs. Hornemann was soon to face similar perils from this quarter as the Christian communities in Cairo were threatened by the French invasion under Bonaparte. After the battle of the Pyramids on 25 July 1798, Hornemann was introduced to the General himself and received protection and help with a further passport in French from him. His letters to London were guaranteed a safe passage provided they too were written in French. This help was due to the good offices of the French scientists in the Bonaparte entourage, particularly Claude Louis Berthollet, the chemist and Gaspart Monge, the geometer. Hornemann's last letter to Banks from Cairo was on 1 September and four days later, disguised as a Muslim trader, he set out with a caravan travelling one of the old routes through Siwa and Augila to Murzuk and the Fezzan and so north to Tripoli. There was then almost a year of silence until it was broken by a letter dated 19 August 1799 to Banks, to be followed some weeks later by a copy of his journal in the original German, evidently that from which a translation into English was later printed. Hornemann wrote to Banks again on 29 November 1799 with another copy of the journal, but now in its English form which he designated 'the most correct and better', sent from Tripoli to Malta by Simon Lucas on his behalf. He then set out on 1 December for Murzuk again and from there his last letter to Banks was written on 6 April 1800. Thereafter – silence.

His plans had been to travel south with a caravan to Bornu and the vicinity of Lake Chad and, if possible, then to journey west to Katsina in the hope that from there he might find the Niger. Banks, for some reason, was led to expect that he might hear again from Hornemann about April 1802 but nothing came. A rumour of his progress emerged on 21 December 1804 when, dining with Banks at Soho Square, Mr Macdonough, a former surgeon in the Consulate at Tripoli, said that 'Jussuf' or Hornemann in the guise of 'a very respectable Moorish merchant' had been seen safe and well at Katsina about June 1803. It was not however until 1808 that any real anxiety for his fate was expressed. By 1809 hope had begun to fade, though it was not until 1817 that there was any real clue to what had happened. Since then everything has pointed to his death early in 1801 from dysentery at Bokani, not much more than a day's march from the Niger near Jebba and about 70 miles from the presumed site of Mungo Park's death at Bussa.

The original text of Hornemann's first copy of his journal was translated into English from the German by a compatriot in London and edited by the Association's Secretary, William Young. In this form it was set by William Bulmer, and published for the Association under the imprint of G. and W. Nicol in 1802. In scope it was a modest successor to the journal of Mungo Park, published three years earlier by the same hands, but it was no more than an interim report from an author who was still absent on his mission. Moreover it was a translation to another language by another hand from the original, a transformation it was to suffer yet again. A copy of it was presented by the British Ambassador in Paris to the First Consul of France, as a courtesy to the man who had, after all, extended his protection at a critical point to the young author. Napoleon ordered its immediate translation from English into French under the editing of L. Langlès of the Institut National and in Paris in 1803 it appeared as *Voyage de F. Hornemann dans l'Afrique Septentrionale*, inspiring thereby the formation there of the Société de l'Afrique Intérieure, et de Découvertes.

The full English title – *The Journal of Frederick Horneman's Travels, from Cairo to Mourzouk, the Capital of the Kingdom of Fezzan, in Africa in the years 1797–8* – for all its fine explicit tone – conceals more than it reveals of the first stage only in one of the great feats of travel and exploration. We shall never know the end of the story but enough may now be deduced from the desultory scraps of information salvaged since from the desert caravans and other travellers to place the young Saxon 'missionary' of the Association among its greatest figures.

V

The 18th Brumaire had come and gone. General Bonaparte had deserted his army in Egypt and had overthrown the Directory on 9 November 1798 to emerge as the dictator Napoleon thinly disguised as the First Consul. By the end of December the French had overrun the entire Kingdom of Naples, and Ferdinand with the royal family, Sir William Hamilton the British Ambassador, and his wife Emma had fled from Naples under the protection of Nelson of the Nile on board HMS *Vanguard* to Palermo in Sicily. Here they landed on 26 December after four days of the worst gale Nelson had ever known. A month later, secured by the military success of General Championnet, Naples had been declared part of the Parthenopean Republic and a satellite of France. Two days later Ferdinand, from Palermo, had conjured a most unlikely resistance into life. His commission to Cardinal Fabrizio Ruffo as 'vicar-general' with full powers to raise his fellow-countrymen against the French, created the Christian Army of the Holy Faith, a frightening mob of 17000 volunteers mainly from Calabria. Somehow between the White Terror of this undisciplined army of patriots and the Red Terror of the invading Jacobins, the unfortunate French geologist Déodat de Dolomieu fell victim to the confusion. Returning from his Egyptian studies in the scientific train of Bonaparte, he was captured at Taranto on 20 March 1799 after his shipwreck on the nearby coast. As a Knight of Malta he was falsely accused by the fanatic Calabrians of complicity in the loss of Malta to the French and flung into a Messina prison. For nine months he was subjected to a harsh regime more as a common criminal than as a prisoner of war. On 18 September however, apparently due to the persistence of some of the English residents in Messina, the story of his sufferings had emerged and been brought to the attention of Sir Joseph Banks by the Institut National through Nion, the French commissioner who was Charretié's successor in London. Banks now became the focal point for pleas from the European academic world seeking the release of Dolomieu, but there was little that he or any one then could do in the face of the revengeful fury of the Neapolitans against the invading French. What small hope of aid existed for the prisoner Banks certainly explored, writing again, as so often now, from his sick bed.

On 8 January 1800 he assured Nion that not only had he written to Naples with the Government despatches but had also sought the intervention of Sir William Hamilton, now near the end of his long term of office there. He had invoked also the persuasive charms of Lady Hamilton as support in swaying the royal family toward clemency unaware how far these had lost their potency. From them both he sought their influence with Lord Nelson to press the case with His Sicilian Majesty. It is clear that Banks knew a great deal about the events in Calabria that had ensnared Dolomieu and had no intellectual difficulty in disassociating the French scientist from complicity with the military crimes of Bonaparte and the political excesses of the Jacobins. He emphasized the widespread concern over the fate of Dolomieu, expressed, as he put it, even 'in my little way of correspondence' by the 'more than 30 signatures of men of Letters anxiously enquiring whether it is possible anything can be done to save him'. His letter to Emma Hamilton on the same day did not trouble her with the details of the case as he had no doubt that Sir William would show her his letter to him. He appealed rather to her vanity and what he had ever been convinced was her 'friendly disposition' toward himself, and exploited without a qualm his knowledge of the nature of her influence with Nelson. He was sure the liberation of Dolomieu could not be effected without her. He put it in this way: 'If it is possible to engage the Gallant Admiral to join the Trio, which is in the power of no one but yourself, what may I not hope in everything from the warmth of your friendship? If the debilitating climate which you have lately inhabited has not damp'd its ardor'.His appeal for her to undertake the business with her 'usual spirit' assured her, with a rousing finale, that it would 'be for the honor of the court of Naples, for the advancement of Science, for the benefit of humanity' and would fix an indelible obligation upon himself. None of this was to any avail for 'the Trio' had their own preoccupations and were soon to leave Naples. The best that seems to have been achieved was some easement in the conditions of Dolomieu's confinement, as he was to record after his release more than a year later. The Hamiltons and the 'Gallant Admiral' set off homeward on 23 April 1800 to land at Yarmouth on 6 November.

Evidence of the sincerity of Banks and his active pressures for Dolomieu's release was passed by various official and other means to the Institut in Paris. On 16 May 1800 this brought a letter of recognition and thanks from seven distinguished members: Antoine Laurent de Jussieu, Camus, the venerable Louis Antoine Bougainville, Laplace, Fleurieu and Lacépède. It was coupled however with a request for Banks to use his influence in securing passports or safe-conducts for two ships about to set out on yet another voyage 'utile au progrès des connaissances humaines', in other words for the expedition of Nicolas Baudin with *Géographe* and *Naturaliste*. This, dated 9 June 1800, was sent through the new French commissioner in London, Louis Guillaume Otto. Banks replied favourably on 13 June and on 27 June, Otto informed the French Minister of Marine that he had now received the safe-conducts from the British Foreign Office. This good news was read at a meeting of the First Class of the Institut on 8 July 1800 but there was nothing to add about the fate of Dolomieu. The pressure on Banks continued with an evident touching faith in what he could accomplish – among others from L'Héritier, Thouin, van Marum, relatives and close friends of Dolomieu, and at last from Marc August Pictet at Geneva, with news direct from Dolomieu himself of his release by a special stipulation under the Treaty of Florence of 18 March 1801. Finally, from Paris on 30 April 1801, Dolomieu himself wrote direct to Banks expressing his thanks to the Royal Society of London for its efforts on his behalf, his appreciation of what the British residents in Messina had done at some risk to themselves and, finally, to Banks himself for his part in the affair. To this Banks sent a long reply, dated 16 July 1801, by the hand of Dolomieu's brother-in-law, Etienne Gilbert, Marquis de Drée. It gave a fair summary of the measures he had been able to take in company with many others, including Fellows of the Royal Society. The Fellows, he was careful to emphasize, had done so 'all of them in their private capacities' for the Royal Society as a body took no measure whatever, or indeed ever publickly took cognizance of your situation'. He was firm in dissociating the Royal Society from having taken any political stance in the matter as an institution and hoped that Dolomieu had not made any public statement expressing a belief that it had. This reproof merely repeated the essence of a code to which the Royal Society adhered in more ways than those that touched the sensitive field of politics. On this he spoke as the President of the Society. He concluded however, as an individual Fellow and as a private Englishman, on a note of some generosity which concealed his otherwise strongly expressed views on the enormity of the First Consul's crimes against humanity at large:

> ... We English tho' much attached to Science, have not, as your Chief Consul did, sent learned men with our Army; our successes therefore, if Heaven should favor us with success, will be productive of political advantages only, while Science, unthought of by Rulers, must look to France alone for having blended Learning with her Arms and gathered knowledge beneficial to the whole race of men with those Laurels which to our Commanders will be the fruitless ornament of successful valor ...

Dolomieu did not long survive his imprisonment in his tenure of the Chair of Mineralogy at the Muséum d'Histoire Naturelle left vacant by the death of Louis Jean Marie Daubenton in January 1800. Toward the end of 1802 Bernard Lacépède himself brought Banks in London a copy of the *éloge* on Dolomieu read before the

Institut. For many years thereafter the strenuous but abortive efforts of Banks toward the release of the unlucky geologist were remembered with gratitude by the French, yielding occasional favours for British prisoners and internees in the Napoleonic wars ahead.

CHAPTER 17

INSTITUTIONS, REGAL AND REVOLUTIONARY
1796–1803

After the upheaval during the summer and autumn of 1791 in the library at Soho Square, with the building of a gallery and the raising of a lantern roof, the scene was ready for the preparation of the catalogue in some final form by Jonas Dryander. The seven years or so of steady work on the *Hortus Kewensis* had established a discipline for both Banks and Dryander as editors and publishers. Banks had exercised his prentice hand ten years earlier with his private printing in quarto of the *Reliquiae Houstounianae* 1781, and had flexed it more recently with his folio presentation of the *Icones selectae Plantarum quas in Japonia collegit et delineavit Engelbertus Kaempfer . . .*, 1791, with 59 engravings by Daniel Mackenzie, as a more thoroughgoing Soho Square specimen of fine printing. Now he was ready to launch into an extended use of William Bulmer's typographical resources in the same way that he had persuaded the Royal Society to put the *Philosophical Transactions* in the hands of a man 'whose Printing is acknowledged as the best in the Country'. In Dryander he now had not only the useful botanist he had induced him to become, but also the exacting eye and pigeonholing mind on whom the security and smooth operation of his library could depend. With the books rearranged in the enlarged premises the serious work of a full catalogue could begin.

From his undergraduate youth Banks had been an assiduous and discriminating collector and his far-ranging library at New Burlington Street was already sufficient to attract such literary bees as Thomas Pennant. On this he built steadily from the ever-widening circles in western Europe to which he sent his desiderata by letter or through his international visitors. The yield of wanted titles greatly increased after his return from the *Endeavour* voyage as the true measure of his scholarship attracted the works of other scholars as gifts and hopeful presentations. He was intrinsically orderly in all his arrangements with or without benefit of servants and probably organized his shelves properly in his early days, but when Dryander arrived in the late summer of 1777 Banks knew he had found in him a secretarial treasure of great price, both as a bibliophile and as a botanist. The atmosphere between the two men seems to have been one of mutual academic respect, affection as friends, and a patient working relationship. The memorial of this partnership stands in the *Catalogus Bibliothecae Historico-naturalis Josephi Banks* quite properly in the name of Jonas Dryander, Librarian of the Royal Society, from whose pen it emerged over the decade of its gestation but nourished by consultation with the scholar whose wealth and knowledge had conjured the collection into life and use.

It took time to prepare the catalogue for printing and was under constant discussion at Soho Square. But by the autumn of 1795 there is in Dryander's letter of 14 September an indication of what was impending as he sent specimen sheets from Bulmer to Banks at Revesby Abbey for comment and a few decisions. Dryander put forward his plan for the style of each entry with the author's name set in italics and small capitals and roman for the reference. This was how it finally appeared, though it was not the arrangement favoured by George Nicol. Banks was content and the Dryander distinctions prevailed.

The first volume to appear was the second, II *Zoologi*, in 1796. Then, in order, III *Botanici*, 1797; I *Scriptores Generales*, 1798; IV *Mineralogi*, 1799; and finally, V *Supplementum et Index Auctores*, 1800. In all there were about 15 000 titles from nearly 8000 authors of whom about 300 were anonymous, as recorded at this stage, in 11 main languages – English, French, German, Italian, Spanish, Portuguese, Norwegian, Swedish, Danish, Latin and Greek. There were 144 periodicals as the proceedings of academies and societies and 44 others, nearly all of them complete from volume I in each series. There were approximately 18 000 single titles or papers and dissertations. Under the head of 'Natural History' these items could be grouped thus: general, including travels and voyages, about 15 per cent; zoology 26 per cent; botany 25 per cent; geology and mineralogy 18 per cent; materia medica 7 per cent; and what might be termed economic biology 9 per cent. More than 300 years of printed works were represented, including an impressive array of incunabula, now one of the treasures of the British Library. The system of the catalogue throughout was in Latin and the arrangement, where it applied in the plant and animal kingdoms, was Linnaean. Otherwise the plan of classification with its many sub-divisions was a compound of Dryander infused with Banks. Though it had its critics as to bibliography, method and presentation at the time of its appearance and since, the *Catalogus Bibliothecae Historico-Naturalis Josephi Banks* ... 1796–1800, remains a distinguished pioneer work in the growth of library practice. The system was fast and efficient in yielding its information from both the herbarium and library and the Banksian correspondence during the whole of Banks's lifetime and this was an advantage freely enjoyed by the visitors of good reputation and serious intent but especially when Dryander was present. Only one edition of 250 sets of the *Catalogus* ... was published. An interleaved series of volumes, with the octavo printed sheets mounted on large quarto pages, it was kept in the library and the accessions added in Dryander's small script and later in Robert Brown's less tidy hand. How many titles were added and recorded after 1800 has never been estimated, but the manuscript accessions probably aggregated 3000–4000.

The printed *Catalogus* ... records only part of the collection kept at 32 Soho Square. Certainly what was regarded as natural history for the purpose of the *Catalogus* ... constituted most – at least 85 per cent – of what lay on the shelves concentrated in the back premises over Dean Street. But there was also Banks's own small study with its passage anteroom and other nooks and crannies before ever the shelves, cupboards and wardrobes of the main house upstairs were reached. There were between 3000 and 4000 titles of which some 750 were devoted to astronomy, navigation and surveying, chemistry and physics, more or less as we would assess them now. About another 750 ranged over various aspects of agriculture apart from those which fell under the general head of economic biology in the *Catalogus* ... Over 1200 volumes covered the antiquities of Great Britain and Europe, 100 or so treated the subject of religion, and as many again were concerned with medicine. There were some hundreds of catalogues of libraries and museums, directories, bound volumes of reports, Parliamentary papers and acts, Chinese manuscripts and, of course, literary periodicals. This store of information was rounded off with maps, ordnance surveys, charts, rolls of drawings and other miscellanea. It was reckoned that some 22 000 titles were eventually acquired by the British Museum under the terms of Banks's will, according to the inventory of Henry Baber of what was delivered on 24 January 1832. It is probable that the library of natural history may account for about 18 500 of which most seem to survive today in the British Library, though some were destroyed by enemy action during the Second World War. By no means the largest of private libraries in its day in Great Britain, it was by most standards a distinguished collection. However as a specialist gathering in natural history texts as the life work of a private gentleman it had few if any close rivals even in Europe. The *Catalogus Bibliothecae Historico-naturalis Josephi Banks* remains to this day one of the most useful repositories in which to delve for a first search in the literature before 1800 of the plant, animal and earth sciences and the geographic explorations of western European man.

Dryander was also Honorary Librarian of the Linnean Society until 1796 and during those first eight years particularly the infant library of the new society was nourished with donations of duplicates from Soho Square or other presentations from Banks as none but the conscientious Swede could select and choose apart from his master. The Royal Society also benefited similarly from time to time as Dryander stood *in loco custodiensis* for all three collections.

After the reorganization of 1791 the library at Soho Square increasingly became a centre for tutorials and a modest employment agency for hopeful young men seeking to extend their education in natural history. Exactly how many served as assistants to Dryander and later to Brown we do not know. But first from about 1780 to 1792 there seems to have been John Swan of whom little is known. Then, on the recommendation of Olof Swartz, came Samuel Toerner (1762–1822), an MA and botanist from Uppsala with a special interest in insects, at the end of 1792. In 1797 he seems to have been followed by another Swede, Frederick Schulzen (1770–1849) until 1801. Thus the passage of the *Catalogus* . . . into print probably rests heavily on Swedish academic aid. Thereafter German scholarship became predominant when Karl Dietrich Eberhardt König, otherwise Charles Konig, FRS (1774–1851), educated at Göttingen, came to Soho Square from 1801 to 1807. Within that period he joined John Sims, FRS in founding and editing the *Annals of Botany* before entering the British Museum as Assistant Keeper in 1807 to become eventually Keeper of the Natural History Department and finally of Minerals. After the death of Dryander when Robert Brown became curator and librarian, John Tiarks, FRS (1789–1837) from Göttingen served as his assistant from 1810 to 1818 before leaving to join the American Boundary Commission sponsored by Banks and the Astronomer Royal. Finally, his place was taken briefly by the young John Lindley, FRS (1799–1865) who became the torch-bearer of the new generation and whose report in 1838 would rescue the Royal Botanic Garden at Kew for the service of science. For the most part these young men commanded several languages other than their native tongues and acted as translators and interpreters.

II

When Banks returned to Soho Square from Revesby Abbey in the first week of November 1795 he found Dryander ready with the first trial sheets of the *Catalogus* . . . in the typography and on the paper from William Bulmer that he had approved the month before. He also found the newly created Count von Rumford, just returned from Bavaria and his 11 years of service to the Elector, ardent now on the efficient use of fuel in the home. As Banks put it to Sir William Hamilton on 17 November

> ... We have Count Rumford here who is to Reduce the value of Newcastle coals to half its Present Price by enabling us to Cook our Kettles with ¼ of the fire we now use he had threatend my Kitchen & I am submissive but I Seriously hope he will find some one better suited for his Practice than mine

Sir Benjamin Thompson, Count von Rumford, FRS. Portrait after Moritz Kellerhoven.

So opened another stage in the long association between Banks and Benjamin Thompson, the American loyalist latterly from Rumford (now Concord) New Hampshire. It had begun in 1777 and had continued steadily from a distance as papers on thermometry and problems of heat and heat exchange travelled from Munich for the Royal Society, earning him in 1792 the award of the Copley Medal. In March 1793 Banks transmitted to the King the papers by Thompson on the boring of cannon and mechanisms for firing them with the accolade that 'his ingenuity as a Philosophical reasoner is allowd to be above par'. And now, in the summer of 1796, the name of Rumford was to be established in another form, as Thompson wrote to Banks on 12 July with his offer to the Royal Society of 'one thousand pounds stock in the funds' at three per cent interest to provide every two years one gold and one silver medal of the combined value of 60 pounds

> ... as a premium to the author of the most important discovery, or useful improvement, which shall be made or published by printing, or in any way made known to the public, in any part of Europe, during the preceding two years, on Heat, or on Light; the preference always being given to such discoveries as shall, in the opinion of the President and Council, tend most to promote the good of mankind.

In accepting this gift the Society asked Banks to seek from its donor his views about 'discoveries in Optics, and improvements in Chemistry' and their relevance to the purposes of the award and Rumford made this clear in his letter of 20 April 1797. The committee consisted of Sir Charles Blagden, Joseph Planta and Taylor Combe who were already at work 'to consider and report upon a design for a medal'. Later the committee, to which Banks, Edward Gray and Rumford himself were added, reported on 4 April 1799 recommending the design of John Milton, assistant engraver at the Royal Mint, and the sinking of the dies by him – not Matthew Boulton as Banks had at first proposed – at the expense of the Royal Society.

The choice of the design of the Rumford Medal took place a month after the first general meeting of the Proprietors and original subscribers of the new Institution had been held at 32 Soho Square with Sir Joseph Banks in the Chair and Rumford as its moving spirit also present. The intention of the medal and the purpose of the Institution were both due to Rumford's philanthropy and its expression as 'the application of science to the useful purposes of life'. In Banks he had a kindred soul but there were others who had been evangelized by his approach to domestic economy in the use of fuel, the problem of smoking chimneys, and the heating efficiency of kitchen ranges. One such was Thomas Bernard, Treasurer of the Foundling Hospital in 1795, who effected great savings in the kitchen there by the use of Rumford's designs installed under the inventor's supervision. From Bernard's enthusiasm grew the Society for Bettering the Conditions and Increasing the Comforts of the Poor, nourished by his correspondence with Rumford during 1796–8. When Rumford returned as putative minister in London from the Elector of Bavaria in September 1798, the 'Bettering Society' was in full spate with Rumford's idea of an accessory 'scientific establishment' much in mind. In the end a Select Committee of the Society was appointed including Thomas Bernard, William Wilberforce and the Earl of Winchelsea to consider the notion of a separate scientific institution. Rumford met this group on 31 January 1799 to discuss the *Proposals* he had drawn up. On 23 February a list of 32 original subscribers had been printed with Banks and Bernard at its head in alphabetical order above an impressive series of names ranged about the key figure of Rumford. It seems to have been Bernard who secured Banks's permission to hold the inaugural meeting at 32 Soho Square on Thursday 7 March.

> ... at one o'clock precisely; to take into consideration a proposed application to his MAJESTY for a Charter for the Institution, and other matters preparatory to the opening of the Institution.

With Banks in the Chair, the enlarged list of 58 proprietors and original subscribers of 50 guineas was read; the plan proposed for submission to the Prime Minister and the Home Secretary; and a Committee of Managers elected to solicit a Royal Charter for the Institution 'conformable to the Proposals'. On 23 March a meeting of the managers was held at Soho Square with Banks in the Chair, the others being the Earl of Morton, the Earl Spencer, Count Rumford, Thomas Bernard, and Richard Sulivan. It is not clear what happened at this meeting but during the next week Rumford evidently nursed a grievance which Banks attempted to clear. Then on 29 March Rumford told Banks why he disputed the need for the immediate election of a secretary and treasurer, having offered his own services for that combined office and found them refused by his fellow Managers. He had wished, he said

> ... to regulate the manner of proceeding at the election of those Officers – namely to prevent the Managers from proposing either their relations or their dependants.

His resolution had found no seconder. None of this however, he assured Banks, 'whatever may be the fate of our present undertaking' could diminish in any way the regard he felt for him personally. There are signs even at this early stage that they both felt the Institution to be drifting away from a scientific anchorage as the first years would indeed show.

Then, on 20 April 1799 the proprietors gathered for a plenary meeting for the last time at 32 Soho Square to elect the Committee of Visitors and to present the draft of the Charter for presentation to the King. On 4 May the full details of the Institution in being was printed by order of the managers – its two committees, its list now of 128 proprietors, 58 subscribers for life, and 54 annual subscribers; its Secretary, the Revd Samuel Glasse, DD, FRS, a prebendary of St Paul's, and its Treasurer Thomas Bernard, both offering their services *gratis*. By this date also a commodious house belonging to the late Mr Mellis of Albemarle Street had been bought by the proprietors, having been surveyed without charge by two of them, Henry Holland and John Soane, architects.

On 6 May Banks wrote to Lord Spencer about the changes made necessary among the manager and visitors by the Earl's withdrawal from an over-active role in the Institution because as First Lord of the Admiralty of pressure of naval business in the French war. The 8th Earl Winchelsea had been elected a manager in Lord Spencer's place in order to be President of the Institution in due time, but the First Lord agreed to leave his name among the managers until the Charter should be completed. Of Count Rumford Banks had this report for Spencer:

... Count Rumford has of late kept himself intirely in the background nor do I think he will ever venture forward again if it has cost him a Fit of sickness to find his way from the Ideal preeminence of his Character to his actual situation in the opinion of this country but I believe he has now satisfied himself & will be as he ought to be an extremely usefull inventor of machines & governor of machine makers ...

The first meeting of the managers was held on 5 June 1799 at the house in Albemarle Street with Banks continuing in the Chair until Earl Winchilsea took office on 22 June. A week later it was announced that the King had accepted the Charter and accorded the new body his patronage as the Royal Institution. The Charter received the Royal Seal on 13 January 1800. By this time Rumford had emerged from his gloom and as a manager under the authority of the Committee of Managers, he now flung himself into the problems of converting the premises at Albemarle Street into the edifice and working institution more or less as it remains today. Throughout he kept in close touch with Banks, of whose approval and support he seemed continually in need, as his letter of 19 June 1800, addressed from the 'Royal Institution', clearly shows. He reported the new building as advancing rapidly – 'the foundations are already out of the ground' – but for the rest it was a matter of seeking Banks's approval for items of expenditure to workmen and staff, for instruments, and for the expenses of the unfortunate first 'professor of natural philosophy and chemistry' Dr Thomas Garnett. By September 1801, however, Rumford was being tempted by the Elector of Bavaria to return to his service and in October he was again in Munich. He subsequently left for Paris and a year later he was still there, a devotee of its scientific community. On 22 November 1801 he was the first discreetly to tell Banks that he had been proposed by the Section of Botany as a candidate for foreign membership in the First Class of the Institut National and at the ballot had been placed at the head of the list of ten. Rumford himself on the same occasion had been proposed by the Section of Political Economy and elected into the Second Class. He returned to his house in Brompton Row on 20 December to see the fourth volume of his essays into print and to oversee some of his final touches at the Royal Institution. On 9 May 1802 he left England for the last time to reach Paris on 19 May where Blagden was only too delighted to receive him as a social and scientific lion in the city as they both luxuriated in its pleasures before they set out together for Munich. Here in time he was joined by the widow Lavoisier who was still with him when he returned to Paris in 1803 where he settled at last.

Throughout Rumford's travels Banks kept him informed about the affairs of the Institution, hoping for his return, but increasingly inclined to feel that he had been deserted. On 2 May 1803 he had been appointed to a Committee of Science

... to regulate the lectures and public experiments; to direct the publication of the Journals; and to report as to any experiments, or additions to apparatus, or models ...

With him on the first committee was Lord Spencer, Henry Cavendish, Charles Hatchett and John Symonds, and within the Institution there was at first sight a promising foundation. Thomas Young, FRS was Professor of Natural Philosophy and Superintendant of the house, appointed in July 1801 in place of the unhappy

Garnett. He had been joined by the young Humphry Davy, appointed in the same month at the instigation of Rumford, as Assistant Lecturer in Chemistry, Director of the Chemical Laboratory, and Assistant Editor to Young of the Institution's 'Journals'. Both men had established brilliant courses of public lectures. Young's yielded little in popular appeal and were better in their printed form in later years. Davy's were delivered with the flair of 'the young Roscius', as he was dubbed, and were popular science close to the first aims of both Rumford and Banks. But in July 1803 Thomas Young resigned to concentrate on his practice as a physician. So on 18 July the Committee of Science proposed that John Dalton be invited to lecture. But there were changes impending in the management at the Institution not greatly to the liking of Banks however pleased and supportive he was of the steady productiveness of Humphry Davy. He had been one of the five reporters on 28 November 1803 on the lecture courses and experiments proposed for the ensuing year. His companions had been Henry Cavendish, Sir John Hippesley, Thomas Bernard and Richard Sulivan – Science heavily outweighed by the Bettering Society and the Foundling Hospital.

In February the printing office was dismantled and the publication of the journals discontinued. Among others, the egregious Revd Sydney Smith was engaged for two courses of lectures on moral philosophy, a clear sign of the cleavage now apparent between the promoters of scientific knowledge as the prime goal of the Institution and those who sought for fashionable popularity. In March 1804 Rumford wrote to Banks in some perturbation about 'his beloved child', the Institution, which he said was as much Banks's as his. In April Banks replied that he could not disguise his disappointment that Rumford had not returned to England. A personal loss to himself it had also been greatly to the detriment of the Royal Institution.

> It is now entirely in the hands of the profane. I have declared my dissatisfaction at the mode in which it is carried on and my resolution not to attend in future, Had my health and spirits not failed me, I could have kept matters in their proper level, but sick, alone, and unsupported, I have given up what cannot now easily be recovered.

and in the summer of that year his despondence was manifest as he wrote to Rumford:

> . . . the Institution has irrevocably fallen into the hands of the enemy, and is now perverted to a hundred uses for which you and I never intended it. I could have successfully resisted their innovations had you been there, but alone, unsupported, and this year confined to my house for three months by disease (gout), my spirit was too much broken to admit of my engaging singly with the host of H[ippesley]'s and B[ernard]'s who had possession of the fortress. Adieu, then, Institution: I have long ago declared my intention of attending no more.

For the next two years the outward and visible expression of the Royal Institution may have deviated from the first bright hopes of its scientific founders and, with Rumford away in the arms of Mme Lavoisier, at home Banks was enduring one of his longest periods of bedridden torture. But within the Institution the seed was germinating, away from the public furore and dramatized performances at the lecture

385

bench, in the steady work of Davy building toward the flowering of his investigations in the Bakerian Lecture to the Royal Society 'on some new Phenomena of chemical Changes produced by Electricity, particularly the Decomposition of fixed Alkalies', on 19 November 1807. At this moment of triumph for the working facilities of the Royal Institution, with Davy submitting his papers to the Royal Society and delivering his lectures on agricultural chemistry to the Board of Agriculture based on his continuing work at the Royal Institution, Banks knew that all was not lost. Beneath a flush of weeds the plant was forming well.

III

After the release of Dolomieu in March, the year 1801 for Banks had been a period of improving communication with France. So much had the tension of the war lessened that after the meeting of the Institut National of 26 December 1801 Banks found himself at the head of an impressive roll of those elected as foreign associates by the First Class of Mathematics and Physics: – Henry Cavendish, Nevil Maskelyne, William Herschel, Joseph Priestley, Peter Pallas, Alexander Volta; among those proposed by the Second Class were Rumford, Thomas Jefferson, the President of the United States, James Rennell and Joseph Haydn. The certificate reached Banks in January 1802 as he lay in the grip of another gout attack. In this state he had time enough to compose a reply and he prepared two drafts before he sent the final text to France, dated 21 January 1802. A translation into French then appeared in the *Moniteur* of 18 March, before the Preliminaries to the Treaty of Amiens were signed on 25 March.

Almost immediately came that virulent public attack on Banks which appeared in the first volume of Cobbett's new *Weekly Political Register*, a letter evidently written in hot blood before the end of March 1802 by the anonymous 'Misogallus'. It was a frothing brew of Gallophobia, taking as its text an English translation of the French translation of the original English document sent by Banks. His personal acknowledgement of the honour conferred by the Institut had much in common with the sentiments expressed and the terms used by Edward Jenner in July 1801 when he presented to the Institut a printed copy of his paper 'History of the Origin of Vaccine Inoculation', but Jenner's letter was not exposed in the British press at the time. It was the misfortune of Banks that, in one sense, he was to be a victim of his own virtues, a sacrifice in the French drive to make some capital gain from a merely formal acknowledgement of an academic honour. In the ordinary way such papers lie in the archives of the institutions concerned as, indeed, did that of Jenner. The position of Banks, however, was that after the traumata of the Revolution, France sadly needed some evidence of her return to international respectability and he, as a person, was perhaps the most prominent and universally acceptable bridge in the restoration of academic relations. Banks himself had no reason to expect the publication of his letter nor perhaps would he have greatly modified its terms if he had. Almost any expression of thanks by any Englishman to any French honour as a matter of civilized etiquette was vulnerable to the smears of the rabid English nationalist in the state of Anglo-French relations then. Such a one was William Cobbett and such too was 'Misogallus'. Under this pseudonym the letter was published in April as a pamphlet, *A Letter to the Right Honourable Sir Joseph Banks K.B.*, by the firm of Cobbett and Morgan, and for the rest of the year the debate boiled merrily away.

As the annual elections of St Andrew's Day approached the occasion was seized by 'A Fellow of the Royal Society' to belabour the President as a disgrace to the Society in another long letter to the *Weekly Political Register*, dated 4 November 1802. Shielded by his anonymity, the Fellow took self-righteous offence at the implied insult to the standing of the Royal Society which Banks's letter to the Institut appeared to express, theorized that Banks could only have been intoxicated when he wrote it and urged his unfitness for the presidential chair. Cobbett added his own voice in the same issue with his 'Letter to the Right Hon. Lord Hawkesbury, His Majesty's Sec. of State for Foreign Affairs' whom he was prepared to tar with the same brush as a culprit for his role in negotiating the recent treaty. Banks's silence and his re-election to the Chair of the Royal Society on 30 November brought a final burst of sarcasm from 'Misogallus' on 7 December, professing a modest pique at the 'unmerited neglect' by Banks of his first diatribe. In the view of 'Misogallus' the renewed tenure of Banks as President only demeaned the whole Society. It should merge, he thought, with the Institut under some new name such as the Philogallican Club or the Regicide Academy 'the metonymy to commence on the 21st January, the anniversary of your incomparable letter and the murder of Louis XVI – a transformation in which he thought Charles James Fox, a more recent foreign associate of the Institut, would be a suitable accomplice.

As far as the public was concerned there was no overt sign of any response from the target in this affair who, when the first shot was fired, had been convalescing from a period of more than three months' illness. This had produced a languor and debility he had not experienced before which had made business irksome to him, as he confessed on 12 April 1802 to John Parkinson sen. At this time, however, Banks was not without some measure of private support as Samuel Purkis, his tanning correspondent at Brentford, had indicated in his letter of 10 April. Purkis had recently seen the new periodical 'published weekly by Peter Porcupine, alias Mr. Cobbett' and described it as 'a sort of *mongrel* production, which seems to have been begotten by a *consumptive Newpaper* out of a *puny American magazine*'. In his view 'silent contempt' was the way in which the 'silly Paper' in Nos. 10 and 12 'of this motley work' should be treated and he apologized for even mentioning it. Much the same was echoed by James Edward Smith from Norwich on 16 December. He, however, delicately withdrew the hem of his garment from 'such sort of political writing on either side', though he was quite prepared to retail the gossip he heard in April and May implicating William Windham, member for Norwich, and Captain Woodford and their 'connection or acquaintance with the man called Peter Porcupine, Cobbet I think is his name' and 'their wonderful antipathy to everything relating to France, and their peculiar displeasure at your letter to the Institute'. Smith had no doubt that the attack on Banks had come from that quarter. A week later, Banks, in writing to Aiton on 21 December about plans for the future of Wiliam Kerr as a collector for Kew, was quite explicit and firm in his view that 'Misogallus' was in fact 'Mr. Woodford who was Christend Emperor'. He assigned the real reason for the bilious letter to Woodford's anger with himself for restoring the La Billardière collections to France at a time when, as paymaster of the emigrés' allowances, Woodford had access with a tacit licence to plunder them from the Duc d'Harcourt. Indeed Banks suspected that Woodford still retained some of the bird specimens 'without pretence of having a property in them'. In all this there was nothing to suggest that the old antagonism to Banks of Dr Samuel Horsley, surviving from the days of the Royal Society 'dissensions', was involved in any way directly. Horsley, as Bishop of Rochester and a splendid example of the church militant, had certainly fulminated at great length in the House of Lords against the peace with France but Banks set the authorship at a more plebian level as merely an outburst of phlegm from the 'Emperor'.

The withering of the Peace of Amiens gradually produced evidence of the sour centre even in the brave notion that 'the Sciences were never at War'. A reminder of the darker side came to Banks in January 1803 when Fourcroy, now a senator and Minister for Public Instruction, sought his help to secure freedom of travel in India for *Citoyen* Godon de St Mesmin, 'a young man filled with zeal and actuated by the desire to be of use to the progress of natural history and particularly of mineralogy'. There was an unusually long pause before Banks replied. Perhaps there he recalled the part played by Fourcroy as one of the investigating committee in 1794 which hastened Lavoisier's execution. Perhaps also there was more than a whisper of change in the atmosphere of scientific amity reflecting the general British distrust of Napoleon. Banks could, however, point with an emphatic finger to a recent cause for concern in the publication of Sebastiani's mission to Turkey and Syria in which 'the appointment of Engineers under the character of commercial agents, had destroyed all confidence in the recommendation of a Frenchman'. Neither the East India Company nor the government would listen to him, said Banks, in spite of his endeavours to refute all suspicion that Godon might be 'a person enabled by education to Communicate intelligence of the strength or weakness of Military posts'. British fury at what was seen as 'the conduct of your chief Consul in continuing to violate the spirit of the treaty of Amiens' had left him with little hope of success. In spite of this he ended with an attempt, once again, to disassociate the armed conflict of the two nations from communication with his 'literary friends' which he hoped to be able to continue as they had been 'so happily kept up during the later Period of the Last War'. For this fond hope he was poorly repaid by Fourcroy as the peace ran out and the war resumed to obliterate much of what Banks had gained in the case of Dolomieu the year before.

A measure of the hardening of Anglo-French antagonisms and of the curdling of Banks's attempts to keep the flow of human kindness where he could, is well defined in his remarks to Thomas Coutts, the banker on 24 December 1803. The issue was how far he could help toward the release from internment in France of Robert Ferguson of Raith, Scotland. Coutts had found Banks unusually depressed and almost deaf on the subject. His bitterness came from his astonishment at learning that having kept himself 'free from all sorts of political intermeddling', he had been denounced by Fourcroy as 'having under the Mask of a literary Correspondence maintain'd Spies in different parts of France'. When his other friends in the Institut remonstrated with Bonaparte on the falseness of such a charge, the First Consul had answered that he had the proofs in his pocket. Banks was sure that Coutts, in this situation, would not advise him to humble himself before 'the villainous Corsican Consul' nor expect him to have any success were he to do so. The ghost of Lavoisier haunted this brief exchange but in the early New Year Banks had salved his feelings enough to write to Delambre repeating his desire 'to promote the scientific intercourse between nations, notwithstanding any political divisions which subsist between them'. He warned however that this could not be done if he and other 'Gentlemen of known reputation and honour' were subjected 'to the vile imputation of acting as spies'. He then sought the release of Robert Ferguson through Delambre and the Institut as an expression of the 'constant intercourse of good offices between men of science in the two nations' and, speaking as an Englishman, 'as a favor to scientific men, and a great compliment to the Royal Society.' Of this the Institut took official note on 27 February 1804 and, by the force of its intercession, Ferguson was able to return home and duly be elected a Fellow of the Royal Society in 1805.

On the same date as this letter to Delambre (30 January), Banks had written to him on quite another matter, a vivid example of the dichotomy in attitudes among the scientific bodies of that period. Banks wrote:

> . . . I have great pleasure in obeying your Command by sending the nautical almnanac for 1807 the last that has been published. I will not fail to furnish you with the future ones as they shall be published. I am oblig'd to you for the correction you have been so good as to furnish me with in that of 1806 which has been communicated to the Royal Observatory . . .

However important this kind of data may have been to the planning of Bonaparte with his armies poised near Boulogne for the invasion of England or for the movements of his navies at sea in the year before Trafalgar, it could not negate the service which this publication gave to all nations whose ships sailed the oceans of the world. Its continuity and correct enumeration was one justifiable expression of supra-national science. The ostensible neutrality of voyages of discovery alone set a background to this apparent paradox. No one knew more clearly, however, than Banks where the defence lines of scientific intelligence were drawn and should be manned in the interest of Great Britain.

IV

The indictment of Banks by 'Misogallus' with its attempt at his public disgrace as an abject Gallophile calls for an examination of his attitude during the previous decade of Anglo-French relations. The events of 1789 did not immediately disturb the cordiality between the savants of the two nations nor the equable flow of communication. However Banks was to glean clear warnings of what was to come through the letters he received from Lord Sheffield visiting Edward Gibbon at Lausanne in the summer of 1791. He gave him a first-hand view of the temper of the Paris mobs and of the new National Assembly at the time of the abolition of the French monarchy. The approaching gloom was more apparent to him a year later in the experiences of Charles Blagden, who was attacked by a Paris mob and narrowly escaped the movements of the new French armies in their campaign into Savoy. The execution of Louis XVI in January 1793 left no further doubt that the times had changed and the declaration of war by France on 1 February set the final seal. The abolition of the old Académie des Sciences on 8 August 1793 by the Convention and the obliterating snarl that 'the Republic has no need of science' brought the nadir of despair among the French savants and a rupture in their exchanges with their outraged British correspondents. The *Philosophical Transactions of the Royal Society* for 1791 and 1792 were held in limbo for there was no recognizable body to receive them

389

in France. The malicious twisting of Lavoisier's correspondence with his English friends into the shape of a 'conspiracy with the enemies of France against the people' and his summary execution on 8 May 1794 was a warning to any who might toy with the notion of some scientific détente with the new regime.

England had not escaped from the tremors of the Revolution and Banks as a citizen of London and a landowner of Lincolnshire, had his own problems resulting from those threats to civil peace conjured into life by Tom Paine 'the staymaker' and his *Rights of Man*. The parish of St Anne, Westminster, was so perturbed that on 5 December 1792 at Jack's Coffee House in Dean Street, with Sir Joseph Banks, Bart., in the chair, its representatives unanimously resolved on a plan for an Association for the Preservation of Peace, Liberty and Property.

> ... being duly sensible of the blessings of the British Constitution, consisting of King, Lords and Commons, in securing to all British Subjects the full enjoyment of Liberty and Property, equally protected, by Law, from the oppressions of Despotism and the depradations of Anarchy ...

They declared moreover their determination to pay obedience to the laws and to support the civil magistrates in carrying them into execution against all disturbers of the public peace. Banks headed the committee of the St Anne Association, which for the next few years, devoted itself to this task as a counter to the rampant 'democracy' in the activities of the London Corresponding Society and other such bodies of suspected Jacobin tendencies.

The following day, on 6 December 1792, at a meeting of noblemen and gentlemen at St Alban's Tavern, Pall Mall, Banks was appointed one of a committee of 13 MPs and men of influence who bound themselves to the terms of a comprehensive resolution 'to afford by our individual exertions, that active assistance to the authority of the lawful Magistrates, and to the maintenance of the established Government, which is at all times due from the subjects of this Realm' within the bounds of the City and Liberty of Westminster.

These preoccupations with the civil order led to the legal restraints embodied by the British Government in 33 George III c.27, 'An act more effectually to prevent during the present War between *Great Britain* and *France*, all traitorous Correspondence with, or Aid or Assistance being given to, His Majesty's Enemies', passed 7 May 1793, and a further more sweeping measure, 34 George III c.9, passed on 1 March 1794. Although the specific mention of letters and books does not appear, the general terms indicate the dilemma which faced Banks if any form of scientific communication was to be pursued. For several years then a brooding quiet fell across the Channel frontiers until, under the Directory, the old Académies were reconstituted in a new form under the Institut National of which the First Class, covering the mathematical and physical sciences, was the reincarnation of the former Académie des Sciences. The new Institut was promulgated on 22 August 1795 and the First Class held its first meeting in the Louvre on 4 April 1796. The glimmer of a new civilized dawn seemed to have appeared and on 4 February 1797 Banks groped cautiously forward in the half-light. Through the person of Josef Charretié, the French commissioner in London for the exchange of prisoners of war, he hoped to gain some 'knowledge of our Brethren in Paris, who are, like us, laboring in the Vinyard of science'. Somehow also a copy of the zoology volume, the first printed, of his own *Catalogus Bibliothecae* . . . had found its way to Paris and elicited a letter dated 18 February 1797 O.S. from Jean Claude de Launay, librarian of the Muséum National d'histoire Naturelle, asking for further copies and promising library exchanges. The moment seemed to have come for clearance from the highest political level for this traffic to resume and Banks seems to have arranged this in an interview with William Pitt in March before sending the back-numbers of the *Philosophical Transactions* and the *Nautical Almanac* to Lalande and of which he received acknowledgement at the end of September 1797. The lines of communication had been partly restored. In a fair trade Banks had secured for the scientists of Great Britain access to the main 'philosophical' publications of the new guard of French science, which comprised a galaxy of talent and genius that no one of good judgement could afford to ignore. Banks yielded to no one in his contempt for the excesses of the Revolution and the devastations of its armies but he kept a smooth diplomacy in the controlled politeness of his correspondence through which ran the steel reinforcement of his devotion to the national interest of Great Britain.

CHAPTER 18

THE EARTH AND ITS PRODUCE
1797–1807

No sooner had Banks been appointed a Privy Councillor than he suffered his longest and most disabling episode of gout during the spring and summer of 1797 after almost a decade of sharp fencing with the disease. It brought an end to what he termed 'the Fatiguing Pleasure' of fishing the Witham and, likening himself to a foundered horse, he cancelled the tour of Lincolnshire with Arthur Young which they had both hoped to make together in the interests of the Board of Agriculture. So Arthur Young roamed over the north of Lincolnshire during August alone, 'like a comet', said Banks, before coming to Revesby Abbey in September to mine the resources of the estate office and its master for guidance over the remainder to the south. It is plain that without this visit to Revesby Young's *General View of the Agriculture of the County of Lincolnshire*, 1799 and 1813, would be relatively anaemic. Apart from the contents of the 156 drawers of the estate office cabinet and the maps and plans there were also the volumes of reports, enactments and historical documents about the country as a whole which Banks had gathered. He was assisted by John Parkinson as steward of the Revesby Abbey and South Holland estates, a Commissioner of the Fourth District under the Witham Navigation and Drainage Act of 1762 to which Banks had made his first subscription as an improving landlord of the fens. Now, with the publication of Young's *General View . . .* in 1799, Banks was able to press forward his ideas on the drainage of those 'horrid fens' which had so affronted the earnest Secretary of the Board of Agriculture. The 'great bull at Revesby', so vilified as an obstacle to their improvement, appeared now through Young's pages to have 'the most liberal ideas upon the subject of reclaiming the Fens'. Indeed during his visit Banks had himself conducted Young by boat to the heart of the East Fen where, in many ways, the crux of the problem lay. Thus in 1799 Lady Banks was able to give in her letter to Miss Mary Heber of 1 November an impression of the first moves in the attack

> . . . Sir Joseph has had a great many Public Meetings to attend & this Year has had very important Business in agitation, a Plan for the enclosure of the Fens, & Sir Joseph has had the satisfaction of finding the Country in general very propitious to his wishes & desirous of promoting the undertaking.

The undertaking in question arose from the meeting in Horncastle of the proprietors of Wildmore Fen, of whom Banks was the most prominent, where it was decided to commission the young Scottish engineer, John Rennie, to undertake a survey of the Wildmore, East and West Fens, and to report on the best mode of draining them in one scheme. The surveys were actually done by Anthony Bower, resident engineer at Lincoln, assisted by James Murray, and Rennie's reports were dated 7 April and 1

John Rennie sen., FRS. Portrait by Sir Henry Raeburn, RA.

September 1800. There were objections, of course, and these were considered in conjunction with Rennie's first report in April at the Town Hall in Boston under Banks as chairman, and after his second report in September. Subscriptions were entered into under Rennie's scheme to promote three bills in Parliament, one for draining the East, West and Wildmore Fens; one for dividing and enclosing Wildmore Fen; and a third for dividing and enclosing the East and West Fens. The first and second of these became Acts in 1801 as 41 Geo.III, c.135 and 41 Geo.III, c.142 respectively, with later amending Acts in 1802 and 1803. The division and allotment of the East and West Fens, however, was not enacted until 1810 under 50 Geo.III, c.129, just half a century after Banks had made his first public subscription towards the Witham drainage.

John Rennie sen., FRS was the latest in a line of distinguished civil engineers with whom Banks was associated in the improvement of drainage and navigation in Lincolnshire – from John Grundy, Langley Edwards and John Smeaton in 1762 over the course of the Witham; John Smeaton in 1782 and William Jessop in 1792 over the Fossdyke navigation; with Jessop again and, at last John Rennie himself in the development of the Horncastle and Sleaford Canals, 1792–4. It is more than probable that Banks first met Rennie about 1785 through Matthew Boulton and James Watt, when he was active in the establishment and operation of the new engine at the Gregory Mine in Derbyshire and Rennie with the installation of a similar Boulton and Watt engine at the Albion Flour Mills, Blackfriars. All forms of 'fire engine' and the use of steam power were of close interest to Banks, and Rennie's new iron shafts and framing at the Albion Mills had their own appeal. Then in March 1798 Rennie had been elected a Fellow of the Royal Society, with his impressive reputation in civil as well as in mechanical engineering. As the last great peatland of Lincolnshire, the East Fen, succumbed to Rennie's Hobhole Drain and its related systems, the wisdom of Banks's choice of engineer became apparent.

The first sales of land in the Wildmore and West Fens began in February 1802. By October 1807 some 10 548 acres of fen had been sold for a total of £433 320. These figures may be set against the substance of a paper prepared by Banks in or about September 1806 intended for Young's *Annals of Agriculture* but never printed there. Instead it was used by Young as an extra for his revised *General View* ... in its 1813 edition, supplemented by the details of land sold to the end of 1807.

Banks cited the unpredictable hazards of stocking the waste fen land by the commoners and their tenants and particularly the devastation of 'the Rot' and other diseases as the prime reason for attempting the improvement. He reckoned the area of commons at 40 000 acres and the adjacent private land, little different from the fens themselves, at about 20 000 acres

> ... making in the whole a Total of 60 000 acres of drownd Land Laying between the Marshes on the one hand & the hilly Countrey inland on the other.

These were excellent approximations to the ultimate figures. The cost of draining this great level he estimated at £200 000 but, allowing the for usual excess of real over estimated expenditure, he reckoned that the more judicious proprietors assessed the cost at not less than £400 000. To meet this outlay, it was planned to sell the higher and better lands of the commons at an estimated unenclosed value of £30 to £35 an acre. The first sales in 1802 realized £39 an acre on average and being sown to oats brought an excellent crop in the two succeeding years. Rumours of this spread and in the sales of 1804 the presence of 'some of the most opulent & most Judicious Land buyers in England' raised the average to £44 an acre and, in 1805 to £51 with some exceeding £65 an acre. This was for land marked out only with surveyors' stakes and open to the common, though certainly under the Act the allotments were tithe-free. All in all Banks assessed the 40000 acres of common land when drained within the ensuing five years at £50 an acre, assuming no material calamity within that time. From this ultimate return of £2000000 the probable cost of the enterprise, £400000, when deducted, left £1600000 to be divided among the proprietors. Certainly by the autumn of 1807 this broad reckoning seemed likely to be achieved at least in covering the cost of the far-flung drainage works.

But there was another side to this great change in the primitive landscape stretching east and west below – but not much below – the frontage of the Revesby Abbey manor house. The process of improvement in any form had always been resisted by the fen peoples since before the first Elizabeth, and Banks, with his historical collections of Lincolnshire records, knew well the social changes implied by the Witham Act of 1762. As the naturalist he was he also knew the ecological consequences of what he was doing as his *alter ego*, the improving landlord. So in the gouty gloom of January 1807 at Soho Square, with William Cartlich at his elbow to transcribe his evanescent thoughts, he called up 'The Mire Nymph, A Poem Adressd to the Proprietors of the East West and Wildmore Fens' by 'Martin Mudlark Tide Waiter', a sort of satirical self-flagellation and back-handed swipe also at the Revd Edward Walls of Spilsby, one of his most persistent critics. The naked beauty of his verse with its fancy rhymes is matched by the haunting spirit of the fens he attempts to exorcise. A few lines will suffice:

... From easy Couch of soft alluvial Mud
Unmovd since Noah landed from the flood
Uprose the Murky Naiid of the Fen
Seldom before beheld by honest Men.
Her head was crownd with Sedge, her bosom bare
Eels crawld like Lice among her clotted hair.
Deep were her Eye balls shrunk, her aguish cheek
Shone deadly pale, above her Peat staind neck.
Why will ye, shriekd she, torture my repose?
Am I a prisoner to my deadly foes
Has barbarous Banks prevaild while worthy Walls
In vain to rouse the tardy Sokemen calls,
Patron of Mire, whose economic lore
My Geese my Ducks my Dabchicks all adore
Sure Rennie, aided by infernal Bower
Are come my muddy Dykes and Sykes to scour
To Starve my Geese, banish my water fowls
And seize my Fishes in their native holes
Rip up the bosom of my favorite Slough
With the fell Harrow & detested Plough

And so for some 93 lines he lacerates his conscience with a geographic tour of the main features of Rennie's drainage scheme in a syllogistic way, larded with quips at Edward Wall's expense, but otherwise presenting well a modern conservationist's lament for the rape of the last wetlands.

II

If a tattered copy of John Gerard's *Herball*, 1597 is the putative inspiration to Banks for his first botanical insights, then Gibson's edition of *Camden's Britannia*, 1695 is responsible for much else apart from his devotion to antiquities. It opened the way to Sir William Dugdale's *History of Imbanking and Drayning of divers Fenns and Marshes* ... 1662, 1772, and his wider understanding of Lincolnshire topography and the intricacie of his own estates as lands for improvement. But Gibson, through Camden, also led into more extended vistas for his undergraduate exercises in Robert Plot's *The Natural History of Oxfordshire. Being an Essay towards the Natural History of England*, 1677, and the intriguing buried world of fossils and strata, with Shotover Hill, its ironsands and ochre pits, to become a favourite hunting ground. There was, however, that other territory for geological enquiry in the mining labyrinths below the Overton estate where he probably saw for the first time in the summers of 1762 and 1763 the real complexities of the strata of the earth and the problems of underground water. This Derbyshire insight was followed by the Staffordshire challenges of the drift coal-mines of the Cheadle and Kingsley estate and the Ecton copper mine nearby.

In his youth Banks explored and noted what lay underground as deep as he could penetrate, a practice he kept into late middle age. The mines of Ashover parish never lost their fascination and after his inheritance of the Overton estate in 1792 his geological curiosity was free to grow.

In the autumn of 1795, with detailed information from William Marsden's brother Alexander, Banks sent his fellow land- and mine-owner John Lloyd to investigate the Irish gold find in County Wicklow near Rathdrum, of which an account was to appear in the *Philosophical Transactions* the next year. But, in his letter of 9 October 1795, he also asked Lloyd to visit their mutual friend Sir George Shuckburgh to examine there 'the mineral in the Tunnell which is called Clunch' but in particular to let him know

> ... how many beds of Iron Stone have been seen in this Clunch as they call it & whether nautili which are the genuine Productions of the ocean are found in Strata above the Iron Stone beds which seem by the Flags they abound with to have been of vegetable origin in Short the Peat bogs of a Prior world.

Both he and Lloyd had been interested but critical observers of Joseph Elkington at work, first for the Duke of Bedford at Woburn and Louisa Countess of Mansfield at Ken Wood and later, in 1795 and 1796, for Lord Egremont at Petworth. These operations of field drainage for crop lands, as well as the related search for springs and ground water supplies, raised many questions about the nature of the superficial soil strata and their orientation. Such problems were of general concern among the landholders and farmers of the period, an interest sharpened by the heavy rains and poor harvests of the last two years of the century. Against this background, in 1800, Thomas Willam Coke invited William Smith, known for his successful drainage and irrigation schemes near Bath, to extend his practices in East Anglia. An introduction from Coke to Banks was an easy transition and in 1801 William Smith had established the force of his ideas on 'the Natural Order of the various Strata that are found in different parts of England and Wales' very clearly at Soho Square. On 1 June 1801 Banks entered his first agreement with Smith for financial support and on the same day was dated the prospectus for the descriptions and delineations of the strata in maps and sections. Before the end of the year Coke had introduced William Smith to the Duke of Bedford. Then, at the end of January 1802, young John Farey, land steward to the Woburn estate, made his first field excursion with Smith to absorb his methods and to become their most important exponent over the next decade. On 11 February Farey wrote a long account of this to Banks who had written to him on 3 February with Charles Hatchett's analyses of some soil samples. In his reply, Farey acknowledged the encouragement Banks had given him toward making a geological survey and map of the country round Woburn and exactly plotting them on parish maps prepared with reference data from the levels observed by Captain William Mudge of the Ordnance Survey. Farey had been introduced to William Smith by the Duke in October 1801, having read the *Prospectus* . . . before this. Now he was able, with the man himself, to spend an evening in a close study of Smith's early stratigraphical map of England, (7ft.4in. × 5ft.10in.) – enough to convince himself that Smith's methods in principle had the answer he was seeking for his local parish maps. Smith's engagement by the Duke was primarily to study the strata of Woburn Park 'principally with a view of better Supplying the Abbey with Spring water', much as Banks himself had been doing several years before at Revesby Abbey on the basis of Joseph Elkington's ideas. On this first encounter John Farey had this to say to Banks:

> . . . Mr. Smith has very little of Theory, his constant Maxim is, "I am in search of Facts only; let others hereafter form a correct Theory from them"; you will I doubt not be much pleased at the pains Mr. S. has been at by the peculiar Fossils, or combinations Of them, to identify each Strata in different parts of its course on the Surface . . .

For Banks the trail was now firmly laid and at the Woburn Sheep Shearing in July 1804 he publicly gave William Smith a cheque for £50 as an earnest of his support for the publication of the map of the strata. Again on 18 December 1804 at the dinner of the Smithfield Club he induced Smith to display his map which afterwards he placed on show in his library 'for the information of the curious'. Thereafter by financial and moral support Banks added his weight to others in the long slow process of drafting, engraving by John Cary, and publication on 1 August 1815, as *A Delineation of the Strata of England and Wales, with part of Scotland; exhibiting the collieries and mines, the marshes and fen lands originally overflowed by the sea, and the varieties of soil according to the variations in the substrata, illustrated by the most descriptive names by W. Smith*. Much was implied in its inscription: 'To the Right Honble Sir Joseph Banks, Bart., P.R.S. this Map is by permission most respectfully dedicated by his much obliged servant, W. Smith'.

In the meanwhile John Farey had established himself as a land surveyor and agent at 12 Upper Crown Street, Westminster. In 1806 he had made a public declaration of his conversion to William Smith's practices in his first paper to *The Philosophical*

Magazine, volume 25, page 44, on 31 June. This was in effect the first published account of Smith's discoveries. Between July and August 1806 and February 1807 he made three journeys along a London to Brighton transect applying Smith's principles, and from it produced a section to scale, 5 foot 3 inches long, dedicating 'this Section of the Strata of the Earth which crop out and appear on the surface on the road between London and Brighton' to Banks 'in testimony of his zeal and liberality in promoting every inquiry connected with Natural History'. This 'zeal and liberality' Banks again expressed in the summer of 1807 when he invited John Lloyd to join him at Overton on 2 September:

> . . . we Shall Stay there only a week yet I think it will be worth your Pains to Come to me as I shall have [John] Farey with me who thinks he is so much master of Smiths means of detecting the Stratification of a Countrey as he Rides over it that he has made a Section of the Earth under the Road from London to Brighton
>   I bring him with me in order that he may report to me the State of the outcropping Strata on my Estate for the Purposes of Agriculture & I mean to send him on to Revesby if you approve of his Proceedings which I think [you] will you may accompany him in a Short Jaunt he will make probably into the Coal Country during the time I am at the Races & Come with him to Revesby Abbey . . .

Lloyd did not come but Farey executed his transect of about 90 miles from Matlock edge past Overton Hall through Ashover, Temple Normanton, Pleasley, Mansfield, Hockerton, Newark, Ancaster, Sleaford and Tattershall, past Revesby to Trusthorpe on the east coast near Sutton. From this geological ride there came in February 1808 the first really extended section of British strata in the form of an impressive strip 9 feet long and 7½ inches wide, dedicated to Banks and explicitly noting that it was done at his proposal, implicitly at his expense. During 1808 and 1809 Farey's detailed geological survey of the parish of Ashover and the county of Derbyshire followed. Banks had a plan of the parish with the stratification marked on it drafted by George Nuttall, his Matlock land agent, hand-coloured to Farey's and his own satisfaction 'as a matter of Science' to be shown at Soho Square during the winter of 1808–9. From the parish map grew in time the geological map of Derbyshire which appeared in the two-volume first edition of Farey's *General View of the Agriculture and Minerals of Derbyshire*; . . . , 1811, 1813. The first volume contained all the geology – in depth as to the strata, in extent as to the soils and distribution of the minerals, the mines and the mining processes, coupled with his theory of faults and denudation – with five coloured maps and sections of strata. It was an historic point in geological publication and perhaps in that one volume alone a more significant contribution to knowledge than any of the other county reviews conjured into print by the Board of Agriculture. In the Preface John Farey avowed its origin as

> . . . mostly the result of a survey of the county of Derby and its environs which was undertaken in the summer of 1807 at the instance of the worthy President of the Royal Society in order to examine minutely its stratification and mineral treasures . . . During that autumn and nearly all the next two years I was employed most industriously in prosecuting my survey.

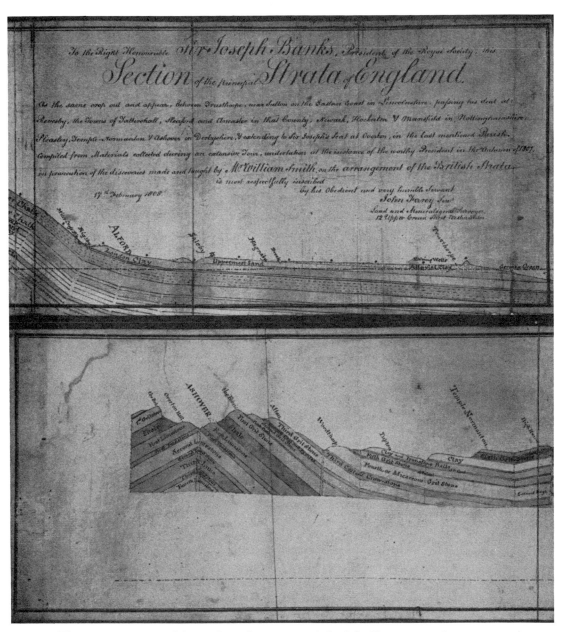

The two extremities of the geological transect made by John Farey sen. in the autumn of 1807 between Trusthorpe near Sutton on the Lincolnshire coast (above) and Overton Hall near Ashover in Derbyshire. The section of the strata is 9 feet long, dated 17 February 1808, and dedicated to Banks who initiated and financed it.

The deep structure of the county of Derbyshire was more thoroughly revealed by Farey's *General View* ... of 1811 under the stimulus of Banks than the topographical changes in the surface of Lincolnshire due to his influence were ever recorded by Young in his *General View* ... of 1813. In the very year that the Gregory Mine effectively ceased to operate, against the trend of all Banks's views, he had, with Farey, opened a new and hopeful partnership in the infant science of geology.

III

Daniel Solander died without ever seeing the letter to him from Sir William Hamilton at Naples about the drawings of the emblems of St Cosmo. This had been enclosed open in a letter to Banks dated 23 April 1782. The emblems themselves Hamilton deposited in the British Museum during his leave in London of 1784, leaving other papers on the same subject with Banks. All were for the attention of the committee of the Society of Dilettanti with a view to publication, and published they were four years later under the editing of their fastidious fellow-Dilettante, Richard Payne Knight, as a matter of antiquarian curiosity. Such was the origin of the limited and now rare edition of the volume entitled *An Account of the Remains of the Worship of Priapus lately existing in Isernia* ... 1786, and such was the chain of events by which Banks came to know the Knights of Downton Castle near Ludlow in Herefordshire.

Richard Payne, the elder of the two brothers, was a Fellow both of the Antiquaries and the Dilettanti, and with him Banks indulged his neo-classical fancies. Thomas Andrew, the shy younger brother and a Balliol man, lived a quiet rural life far from such urban quirks until Banks, as a member of the Board of Agriculture and the experimentalist of Spring Grove, enrolled him as a county correspondent for Herefordshire. Richard Payne introduced them some time in 1794 and almost at once Thomas Andrew and Banks were actively engaged in the production of a stream of papers on a wide range of horticultural activities and new thoughts in plant and animal biology. The first of these emerged in the spring of 1795 as Thomas Andrew Knight's paper, entitled with innocent brevity 'Observations on grafting', was read to the Royal Society in the form of a letter to Banks dated 13 April. The pattern had been quickly established and so it continued, letter after letter and paper after paper to the *Philosophical Transactions*, the erstwhile silent countryman but active and critical observer transformed, confessing to Banks on 14 August 1799

> ... If I become a troublesome scribbler to you, I must claim your pardon on the ground that you have made me such; for without the attention I have been honoured with from you, I am certain I should never (in print) have scribbled at all.

This point had been well made by Banks in the earlier correspondence from which had evolved Knight's second paper to the Royal Society, read on 9 May 1799 and entitled 'An account of some experiments on the fecundation of vegetables', the substance of a letter to Banks dated 25 April. His experiments with peas as early as 1787 were discussed in this paper and showed clearly his observation of many phenomena in plant breeding (dominance, recessive behaviour, hybrid vigour) in the next century to be associated with the name of Gregor Mendel. In the course of these exchanges Banks found occasion on 18 January 1798 to admonish Knight, urging him to persevere with the cross-breeding of annual plants

> ... When you consider your experiments upon the fecundation of plants, and improving the kinds of them by coupling the best males and females of each sort, as unimportant matters, you really act very differently from what I feel myself disposed to do on the occasion. I am loth to speak in a dictatorial style, if my opinion differs from yours; but I do confess, I think no experiments promise more public utility than those for improving the breeds of vegetables.

It was perhaps with this thought that 18 months later, on 28 June 1799, Banks selected from the King's flock at Windsor the Spanish Merino ram No. 130 with a good carcass as well as a fine fleece and sent it to Knight at Elton for cross-breeding with the old Archerfield or Ryeland breed of Herefordshire. This was the beginning of many useful exchanges of breeders' lore in the development of farm livestock, not only in the matter of fat carcasses and fine wool but, notably, on the virtues of the Hereford cattle themselves. But even as he acknowledged the safe arrival of the royal ram in his letter to Banks of 14 August 1799, Knight expanded his thoughts on the ascent of sap in trees, the opening 'scribble' in a course that would beget a sequence of four papers to the Royal Society within the next five years and confirm him as a leader in plant physiology. It also fixed him high in the estimation of Banks when the day came for the meeting at Hatchard's in Piccadilly which launched, at John Wedgwood's proposal, their idea of a Horticultural Society.

Wedgwood had floated the notion first in a letter to William Forsyth, of 29 June 1801, at the same time seeking the general approval of Banks, who, on 31 July, had no difficulty in pronouncing – 'I approve very much the idea'. In expressing his support he had before him Wedgwood's plan for a new society which proposed 'from time to time to publish a volume of papers' specifically on 'horticultural subjects' and so of a kind which, in Knight's contributions, were already finding a place in the *Philosophical Transactions* with his encouragement. Another society was about to emerge which might threaten the eminence of the Royal Society and bleed it of support but yet again Banks helped rather than hindered – indeed, he said he would be honoured to be an original member. So, with John Wedgwood in the Chair, Banks was one of the seven who formed the inaugural meeting at Hatchard's on Wednesday 7 March 1804, with William Forsyth, Charles Greville, R. A. Salisbury, W. T. Aiton and James Dickson, all associates or friends. At the second meeting on 14 March, Banks was in the chair and at the third on 28 March, Wedgwood again as the 'Original Society' of 28 names was recorded, with Banks called upon to assist in framing a set of rules. Thomas Andrew Knight's name was not yet included and it was Banks who that day brought it forward for original membership, as he wrote to Knight on 29 March. Then, on 5 March 1805, a committee of seven was formed with Banks as chairman 'for the purpose of preparing a Prospectus declaratory of the intentions of this Society, to be submitted to the Public'. On Thursday 7 March this met at 32 Soho Square and Knight was asked to accept the task of writing it. Within the month he had done so and Banks read this important paper at the next General Meeting of the Society on Tuesday 2 April 1805. It was headed 'Introductory Remarks relative to the Objects which the Horticultural Society have in view' of which the Council was asked to have 250 copies printed for distribution to members of the Society and to the press. At the same meeting Banks, speaking for the committee, was able also to announce that the Council of the Linnean Society had agreed to permit the Horticultural Society to meet in their apartments, for the sum of 25 guineas a year and from that date Hatchard's ceased to be the venue for these occasions. First No. 10 Panton Square and then, from the autumn of 1805, 9 Gerrard Street, the former haunt of Samuel Johnson's Literary Club, became the home of the two societies until May 1819.

For the first five years or so of the Society's life, Knight was undoubtedly the mainstay of its proceedings with some 19 papers presented and published in the *Transactions* . . ., volume I, of which the first of five parts was published in 1807, a handsome quarto printed by William Bulmer and the last in 1812. His subjects flowed from his experience and experiments at Elton – training and grafting of fruit trees, the construction of hotbeds and forcing houses, new and early fruits, peaches and peach houses, apples and alpine strawberries, onions and potatoes – a series in no way interfering with his contributions to the Royal Society and all of them interlaced with his Banksian correspondence. But Banks, too, in his more desultory way, helped to fatten the first volume with some ten papers derived from his wide knowledge of the academic literature and from the background of his activities at Spring Grove. His first paper to the Society on 7 May 1805 was a blend of the two – an attempt to trace the introduction of the potato into the British Isles and an account of hill wheat in India, of which he had tried several kinds at Spring Grove. His second, on 3 December 1805, was concerned with the acclimatization of tender plants to the British climate, from Spring Grove and the Royal Botanic Garden experiences over many years. His paper on the revival of an old method of managing strawberries, given on 2 December 1806, was a hint of preoccupations to come with Knight on improving the fruit by crossing. His account of the growth and productivity of his American cranberries, *Vaccinium macrocarpum*, at Spring Grove, compared with that of his strawberry beds, given on 1 March 1808, showed his attitude to the economics of horticulture. But his papers to the *Transactions of the Horticultural Society*, volume I, was a late and unusual manifestation in his life, not otherwise remarkable for his contributions to the printed word. It is as if in his correspondence with Thomas Andrew Knight there had been a brief reciprocal stimulation of the kind he had himself imparted in the subjects for which they shared a common enthusiasm.

Another important result of this relationship arose in the spring of 1803 when during one of his visits to Soho Square, Knight was introduced to Humphry Davy by Banks who, as Chairman of the Committee of Science at the Royal Institution, was then arranging with the Board of Agriculture for lectures on the chemistry of agriculture. Was this a happy chance? There were, of course, many such meetings at Soho Square among the galaxy of diverse talents passing that way. But from all that followed it has the mark of a well-planned impromptu. From that year forward the working association between Knight and Davy was close, warmed in the summer of 1803 with the first of many fishing holidays together at Elton and Downton Castle, trouting in the Leintwardine waters of the river Teme. Ten years later the evidence of the 'triangular trade' in scientific ideas between Banks, Knight and Davy, would emerge in *Elements of Agricultural Chemistry in a Course of Lectures for the Board of Agriculture*, 1813, a fine quarto in the typography of William Bulmer, from the philosophic nursery in Soho Square.

IV

In the parish of Little Snoring, about ten miles south of Holkham Hall, at least one alert observer rose in 1804 to state in print what he himself had seen in a wheat field there before the harvest of 1803, as just one case of many he had heard that year. This was another example of 'the miraculous barberry bush' at which John Lawrence had jeered on page 44 of his *New Farmer's Calendar* as a yokel's superstition but which 'Agricola Norfolciensis' now defended as something worth 'a little stricter investigation', something with light to shed on the origin of the black rust in wheat. He had seen a concentration of rust fanning out as a wedge in a wheat field from a single barberry bush at its point in a hedgerow, the shade darkest toward the bush itself of which there was no other specimen in or near the affected field. He let his observations rest as a recorded fact, not as a countryman's superstitious fancy, without arguing whether or not the barberry was the 'cause' of the mildew in question. It was to be many years before the complicated life cycle of the rust fungi in wheat and other species was made clear and understood, but the barberry (*Berberis vulgare* L.) had for centuries been a mystery even to the extent of being decreed for eradication at Rouen in 1660 as a malign influence in the rusting of wheat. Agricultural interest rose and fell as the plant disease itself fluctuated among the crops in the corn lands of Great Britain but now, in the seasons of 1803–4 with its devastations diminishing the harvest, its importance was enhanced as the war with France was renewed and imported grain supplies were threatened again. The subject was certainly a talking point at the Holkham Sheep Shearings which Banks had attended in 1803 and 1804 and the conundrum of 'the miraculous barberry-bush of Norfolk' must have concentrated his thoughts on the cause of blight, mildew and rust, or the 'causes', for the notion of anything singular was contentious.

There were, however, many distractions that year apart from the founding of the Horticultural Society. There was, of course, the change of administration as Henry Addington gave way to William Pitt in April involving Banks in personal adjustments to the new men in office when the Cabinet formed in May. This touched closely on his work with Lord Liverpool on the copper coinage for Ireland as things changed at the Board of Trade but still left him much involved with its former President as they laboured together on the substance of *The Coins of the Realm* which the noble Lord would publish in 1805. There was the nagging matter of the imprisonment of Matthew Flinders and the need to brief and urge on the new Secretary for War and the Colonies, Lord Camden, and later to bring forward with him the second expedition of Mungo Park. In spite of intermittent gout at the end of June he attended both the Woburn and Holkham Sheep Shearings and on his return faced the complexities of arranging the first public sale of the King's Spanish Merinos on 'the field south of the Pagoda' at Kew on 15 August. On this occasion Franz Bauer was much in evidence as he and Banks examined specimens of rusted wheat brought for their opinion and as a challenge to Bauer's developing art of drawing with the aid of the microscope. Then, on the morning of Friday 17 August, Banks had the pleasure of inspecting with the King himself the cargo of plants from China which had come to Kew on the evening tide the day before – the first offerings of William Kerr, His Majesty's collector at Canton.

Within the next week his mother, living then with him, fell ill at Soho Square and

403

on 27 August she died, to be followed a week later by her sister Arabella, at Gough House, Chelsea. With these bereavements in such short order the northern migration of the Banks family was in disarray. For ten days everyone lived at Spring Grove until the body of Mrs Banks left Soho Square for its burial in the family vault at Revesby church on Friday 7 September. Then Banks reverted to his earlier arrangements, setting off first to inspect the Duke of Marlborough's china collection at Blenheim Palace and then to spend one day with Matthew Boulton at Soho, Birmingham, on 11 September. Here he had the tricky task of inducing Matthew Boulton to meet John Rennie and collaborate with him in transferring his coining machines to the Royal Mint at the Tower of London to work there under contract with the Treasury. There was also the progress of minting the copper coinage for Ireland at Boulton's Soho factory to be reported on. When he wrote to Sir Stephen Cottrell about this from Overton on 14 September he ended on a surprisingly cheerful note

> ... At present I can proudly say, that my Foreign Correspondence which has not for some years been free from heavy Arrears, is brought up to the present time, and that I now have leisure, which I have long wanted, to pursue my speculative Amusements.

Perhaps it was in this spirit that he had set Franz Bauer to record the lesions on specimens of blighted wheat and their microscopic details during the summer, and in the same way diverted Lord Liverpool's thoughts from coins of the realm with a first draft of his own 'speculative Amusement', the cause of blight, mildew or rust in corn, soon after his return fro Lincolnshire in November. By 27 November he was ready to trouble Arthur Young for references to the best writers on blight in wheat and specifically to any who attributed the disease to the presence of a parasitic plant. This is interesting for it was more likely that his own library would, on the face of it, have held such material than Young's. But it is even more curious that in the final paper as it was published, he cited the Italian version of the *Osservazioni sopra la Ruggine del Grano*, 1767, of Felice Fontana from his own library with no reference to the more useful English translation 'Observations on the Mildew of Corn' printed by Arthur Young in his *Annals of Agriculture* 1792, volume 17. He submitted an advance version of his own paper before the end of the year to Thomas Andrew Knight who returned it on 29 December with approval and demands for more information. With two plates of drawings by Franz Bauer, engraved by F. Sansom, Banks dated his text 30 January 1805 and had a first quarto edition of 500 printed as a separate pamphlet by William Bulmer.

It was entitled *A Short Account of the Cause of the Disease in Corn, called by the Farmers the Blight, the Mildew, and the Rust*. From February 1805 Banks distributed some 83 copies with coloured and 389 with plain engravings to 249 individuals, mostly the landowning gentry and farmers but also to royalty and the titled landowners, with about 50 to professional men, including fellow-botanists and foreign scientists. In March 1805 it was being set up by Bulmer for Arthur Young in *Communications to the Board of Agriculture* and by May 1805 an octavo version, with a single rearranged engraving, had been printed by John Harding. Printed also in the *Annals of Botany*, *Philosophical Magazine*, and *Journal of Philosophy*, Banks reckoned that some 4850 copies including his own privately issued pamphlet would have been available to the public. This was agricultural education on an impressive scale, intended to 'awake the energies of reason' among farmers and agriculturalists willing and able to study the day-to-day progress of their crops, such as Thomas Knight, who pursued the relation of the barberry to the disease and, in later editions of the paper, his letter of 20 March 1806 was printed with it. This contained his observations during the summer of 1805 establishing the connection between the rust on the barberry and its ability to light up the infection on wheat. It is probably through Knight that Bauer received the barberry specimens from which he completed his magnificent illustrations of this piece of plant pathology even though they were never published as engravings but lay in notebooks at the disposal of Banks and his scientific friends. It would be another 120 years before all the complications in the two sexual phases of the fungus *Puccinia graminis* Pers. residing separately on the wheat plant and the barbery would be elucidated, although in 1807 Candolle had already agreed with Banks that they were related and there were other scientific bloodhounds on the scent. But Banks had publicly and widely posed the key question

> ... Is it not more than possible that the parasitic fungus of the barberry and that of the wheat are one and the same species, and that the seed is transferred from the barberry to the corn?

His challenge was instantly taken up by reviewers and anonymous correspondents in the agricultural press, critical not only of the central theme but on other arguable points. One of the most comprehensive and withering blasts came early in May 1805 from the anonymous reviewer in *The Farmers' Magazine* at Edinburgh in eight pages of analysis which could be condensed into one of its own sentences

> ... We are free to say, that, if the author were not a man high in rank, and at the head of the Royal Society, his publication would have been disregarded by every farmer in Great Britain.

In this and other correspondence the suggestion of a parasitic fungus as a possible cause was dismissed as immaterial to the problem. But in November 1805 a more sober and constructive approach appeared from the pen of 'Agricola Northumbriensis' in the *Agricultural Magazine*, volume 13, dissenting from many views of 'the learned Baronet' but prepared to take a longer one

> ... I cannot refrain from expressing my disapprobation of the *terms* and the *ridicule* which some agricultural writers have employed against them. Such conduct must operate so as to prevent that aid which the cultivator of the soil evidently requires, from the profound naturalist, in his endeavours to discover the causes of these disorders. The discovery of these causes to the satisfaction of all, will require, for a great length of time, the united efforts of the philosopher and the farmer – the wisdom of the former and the most accurate and minute attention (to various phenomena) of the latter.

But whatever the failings in logic, observation, interpretation or practicality of the 'learned Baronet', he had, with his brochure, lit a torch of enquiry among his philosophic friends as well as his bucolic sceptics which time would justify in the end.

V

There were signs in 1802 that the collecting years of Francis Masson were coming to an end. As early as February Banks had remarked on the paucity of plants in his last consignment from North America and pointed out that the King might be difficult to convince of his continuing zeal. There were signs too that Banks himself was casting his thoughts elsewhere for he had been commanded to confer with Baron Hawkesbury, then Foreign Secretary, that when a resident minister from Spain should be appointed he was to seek permission from him for a gardener from Kew to be established for a time at Buenos Aires as a collector. He was suggesting the status of a gardener to avoid the Spanish taking 'political umbrage', hoping that the Court of Spain would treat him as favourably as the Dutch had in their time treated Masson at the Cape. He initiated this move from Revesby Abbey and kept W. T. Aiton informed of progress and, through him, the King. William Kerr, 'a well-behaved and considerate young man' was the gardener from Kew proposed, a Scot from Roxburghshire and the son of a nurseryman at Hawick. But as the year ended, the diplomatic niceties had not been concluded, in spite of Lord Hawkesbury's optimism 'that the Renewal of Confidence between the two Nations' would take place, and on 21 December Banks told Aiton that he was on the point of recommending to the King that Kerr should make a voyage to China before going to the Rio de la Plata. Lord Hawkesbury however had dissuaded him from this. Meanwhile Banks hoped that seeds collected near the River Hawkesbury in New South Wales would soon be arriving for Aiton to plant at Kew but with the renewed approach of war the South American plant hunting ground as a field for Kerr was dropped for a decade to come.

Banks now played the China card with the King's approval, and, in the first week of April 1803, approached Jacob Bosanquet, Deputy Chairman of the East India Company, to sound the feelings of the directors on his scheme for Kerr's employment in Canton as a plant collector for Kew. By 12 April the Court of Directors had approved the sending of Kerr under the control of David Lance, superintendant at the Company's Canton Factory. On 18 April Banks had drawn the threads together. David Lance and Kerr met at India House to arrange the formalities of the passage. Kerr had already received from Banks the details of his instructions relating to plant collection and the botanical and agricultural enquiries he was to pursue, supplemented with generous extracts from Grosier's *A general description of China*, 1788, translated from the French. Aiton had also seen Kerr's instructions which he had found, much to his satisfaction, quite explicit. On 20 April he proposed to put the plants for China on board the ship – the first of a series from the Royal Botanic Garden and London plant nurseries to attempt the long oriental voyage in the modified 'plant cabins' during Kerr's period in the Far East. At the last moment Banks visited Bosanquet in Leadenhall Street to confirm the Company's undertaking at his suggestion to pay all Kerr's expenses, except his salary. Banks saw the King on 21 April and arranged that Kerry should receive £100 p.a. from the Privy Purse as from Lady Day, 25 March, for which he had already been given advances by Aiton. On 23 April Banks armed Lance with further details of what was wanted from China and its vicinity in the way of fruit species, especially as Malta might be lost to British occupation, the very nub of the problem on which peace with France would crumble within the month. On 28 April he conveyed to John Roberts, the East India Company Chairman still, how pleased the King was with the Company's collaboration and its proposal to bear the expenses of his plant collector in China which he was prepared graciously to accept. And on this note William Kerr left his country for ever to carry the torch as Kew collector on the China coast. For seven years Kerr struggled with the complexities and limitations of life on the edge of the Middle Kingdom, never penetrating far into the countryside or the enigma of the Chinese mind, but somehow managing to send useful cargoes home of botanical delights through the hazards of shipboard management and the temperamental vagaries of the East Indiamen captains.

The Indiaman *Henry Addington* returning with Kerr's first plant consignments for Kew, also brought home John Allen, the young Derbyshire miner from Banks's Overton estate, (who had been with HMS *Investigator* under Matthew Flinders), and through whose care so many of the plants survived. The King and Banks inspected them together in the Royal Botanic Garden on 17 August 1804, two days after the public sale near the Pagoda when John Macarthur bought so many Spanish Merinos from the royal flock to return with him in the *Argo* to New South Wales. The name of Kerr himself at last achieved its own place from this first shipment in the *Corchorus japonica* transformed by Candolle to the *Kerria japonica* of today. And two years later the small species rose was sent by Kerr to find a place in our gardens through its cultivation at Spring Grove under Isaac Oldacer after finding its identity as *Rosa banksiae* in the *Hortus Kewensis* of 1811, the Lady Banks's rose.

But Lady Banks had more to gain than a botanical commemorative from this revived Chinese connection. David Lance had been commissioned by her to collect Chinese porcelain for the shelves of her dairy at Spring Grove. Sir George Thomas Staunton, FRS, now a supercargo at Canton, whom Banks had asked to assist Kerr with his deeper knowledge of the Chinese character, also contributed to Lady Banks's hobby and to her husband's pursuits of the history of porcelain. Staunton was of more direct help in this than in assisting Kerr. Even after five years in the Factory, with his exceptional knowledge of the Chinese language, written and spoken, he found himself still ignorant of the country and the people, hedged in at Canton and 'embarrassed by the jealousy of the upper ranks of Chinese and the ignorance of the lower'. But with the support of the three supercargoes, Lance, Drummond and Staunton, somehow Kerr made progress. He gained the goodwill of Puankhequa, President of the Company of Merchants, the Co-hong, through whom the Emperor kept a tight rein on trade with the foreigners. An elaborate exchange of presents between Banks and this influential Chinese dignitary ensured the flow, albeit restricted, of requirements for the Royal Garden at Kew. On the other hand Kerr incurred a mild reproof from Banks when he went to Luzon in the Philippines at the suggestion of David Lance and James Drummond

> ... These gentlemen do not seem to have considered that in a cold climate like England one Plant from the temperate Climate of the north of China is worth a hundred from the Burning heats of the intertropical Countries ...

And so he urged Kerr to concentrate on plants from northern China and Tartary as long as he had any hope of receiving these through the Co-Hong merchants. In this

407

he spoke more as a practical gardener, but in Kerr's plants and journal from Manila, when they came to hand, he found enough to satisfy his botanist's curiosity. So from 1806 to 1810 the plant cargoes in the modified plant cabins that became a fairly regular feature of the East Indiamen sailing to and from the Thames managed to fulfil the general intentions of Banks and the King in spite of the studied neglect by some of the more intransigent captains.

CHAPTER 19

THE DILEMMAS OF DISCOVERY
1800–1806

In 1785 the French botanist Jacques Julien de La Billardière had visited Banks at Soho Square and carried back to Paris various items as gifts to La Pérouse for the voyage of the *Boussole* and the *Astrolabe*. In the heady and uncertain political climate of 1791 the National Assembly had responded to a resolution of the Société d'Histoire Naturelle on 22 January that an expedition be mounted to search for the missing Lá Perouse, and on 29 September the *Recherche* and *Espérance* sailed from Brest under the command of Bruni d'Entrecasteaux. The senior botanist was the touchy La Billardière, now pro-revolutionary, and with him as naturalist the more obscure and gentler Louis Auguste Deschamps. During the preceding summer La Billardière had received from Banks a set of the *Icones Kaempferi* ... engravings. Acknowledging these on 25 July he had asked for advice and help in his preparations for the voyage. From Spring Grove on 22 August Banks replied in French, demurring at the notion of instructing someone who was certainly no novice but emphasizing the importance of drawing the flowering parts from very fresh specimens, the need for large supplies of drying paper and with some hints on spirit preservation. He directed attention especially to New Caledonia as a region to be visited if possible to repair J. R. Forster's neglect on Cook's second voyage. Then came the usual long hiatus until, on 4 February 1796, Banks received a letter from Samarang dated 9 April 1794 in which La Billardière gratefully acknowledged this advice in the collections he had made in New Holland, the Friendly Isles and New Caledonia. But the expedition had disintegrated after the death of d'Entrecasteaux at sea among the Manus Islands and the reversion of command to the Royalist d'Auribeau. At Surabaya debility, disease, and the penetrating virus of the Revolution completed the dissolution of a brave venture, a failure in its first aim, but rich in the rewards of discovery and its collections of natural history.

The royalist element for a while prevailed. La Billardière and Deschamps with others were interned by the Dutch. The collections from the *Recherche* were transferred to a Dutch ship under the control of Edouard de Rossel and were captured off the Shetlands and brought to London on 1 November 1795. La Billardière, Deschamps and other scientists were released in March 1795, the former to find his way safely back to France by way of Mauritius in March 1796; the latter, with Dutch permission, to remain in Java exploring and collecting for another five years. The mystery of La Pérouse's disappearance remained.

In London the natural history collections, subject to the protest from Rossel, who was unaware that Holland had been annexed by France and so was at war with Great Britain, were placed at the disposal of Louis XVIII, set in order by the Comte de Bournon as a protective measure against damage by storage in the Custom House, and finally offered by the French King to Queen Charlotte, through the royal French

Ambassador, the Duc d'Harcourt. At this point Banks was commanded by the Queen, through a letter from the Duc on 29 March 1796, to inspect the collections and advise her accordingly. The next day he visited Harcourt House where he saw the plant collection, the bird skins, the reptiles and fish but not the insects which were at the house of Comte de Bournon. On 31 March he conveyed his impressions to Major William Price, Vice-Chamberlain to the Queen for her consideration. His impression of La Billardière's contribution to natural history was generous however much he disapproved the revolutionary set of his politics

> ... The collection of Plants bears testimony to an industry all but indefatigable in the Botanists who were employed, the chief of whom I am sorry to say was the principle fomentor of the Mutiny which took place in the ships built upon the strongest Jacobin Principles
>
> I counted near 350 quires of paper containing specimens, and there are 3 or 4 large boxes besides in which the dried Plants are packed together so close that they probably contain as many specimens as the quires of paper, the largest part of these are in good preservation, and doubless would form a very valuable Herbarium, as many of the Countries that have been visited are almost or entirely unknown to Europeans.
>
> As the duplicates, which are in a manner innumerable, would serve no purpose but to encumber Her Majesty, I shall with pleasure if I am honoured with her Royal commands, undertake to select for her Majesty a complete collection of one good specimen of each species; but as the individual specimens from whence they are to be taken cannot consist of less than 10,000, every one of which must be separately examined, I dare not undertake to complete the work in less than a year from the present time.

On 1st April the Queen, through William Price, readily accepted the offer of a selected plant collection but wished for no other part. On 2 April Banks expressed his readiness to receive the plants at Soho Square for the long task that seemed to lie ahead. It seems to have been decided that the faunal specimens and the minerals were best presented to Banks as a token of what the French emigrés felt they owed to him. But none of this was to be.

In March the French Directory applied to the British Government for the collection to be released. This called for a reversal of the official decision already made in favour of Louis XVIII, the King in exile, and on this count could not be made. Both the Directory and La Billardière then appealed to Banks, never doubting, according to Bournon, for one moment that his influence would be decisive. Their faith was justified but it required time. On 9 June he could do no more than assure La Billardière that he had gained some sympathy in the Cabinet and that he had hope of a favourable decision, bearing in mind how France had extended protection to Captain Cook, and so providing an axiom 'that the science of two Nations may be at Peace while their Politics are at War'. He was able to press his argument home with Lord Grenville, the Foreign Secretary during the latter part of June, gaining a verbal agreement that the collections might be restored – 'unless the late King of France had any personal interest in M. La Billardière's journey', as he told the French commissioner in London, Josef Charretié, on 24 June. Nearly another month passed without any sign of the answer Grenville had promised and Banks gathered all his arguments into a forceful letter to him 'to request a speedy answer to this interesting subject, and to deprecate a refusal'. It was a masterly combination of morality and expediency and on 31 July Banks had the satisfaction, when he met Grenville at Windsor Castle that morning, of securing his promise for the return of the collections and an appointment in Whitehall for 4 August to finalize the details. In the formality of the Foreign Office Grenville readily confirmed his Windsor promise but insisted that the Government's name should be kept out of the business when the return was made through Charretié in the next cartel of prisoners. Banks then faced on the same day the delicate task of explaining to the Queen, through Price, her Vice-Chamberlain, what had been decided and why. At the same time he sought her permission for the transfer to proceed, softening the loss of an exciting plant collection with a substitute 'as valuable at least as the one in question' – presumably duplicates from the Pacific gatherings of Archibald Menzies lodged the previous autumn at Soho Square. By 10 August the way was clear on all counts, as Banks called the French commissioner to Soho Square to arrange the packing and transport of the whole collection – except for one discordant bleat from John Woodford, known as 'Emperor', claiming the bird collection as a gift for his services to the French nobility. In the end this was refused except for the gift of one duplicate and Banks had made an enemy.

On 10 August also Banks told Antoine de Jussieu that he had secured from the Foreign Office a passport for the West Indian voyage of Nicolas Baudin as well as the return intact of La Billardière's collections

. . . a monument to his indefatigable industry that does him immortal honor

But it was late in the year before La Billardière acknowledged the arrival of his cases, complete except for the destruction by careless handling of his insect boxes in the journey from Le Havre to the Jardin des Plantes. And it was 16 December before the Scientific Class of the Institut National instructed its secretary to record its appreciation for what Banks had achieved in restoring French property. What it could not fully appreciate was how much Banks had managed alone by force of argument and personal authority in reversing the decision of the British Government for a scientist with Jacobin tendencies, against the interest of his Queen and, most difficult of all, against his own strong scientific curiosity. But in keeping to his personal ethic of fair dealing he had raised a standard for international communication in peace and war which he kept aloft against discouraging odds according to his lights as 'a man of honor'. He put this in so many words when he wrote to La Billardière on 15 July 1797

. . . I hope you have by this time made some progress in arranging the Glorious Collections which I had the Good Fortune to send over to you, I Envy you the posession of Some of them which I Saw accidentally & hope when Peace returns to Procure from you some duplicates, for I can assure you as a man of honor that not a single Specimen was on any account retaind here, Either by my self or, I firmly believe, by any other person here, the whole intire Quantity was transmitted under my Seal to the hands of Mr. Charretié. I hope we shall soon hear of your Publications.

His hope was realized when La Billardière on 5 March 1800 sent him the two volumes of the *Relation du voyage à la recherche de La Pérouse* ..., 1799, with the attendant atlas, in time for inclusion in volume 5, the Supplement and Index, of Dryander's *Catalogus* ..., 1800. Then from 1804 came the sequence of fascicules illustrating the flora as outline engravings with the flowers and the fruit finished in more detail according to the broad advice given by Banks in July 1791. The first four of these, a total of 40 engravings, were reviewed in the *Annals of Botany* in 1806 as La Billardière's *Novae Hollandiae Plantarum Specimen*, commending the plan and the method of illustration but confessing 'that the descriptions are often more concise than we could have wished', reduced as they were mostly to a one-line diagnosis. But the anonymous reviewer politely made another point. In his preface La Billardière had acknowledged the two French ministers, Chaptal and de Champigny, under whom the work had been published but, said the reviewer

> ... Time and circumstance probably prevented M. Labillardière from making the acknowledgements that were due in another quarter; for we know that both for the appearance of the journal of his voyage, and whatever has hitherto resulted from the scientific researches made on that expedition, the public are entirely indebted to the disinterested liberality of the President of the Royal Society ...

So La Billardière had his collections, his public acclaim and his botanical priorities in the international nomenclature of Pacific plants. While these accrued in Paris his younger companion, Louis Auguste Deschamps, botanized industriously among the mountains and hills of Java working toward the 'Flora Javanica' that would never appear to commemorate his name.

After five years in the field and two years as a resident physician under the protection of Governor van Overstraten, he took ship for Mauritius and from thence sailed in *L'Union* for France. Approaching the Channel the vessel was captured by HMS *Jupiter*, Captain Lossack and taken to Portsmouth in May 1803. At the same time the *Naturaliste* Captain Hamelin, returning from the Baudin expedition, was under detention after interception by HMS *Minerva* in the Channel on 27 May. Both these posed problems for Banks to resolve at the same time. Deschamps wrote an explanatory appeal from the *Jupiter* to Banks on 28 May seeking release as a non-combatant survivor of the d'Entrecasteaux expedition on the precedent of La Billardière and permission to return to France on the *Naturaliste*, or at least to have his collections sent on her. Banks immediately secured an order for his release from the Admiralty to be sent to Portsmouth, and by 11 June Deschamps was free in the care of William Cole of the Customs and the Revd Richard Bingham, a magistrate of Gosport, who provided him with a passport for travel to see Banks in London. By 25 June Deschamps was home among his people at St Omer but his personal effects and the collections were in a state of some confusion as William Cole tried to land them though the tentacles of the Prize Agents. On 17 June Cole reported to Banks that he had possession of everything on board *L'Union* belonging to Deschamps, the captors having agreed to relinquish any claims on their part, but that he was ordered to deliver it all to the Custom House in London. On 24 June Banks applied to the Treasury for an order to receive Deschamps's clothes, collections and papers duty free in order to send them on to him in France at the first opportunity by a neutral ship, and a warrant was granted on 28 June. Two trunks went astray by mistake to some Frenchmen on parole at Bishop's Waltham but were recovered by William Cole on 18 August in the midst of his frantic activities raising a Defence Corps of 250 men against the threat of an imminent French invasion. The vagrant trunks were sent to join the rest, which was safely housed in the Baggage Warehouse of the East India Company in Great St Helen's, under the charge of William Maclean. With everything now in hand Banks wrote to Deschamps on 18 August explaining once again the reasons for the delays. For a month every attempt had been made through George Christopher, the English agent of M. Pigault-Maubaillarcq, whom Deschamps had named his own agent at Calais, but without effect, as no ship could be found that would sail for France nor would the French allow any ship to enter Calais from England. On 21 September Deschamps acknowledged this news and confirmed that communications were interrupted. He was also concerned that in the list of the collection sent there was no mention of six wooden cases with dried plants. Nor indeed is there in the inventory taken by Banks's servant John Gold on 22 November 1803, beyond the two damaged trunks containing specimens of plants. But William Cole on 17 June had already taken a gloomy view as he inspected what he found on *L'Union*

> ... The Hortus Siccus, from not having originally been properly packed is much mutilated and many Specimens destroyd in all probability: and thus I fear will be lost to M. Deschamps & History, a great deal of his Herculean Labors ...

For more than ten years no more was done, or perhaps could have been done. Then, with Napoleon confined on Elba and a king on the throne of France again, Deschamps was moved on 14 June 1814 to write to Banks again seeking his lost collections, though the letter did not arrive at Soho Square till the winter by the hand of a Mr Timothy Topping. It was through Topping that Banks sent a reply on 7 April 1815, the last he ever sent to Deschamps on the subject and the last word that perhaps Deschamps himself ever had on the fate of his possessions. Banks had organized a search in the warehouses of the East India Company Custom House without result. Hearing no more from that quarter on the matter he had assumed that all was well. Not all was lost, however, for at some time after his return from China in 1831, John Reeve of the East India Company, bought at a sale in India House the diary, drawings and other manuscripts belonging to the Java years of Louis Deschamps. Today some 271 drawings with the manuscripts lie in the British Museum (Natural History) but of the plant specimens nothing now is known.

II

As HMS *Investigator* sailed down the Channel in July 1801 in pursuit of Nicolas Baudin and his small army of French savants aboard the *Géographe* and *Naturaliste*, the administration of Henry Addington was posing Banks with new problems. Changes at the Home Office bearing on the future course of the British expedition were underway, as Charles Greville hinted in his letter to Robert Brown sent by HMS *Buffalo* on 14 January 1802

> ... the confinement of S[ir] Jos. B[anks] to his bed for this month past has prevented him from setting the new department of State, to which the colonies are since Mr. Addington's administration alotted, to work ...

But these were only the first of many departmental hazards through which Banks had to navigate a passage at home before the *Investigator* expedition could fulfil its purpose. For 30 years the Banksian correspondence had been deeply concerned with the future of British settlement on the Australian continent and especially from 1800 to 1810 during the chequered course of the command vested in Matthew Flinders – the voyage itself, his long imprisonment on the Isle de France (Mauritius), his return and publication of *A Voyage to Terra Australis* . . ., the work of his civilian associates in the fields of art and science leading especially to the *Prodromus Florae Novae Hollandiae* . . . of Robert Brown. This burden stemmed primarily from the two important documents Banks had drafted in 1801 as the expedition was being mounted: first, the 'Hints, respecting the Rout that may be pursued with advantages by the *Investigator* discovery ship' for Lord Spencer, First Lord of the Admiralty, in late January 1801; second, the 'Memorandum of agreement signed by all the persons employed as scientific assistants on board HM Ship the *Investigator*, for the purpose of exploring the country of New Holland' at Soho Square on 29 April 1801 in his presence as the official witness.

The first paper contained the eight salient points which were incorporated almost verbatim in the Admiralty's 'Instructions for the Voyage of H.M. Sloop *Investigator*' signed by the three commissioners, St Vincent, T. Trowbridge, and J. Markham, on 22 June 1801, supplemented by Banks's later detailed instructions relating to the fitting up and use of the plant cabin on the quarter deck. There was however a preamble in which Banks analysed the probable intentions of the Baudin expedition, the passport for which he had negotiated with the British Government during June 1800. He had been highly suspicious of the intentions stated by the French in their application for safe conduct, which he said was

> . . . to be the discovery of the N.W. Portion of New Holland, a part of the Coast better known to navigators than any other . . .

and this, in short, he assumed to be a 'political manoeuvre' to conceal the real purpose of the voyage. He then speculated on the possibility that Flinders could reach his destination along the southern coast of New Holland before the French, late though his start would be, assuming that Baudin had orders 'to touch at the Isles of France & Bourbon'. In this Banks's judgement was shrewd, for by the six weeks spent at Mauritius among the unsettled and unhelpful colonists Baudin lost vital time which in the end delayed his appearance along the southern Australian coast. This, with other changes in the French plan, left Flinders uninterrupted in his charting until the shock of the meeting in Encounter Bay on 8–9 April 1802. In a sense the long gamble had succeeded and the *Investigator* had balked the French of all but some 400 miles in their charting of the southern coast westward from about Cape Banks – the interval between what Lt James Grant had covered in the *Lady Nelson* in 1800 and what Flinders had completed from January to April 1802. The French had also been preempted by the English in settling that vexed geographical conundrum common to the instructions of both expeditions, as Banks had suspected, to investigate that part of the southern coastline, in the words of Baudin's orders

> '. . . where it was supposed that a Strait existed communicating from the bottom of the Gulf of Carpentaria, which in consequence, would have cut New Holland in two great islands of practically equal size.'

For the *Investigator* there was much more to be done about the Australian coasts, as also for the *Géographe* and the *Naturaliste*, but effectively by that brief April meeting in 1802 the strategic race had been run and any French hopes for settling on the west of New Holland, whether an island or not, had greatly dimmed. The magnitude of their scientific discoveries however remained a rich and increasing harvest to the credit of the planning committee of the Institut National. It was, nevertheless, only to survive and return to France intact partly by the saving hospitality of Governor King to the *Géographe* at Port Jackson between June and November 1802, and partly by the intervention of Banks in securing the safe passage of the captured *Naturaliste* and its collections during May 1803.

The second document was altogether a more unusual affair. In framing it Banks had Evan Nepean as Secretary to the Admiralty, the key official with whom he had to deal. Nepean for his part had in Banks a man with whom he had long been accustomed to work during his years as under-secretary in the Home Department and to whom he was now ready to delegate the main decisions relating to the voyage as far as this lay within his power and status in the Admiralty. This unorthodox place of unique trust Banks occupied discreetly, always observing with care the forms of Admiralty practice in courteous deferment to Nepean and his staff even though in effect the final decision was his own. Thus, the draft of the 'Instructions . . .' for Flinders was submitted for his approval and suggestions, based as they were on his own 'Hints . . .' to the First Lord and supplemented as they were with his own additions about the management of the plant cabin during April made to Nepean:

'. . . I have added at the End my Ideas about the management of the Plant Cabbin & I submit that it will not be improper to [include] Either that or something Else in the orders You remember how the King's interest & that of Science which were Embarkd together in a Plant Cabbin on board Vancouvers Ship was abusd'

So when it came to establishing the terms and conditions of engagement 'in the undertaking of the Scientific men to be employd' Nepean replied to Banks's customary enquiry

Any proposal you make will be approved. The whole is left entirely to your decision.

Thus by 16 April Banks had fixed the status and salaries of the five civilian 'scientific people': Robert Brown, naturalist, £420; William Daniel (replaced before sailing by William Westall), landscape and figure draughtsman, £315; Ferdinand Bauer, botanic draughtsman, £315; Peter Good, gardener, £105; John Allen, miner, £105. On 28 April the final 'memorandum of agreement' was ready for signing on Banks's terms. Apart from making clear the chain of command and the level of co-operation expected it stressed that the salary paid to each person was in full compensation for his time and that all journals, drawings, collections of all kinds, as well as notes and sketches, were to be delivered on the return of the expedition 'to such Persons as their Lordships shall direct to receive them'. But the memorandum also contained sections relevant to the commander as well as to the 'scientific people', drawing the personnel together under one mantle

That if the information collected during the Voyage is deemed of sufficient importance, it is their Lordships intention to cause it to be published in the form of a Narrative drawn up by the Commander, on a Plan similar to that pursued in the Publication of Captain Cook's [third] Voyage and to give such pecuniary assistance as their Lordships shall see fitting for the Engraving of Charts, Plans, Views, Figures &ca. and that in such case the most interesting observations of Natural History & the most remarkable Views of Land & delineations of People &ca. will be inserted therein –

It was further stated that the profit from the sale of such a publication would be divided between the commander and the assistants

... in proportion to the good Conduct each shall have held during the Voyage, and the comparative advantage the Publication shall in the Opinion of their Lordships derive from the Labours of each individual –

Thereafter when all the official demands had been met and the Admiralty thought fit, and provided everything was considered public property

... the remainder of the descriptions of Plants and animals &ca. and the Scetches of all Kinds shall be at the disposal of the Persons who made them, for the purpose of being Published by them whenever it is thought proper at their own risque, and for their own advantage ...

Peter Good raised one slight note of dissension at Kew on 6 May saying that, by his recollection of what had been read and explained at Soho Square the week before, he and John Allen were supposed to deliver all their collections to Robert Brown whose immediate property they would become. The misunderstanding was resolved and the expedition set out with a reasonably well laid foundation of mutual understanding.

During the course of the voyage Banks was kept as well informed of its progress as the Admiralty could manage within the limitations imposed by such distant and unfrequented waters. The first reports were from Flinders at Cape Town in October 1801, the next from him at Port Jackson in May 1802, supplemented by reports from Governor King about the *Investigator*'s arrival and the concurrent presence of the *Géographe* and the *Naturaliste*. From Robert Brown to Banks came his first letter of the voyage dated 30 May with his progress in collecting, and that of Ferdinand Bauer in illustrating, a commendation of Peter Good but silence on William Westall and John Allen. However he had much to say about his conversations with the French on *Naturaliste*, especially Jean Leschenault de la Tour the botanist, of whom he gave a glowing account and from whom he sent a list of those remaining on both ships, the dead, and those who had disembarked at Port Louis. Leschenault was the only botanist on either vessel still aboard. This check-list Banks eventually sent in a letter to Louis Dufresne at the Jardin des Plantes on 8 February 1803. On the subject of his own plant collection Brown was inclined to be gloomy, with no more than 300 new species to report among 750 observed. He was even more concerned about his depleted paper supply and the impossibility of getting more at Port Jackson. So he begged Dryander to send him eight reams of Imperial brown which he had found superior to cartridge.

From Flinders Banks received a long letter dated 20 May, struck off while he laboured to complete his charts for the Admiralty, setting out their main features, assessing the extent of the French discoveries, commending Governor King for his helpful preparations in refitting the *Investigator* for the northern survey with the *Lady Nelson*, and especially praising Robert Brown and Ferdinand Bauer for their abilities and application. The first phase of the expedition was now ended.

On 22 July 1802 Flinders left Port Jackson with his two vessels to pursue the survey for which the partnership had been designed in principle four years before by Banks, Governor Hunter and the Admiralty. It was not to survive more than three months. Flinders in an analytical letter of 18 October to Governor King explained the technical reasons, apart from the damage to her main sliding keel which had so changed her sailing qualities, why he sent the *Lady Nelson* back to Port Jackson. Brown also took advantage of this to send a short report to Banks as the vessels parted near the Cumberland Isles. The voyage to Timor was a sequence of hard decisions as the important survey of the Gulf of Carpentaria was made during November, a race against the expected north-west monsoon with a ship that was now too evidently rotting away. When the *Investigator* reached Timor on 31 March 1803, after Flinders had reluctantly left the Australian coast at Cape Arnhem, the health of the expedition was as much at risk as the fabric of the ship. Apart from the heat of a tropical summer, scurvy had now appeared after nine months on the Spartan rations that were all that could be supplied at Sydney. Flinders then spent eight days at Koepang gathering what provisions he could and then sailed on a long sweep west and south into the Australian Bight, pausing only at Middle Island in the Recherche Group before reaching Port Jackson again on 9 June 1803. Dysentery had added its ravages and among its victims was Peter Good on 19 June, while Flinders and Brown slowly recovered from their scurvy. The second and last phase of the *Investigator*'s voyage, under the command of Matthew Flinders, ended with the ship being condemned as unfit for sea and the striking of the pennant on 22 July 1803. The *Investigator* had not lasted the course as Flinders had warned Banks before the voyage and as he could not forbear repeating in his letter to Soho Square from Timor on 28 March 1803. But the notion of waiting for second ship from England was not acceptable and after discussions over alternatives, Governor King put HMS *Porpoise* at Flinders's disposal for the passage home, with Lt Fowler of the *Investigator* in command. Of the civilians, only William Westall elected to sail with Flinders and so experience the rigours of survival on Wreck Reef, with the slight damage and loss among his drawings before returning by way of China and India in February 1806. Robert Brown, Ferdinand Bauer, John Allen, and Inman, the astronomer, who had replaced Crossley, elected to remain in the colony for the time being. Allen soon found his stay unprofitable and elected for Canton in the *Rolla* with Westall, eventually to reach England in the *Henry Addington* on 17 August 1804 in charge of the plant collection from William Kerr. Ferdinand Bauer took advantage of a passage in the *Albion* whaler to visit Norfolk Island where he stayed from September 1804 until February 1805. Robert Brown in November 1803 made what he thought was to be no more than a three-month's visit to Tasmania in the *Lady Nelson* but found it stretched to nine months before he could return to Sydney in August 1804, having botanized along the Tamar River in the north, the Derwent in the south, the Kent Group in Bass Strait, and along the margins of Port Phillip. From Sydney, in spite of ill-health, Brown visited the Hunter River to the north and the Hawkesbury and the

Government House at Sydney, 1802, as it was during the terms of Governors Hunter, King and Bligh. Drawing by William Westall, ARA made at the time of the first visit of HMS *Investigator*, May–July 1802.

Grose rivers to the west, before settling to the arrangement and packing of his specimens in readiness for the sailing of the strangely reincarnated *Investigator* in May 1805 under Captain William Kent. After nearly five months of unbroken sailing from Sydney, Brown and Bauer landed at Liverpool on 13 October 1805, one week before the battle of Trafalgar, with their collections and drawings in good order and George Caley's journal of his Blue Mountain exploration as far west as Mount Banks.

III

The frustrations, the losses and the discomforts of the civilian complement of the *Investigator* were minor themes beside the tragic last decade in the life of its young commander. For Matthew Flinders there was to be no easy return to quiet cartography. The Peace of Amiens, which Banks had assessed as 'merely an armed Truce & a very Troublesome one', had broken down, as he wrote to Flinders on 10 April 1803

> ... I think therefore I may fairly give you hopes (however little I may wish it) that when you return we shall be at war & a chance of Employment in the Favorite Capacity of a Seaman will be waiting for you

418

But none of this was seen by Flinders before he sailed from Sydney in the *Cumberland* after his hopes and the course of his life had shattered in the wreck of HMS *Porpoise* on 17 August 1803. The ship that had brought the young Suttor family to a successful if arduous future based on the garden plant survivors in its greenhouse had now, by its loss, darkened the future of another young married man. Most but not quite all the careful charts and all the logs were saved, most of the drawings, but none of the growing plants, none of Brown's first selection of dried specimens in their puncheons, nor any of the seeds in their marked boxes. All but three of the crew had survived to be rescued and the leaky 29-ton substitute set out for the precarious return to England carrying the papers that were enough in the state of war revived on 17 May 1803 to ensure the end of its voyage at Port Louis, Mauritius, when Flinders arrived there five months later. From 17 December began the long years of confinement and frustration for Flinders, torments beyond the expectations of those whom Banks conjured into expeditions under the shelter of the passports he managed to provide.

Within six months of the first encounter between Decaen and Flinders, Banks had deduced from a variety of sources that something had gone wrong with his strategy for the cartography of the land mass known as New Holland. Flinders had written several times to Banks from Port Louis but none of these letters had reached Soho Square with a first-hand account of what had occurred when Banks attempted to ease Ann Flinders's distress at the rumours she had heard. In his letter of 4 June 1804 Banks gave her a good picture of what in fact had happened, based on conjectures from the official papers he had seen, but not with any final detail of how her husband came to be in the hands of the French. There was every reason, he said, to believe that he would be well treated and would soon be returnd on one of the prisoner cartels slowly becoming a practice in those eastern seas, adding

> . . . I am as anxious to see your Gallant & Excellent husband as any of his best
> Friends can be, he has done much since he was employd in his Last expedition to
> increase my Regard for him & nothing which can in any way diminish it
>   his Present Misfortune is one of the Calamaties of war which you & I must bear
> with as much patience as we can muster . . .

In this new ordeal, these were some of the first words of continuing comfort which Ann was to receive from the man who had, on the face of it, so heartlessly intervened in her romantic flight of fancy three years before when she had hoped to sail with her new husband in the *Investigator*, but was obliged to leave the ship at Spithead. They were the first of a long line of warm gestures which never failed as Banks bent all his energies toward gaining the release and later the professional advance of her husband.

As he wrote to Ann Flinders, Banks himself was at a low ebb. He had two days before revealed to Lord Liverpool his intention to retire from all public business and in particular from the Privy Council Committee for Trade. However his hope to remain useful to science, agriculture, horticulture and the management of his own estates was underlined by his visits immediately after to the Sheep Shearings at Woburn Abbey and Holkham Hall, his preparation of the printed report on the King's Spanish Merino flock and the arrangements for its shearing as well as the sudden decision for a public sale at Kew on 15 August. But he was not deflected from active concern with the problem of Flinders's captivity, made more difficult now by the changes in the administration as William Pitt came to office for the last time. William Marsden had replaced Evan Nepean as Secretary at the Admiralty but on 6 August he had nothing to add to what Banks already knew. Lord Camden had replaced Lord Hobart as Secretary for War and the Colonies and when Banks approached him on the subject, was content on 10 August to allow him a free hand in his attempts to obtain the liberation of Flinders by a direct request through the Institut National. So on 22 August Banks put the case to the Secretary Jean Delambre, in a plea, apart from more formal arguments, for the release of Flinders as an act of reciprocity for the hospitable treatment accorded by Governor King to Baudin and Hamelin at Port Jackson. It was the start of a six-year tussle to free the man who, from his captivity even then was writing to him in these terms

> ... although I cannot rival the immortalized name of Cook, yet if persevering industry, joined to what ability I may possess, can accomplish it, then will I secure the second place, if you, Sir Joseph, as my guardian genius will but conduct me into the place of probation. The hitherto obscure name of Flinders may thus become a light by which even the illustrious character of Sir Joseph Banks may one day receive an additional ray of glory. As a satellite of Jove I may reflect back splendour to the gracious primary who, by shining upon me, shall give lustre to my yet unradiated name.
>
> But this is visionary ... the thought is bitterness.

Such hyperbole, proportional to the frustration of caged ambition, was unnecessary even had it reached Banks before he had taken action. Banks did not receive Delambre's letter of 5 March until 10 April 1805 conveying the Institut's recommendation for the release of Flinders, nor was it until 22 October that the captive himself had it from Banks in a letter of 20 June.

By degrees however the charts, the papers and the letters found their way through the obstructions of Decaen and the repatriated civilian detainees to Banks and the Admiralty in London and to King at Port Jackson. At some time during 1805 Banks had received a letter from Flinders dated 31 December 1804 recording the despatch of 'my general chart of Australia' some two months before. This had gone, with letters for William Marsden at the Admiralty, by the hand of Walter Robertson, a surgeon of the East India Company, released from internment to return to England by way of America. In the chart and the letter Flinders had now presented in the one word 'Australia', perhaps for the first time, the geographical reality of the island continent which it had been the intention of his voyage and that of Baudin to resolve. New Holland and New South Wales were one land mass. There was no dividing strait, and all the relevant charts that came to Banks he passed on to the Hydrographic Office at the Admiralty under Alexander Dalrymple. But there was food also for the Royal Society and printing for William Bulmer in the *Philosophical Transactions* in the letter from Flinders to Banks dated 5 March 1804 and that dated 19 August 1805, to be read on 28 March 1805 and 27 March 1806 respectively, and to appear to the world in successive volumes as 'Concerning the differences in the magnetic needle, on board the Investigator, arising from an alteration in the direction of the ship's head' and 'Observations on the marine barometer, made during the examination of the coasts of New Holland and New South Wales, in the years 1801, 1802 and 1803'. Then at last

420

there seemed also, as the year 1806 ended, a definite prospect that Flinders would be released as Banks conveyed the hopeful news to Ann on 29 December. After many refusals Napoleon had put Flinders's case to the Council of State, and on 11 March an order for his release had been signed. Three copies of the order were sent from Paris on 21 March 1806 for despatch to Mauritius at the first opportunity and later in the year Banks himself had received a fourth copy which he had placed with the Admiralty to be sent to the English commander in the eastern seas for operation under a flag of truce should the other fail. The long wait seemed about to end.

IV

From Revesby Abbey on 19 October 1805, Banks commented briefly to William Marsden at the Admiralty on the substance of what Robert Brown had announced to him on 13 October from Liverpool

> The Cases of natural history Sent home by our adventurers are sufficiently numerous to do credit to their diligence, They have been Employd to gather the Harvest from the Boundless Fields of nature & have reapd plentifully, I am much mistaken however if some of the indefatigable Sons of Revolutionary France have not sent home more Tonnage in Collections from Small Countries than ours have done from the immense & untrodden Continent of New Holland . . . Those taken from the Circumnavigators who went in Search of La Peyrouse & afterwards restored to them, were Certainly much more extensive as I well know who had them some time in my Custody . . .

From this point he advised Marsden to entrust the care of the collections to Brown and Bauer for the time being until inventories had been made, a business he was prepared to superintend if it was approved. He then drew attention to the precedents of the draughtsmen for Cook's second and third voyages who were retained for some time in the public service after their return until they had finished and delivered the pictures required by the Admiralty. On this basis he then proposed that Brown should be employed to work on the natural history collections and Bauer in finishing the most interesting of his sketches. He was still at Revesby Abbey suffering from gout when Dryander, on 7 November, announced that Brown and Bauer had arrived at Soho Square, that the collections were on the road from Liverpool under the care of Brown's servant and were expected to arrive on Monday 11 November. They had reported at the Admiralty but saw no one 'as the good news yesterday would too much occupy them'. This was plausible enough as the 'good news' was the arrival of despatches with the first word of the victory at Trafalgar, overshadowed though it was by the loss of Nelson.

By the middle of January 1806 Brown had settled into residence at 9 Gerrard Street in his triple capacity of librarian, clerk and housekeeper to the Linnean Society while Banks was slowly recovering from his long attack of gout. So it was not until 25 January that Banks was able to give Marsden his first full assessment of what the civilians had brought back from the *Investigator* voyage. Under Brown's supervision the collections were at the first estimate: 3400 plant species from New Holland and New South Wales, 200 from Timor or 3600 in all; dried skins of birds, about 150; quadrupeds, most damaged by insects or lost in the wreck of the *Porpoise*; insects, one

421

case; minerals, 3 boxes. From Ferdinand Bauer, under Brown's supervision also, had come 1541 plant drawings from New Holland and New South Wales, 80 from Norfolk Island, 60 from Timor, and 89 from the Cape of Good Hope; of animals some 273 from New Holland and New South Wales and 40 from Norfolk Island; altogether an array complete with the fine detail from plant dissections and a colour chart prepared for the sketches to be finished accurately at leisure; a body of recording art which Banks, with his memory of Parkinson's industry, assessed as beyond what he thought it possible to perform.

In placing his scheme before the Admiralty 'for bringing to public use' Brown's collections and Bauer's drawings, Banks reckoned that three years would be required for arranging the plants 'properly in systematic order' and to finish the 'most interesting of the Scetches'. However he recommended that the salaries of both men should be continued without a stipulated term, reserving the power to extend or terminate as circumstances dictated. All Brown's collections were then at Soho Square but Bauer, during Banks's illness, had taken his drawings away.

> ... I must therefore request their Lordships to give particular orders to Mr. Bauer to return these Scetches to me, that they may be kept in my House, not only for the sake of secure Custody, but because it is absolutely necessary that Mr. Brown who does all his business in my Library, should have before him the Scetch of every Plant during the time it is under Examination, lest some misunderstanding of the Structure of those minute parts, on which systematic arrangement depends, should have taken place either on his part or that of Mr. Bauer, as not infrequently happens to the most expert naturalist, in such case Mr. Brown & Mr. Bauer must consult together till they agree in the same opinion, which can never fail to happen with Persons well versd in the Science of Botany. this is the only mode by which it is possible to prevent an occasional variation between the Drawings & the Description, which never fails to throw a great deal of discredit on all the parties concerned.

Aware also that Bauer would be reluctant to be parted from the creations of his hand and eye for the handling that this would imply, Banks pointed to the fact that the Parkinson and other drawings from the *Endeavour* voyage had sustained and survived 33 years of such use in a satisfactory state.

Then, as to the matter of publication envisaged in the original memorandum of agreement, he recommended that Brown and Bauer should join in preparing periodical groups of engravings and descriptions

> ... there being every reason to hope that such a work will, if conducted with prudence & economy be a source of profit to these Gentlemen as long as they are able to supply new Subjects either beautiful to the Eye or interesting to Science, and as such an undertaking may be at any time abandoned whenver it shall appear by a decrease of its Sale, that the Public ceases to take a proper interest in its continuation.

With this submission he presented his account for the carriage of the specimen collections, drawings and personal effects of Brown and Bauer from Liverpool to London with the Custom House and other incidental charges – a sum of £87.8s.od.

These were approved and minuted under the signature of William Marsden on 25 January 1806 – the Navy Board to reimburse Sir Joseph; Brown and Bauer to receive their respective salaries until further order, subject to certificates being produced from time to time by the President of the Royal Society; and their Lordships generally agreeing to all the arrangements that Banks had proposed.

The drawings of William Westall, damaged with the salt water on Wreck Reef, had come home in the care of Lt Robert Fowler in August 1804 with 12 puncheons of Brown's dried plant specimens. Both collections were delivered to Banks for unpacking and inspection. The drawings were passed to Westall's elder brother, Richard Westall, RA for such conservation as he thought necessary and then returned to the Admiralty to await the artist's return the next year. Thus by the summer of 1806 all the civilians were at work under the supervision of Banks at Soho Square. Only the commander of the *Investigator* remained a lonely prisoner on the Île de France with not one but four orders for his release signed and by various paths on their ineffective way. The essense of his work had come home by the hand of Aken, the ailing master of the *Investigator*, in his long memorandum 'A Memoir explaining the marks used in the Charts of Australia constructed on board his Majestys ship *Investigator*, ... With some new facts and additional observations upon these and other nautical subjects connected with Australia', in five chapters with another three by a different route later. Of these the fifth and the eighth, as letters to Banks, had claimed their places in the *Philosophical Transactions* of 1805 and 1806 while the first, 'Of the restitution of the name Australia or Terra Australis . . .', had set its seal on the shape of maps to come.

V

In the peace of the Scottish Border hills there was to be no peace of mind for Mungo Park. The soft arms of his Ailie and 'a life of indolence' on the proceeds of the book of his first journey to the Niger receded against the lure of a distant fame through the patronage of Banks. In 1800 Britain had acquired Goree Island near the modern Dakar and Park lost no time in reminding Banks of its importance as a portal to the African interior. But a year earlier on 29 May 1799 Banks had formulated the strategy of the West African coast to the African Association and presented it on 8 June to Lord Liverpool for the Cabinet as a memorandum composed by Lord Moira and himself. It was a curious amalgam of theories on river gold recovery based on the Wicklow Mountain finds of 1795 and similar wealth from African streams, the establishment of a trading company with a Christian mission and the reduction of slavery founded 'upon the principles of natural justice and commercial benefit'. He concentrated the issue to Lord Liverpool

> . . . Should the undertaking be fully resolved upon the first step of Government must be to secure to the British throne, either by Conquest or by Treaty the whole of the Coast of Africa from Arguin to Sierra Leone; or at least to procure the cession of the River Senegal, as that River will always afford an easy passage to any rival nation who means to molest the Countries on the banks of the Joliba . . .

Of the military hazards with a 'rival nation' he had his own involvement to recall in the experiences of the Sierra Leone Company and of his Swedish protégé, Adam

423

Afzelius, in the French attack on Freetown in April 1794. Now, in effect, the British attack on Goree in 1800 had declared the unity of the Government with Banks as the voice of the African Association. The colonialism of trade expansion and the exchange of natural resources with manufactured goods in the struggle for national survival was developing into imperial rivalry with motives far removed from earlier pretensions. If Flinders was in some measure a sacrifice on this altar in the South Pacific then Mungo Park was its victim in Africa and Banks their high priest. Each young man was a willing devotee of the faith which killed him and both were in part consumed by their own ambition for a hero's fame. Mungo Park had tasted some of this pleasure and some of its material rewards in the accomplishment of his first journey. Matrimonial bliss however could not smother his ambition and his attempted compromise with Ailie early in 1801 as emigration to New South Wales failed. Banks still viewed Park and Flinders as a partnership in the exploration of New Holland and the solution of its geographic mysteries, but shared fame has an insipid flavour for aspiring heroes. The qualified picture which Banks sketched of life in the new colony may have been partly responsible for his return to Scotland in October 1801 'a little down-hearted', with the romantic village of his fancy in New Holland for himself and his family quite expunged. He now found himself as a country surgeon for a year or two in a small house just off the market centre of Peebles but still looking to Banks as his 'particular friend' from whom he yet hoped he might achieve 'a more eligible situation'.

Then in 1802 the literature of France, with which Banks was on terms of easy familiarity, yielded a spark to the prepared tinder at Soho Square. Banks had already been in discussion with the Colonial Office about the course of African discovery and the prospects of colonization when he encountered Sylvester de Golbéry's *Fragments d'un Voyage en Afrique*, 1802. Written by a former aide-de-camp to the Governor of Senegal, this was, in the view of Banks as he wrote on 1 August to John Sullivan, under-secretary at the Colonial Office, intended to encourage the French to colonize the whole region of Senegambia. This aim Banks thought the book would certainly promote if not actually bring about. In it de Golbéry laid down a French claim to the whole coastline of West Africa from Cape Blanco to Cape Palmas based on its discovery and settlement by the Normans in 1364. Banks concluded with a heavy emphasis

> ... I am clear that His Majesties Ministers should be aware of the contents, and hold in mind what will happen, which is that whoever Colonizes in that part of Africa with Spirit will Clearly be able to sell Colonial Products of all kinds in the European market at a Cheaper price than any part of the West Indies can afford it ...

This stimulated a memorandum prepared by John Sullivan on the development of British trade to foil French intentions in the area with the establishment of factories at the navigable limits of the Gambia. Then, as a Privy Councillor, Banks was called away from Spring Grove to a meeting at Weymouth where the royal family was in residence for the summer. The Council met on Monday 16 August and it is probable that West Africa was on the agenda. The occasions were few on which Banks posted so far on the King's business.

Plans for an armed expedition seem to have been laid but no firm decision reached until May 1803. In October Lord Hobart wrote to Banks asking him to summon Park to London for a discussion in Downing Street. On 10 October Banks sent this message on to Peebles with a broad hint that an expedition likely to be much to Park's taste was afoot. On 20 October Park had been to London, had been offered the leadership of another expedition to the Niger and was then able to write to Banks from Stilton on his way to Scotland to consult his Ailie once again before deciding on another long and dangerous separation. But any such scheme was cast in abeyance by the fall of the Addington administration in the spring of 1804 and it was not until the autumn that Lord Camden as the new Secretary for War and the Colonies revived the subject with Banks and the encouragement of William Pitt, on 28 September. The Hobart plan was reduced under Camden who said to Banks

> . . . It bears so much the description of a Journey of Enquiry without any military attendance upon it, that it seems to me more fit that Mr. Park should be instructed as to his Enquiries and Researches by those who have turned their Mind to this subject as much as you have done than by me; . . .

In October Park returned to London where he developed a memorandum expounding a new theory of the Niger's course involving its confluence with the Congo. This was derived from the ideas of George Maxwell, a former African trader at the mouth of the Congo, and it had the support of Banks but not of Major James Rennell who did his best to dissuade Park from the expedition altogether as too dangerous. But Banks, in his annotations on Park's paper, had his own stern philosophy

> . . . I am aware that Mr. Park's expedition is one of the most hazardous a man can undertake; but I cannot agree with those who think it too hazardous to be attempted: it is by similar hazards of human life alone that we can hope to penetrate the obscurity of the internal face of Africa: we are really wholly ignorant of the country between the Niger and the Congo, and can explore it only by incurring the most frightful hazards . . .

Of all this Mungo Park himself was under no illusion and it was perhaps with a prevision of his fate that he shirked a formal parting from his family when he left for London pretending that he was bound only for Edinburgh twenty miles away. Park and the nucleus of his party did not sail until 31 January 1805. They left Portsmouth on board the troopship *Crescent*, with his young brother-in-law, Alexander Anderson, as second in command. At home another brother-in-law, James Dickson, had their power of attorney. Helped by Banks, he had submitted a memorial to the Treasury covering the payment of the sums on which the Government had agreed should nothing be heard of the party in two and-a-half years – £3000 to Aileen Park and £1000 to Dr Anderson, her father on behalf of Alexander.

The tragedy of Mungo Park's second and last expedition to the Niger is entrenched in the history of West Africa, embroidered with a few myths, its visible relics only an Emir's staff in Nigeria and a *Nautical Almanac* in Kensington Gore. Unlike the story of Flinders this was not an account over which Banks would preside as the guardian of its publication, nor the African Association as the midwife at its birth. Its story, incomplete and uncertain to the end, came to the public a year after *A Voyage to Terra Australis* . . . as the *Journal of a Mission to the Interior of Africa* . . ., 1815, confided by the Government to the auspices of the African Institution, the descendant of the Sierra Leone Company, under the mantle of William Wilberforce, a foster-parentage with which Banks expressed himself content.

CHAPTER 20

FINE WOOL AND FAR PASTURES
1801–1812

The summer of 1801 was marked by a small event that heralded the beginning of
Great Britain's rise as the mistress of the nineteenth-century world wool trade. On 9
July Banks delivered to Henry Lacocke, wool stapler of Bermondsey, '8 Fleeces from
N.S.Wales to be examind and Reportd upon'. Together that day they had examined
the first few pounds of authentic fine wool to come from Australia and the sheep of
Captain John Macarthur, under the care of the retiring Governor John Hunter in
HMS *Buffalo*, sent by Governor King 'for the opinion of Sir Joseph Banks, President
of the Royal Society'. In the form of Henry Lacocke's report, this 'opinion' had been
sent out in HMS *Glatton*, Captain James Colnett to be published in *The Sydney Gazette
and New South Wales Advertiser*, volume I, No. 4, 26 March 1803. Of this the essence
was

> . . . if they could preserve Nos. 1 and 2 for their breed in the colony, I think they
> may make good progress in their breed and wool.

These were from one old ewe imported from the Gordon flock at the Cape of Good
Hope in 1797 'said to be of the Spanish Breed' and her one-year old ram lamb and, as
fleeces, Henry Lacocke matched them closely with those of the Spanish Merino flock
at Kew and Windsor. A standard had been set for the colonial breeders on which
selection could be made.

Meanwhile the turbulent owner of these sheep was himself on his way to England
with other fleeces from his growing flock, to astonish the sceptical manufacturers of
Yorkshire and the West Country and the wool importers of the City. Captain John
Macarthur was returning under arrest for wounding in a duel at Parramatta his
commanding officer Lt-Col. William Paterson, FRS on 14 September 1801. Until his
arrival in London on 21 December 1802 he could not have known of the favourable
judgement which Banks and Lacocke had made on the wool from his flock at
Elizabeth Farm near the head of the harbour of Port Jackson. He had returned on
board the *Princess Charlotte*, Captain Richardson from Amboina in the Moluccas,
where he had taken charge of six cases of plant specimens from Christopher Smith
for delivery to Banks, another good reason for a meeting between the two men. They
did not meet because Banks was bed-ridden in one of his worst periods of gout. But
there was John Maitland of Basinghall Street as the knowledgeable importer of
Spanish fine wool and Banks's trusted helpmate in that field; and Henry Lacocke, by
now Banks's faithful disciple and custodian of the King's Spanish wool clip. With
their favourable opinions and their introduction to the clothiers from Yorkshire and
the western counties, Macarthur had ample encouragement to develop his plans. By
26 July 1803 his *Statement of the Improvement and Progress of the Breed of Fine-woolled*

Sheep in New South Wales had been prepared for John Sullivan in the Colonial Office. On 21 September this document, with the collected memorials of the wool manufacturers, was sent to Banks for an opinion by William Fawkener, the Privy Council's senior clerk. On 22 September from Revesby Abbey Banks sent his qualified reply to Fawkener, critical of what he thought were Macarthur's over-sanguine estimates of the fine quality of the pastures of New South Wales but suggesting that

> ... in the meantime their Lordships [of the Privy Council] may, if they see fitting examine such persons now in London as have been in N.S.Wales on the subject, & order Letters to be written to the governor, requiring from him the best information he shall be able to procure in the Colony, relative to the nature of the luxuriant pastures described by Capt. McArthur & their fitness in their natural state for the Pasturage of fine wooled sheep ...

The Privy Council Committee duly took evidence during the summer of 1804. Macarthur presented his *Memorial* ... of 4 May 1804, and on 14 July Stephen Cottrell, Clerk to the Privy Council, sent the Committee's judgement to Edward Cooke, under-secretary at the Colonial Office firmly entertaining

> ... no doubt that it is well deserving the attention of His Majesty's Government to encourage the produce of fine wool in the colony of New South Wales ...

However it conceded only the possibility of a conditional grant of lands to Macarthur or any joint company associated with him or any other individual, and then only with the benefit of more knowledge than was at hand. This was in line with the caution with which Banks continued to approach the question to which he was by instinct well disposed, in spite of ideas held to the contrary. He had in March 1804 expressed his view of the proposal to form a land company in which John Maitland and others were concerned with John Macarthur to cultivate the breed of fine-woolled sheep on a large scale, with a capital of £10000. He thought

> ... The Success of the Enterprise will manifestly be an advantage of no inconsiderable importance to the manufacturing interest of this Kingdom & Even in the Event of its Failure much benefit must arise to the infant Colony by the money that will be sent there for the purpose of trying the Experiment ...

The paths of the colony and the King's Spanish Merino flock were, under the influence of Banks converging rapidly as the day for the first public sale of the sheep was set for 15 August 1804 in 'the field south of the Pagoda' at Kew. Here out of the 44 sheep offered, Macarthur bought seven young rams and three old ewes. In doing so he had been warned by Banks of the provisions of the act 28 Geo.III, c.38, once the contentious Wool Bill of 1788, which laid an embargo on the export of sheep from the kingdom. This obstacle was surmounted on 5 October, when Lord Camden applied to the Treasury to allow their export, strongly supported by the Privy Council. He also recommended that a tract of land be granted to Macarthur specifically for the breeding of fine-woolled sheep. On 31 October Camden sent a direction to Governor King

... I am commanded by His Majesty to desire that you will have a proper grant of lands, fit for the pasture of sheep, conveyed to the said John Macarthur Esq., in perpetuity, with the usual reserve of quit rent to the Crown, containing not less than five thousand acres ...

With this negotiation complete, Macarthur sailed on board the *Argo* whaler on 29 November 1804 to enter Sydney Harbour on 7 June 1805 with his small nucleus of true Negretti Merinos of which only five rams and one old ewe survived to reach Elizabeth Farm.

Then, and only then, was the second part of Banks's advice to the Privy Council set on foot as Governor King on 27 July 1805 published his General Order

... Requiring the fullest Information being transmitted for the Lords Committee of the Privy Council for Trade and Plantations, Respecting the Increase and Improvement of the Breeds of Sheep with Growth and Improvement of Wool raised in this Territory; His Lordship [Camden] having also in the strongest manner recommended a general attention to that important national object ...

This first field survey of Australian livestock was made by the Revd Samuel Marsden, John Macarthur, and Edward Wood, the wool stapler who had come out on the *Argo*. On 10 October the Governor sent Lord Camden a full report satisfying the terms of enquiry which Banks had set out in his letter to William Fawkener just over two years before. And on 13 October King saw his way clear to order the convict assistant-surveyor James Meehan to measure out, in the vicinity of Mount Taurus along the Nepean River, the 5000 acres for John Macarthur as directed by the Secretary of State for War and Colonies.

There were also others who responded to the stimulus of the Golden Fleece emanating from the partnership of the King and Banks when *A Project for Extending the Breed of Fine Wooled Spanish Sheep, now in the possession of his Majesty* ... appeared in print in 1800. In New South Wales Marsden was assiduous in wool improvement and had written to Banks on 7 April 1803 with details of his flock and the opinions of others in the colony. He would be faithful to the task in his own way, less a pastoralist more a committed farmer than Macarthur, but a no less difficult character. At home the message was being read in Sussex by young Gregory Blaxland who, on 15 September 1804, had responded to the success of the public sale at Kew by seeking from Banks some old ewes and one or two ram lambs of the Spanish breed to cross among his flock of 300 Dorset sheep. Banks could only refer him to the next public sale but, in the interim, the vision changed for Blaxland. On 1 September 1805 he sailed for New South Wales as a free settler to occupy a grant at South Creek on the western fringe of the colony almost in the shadow of those blue mountains whose crossing he would be able to effect and report to Banks some ten years later.

II

Before Gregory Blaxland sailed in the *William Pitt* or John Macarthur had arrived in Port Jackson another man had been influenced by Banks in a way that would affect them both. As far back as 5 June 1802 Governor King had indicated to John King, under-secretary at the Home Office, that if Macarthur were allowed to return to the colony and rejoin the other 'turbulent characters' among the officers, then his own recall or permission to return might become necessary to avoid a worse situation. Now the point had filtered through to Lord Camden and on 21 April 1805 he felt constrained to tell King George that

> ... it might be advantageous to your Majesty's Colonies in New South Wales to permit Capt. Gidley King, the present Governor, to return to England when a proper successor should be found ...

He had not been successful in selecting any person fit and willing for the post until he had heard from Sir Joseph Banks 'so high a character of the ability and integrity of Capt. William Bligh' that he now presented him for consideration. On 22 April the King approved the choice of Bligh as Governor of New South Wales and ordered Camden to prepare the commission.

No one was more keenly aware than Banks of the cumulative stresses which had weakened King's resolve to remain at Port Jackson. Perhaps no one else either was as well informed about colonial society or so alert to the extra burden that John Macarthur would impose on his return, however laudable his intentions as a pastoralist with the Spanish breed. The nomination by Banks of Bligh as the next naval Governor was based on a variety of reasons but one at least seems to have been his recognition that a stronger character than the tiring King was likely to be needed in his place. Bligh had many qualities, apart from his wide Pacific experience which marked him as a reasonable choice in a war-torn world just before Trafalgar, but there were also elements in his personality, in the final terms of his commission, and in the curious social amalgam of the Sydney settlement, that concealed prospects of fulmination perhaps beyond the vision of a preoccupied administration so far away.

After an earlier conversation Banks received Lord Camden's agreement that Bligh should be offered the place of governor by a letter received on the morning of 19 April. He immediately clarified details about the payment of salary in a letter to James Chapman, under-secretary in Camden's office, and later the same day wrote to Bligh with a firm and specific offer. He had already cleared the way through the Admiralty by discussion with William Marsden through whom now he passed the letter to Bligh then commanding HMS *Warrior* at Torbay. Its terms were practical and their presentation compelling:

> ... I have always, since the first institution of the new colony in New South Wales, taken a deep interest in its success, and have been constantly consulted by His Majesty's Ministers, through all the changes there have been in the department which directs it, relative to the more important concerns of the colonists.
>
> At present, King, the Governor, is tired of his station; and well he may be so. He has carried into effect a reform of great extent, which militated much with the interests of the soldiers and settlers there. He is, consequently, disliked and much opposed, and has asked leave to return. In conversations I was this day asked if I knew a man proper to be sent out in his stead – one who had integrity unimpeached, a mind capable of providing its own resources in difficulties, without leaning on others for advice, firm in discipline, civil in deportment and not subject to whimper and whine when severity of discipline is wanted to meet emergencies. I immediately answered: As this man must be chosen from among the post

captains, I know of no one but Captain Bligh who will suit, but whether it will meet his views is another question.

He then laid out the income – £2000 a year – the possibility of savings, the marriage prospects for Bligh's daughters should the family go with him, and the prospects of a pension at the end of his service. The circumstances and the details were different but in principle Banks was presenting the same assessment of a task and its possibilities that he had applied so often before, – a statement of the facts, a realistic view of the future, and nothing more than he was prepared to defend and support until it was accomplished. Bligh knew from his past experience how well he could depend on Banks. The last paragraph condensed it all:

> . . . Tell me, dear Sir, when you have consulted your pillow, what you think of this. To me, I confess, it appears a promising place for a man who has entered late into the status of a post-captain, and the more so as your rank will go on, for Phillip, the first governor, is now an admiral, holding a pension for his services in the country.

One of Lord Camden's last acts in Bligh's case, before the advent of Visc. Castlereagh, was to confirm with the Admiralty on 4 June that

> . . . it is His Majesty's pleasure that your Lordships should grant him such powers as have been usually granted to the Governors of the rest of His Majesty's colonies and plantations.

But with Castlereagh there were some changes in detail and neither Bligh nor Banks were satisfied with the new conditions of the appointment. On 3 September Bligh warned Banks of possible dangers in the establishment of the post as that of a civil not a naval governor. Banks was sure that Lord Camden had given no such hint when he had first approached him for a nomination, and on 17 September 1805 replied from

> . . . Had I been aware that the naval command was not to be continued to the new Governor in the same extent as had been done in the cases of Phillip, Hunter, and King, and had I not perhaps speculated on the probability of more being entrusted to a man of your standing as a post-captain than was done in Governor King's case, I certainly should not have advised you to give up your ship for the appointment; in truth I have too high an opinion of your talents in arranging naval service to have advised you to a step which may in future be interpreted by our Admiralty into a dereliction of your chance of a flag.
>
> I trust, however, that if this is a measure of Cabinet which cannot be altered, that so much justice at least will be done to you as to preserve intire your claims to future promotion, which in the case of Governor Phillip has actually taken place . . .

Unable to do more from Revesby Abbey, Banks advised Bligh to consult Evan Nepean and Edward Cooke as men on whose friendship he could depend. But Bligh found the haunting of the offices in Whitehall fatiguing even though his case had the vigorous support of Earl St Vincent.

While Banks languished at Revesby Abbey 'in Gout', the battle of Trafalgar had been fought and the despatches announcing the victory had arrived at the Admiralty on 6 November. Dryander had sent this news to Banks on 7 November, telling him also of the arrival of Robert Brown and Ferdinand Bauer at Soho Square that day. On the same date Bligh also sent Banks an abstract of the official despatch with his own comment on the death of Nelson. But this was only a brief respite from the worried forebodings about the terms of the new governorship which continued intermittently until Bligh sailed, after long and irritating delays, from Spithead in February 1806 on board the *Lady Madelaine Sinclair* transport, under the convoy of yet another HMS *Porpoise*, Captain Joseph Short. The unhappy voyage – its quarrels well documented by Bligh's redoubtable daughter, Mary Putland – ended on 6 August. For Bligh the ordeal of the Rum Rebellion was close at hand. For Banks the ordeal of the 'Ministry of all the Talents' was already in full spate.

III

While Bligh swung at anchor off Spithead, cursing the French, the weather, and some of the terms of his governor's commission, William Pitt was dying. As the convoy for New South Wales at last set out, Pitt was dead and, on 10 February 1806, the administration under Lord Grenville had come to power. Charles James Fox was now at the Foreign Office; Charles Grey, soon to be Visc. Howick, was at the Admiralty; William Windham was Secretary for War and the Colonies; Earl Spencer was at the Home Office. With this array in the critical ministries the atmosphere for Banks had grown cold; only Lord Spencer remained as a warm centre. The change in the administrative climate was condensed in Banks's reply to Captain William Kent on 12 March 1806 regretting his inaction on Kent's petition for a land grant near Sydney

> . . . The reason was that I have not yet ventured to present myself at the Office for the Colonies since it has been occupied by its new inhabitants nor probably shall, not till I have some good reason to give for intruding myself or till they manifest a wish to see me. To do otherwise might be very detrimental to my hopes of Establishing with Mr. Windham the same sort of confidence in me as Ld. Camden Ld. Castlereagh & their Predecessors have favord me with.

Banks could not say that in William Windham he was faced again with the man who had over the years been his frequent opponent; however Windham soon sought Banks's advice, for the year 1806 saw a profusion of notes and memoranda relating to the colony of New South Wales.

Banks had in May 1805 submitted, through the Privy Council, a proposal for supplying a coinage, struck in silver and copper, as a circulating medium in place of the 'spirituous liquors' and the notes of individuals. With this he had recommended 'the establishment of a Government Bank of Exchange', the whole plan being conceived to prevent 'the depreciation of paper Money by the excessive issue of it' and to 'establish a depository of unquestionable security for monied property' which

432

would 'encourage individuals to open stores for the Sale of European Goods at a fair price & relieve Government of the unpleasant necessity of being Retail Traders' which was then unavoidable. He had also, during the same year, been drawn into the question of colonial trade by the customs seizure of the *Lady Barlow* in July 1805 and its cargo of 14000 seal skins, 260 tons of 'elephant' oil, and 100 tons of beefwood for cabinet making, the whole being the property of Robert Campbell and the first produce entirely gained by the enterprise of the colonists. Eventually the cargo was released – but for export only – by an agreement with the contesting East India Company and the tacit approval of the South Sea Whalers, the Enderbys and the Matthews. The debate, which stemmed from a reading of the original instruction in Governor King's commission about colonial trade, carried on into the new administration as the *Honduras* arrived in June 1806 with some 35000 fur seal skins, the property of Simeon Lord, emancipist merchant and shipbuilder. It continued over the ship *Sydney*, another Campbell property, expected to arrive with 50000 seal skins, 600 tons of oil, 300 tons of timber for ship building cabinet wood, and 4 masts for frigates. These three cases focused attention on colonial trade and its scope for growth against the restrictions which the East India Company imposed and sought to maintain. It faced Banks, both as an individual and as a member of the Privy Council, with questions of principle in international law and facts relating to the activities of colonial entrepreneurs such as Robert Campbell, Simeon Lord, and John Macarthur. He acquired his information on Robert Campbell from Captain William Wilson of Monument Yard, agent also for the Revd. Samuel Marsden, and a petitioner to the Privy Council for the admittance of the *Sydney* as a recognized trading vessel for customs purposes in London. On Simeon Lord and the background of the *Honduras* there was Captain Henry Waterhouse, RN (retd.), late commander of HMS *Reliance* and, until May 1805, owner of The Vineyard, a 200-acre farm on Duck Creek near Parramatta with its small flock of Spanish Merinos. On John Macarthur, apart from Waterhouse, there was also Captain William Kent, late commander of HMS *Investigator* on its last voyage home, an aspirant grantee as well as an owner of 1200 acres of well-stocked land in the colony.

It was fast becoming clear to Banks and others that the small penal settlement was moving into a new phase, that its material survival was assured but that its future was uncertain – apart from any wartime hazards or the increasing mercantilism of the Americans in the Pacific. Banks, under the mantle of the Privy Council on 30 June 1806, had intervened successfully in favour of William Wilson's plea for the admission of the *Sydney*'s cargo when it should arrive. In the process he had occasions to consult John Reeves, the King's printer and law clerk to the Board of Trade, on the shipping and navigation laws and the status of New South Wales as a crown possession in relation to their operation. He had excused himself to Reeves on 10 July

> ... I have taken some pains to gain a Superficial Knowledge of the Common & Statute Laws of the Kingdom but I have never Studied in any Shape the Practice of them. This I Leave to the Professors well knowing, as Politics with me is only allowd to fill up the intervals of Science, that I have no chance of finding Time Enough to make me even a bad much less a good lawyer.
>
> The Question I apprehend to be how far may the inhabitants of the new Settlements in N.S.W. navigate Ships built there according to Law in the atlantic &

as much of the Indian & Pacific oceans as the [East] India Company will allow them . . .

But he had already organized his thoughts on 7 July as 'Some observations on a bill for admitting the Produce of New South Wales to Entry at the Custom houses of the United Kingdom'. He had also, in the Privy Council submission to the Treasury on 30 June, lodged notice

> . . . that their Lordships intend without delay to Propose instructions for the future Government of the Shipping concerns of that Colony on a Plan suited to provide the inhabitants with the means of becoming by degrees Less & Less burthensome to the mother Country & Framd in such manner as to interfere as Little as Possible with the Trade the navigations or the Resources of the East India Company

This passage was already embodied and waiting in the manuscript hand of William Carlich with insertions and corrections by Banks dated 4 June 1806 and entitled: 'Some Remarks on the Present State of the Colony of Sidney, in New South Wales, and on the means most likely to render it a productive, instead of an expensive, settlement'. As such, by August it had passed into the hands of the Board of Trade presenting a plea for an indulgent policy towards the colony's commercial growth – in the seal fishery for fur and oil, in the trade possible with coal, *bêche de mer* or trepang, with sandalwood, with the production of fine wool, and eventually in the southern whale fishery. It was a moderate and well-argued defence of the colonial interest against the restrictive monopoly claimed by the East India Company with its exaggerated fears of colonial pirates, and it epitomized in its closing lines 'the future prospect of empires and dominions which cannot now be disappointed' with which, as a vision, he had rallied Governor Hunter over nine years before. Now he rallied the Government

> . . . It will give an opportunity to our countrymen to occupy in succession every desirable situation which might tempt other nations to colonise and lay the foundation of a claim which the lapse of time may hereafter mature of resisting the attempt of other countries to participate in the sovereignty of a mass of land great enough in point of extent to satisfy the ambition even of a French Emperor; and it must be remember'd that the district now propos'd to be open'd to the investigation of British adventure is about as unknown to civilis'd nations as an equal portion of the moon, and probably hides within its broad bosom objects of commerce, materials for manufacture, and sources of wealth of the utmost importance for the future welfare and prosperity of the United Kingdom.

What one of those 'objects of commerce' could be had by now become clear to Banks as he gathered information about the origins and progress of wool-growing sheep in New South Wales and of the Spanish Merino type and its derivatives. In his dual capacity as a Privy Councillor and sheep-breeder he was the point to and from which information in this field flowed. There is therefore no special animus in his gathering together from his enquiries, on 20 July 1806, of 'Some Circumstances respecting Capt Macarthur Late of the New South Wales Corps & of his Pretensions to extraordinary indulgence from Government on the Plea of having Raisd a Flock of fine woold Sheep at Sydney'. From many quarters it was becoming evident that Macarthur was now an important figure in the Sydney population of some 7000 and the very small group of rising merchants and pastoralists whose activities held the promise of rendering the colony 'a productive, instead of an expensive, settlement'. Macarthur had achieved an 'extraordinary indulgence', both in his permission to export the Spanish sheep from the royal flock and in the grant of 5000 acres near Mount Taurus along the Nepean River. Now there were other claimants for similar indulgences, such as the Blaxlands, both Gregory and John, and hence an urgency in establishing as many facts as possible for the guidance of the Government in London and Sydney. With Henry Waterhouse and William Kent both close at hand Banks had two of the most important sources of first-hand information about the recent state of the colony. Both had been the skilful seamen and the entrepreneurs who together in HM Ships *Reliance* and *Supply* had brought the small nucleus of Spanish Merino type sheep from the Gordon flock at Cape Town in 1797. As such they had been the sources from whom Macarthur and a few others had drawn their first fine-woolled stock. Both had been farmers in a moderate way and so were well-grounded in the practicalities of what Macarthur was now preaching with such force. Both were well-informed on the personalities important to the immediate future of the settlement under the terms in which Banks was attempting to assess it.

From this study emerged his paper on August 1806 – 'Observations on Sheep in New South Wales' – elaborating the reasons for his qualified but certainly not vindictive views on Macarthur's claims 'respecting fine wool', warning the Government that expectations might have been pitched too high. In his 'Remarks on the Present State of Sidney . . .' he had made clear his confidence that the true Merino breed would retain the superiority of its fleece and produce wool worth six shillings a pound when washed and scoured or £672 a ton and that

> . . . there can be no doubt that it will bear the necessary charges of freight, insurance, &c., and become in due time a profitable article of investment for a cargo from Port Jackson to London.

But he now analysed what could be expected from the approximate 21 000 sheep in the colony, compounded as they were of stock mostly derived from the Cape or the Indian sheep covered with hair rather than wool. Three or four generations at least, as he knew from his experience at Spring Grove, would be needed in crossing with the Spanish ram to attain a reasonable standard of fine wool and he reckoned that no real Spanish Merino had reached Sydney until the *Argo* brought the Negretti rams and one old ewe from the King's flock in June 1805. He therefore estimated that until the sheep had been much improved and their numbers greatly increased, no quantity sufficient materially to benefit British manufacturers could be supplied from the colony for many years. However he was confident that in time this could be done and therefore thought that small quantities should be sent to Europe annually for its quality to be assessed. But he postulated that another serious limiting factor would be the number of good and reliable shepherds available to care for the flocks in the unfenced open country to guard them from the attacks of the native dogs. And although the first tightly crammed cask of fine wool from Elizabeth Farm as a commercial venture reached London in September 1808, under the care of young Edward Macarthur on his father's whaler *Dart*, to astonish the trade with its high quality, Banks himself would be dead before the annual shipment of washed wool of adequate quality exceeded 100 000 pounds, the produce of perhaps 30–40 000 sheep or about one-tenth of the colony's flocks.

IV

Banks heard of the chequered course of the colony's development not only from Governor Phillip Gidley King but also from George Caley. Caley, in addition to collecting for Banks, was also a restless and well-intentioned if limited amateur explorer through whom there filtered a stream of quirky and independent observations on the harsh realities of life within the 60-mile radius from Sydney Cove. For seven years from his arrival with King on 14 April 1800, no one had probed the land-locked terrain of County Cumberland more widely and persistently than he. He had been introduced to its botanical opportunities by Lt-Col. William Paterson during his first Australian spring in September 1800. He had been sent by King with Lt Grant on board the *Lady Nelson* to sample the botanical peculiarities of Jervis Bay and Westernport in the autumn of 1801 having in the spring of that year made his first independent foray west from Prospect Hill to the Nepean River. With that same classic landmark as his point of orientation and departure during 1802, with one companion and a mare for transport, he made a series of short week-long excursions to the south and west through the 'Cow Pastures' along the Nepean as far as Picton Lakes beyond Mount Hunter and north-west to South Creek and the Hawkesbury. In 1803 he penetrated the Blue Mountains along the Grose Valley with Colonel Paterson and during the winter made a profitless visit in HMS *Porpoise* to Bass Strait without ever making the land. In November he gathered his pride and made a field trip to Mount Hunter with Robert Brown, who spoke well of him as a collector whatever his failings may have been in the subtleties of the Linnaean system and its Latin conventions. In 1804, with one man and his faithful mare, he spent ten days among his favourite Cow Pastures before setting out on the small colonial sloop *James* in company with Ferdinand Bauer on the *Lady Nelson* for the Hunter River where he spent the next four months. Then in November 1804 on foot, with three convicts as his party and what food they could carry, Caley made his assault on that part of the western range still known to the colonists as the Carmarthen Mountains. Here he penetrated as far as the point he named Mount Banks, (as it now is again after a period with the title of 'Mount King George') and so came as close as any man had done so far to finding that westward passage across the vast sandstone barrier to inland settlement. In 1805 after short visits to the George's River and along the coast north to Narrabeen he spent nearly four months away on board the *Sydney* from 5 October 1805 in a voyage to Norfolk Island, Hobart, Sloping Island, Adventure Bay, and the Kent Group in Bass Strait. In the winter of 1806 he retraced the course of Ensign Barrallier's route past the Nattai into the Burragorang Valley with his aboriginal companion Moowat'tin, or Dan, as a guide. In 1807, and in the same company, he explored the dissected country of the coastal escarpment beyond the Appin Falls, and again to the south-west searched for the junction of the Wollondilly and Nepean rivers. These were his last excursions before the colony effervesced into the disturbance of the 'Rum Rebellion' with the deposition of Governor Bligh in 1808.

The record of these wanderings Caley dutifully sent to Banks, and Banks alone, as to the man who paid his modest salary. By every reasonable opportunity, seldom more than once a year, he sent his dried plant specimens and seeds, occasionally living plants, dried bird and marsupial skins, various woods and other 'curiosities', supplemented with his descriptive notes, journals and his own peculiar maps. It was a continual struggle to find adequate supplies of paper and of suitable wood for the packing cases and other containers. These years were not without their record of episodes where Caley's tough Yorkshire independence and personal loyalty to Banks resulted in conflicts and misunderstandings with King and Bligh as well as such others as the Revd Samuel Marsden. His essential honesty, if not always his good judgement, made his letters and journals a valuable counterpoint to the other private and official correspondence which fed the intelligence centre in Soho Square. His essay entitled 'A short account relative to the proceedings in New South Wales from 1800 to 1803, with hints and critical remarks, addressed to Sir Joseph Banks', penned about March 1804 was invaluable as one such supplement on the first years of King's regime. So too were his long letters after the deposition of Bligh, beginning with that of 7 July 1808. Critical of Bligh as a person, it had its importance as a comment from one who stood apart from both sides, while remaining loyal to the Governor as the only legal authority. His letter to Banks of 28 October 1808 served also as a channel of information from Bligh himself before he could write with any certainty that his letters would reach London.

Another view of the state of the colony came less often but more poignantly from that young free settler from Chelsea, George Suttor. His grant, No. 118 in the parish of Castle Hill had been gazetted on 31 March 1802, in all 186 acres somewhat awkwardly straddling the roads (or tracks) near their divergence north-west to the Hawkesbury River settlements and north to No. 2 Convict Prison Farm four miles away. His cottage had been built on the former, now the Windsor road from Baulkham Hills, but it was near enough to the convict farm to the north with its nucleus of dissident Irish to be a source of worry to Suttor with his young wife and infant children. They had scarcely been settled on the grant before, on 15 February 1803, 15 Irish convicts broke out of the farm area to attack the house of Verincourt de Clambe, a former French Indian army officer and the first white settler in the district. Other farms were attacked in the near neighbourhood but all the convicts were caught and 14 sentenced to death. Only two were in fact executed and these were hanged near Clambe's cottage. This terrifying episode was the prelude to the serious outbreak of 4 March 1804, in the course of which the Suttor's cottage was entered and the two young people narrowly escaped being shot. For three days the district north and west of Parramatta was terrorized by the rebels led, it is said, by two Irishmen who had been soldiers. The band was defeated along the Hawkesbury road by Major Johnston and a detachment of the New South Wales Corps. Under the stress of this precarious start George Suttor wrote on 10 March 1804 to Banks in despair for the future.

... When such is the state of the country, what prospect is there for a settler and his family? His business he cannot properly attend, for he never lays down but in the fear of being broken in upon before morning. Should he by successful industry get forward his very property exposes him. Surrounded by all these evils, no prospect for my wife and growing family but penury and want, with spirits depressed, and broken in mind. With these ideas, I have no resource, sir, but in

your goodness, and to implore your advice what course to pursue. I have
sometimes thought if I could have procured a passage Home I would have
returned to England with my family; but a step of this kind, had I it in my power, I
should not have taken till I had first made you, sir, who have been so much my
friend, acquainted with my situation and asking your advice. I hope I shall not give
you offence by this intrusion . . .

But whatever words of comfort from Soho Square reached Suttor, the black mood
evidently soon passed with the return of peace to the hills, and on 20 May he was
sufficiently restored to advertise for sale a wide range of young fruit trees from his
Chelsea Farm nursery.

During that other very rum rebellion in 1808, however, he paid some price for his
loyalty to the legal authority of Bligh, an attitude he shared with his other neighbours
among the Baulkham Hills – John and Robert Smith, Andrew McDougall, John
Hillas, Michael Hancy, Matthew Pearce – all of them signatories to the petition
against the actions of Major Johnston and John Macarthur. For remaining firm in his
support of Bligh and refusing to recognize the legality of the usurpers, he was
sentenced to six-months' imprisonment. He joined Caley and together they returned
to England in that convoy whose departure from Sydney marked such a turn in the
affairs of the colony. On 12 May 1810 Bligh sailed on board HMS *Hindostan* and with
him were George Caley and George Suttor who rambled together ashore at Rio de
Janeiro through country which Banks had once vainly tried to reach in 1768. With
them also was Moowat'tin of whose arrival in London Banks so firmly disapproved.
On board HM Ships *Dromedary* and *Porpoise* was the New South Wales Corps, thinly
disguised now as the 102nd Regiment, recalled at last. Its oldest serving officer, Lt-
Col. William Paterson, died off Cape Horn, thereby setting a period to 20 years of
correspondence with Banks.

CHAPTER 21

OLD CHINA AND NEW HOLLAND
1805–1813

During 1807 Banks, although in his sixty-fifth year and feeling the burden of his infirmities and the public demands on his time and good nature, turned aside to indulge his wife Dorothea with more than his usual support in her hobby of collecting old china ware. In the previous ten years this had grown to form an impressive display on the slate dresser and shelves of her 'lofty and cool detached Dairy' in the enclosed carriage-yard at the rear of the Spring Grove house. Plagued by the gout that winter, Banks had been diligent both in prose and verse and, as the anniversary of their marriage passed in March, he dedicated to her his

> ... little Essay founded entirely on her correct Judgment in Collecting & her excellent Taste in arranging & displaying the Old China with which she has ornamented her Dairy at Spring Grove ... as the pure tribute of a Husband's affection unabated during an Union of 27 Years Marriage

Behind this literary effort, of course, lay more than 25 years of his own working association with the Far East fostered in his correspondence on East India Company affairs and his endless plant hunting for the Royal Botanic Garden. His Chinese scholarship had expanded from 1791–7 in his work with the abortive Macartney embassy and the published account by Sir George Leonard Staunton. It had been further consolidated when young George Thomas Staunton began his service at Canton in 1798. The china ware collection at Spring Grove had therefore been established on a sound basis. But it was when William Kerr went to Canton with David Lance in 1803 as a botanical collector for Kew that the subject of old porcelain became something more than 'the whim of ornamenting Dairies' then not so uncommon with 'the Ladies of old & opulent Families' who had gathered hoards of it during the past century at such great expense.

In that year, as Kerr and Lance sailed for China, hostilities with France were renewed on 18 May. By contrast the next day Banks was installed as a Knight of the Bath in the chapel of Henry VII at Westminster Abbey. Six weeks before one of Banks's oldest friends, Sir William Hamilton had died with his hand in that of Visc. Nelson, Duke of Bronte, also a Knight of the Bath but who on the day of installation was on board HMS *Victory* about to sail on his last voyage. The link of the Red Ribbon however still held, for in July Nelson commended a French prize with Greek antiquities on board to the care of Banks and possible sale to the Government at a value rewarding to the seamen who had taken it. Meanwhile Banks had been struggling with the accounts of the Order for the charges incurred for the Abbey ceremony and the subsequent Dress Ball at Ranelagh on 2 June and the tickets for the design and the engraving of which he had been responsible. This then was the prelude to a round of visits with china collecting at its centre, in spite of the war clouds and threat of an imminent French invasion.

On 13 August Banks and his ladies visited Windsor Castle to view the china collection made by Queen Caroline and arranged in a small room by William Kent about 1730 with a taste of which they all approved. Then a week later the family set out for Overton, in the great coach taking with them, as guest, Jonas Dryander. On 23 August they stopped at Woodstock to view 'the superb Collection of old Porcelain' deposited by Mr Spalding at Blenheim in the special gallery built for it by the Duke of Marlborough. The next day, with Lord Spencer at Althorp, Banks specially noted a pair of large Japanese porcelain jars each three feet tall and two beakers of the same pottery each two feet tall – a group for which Sarah Duchess of Marlborough was said to have paid 'the Enormous price of £1500'. Three days later the family called at Phillip Gell's Hopton Hall near Wirksworth where they studied more very good Japanese ware over a century old showing some evidence of Dutch European influence. The next day the family was settled at Overton Hall. Then after six days with Banks, Jonas Dryander returned by the stage coach from Chesterfield alone to London.

When Banks set about his dedicatory essay 'Collections on the Subject of Old China and Japan Wares with some Remarks on these interesting Manufactures ...', it was probably under the immediate stimulus of the gifts received late in 1806 from Puan Khequa, otherwise P'an Yu-ti, chief of the Co-hong from 1796 to 1808. These were an amicable return for those which Banks had sent by the hands of Lance and Kerr and included much interesting porcelain among the lanterns and lacquer, the 'ancient dwarf Tree' and the eight pots of moutans or tree paeonies. As a 'dissertation on the history and art of the manufacture of porcelain by the Chinese', it supports the authoritative praise of which Sir John Barrow in later years had only heard. It is also one example among many of silent rebuke to that bleak and pejorative comment of Sir Humphry Davy – 'He had not much reading, and no profound information'. Indeed in principle it is the epitome of that study of all available sources which Banks continuously exercised. In practice it was a spirited plea for the study of Chinese technology by British potteries in design and manufacture.

> ... could we combine the solidity the toughness & the brilliancy of the Chinese Porcelain, with the forms of the Etruscan Vases & the Painting of our Modern Artists, who can say to what extent the Sale of the Article would be increased

Here he combined applause for the dedication of Sir William Hamilton and the influence of his Etruscan collections on the wares of Staffordshire with that for the female practicality and taste of his wife in displaying for close study and emulation 'the pure white, the beautiful colors & the semitransparent brilliancy of the glaze of China Ware' so well adapted also 'for the purpose of domestic economy'. In pursuit of his subject he burrowed deep in the literature, mostly within his own library, and extending back for some 150 years almost to the origins of European contact with the Far East. His earliest sources were the *China monumentis ... illustrata* of Athanasius Kircher, 1667, and John Ogilby's English version of *An Embassy from the East India Company of the United Provinces ...* of Johannes Nieuhoff, 1673. He drew much from the fifth fascicle of Engelbert Kaempfer's *Amoenitates exoticae*, 1712, but undoubtedly leaned most heavily on the writings of the French Jesuits notably Jean Baptiste du

Halde and his four folio volumes *Description de l'empire de la Chine . . .* , 1735, and the *Lettres Édifiantes et Curieuses des Missions Étrangères* in the edition of 1781. There were also the 15 formidable quarto volumes of the *Mémoires concernant l'histoire . . . &c des Chinois*, 1776–91, of the Jesuit missionaries to Peking which Banks had used to instruct Lord Macartney in 1792. These threads were gathered into a broader context with Adam Anderson's *An Historical and Chronological Deduction of the Origin of Commerce*, 1787–9, and capped by the relevant articles in the *Encyclopaedia Britannica*, 1797. There is evidence of his other reading in quotations from Shakespeare's *Measure for Measure*, 1604, and from Ben Jonson's *Epicoene or The Silent Woman*, 1609. Whatever the language of his original sources – English, Latin or French – clear concise English notes and abstracts written at speed in his cursive script emerged from them.

For the embellishment of this little labour of love he enlisted Franz Bauer as draughtsman for the black-and-white figures selected to illustrate the dragons, the kilins, the foo, and other emblematical animals from the printed books for comparison with the actual figures on pieces in Lady Banks's collection, amplified by those of gods, goddesses and men in the Spring Grove display of Japan and China ware. The manuscript with an ample appendix and its illustrations survives as a gentle testimony of one facet of life in the Banksian household known only to a small circle of relatives and kindred spirits. It was finished in a year when Banks had more than usually indulged himself in versification – for example his stanzas in praise of Thomas William Coke at the Holkham Sheep Shearing of June 1807; his 'Elegy' directed at the Dean, Dr George Gordon, on the demolition of the spires of Lincoln Minster in September 1807; and his lines 'to the memory of the late Duke of Bedford, 21 December 1807'. So it is in this context that we may note his reply to Henry Francis Greville in June 1807 politely refusing an invitation to become a member of a new literary society:

> . . . I am sorry I cannot accept your obliging invitation to dine on the 28th, as I shall then be in the country. But this is of no moment, and I know myself too well to suppose myself a proper member of a Society for Belles Lettres. I am scarce able to write my own language with correctness, and never presumed to attempt elegant composition, either in verse or in prose, in that or in any other tongue. It is fitting, therefore, that I continue to confine myself, as I have hitherto done, to the dry pursuit of Natural History, etc.

This detached view of his own literary abilities was not one of false modesty. Writing was a necessary and practical business whether in 'the dry pursuit of Natural History' or the management of other affairs. For Banks, 'elegant composition' was subordinate to plain speaking but it did not prevent him indulging his fancy now and then with various forms of verse; one such occasion was his gathering into an organized essay from his gleanings on the subject of porcelain. His prose dedication to Dorothea Banks we have seen as a preamble to the manuscript. More occult was his 'Sonnet adresd to Lady Banks' of which the fourth and last verse epitomized so much

> Take from his hands this Little Quire
> Written by him at thy desire
> 'Twill serve at Least to Prove

> a husbands wish his wife to Please
> Abates not as the years increase
> if it began in Love

II

Nearly three months before the *Investigator* sailed from Spithead Banks had committed the Admiralty, Flinders and the civilian group, notably Robert Brown, Ferdinand Bauer and Wiliam Westall, to a plan of his own devising for the eventual publication of the voyage and its results. The terms were framed in the articles 4 to 7 in the memorandum of agreement signed on 29 April 1801, the document he had drafted declaring their Lordships' intention, if the information were deemed of sufficient importance

> . . . to cause it to be published in the form of a Narrative drawn up by the Commander, on a Plan similar to that pursued in the Publication of Captain Cook's Voyage and to give such pecuniary assistance as their Lordships shall see fitting . . .

Five years later the time had come for Brown and Bauer to prepare their part as Banks in January 1806 cleared the way with William Marsden at the Admiralty for their work on the natural history of the voyage to begin the in back premises at Soho Square. Banks had insisted on the pair in double harness for practical scientific reasons with his own light hand on the reins. Beside him as a guide was Jonas Dryander to whom Brown in his first progress report in June 1807 paid acknowledgement: 'from whose extensive knowledge he deriv'd the greatest assistance' in examining and arranging the plant collections and in selecting the specimens destined for the British Museum. Banks had chosen with Brown and Bauer over 200 species to be finished as coloured botanical drawings for the official record from among the 1500 or more sketches 'of Plants made on the Coasts of New Holland and New South Wales'. Banks had given the Admiralty an estimate of three years for the systematic arrangement of the plants and the finishing of sufficient botanical drawings. In January 1810 the Navy Board impatiently enquired what four years' work had achieved and on the 5th Banks called Brown to an accounting. He was told on the next day that of the 3400 odd plants some 2800 had been arranged and specimens selected for the British Museum. Of these nearly 2200 had been described of which over 1700 were new species comprehended in 140 new genera. Whatever the Navy Board might have thought, Banks knew that Brown had been no laggard. The technical problems in botanical systematics even under the well-worn Linnaean classification were sufficiently daunting but Brown now, with the support of Banks, adopted the natural system of Jussieu proposing some new orders and re-defining others. This recognition of the virtues of French systematics was wedded to an over-riding drive to publish before the French botanists themselves. Brown had been able to judge their abilities in the brief encounters on the voyage itself while the French nationalistic fervour for scientific priority was nowhere more evident than in the library at Soho Square. His plan, on which he had embarked, for a 'Prodromus' of the New Holland flora was consistent not only with article 7 of the 1801 agreement

442

but also with the implicit object of the whole voyage as Banks had conceived it in general and Brown now interpreted in particular, as

> ... to prevent anticipation, especially on the part of the French Botanists who lately visited the same Country ...

This had been stated in his report to Banks of 2 June 1809. In that of 6 January 1810 he recorded that his plan had been to include the generic and specific characters of *all* the plants known to be native to New Holland. Of this half had been prepared for the press of which half was already printed in its octavo format, or about a quarter of the 600 pages envisaged. The printing was completed in March and in the first week of April 1810 the publication could be recorded of *Prodromus Florae Novae Hollandiae et Insulae Van-Dienan ... Vol. I*, dedicated 'viro illustri Josepho Banks ...' in whose library and herbarium the work had been composed, and without whose direction and advice it could not have been prepared so thoroughly in so short a time. Apart from the range of the Banksian herbarium with its first extensive gathering of Australian species by Banks and Solander and others by Nelson, Menzies, Paterson and Caley, there was Dryander with his incomparable knowledge of its contents in addition to the orderly annotated pages of the interleaved working copy of the *Catalogus Bibliothecae Historico-Naturalis Josephi Banks*. All Brown's citations of the botanical literature were to be found on the shelves of the library and there can be no doubt that Dryander in his last years gave Brown as freely of his guidance as he was affording W. T. Aiton in preparing the first two volumes of the second edition of the *Hortus Kewensis* at the same time.

For Ferdinand Bauer the years after his return passed without interruption preparing the 205 exquisite coloured drawings of the plants selected by Banks and Brown to represent the genera and species established in the *Prodromus*. Collaborating with Brown over the minutiae of his subjects, he probably worked in the engravers' room, a facility now almost unused since the death of Daniel Mackenzie in 1800 but still the storehouse, in its seven large presses, of the copper plates of the *Endeavour* florilegium. The Parkinson drawings too were open for his inspection but Bauer had little to learn from them. Brilliant as they were for their time and circumstance Ferdinand Bauer by his industry, precision and scientific completeness had now carried the art of botanical record beyond that attained by any of his predecessors and close to Banks's long-fostered vision. Only Franz at Kew would match his younger brother in his quiet years at Soho Square. Banks, in his letter to William Marsden in January 1806, had suggested that Brown and Bauer might join in the publication of engravings and descriptions 'of the most interesting Objects of Natural History they have collected in a hansome form as a Periodical Work'. Ferdinand had immediately issued, a small fascicule of five botanical subjects during 1806, engraved and coloured by himself. Five years earlier he had engraved one plate from his brother's drawing of *Erica Banksii* to help complete the third part in 1801 of the *Delineations of Exotic Plants* ... which Daniel Mackenzie had not lived to finish. So the engravers' room at Soho Square was already familiar to him and would remain so for another seven years, until the third small fascicule of his own engravings appeared in 1813 to complete the 15 subjects which were all he ever published as the *Illustrationes Florae Novae Hollandiae*, 1806–13. It was abandoned, as Banks had allowed it could be in his letter of 1806

(a) — *Didelphis ursina.*

(b) — *Didelphis cynocephala*

The drawings, of which these are the engravings, with the descriptive paper were sent under cover of a leter to Banks from George Prideaux Harris, dated Hobart Town, River Derwent, Van Diemens Lans, 31 August 1806. Received by Banks in London on 28 March 1807 the paper was read by him before the Linnean Society on 21 April 1807. Edited by Alexander Macleay it was published in the *Transactions of the Linnean Society of London*, IX: 174–178, 1808, with the engravings as tab. 19, p. 174. Today the MS. of the paper is in the archives of the Linnean Society of London; the covering letter is in the National Library, Canberra, as Banks MS.9/84; but the original drawings are lost. The animal at (a) *Didelphys ursina*, then called Native Devil, is now the Tasmanian Devil, *Sarcophilus Harrisii* Boitard, 1841; at (b) *Didelphys cynocephala*, then called Zebra Opossum or Zebra Wolf, is now the Tasmanian or Marsupial Wolf or Tiger, *Thylacinus cynocephalus* Harris, 1808.

The specimen from which the drawing of *Didelphys ursina* was made by Harris was a male in the possession of Lieutenant-Governor David Collins. It was put on board the *Ocean* transport as a present to Sir Joseph Banks but died before the vessel left New South Wales.

444

... whenever it shall appear by a decrease of its Sale, the Public ceases to take a proper interest in its continuation.

The times were against the luxury of botanical publication, but the coloured drawings for a public record had been finished as Ferdinand Bauer in 1814 returned to Vienna with the residual drawings and specimens from the *Investigator* voyage that were his to claim under the original agreement.

Brown and Bauer had dutifully conformed to the terms of the memorandum they had signed despite their disappointment in its material outcome as the *Prodromus* and the *Illustrationes* failed to win financial rewards. William Westall, 'the Draughtsman employed for Landscape and Figures', the young probationer from the school of the Royal Academy, conformed less to the Banksian intent. He had certainly signed the memorandum which required him 'to pay regard to the Opinion of the Commander in choice of Objects most fitting to be delineated'. Coastal profiles, topography, the human figure and various artefacts were to be his special field under the direction of Flinders. But it is clear that from the beginning he had no such limited view of his duties nor any true understanding of the purpose of the voyage, or so it would seem from his letter to Banks of 31 January 1804 from Canton:

... I was not aware the voyage was confined to New Holland only had I known this I most certainly would not have engaged in a hazardous voyage where I could have little opportunity of employing my pencil with any advantage to myself or my employers.

But however much Westall bemoaned the dullness of the Australian landscape to which he was committed in place of the romantic South Seas of his misguided hopes his pencil served the primary intentions of both Banks and Flinders well. For Flinders, Westall's coastal profiles made as a navigational aid for inshore work were admirably done and remain unexcelled. For Banks, the topographical views which Westall captured in pencil *au premier coup* had an atmosphere and well-selected detail more than enough to justify the young man's place as a recording artist. Though much was lost under the engraver's hand the originals came to life in paint as Westall himself translated his early sketches into finished works for the Admiralty. But it was not until about June 1809 that Banks was able to harness Westall again to the task for which he had been appointed. In his search for the romantic Westall had seized his chance abroad to travel slowly home from Canton by way of India and then to explore Madeira and Jamaica before resigning himself to the English scene again in 1806 and the ultimate fulfillment of his obligations to the *Investigator* voyage. For this the final pressure came with the return of Flinders at last on 28 October 1810.

III

The French order of 11 March 1806 which Banks had secured for the release of Flinders remained a dead letter. From year to year Banks pressed for its execution whenever possible, keeping Ann Flinders informed about what was in hand. He tried to persuade the Admiralty that Flinders should be promoted to post-captain in spite of its policy against preferment for imprisoned officers but against the obdurate

Decaen at Mauritius, the shifting sequence of First Lords, and the Admiralty practice on promotion Banks was ineffective. He and Ann Flinders had to wait four years before British naval pressure in the Indian Ocean at last enabled Flinders to sail on parole from Port Louis on the *Harriet* in a cartel on 13 June 1810 after a captivity of nearly six and-a-half years. Transferred at sea to HMS *Otter* he reached the Cape on 10 July but not until 28 August could he sail on the fast *Olympia* cutter to anchor at Spithead on 24 October. Next day, from the Norfolk Hotel in London, he wrote to Banks, away at Revesby Abbey, announcing his arrival – and his discontent with the dating of his promotion. But Banks was aware of his release from despatches received a month before from Cape Town, news which he had relayed by letters of 25 and 28 September to Ann Flinders accurately estimating the date of her husband's arrival. John Barrow, now second Secretary at the Admiralty, had kept him informed of what Whitehall had thought and done in Flinder's case and on 24 October Banks had replied with acid politeness, grateful for the First Lord's

> . . . Kindness to Flinders as far as it goes & Shall always feel a proper French degree of Gratitude, but as I am of opinion he has not gone nearly so far as he might have done, I must attribute the Late date of Flinder's Commission to his General Conduct being appreciated at the admiralty at a Lower Rate than that his Friends put upon it . . .

He then argued that Flinders had never been a prisoner of war within the scope of the Admiralty's rule and that the captain's commission should have been dated from that of the official French order for his liberation in March 1806. To do so

> . . . would mark our attention to our officers when under misfortune & Shew how little the office [is] inclind to take advantage of that harsh Rule which interdicts the Promotion of a Brave man however well he had Fought if the Fortune of war has placd him in the hands of his Enemies, till his Enemies are Pleasd on their own mere motions to Restore his Liberty Surely this Rule is more like a French one than an English one . . .

But, French or English, the rule was inflexible and Flinders's commission as Post-Captain of the *Ramillies* was only back-dated to 7 May 1810, a compromise between the First Lord's date of accession to office and Flinders's release. And yet Banks four days later, depressed and shaken by the death of Dryander of which he had just heard, seems to have accepted Barrow's extenuation of the dating of Flinder's preferment as compounded of reason and good sense, even 'liberal in the extreme', although there was a reproach that more generosity had not been shown. If Banks could do no more for Flinders's commission, there was everything to be done for the chronicle of the voyage. On 13 January 1811 Banks set the official wheels turning again with his letter to John Barrow, refreshing the Admiralty's memory on the agreement of 1801 and offering their Lordships

> . . . in case they stand in need of it, the same Superintendence in the management of Engravers, Draughtsmen &c. &c. as I had the honour to execute under the direction of the then Board of Admiralty, in the Publication of the third Voyage of Capt. Cook . . .

446

The haunting shade of Dr Hawkesworth had been averted, for Banks was confident in the ability of Flinders to manage the narrative and other parts of the writing himself. Two days later Barrow, from the Admiralty Office, wrote with their Lordships' fervent thanks and full acceptance of the offer made by Banks giving him unequivocal authority for the publication to start. Barrow condensed it in one paragraph.

> ... I am, therefore, to convey to you their Lordships' request that you will take charge of the sketches, charts, journals, and other manuscripts now in the Admiralty, which I am directed to deliver up to your self, or to your order; and, further, that at your convenience you will make out and transmit to me for their Lordships' information and approval, a list of the subjects which you may deem it expedient to select for the embellishment of the publication, it being their Lordships' intention that, as in the case of Captain Cook's third voyage, the drawings and engravings shall be prepared at publick expense, and the paper, printing, &c., paid for out of the proceeds of the work.

For Banks there now ensued a period of activity at Soho Square in some ways perhaps more satisfying than at any time before, certainly more distracting from the physical burden of his gout than he had experienced for more than a decade. The *eau médecinale* had undoubtedly afforded great relief since Lord Spencer had persuaded him to try it in February 1810 but there was also perhaps a healing element somewhere in the evidence of achievement slowly gathering after long years of frustration. Flinders was home at last with a task not quite complete but marvellously well done. Bligh was home again, his reputation under a cloud indeed, but his conversation full of detail about the colony whose future seemed now assured in spite of – even because of – the rebellion which had caused his return. Caley and Suttor were home together, each with a ten-years' tale to tell. Brown and Ferdinand Bauer were home and well forward with their labours. Westall was at last roped down to his easel and his board. Dryander, alas, was dead. The King was also lost to him, a mental invalid behind the walls of Windsor Castle, but the Royal Botanic Garden flourished and the Spanish flock had been vastly augmented. The Admiralty now, at long last, had recognized his vital part in South Seas exploration by conceding to him the management in detail of the published account of the *Investigator* voyage. With Flinders in rented rooms at 16 King Street, Brown now in charge of the library and collections at 32 Soho Square where all the documents of the voyage were concentrated Ferdinand Bauer in the engravers' room below, and with Aaron Arrowsmith across the Square at No. 10, all the essential elements for the final planning of the volumes and atlas to come were at Banks's command. His place on the Board of Longitude facilitated the unfortunate but necessary re-calculation of Flinders's longitudes by John Crossley, the first astronomer to the voyage, and by Flinders's brother Samuel. Thus the engraving of the charts by Arrowsmith was delayed until 1813 but in the meanwhile Flinders had drafted the text for the first volume of the narrative with its long historical introduction, and had completed his observations on the magnetism of ships and the circular on this theme which Banks had recommended to the Admiralty for distribution to the Royal Navy.

A glimpse of the atmosphere at Soho Square during the writing and production of Flinders's *Voyage to Terra Australis* ... emerges in the pages of John Lloyd's diary of his visit to London in April and May 1811. On Easter Saturday 13 April he breakfasted at Soho Square with the Banks family, Captain Flinders, Governor Bligh, Robert Brown, Charles Konig, and Ferdinand Bauer whose drawings of some New Holland plants were the focus of particular interest. Other visitors after Easter included Captain James Burney, William Marsden, Archibald Menzies, Major James Rennell, John Rennie and Dr James Edward Smith. There was one other important addition to the library staff in Brown's assistant, Dr Johan Tiarks, the young German mathematician and astronomer who was to spend seven years at Soho Square. A glimpse of the spirit of the working partnership also emerges in the note from Banks to Flinders on 13 August 1813, that same wet day when Queen Charlotte had lunched with the family at Spring Grove:

> I have Perusd the Sheets of your work which I send back with this & I Find nothing in them which I do not approve a good beginning they say gives fair hopes of a Good Ending & yours I Really think is a good beginning God Speed your Progress

It was perhaps inevitable that under the direction of Banks George Nicol should be the publisher and that William Bulmer should be the printer. This was a working triumvirate of nearly 20 years' standing with Bulmer a proven fine printer. Of the engravers for William Westall's & views and 28 coastal profiles only Samuel Middiman had been used by Banks before. The other six – J. Byrne, W. Finden, I. Pye, J. Pye, L. Scott and W. Woolnoth – were new recruits. For Bauer's ten botanical plates Banks was fortunate to capture F. Sansom, one of William Curtis's regular engravers, but Elizabeth Byrne and I. Pye were new names. It is notable that Ferdinand himself did not execute any engravings from his own drawings for the official volumes. The 16 charts were engraved under the eye of Aaron Arrowsmith at No. 10 Soho Square and regularly submitted to Flinders during the last year of his life. These 'embellishments' were paid for by the Navy Board under an arrangement made by Banks on 1 March 1811 with John Wilson Croker at the Admiralty. Each artist or engraver received payment after the items had been checked and certified in writing by Banks expressing his formal approval.

On 27 April 1814 Banks, from his wheelchair, wrote to Flinders in his sick bed

> ... I Continue intirely to approve of your original Intention of Dedicating your work to the three who have Countenanced it I do not Know that a more Proper use could be made of a Dedication of work like yours
>
> I greived to hear of the bad health you have lately experienced but as I hear that you have now discoverd the Solvent Suited to your Case I Flatter myself that you will have more Ease in Future

But when Flinders wrote his final dedication on 20 May 1814 there were four names – Earl Spencer, Earl of St Vincent, Charles Yorke and the 2nd Visc. Melville – as the four sympathetic First Lords during the *Investigator* voyage. Then, some five weeks later on 26 June, Flinders recorded that Robert Brown had called to say that he had collected the two printed volumes and the atlas of charts of the finished *Voyage* ... to be shown that same Sunday evening by Banks in the library at Soho Square. Four

William Bulmer, fine printer, of the Shakspeare Press, Russell Court, Cleveland Row, St James, *Gentlemen's Magazine*, October, 1830.

days later, Aaron Arrowsmith presented to John Croker his final set of chart proofs, with his account for £940 certified by Banks

> . . . This Compleats the whole Expence of The Voyage which altho it has somewhat Exceeded the Sum intended will I think be found Rather deficient Than otherwise in decoration when Compard to Similar Voyages Publishd under Similar Protection

It is reasonably certain that at least three weeks before he died on 19 July 1814 Matthew Flinders saw and handled the finished work, printed and bound – *A Voyage to Terra Australis; undertaken for the purpose of completing the discovery of that vast country, and prosecuted in the years 1801, 1802, and 1803, in His Majesty's Ship the Investigator . . .* It was probably carried to Fitzroy Square, a ten-minute walk, by Robert Brown as the courier from Soho Square and the author of its stimulating botanical Appendix No. III, 'General Remarks, geographical and systematical, on the Botany of Terra Australis'. But of the man who in the course of more than 20 years had steadfastly worked to bring it all about and sustained it to the end through the tangles of political change and the hazards of a world so long at war there was little obvious trace in its

449

pages. As in the case of Bligh's *Voyage to the South Sea* ... the directing hand had ensured its own obliteration from the printed record.

IV

For nearly seven years Matthew Flinders had been confined on Mauritius as Banks battled for his release. Within that same period Banks also engaged himself against British obduracy and the cussedness of agricultural conservatism to secure the release onto the fields of Great Britain, by a series of public sales, of the fine wool genes of the few authentic Spanish Merino stock gathered from the well-guarded Spanish *cabanas* and propagated on the Royal farms at Kew, Richmond and Windsor. These sales were regularly held about mid-August from 1804 to 1810 in 'the field south of the Pagoda' at Kew, now the Surrey cricket ground just outside the Gardens. The ewes and rams for sale came from the descendants of the Negretti importation of October 1791. From the week of arrival of that small historic flock from the Alanges, 36 ewes, 4 rams and a *manso* or bellwether, Banks had been the guardian of their progress as a foundation stud of potential importance to the wool growing and wool textile industries of Great Britain. To his unpaid and unpensioned role as Groom of His Majesty's Botanic Garden (in effect) he shouldered in addition the burden of Groom of His Majesty's Spanish Flock and with it a great increase in the volume and complexity of his correspondence as well as in the demands on his time and physical energies, especially during the spring and summer. Not only was he faced with the delicate task of directing the details of flock management by Richard Stanford, the royal shepherd at The Orange Tree Cottage, Kew, but had to do so with the approval and help of the superintendent of the royal parks and farms, Alexander Ramsay Robinson until 1802, and thereafter Richard Snart. Even though he had, at his own expense, the loyal assistance of the old wool stapler Henry Lacocke from 1798 to 1809, he was for the most part his own sheep classer, salesman, wool expert and scientific consultant on all matters touching the selection and breeding of the Spanish Merino. His knowledge of the breed, grounded on the establishment of his own small flock at Spring Grove from 1785 to 1791 was practical and at first hand. It was also academic in his pursuit of the subject by correspondence and the hunting down of relevant literature at home and abroad. As a sustained investigation over many years it is a good example of the enquiring Banks at work building from a state of ignorance to one of highly competent authority.

As the new century opened Banks, in the spring of 1800, at first visualized a ram show and sale at Spring Grove as a step in spreading 'the breed of Spanish sheep' in accord with the spirit of 'His Majesty's Patriotic Plan'. On reflection he favoured a system of private sales from the royal flock to suitable breeders. In the early summer, with the King's approval, Banks then published a pamphlet, printed by William Bulmer entitled *A Project for extending the Breed of Fine Wooled Spanish Sheep, now in the possession of his Majesty, into all parts of Great Britain, where the Growth of Fine Cloathing Wools is found to be profitable*. This paper was a potent stimulus at home and abroad. Arthur Young printed it in his *Annals of Agriculture*. Lord Sheffield made it an appendix to his *Observations on the Objections made to the Export of Wool from Great Britain to Ireland*. The *St. James Chronicle* and the *Philosophical Magazine* followed before the end of the year, and in its French translation it appeared as part of the text in 1802 of C. P. Lasteyrie's *Histoire de l'Introduction des Moutons à Laine fine d'Espagne dans les divers Etats de l'Europe et au Cap de Bonne Esperance.* It was supplemented ably by those luminaries of the Bath and West of England Society, Dr Caleb Hillier Parry, a beneficiary of the King's largesse in donating rams, and John Southey, 15th Lord Somerville, and Gentleman of the Bedchamber, who had independently responded in his own way to the 'Patriotic Plan'. With further published reports by Banks on 'the State of His Majesty's Flock of Fine Wooled Spanish Sheep, in 1803 and 1804, the period of private sales to patriotic breeders ended and the public sales began with the notable occasion when John Macarthur purchased heavily for his flock in New South Wales. By 1807, however, in the autumn Banks succeeded in his plea to the King for release from the charge of the Spanish Merino flock on the grounds of the 'extreme Feeble State' of his health, and the management passed in principle to Richard Snart. In practice Banks remained as a continuing point of reference as difficulties arose. But other patriots of the breed were emerging in the wake of Banks, Dr Parry and Lord Somerville. George Tollet, of Swinnerton near Stone in Staffordshire, had inscribed his tributes in Young's *Annals of Agriculture* of 1806. Nehemiah Bartley had published his *Essays on Extending the Growth of Fine Clothing Wool by Interbreeding with Spanish Rams and British Ewes* in 1807. In the same year Benjamin Thompson, of Redhill Lodge near Nottingham, had developed the subject in his letters to the *Monthly Magazine*. But the scene was suddenly to change with the rising of the people of Madrid against the French invaders on the memorable *dos de Mayo*, 2 May 1808.

Out of this Spanish upheaval suddenly on 30 October 1808 the refugee remnants of the famous Paular *cabana* came flooding into Richmond Park to the dismay of Richard Snart and Richard Stanford. They were some 1500 worn and emaciated little Spanish sheep, a gift from the Junta of the Asturias to the King of England in the hope of aid for the Spanish patriot rising against Napoleon. Again the solution of the problem was sought from Banks and in the emergency he turned again to authorship. Bed-ridden and gout-stricken at Soho Square during the winter of 1808–9, he wrote the paper to appear as a pamphlet under cover of a letter dated 18 February to Sir John Sinclair as President of the Board of Agriculture and entitled *Some Circumstances relative to Merino Sheep, chiefly collected from the Spanish Shepherds who attended those of the Flock of Paular, lately presented to His Majesty by the Government of Spain ...*, 1809. Printed in the first instance again at the expense of Banks by William Bulmer, it was spread abroad also in the pages of the *Communications to the Board of Agriculture*, the *Philosophical Magazine* and, as an Appendix with other Banksian reports to Sir George Steuart Mackenzie's *A Treatise on the Diseases and Management of Sheep*, 1809.

Still confined with gout during March and April 1809 Banks prepared a plan to resolve to the national benefit the problems posed by the sudden accession of so many Spanish fine-woolled sheep after so many years of struggle for so few. Entitled 'A Project for the Establishment of Merino Flocks in various parts of the Kingdom under the immediate superintendence and control of the committee of the Privy Council for Trade', it owed much to the working example operating to effect the complete *mérinisation* of the sheep flocks of France by Napoleonic decrees. As an idea it was still-born, aborted in the stress of a new crisis from the south of Spain. Its harbinger was in the letter written by Andrew Cochrane-Johnstone from Seville on 3 May to Sir John Sinclair. This announced the acquisition of the Negretti *cabana*, some 12000 head, their proposed despatch to England in government transports as a matter of national importance, and his nomination of William Cobbett, as the organizer for the sale of half the number at Botley in September. Sinclair passed the

A Spanish Shepherd, Antonio Gonzales, with his dog Montiero, who arrived in England in September 1810 with 200 Spanish Merinos from the Nunez *cabana*. He was later a shepherd with George III's flock at Kew and Richmond. Painting by Samuel Woodforde, RA, 1811.

452

problem to Banks in a letter of 25 May and promptly escaped to Scotland. Lord Bathurst, as President of the Board of Trade, in desperation appealed to Banks in letters of 30 May and 1 June. Lord Castlereagh, as Secretary of War and the Colonies, appealed to Sir Arthur Wellesley to countermand the order for the transport of the sheep but to no avail. Lord Bathurst's distraught cry 'What can be done with them?' elicited from Banks on 10 June the sobering response 'The die is thrown & H.M. Ministers must abide by the hazard of the Casts . . .' followed by a plan for operation should the sheep arrive. In the end fewer than 1500 were disembarked from the transports at Deptford to wend their bleating way past the War Office as they grazed through St James's Park to the care of Richard Stanford at Kew – too late and too ill-conditioned for the sixth public sale of the King's Merinos on 26 July 1809.

This drama with Merinos as the spoils of the Peninsular War ensured a public interest that seemed to bear – deceptively – the trappings of success in the 25-year campaign which Banks had followed to gain acceptance on British farms for the odd little Spanish stranger. Benjamin Thompson, minor playwright and translator, had produced an English version of C. P. Lasteyrie's work of 1802 under the title of *An Account of the Introduction of Merino Sheep into the Different States of Europe . . .*, 1810, with a dedicatory letter to Banks dated 1 December 1809. This enthusiasm brought him to the post of Secretary of the Merino Society of which Banks was the elected President from its foundation on 4 March 1811 until his death in 1820. Thomas Young, FRS evolved, from his study of the diffraction of light in its passage through a simple grating what he termed his 'agricultural micrometer' (an eriometer) for determining the thickness of very fine fibres such as those from the Spanish Merino fleece. He explained to Banks the theory and practice of this device in his letters of 10 September and 6 October 1810 tracing its origin to his lectures at the Royal Institution in past years. But Banks's paper on *Some Circumstances Relative to Merinos* , 1809, had yet one more effect before the whole theme began its slow decay as an active issue in British agriculture. In 1811 a devotee of the breed printed anonymously a small work dedicated to Banks on the etymology of the Spanish pastoral terms related to the sheep and its husbandry under the title *On the Name and Origin of the Merino Breed of Sheep*, a subject on which speculation is as rife to day as it ever was in the years of Banks's pioneering study of the animal. Sinclair's Society for the Improvement of British Wool at Edinburgh ended its brief life under the weight of its author's competing enthusiasm for the old Board of Agriculture. Banks's Merino Society at London flooded the Midland and southern counties with its members but died soon after its author's death as the South Sea colony he had fathered began its rise as a grower of fine wool in a measure far beyond his dreams.

V

In the early spring of 1803 Banks was grappling with the demands for Spanish rams from the royal flock created by his pamphlet *A Project for Extending the Breed . . .* In particular there were the pressing enthusiasms of the two Gloucestershire clothiers and farmers, Edward Sheppard and David Lloyd of Uley, eager to breed as well as manufacture an improved home-grown fine wool for their looms in the Cam valley. But in the midst of these distractions during April 1803 he raised with W. T. Aiton the idea of a second edition of the *Hortus Kewensis* again, as in the first, with the help of Jonas Dryander. With the library at Soho Square now in full working trim and its use facilitated by the five volumes of the *Catalogus Bibliothecae* . . . since 1800, the task which Banks now envisaged for Dryander and Aiton was a natural application of its resources and the academic skill of its curator. So when Aiton wrote to Dryander on 25 April 1803 proposing the new edition as a working collaboration between them there is little doubt that the ground had already been prepared. Dryander responded after a brief interval accepting the invitation, disclaiming any interest in 'pecuniary consideration', but making the whole project contingent upon a conference with Banks

> . . . to determine upon what alterations the edition of Willdenow's *Species Plantarum* and other new books may make expedient particularly in regard to synonyms and differentiae specificae, and also on what is most proper to be done in regard to the adoption of new genera cut out of the old ones, and to the placing of some of the old genera, which have of late been thrust from one class into another, so as to steer cleer between too close adherence to old errors, and too great readiness to adopt new whims . . .

Dryander noted that there might be some delay before Banks would have the leisure for such discussions and that he himself was 'not au courant as the french call it' with the most recent botanical literature because for the previous six or seven years he had attended to other fields of work – presumably the *Catalogus Bibliothecae* . . . Thus after 14 years of library organization and management and the more general bibliography of natural history, Dryander cautiously prepared to gather again the loose botanical strands of the first edition of *Hortus Kewensis* into a tighter scientific discipline. He was also setting in operation at Soho Square a pattern of work in systematic botany which his future colleague and successor, Robert Brown, would bring to fruition not only in the *Prodromus Florae Novae Hollandiae* . . . but also in the final volumes of the second *Hortus Kewensis* ten years later. It is a measure of the changes impending that, even as Dryander was reaching out toward the new taxonomy, Brown from Sydney in New South Wales in his letter to Banks of 3 August 1803 was still groping for a systematic foundation on which to build the classification of his New Holland collections when he noted

> . . . In arranging the collection I at first follow'd Jussieu's Ord's Naturalis; but I soon found the plants of doubtful affinity so numerous that I judg'd it better to use the Linnaean method. The part sent, however, was in some degree arrang'd according to the former plan, and on the present occasion I had not time to alter it.

As these words were written Dryander had already spent days in July with Aiton at Kew and Banks at Spring Grove, days no doubt of 'leasure for attending to this business' of the new *Hortus Kewensis*. But there was more opportunity to come for the development of plans for this work as Dryander set out with the Banks family on 21 August 1803 for Overton and a quiet week in the Amber Valley. Here was leisure enough for thoughtful discussion such as Banks and Dryander would never enjoy together again in the seven years that remained. But from the autumn of 1803 nevertheless it may be accepted that the work toward the second edition had properly begun.

Two years later the return of Robert Brown and Ferdinand Bauer and their work on the *Investigator* plants and botanical drawings at Soho Square brought an exciting interruption and a challenge to Dryander's ordered academic world. He had already emphasized to Aiton his own queries on the system of classification to be followed for the new *Hortus* and was now fully aware of Brown's search for a suitable taxonomic framework on which to cast his arrangement of the New Holland accessions. Another disturbance to the Linnaean calm had appeared the year before in the first fascicules of La Billardière's *Novae Hollandiae Plantarum Specimen*. With Charles Konig at his elbow in Soho Square Dryander responded with his own modest contribution to the *Annals of Botany*, 1806. This took the form of his *Chloris Novae Hollandiae . . .*, a catalogue of the species from New Holland and Van Diemen's Land of which illustrations and/or descriptions had been published to that date as far as they had come to his own unexcelled knowledge in this field – some 424 in all. It was dominated by the authorship of La Billardiere, Cavanille, Ventenat, Smith and Willdenow, a useful if unmarked stone in the foundations of Brown's *Prodromus . . .* to come. So with W. T. Aiton and the expanding *Hortus Kewensis* on one side and Robert Brown with the evolving *Prodromus Florae Novae Hollandiae . . .* on the other, Dryander in his last years was fully engaged as a point of reference in taxonomy and bibliography and as an editorial adviser. To the end he remained a practising but sceptical Linnaean of which his *Chloris . . .* was the last example. As to the new *Hortus . . .*, his work extended no further than Volume 2 when death overtook him. It was not until 1813 when Volume 5 was published that his part in it was acknowledged by Aiton

> . . . This estimable man exerted his best talents not only in improving the plan but in arranging the materials of this Catalogue for the press, and correcting the proof sheets during the progress of the printing until a few days previous to his death; endeavouring at the same time to instil into the mind of the Author some portion of that extensive scientific information for which he was so universally esteemed

In October 1810 while Dryander was engaged in this work of scientific altruism Everard Home gave Banks in a letter to Revesby Abbey grounds for optimism in his reading of the symptoms which had already cast a long shadow over his devoted librarian. That he was suffering from something other than piles was apparently clear, and that it lay within the competence of Home to cure was apparently also fairly definite, but what it was remains obscure. Its seriousness is evident in the firm directions which Banks gave Home on 11 October for the accommodation of Dryander in the house at Soho Square in the bedroom in which his mother had died, and for the special attentions by the staff in executing his wish 'that Every Kind of accomodation the house can afford be given to my Good Friend'. It would seem that there was no cause for immediate alarm since Banks then turned his pen to speculations on the intestinal tract of birds, its relative shortness and its digestive powers, with its bearing on the germination and dissemination of plant seeds. But within the ensuing week the industrious almost cloistered life of Jonas Dryander had reached its painful end. The details of his last few days are buried in the lost letter from Home with the news which so grieved Banks that for a day or so he could not reply. When he did so on 19 October it was with awkwardly and almost unwillingly expressed emotions as on other occasions when his inmost feelings were deeply touched. There can be no doubt that he mourned the loss of Dryander as an old and valued friend, as one indeed who was almost a part of his immediate family, but as he struggled to convey this to Home it was a sharpened sense of his own mortality that seemed to prevail:

> ... I have lost my right hand, & can never hope to provide anything as a substitute that can at all make amends to me: my chief pleasure, that of my Library, is reduced almost to a Shadow when I consider the many points from whence I derived satisfaction in the possession of it.
> ... For me I console myself in Feeling that my departure cannot be long delayed; & that, should I linger, I must soon be deprived of all those enjoyments to which he used to administer while he participated in them; my hearing begins to Fail; one eye, as I told you before, is of little use: in short the infirmities of age overtake me fast: ...

Banks had always hoped that Dryander would survive him, and had made provision for him to have the use of the library and the breakfast hospitality of 32 Soho Square for himself and his friends as long as he lived – '. . . but heaven's will be done'. Banks also attributed Dryander's premature death to a concealment of the true nature of the disease from Home for so long and he thanked the physician for all that he had done at the end. To Robert Brown also he wrote with his thanks for all that he had done in those last weeks, instructing him to arrange the proper burial of a colleague whose friendship they shared and valued. For the time being the library was to be closed to outside visitors until he returned to London and could make new arrangements.

An outside view was expressed by his old Christ Church friend and contemporary, Samuel Goodenough, elevated at last by the Duke of Portland to the Bishopric of Carlisle, about the loss of his fellow Vice-President of the Linnean Society. This was focused on its effect on the production of the second edition of the *Hortus Kewensis*, a work which he applauded. He wrote his own form of an epitaph for their lost colleague to the President of the Society, James Edward Smith, on 9 November:

> ... What a dreadful loss will the death of poor Dryander be! I do not think he is to be replaced in all his bearings. Possibly he was a dull plodding genius as to brilliant and classical effusions: but that said genius fitted him for every other situation which he filled. Plodding is the first quality of a librarian. None but he could have worked up the *Bibliotheca Banksiana*. Who so fit to investigate *dried* plants, and trace out synonyms in the musty journals of foreign Academies. Then he was a walking Dictionary, or rather Repertory, for all inquiries into natural history. Then also his usefulness as a patient drudge in all matters which were proposed to him, was an excellent quality. His bluntness had its great effect with innovators, impertinents, and popinjays. He had a consciousness of his real worth also, which made him a very independent character. I really am quite sorry to have lost him. What will Sir Joseph do?

Smith, from Norwich on 3 December, said he mournfully agreed. He could however settle the Bishop's query about Sir Joseph's problem. Robert Brown was now settled in Dryander's place at Soho Square and it was hoped that the second edition of *Hortus*

456

Kewensis could now proceed. As to Robert Brown himself, compared with Dryander, Smith expressed the view that

> ... his manners will be more *suaviter*, but not less *fortiter* with coxcombs and blockheads!

Next evening, on 4 December, the Bishop took the chair at the Linnean Society to announce the death of Dryander and the Vice-Presidential vacancy created. In his valedictory address he embroidered the opinions he had already written to Smith. Nowhere, he said, possibly in the whole world was a man to be found to fill the place of Dryander in the department of natural history, though Robert Brown would manage the botanical side at Sir Joseph's 'admirably well'. A Librarian for the Royal Society, a Vice-President for the Linnean Society, a collector of medals and coins for Mrs [i.e. Sarah Sophia] Banks – these could be found. But someone with Dryander's bibliographical erudition and detailed knowledge of the Banksian collections did such a man exist? Then too there was his sterling part in the founding of the Linnean Societ and his care for its progress as a gathering point for scientific men rather than 'Society-hunters'. This was a service to the infant scientific community of London not to be overlooked and the Bishop expressed what seems to have been its collective view of what had been lost in the departure of Jonas Dryander from 32 Soho Square, but not from the parish of St Anne's. He lies buried by the gutted ruins of the church in Dean Street still close by the site of that establishment to which he gave the long years of his maturity in England, the expatriate Swede to whom, in his modest way, British science owes so much.

457

CHAPTER 22

THE PROTECTOR OF ICELAND
1801–1813

I

The broad reach of the influence radiating from Soho Square is nowhere better shown than in the troubled affairs of Iceland during the long years of war with France. Late in January 1801 Banks had drafted his 'Hints respecting the Rout . . .' as guidance to the Admiralty in framing the instructions for Matthew Flinders and the voyage of HMS *Investigator*. Within the same weeks he had also penned and dated 30 January 1801 his 'Remarks concerning Iceland' that desolate appendage of Denmark with its impoverished and dwindling population just below the Arctic Circle, but of which he held fond memories of his visit in 1772 and the warm friendships then formed and surviving still in his correspondence. Refreshed briefly at second hand by the visit in 1789 of Sir John Stanley, the British connection which Banks had so firmly grounded in his own roving scientific curiosity was reinvoked under the military expediency of the War of the Second Coalition when Russia, Sweden, Prussia and Denmark formed the Armed Neutrality of the North on 16 December 1800. The British response on 14 January 1801 was to impose an embargo on all vessels of the Armed Neutrality and by this to sever the meagre but life-preserving trade between Denmark and her colonies of Iceland, the Faeroes and Greenland. Thus, almost certainly at the instance of the Foreign Office under Grenville, Banks was induced to present his views on Iceland as a target of British strategy in the north. On its value as a bargaining counter toward a subsequent peace or, preferably, as a permanent accession to the British Crown Banks at this time seems to have been convinced. This was an opinion which drew heavily on his recollections of what the Icelanders themselves had so often during his visit in 1772 seemed to propose as a desirable release from their Danish overlords. Now, more than 28 years later, he was sure that with no more than 500 men and a few guns the whole island could be easily mastered if, in the light of the facts he had assembled, this was decided on by other 'people better versed in the political interests of the United Kingdom' than he pretended to be. It was implicit in all he had to say, however, that he wished the steps toward annexation to be as peaceful as could be contrived, a process which the Pitt administration was evidently content to accept.

The plan conceived – but never executed – was to send British warships to Iceland, to capture immediately the Danish Governor, Trampe, and the Lt-Gov. with several of the more important Icelanders, including Magnús Stephensen the Chief Justice and son of Banks's old friend Ólafur Stephensen. Thereafter the British force was to wait quietly at anchor until, it was hoped, the Icelanders would peacefully declare their 'acknowledgement of homage and fealty to the Crown of the United Kingdom' and their desire 'to participate in British Freedom'. This was embodied with much dulcet argument in a letter to Magnús Stephensen from Banks, evidently as an official document to be presented by the commander of the expedition which was never despatched. It remained therefore a dead letter as political and military events quickly rendered obsolete any plan for the annexation of Iceland at that stage. On 3 February 1801 Pitt resigned and on 14 March a new government was formed under Addington with Hawkesbury as the new Foreign Secretary. On 24 March the Russian Tsar Paul I was assassinated and his successor Alexander I withdrew from the Armed Neutrality which disintegrated further under the British attack on Copenhagen on 2 April 1801 with the destruction of the Danish fleet. The Northern Convention finally dissolved in the treaty between Britain, Russia and Denmark signed on 23 October 1801 leaving the status of Iceland undisturbed as a Danish colony.

For six years the matter rested until the agreement of Tilsit between Alexander I and Napoleon in July 1807 involved Denmark again in hostilities with Britain. Again Copenhagen was besieged and again, on 7 September 1807, the Danish fleet was captured. But of this no news had reached Iceland before, in the late summer, the merchant fleet had sailed for Denmark to be captured for the most part by the British and brought as prizes to Leith and other United Kingdom ports. Among the victims was Magnús Stephensen, Chief Justice of Iceland, captured on board the merchant ship *De trende Søstre* off Norway on 19 September and brought to Leith from where he was allowed to sail on a British warship to Copenhagen, arriving there on 10 October. From this point the subject of Iceland and the manifold distresses of its people was to be a steady drain on the diplomatic and conciliatory resources of Banks, a period opened now by Magnús Stephensen's letter of 17 October from Copenhagen pleading for his intervention on behalf of the captured merchants and their vessels. Banks sent Stephensen's letter immediately to Hawkesbury (now the Home Secretary), who responded favourably and asked Banks for a written statement on the Iceland problem in general. So on 30 December 1807, Banks for the second time, provided for the British Government a brief with benevolent intentions towards the Icelanders but now advising against any expedition to acquire the island by such means. Instead he proposed a plan to offer the Icelanders an option peacefully to recognize the Crown of the United Kingdom holding meanwhile the captured merchant ships and their cargoes as a pledge and their owners and crews in Britain 'as hostages for the conduct of their countrymen in Iceland'. Realizing that the Government was in favour of this rather than the plan of 1801 for an armed expedition, Banks now concentrated his efforts on securing the release of the 13 or 14 merchant vessels from the tentacles of the Prize Court and getting for them a distinctive licence to trade from Iceland free from the British blockade in the northern seas. To this end he wrote on 2 January 1808 to the Secretary of State for War and the Colonies, Castlereagh. But weeks passed without decision, the obscurities of government hesitation visible only in the rock-like obstinacy of the King's Proctor in refusing the order for the liberation of the 11 vessels now in question. Again Banks taxed Castlereagh on 24 February with the long delay, the obduracy of the King's Proctor, and the increasing jeopardy in which the Icelanders were placed by the threat to their seasonal supplies. Meanwhile he did all he could to allay the worst fears of the owners, Silvertsen, Petraeus, Bredal, Knudsen, Clausen and others as he struggled with the departments in Whitehall. At last he wrote to Edward Cooke, under-secretary at the Department of War and the Colonies, on 7 April reminding him that though he had told him of the decision to release the Icelandic ships as far back as 26 February the King's Proctor had not yet received the necessary orders. With this preamble Banks then proposed to call on Cooke in person in a few days – 'I have much indeed that I wish to consult you about'. The subdued rumble in these words and, no doubt, the Banksian visit itself seem at last to have had effect though too late to allow sailings to Iceland that summer, or to prevent great losses on the cargoes of the former prize vessels when these eventually came to sale in Britain. The freedom for a licenced trade between Great Britain and Iceland which Banks had done so much to effect was vital to the well-being of the fast-declining population of Icelanders. But there were other consequences, unpredictable and peculiar.

As a logical step in the matter of Anglo-Icelandic trade on the best principles of Adam Smith, and with a side glance toward improving life for the English poor, Samuel Phelps, a soap dealer of Lambeth, had in December 1808 secured a licence from the Board of Trade for his company, Messrs Phelps, Troward and Bracebridge, to send a food ship to Iceland. But his philanthropy was tinged with self-interest by the large quantities of marketable tallow in Iceland, an attraction pointed out to him by a devious clerk, James Savignac, and a questionable Danish adventurer and privateer captain on parole, Jorgen Jorgensen. With these two murky gentlemen aboard, Phelps's ship the *Clarence*, Captain Jackson reached Hafnarfiord on 12 January 1809. Illegally exercising its Admiralty letter of marque in Icelandic waters, the *Clarence* seized a Danish brig and, in the absence of the Danish Governor, Trampe, forced his deputy to allow the landing of its cargo and its storage in the warehouse where Banks and his party once had found accommodation. The voyage was ill-judged for in the depth of winter, the native Icelanders were averse to visiting Reykjavik for trade. So at the end of March the *Clarence* returned to Liverpool in ballast with Jorgensen aboard while Savignac remained at Reykjavik to guard the cargo, an investment of some £8500. On 14 April Jorgensen sent Banks an account of the venture and on 16 April Banks relayed it to William Wellesley-Pole, successor to William Marsden as Secretary to the Admiralty. On 21–22 April Samuel Phelps himself sought protection for a new venture by a petition to the Treasury and succeeded in gaining the despatch of HMS *Rover*, Captain Knott to Reykjavik in June specifically to protect 'British ships licensed to trade'. On 16 June Trampe was persuaded to sign a convention recognizing unimpeded British trade with Iceland during the period of Anglo-Danish hostilities. The path had now been cleared for the second attempt by Samuel Phelps prompted by Jorgensen to reap a profit from the Iceland trade.

Sailing from Gravesend on 2 June 1809, the 10-gun letter of marque *Margaret & Anne*, Captain Liston with Phelps and Jorgensen on board, sailed into Faxafiord and dropped anchor in Reykjavik harbour on 21 June. But despite the recent convention signed with Captain Knott by Trampe, the Danish Governor had posted placards prohibiting trade with the English under pain of death. Whereupon Phelps, Savignac and Captain Liston, with an armed party from the crew of the *Margaret & Anne* seized Trampe at the Governor's house. Trampe's ship, the Danish merchantman *Orion*, was boarded and declared a prize, and its owner imprisoned below decks on the *Margaret & Anne*. With no authority to annex the island to the British crown, Phelps and his party foisted Jorgensen, as the only Dane among them, into the role of new governor supported by a small group of Icelanders. On 26 June proclamations were issued in Reykjavik in Jorgensen's name, ending Danish rule and creating a republic as a British protectorate, and for a while. Magnús Stephensen, and his brother Stephan, Bailiff for the west of Iceland, the Bishop and many of the clergy acceded to the new regime. On 11 July, in the euphoria of the moment, Jorgensen elevated himself as Protector and for almost a month made serious play with this fictitious authority. However, throughout July the Icelanders, free from the Danish prohibitions brought in their tallow and eiderdown to the trading satisfaction of Phelps and Savignac. But by the middle of August the tide turned with the arrival of the British protecting sloop HMS *Talbot*, Captain Alexander Jones, and the flimsy republic disintegrated. Phelps's attempt to justify the position under the terms of his letter of marque carried no weight with Captain Jones who preferred the testimony of Trampe and the Stephensen brothers, who, for personal reasons, appealed to Jones to restore the previous form of government.

Thus, on 22 August, Jones, Phelps and the Stephensen brothers signed yet another agreement restoring Iceland to its former status as a Danish colony, but confirming its freedom of trade with Great Britain, and leaving its administration for the time being in the hands of Magnús and Stephan Stephensen. Curiously, Phelps was allowed to keep Trampe as his prisoner and the *Orion* as his prize when, on 24 August in the *Margaret & Anne*, he set sail from Reykjavik. The late 'Protector' Jorgensen, identified by Captain Jones as a prisoner-of-war who had broken his parole, was in custody on the *Orion* as, on Tuesday 29 August, the ship returned alone to the Icelandic capital. In the interim, the *Margaret & Anne*, with its highly combustible cargo of tallow and eiderdown, had mysteriously caught fire at sea. All on board had been saved, largely by Jorgensen's brave seamanship even though technically he was a prisoner. It was not until 20 September that the *Orion* and its company reached Leith, and Jorgensen was lodged in prison at Chatham as a parole-breaker, in the estimate of Captain Jones a 'good natured mad man, nobody's enemy but his own', an adventurer of the South Seas who would return as a convict to die many years later in Tasmania.

For Samuel Phelps the Iceland venture was a financial disaster in the loss of the ship and its cargo valued at £40000, but otherwise fortunate for no serious attempt was made to bring him to account for his freebooting actions. He drew some wry comfort from his experience, however, in observing that it seemed to prove Adam Smith's dictum 'that governments should interfere as little as possible in trade and commerce' or at least that 'their *agents* should be careful how *they* meddle in those matters', pointing an accusing finger at Captain Jones.

These events came swiftly to the attention of Banks as the various actors in this little drama called at Soho Square on their return, only to find him far away at Revesby Abbey, but still, as always, accessible by the mail service so well mediated by Dryander. Jorgensen was the first suppliant in his few days of freedom before Chatham prison claimed him but Banks found him less than admirable and more than a little to blame. Trampe however was released almost immediately on reaching England and lost no time in making contact with Banks who found him and his account of the 'revolution' altogether more acceptable. In time Trampe came to accept that a proper agreement under which he could work should be made with Great Britain and, with Banks, he achieved this by the Order in Council of 7 February 1810. This established freedom of trade between London, Leith and Iceland and protected Icelandic shipping engaged therein. For the rest of the war until 1814 the Icelanders gained some benefit from the limited commerce that now ensued, but the events of 1809 and the ill-starred voyage of the *Margaret & Anne* had other items in the profit and loss account of the enterprise to appear on its balance sheet.

II

As chance would have it the most important figure on board the *Margaret & Anne* in that summer voyage to Iceland was a young man, almost 24, a gifted botanical draughtsman but now committed to the science of his art and recently proposed for election to the Linnean Society, recommended as 'A most zealous Botanist & Entomologist, as deserving of that honour, & as likely to be useful to the Society'. For William Jackson Hooker this was a voyage of scientific curiosity, its impulse distant from thoughts of mercantile gain, an adventure whose prospect had been opened to him by Banks who had summoned him to a breakfast at Soho Square in April 1809. It was then more than three years since Hooker had been first introduced to Banks in February 1806 by Dawson Turner, his hard-driving taskmaster in botanical art, his chief sponsor now to Fellowship of the Linnean Society but now also his chief dissuader from the Iceland excursion. But there was nothing Turner could do to counter the spell of that powerful influence to whom he had introduced him. In 1806 Hooker's introduction to 32 Soho Square fortuitously occurred within the first weeks of settled work there by Robert Brown and Ferdinand Bauer on the plant collections and the associated drawings from the *Investigator*. For a receptive mind there could have been no greater stimulus toward botanical science as a life-work than this vision of a strange and remote plant world unfolding in the hands of its collector, recorded by one of the supreme artists of his day, and systematically classified in that cheerful but critical atmosphere. Another conversion had been made and Hooker, returned to his drawing-board at Great Yarmouth to note in a memorandum to himself: 'I was now determined to give up everything for Botany'.

In July 1806 Hooker was back in London with rooms in 58 Frith Street, Soho, at the very centre of that well-trodden axis of half a mile with the British Museum at its northerly end, the Linnean Society at 9 Gerrard Street a few hundred yards to the south, and the pulsating hive in 32 Soho Square a few steps round the corner. The conversion was complete but, for two years, the young gentleman of uncommitted means ranged from the delights of field botany in Scotland to the sober discipline of the drawing board in the Dawson Turner menage at Great Yarmouth. Then at the end of 1808 the distant floral mysteries of New South Wales and the notable example of Robert Brown revived the spell of Soho Square and again polarized his vague ambitions but still left him fumbling for a plan. Suddenly all indecision was at an end as Banks, about mid-April 1809, offered him a berth on the *Margaret & Anne* with all expenses paid for a voyage to Iceland. The final tug had come and he did not hesitate. On 24 May he came to London with Dawson Turner beside him pleading against the expedition and for the finishing of the drawings for his own *Historica Fucorum*. But Hooker had caught the scent of a wider future and on 29 May he was at Gravesend ready for its pursuit.

Of the 'revolution' in Iceland he was a bemused spectator but after the first few days he was free to pursue all the openings among the Icelanders which the introductory letters provided by Banks unlocked for him, releasing a flood of warm recollections and tearful gratitude to the man whom the old Stiftsamptman, Ólafur Stephensen, epitomized as 'the great benefactor of Iceland'. His botanizing and

462

William Jackson Hooker *aet. c.* 25. Drawing by John Sell Cotman, 1811.

sketching was fruitful but his hopes of following the trail of Banks in the ascent of Mount Hekla were blighted in the refusal of his guides at the last moment to make the attempt. He finally embarked with a rich harvest on Saturday 26 August when the *Margaret & Anne* set sail about four o'clock in the afternoon. But 60 miles off-shore and barely 12 hours later, the vessel was on fire, ignited by the Danish prisoners on board, and within a few hours it had become a spectacular and total loss. No lives were lost due to the prompt arrival of the accompanying prize *Orion* and to the brave exertions of Jorgen Jorgensen, for whom William Hooker steadfastly thereafter expressed a personal regard as the man to whom he felt he owed his life. But of his collections and sketches Hooker could save nothing and only two-thirds of his notes. Bereft but unbroken by this disaster Hooker returned to settle in his newly acquired Brewery House at Halesworth in Suffolk, to his botanical art and slowly to his work on the *Jungermanniae*. From Revesby Abbey Banks, on 1 October 1809, had sent Hooker, within a few days of his return, a letter of warm condolence on the losses sustained with hopes that their friendship would continue unimpaired. But he added a stimulus to further action in mentioning 'the cargo of Scotsmen' with Sir George Steuart Mackenzie of Coul near Dingwall at their head, who proposed an Icelandic visit and whom he had advised to wait another season until the summer of 1810. In December Hooker came to London in defence of Jorgensen, and who he feared was suffering from the impressions that Banks was receiving from Trampe. But dining with Banks that month he found the subject of Jorgensen of less weight with his host than that of Iceland itself and pressure from him for the writing of a book. For this Banks placed his own journal at Hooker's disposal confirming the loan on 16 June 1810:

> ... The papers containing memorandums of some matters I saw in Iceland you are welcome to use as remembrances, but as I have declined to publish them myself you will easily understand that I had no view when I put them into your hands of their being published in my name or with any kind of reference to me; as far as they may be useful to you in your own work, they are entirely at your service. I meant them as some recompence for the loss of your own papers, and in this point of view I am in hopes they may be of some use.

So indeed they were as Hooker was to acknowledge with his use also of some of drawings of 1772 and the continuing assistance of Banks in the two publications, notably the engraving of the maps of the island. First came the private printing at Yarmouth in 1811 and then in 1813 the public edition of *A Journal of a Tour in Iceland, in the Summer of 1809*.

However while the first edition was in preparation, his pleas on behalf of Jorgensen made no headway against the evidence of the Dane's behaviour before and during the Iceland 'revolution'. Banks with his wide sources of information as well as his intuitive judgement of men, had formed a less favourable view of Jorgensen. In this he balanced Trampe's account of events which he summarized in May 1810, as 'A Brief Recital of some of the enormities lately committed in Iceland, by the crew of the Letter of Marque, Margaret & Anne ...' against Jorgensen's verbal account to him in October 1809 supplemented by his later written version sent to Banks by Hooker to whom he returned it on 15 June 1810 with a severe condemnation of both Phelp and

Jorgensen. Two weeks later on 29 June, again to Hooker, Banks pronounced a sort of final anathema:

> ... Whether the merchant or the usurper best deserve to be hanged is a matter that may be doubted, but that both of them deserve it richly for hazarding the destinies of an innocent nation in order to facilitate their trade, is what I do not doubt, and a matter of which I think you will in due time be convinced if you are not already.

But Hooker continued in support of Jorgensen, and his published account remained partial to the Dane and his part in events, while the volume as a whole was dedicated to Sir Joseph Banks. Jorgensen was in time released and several years later, while Banks was ill in bed at Spring Grove, he sent him one of the long manuscript accounts he had composed as an 'Account of the Revolution in Iceland 1809'. Banks found it prolix and unamusing, with 'little indeed of that plain unvarnished narrative which truth best loves to be clothed in', as he told Hooker on 2 September 1813. A month later Banks dismissed Jorgensen from his life in a further letter to Hooker on 2 October:

> ... Respecting Jorgensen all I can say is, that I do not mean to give myself any further concern about him, his good or evil for hence will be alike indifferent to me; it is not my wish to exercise the office of an avenger and I thank God it is in no shape my duty to interfere in his case further than I have done.

This was quite unlike the relationship between Banks and Hooker for, to the abiding distress of Dawson Turner who wished Hooker safe at home and bound to his desk and drafting board, the subject of distant travel continued to come forward at Soho Square.

In May 1810, the prospect of a voyage to Ceylon, by way of the Brazils, had somehow intruded as Banks and Hooker discussed Icelandic affairs together over breakfast. This was not unreasonable for Banks had just convinced the King that the establishment of a Royal Botanic Garden in Ceylon would be an advantage in the transfer of new species from the Far East as a staging post in their gradual acclimatization. William Kerr was to be transferred from Canton to set this new garden in operation. Moreover Banks had just prepared guidelines for Sir Gore Ouseley, recently appointed as Ambassador to Persia, with the Botanic Garden in Ceylon as an important recipient of desirable Persian species of horticultural, especially culinary, importance. Again Hooker was seduced by the Soho Square ambience into volunteering for a journey to Ceylon. Again Dawson Turner was shocked, though somewhat eased by the delay which Banks had counselled until the following year. But Hooker, inspired by the prospect, returned to Halesworth to labour hard at his *Jungermanniae*, Turner's *Fuci*, and especially his *Journal of a Tour in Iceland* for the first private circulation, spurred by the rising competition of Sir George Mackenzie's visit to the island that summer. By March 1811 his *Journal* ... was finished and ready for printing. In May, by the arrangements which Banks had promised, he settled at the India House to study the flora in the drawings by the native artists whom Dr William Roxburgh had so competently mobilized over the years in association with Banks who was then supervising the third volume of the engraved *Plants from the Coast of Coromandel* which he had selected. Hooker now

465

began the long process of making his reduced copies of the drawings and under this stimulus made his first visit to the Royal Botanic Garden at Kew to view the living plants themselves – a first view, indeed, of what he would come to 30 years later as the first official Director. His Iceland *Journal* . . . was privately published in August 1811 and the first volume of *British Jungermanniae* in April 1812, but his ambitions for Ceylon were blighted by the complications of his estate affairs, not eased until May 1813. Now the spectre of the Far East took a new form.

The ramifications of global war had recently brought the Dutch East Indies into British possession under the governance of Stamford Raffles and from this change had emerged a report from Dr Thomas Horsfield directing attention to the claims of natural history in the island of Java. If Hooker was willing to go Banks was now ready to approach Earl Bathurst, President of the Board of Trade, for finance covering an expedition to that island to gather living plants for Kew and knowledge about the spice trees of the Indies. Again, and for the last time, the torch of adventurous travel in the service of botany raised its beckoning glow for Hooker but the family clamour urging a quieter domesticity, abetted by the voice of Dawson Turner, in the end prevailed. For Banks in his bed at Spring Grove, the news was unwelcome but grudgingly accepted, as the young man he had done so much to inspire and help receded from him. The ghosts of the dead men of the *Endeavour* voyage from the fatal stay at Batavia still haunted the public memory but Banks, the old survivor, could not forbear to press his case for courage in the pursuit of natural knowledge whatever the known risks. In his letter to Hooker of 19 June 1813 his final thrust, unavailing in its challenge, condensed the essence of his own life and purpose:

> . . . Let me hear from you how you feel inclined to prefer ease and indulgence to hardship and activity. I was about twenty-three when I began my peregrinations. You are somewhat older; but you may be assured that if I had listened to a multitude of choices that were raised to dissuade me from my enterprise, I should have been now a quiet country gentleman ignorant of a number of matters I am now acquainted with, and probably have attained no higher rank in life than that of country Justice of the Peace.

This clear-sighted recognition by Banks of the *Endeavour* voyage as the turning point in his own life stands well in the light of all we now know about the man. But neither he nor Hooker could know in 1813 how critical for the future was the younger man's decision to remain at home. The path of 'ease and indulgence' led, not to the grave, but the Regius Chair of Botany at Glasgow on the advice of Banks and to the vast herbarium and library for Kew. The path of 'hardship and activity' was reserved for the next generation born in the comfort of the Brewery House at Halesworth in 1817, as Joseph Dalton Hooker.

III

The 'cargo of Scotsmen' whom Banks had deterred from visiting Iceland in 1809 were in fact three youthful students of the University of Edinburgh but only one of them a Scot – their leader, some eight years the eldest, Sir George Steuart Mackenzie, 7th Baronet of Coul, Strathpeffer, in Ross and Cromarty. A gifted mineralogist and pupil of Robert Jameson, he was already known to the scientific world by his demonstration, at the age of 20, that diamonds were a pure form of carbon. He had since moved into the orbit of Banks as an enthusiastic proponent of the Merino breed of sheep in Scotland and a beneficiary of the King's flock by his purchases at the public sale of 1807. As a serious landholder he had been influenced toward the Spanish breed directly by the published reports of Banks and Caleb Hillier Parry in the south and the experience of Sir James Montgomery of Stobo in Peeblesshire and General William Robertson of Lude near Blair Atholl in Perthshire. In 1809 he distilled the essence of his sheep lore into a small but important *Treatise on the Diseases and Management of Sheep* . . ., adding greatly to its value with a 53-page *Appendix, containing documents exhibiting the value of the Merino Breed of Sheep, and their progress in Scotland.* For the first time this gathered in one place the succession of reports printed by Banks since 1800 on the royal flock including the latest on *Some Circumstances relative to Merino Sheep* . . . of January 1809. Now with the approval and support of Banks, he had proposed a summer expedition to Iceland primarily as a *curioso* with a special interest in geology, supported in other fields by his younger companions Richard Bright and Henry Holland, still in the throes of their medical education at Edinburgh. So in May 1810 this party of future Fellows of the Royal Society landed at Reykjavik to be briefly caught in the aftermath of the 'revolution' of the year before.

Mackenzie brought the first copy of the Order in Council of 7 February 1810 which Banks and Trampe had managed to negotiate for the liberation and protection of Icelandic ships trading with London and Leith. William Hooker apparently had hoped to return with Mackenzie somehow to retrieve his botanical losses but had withdrawn as the Edinburgh party promised to collect for him. As a base Mackenzie occupied Trampe's house in the absence of any other, sending his apologies in his letter of 20 May 1810 to Banks for the liberty he took but hoping that some good was done by keeping a fire in it. The heavy losses among the island's horses during the previous winter made it difficult to find sufficient mounts but in the end the three young men returned, after a successful summer tour, with an ample harvest of specimens for themselves and enough to offset some of Hooker's losses.

Mackenzie's account of his *Travels in the Island of Iceland during the summer of 1810* was a composite affair with chapters on the botany and zoology by Richard Bright and those on the history, literature and diseases of the Icelanders by Henry Holland. The first edition in 1811 carried no reference to the 'revolution' as a matter of legal discretion during the course of Samuel Phelps's litigation but in the second edition of 1812 Mackenzie's version of the events of 1809 appeared, with its criticism of what Hooker had put before the public on this theme. In the resulting tension between these two young men Banks kept tempers fairly cool though Mackenzie's view was perhaps closer to his own. At one point it seems Mackenzie had some time before his actual visit suggested that Banks might recommend him as Governor of Iceland. That this notion had not wholly died was evident in the letter Mackenzie sent to the Marquis of Wellesley, the Foreign Secretary, and which was passed on to Banks at Revesby Abbey by Charles Smith, the under-secretary, on 15 October 1810 for comment. Banks returned the document marked 'Secret' on 18 October commenting that

. . . Sir G. would not in my judgment have made so good a Governor as any one of the Junior Clerks in your office.

Official British representation in Iceland from 1810 was limited to that of the consul, John Parker, who held the post until the war ended. Banks and Mackenzie continued a friendly relationship on Icelandic matters as late as October 1815 when Rasmus Christian Rask, the Danish philologist, returning from two years' study of the language in Iceland, proposed the formation of a society to preserve the culture of the island. Both Rask and Mackenzie independently sought the support of Banks but, while they must, with little doubt, have had a sympathetic ear in Soho Square, there is no evidence that any action followed from that quarter. The ending of the war and the banishment of Napoleon in 1815 had released a flood of new demands global in their range and taxing enough in their variety on the waning physical powers but not on the enthusiasm of Banks nor on his abiding sense of duty.

IV

The Order in Council of February 1810, which Banks had done so much to promote and which Mackenzie had carried to Reykjavik in the spring that year, declared Iceland and the other Danish possessions in the North Atlantic to be neutral for the purposes of trade. Intended essentially as a humanitarian safeguard to the survival of the isolated colonies in time of war, the Order was less successful in practice than was hoped. Imports from Iceland did not escape the high protective duties at the British ports. The ships accordingly failed to dispose of their cargoes and were often detained for long periods. Under strong pressure from Banks, Mackenzie and others, the Board of Trade finally agreed as a special dispensation that the cargoes could be sold in Denmark. But the problem of survival among the Icelanders remained a haunting threat and Banks was again induced by events to contemplate annexation of the island as a practical solution offering relief to its inhabitants and some measure of gain to Great Britain. His thoughts focused on the rich fishing resources of Icelandic waters as the leading benefit to be expected by the United Kingdom, an argument he had previously raised but which he now developed. In late March or early April 1812 he sat down to state the case, possibly soon after his return from chairing meetings of proprietors at Spalding and Holbeach early in March opposing the Commissioners of the South Holland Drainage. In the last days of the Perceval administration Castlereagh had become Foreign Secretary and it is possibly to him that Banks addressed his 3000-word paper entitled: 'Some Notes relative to the ancient State of Iceland, drawn up with a view to explain its importance as a fishing station at the present time, with comparative statements relative to Newfoundland.' Over the triangular relationship between Great Britain, Denmark and Iceland, Banks cast his net wide. The document assembled a chronology of significant events from the first Norwegian settlement of Iceland about AD 860 to the most recent happenings. Point by point he invoked a range of authorities, historical and geographical – Richard Hakluyt's *Voyages* . . ., Thomas Rymer's *Foedora*, Johannes Meursius's *Historia Danica*, Anton Büsching's *Erdbeschreibung*, Thomas Hearne's *Liber Niger Scaccarii* the *Itinerary* of John Leland, William Camden's *Britannica*, the *Chronicles* of John Stow, and so on. These classical sources were engrafted with his own direct experiences of Newfoundland and Iceland and capped by his most recent reference, the chapters of young Henry Holland in Mackenzie's *Travels* . . . published in October 1811. The conclusion was that, with the Newfoundland fishery now largely in the hands of the United States, the Iceland fishery managed by Denmark threatened to become a formidable rival to that of the United Kingdom. This could be averted and the Icelanders safely fed from British sources if they could be induced to cede their country 'to partake of the blessings of British liberty' with their private property respected and their ancient laws retained. In short his view was

> ... That the island be ceded to the Crown of the United Kingdom as a Royal fief to be held as Alderney, Guernsey &c. are held, the King having the same power in the island, as the king of Denmark had before its annexation.

But however much the Cabinet may have been better informed on the place of Iceland in the world by this essay, their collective political wisdom, for which Banks always professed an outsider's respect, dictated otherwise. The political principle of expedient inaction prevailed. This was the last explicit proposal by Banks on the subject to the Government and presumably the Danes knew nothing of it at the time, for during the same weeks there was much correspondence between Count Reventlow, the Danish Ambassador to London, and the Danish Foreign Office on the matter of reward to Banks and Mackenzie for their humane efforts to relieve the distressed Icelanders. On 12 May 1812 Reventlow had written on behalf of the Danish Government thanking Banks for all that he had done. On the same day he wrote also to Joachim Castenschiold, who had succeeded Trampe at Reykjavik as Governor of Southern Iceland, urging him to write in the same vein also to Banks. In June Banks thanked Reventlow and assured him of his continued concern for the Danish colonies of Iceland, the Faeroes and Greenland and on 22 August Castenschiold added his own appreciation of all this philanthropy.

   This last encomium proved more than Banks felt able to accept as properly his due. He replied some time in November after his return from Revesby Abbey somewhat pained to learn how much his services seemed to be overrated by the Danish Government and the Court, but anxious to set the record straight:

> ... It would be a silly presumption in me to take to myself the merit of a line of conduct which flows from the natural humanity of the English nation carried into effect by the wisdom and moderation of my Sovereign & his Ministers; I do not wonder that the Merchants who see me often on their business attribute to me more than belongs to me; in my Station as one of the Committee of Privy Council for Trade it is my duty to attend to such Points as my Fellows intrust to my Especial charge. among these are the affairs of Iceland Greenland &c. I hear & represent to the Comm[itt]ee the cases that occurr, but Sir it is from the benevolence of the British Cabinet & in no shape from me that the Regulations made in favor of the unoffending Colonists have originated & brought to maturity. I am merely the organ and engine of promulgating their good works. To them then & not to me must the Credit of having acted with humanity wholly attach.
>
> It grieves me to be under the necessity of destroying the good opinion which your Gracious Sovereign & his Excellent Minister have entertained in my favor, but truth renders it necessary for me to state the Facts above mentioned ...

This plain disclaimer of any special merit did not prevent the Danes, some five years later, from setting the seal on their appreciation of what they knew to have been his part in helping Iceland and the other colonies to survive the rigours of the long conflict which had so disturbed their friendship with England. This was conveyed by the King of Denmark, Frederik VI himself, in a letter dated 7 September 1817 and the gift of three cases of books, including the *Flora Danica*. These arrived at Soho Square to find Banks deeply involved in plans to resolve the uncertain geography of the Greenland coast and to penetrate the Arctic as far beyond as man could go.

CHAPTER 23

THE MASK OF ISLAM AND LAST SERVICES TO KEW
1807-1820

After the departure of Mungo Park on his second expedition in January 1805 there was a lull in the affairs of the African Association until news of the death of its other missionary, Henry Nicholls, on the coast at Old Calabar. This was announced at the General Meeting in the Thatched House Tavern on 3 May 1807, some two years after the event. The return of Brown and Bauer with the *Investigator* collections in 1805 had injected a new stimulus at Soho Square in botanical science and art. This was reinforced by the return of William Roxburgh from the Garden at Calcutta on sick leave bringing Indian botany much to the fore in direct discussions with Banks. In the summer of 1806 William Hooker had settled in nearby Frith Street and in July 1806 a young Swiss alumnus of the universities of Leipzig and Göttingen arrived carrying a letter from Professor Johan Blumenbach to Sir Joseph Banks. Although he did not know it then, Johan Ludwig Burckhardt, at 22, by those few short steps had taken a long stride toward immortality in Middle East and African exploration.

He was immediately accepted by Banks who took him under his wing. For a year Burckhardt hunted his fortune in London but the political wind was not favourable in those civil service departments where he sought employment as a protégé of Banks. At last, almost in penury from a firm refusal to tap the family wealth in Basle, he succumbed to Banks's subtle intellectual indoctrination. For him the future was dedicated to that same African vision for which Park and Hornemann had, unknown to him or anyone else, already given their lives, but whose long silence tempted emulation; Banks and the African Association had found in Burckhardt not the last but perhaps the greatest, most dedicated and erudite of the young 'missionaries' sacrificed in the cause of African exploration. As a first step Burckhardt during 1807 studied Arabic at Cambridge under the wing of that inveterate traveller and mineralogist, Dr Edward Clarke, late senior tutor of Jesus, present Vicar of Harlton, future Professor of Mineralogy, university librarian, and ultimately custodian of the Burckhardt manuscripts from the Middle East. In London he had the benefit of the oriental wisdom of W. G. Browne during his scholarly interim from hazardous travel in those very regions that Burckhardt was to enter in a similar disguise; and, as always, Banks. The African Association now woke to action again round that small nucleus of men with Banks at its heart.

He had ceased to be Treasurer of the Association in 1804, his place being taken by Dr Anthony Hamilton, FRS, Vicar of St Martin-in-the-Fields. But he remained effectively as Secretary and certainly as the centre of active inspiration with Francis Rawdon-Hastings, FRS, 2nd Earl of Moira, as his longest serving companion in their small committees. On 21 March 1808, a committee of five – Sir Joseph Banks, the Earl of Moira, Roger Wilbraham, William Morton Pitt, Dr Anthony Hamilton – accepted Burckhardt's offer as a volunteer for African exploration under its direction.

In April this was confirmed in a meeting of the Earl of Moira, Banks and Hamilton, noting that Burckhardt remained firm in his decision and ready to accept 'half a Guinea per Diem' as recompense 'from the time of his departure from England' with books and instruments provided by the Association. During the year Burckhardt continued his studies, growing a beard, becoming accustomed to oriental dress and enuring himself to foot travel in hot sun with rough living, mostly in the Cambridge countryside. On 20 January 1809 his instructions were framed by Banks and Hamilton in general terms, based on those to Park and Hornemann with which he had become familiar, and were given to him on 26 January 1809 when the terms of his engagement were made final.

For his clothes and outfit he was to receive £70 with £55 allowed for his passage to Malta. From the date of his leaving England and during the period to be spent in Asia Minor and Syria his salary was to be 10s.6d. per day. From the day of his arrival at Cairo this was to become one guinea per day which was to cease if, after a year from the receipt of his last letter, there was no further news of him. If he had not been heard of by the beginning of 1819 his salary was to be at the disposal of the Treasurer of the Association but in no case was Burckhardt to have a claim on the Association for more than six years' salary, though he could claim on its generosity if the funds permitted. Finally £150 were to be lodged immediately to his credit in Cairo for 'the purchase of beasts of burden and goods' when he was ready to set out for the interior of Africa.

Five weeks later, on 2 March 1809, he left England and passing through Malta by an arrangement with the Colonial Department, which Banks had engineered, reached Aleppo on 14 July. For the next three years he travelled and studied Arabic and the Arab culture in Syria and the Arabian Peninsula uncovering, among other places strange to European eyes, Petra the 'rose-red city'. Between September 1812, when he reached Cairo, and the summer of 1815 when he returned to that city, he travelled through the Nubian Desert to Upper Egypt and the Sudan, across the Red Sea as a pilgrim in the guise of 'Sheikh Ibrahim' to Mecca and Medina. But for one brief excursion to the Sinai Peninsula during a bout of plague in the summer of 1816, he lived the last two years of his life comfortably but quietly in Cairo, waiting for that pilgrim caravan returning from Mecca under whose cover he would hope to travel west across the Fezzan or the Maghrib in search of the elusive Niger and its true course.

For the eight years of his wanderings since March 1809 he had kept a steady correspondence with Banks sending some 26 letters until late in 1817. In Cairo he completed the journals of his travels in Syria, Nubia and Arabia, extended his collection of Arab manuscripts, gathered Egyptian antiquities and, most notably, with Henry Salt and Banks (in his role as a Trustee of the British Museum), organized the transfer from Egypt to London of the head of the 'young Memnon', that of Rameses II. Salt was another scion of the African Association; the sum of £500 had been voted to him at a Committee meeting on 26 December 1808 to cover whatever opportunities for finding the source of the Niger might emerge during his journey to the upper Nile and Abyssinia on his mission to the Emperor from the Secretary of State for Foreign Affairs. Now he was British Consul in Cairo and in this capacity as well as that of African traveller he attended Burckhardt as he lay dying on 15 October 1817 from dysentery. The last phase of the north African crossing, for which he had so long prepared, was unfulfilled even as it was about to begin. As

Sheikh Ibrahim he died and according to Muslim rites so he was buried. This news was sent to Banks by Salt in a letter of 21 October 1817 noting the bequest by Burckhardt of his Arabic manuscripts to the University of Cambridge. Early in 1818 these passed through Banks's hands to Dr Edward Clarke, now the university librarian. More than a year later in 1819, the Association for Promoting the Discovery of the Interior Parts of Africa, published under the imprint of John Murray *Travels in Nubia; by the late John Lewis Burckhardt*, preceded by the long series of letters to Banks between 22 April 1809 and 18 May 1817.

II

There were other frontiers and other obstacles to European curiosity than the north African mysteries which Park, Hornemann and Burckhardt set out to penetrate. Three months before Johan Burckhardt entered, another young man, under the stimulus and advice of Banks, had landed in Sydney on 11 April 1806 from the female convict ship *William Pitt*, replete with all the appurtenances of a free settler hoping to farm and rear livestock in the new colony. Gregory Blaxland had first approached Banks in September 1804. Within six months he and his elder brother John had been converted from farmers in Kent and Sussex into aspirants for extensive land grants in New South Wales and hopeful breeders there of the fine Spanish Merino fired by the practical example of John Macarthur returning to Elizabeth Farm with his expensive prizes from the royal auction in August 1804. But it was not until 1 September 1805 that the younger Blaxland sailed to take up at South Creek near Penrith the first grant toward some 8000 acres. Thus the first Blaxland acres lay almost within the shadow of that deceptive sandstone barrier to western expansion known to Governor Phillip as the Carmarthen and Landsdowne Hills but which by 1793 had become the more familiar Blue Mountains.

From the first year of the infant settlement at Sydney Cove, Banks had been kept informed on the slow struggle to extend the area of useful occupation beyond the limits of the undulating eucalypt savannah and patchy fertility of the Cumberland Plain. Phillip had told him much about his first tentative explorations; Major William Paterson, had attempted the passage of the mountain barrier by the Grose River valley in 1793; George Bass had attempted to scale the modest heights in 1796; Wilson, Hacking and Barracks had tried a southern route in 1798; Ensign F. L. Barrallier had found the Kowmung River and Kanangra Walls in his path in November 1802, as far as Banks could discover from the charts and journals brought home in HMS *Glatton* with their author in May 1803; George Caley had followed the 'cow pastures' south and the foothills to the west of them in October 1802. In February 1804 Caley had penetrated as far west as Mount Banks on the north side of the Grose River, sending his journal and maps of these attempts home to Banks by Robert Brown in the *Investigator* in 1805 – too late for Gregory Blaxland to have seen before he left England, but timely enough for Banks to have discussed their significance with John Blaxland as he prepared during the summer of 1806 to join his younger brother in the colony. As he sailed in his whaler *The Brothers* in September, he carried from Banks not only his good will but introductory letters to both governors, the departing King and his successor Bligh. Banks may also have planted the idea that the woodlands or 'forest' country of the Cow Pastures and its like elsewhere might be 'more fitting for Neat Stock than for Sheep', a thought he had

473

noted in his enquiries of Captain William Kent, possibly prompted by Caley's description. Certainly the elder Blaxland must have carried a large measure of inspiration from Banks who was labouring hard that summer with the new Portland administration and especially, perhaps, in the education of William Windham as Secretary for War and the Colonies. On 4 June he had completed his long paper headed 'Some Remarks on the Present State of the Colony of Sidney, and on the means most likely to render it a productive, instead of an expansive settlement'. There may well have been some echo in the ears of the Blaxland brothers of the rallying call of its last lines

> . . . and it must be remember'd that the district now propos'd to be open'd to the investigation of British adventure is about as unknown to civilis'd nations as an equal portion of the moon, and probably hides within its broad bosom objects of commerce, materials for manufacture, and sources of wealth of the utmost importance to the future welfare and prosperity of the United Kingdom.

But the first acres, granted without enthusiasm by Bligh to the Blaxlands, near the present Luddenham lay at the western limit of that 'district now propos'd to be open'd', in the rain shadow of the Blue Mountain barrier rising less than five miles away across the River Nepean. In the hottest and driest fringe of the small colony the Blaxland grant was vulnerable to the worst effects of drought in the years 1810–11 exacerbated by the caterpillar plague of September 1810. A further plague in the southern spring of 1811 and the prolonged dry seasons of 1812–13 altogether implied a devastation of crops and pastures more than enough to drive Gregory Blaxland to seek new land for the cattle which the brothers favoured on their holdings.

Thus, in the summer of 1810–11 Gregory Blaxland probed the country south and west of the Cow Pastures along the Warragamba valley in search of an outlet, much as Caley had done in 1802. In 1811 he tried the same 'Western' river by boat as far as he could go without success but with a new insight into a more hopeful method of attack. In essence the plan called for a bold ascent to the high land directly visible west of the Blaxland grant and then to follow the ridges, leaving the Warragamba to the south and the Grose River to the north. He revealed this to Governor Macquarie after a dinner with him several days before starting but received little more than a reserved approval and permission to proceed. Then, on 11 May 1813, Blaxland started from his Luddenham farm with his party – Lt John Lawson, the young colonial-born William Charles Wentworth, four convict servants, four horses and some dogs. By 28 May, after an arduous passage through the dry mountain scrub, it was clear that a way through to the interior had been found even though the main range had not been passed. This was soon attained by the surveyor George Evans in December 1813 when he penetrated 100 miles beyond Blaxland's furthest point. The first road was built by William Cox with convict labour during 1814 and in April 1815 Macquarie himself was able to travel over the range some 135 miles in nine days to the site of the present city of Bathurst. The hinterland was, in Banks's words 'open'd to the investigation of British adventure' at last.

The first account of this expedition by its leader came to Banks under cover of a letter dated 10 November 1816, a modest octavo manuscript of 38 pages entitled 'A Journal kept by one of a party whilst passing the Blue Mountains in New South Wales . . .'. This came to Soho Square about April 1817 at the same time as the first deep penetration of the silent western plains was about to begin under Lt John Oxley, RN. It was he who provided the novitiate in Australian botany for Allan Cunningham, the Kew collector sent by Banks, engaging his time profitably on the expedition, until fresh orders came from London, and was the flowering of a new career. But for Gregory Blaxland his letter to Banks was a last cry for recognition, denied him by Macquarie; never accorded him from Whitehall.

> ... May I request Sir that you will have the goodness to explain to His Majesties Ministers how far I have endeavoured to be of service to the Colony since I have been in it and how far in your opinion I have succeeded and how far it may be considered I have been able to make a return on my part for the expense incured [sic] by Government in the first instance. I have Memorialised Lord Bathurst on the subject and offered to explore the interior of the Country further in any direction possible that might be required but I have heared [sic] nothing further respecting it nor have I received an answer ...

But Banks himself was a very sick man in 1816 and he too may never have replied. Blaxland's enthusiasm for further exploration withered in the chill of official lack of interest; he never settled beyond the Blue Mountains himself, but rested content as the vigneron of Brush Farm on the Parramatta River and the pioneer of Australian wine. It was his brother John who exploited the pastoral future of the colony as the pioneer of cattle breeding but, again, not west of the Blue Mountains but north of the Hunter River.

III

The spring of the year 1814 held the promise of peace at last. Napoleon had abdicated on 11 April and had been banished to Elba. During that month Banks, with the aid of the *eau médecinale*, had recovered from a short fit of gout. By the first week in May he was well enough to face the pleasures of his Sunday *conversazioni*. These were heightened now by the presence of those who had recently come from Paris with optimistic news. At Kew something of this euphoria stirred the blood of W. T. Aiton. On 29 May he wrote to Banks reviving the idea of the Kew plant collectors whose despatch abroad had in the past four years languished because of the King's illness, the Regency, and the war. Now Aiton had several good men fit for plant hunting abroad and he suggested that Banks approach the Prince Regent to allow them to go. South Africa, America and New Holland were territories he had in mind. On 7 June Banks rose to the challenge ready, he said, to resume the indulgence he had formerly enjoyed 'from the gracious kindness of our beloved & afflicted Monarch' in directing the activities of the collectors from Kew. Moreover, he assured Aiton, now that the seas were safe again, he was anxious to see the process of foreign collection for Kew resumed if only to meet the serious competition of the Emperor's garden at Schönbrunn. He nominated the Cape of Good Hope and New South Wales as his prime choices for the gathering of conservatory plants and had no doubt he could issue such instructions to the governors at these places that His Majesty's collectors would be able to work effectively in areas hitherto unexplored. He would have liked to recommend Buenos Aires as a hunting ground also but this could not be considered until Spain had regained possession of that rebellious colony. But he turned the matter of the Prince Regent's permission back to Aiton as something he must first obtain, and this followed in due time.

Then, leaving late for Revesby Abbey this year, Banks sent George Harrison, assistant secretary at the Treasury, a long memorandum for the Prime Minister dated 1 September. In this he set out the background of the Royal Botanic Garden, the importance of its foreign collections, specifically recommending the two men Aiton had nominated, James Bowie and Allan Cunningham, as collectors in the regions proposed, and offering to resume his former role as director of their operations. Harrison acknowledged this on 2 September regretting he had missed Banks on his visit to the Treasury with the memorandum. However they arranged to meet and discuss final arrangements on Thursday 7 September. On 9 September Cunningham and Bowie were sent their formal commissions to be collectors of plants 'for H.M. Botanic Garden at Kew' at £180 per annum and such allowances as Banks should approve, and whose instructions, direct or through Aiton, they were to obey. For the rest, Harrison proposed that the Treasury should issue Aiton with such sums as Banks from time to time should approve to finance the work of the collectors and that when Aiton submitted his accounts they would be passed when certified by Banks. This was the same practice which Banks had followed with the Admiralty in directing Flinders over the *Investigator* voyage.

The official seal was fixed on these arrangements when Harrison on 13 September sent word to Banks, now at Revesby Abbey, that Lord Liverpool and the Lords of the Treasury had accepted the recommendations made by Banks in his letter of 1 September. The plan had now been made to cover a period at Rio de Janeiro, then the Cape and so to New South Wales. The collectors would travel by the first King's ship to Brazil and Lord Bathurst would instruct the Governor at the Cape to provide a wagon and oxen when the time came. Harrison also, on 15 September, sent Banks a document for each collector in official form for use either as a sort of passport or letter of introduction as they travelled. On 18 September Banks sent these on to Aiton and to Harrison in his own 'not very Clerkly' handwriting the draft of his own instructions for Cunningham and Bowie for approval and despatch also to Kew. By 1 October Aiton was able to report that the two gardeners had been assigned berths on HMS *Duncan* and that, as Banks had directed, the Foreign Office had provided a letter to Lord Strangford, British Ambassador at Rio de Janeiro.

The *Duncan* sailed from Spithead on 3 October with Cunningham and Bowie and on 28 December was at anchor in the harbour where the *Endeavour* had been so unwelcome in 1768, and to which Banks had found himself so rigidly confined. His expectations that times had changed with the presence now of a sovereign in place of a mere viceroy were only partly fulfilled. The Portuguese dallied for two months before John the Prince Regent of Portugal and King of Brazil granted the two collectors their passports for travel in the hinterland in 'the Three Captainships of Rio Grande, St. Paul's and Minas Geraes', but declined any further useful hospitality to ease the cost in any way to the British Government. In passing this information to Banks, William Hamilton, under-secretary at the Foreign Office, said

. . . You will see that the Portuguese have not improved in their ideas of Liberality.

For real help Cunningham and Bowie depended on the advice of Henry Chamberlain, British Consul at Rio de Janeiro, well known to Banks but whom he overlooked, when he wrote his instructions, as someone to whom they could turn. On 10 June 1815 Banks expressed his thanks to Chamberlain with apologies for his own forgetfulness and by the same despatches approved what Cunningham and Bowie were doing in their journey along the coastal hills south to Sao Paolo, delighted with the specimens he had already received from them. Concluding that his letter would reach them about the time of their return from the south, he included this brief reminder of the purpose of their mission:

> ... We must however continually recollect that one Plant from the Cape of Good Hope or from N S Wales that will live in the dry Stove or perhaps in the Green House is worth in Kew Gardens a score of tender Plants that require the Hot house or Roaster. I trust however that some Plants may & will be found capable of Greenhouse cultivation. In all cases where you suspect a Plant to be hardy you will note it especially in your Journal which will be an useful memorandum for us here.

But he urged them to take the first passage possible for the Cape, noting that

> ... the reception you have met with does not encourage us to wish for any further connexions with the Government of Portugal in the Scientific line ...

And he ended this first of the long sequence of his letters to these two men with a studied reply to their complaint about the discomforts of their situation on board HMS *Duncan* in the Warrant Officers' mess

> ... you must remember your situation is better than that of the Midshipmen who are Gentlemens Sons & that Masson Kerr &c were quite contented with the same provision as you have.

The promise of an enduring peace had not lasted and even as Banks wrote these words the opposing forces were gathering that were to end in the battle of Waterloo one week later. Meanwhile Bowie and Cunningham, more familiar with the Portuguese language and the problems of travel in wild regions after their six months' expedition to Sao Paolo, had become hardened to worse conditions than those of which they had complained. Cunningham, the more sensitive and intellectual of the pair, was now more ready to impose his mark on the correspondence home which at first Bowie, the less literate, had tended to monopolize in replying to the joint letters which Banks addressed to them. The brief intentions for Brazil became a stay of nearly two years as the collectors travelled in Minas Geraes until September 1816. Then within the same week on 25 September 1816 the two collectors left Rio de Janeiro at last on the separate paths which Banks had determined for them.

Bowie, on the *Mulgrave Castle*, reached Cape Town in time to send his report and packages on 12 November but Cunningham, on the convict ship *Surrey*, could not send Banks the first brief word of his movements until, at the entrance to Bass Strait on 3 December, a passing ship bound for Batavia uplifted homeward mail. Then on 20 December 1816 Cunningham, from the ship at anchor in Port Jackson, had his first sight of the vegetation, so deceptively dull to the ordinary eye, so rich in botanical variety to the perceptive collector.

Allan Cunningham *aet.* 41. Drawing by W. Brockedon, 1832.

For James Bowie the future lay in extending the work of Francis Masson as far as possible and this he diligently pursued until several years after the death of Banks when the funds for Kew collectors had shrivelled, and he was recalled in 1823. But at the outset he earned the disapproval of Banks for expenditure rather beyond the limits he had been set by buying slaves to help in the garden he had impetuously established with the best of botanical intentions. These strictures had been written by Banks on 26 March at the end of a gouty winter but his views on the economics of collecting had also been stimulated as a Trustee of the British Museum and the sight of the extraordinary mass of specimens in natural history recently brought home by William Burchell whose example he now held out to Bowie. For future journeys into the interior Bowie was pressed to study Burchell's example as a traveller and as a collector, in Banks's view unexcelled. But in the short view Banks set a specific objective, confining Bowie to the neighbourhood of the Cape or to brief excursions to places which Masson had already visited for

> ... the first business expected to be done by you is to replace the Plants sent home by him which have perishd without having been increasd, their Names stand in the *Hortus Kewensis*, it is therefore most important to the credit of the Garden to replace the Plants & make the Garden correspond with the Catalogue.

478

However he applied a balm in reminding Bowie of the excellent character he bore from his South American performance and reporting the abundance of new species already flowering at Kew that spring for which he and Cunningham were owed a great debt. It could not be said on the other hand that the advance provisions attempted by Banks through the office of Earl Bathurst with the Governor at the Cape, Lord Charles Somerset, were immediately effective for James Bowie. The Governor 'did not remember' any letter from Lord Bathurst directing official aid to the Kew collector but in the end various easements were provided to the satisfaction of both Banks and Bowie. The situation between Cunningham and the other Colonial Governor, Colonel Lachlan Macquarie, at Sydney, New South Wales, suffered also but more awkwardly from a failure of understanding by the Governor or from a failure of communication from the official hand at home in spite of the effort by Banks to establish the status and needs of a collector from Kew on His Majesty's business.

Cunningham's first meeting with Governor Macquarie was at Parramatta on 21 December 1816 – the day after his arrival from the long passage from Rio de Janeiro. Macquarie received him with courtesy, disclaimed having been sent any special instructions concerning him, but promised such help as he himself deemed necessary in the making of his collections. The Governor however, in the absence of specific instructions otherwise, strongly advised Cunningham to join the expedition being mounted under John Oxley to cross the Blue Mountains for exploration beyond the limits established by George Evans over a year before. In his first letter from Sydney on 2 January 1817 Cunningham told Banks of his intention to join this expedition as one promising 'an immense number of new & interesting specimens of Plants' in the exploration of virgin territory – unless he received other orders from Banks before he set out. Then on 3 April 1817 Cunningham started from Parramatta with George Evans in advance of the main party to be joined at Bathurst by the leader John Oxley on 15 April. On 8 September 1817 Cunningham returned to Parramatta having been one of a party which had penetrated more deeply into the interior than any before them – some 400 miles from the coast after a journey on foot with led packhorses of over 1000 miles, relieved in part by boat travel, in a first attempt to trace the course of the Lachlan and Macquarie rivers.

On 20 September Cunningham condensed his own account of this first extended 'British adventure' into the Australian interior as a six-page letter to Banks, in advance of his journal which followed in two parts on 1 and 13 December. In five months with the Oxley expedition Cunningham had matured as a botanist-explorer 'through a perfectly Wild and rather difficult Country' and, with the limited transport available to him' had gathered more than 400 specimens and some 150 packets of seeds from a wide range of plant genera, in the course of a very wet season. No immediate 'objects of commerce, materials for manufacture, and sources of wealth' had sprung to the attention either of Oxley or Cunningham on the way but they had traversed that great belt of red-brown earths of the wheatlands-to-be and the wide stretch of temperate short grass and eucalypt savannah to the edge of the saltbush shrub steppe over which the fine-woolled descendants of the old Spanish Merino would roam in numbers enough to render the colony 'a productive, instead of an expensive, settlement'. Moreover, Cunningham in his transect over the Blue Mountains and inland 400 miles west from the coast had crossed botanical territory dominated by five great Australian plant families – Proteaceae, Epacridaceae,

Rutaceae, Leguminosae and Chenopodiaceae – a liberal education in readiness for the years of his northern land journeys.

On 9 September 1817, the day after his return, Cunningham was invited to dinner by Governor Macquarie who gave him the letters from Banks of 13 and 20 February and the associated order for him to join Lt Phillip Parker King

> ... in a Voyage of discovery on the W. & N.W. Coast of New Holland in which it is very much wished that he may anticipate the French who are fitting out a Ship for the same purposes.

Here was the same note of urgency with which Banks had pressed forward the *Investigator* voyage under Flinders to meet the challenge of Nicolas Baudin already at sea with the *Géographe* and *Naturaliste*. Now, 16 years later and the war just over, it was the vision of a voyage preparing under Louis de Freycinet on the *Uranie* that was haunting Banks, anxious for the British to fill the gap in Flinders's cartography and to explore the coastline unvisited by Brown. Banks passed this new challenge on to Cunningham:

> ... this will give you an opportunity of collecting Plants which could by no other means be obtained & of enriching the Royal Botanic Gardens at Kew with Plants which otherwise will have been added to the Royal Gardens at Paris & have tended to render their collection superior to ours.

Flinders and Brown had sailed under orders from the Admiralty; P. P. King and Cunningham were to operate under the Colonial Office; Banks was the common denominator. So it was to Banks that Cunningham turned when he found somewhat less than the help he hoped for from Governor Macquarie or had been led to expect from the tenour of the documents he carried. So it was also to Banks that Macquarie turned on 18 December 1817 taking umbrage at what he conceived to be unmerited complaints gleaned at second-hand from the gist of Cunningham's letter to Banks of 13 December. There were faults on both sides – a blinkered officiousness in Macquarie; an insecure inexperience in Cunningham – but Banks wrote to the Governor in firm but polite defence of the younger and more vulnerable man who had further appealed to him on 20 December. In his reply to Macquarie in July 1818 Banks struck a delicate balance, softening the element of reproof with judicious praise and cooling the whole dispute by directing the vice-regal mind toward the mysteries of reproduction in the duck-billed platypus. The first hard pill he administered in this way:

> ... willing to exculpate Cunningham as Clearly as Possible from the charge of discontent or dissatisfaction at your Conduct I Read to Lord Bathurst the Paragraph in which he states to me the Facts of your having given to him the indulgences of a Servant & Rations but withheld from him the house & the horse he would have been glad to have receivd, his Lordship on hearing it agreed with me that it bore no Resemblance to a Complaint against you & we both suppose that you must have been Greviously misinformd in beleiving so ...

Then came the sugar coating:

... I Seize with Pleasure this opportunity of acquainting you that your enlightened activity in Causing the Country beyond the blue mountains to be explord has securd to you the approbation & gratitude of all Scientific Persons here, we wait with impatience for the Publication of the Journal in order that we may profit by the Fruits of your activity & we Feel Certain that the interesting business of discovery will never cease to be Prosecuted while you Continue to Govern the Colony

While these slow communications were pasing between London and Port Jackson, Lt King had commissioned HMS *Mermaid*, an 84-ton cutter bought for some £2000 at Sydney, and between 22 December 1817 and 28 July 1818 had made his first survey voyage of the north-west coast via King George's Sound with a brief re-fit at Koepang. From here Cunningham wrote to Banks on 9 June 1818 with an account of the voyage which, in spite of the discomforts on the *Mermaid*, he had found congenial both in the company of King and his officers and in the botanical attractions along the 500 miles of strange coast so far surveyed. Then, while King at Sydney settled to his chart work, Cunningham set out by land for a two months' botanical study of that fertile small coastal plain called Illawarra and the Five Islands which were the Red Point of Cook in 1770. For this journey Macquarie had relented in his official parsimony and allowed Cunningham a government horse with both a pack saddle and a cart. With these Cunningham was able to study the vegetation and topography of that steep escarpment which had been the backdrop to the first attempt by Cook and Banks to land on the east coast of Australia more than 48 years earlier. Descending some 1500 feet down the Bulli Pass he reached the foot of the escarpment not much more than a mile from the very beach whose restless surf had so deterred Cook and Banks from landing. Then on 19 December 1818 he followed the journal of the *Mermaid* voyage, sent to Banks on 3 October, with a letter describing the botanical delights of the moist gullies and their sub-tropical rain forest vegetation which had been visible only through a Dollond telescope mistily from the *Endeavour* yawl off-shore. In the last year of his life Banks would see specimens from the site of his first close view of the continent whose exploration he had done so much to set in train. In April 1819 four cases of specimens for Kew would carry the yield from this excursion and the subsequent short voyage of the *Mermaid* in January and February to Hobart in Van Diemen's Land.

Then came the last voyage of HMS *Mermaid* of which Banks was to hear or know anything. On 8 May 1819 King put to sea in company with Lt John Oxley, the Surveyor-General, and the *Lady Nelson*. King and Oxley together surveyed the harbour of Port Macquarie and on 21 May Cunningham reported this to Banks with an account of his own collecting journeys ashore and along the river Hastings. Then the two vessels parted company and King continued on his second northern voyage with a running survey along the Queensland coast, sounding in places where neither Cook nor Flinders had been able to touch land. Then, almost exactly 49 years after the *Endeavour* had been beached in the river of that name, the *Mermaid* came to anchor at the same point and Cunningham became the first botanist to return there since Banks and Solander. But he was prevented from extending their work by the hostile aboriginals although more than a year later on his second visit he was able to botanize more freely. After leaving the Endeavour River the *Mermaid* was beset with troubles but Cunningham kept assiduously at work in spite of his steady debilitating weakness. When King at last was able to bring the leaky *Mermaid* into Koepang on 1 November 1819 he had added 540 miles of coastal survey to the 500 miles of the first northern voyage while Cunningham had gathered over 400 specimens, 200 packets of seeds and bulbs, and had made important observations on the relation between some of the Australian and Indian flora. From Timor then, on 8 November 1819, Cunningham sent to Banks a full account of the voyage up the east coast of Queensland, the completion of the northern survey, and the substance of his botanical and consequent deductions. Then on 20 January 1820 the *Mermaid* anchored again in Sydney Cove. On 13 July King and Cunningham were at sea again on the *Mermaid*'s last voyage to the north and on 9 December 1820, after a hazardous and circuitous return through Bass Strait, reached Sydney with a vessel now unfit for further service.

When Cunningham landed he was no longer the diffident young man, the gardener from Kew. He was now a botanical collector toughened by five years of sea and land travel in some of the world's most remote places and with a quiet assurance achieved by his acceptance among his fellow travellers as a good companion under arduous conditions. He was prepared for the explorations to come as a self-reliant bushman whose capacity for endurance in lonely places had been well tried but he was not prepared for the blow that fell as he scanned the accumulated mail waiting for him on shore that Sydney summer day. Sir Joseph Banks was dead – and had been for the duration of that last precarious voyage of the *Mermaid*. But he had lived to receive Cunningham's letters of 8 November 1819 from Koepang and all the specimens that had gone before, with energy enough to reply on 14 April 1820 in some of the last few lines he would ever write:

> I have receivd safe and in good condition the numerous things you have sent me, and the Royal Gardens have materially benefited by what we had from you. I write you a short letter because I am not well. I know of nothing more to say to you than that I entirely approve of the whole of your conduct, as does also our worthy friend, Aiton at Kew.

Few though they were, these last warm words from the man who had guided his path from afar for so long remained with Cunningham as a sheet anchor of comfort and inspiration in the arduous, productive, but lonely years ahead. Of all the young men whom Banks enlisted to the service of botany on the frontiers of European expansion Cunningham probably stands next to Robert Brown as his most successful proselyte, certainly in his work with the Australian flora.

IV

The establishment of the Botanic Garden at Calcutta had been almost coincident with that of the first settlement at Sydney Cove in New South Wales. As Banks in 1806 grappled with the flood of demands for his opinion on many themes by the short-lived Grenville ministry of the 'Talents', both the garden in India and the colony in the south Pacific were well forward in their development as matters for concern in Soho Square. But it was almost certainly at Spring Grove on Saturday 2 August 1806 that Banks drafted his views on the management of the Botanic Garden at Calcutta for the Court of Directors of the East India Company. Since 1793 William Roxburgh had been assiduous in its supervision and now, for the second time, was home on sick leave consulting with Banks but uncertain whether to return to a climate that was draining his physical reserves but not his botanical fervour. In this quandary Banks seized the occasion to remind the Court of Directors of the twin pillars on which the 'Liberal Plan' of Colonel Robert Kyd for the Garden had rested – first, an increase in food resources and raw materials for trade and manufacture for the Indian population and an insurance against drought and famine; second, the advancement of knowledge in the natural sciences, especially of botany. Both these purposes had been well served by Roxburgh and, in Banks's opinion, would continue if he chose to return. But if he chose retirement, then Banks was prepared to recommend Dr Francis Buchanan, already a candidate, as the most proper person the succeed him. But Banks carried the matter much further:

> My principal Object however in this Letter is to make a Trial whether I have
> sufficient interest with the very respectable body to whom it is addressd to be
> permitted to Lay the foundation of a Proper Succession in future to an
> establishment in the welfare of which I feel a deep interest. I am bold in pleading
> this Cause because it is in favor of a Science to which I have devoted the best part
> of my Life & for which I have voluntarily Exchanged my prospects [of]
> Parliamentary consequence & possibly of high office & I am the more so as I write
> to a body of men [of] whose good will I have receivd Repeated & Continual
> Testimonies & which I have Every Reason to believe I shall Continue to Enjoy . . .

He then emphasized the qualifications necessary in an assistant who could be appointed and who could in time succeed to the Superintendent's post – 'a young man Regularly Educated in Europe to the Science of natural history' but also someone who was 'able to communicate the Knowledge he may acquire in India in a perspicuous & Correct Style'. Such a man, he said, was available in Charles Konig who had been an assistant in his library for the past five years and from whom he would part with regret. Then he concluded with a form of persuasion he seldom used, threatening 'to withdraw all concern in the Plan for the advancement of the Public interest . . . by the Company for the advancement of natural Knowledge' unless proper provision were made for Roxburgh and his son in the Company service. Whether this form of blackmail or the light of pure reason prevailed, the upshot was that Roxburgh returned to Calcutta in 1807 and the management of the Botanic Garden went on as before.

Roxburgh had learned much during his leave in England about the growing standards of botanical illustration. He would, for example, have seen what Ferdinand Bauer had done with the New Holland flora as he worked with Robert Brown whose diagnostic precision also had a lesson. But he had also been prompted to imitate Gaertner in improving the figures and description of the fruits. Daniel Mackenzie was dead, however, but he had left 250 of the planned 300 figures for the *Plants of the Coast of Coromandel* complete, of which 200 had been printed up to May 1805 as Volumes I and II. A further 25 Mackenzie engravings appeared as Part 1 of Volume III in July 1811 but the last 25, as Part 2 in May 1815, Roxburgh would never see in print. Banks himself lived just long enough to see the last 50 engravings of Parts 3 and 4 finished and published by March 1820, produced from the copper plates of Girton, Peake and Weddell. For many years these were all that were published of the work of

Roxburgh's diligent Indian artists until Robert Wight's *Icones Plantarum Indiae Orientalis*, 1840–53, added another 400 from the grand total of 2512 numbered drawings which survive at Kew from the batches sent home to the East India Company over the years 1790–1813. Of the original 300 Indian drawings engraved by Mackenzie and the others for the *Plants of the Coast of Coromandel* some 273 survive but without the Company stamp, no doubt because they were in Banks's keeping for so long at Soho Square.

During the summer of 1813 in India Roxburgh's health broke down and he retreated to the Cape of Good Hope as he had done before in 1798 seeking relief, but without effect. Travelling on to St Helena he remained there from June 1813 to February 1814 when he sailed for England bearing with him the manuscript of his 'Flora Indica' intending it for the press, having left a full copy with Dr William Carey, his missionary friend at Calcutta. Soho Square became his haunt in the spring and summer of 1814 as he worked with Robert Brown checking, correcting and adding to the 2579 numbered descriptions of the full 'Flora' in the three volumes which now lie in the British Museum (Natural History). Here is a record of over 25 years of diligent plant collecting, mainly in the provinces of Madras and Bengal, a check list of the species which were for so long, as dried specimens for Soho Square or living plants and seeds for Kew, the subjects of the steady correspondence between Banks and Roxburgh. But this revised and extended 'Flora Indica' never came to press as Roxburgh's health rapidly declined and he returned to his native Scotland to die in Edinburgh and be buried in Greyfriars Churchyard on 18 February 1815. Only the less complete version with William Carey in Calcutta became the published *Flora Indica* of 1820–4 and 1832, with some additions by Nathaniel Wallich.

After Roxburgh's retirement, his place was briefly taken at the Botanic Garden by Dr Francis Buchanan, in 1814, before his return to England in 1815. Buchanan had been Banks's preferred candidate in 1806 had Roxburgh not then returned to Calcutta. Another Scottish medical man, Buchanan had been known to Banks since the expedition of Captain Michael Symes to 'the Kingdom of Ava' in 1795. From this Banks had received Buchanan's collection of Burmese plants for the Soho Square herbarium where Daniel Mackenzie had prepared the illustrations for Symes's *Account of the Embassy to the Kingdom of Ava* . . .

Last of the superintendents of the Garden at Calcutta within the lifetime of Banks was his nominee Dr Nathaniel Wallich, formerly of the Danish medical services at their settlement at Serampore but, after its capture in 1813, an officer in the same service for the East India Company. Appointed in place of Francis Buchanan in 1815, he was displaced by competing aspirants during a troubled period of two years among whom, briefly, was Henry Thomas Colebrooke, the first great Sanskrit scholar who as a small boy had been tutored in the library and schoolroom in the back premises of 32 Soho Square. But, pressed by Banks, the Court of Directors reinstated Wallich in 1817, and for the next 30 years he reigned over the Botanic Garden and accelerated the rise of Indian botany on Roxburgh's solid foundations. Convalescing at Spring Grove from his carriage accident on 25 August Banks commended Wallich warmly in a letter of 28 August 1818 for services already rendered:

> When I took upon myself to Recommend to the Directors of the East India
> Company to Reinstate you in the charge of the Botanic Garden at Calcutta, I was

Conscious that I was doing a Good & a Proper thing, from the activity intelligence & Zeal you had so amply Evincd while the Garden was under your administeration, but I confess I was not aware [of] the increased Energies which have been this year Exercisd in Favor of my Favorite Establishment The Royal Gardens of Kew . . .

And indeed throughout 1818 and 1819 scarcely an Indiaman sailed from Calcutta that did not carry consignments of growing plants and seeds from Wallich directed through Banks to Aiton at Kew. The losses were heavy in the passage but the gains were great enough, especially in species from Nepal and Sylhet, and the herbarium at Soho Square was continually enriched with dried specimens from the same regions. About these on 1 March 1819 Banks had this to say to Wallich:

. . . We are very busy in my Library with your Specimens none of them however Shall be Publishd here as I Consider the Publication of them to be the Property of you not of myself . . .

So it continued, ship by ship, for the enrichment of Kew and the last months in the life of the man who had made it possible until the final letter from Calcutta of 20 January 1820 announcing the consignment by the Indiaman *Carnatic* of a musk deer, a Madagascar turtle, with seeds for Kew and Spring Grove, none of which Banks would live to see.

V

The summer of 1810 was the last in which Banks and the King had any botanical communication at Windsor Castle and William Kerr was the last collector to benefit from that long collaboration. On 30 June 1810 Banks told Kerr that the King had agreed to the founding of a botanical garden in Ceylon and that he had been appointed Superintendent there in recognition of his diligence at Canton and the many valuable additions to Kew he had provided. For seven years Banks had managed the affairs of Kerr through W. T. Aiton who regularly submitted at Soho Square his accounts and lists of plants being sent to China and from Banks frequently drew advances of money to cover immediate expenses later to be recouped from the Privy Purse. Similarly from Canton at intervals Kerr drew bills on Banks for his expenses as emergencies arose according to the working agreement between them. Only once did Banks show any displeasure with Kerr. This was his muted grumble when Kerr, after exploring Macao and its vicinity, made a hurried visit to Luzon in the Philippines in January and February 1806 against his advice, a mild rebuke softened by his agreement that the results justified the effort made. Kerr's 'Manila Journal' and the catalogue of Philippine plants were sent home on the *Ganges* in March 1806 and duly came to rest at Soho Square. Now in 1810 this virtue was rewarded in the liberal salary and retirement pension that Banks had secured from the King in the last months of their working association, a delicate negotiation with a blind monarch, ailing himself and deeply worried about the failing health of his favourite child, the Princess Amelia. During 1811 William Kerr reached Ceylon on a ship of the East India Company, facilitated by Sir George Thomas Staunton, chief interpreter as he now was at Canton among the supercargoes. Staunton also advanced Kerr his salary for his last months in China which he reclaimed in May 1812 as a bare repayment but to which Banks insisted he should add interest and exchange for the friendly loan. Kerr lived long enough to establish the Botanic Garden at Peradineya near Kandy in 1813 before he died there in November 1814. This news was received by Banks in the spring of 1815 in a letter from Sir Alexander Johnston, FRS, the distinguished President of the Council in Ceylon, dated 12 January, hoping that a successor would be found and sending to Soho Square all Kerr's papers relating to his botanical work. These covered a tour of northern Ceylon and the area of the majestic Adam's Peak.

On 25 June 1816 Banks replied to Sir Alexander Johnston regretting the delay in finding a successor to Kerr. William Huskisson, Chief Commissioner of Woods and Forests, knew nothing of Kerr's affairs but through Earl Bathurst as Secretary for War and the Colonies Banks had at last obtained a passage on HMS *Minden*, Captain Patterson for Alexander Moon, 'a smart young man trained at Kew'. The next day he also wrote a letter of introduction for Moon to Sir Robert Brownrigg, Governor and Commander-in-Chief of Ceylon, who had recently pacified the turbulent kingdom of Kandy. In July Alexander Moon sailed on the *Minden* to be landed at Gibraltar while the battleship joined Lord Exmouth's squadron in action against the pirates of Algeria. During this interval Moon collected plants in southern Spain and round Tetuan in Spanish Morocco until he joined the *Minden* again at the end of October for the voyage to Ceylon. He sent his 'Plants & Seeds Collected in the neighbourhood of Gibraltar, St. Roque, and Tetuan' under the care of General Dunn to Banks before sailing from the Rock, to reach Colombo early in 1817. For the next eight years Moon evidently satisfied the criteria which Banks had laid down in 1811 for the Superintendent at Peradineya as 'a Botanist ... not only skilled in horticulture but also in the names of plants &c.' As such he also ranged widely over the island and his last letter to be read by Banks dated 8 May 1819 recorded the end of his exploration of the province of Kandy, listing 373 kinds of seeds for Kew and some 50 skins of birds and mammals for the British Museum. He developed a herbarium supported by botanical drawings in much the same mode as the practice established at Calcutta and in 1824 produced a *Catalogue of Indigenous and Exotic Plants ... in Ceylon*, cross-checked no doubt, as Banks had also insisted in 1811 with '. . . a person in England ... appointed correspondent to the Garden in order to keep nomenclature consistent &c.' – in other words most probably Robert Brown.

As Banks drafted the plan of the botanical garden for Ceylon, Dr Alexander Anderson of the Botanical Garden on St Vincent resigned his post in July 1811 and died there on 8 September the same year. Ever since April 1772 when his friend Valentine Morris had sought his interest for the introduction of the bread-fruit, the island had been a matter of concern for Banks. The Botanical Garden had come under his notice during the years of his close association with its venerable founder, General Robert Melville, who had dined so frequently under the 'perpetual Dictatorship' of Banks in the 'rebellious dining club'. In 1785 Dr Alexander Anderson had been appointed superintendent of the Garden, under the jurisdiction of the War Office and since then had been an intermittent correspondent of Banks. In June 1807 General Melville submitted proposals to Banks that proper financial provision should be made by the War Office for Dr Anderson and his family. For Banks this was not easy during the vagaries of the Grenville ministry but by 26 March 1809 he had framed a 'Memorial in favour of Dr Alexander Anderson' and submitted it to Sir

James Murray Pulteney, Secretary at War, who, having lost the original, passed a second copy from Banks on to the Lords of the Treasury. This recorded Anderson's long service on the island, collecting and distributing useful plants through the agency of the Botanical Garden of which the bread-fruit was a prime example. It recommended a retirement pension as the continuation of his salary of £1 a day and its reversion unchanged to his widow. But the operation of this War Office benevolence for Anderson himself was a mere three months. Thereafter under William Lockhead the Garden languished for some four years until his death about the time of Waterloo. This same period had also been a sort of limbo for another botanical associate of Banks – George Caley.

Unaware of the actual state of turmoil which had emerged in New South Wales under Bligh as far back as 25 August 1808 Banks had written to Caley:

> ... I have grown of late years very infirm. My eyes fail me much and I have not of course the pleasure I used to have in the pursuit of natural history. I have not, therefore, any longer occasion for your services in the extensive manner in which you have been employed yourself of collecting great quantities of articles. You deserve, however, some reward from me for your diligence and activity.
>
> You have I understand the lease of a farm from Governor King. If you wish to employ yourself in the cultivation of it, or if you wish to return home, I am willing to settle £50 a year upon you for your life and to release you from all services to me beyond what you voluntarily wish to perform. You would probably chuse, if anything new should fall in your way, to send it to me; but as I mean your annuity as a recompense for past services, I shall not bind you to future ones.

But Caley, under more complicated circumstances, returned with George Suttor on board the *Hindostan* with Governor Bligh, as favourable but not wholly uncritical witnesses on his behalf, in the court-martial of Major Johnston yet to come on 7 May 1811 at the Royal Hospital, Chelsea. But Caley was not called. Instead, after hankering awhile for the warmer climate and 'primitive scenes of nature in the wilds of the colony' he returned apparently to his old haunts in Manchester, supported by the annuity of £50 from Banks, supplemented by further monetary gifts from the same source from time to time. Then in 1815 Banks proposed Caley to Earl Bathurst, Secretary for War and Colonies, as Superintendent of the Botanic Garden at St Vincent. In September 1815 he drafted Caley's instructions for the post and on 1 August 1816 Caley had reached his second arena of trial and tribulation but now, at 46, a married man. His salary at £1 a day with rations was identical with that of the late Dr Anderson and over six times the annual wages of his collecting days for Banks in New South Wales – and there is nothing to suggest that Banks did not continue the £50 annuity 'as a recompense for past services'. But from the frying-pan of a convict society in New South Wales he had come to the slow fire of a slave economy in the tropics and a position of sedentary responsibility. For neither, perhaps, was he fitted in personality or temperament but at least in the convict colony he had, the greater liberty of a frontiersman. At St Vincent he was imprisoned with a mere 20 acres as his stamping ground within the confines of a small island. Within two years his wife was dead and within four his old master and patient benefactor had died at Spring Grove. Two years later he resigned from the Botanic Garden and returned to London, a lonely man to the end, dying in Bayswater in 1829 subsisting still on his pension from Banks and the interest from an investment of £100 made for him from the same source in the spring of 1818.

VI

As the tides of war ebbed and flowed across the oceans of the world and the correspondence of Banks for the most part reached its far-flung destinations, a less troubled line of communication was quietly sustained at home. From Soho Square and Spring Grove the Ludlow wagon and the Ludlow and Worcester coaches variously bore letters and packages to the Teme valley, first to the Elton house and, after February 1808, to Downton Castle, bringing in return a steady flow of papers from Thomas Andrew Knight with the results of his horticultural and agricultural observations and experiments. Knight had been elected to a Fellowship of the Royal Society in 1805 for his studies of grafting in trees, cross-pollination on vegetables and the seasonal movement of sap. With further papers on the reproduction of buds and the orientation of the structure of seeds, he had been awarded the Copley Medal in 1806, after the publication of nine papers in the *Philosophical Transactions of the Royal Society*, 1795–1806. All had emerged from the encouragement of Banks and each paper appeared from Elton in the late winter or early spring as a long letter to the President of the Royal Society with whom its form and substance had been discussed. Banks was the anvil on whom Knight shaped his ideas, a critic on whose honesty he could depend, a gardener and agriculturalist with a practical insight like his own. But for ten years or so from when they first met in the spring of 1803 Humphry Davy was also involved with them. From Knight, as also from Banks, in developing the course of his lectures on agricultural chemistry at the Royal Institution, Davy drew much material for his analyses, such as an array of barks for the estimation of tannin as well as from the substance of Knights papers in the *Philosophical Transactions*. Later Davy joined Banks as a referee and critic as in the publication of Knight's paper on the origin and function of sap-wood in August 1808. Until Davy's capture by the widow Apreece in 1811 and their marriage in 1812 there is no doubt that the working association of Banks, Knight and Davy enhanced the value of the published *Elements of Agricultural Chemistry*, 1813. There were however many more by-products of the Banks-Knight correspondence of importance in the origin and growth of scientific ideas than ever found their way into print during the lifetime of the writers, or indeed ever under their own names – even as footnotes in the work of other men. Some 144 letters by one or the other survive – 80 by Banks; 64 by Knight – well over 100 000 words in all. From this material some 22 were published as papers in the *Philosophical Transactions of the Royal Society* before Banks died. These occupied some 200 pages of the *Philosophical Transactions*, in sum therefore about 80 000 words. They form about 2.3 per cent of all the papers published in that journal during the tenure of Banks as President of the Royal Society of which no more than about 3.8 per cent were devoted to general botany or the plant sciences, a field in which Knight was clearly the major contributor. The accusation laid against Banks that 'his favourite science' was excessively represented in the papers submitted to the Royal Society and published in its *Transactions* is certainly not supported by the facts.

The brief life of Lord Grenville's Whiggish ministry had been a troublesome period for Banks and when Grenville resigned office on 25 March 1807 and the new administration dissolved Parliament it was to his evident satisfaction. This leaked through as an unusual expression of his political views in his letter to Knight of 9 May acknowledging the arrival of the paper 'On the Economy of Bees'

> ... The present Tone of the Countrey Promises a Stable Administration The cry of no popery be it ill or well founded never Fails to produce the most powerfull effects on whose against whom it is levelld I do not expect Ever to See a Grenville again in the Service of Geo. 3d ... I hope very Soon to Lay aside the irksome Trade of a Politician & Resume my old habits

But even as he wrote this he was not entirely free from demands on his time far removed from botany. As a member of the Committee of the Privy Council for Coin he had just drafted a 5000-word paper on re-coining the currency for Earl Bathurst, President of the Board of Trade in the new Portland government. This was perhaps his last major advisory paper as a Privy Councillor but not his last service in relation to the Royal Mint with whose re-organization several years later he was concerned. Nor was it his last exchange with Lord Bathurst on the subject, for on the same Saturday, 9 May 1807, he wrote to Knight that he was troubled by William Fawkener, clerk to the Privy Council, for an opinion by Monday morning on what he duly pronounced was a 'Silly & half informed' paper unlikely to impress the Governors of the Bank of England with his Lordship's knowledge of Mint affairs if it were submitted to them.

Before the year 1807 was out Banks and Knight had exchanged ideas on subjects as various as the growing of hautbois strawberries, the depressing effect of Napoleon's advancing Continental system on the price of combing wools, the value of horse-chestnut husks for tanning and of malted grain for fattening livestock, the occurrence of lactation in castrated males of various species, the management of bees in glass hives, the colour variegation of foliage in plants and its transfer by cross-pollination, John Hunter's ideas on the primitive colouration of animal species, and 'a most curious discovery' the frozen carcase of 'the Siberian Elephant or Mammont a Lost Species' near the mouth of the Lena River in Siberia, about latitude 72° North, with 'very Long & very thick hair & Fur' as, indeed it should have been, said Banks, for

> ... we Know that the Coverings of other animals increase [as] the Climate they inhabit is Colder & diminish in hotter Countries

Then too there was the subject of the young Hereford bull at Revesby Abbey, which had come from Knight's herd at Elton as a pioneer of Banks's enthusiasm for the breed in the north, but who seemed to belie the placid reputation of his kind for though, as Banks wrote,

> ... Your young Bull is an angel in my Eyes & our people begin to admire him, ... he has some views of becoming an angel of destruction as well [as] of renovation for he has made some attacks, but the Ring we have put in his nose will we beleive reduce him to Reason ...

But early in September 1808 the animal had turned so dangerous that reluctantly Banks had him slaughtered, a loss somewhat eased by the progeny he had already sired in the Revesby herd among whom his better qualities prevailed. These included one out of a Holderness cow, a gift from the King. And the following year in December the young bull was replaced with another from Elton with three in-calf Hereford cows, all of them droved together the 140 miles across country from Ludlow to Revesby. Knight had arranged that the cows were in calf to three different bulls of the best blood in the county and for the four animals charged Banks £125, though he did this only at the baronet's firm insistence that a gift would be too generous.

The exchanges of 1807 between Banks and Knight were overshadowed in the autumn by the sudden and severe illness of Humphry Davy, an infection incurred it was supposed during his attempt at the disinfection of Newgate Prison. The event followed Davy's brilliant Bakerian lecture on 19 November – 'On some new Phenomena of chemical Changes produced by Electricity, particularly the Decomposiion of Fixed Alkalies . . .' – recording his work with the voltaic battery since 1800 which had now culminated in the recognition of the elements potassium and sodium. The illness of Davy prevented Banks from discussing with him the ideas which Knight had recently put forward on the possible chemistry of discolouration in apples after exposure to air. But for Banks himself it was also something much more, the possible loss of one

> . . . who is the man most willing of all my acquaintances realy to Consider a Question Stated to him Several of my friends will Converse about such matters & tell me what occurs at the moment, he is the only one who will think in my absence & if anything occurs tell me the next morning . . .

Indeed so much did Banks value Davy's Bakerian contribution on electro-chemistry that, as he sat for his portrait to Thomas Phillips, RA in the spring of 1808 as Davy convalesced, he wrote to the artist on 1 April expressing a wish that the manuscript in his hand should be the paper in question as 'This will mark the time when the Picture was painted'.

In 1809 an exceptionally wet August was followed by a hurricane on 26 September which blew down 103 oaks in the estate woods near Revesby. This gave Banks an opening on the subject of transplanting large trees in his letter to Knight of 25 October when he had selected some 50 fallen oaks for re-planting in the Park by a method he had used for over 30 years and had described to Knight on 16 September the year before. He had begun with limes and maples 80 to 100 years old about six feet in girth and had succeeded also with elms and oaks of the same order of maturity.

> . . . Thus I intend to do Justice to Posterity to whose use all these Trees had been abandond as they grew in those parts of my woods which had been lately Cut in a 21 years Course, if they grow in my Park it is well, if now the wind will have Compelld me to apply to my own use a Sum of money the value of those Trees which posterity ought to have receivd

In September 1809 also he sent to Knight a parcel of roots of the stoloniferous fiorin grass *Agrostis alba* L. which he had got from Dr William Richardson at Armagh. At the same time he reported the delay of the 'new' Negretti flock of Spanish Merino sheep at Portsmouth from which no stock could be distributed until they had recovered some condition from their ordeal. It was therefore not until the summer of 1810 that Banks could announce on 4 June the despatch of two rams and five ewes of true Negretti blood to add their genes to those crosses with the old Archenfield breed which Knight had developed from the King's ram No. 130 over ten years earlier. This was some two months after Banks had read his little *éloge* to the Horticultural Society on the Spring Grove Codling, an apple of Knight's improvement at Elton to which Banks had accepted 'the honor of being Godfather' on 3 April 1810. This was a month in which Banks had also confessed to Knight how deeply he was puzzled by the problem of when sex was determined in the developing animal:

> I confess I am in a wood so thick that that I cannot see the trees when I take in my head to attempt to think on the subject of the time at which nature decides the sex of entities destined to propagate their species; the whole question appears to me encumbered with mysteries & clouded by obscurities, that my poor head is by no means a match for them. It does not follow that because an anatomist cannot distinguish the sex of a young foetus that the sex has not been already determined altho' it is not developed: here then I am impaled upon a difficulty from whence I can never extricate myself unless the anatomists shew me better reasons than they have yet done to prove that because the sex is not evident to them it is not determined. After this acknowledgement of my dulness I conclude you will not expect to hear any more from me on the sexual question . . .

But the whole problem of sex and organ differentiation in plants and animals, in the seed and the egg, remained an active topic between them. The mysteries and the obscurities, however, were to remain until the clouds began to lift with Robert Brown's recognition of the cell nucleus 20 years later, but still at 32 Soho Square, and in a further 50 years when the place of the chromosomes in cell division had been established by Walther Flemming, toward the end of the century.

In 1811 Knight became President of the Horticultural Society and in the same year appeared as the author of *Pomona Herefordiensis*, printed by William Bulmer. It was handsomely illustrated with 30 engraved plates by the other William Hooker, a pupil of Franz Bauer whom Banks and Roger Wilbraham pressed on the Society as its horticultural artist. In 1812 Knight again honoured Banks by naming a new peach after Spring Grove. Banks reciprocated with practical help in the study of the fungus affecting pears. Specimens received from Downton Castle were submitted to the discriminating eye of Franz Bauer under his compound microscope and his observations eventually incorporated in the paper by Knight some three years later 'On the mode of propagation of the *Lycoperdon cancellatum*, a species of fungus, which destroys the leaves and branches of the pear tree', printed in the *Philosophical Transactions* for 1816. Within this span of time Banks himself had established his Malta orangery at Spring Grove and engaged the services of Isaac Oldacer during 1814 to build an improved mushroom house there also against the north wall of one of the hothouses. This was inspected and highly approved by a committee of the Horticultural Society on 7 July 1814, reflecting as it did the design and methods used by Oldacer for many years in the Imperial Gardens 'near St. Petersburgh'. Then in August 1816 Oldacer became head gardener at Spring Grove. The following year the *Transactions of the Horticultural Society*, volume II, No. 6, carried an 'Account of the Method of growing Mushrooms in Houses' by Mr Isaac Oldacer, gardener to his

Majesty the Emperor of all the Russias, &c. This paper, with the plan and elevation of the Spring Grove mushroom house, had been prepared for the press by Banks as one of the last few manuscripts to be set out in fair copy by his faithful clerk, William Cartlich.

There were however many other strands in the exchanges between Banks and Thomas Andrew Knight than such horticultural felicities. There was the abortive matter of Broad the rat-catcher and his 'secret' method, but there was also the intrusion of a new element in the evolution of animal as distinct from plant experiments. During 1815 Knight submitted to Banks a paper for the Royal Society by the physician to the Worcester General Infirmary, Dr Andrew Wilson Philip, the first of a series designed to study the effect of cutting the pneumogastric innervation of the stomach on digestion in rabbits. The paper came to Banks at the end of November 1815 and on 15 January he told Knight that it had been accepted for printing. He was away from the chair in Somerset House, however, in bed with gout when the paper was read, and heard the next day from the Vice-President how it had been received. On 16 February 1816 he told Knight that the paper was now unlikely to be printed and on 23 February that Philip had been rejected as a Fellow at the meeting of the previous night, a decision which greatly surprised Banks. The circumstances were clearly put in his own words to Knight:

... The numbers were 56 in favour & 32 negatives but our statutes require full 2/3 of the votes present to make an Election it requires therefore 64 balls to elect him & this notwithstanding the Austrian Archdukes were present as Fellows & no doubt voted for the candidate as did those fellows who attended their imperial highnesses who would not otherwise have been at the meeting.

The cause of this has been the style in which his Paper on the Experiments tried on Rabbits by severing the nerves on which digestion &c depends. These cruel experiments were detailed with all particulars of the tortures experienced by the animals exactly as if the audience were to be composed of none but Butchers & Surgeons. I was in my Bed when the Paper was read but the Vice president in the chair told me the next day that the disgust expressed by the audience was marked by more than half of them leaving the room in succession one at a time the Paper was not concluded but at the next meeting we suppressed the continuation of the experiments & read only the results.

I am sorry for the event though it is a victory of humanity over science. Our comparative anatomists here are careful in the extreme to pass over in their descriptions all that can possibly be availed of the effects of their knives on the sensations of their victims but I suspect that this check will suspend for a time at least their communications to the Royal Society. in fact these matters are better suited to medical & anatomical publications than to the audience as it certainly is of the Royal Society.

I have told you before that the Doctors deduction is held in extreme doubt by our operators. of course I conclude his Paper will not be printed in the Phil. Trans. he will however of course print it in some other way to vindicate his opinions & controvert those of our Physiologists.

I am sorry we have lost so good a Philosopher as Dr. Philips certainly is as an associate but I trust we shall not be deprived of his future endeavours to scrutinize the secrets of nature. If you write to him I pray you to assure him that I grieve at his disappointment but that the conduct of my too humane colleagues have not abated an atom of the esteem in which I have hitherto held [him]. There seems to be a spirit rising against experiments tried upon living animals. I was astonished to hear the other day that [Anthony] Carlisle in his lecture to the Royal Academy [who] had introduced rather abruptly an attack on these experiments concludes by an assertion that anatomists ought to confine their researches to the bodies of dead animals.

Vivisection on the living plant, as in so many of the experiments of Knight himself, held no such emotive overtones. Philip took umbrage at the rejection of his paper and threatened to publish it elsewhere, with an attack on the Royal Society. Banks advised him against the latter but encouraged him in the former course, drawing his attention to the recent action of Dr Caleb Hillier Parry in a similar case. This was an important paper by Parry, rejected by the Royal Society, but now in print under its own title without any hint of what had gone before. As *An Experimental Inquiry into the Nature, Cause, and Variation of the Arterial Pulse; and into Certain other Properties of the Larger Arteries, in Animals with Warm Blood*, 1816, it was indeed dedicated to Banks himself. The 'Animals with Warm Blood' of the experiments were in fact sheep, for the most part, from the Merino × Ryeland cross-bred stock developed by Parry on Sion Hill at Bath into the Anglo-Merino breed derived from Spanish Merino rams from the royal flock. But Philip, rejected again in 1818 from Fellowship of the Royal Society, though he still had the support of Banks, could not forbear to launch his grievance with the Society. He incorporated it in the second edition of his *Experimental Inquiry into the Laws of the Vital Function*, 1818, which Banks deprecated as a misrepresentation of the facts in his letter to Knight of 19 January 1819 though he expressed his willingness to set Philip straight on the matter. For Banks the matter ended there. For Philip time healed the wound with his ultimate election into the Royal Society on 11 May 1826.

For Knight the long correspondence with Banks ended late in 1819 with a last letter from Soho Square on 24 September on pineapples and the virtues of liquid manure but especially those of bone meal as fertilizers, with a last diagnosis on an aberrant form of cherry blossom from Downton:

> Mr. Brown to whom I submitted your premature Cherry blossom, my Eyes having long ago refused to be aided by a microscope, has examined it with his usual care & he declares it not to be a flower but a group of leaves that have assumed the colour of petals. he finds neither Calix Corolla Stamina or style in their proper places & has not therefore a doubt of his conclusion being correct. I rejoice therefore at your having sent up the specimen as it has led to the development of an error which had it not been explained might have led to an abundance of false conclusions . . .

One pair of observant eyes at Soho Square had lost their power to discriminate such things. But in Brown another pair remained acute for many years to come, resolving such problems and opening a new future for botany and the biological sciences at large.

493

VII

The long and close association between Banks and the royal family had been sadly but not finally disrupted by the illness of the King in the late autumn of 1810 and the uncertainties of the restricted Regency in the ensuing two years. The King himself had receded almost completely from ordinary contact with his family and the outside world into the 'Lower Suit of Rooms' at Windsor Castle. Beyond his physicians and his personal staff he was seen by few others. Of his family the Queen alone saw her 'cher Objet' in his isolation. For her these interim months, before the Regency Act became effective after 19 February 1812, were distressing as she faced the new realities of life without the King. Gone for the time being was the Court of St James's. In its place two new Courts had grown at opposite ends of the Mall – her own at the Queen's House and the Prince Regent's at Carlton House.

At a good baiting distance between Windsor and London the villa of Spring Grove always held a welcome for the Queen. Within its precincts increasingly now was to be found the man who so long ago had named a flower and a ship in her honour and who had remained a steadfast friend to the King and herself. Banks would never see the King again and the Queen alone remained a link between these two old men. From the summer of 1813 the Queen found occasion from time to time to pause for a few hours in the warmth of Spring Grove hospitality and the delights of its garden near the royal establishment at Kew. These occasional visits began on Friday 13 August 1813, a persistently wet day, 'to see some very curious & beautiful Plants' as she had arranged with Banks. The constant rain defeated her botanizing but not her enjoyment of the company of her host and his conversation. She found him 'in excellent spirits, looking like Ivory, free from Pain, but quite helpless in point of legs'. Confined to his wheelchair we have her record that he was 'roled about both within and without doors', a stricken giant but one who yet found 'hardly time enough for the variety of his pursuits'.

The weather being unkind to the study of field botany in the garden the Queen was introduced instead to the more recondite mysteries of etymology and the 'world of old books and dictionaries' in which Banks had come to live as crippling illness set tighter bounds to his free movement. It is more than likely on this visit that the Queen was introduced to one of Banks's favourite authors at this time, Thomas Tusser and his *Five hundred points of good Husbandry* . . ., in which he was busy collating the edition of 1610 with that of 1585. For all that the Queen was impressed with the outward evidence of Banks's scholarship he himself was apt to set the standard much lower. The composition of his notes were to him, he said,

> . . . merely a matter of amusement, incompatible with the Labor of Consulting the Historical and other authorities necessary for the Complete illustration of the manners and times in which Tusser wrote . . .

He gave as his sole reason for committing to paper his thoughts on a favourite author the desire

> . . . to Fill up the abundant Portion of Leisure Time which fell to the Lot of the writer, when his Legs became, by Excess of Gout of Little use to him; & to make Time Pass Pleasantly on, by a due admixture of writing with his Reading . . .

Roger Wilbraham, his erudite neighbour near Spring Grove, who read them the following year, rated them if they were to be published as 'the most compleat & perfect illustrated & commented Edition we have of any of our old Poets'. Some of this feeling the Queen could evidently sense as fair when she found herself regaled with the delights of ancient whimsical words rather than the beauty of 'very curious and beautiful Plants' on that wet summer afternoon. She promised to return on 'the first Sun Shining Day'.

Shining days were few that year and in the autumn heavy rain again thwarted her intention of 'viewing the choice plants in Sir Joseph's garden and pleasure grounds'. Setting out from the Queen's House about midday on Monday 4 October 1813 in her travelling carriage, with a Sergeant's Guard of 11 men, the Queen and her party reached Spring Grove about an hour later attended by the Princesses Augusta and Mary and the Dowager Countess of Ilchester. Her retinue was completed by the head coachman, the second coachman, the hobby groom, two postilions, and two footmen.

On this occasion again there was to be no gentle stroll through the garden and greenhouses. The rain fell incessantly and conversation indoors was the sole amusement, before 'the Royals' gathered in the dining room for an early dinner about half-past-one attended only by Sir Joseph and his ladies. The table was set across the room lengthways and Her Majesty sat alone on the long side facing the front windows. The Princesses were placed at the opposing ends until Princess Mary with her back to the fire retreated from its heat to join the Countess of Ilchester on the long side opposite the Queen and with her back to the garden view. No servants waited in the room itself. Lady Banks and Sarah Sophia had that honour. The door was left ajar so that when the bell rang for plates to be brought or dishes to be removed no servant need actually appear in the room. Sir Joseph, immobile in his chair, was tactically placed by a side table in the corner between the fire and a front window. Here he managed the wine – a choice of hock, sauterne, madeira and port. In due time he made the coffee and the tea – a choice of the dark Bohea and his own favourite green. Here also on the side table were rolls, brown bread and butter.

The main table itself was spread with a hot pheasant, crumbed sweetbreads and white sauce, light pastry and a Spring Grove cranberry tart, for as Banks told Knight 'My Cranberries this year have performed wonders'. For dessert there were peaches, nectarines and grapes, but outstanding at this late season were the hautbois strawberries and Coe's Golden Drop plums. The plums were there by the suggestion as far back as 1809 when Knight drew Banks's attention to the kind which, as Banks later told him, 'originated with a gentleman of the name of Coe at Bury St. Edmunds' supposed to be the plum dried by the Portuguese and sent to England in boxes. The fruit were on the table also by virtue of the successful method of culture devised by Knight and performed by Banks 'on a South wall with Flues behind to counteract the effect of autumnal frosts'. The strawberries were there as evidence of the active collaboration in their breeding by Banks and Knight, but this also, said Banks:

... by a remarkable accident in my Garden which I think may lead to useful consequences my hermaphrodite hautboy Strawberries bore a large crop in the season & to my surprise as well as that of my Gardener producd a second crop in October not very abundant but if possible of a higher flavour than those in June & certainly fairer & larger fruit.

495

From this array the Queen, Princess Augusta and Lady Ilchester selected the sweetbreads and white sauce. Princess Mary chose the pheasant. Warm port wine and water was evidently the Queen's tipple on these occasions. Princess Mary was more inclined to 'a dish of green Tea' prepared by Sir Joseph who was disconcerted by a delay of ten minutes before the water was at the boil. As to the remarkable out-of-season hautbois strawberries it was Princess Augusta in particular who indulged herself with these and much cream.

Two days later, on Wednesday 6 October, the Banks family paid a visit to Frogmore where, undeterred by the discomforts of the last visit, the Queen repeated her intention of 'calling some fine day at Spring Grove soon' and added, with consideration: 'Don't get much a sandwich will do'. But as an expression of hospitality at Spring Grove she must have known well that a sandwich would never do.

A week later the weather was kind at last and on Thursday 14 October the Queen came again to Spring Grove with the Princesses Elizabeth and Mary. This time they spent a pleasant hour walking in the garden where, as the *Morning Post* reported, 'They were more fortunate in the weather than on the late former visit'. In particular they were able to admire the new Malta Orange House where, as Banks told Knight: '. . . My Oranges look well they are now yellow & firm with the dark green foliage of the trees a beautiful show'.

The arrangements for lunch inside were much as before and much as they were to continue. Again the royal guests were waited on by the ladies with Sir Joseph in his place managing the wine, the tea and the coffee. On this visit the Queen 'eat Bechemel (of Fowl) & afterwards Coffee'; Princess Elizabeth showed a marked preference for the potatoes, brown bread and butter, with coffee to follow; for Princess Mary it was the cold partridge and the green tea. Again there was the display of the remarkable second crop of hautbois strawberries and the successful Coe Golden Drop plums.

In succeeding visits over the next five years on these late summer or autumnal occasions, the main course remained essentially avian, variously disguised as 'Sauté de Perdrix' with 'Sauce piquet' for the partridge or for the chicken even the ultimate dignity of appearing as 'Un Blanquet de Poulet au Supreme'. Occasionally a 'Hare Pye' or a roast hare would intrude, diversified once or twice with mushrooms, cucumbers and pineapples, much to Her Majesty's delight, as Sir Joseph's special houses for their culture became more efficient after the advent of Isaac Oldacer. Warm port for the Queen, warm lemonade for Princess Elizabeth, green tea for Princess Mary were the regular choices. Always there was a fine display of fresh fruit in season – peaches, pears and plums, apricots, nectarines and apples, grapes both white and black, strawberries both hautbois and wood – their quality and abundance all in some degree enriched by the steady cross-fertilization that flowed as letters and parcels between Downton Castle and Spring Grove.

In return for these hospitable interludes there was always a welcome for Banks and his ladies in the Queen's own garden creation, her retreat at Frogmore. Between the Middlesex villa of the gentleman commoner and the 'little Paradise' in Berkshire of his Queen there were strong links. Indeed the chain stretched far back beyond the time when she had bought the lease of Frogmore Farm to their youth when the King and Queen, on that Saturday 10 August 1771 at Kew, had first received Mr Joseph Banks and Dr Daniel Solander on their return from the South Seas. In the creation of

Frogmore, behind the names of the Aitons, father and son, of William Price her Vice-Chamberlain, and of Franz Bauer 'Botanick Painter to His Majesty', there lies the pervading influence of Banks extending beyond the social pleasantries of dutiful hours at Windsor Castle and now in the garden itself.

The year 1818, for royalty and commoners alike, broke the long friendship and ended the visits to Spring Grove. Two of the middle-aged princesses had found husbands. Mary in the summer of 1816 had married her cousin William of Gloucester and her elder sister Elizabeth became the Land-gravine of Hesse-Homburg in April 1818. Of the trio only Augusta remained unmarried and in time to inherit her mother's estate of Frogmore. In September 1818 the close union of the Banks household was broken in the death of Sarah Sophia leaving her brother shattered and grief-stricken as he had never been before. Two months later at Kew in November 1818 the link between the Banks trio and the royal family was at last almost severed in the death of the Queen. Only a slender bond between the families now remained. For Dorothea Banks there lingered on the decade of her correspondence with the Princess Elizabeth as a terminal diminuendo. For the Princess, a recent bride and soon to be the Landgravine of Hesse-Homburg, there was her own memento in the copy she had herself laboriously made of 'Sir Josh. Banks's Private Journal round the World' with Captain Cook.

CHAPTER 24

CONGO HEAT AND ARCTIC ICE
1813–1820

For the inquisitive European the obscurities of the African interior, and especially the true course of the Niger and its relation to that of the Congo, remained much as they had been before the tragic last journeys of Hornemann and Mungo Park when the war ended at Waterloo. Nor was the elaborate preparation of John Burckhardt for yet another trans-Saharan attempt any closer to its goal. But by the end of June 1815 the sea lanes of the west African coast were at least safer for mercantile shipping and the more peaceful employment of a British navy. The pattern of the slave trade too was changing under the pressures of Wilberforce and his associates. For the British colonies in the West Indies the Slave Trade Felony Act of 1812 had broken their direct trade from west Africa and abolition of the Portuguese trade from the coast north of the Equator had been bought under treaty for £750000. Spain had yet to conform and the Bourbon restoration in France was equivocal in the application of its own anti-slavery legislation. So the trade continued but under the spreading stigma of illegality and the increasingly firm police action of the Royal Navy. There emerged in July 1815, from the Department for War and the Colonies under Lord Bathurst and his under-secretary Henry Goulburn, a proposal to explore the Congo upstream from its mouth to determine whether it was in fact confluent with the Niger. For this a naval expedition was logical and the Admiralty had in John Barrow, its Second Secretary, an eager exponent of the idea to Banks on the premise that nothing effective could be done without his active engagement. The subject seems to have opened officially from the Admiralty on 29 July 1815 as Barrow put it to Banks, with the notion of a steam-driven vessel with paddle-wheels as part of the plan. Subsequently as the expedition evolved all the important documents were channelled to Banks, even though on 6 August he declared himself concerned only with the natural history.

On 2 August James Watt jun. of Boulton and Watt advised the Admiralty that an engine of not less than 20 horsepower would be necessary to face the expected Congo current and that such a machine was in fact being built for the Tyne Packet Company, though a second with its paddle-wheels could not be produced in less than two or three months for a cost of some £1700. This paper was sent to Banks by Barrow on 5 August at the request of William Murdock, Boulton and Watt's supervising engineer. At the same time he was told that the leader of the expedition was to be Commander James Kingston Tuckey, not long returned from ten years as a prisoner in France, and that Robert Seppings, the naval architect, would design and construct a vessel suitable for steam propulsion in six weeks. Tuckey was well known to Banks for his able survey of Port Phillip as Lieutenant of HMS *Calcutta* in 1802, on which Flinders had not improved, and his subsequent *Account of a Voyage to establish a Colony at Port Phillip in Bass's Strait ... in the years 1802, 1803–4* (1805).

Seppings was a naval designer in whom Banks had great confidence and for whom he had been the channel of a paper to the Royal Society 'On a new principle of constructing His Majesty's ships of war', read on 10 March 1814. However, although he had great confidence in both men, Banks had reservations about the expedition and the difficulties to be overcome. He called for the opinion of his favourite engineer, John Rennie sen., on the question of the engine and the performance required which he received on 11 August. Then on 12 August to Barrow he elaborated his views.

He saw the enterprise for exploring the lower reaches of the Zaire [the Congo] as subject to an unique difficulty. There was no place on the river safe enough for a base from which it could start or to which it could return, for the Portuguese, whom he knew to be jealous of strangers, were now more likely to massacre than to assist any English intruders being 'irritated almost to madness by our interference with their Slave Trade'. The time as well as the place was inauspicious. On the other hand he saw in the development of a steam boat for the river navigation a means of establishing a mobile headquarters capable of being strongly defended if properly organized, and of being taken upstream as far as the first falls, a distance of some 85 miles. He thought it inconceivable that 'a rich & a powerful Nation', having newly discovered steam power as a method of navigating against strong river currents, should neglect its use 'as a public measure' when it was being adopted by private enterprise. For the armed defence of the expedition he deprecated the enlistment of black Africans who were likely to desert at the stage when they would most be needed that is, in the territories of the 'black Monarchs themselves'. But over all he was firm in advising that, if the expedition were to be mounted as a naval operation, it should be well provided from the beginning.

In assembling his arguments there was no hint of irony as he reminded the Secretary of the Admiralty of the lessons to be had from past naval expeditions, beginning with his own voyage in HMS *Endeavour*, 'a Ship fitted out for Discovery in an Economical Way' sent to sea without an escort and the whole enterprise nearly foundered on a coral reef. Thereafter, as he put it, the Admiralty 'relaxd their System of Economy' and always sent two vessels in company on such voyages of discovery. Here he chose to overlook the long history of the *Investigator* with the *Lady Nelson* as a failure of this principle. The exigencies of war could perhaps be made to bear some blame. But he could not neglect that other famous case in which he had been so closely involved and we may wonder what effect on Barrow, the aspiring naval historian, this masterly down-beat summary of the bread-fruit voyages of Captain Bligh may have had:

> ... I was many years ago employd by Mr. Wm. Pitt to arrange for him a Plan for bringing the Bread Fruit from the South Sea Islands to our Western dependancies, but was strictly requird to use every possible degree of Economy. I proposd a Lieut. Commander a Master's Mate as his Lieut. &c. &c. &c. this niggardly arrangement produced the Mutiny which began by turning the Commander adrift & ended in the Peopling of Pitcairn's Island. a less Economical Outfit succeeded & the business was happily effected.
>
> Hence I deduce that in all matters of Naval Equipment it is better to adopt a Plan of sufficient extent at first than to do it after a failure, which if attributable to parsimony will in a country like this meet with censure.

This was written soon after Banks had seen the letter from Sir Thomas Staines of HMS *Briton* describing his meeting with the Pitcairn Islanders and which he had sent to Barrow, who in return sent Banks a copy of the longer account sent by Captain Pipon of the *Tagus*.

Banks felt he had discharged his conscience and professed himself ready to submit to the judgement of others 'well aware how fallible the judgment of an individual has frequently provd to be'.

> . . . I am now ready without further Remonstrance to do all in my power to promote the success of the Undertaking. I am busily employd in searching for a Naturalist properly qualified to give an account of the Productions of a Country wholly new to European Investigation. I have met with one disappointment, but have no doubt that I shall succeed.

But before the expedition could leave Banks had to sustain another disappointment. His fine plans for the application of steam power to a vessel designed both for the open sea and river navigation foundered on the technical incompatibilities of the problems posed. Robert Seppings had embarked in August on the design of a 100-ton vessel to draw no more than four feet and yet contain a 24 horsepower engine of some 30 tons weight and 20 feet in length across the whole breadth of the small ship which had also to be strong and stable enough under sail to be navigated safely across the Atlantic to the mouth of the Congo. By the end of January 1816 the ship had been built, the engine had been installed, and the trials had shown that for the consumption of about three tons of fuel a day the best rate of going was five and-a-half knots while holding a draft of 4 feet 3 inches. This performance in no way compensated for the great burden of an engine which alone occupied one-third of the vessel. So with Seppings and Tuckey in close agreement the engine was removed to serve its working life ashore in the new dockyards at Chatham. The ship itself, as HMS *Congo*, was successfully converted to operate by sail alone schooner-rigged and with three parallel keels. In this form she completed the voyage as a dry commodious vessel, out-sailing her companion 'that brute of a transport' the 350-ton *Dorothy*, and returning to serve as a survey ship well adapted to the conditions of the North Sea. In the *Congo* Banks had at last found the vessel for inshore and estuarine survey that he had hoped for in the *Lady Nelson* with her sliding keels designed by Schrank but rejected in the end by Matthew Flinders.

Of Captain James Tuckey, the commander proposed, Banks agreed he knew 'nothing but what is very interesting in his favor' and that he was a man eminently suited for the task in hand. But what he did not know perhaps, nor did anyone seem to consider, was how far Tuckey was an ailing man before the voyage began, suffering from the recurring illnesses of his eastern service and more recent captivity in France. At the age of 40 he was, like Flinders, already a victim of long years of arduous naval service and wartime imprisonment, but stubborn always in rejecting the cloak of an invalid. He was to carry with him in his commission

> . . . for an expedition of discovery up the River Zaire into the interior of Africa, by command of His Royal Highness the Prince Regent, signified to us by Earl Bathurst:

orders to receive on board four civilian supernumeraries supplemented by a 'memorandum of an instruction' longer and more detailed than any with which Banks had been previously associated. It was not easy to find this small civilian complement and, like the problem of the steam engine, it was late in the preparations before the matter was resolved.

Barrow had tinkered with the question when he suggested to Banks on 30 November that the young gentleman volunteer, Edward Galwey, with two young Scots, Goldie and Syme, in association with the two surgeons Tudor and McKerrow, might collectively serve the purposes of natural history. Banks rejected the whole idea. The Scotsmen were poor artists and their knowledge of botany was limited to Scotland, and as for a naturalist he was waiting for the return from Paris of Dr William Elford Leach, of the British Museum, to consult him on the subject. So it was through Leach that John Cranch of Kingsbridge, Devon, joined the expedition as a 'Collector of Objects of Natural History', described by Barrow as

> ... one of those extraordinary self-taught characters, to whom particular branches of science are sometimes more indebted, than to the labours of those who have had the advantage of a regular education.

William Tudor the surgeon was appointed as 'Comparative Anatomist' at £250 a year, as was John Cranch, rising to £300 on their return. The other two civilians came as late additions.

During 1815 the German geologist, Baron Leopold von Buch, had travelled in Madeira and the Canary Islands with Christen Smith, Professor of Botany at the University of Christiania [Oslo]. On 8 December they reached Portsmouth and it had been Smith's intention to prepare his 'Flora' in London for publication before returning to Norway. Banks however was able to induce the young professor to join the Congo expedition at a salary of £300 a year rising to £400 and to take with him as an assistant and a plant collector for Kew one of the gardeners, David Lockhart, probably at £180 a year, the same scale as for Allan Cunningham and James Bowie just beginning their work in Brazil.

On 16 February 1816 HMS *Congo* and the *Dorothy* transport left Deptford but not until 19 March did the expedition clear the Channel. Professor Christen Smith and David Lockhart each had received from Banks some of the last direct instructions that he ever wrote, some details of which survive apart from the terms he incorporated in the official memorandum. To Smith he merely ventured 'to offer a few hints' of the services expected from him by the Lords of HM Admiralty 'under whose protection the Expedition in which you are Engagd is Fitted out', but these were ample enough. He made one special point:

> ... you will have a Peculiar advantage in this Expedition which very few Botanists have hitherto been so Fortunate as to Enjoy the demand of Firewood for the Steam Engine on Board your vessel, will make it necessary to Cut down Trees on the Banks of the River very Frequently. in the hot Climates Trees are seldom accessible to Botanists on account of the Labor of Felling them. you will have them Felld to your hands, & their Flowers and Fruits laid at your Feet. of this valuable Privilege you will I am Sure make Good use in which Case your Herbarium will probably Contain a greater Proportion of arborescent Specimens than has Generaly been brought Home from any intertropical Countrey.

The late removal of the engine from the overburdened *Congo* negated the intentions of this important note but the point had been stressed and some results accrued in the end. Smith was, of course, enjoined to keep a proper journal to be delivered in time to the Admiralty for publication if it was thought necessary. No account of the expedition was to be published by any of its members until the public narrative was printed or officially abandoned. Thereafter each person would have his papers returned to be used as he wished.

To David Lockhart the instructions from Banks were more brief, being directed to him as someone enrolled in 'the Company of His Majesties Discovery Vessell the Congo' and thus bound to obey the commands of its officers. His station, however, was that of 'assistant Gardiner to the Botanist of the Expedition Professor Smith', under whose immediate direction he was 'to do all things conducive to the attainment of a Perfect Knowledge of the Vegetables in all Places you Shall visit'. There was the usual injunction:

> . . . as it is deemd Proper that the new Plants discoverd in your voyage Should first appear in the Royal Botanic Gardens at Kew you are not on any Pretence to Furnish any Person with any Part of your Collections of Seeds Bulbs or Succulent Plants

The brave intentions of the voyage of HMS *Congo* and *Dorothy*, partly realized, foundered in tragedy. Of the 56 who sailed out of Falmouth on 19 March 1816, Tuckey and all his officers were dead by the end of October and of the civilian supernumeraries only David Lockhart was alive – a total mortality of 21. The expedition had penetrated as far up the river as the Yellala Falls from where it had begun an overland march to circumvent the gorges but, before the river was reached again, it had been forced to return by the failing health of all. Lockhart, who had worked hard and valiantly throughout the river journey, was, with the sergeant of the marines, the last to succumb to the prevailing fever and, after a convalescence at Bahia, the only one to survive of the party which had penetrated beyond the Yellala Falls. From here he returned to London on the brig *Regent* with Christen Smith's journal, notes and specimens, reaching the Thames in June 1817. Barrow told Banks of his return on 29 June and in time Lockhart delivered his botanical relics and the journal to 32 Soho Square.

The zoological collections of John Cranch reached London before the return of Lockhart. In the hands of Dr W. E. Leach at the British Museum and of Sir Everard Home they contributed the substance of papers read before the Royal Society on 5 and 7 June, 1817 to be printed in the *Philosophical Transactions* and as Appendices II and III in Tuckey's *Narrative of an Expedition to Explore The River Zaire, usually called The Congo, in South Africa, in 1816* . . ., 1818, with an anonymous introduction by John Barrow as its editor. Franz Bauer made two drawings distinguishing the fine details of the ova in the two marine species described by Home and these were engraved by James Basire II. William Marsden presented the 'vocabularies' of the Malemba and Embomma languages as Appendix I. By the studies of Leach in later years, the name of that 'extraordinary self-taught character' John Cranch is extensively commemorated, especially among the crustacea and mollusca from these first gatherings in marine biology in the Gulf of Guinea.

As with the narrative of Tuckey so too with the journal of Professor Christen

Smith what was published in the official volume of the expedition was the best that could be salvaged from the unrevised scrawls of sick and dying men in small notebooks of which much was scarcely legible. Smith's journal was translated from the original Danish of his notes by a Dr Rydberg of the Danish Embassy and edited into a printed text covering pages 229–336 of the final work, equal to somewhat more than half of Tuckey's contribution. For the African Association Banks arranged a separate publication of the translated journal and this elicited in January 1819 a request from Jens Hornemann at Copenhagen for permission to print it in the original Danish to clear some obscurities in the English translation important to him as a botanist. But for botanists at large, of greater value, in spite of the haste with which it had been compounded, was the substance of Appendix V – 'Observations, Systematical and Geographical, on Professor CHRISTIAN SMITH'S Collection of Plants from the Vicinity of the River Congo, by ROBERT BROWN, F.R.S.' This formed the material of pages 420–485 and, as an Essay, followed closely the pattern of his 'General Remarks ... on the Botany of Terra Australis', Appendix III of Flinders' *A Voyage to Terra Australis*, 1814. pages 533–613. Again, as for the Australian flora, Brown was well placed at Soho Square with the combined resources of the herbarium and the library to make a first scientific assessment of the plants gathered along the Congo.

He was generous to the percipience and industry of Christen Smith and the intelligent hard work of David Lockhart, his sole living witness of the habitats explored. From no more than two months' field collecting Brown reckoned that from 36 natural orders some 620 species of which 590 were certain had been gathered along the banks of the Congo, about 250 of them new; while of the 32 unpublished genera, in his view some 12 were new. In reaching these conclusions in so short a time he had among much else at his elbow in Soho Square, he said, such specimens collected for Banks as: some 250 from the Cape Coast gathered by William Brass; 450 from Sierra Leone by Henry Smeathman; and many from among the 1200 in the collection of Adam Afzelius taken in the same region. Moreover, on a wider front, he had before him the unpublished 'Flora Indica' of William Roxburgh with related specimens, and, most exciting as a background to botanical geography, the recent volume of Bonpland and Humboldt, *Nova Genera et Species Plantarum, quas in peregrinatione orbis novi collegerunt*, 1815.

In these Congo specimens of Christen Smith and David Lockhart, the herbarium of Sir Joseph Banks received one of the last important accessions during his lifetime, certainly the last to attain a place in the printed literature within his span of days. For Robert Brown, in his systematic and geographical analysis of the collection, it was but the second of a series yet to enter Soho Square from the exploration of distant lands and to be sifted, classified and summarized in print there.

II

While Banks was at Revesby Abbey on his last but one visit John Barrow wrote to him on 3 October 1815 with details of the Admiralty's arrangements for the civilian complement to go with Captain J. K. Tuckey on the expedition with the proposed steam vessel HMS *Congo*. He expressed his view also, as an old China hand from the Macartney Embassy of 1792–4, that the new mission under Lord Amherst then preparing did not promise well as no member of it was competent in the Chinese language. As advice to Banks this was not needed and when the time came the gap would be well filled. Meanwhile the directors of the East India Company, conscious of their failings in the mounting of the Macartney Embassy, conceived it their duty now to make better provision for the new opportunity in Chinese natural history. In this laudable conversion Banks was the natural agent of mediation with the ambassador to whom he wrote on 9 December. Dr Clarke Abel had already been appointed chief medical officer to the Embassy and as a competent natural historian he had Banks's recommendation. Abel sought no further salary for this additional burden, merely a gratuity in due time if his contributions to the East India Company collections were judged worthy. A gardener however was necessary, at the rate of £100 a year, to collect and preserve the exotic plants not already at Kew of which specimens would be deposited in the Company's Museum and seeds presented from the directors to the Royal Botanic Garden. Banks himself would undertake to examine and arrange the plants as he had done for the former Embassy and guaranteed, if the British Museum were allowed to share in the collections, that its officers would add their services in naming and arranging the relevant articles.

In the euphoria of the triumph over Napoleonic France this second British Embassy was intended as a strong protest against the arrogance and exactions of the Chinese merchants and mandarins at Canton by a direct approach to the Emperor. It was a forlorn task from the beginning, but at least less over-loaded with the trappings of Western technological pride and presumption than in the former episode of mutual incomprehension. For Banks, however, the aim was still the same limited objective as before which he defined in principle again to Clarke Abel on 10 February 1816 as he had done originally to Sir George Leonard Staunton on 18 August 1792 with his 'Hints on the Subject of Gardening suggested to the Gentlemen who attend the Embassy to China'. This he now brought up-to-date with instructions to Abel on the plants to be sought and preserved against a background of detail on Chinese methods of horticulture, of Chinese species successfully cultivated and those still wanted for cultivation in England. But even as he prepared this guidance Banks was also toying with a matter that Abel himself had raised after being approached by Captain Bowles of HMS *Amphion*, on the point of sailing for the River Plate, as the restless Spanish province simmered towards its independence later in the year. Abel had put forward the name of his friend King, a Cambridge senior wrangler of 1808, who had added medicine and surgery to his mathematics and was prepared to join Bowles as naturalist at his own expense. This revived a possibility that Banks had hoped for in 1814 as a region to be tapped by collectors from Kew and so he took the subject up with John Barrow on 12 February seeking more information about Bowles and the nature of his expedition to South America, offering King as

> ... a Man of Fortune who would be willing to undertake the Voyage on the same terms as I went with Cook, to be allowd to Mess in the Cabbin, & who would provide proper Assistants at his own expence, provided also that there is time for him to prepare or a fair chance of a comfortable passage out to join the Expedition.

Before this matter was resolved however the Amherst Embassy sailed from Spithead on board HMS *Alceste* in late February to reach Canton in early July. After much parleying with the Chinese dignitaries of low status sent to meet him, Amherst was granted leave to sail to Tientsin where the same obstruction at a somewhat higher level was repeated. The focus of Chinese resistance was the British refusal to promise the ritual of the ko-tow before the Emperor. The Macartney Embassy had refused it and the Amherst Embassy followed suit, confirmed in this by the presence as 'King's commissioner of Embassy' of Sir George Thomas Staunton, chief of the East India Company Canton Factory and now interpreter and Chinese specialist to the British mission. As a small boy of precocious ability in the Chinese language he had been with his father on the Macartney Embassy and knew well what was and what was not done on that abortive occasion. Macartney had short shrift with no more than two weeks at the Imperial Court near Jehol. Amherst had even shorter. He reached the palace at Yuan-mien-yuan on 29 August 1816 late at night, was summoned to the imperial presence as he was about to retire from fatigue, refused the command and was dismissed without further parley the same day. Like Macartney he was conducted slowly down the Grand Canal and over the mountains to Canton where on 20 January 1817 he re-embarked for England. Another mission had failed on the score of mutual obduracy.

Botanically the Amherst Embassy was as ill-fated as that of Lord Macartney. HMS *Alceste* on 16 February 1817 struck a reef at the entrance to the Strait of Gaspar off the coast of Sumatra and was totally wrecked. Some of the crew reached Batavia in a boat and the rest were rescued on 6 March by HMS *Ternate*. The whole of Clarke Abel's collections were lost except for a small number of duplicates which he had left with Sir George Thomas Staunton at Canton who returned with them to England later in the year. Hearing of Abel's loss he returned the small duplicate collection and these were all that survived to be described and listed by Robert Brown as a botanical appendix to the doctor's *Narrative of a Journey in the Interior of China, and of a Voyage to and from that Country, in the years 1816 and 1817; containing an account of the most interesting transactions of Lord Amherst's Embassy to the Court of Pekin, and Observations on the countries which it visited.* (1818).

In these two embassies to China the literature of travel had been enriched but as stalking horses for Banks in pursuit of natural knowledge in botany they had proved unsound and broken-backed.

III

The siege of Copenhagen and the capture of the Danish fleet in September 1807 had two results for Banks. First, there came the problems of captured Icelandic merchant vessels and action for their release. But as he drafted the long case on their behalf to be sent to the Home Secretary on 30 December he had during that same week met for the first time a young man returning to Whitby from a short service in the Navy bringing captured Danish warships from Copenhagen to Portsmouth. This was William Scoresby jun. at 18, discharged on 21 December from duty as a volunteer ordinary seaman, free to pay his first visit about Christmas time to Soho Square. For the next ten years, between the intervals of his Arctic and Greenland whaling voyages with his father, and, from 1810 as captain in command, he was a regular correspondent with Banks and frequently a visitor. Under this stimulus Scoresby evolved fast into the serious student of Arctic phenomena and of the natural history of the polar regions, refreshed at intervals with sessions in natural philosophy and chemistry at the University of Edinburgh. Already a pioneer, with his father in 1806, by the achievement of 81°30' as the latitude furthest north, he remained until the end

William Scoresby jun., FRS, *aet.* 22. Drawing by John Sell Cotman, 1811.

of Banks's life as his most intelligent channel of information about the far north beyond the Arctic Circle. In the younger Scoresby Banks clearly saw the man who, in default of national expeditions, could, as a whaling captain of some intellectual weight, probe the polar frontiers in readiness for the grand attack to settle the old question of a 'north-west passage'. Thirty years had passed since Banks himself had first grappled seriously with the challenge of the Arctic, not himself as a traveller far toward the pole but as the organizing base from which Lt Constantine Phipps had much practical help in his summer dash in 1773 with the *Racehorse* and the *Carcass* to latitude 80°37′N., a point unexcelled until the Scoresbys's limit in 1806. From the Pacific side there had been the penetration of the Behring Strait by Captains James Cook and Charles Clerke in the *Resolution* and *Discovery* in 1778 and 1779 as far north as 70°41′. But across the top of the world between the north Atlantic and the north Pacific lay the shroud of a great geographic mystery.

Ever since his own sub-Arctic adventures in Labrador (1766) and Iceland (1772) Banks had kept an abiding interest in the polar regions, freshened at intervals by his visitors and friends from among the fur hunters and whalers of both hemispheres and both the great oceans investing the Americas. As an agriculturalist and gardener and unofficial watchdog of the nation's corn supplies he was acutely alert to the vagaries of the climate and so to the possible influence of Arctic ice movements, sea currents and sea temperatures on the seasons and the trends in the British weather. As a marine biologist, who had dabbled extensively over some 120° of latitude in several seas and two vast oceans, he was familiar with the technical challenge of hydrology and the need for new instruments of physical survey to record sea temperature and sea density at varying depths across the sea lanes traversed both in trade and exploration. In Major James Rennell he had a willing contender in debate and a gatherer of data relating to the winds and sea currents of the world. In Henry Cavendish he had a willing philosopher in the invention and design of instruments. One such device was in manufacture when Cavendish died in March 1810; an apparatus for measuring temperature at very great depths in the ocean. George Gilpin, Clerk of the Royal Society, continued with its development when he too died the same year and the instrument was finally finished by William Cary of 182 Strand, one of Jesse Ramsden's former apprentices. This equipment Banks passed to William Scoresby when he took over the *Resolution* whaler from his father as his first command on attaining his majority in October 1810. A year later, after the whaling season of 1811, Scoresby reported to Banks his first results with the new instrument off Greenland, finding it not wholly satisfactory under the Arctic conditions or fully resistant to pressure at great depths. In time this became Scoresby's successful 'marine diver' with which he was the first to establish in the Arctic that the temperature near the sea floor was higher than at the surface. With the first sea temperature records of 1811 Scoresby sent Banks also his meteorological journal for the Greenland whaling season of 1810. For seven whaling seasons the younger Scoresby fished the waters of the high Arctic and for seven winters brought the fruits of his experience to Banks. Through this channel of scientific news the Admiralty was also nourished with ideas. France was defeated but across the top of the world the shadow of the new ally, Russia, was spreading to the east. To the promptings of geographical curiosity about the frozen north a strong tincture of imperial politics was now added as the Russian trading presence spread along the north-west American coast. The search for a north-west passage was again alive.

The 'polar institute' of Soho Square was manned unusually late in the summer of 1817 as Banks deferred his Revesby Abbey visit until October. On 22 September, before he left, he wrote to Scoresby at Whitby for details of the state of the ice along the West Greenland coast in Baffin's Bay and its rumoured decrease. At the same time he acknowledged the gift to Lady Banks from William Scoresby sen. of two white polar bearskins. When Banks returned from Revesby he had been fed from Whitby with full information on the current state of the Greenland coasts. In reply he told Scoresby of the recent Act of Parliament offering £20000 for the discovery of a north-west passage, the latest renewal of a form of reward which had never yet tempted a whaling captain to any such effort for reasons that the young man, better fitted than any, was able and at pains to explain. He had given vivid evidence of his fitness and knowledge as an Arctic sailor in the long essay on the ice and the currents in the seas between Iceland, Greenland and Spitzbergen which Banks showed to Major Rennell and no doubt also to John Barrow, Second Secretary of the Admiralty. All this was fodder for Barrow's long article in the October number of the *Quarterly Review*, significant evidence that the next determined move toward the pole and the passage was to be a naval affair and at last again a preoccupation of government.

Into this court Banks firmly placed it with his letter of 29 November 1817 to

507

Robert Dundas, 2nd Vis. Melville, First Lord of the Admiralty, proposing that efforts should now be made

> ... to endeavour to correct and amend the very defective geography of the Arctic Regions more especially on the side of America. To attempt the Circumnavigation of old Greenland, if an island, as there is reason to suppose. To prove the existence or non-existence of Baffin's Bay; and to endeavour to ascertain the practicability of a Passage from the Atlantic to the Pacific Ocean, along the Northern Coast of America. These are objects which may be considered as peculiarly interesting to Great Britain not only from their proximity and the national advantages which they involve but also for the marked attention they called forth and the Discoveries made in consequence thereof in the very earliest periods of our foreign navigation ...

With almost ten years of ice-watching through the young eyes of William Scoresby as background, now was the time, said Banks, for such explorations to begin. Not for many years had the Arctic approaches been so open and the prospects of success so high. So Banks framed for British enterprise again the challenge of the north as he would leave it to the young naval officer who, within the month, was to enter his library in pursuit of the task.

At the Admiralty decisions had to be quickly made. Four specially strengthened whalers were to be commissioned to sail as two pairs in the spring of 1818 on a plan conforming to the aims which Banks had clearly defined. In the event the *Dorothea*, Captain David Buchan of 370 tons and *Trent*, Lt John Franklin of 250 tons, were deputed to sail directly north between the east coast of Greenland and Spitzbergen as far as they could penetrate beyond the limits achieved by Phipps in 1773 and the Scoresbys in 1806. The *Isabella*, Captain John Ross of 382 tons, and the *Alexander*, Lt William Edward Parry of 250 tons, were charged with a course through Davis's Strait along the doubtful west coast of Greenland to clear the mysteries of Baffin's Bay and seek an outlet west into the Behring Sea. Of the two young lieutenants, John Franklin at 32 was the elder, the Spilsby cousin and veteran companion of Matthew Flinders on the *Investigator* voyage and thus from his boyhood well-known to Banks. Parry, the youngest of the four commanders at 28, was a late-comer to the Banksian orbit when he entered Soho Square with his uncle Sir Benjamin Hobhouse, FRS on Tuesday 23 December 1817 to meet and breakfast with Banks for the first time. William Edward was the fourth and youngest son of Dr Caleb Hillier Parry, FRS, the Bath physician and Merino sheep-breeding friend of Banks. For more than three years Lt Parry had seen naval service on the American coast but in March 1817 had returned home after his father had suffered his crippling stroke in 1816. In 1816 he had volunteered for the ill-fated Congo expedition under Tuckey but from across the Atlantic had been unable to join it in time. For nine months he had remained in Bath with his distressed family until early in December 1817 he had read in a newspaper of the planned Arctic expedition and, having missed the hot, volunteered now for the cold. Through Barrow the Admiralty accepted him for a command and Soho Square was now open to him for his Arctic briefing. Parry conveyed a vivid impression to his parents of the stimulus he had received:

> ... It is impossible, in the compass of a letter, to repeat to you half of what Sir

Captain John Ross, RN, of HMS *Isabella*, 1818. Portrait by J. Green, 1833.

Joseph Banks said to me upon the subject – much less, to give you any idea of his very affable, communicative manner; he desired that I would come to him as often as I pleased (the oftener the better) and read or take away any books I could find in his library that might be of service to me. . . . Having obtained *Carte blanche* from Sir J. I shall of course go to his library without any ceremony, whenever I have occasions: for his invitations are not those of fashionable life, but are given from a real desire to do every-thing which can in the smallest degree tend to the advancement of every branch of science

Lt William Edward Parry, RN, of HMS *Alexander*, 1818, *aet. c.* 30. Portrait by Samuel Drummond, ARA.

Banks had immediately shown him a map he had recently caused to be drawn of the state of the Greenland ice-fields, lent it to him and directed him to the Hydrographical Office for the latest information deposited there by William Scoresby. Parry soon met Scoresby in person at Soho Square and adjudged him 'a very intelligent, and indeed a scientific man'. Another Banksian symbiosis had occurred in the back premises of No. 32. A second newcomer was added in Captain

Edward Sabine, the younger brother of Joseph Sabine, FRS, by the more formal recommendation of Banks and the Council of the Royal Society, among whom Captain Henry Kater was pre-eminent as scientific adviser on instrumentation, especially the theory and use of his seconds pendulum. There was of course always Major James Rennell at hand, enquiring and critical, but less than optimistic on the prospects of a passage being found so far north.

By the first week of May 1818 the four ships of the expedition had reached Lerwick in the Shetlands and from there both Parry and Franklin wrote to Banks before they parted for their separate adventures in the *Alexander* and the *Trent*. Banks heard no more until the *Dexterity* whaler of Leith brought the despatches from Ross, dated 25 July from HMS *Isabella* 75°45′N. lat. 60°10′W. long. in Melville Bay on the west Greenland coast, reporting the land between 68° and 75°N. some 100 miles further west than the Admiralty charts defined. All the commanders were agreed in their great debt to Banks during the mounting of the expedition but Ross condensed the view into a few words

> . . . you are the father of the Enterprise I have the honor to Command . . .

But even as these words were flying south in the *Dexterity* whaler another stamp was being put on the record of events – that of John Barrow, Second Secretary of the Admiralty, emerging from the anonymity of the *Quarterly Review* to sign on 1 August 1818 the Foreword to his own version of *A Chronological History of Voyages into the Arctic Regions; undertaken chiefly for the purpose of Discovering a North-East, North-West, or Polar Passage between the Atlantic and Pacific: from the earliest periods of Scandinavian navigation, to the departure of the recent Expeditions under the orders of Captains Ross and Buchan.* A new burst of Admiralty scent was working to expunge the trail from Soho Square.

By 21 November 1818 all the ships were back at Deptford; the *Dorothea* and the *Trent* forced back at the edge of the pack ice off the west coast of Spitzbergen by violent storms; the *Isabella* and the *Alexander* returning, after verifying much of the Elizabethan geography of Baffin's Bay, almost at the point of success in the entrance to Lancaster Sound, but defeated for the moment by Ross's strange vision of the obstructing 'Croker Mountains'. The obscurities were not greatly helped by Ross's published account of *A Voyage of Discovery . . . in His Majesty's Ships Isabella and Alexander . . .*, 1819, but there were enough signs in Parry's unpublished journal to mark him as the man to resolve the problem of a passage to the west. So on 11 May 1819 Parry turned north again from the Nore in command of his own expedition in the *Hecla* with the *Griper*, Lt Liddon in company. With him again as astronomer was Edward Sabine. Ahead lay 18 months at high latitudes, one long frozen winter, but, at the end, perhaps the most fruitful of all such Arctic voyages. Behind it, in his garden at Spring Grove, lay the sick man who had done so much to make it possible but who would not now live to see the young men return with so much success to report. He would not know how far to the west Parry had driven his ships – beyond 110° of longitude nor that the land beyond which

> . . . is the Western most land yet discovered in the Polar Sea . . . was honoured with the name of Banks's Land . . .

Captain John Ross and Lt William Edward Parry (the taller naval figure) meet the Inuit Eskimos of Greenland at Melville Bay, 75°45'N and 60°10'W, on their voyage with HMS *Isabella* (the larger ship) and HMS *Alexander*. Here was written Ross's letter to Banks of 25 July 1818 and from here came one of the Eskimo sleds now in the Museum of Mankind, London, by the agency of Banks. This engraving is from the original drawing by the Eskimo interpreter John Sackhouse or Sacheuse, the figure with the top hat just beyond Ross.

And so it would remain for yet another 30 years as close as any man ever came to forcing the north-west passage from the east until McLure at last, in the search for the lost Franklin, drove a passage from the west to chart Banks's Land as the island that we know.

William Scoresby meanwhile was driving his own independent path under the gentle stimulus of Banks, gathering his experiences, his measurements and observations into written order. On 4 February 1819 Banks had secured his paper to be read at the Royal Society 'On the anomaly in the variation of the magnetic needle as observed on shipboard' and to be printed in the *Philosophical Transactions*, volume 109 of that year. In the same month Banks sent him the list of 45 plant species identified for him by Robert Brown to be included in his book as those occurring within 11 degrees of the North Pole. Such observations would also be matched and amplified by Parry and his colleagues with help from Soho Square. Scoresby's *Account of the Arctic Regions and Northern Whale Fishery*, 1820, and Parry's *Journal of a Voyage for the Discovery of a North-West Passage from the Atlantic to the Pacific; performed in the years 1819–20, in His Majesty's Ships Hecla and Griper . . .*, 1821, stand, each in its own way, as tablets to the memory of a bright collaboration between two attractive young men and the friendly sage of Soho Square. But no less enduring as a mark on the historical record of the Arctic studies stimulated and directed by Banks was that letter from Franz Bauer read before the Royal Society on 11 May 1820 on 'Some experiments on the fungi which constitute the colouring matter of the red snow discovered in Baffin's Bay', and published in the *Philosophical Transactions* of that year.

512

IV

The long course of the wars with France, that first great global fracture of international peace, by the winter of 1813–14 was drawing to a close. The spring of 1814 was brightened by the consignment of Napoleon to Elba under the Treaty of Fontainbleau on 11 April and the summer augured well in the Treaty of Paris on 30 May. By mid-July Delambre was moved to rejoice with Banks that freedom in the exchange of knowledge had been restored between the Institut National and the Royal Society. Sir Humphry Davy and his lady were among the many English already in Paris and Sir Charles Blagden was soon to follow. A fresh and final phase in Banks's foreign correspondence had begun as he became increasingly the chair-bound cripple and less the scientific host in Soho Square. No longer would there be the late August and early September visit to Overton Hall in Derbyshire and only three more journeys lay ahead to Revesby Abbey, the last a mere two weeks in early October 1817. The clarity of mind and the abiding enthusiasm was still evident but the sight was losing its acuity and the business of writing becoming more irksome as the letters were reduced more often now to the small octavo in place of the once regular quarto. Only Blagden, across the Channel with the Berthollets at Arceuil, received the old form with any continuity. But though the volume of Banks's letter-writing was less, it was punctuated still with documents of significant record as he kept unswervingly to the course of public duty he had set for himself and the responsibilities of his station, as he conceived it. His visits to the great offices in Whitehall and the City were now few and his absences from Somerset House on Thursdays more frequent. The villa at Smallborough Green confined him for longer periods after 1815, so that even the Prime Minister Lord Liverpool came to him from time to time when letters would not do.

Early in 1814 Banks pressed Lord Liverpool with a strong case for providing the Astronomer Royal, John Pond, with an assistant at £100 a year and an easement in his household expenses by the provision of a proper allowance for coal and candles, and sought a personal meeting to effect this, – in spite of his gout. But the days for such heroics were now few. He was becoming more dependent on Dr Johan Tiarks as his assistant-librarian for outside visits in which he required an intelligent observer or messenger in affairs apart from botany. As to botany itself, he made what seems to have been his last purchase for the herbarium in the collection of Jean François Berger, acquired during the summer through the agency of Blagden in France after the Swiss geologist had returned to his native Geneva at the end of seven years of exile in England. The collection of plant specimens reached Soho Square in early October. In August his contact with Martijn van Marum at Leiden was renewed in the gift received from him of D. G. Keiser's *Mémoire sur l'Organisation des Plantes* with its close affinity to the work of Thomas Andrew Knight. In Paris Charles Blagden was actively mediating arrangements for French scientific visits to come, and plying Banks with enquiries reflecting pent-up French curiosity.

One such, just as the Royal Society year opened, concerned the forward stride in printing machinery in London. This focused on *The Times* and its new production plans, harnessing steam to its printing process with the machine devised by Thomas Bensley and Friedrich König under the patent of 1810. Prevented by his crippled state from viewing the machines himself, Banks depended on Tiarks to gather the details for him to include in his letters to Blagden in November and December 1814. Banks drew Blagden's attention to Sheet 11 in the fifth volume of *Hortus Kewensis*, second edition, as a sample of the printing of König's patent. Three years later in 1817 the first book printed by such machinery would be Blumenbach's *Physiology . . .*, on one of König's presses.

However 1815 opened for Banks on quite another note as the public uproar over the Corn Bill and the debate on the price of corn rose in pitch. On 10 February he again addressed the Prime Minister. He enclosed a statement showing the regional variations in the price of corn in France under cover of a letter expressing his very individual analysis of the state of Britain as it stood at the time. He saw no solution to the post-war crisis in the proposed ceiling price of corn at 80s. a quarter with imported foreign wheat at 66s., relief neither to the farmers, who provided the rent rolls to such as himself, nor to the manufacturers, whose trade depended on their ability to buy. His last paragraphs condensed the dilemma:

> . . . In whatever manner the question is taken up, the Shock to be encounterd is most tremendous; the Farmers used to receive 120s for a Quarter of Wheat will if 80 should be agreed upon be deprivd of ⅓d of their income. All persons who have fixd their Rents at the War price of Corn must lower them to that pitch, but the Farmers & their Landlords who are thus deprivd of so large a part of their late disposable Income, have no means of curing the Evil they will labor under, but by reducing their Purchases ⅓d also, & this must produce a shock to our Manufactures, which will be deeply & widely felt: there is little hope that the Parliament will grant relief further than 80s a Quarter, but it is quite certain that a relief of 100s would not replace the Manufactures in the state in which they have been during the continuance of the Continental System.
>
> We ought however to consider that by purchasing foreign Corn, we do not only hazard the horrors of Famine, by becoming dependant on our natural Enemies for our food, but the probability also of sacrificing the whole Balance of Trade in our favor to the purchase of Corn, & the certainty that the whole of the Sums we pay for Food will not only be withdrawn from the support of our Manufactures, but will become aliment to the Manufactures of the Rival Nations who feed us.

The 'Rival Nation' that had done so much during the war to feed Britain was France, the 'natural Enemy'. Within three weeks of this letter to Liverpool that enemy had risen again as Napoleon landed from Elba on 1 March. Ten days later the problem of the day had been brought to the very doorstep of 32 Soho Square in the attack on the house for which Banks had evidently been prepared in much the same way as in that early June week of the Gordon riots in 1780. Then he had come from Spring Grove with five armed servants and the house had not been attacked. Now, with armed soldiers inside, actual damage was sustained as the mob broke down the front door with a lamp post torn up from the Square and smashed the windows of the entrance hall beyond which they did not dare go. On 13 March Banks, in reply to a letter of sympathy from Lord Sheffield, pointed out that '. . . drilld by Some of King Luds Nottingham Regiment', the mob was well aware of the nature of the crime they committed and never attempted to leave the hall lest they be caught and punished as burglars. In brief, he said:

They never Resist the Soldiers or Constables but on being driven away disperse in Small Parties & proceed to their next Rendevous where they assemble into a mob & Resume their mischief

The Papers they destroyd were Letters on the Subject of my distribution of the Kings merino Sheep which I had turnd out from my Room as being absolutely useless. I am therefore no Further to be Pitied than the amount of the Carpenters & Glaziers bill

That the attack took place at all he attributed to the information gleaned by the mob from gossip with his servants. Although he was not in Parliament where the debate was concentrated, he was certainly known to be 'in the Great Council' and thus, as a prominent Privy Councillor, deeply involved as an adviser on the corn supply to which his letter of the previous month to Lord Liverpool had attested.

Later in the summer another facet of this concern with the feeding of the nation appeared as a letter under his name in *The Times* of 15 August 1815, part of an advertisement by the firm of Donkin, Hall and Gamble, provision contractors of Rotherhithe. Banks testified to the high quality on opening a canister of roast fillet of veal, sealed on 5 December 1812 by the hermetic process of Bryan Donkin, FRS, received at Soho Square on 15 January 1813. Opened on 14 July 1815, after two years and six months in Banks's possession before a group of six gentlemen besides himself, it was pronounced to be in a perfect state of preservation, as was also a small bottle of concentrated consommé of which he asked for more for his own use. As to the tinned veal he wrote:

> ... I consider the process you employ as one of the most important discoveries of the age we live in; it has in the experiment described above, entirely prevented even the first stage of putrefaction for two years and a half. That the same principle will continue to act longer, cannot be a matter of doubt; where then can be the difficulty of supplying all the seamen and soldiers who now eat salted provisions with fresh meat?

From this it was a short step to the decision by which the *Hecla* and the *Griper* were supplied with tinned meats from Donkin and Company for Parry's Arctic voyage of 1819–20.

But as the Hundred Days of Napoleon ended, the course of British technology moved on unchecked. The application of steam power to sea-going vessels continued to engage Banks's close attention as he encouraged the building of HMS *Congo* for Tuckey's expedition to the west coast of Africa. The strata of the earth, and his support of William Smith for so long, were at last displayed in all their 16 sheets on his table as *A Delineation of the Strata of England and Wales, with part of Scotland;* ... dedicated to him 'by his much obliged servant, W. Smith, Augst.1, 1815. Then on 29 August he assured Smith that he was urging the Duke of Bedford and Thomas William Coke to subscribe to the maps with him, adding his intention of recommending the purchase of the collection of fossils, the 'Organic Remains', by the British Museum. At Revesby Abbey on 30 October he had the pleasure of replying to Sir Humphry Davy's letter announcing the discovery of a safe lamp for use in coal-mines, a paper which he promised should be read at the first meeting of the Royal Society after his return, as it was on 2 November. The year closed with Banks introducing William Scoresby the younger to John Pond the Astronomer Royal as a further step in his education.

In March 1815 one of his first French visitors had been Edmé Jomard, geographer, engineer and Egyptologist, harbinger of the succession of his countrymen who were preparing to beat a steady path to Soho Square. In March 1816 Augustin de Candolle was an early and delighted visitor, entranced with what he found at Kew. About the same time from Haiti there came an acknowledgement from the Foreign Secretary, Julien Prevost, of the gratitude of the King, Henry Christophe, for what Banks had done to help his high-flown plans for the education of his people. In helping Wilberforce find recruits to lay the foundations of a school system, Banks had proposed his assistant librarian Tiarks but, as he told Blagden later, he was refused because he had been educated at Göttingen '... which his Saintship [Wilberforce] declard to be an unhallowd Place'. Nevertheless Banks could write to Wilberforce in a burst of supportive sentiment

> ... Were I five and twenty, as I was when I embarked with Captain Cook, I am sure I would not lose a day in embarking for Hayti. To see a set of human beings emerging from slavery and making most rapid strides towards the perfection of civilisation must I think be the most delightful of all foods for contemplation ...

This philanthropy was mixed about the same time with a vigorous engagement on a matter of art and antiquity with Richard Payne Knight.

Benedetto Pistrucci, the gem-engraver and medallist, had come to England in 1815, recommended to Banks by the mineralogist Etienne Gilbert, Marquis de Drée. Early in 1816, while he was modelling a cameo portrait of Banks at Soho Square, he met Knight, who had come to show his fellow-Dilettante what he had bought as an antique specimen from the dealer Bonelli for £100. Pistrucci declared it to be a cameo of his own making some six years earlier in Rome for Bonnelli at less than £5. The affronted connoisseur defended it as a true antique with the subject wreathed as Flora in the blossoms of an extinct species of pomegranate, not roses as Pistrucci claimed and as Banks independently diagnosed. Knight was unmoved, and Persephone of the pomegranates remained for him a true figure of antiquity but this duel of the Dilettanti established Pistrucci firmly in London. Later in the year Banks commissioned from him a jasper cameo head of the King. For this he paid Pistrucci 50 guineas and submitted it as a model for a new half-crown piece to the Royal Mint. The chief engraver's copy was a failure and Banks gave the original cameo to Queen Charlotte. In her letter of thanks on 15 October 1816 she declared it 'one of the best Profils' she had ever seen of the King.

Between August and October Banks received visits from Joseph Gay-Lussac and Dominique Arago. The former was interested in the Ordnance Laboratory, Woolwich, under William Congreve but Banks could not overcome the military resistance to such a visit by a former enemy. This was a contrast to the freedom with which the Admiralty had allowed Charles Dupin, the mathematician to roam over the naval installations and communicate a paper through Banks to the Royal Society, read on 19 December 1816, 'De la structure des vaisseaux Anglais, considerée dans ses derniers perfectionnements'. The visit of Arago was preparatory to that of Biot the following year, developing plans with William Mudge for the northern extension of the west European arc of meridian on which the French had been engaged for some time. It was as Banks reported Arago's visit to his staunch friend and invaluable parliamentary committeeman, Davies Gilbert, FRS, that the repressions and strains of 20 years of war-time correspondence at last broke:

... I greive over the depressd State of the mining interest, which like Every other branch of Commerce Sinks under the Poverty of all Europe causd by the Rapine of Bonaparte, That a wretch who has Entaild such a mess of misery upon a Larger Extent of this Globe & a greater Number of his Fellow men, than any Former Tyrant has Ever held in Subjection, Should be Sufferd to Live, while his dishonourable & dishonest Conduct is Felt so far & so wide is indeed an instance of honorable Feelings gone mad Could not an act of Parliament passed here & a decree of the French Representative body constitute a Jurisdiction & a Judicature on board an English & a French Ship by which he might be Tried & Executed. it would yeild Some Consolation to those who Still Suffer & will Suffer a long time from the Consequences of his Crimes & a Solace to the Souls of the multitudes whose blood he has Spilld that his Execrable Carcase was Sunk in the bottomless ocean & Establish an Example of Terror to Future Tyrants ...

But this furious mood of depression and sick man's tirade, however real its feeling, was a brief cloud over his steady watch on the progress of science. On 3 October he sent Blagden the first and second numbers of the *Quarterly Journal of Science* and the May issue of the *Annals of Philosophy* for 1816, drawing particular attention to the collaboration between Edward Clarke and Newman from which evolved the gas or oxy-hydrogen blowpipe, lauding it as 'Realy the most important instrument that has ever been given to the Science of Chemistry', fearing however that the French would reap more benefit from it than English scientists. He mused gloomily:

... it is a Cursd Consideration That all our Chemists become Gentlemen, who have more Pleasure in dissipation than in Labor

though he took some comfort that one at least, John George Children, FRS had returned to his science recently when the family fortune was lost and he had taken William Alexander's place at the British Museum as an assistant librarian. Moreover he brightened a little further at the recollection:

... From what minute origins do important discoveries originate Gauze Lamps & the new blow pipe owe their promising entry to the Simple fact Communicated to our [Royal Society] Comm[itt]ee by the Gas Light manager that the Flame of Gas Can never Communicate through very Small apertures

The spring of 1817 brought Banks back to a measure of reasonable health and on 11 April he was preparing Blagden with the arrangements in hand for the visit of Jean Baptiste Biot who was to work with William Mudge and Thomas Colby of the Ordnance Survey. He urged Blagden and Biot to come from France as soon as possible with the hope that they would all meet at Soho Square to discuss arrangements before Mudge set off for Aberdeen. On 3 May he assured Blagden that he had arranged through the Treasury for Biot's instruments and baggage to be passed under seal through the customs at Dover, to be taken from the wagon in his own cart to the lodgings he had arranged at Atkinson's Hotel in Dean Street, and there for the seals to be broken by a London customs officer and the whole admitted duty free. This novel request, he admitted, had produced some blushes at the Custom House but every civility had been promised to the French scientist. He had invited William Mudge to a family dinner on Wednesday 7 May and he hoped that Blagden and Biot would have arrived in time to join them. Biot would, of course, be his guest at the Royal Society dining club on Thursday 8 May. On Friday 9 May he had invited the Royal Society Committee for Kater's seconds pendulum to dine at Soho Square, when he hoped also to have the company of Biot and Blagden. So, in this fashion, Banks eased the passage in its difficult early stages for one of the first important post-war exercises in Anglo-French scientific collaboration. In effect it picked up the threads dropped some 30 years before in 1787, when William Roy, with help from Charles Blagden, had connected the first English triangulation at Dover with the French survey at Calais. The future course of the Anglo-French observations at Balta and Unst in the Shetlands was unhappy in the disagreement between Thomas Colby and Biot, with Dr Olinthus Gregory, the successor to Charles Hutton in the chair of mathematics at Woolwich. William Mudge kept his friendship with Biot in spite of the language barrier between; and Arago, when he and Humboldt arrived in November 1817 with the French pendulums for the comparative estimations of gravity, was on excellent terms with all parties. Banks had his own estimate of where the trouble lay and it is perhaps no surprise that Olinthus Gregory held the anonymous pen in 'A Review of some leading Points in the Official Character and Proceedings of the late President of the Royal Society' in Tillock's *Philosophical Magazine and Journal*, of September and October 1820. A somewhat different sentiment was expressed by Biot in that same year for 'ce venerable compagnon de Cook', buried as it was in his paper in volume III of *Memoirs de l'Academie royale des sciences de l'Institut de France, Anne 1818*, describing his work of measurement '. . . sur l'arc du meridien compris entre les Îles pythiuses et les Îles Shetland'.

> . . . Noble exemple d'un protectorat dont toute l'autorité est fondée sur l'estime, l'attachement, le respect, la confiance libre et volontaire; dont les titres consistent uniquement dans une bonne volonté inépuisable et dans le souvenir des services rendu; et dont la possession longue et non contestée fait supposer de rares vertus et une exquise délicatesse, quand on songe que tout ce pouvoir doit se former, se maintenir et s'exercer parmi ses égaux.

Early in December Arago, Biot and Humboldt returned to France leaving Banks in no doubt of their gratitude for the way in which they had been received and of which Biot's tribute in the *Memoirs* . . . later gave full testimony.

The year ended on a note of some botanical interest as he bowed to James Edward Smith's insistence that he should read Smith's article on 'Botany' in the *Encyclopaedia Britannica*, something he had not troubled about before 'conceiving it to be an elementary performance'. He confessed himself more gratified than he thought proper at 'the distinguished situation' in which Smith had placed him, even though he thought the personal reference was superfluous. Writing on Christmas Day 1817 his further comment clearly displayed the critical thrust of the work in hand at Soho Square and the background against which Robert Brown was resolving his taxonomic difficulties. Harking back to his own early roots in William Hudson's *Flora*

Anglica of 1762 and noting the immense advance in botanical science since then, Banks defined his own position after more than half a century in the field:

> . . . I admire your defence of Linnaeus's Natural Classes: it is ingenious and entertaining, and it evinces a deep skill in the mysteries of classification, which must, I fear, continue to wear a mysterious shape till a larger portion of the vegetables of the whole earth shall have been discovered and described.
>
> I fear you will differ from me in opinion when I fancy Jussieu's Natural Orders to be superior to those of Linnaeus. I do not however mean to alledge that he has even an equal degree of merit in having compiled them, – he has taken all Linnaeus had done as his own; and having thus possessed himself of an elegant and substantial fabric, has done much towards increasing its beauty, but far less towards any improvement in its stability.

But towards that greater stability Brown was making his own signal contribution with his *Prodromus Florae Novae Hollandiae* . . . as its first landmark, and with the Banksian herbarium at his service as one of the most comprehensive samplings of the plant world then to be found in one place for such a purpose.

The first months of 1818 were dreary and gout-ridden as Banks engaged himself in one of his last services to Lincolnshire. In December 1817 he had been approached by John Cust, 1st Earl Brownlow and Lord Lieutenant, on behalf of the county, to press for the completion of the ordnance survey. Cust had written to Henry Phipps, 1st Earl Mulgrave, Master-General of the Ordnance, asking for this to be put in hand but had received no reply. Banks took the matter up with Colonel William Mudge as the executive director of the survey, while the county waited for the indecisive Lord Mulgrave to reach a conclusion. This was at first a refusal but Banks, knowing the Master-General would relent in the end, induced Mudge to examine the matter closely and by 8 January 1818 had received from him an agreement to begin the work as soon as he received the necessary authority. Mudge depended on Banks to make the official case and promised, when the work was in progress, to submit proofs of the map engravings to him for approval from time to time. The following day Banks sketched out the procedure to Lord Brownlow and the shape of the case to be made to the Master-General. A month later, on 8 February, Banks sent Brownlow a letter in Robert Brown's autograph reporting that Mudge had received word from the Master-General and was ready to proceed with the survey as soon as 500 subscribers had been found for the maps at the rate of £4.14s.6d. a sheet. Within the next few weeks Mudge called on Banks and together they drafted the public notice to invite subscriptions payable to Cox and Greenwood. On 28 March Banks sent this to Lord Brownlow. Before the end of April Mudge had sent his surveyors into Lincolnshire with orders to finish the survey as speedily as possible although this was in advance of the subscription being filled. This information with further directions on procedure was sent by Banks to Brownlow on 25 April. Under this pressure from Banks the first modern survey of the county was hastened to a finish out of its geographical turn, certainly, but marking a turning point in the whole history of the Ordnance Survey by the new standards set. The process begun from his sick-bed at Soho Square during the winter brought the first proofs from the new engravings to his eyes at Spring Grove in April or early May less than two months before his death. His last view of the county landscape itself had been in the first two weeks of October 1817 but before he died he had ensured for posterity a clear and advanced professional record of lines across its broad surface whose course he had in his lifetime done so much to determine.

With the late spring of 1818 came more men of science from the Continent to find Banks still an invalid at Soho Square – among them Pierre Latreille, the French entomologist; Marc Auguste Pictet, the Swiss physicist and old correspondent of Banks; Jean Baptiste Huzard, veterinarian and publisher of Paris; and, most important perhaps, Georges Chrétien Cuvier, comparative anatomist and ambitious Académicien. Banks was fit enough, however, to have Cuvier as his guest at the Royal Society dining club on 4 June, at the end of one of his longest bouts of continuous invalidism. Later Banks felt he had cause to complain to Blagden of Cuvier's neglect both of the Society and the club when, as one of its most favoured foreign Fellows, more could perhaps have been desired. But could more have been wished for, three years later on 2 April 1821, in the tone and substance of the *éloge* pronounced by Cuvier on his late scientific host in London? As a French tribute before the Académie Royal des Sciences de l'Institut de France from such a man as Cuvier, it was generous and on the whole a fair presentation of the life and scientific place of Banks in western Europe. Not least was this so for its innocent wonder, duly recorded, that for all his influence with the King and government, Banks neither increased his personal fortune thereby nor gratified his vanity, presumably by seeking further titles.

From July 1819, for the ensuing year, Banks performed a last public service in his chairmanship of two committees, both of which met at Soho Square in deference to his invalid state. The first, appointed to enquire into methods of preventing the forgery of banknotes, – Banks, William Congreve, William Courteney, Davies Gilbert, Jeremy Harman, William Wollaston and Charles Hatchett – dated its report from Soho Square, 15 January 1819. The second, appointed to consider the subjects of weights and measures, – Banks, George Clerk, Davies Gilbert, William Wollaston, Thomas Young and Henry Kater – presented its report from Soho Square, 24 June 1819. But these commissions had scarcely begun their sittings before Banks and his ladies sustained a carriage accident on 25 August returning to Spring Grove from a visit to the retired judge, Sir Archibald Macdonald, at his house in Duke Street. His sister Sarah Sophia, though apparently only slightly hurt, died a month later on 27 September 1818. This intimation of mortality seems to have induced in Banks a prevision of his own approaching end but he had, before the accident, moved to divest himself of at least one personal accretion. On 21 August he had written to Wellesley-Pole, Master of the Royal Mint, offering the collection of coins and books relating to numismatics which he had gathered over the years as a foundation for such a collection at the Mint. This was accepted by the Master on 24 August with gratitude for the deficiency it repaired. Then, a month after his sister's death, he offered her collection of coins and medals also to the Mint thinking they had been bequeathed to him. Discovering that they were a bequest to Lady Banks he rescinded the offer that same day but his wife presented it instead. However in the end Sarah Sophia's numismatic cabinets came to rest in the Department of Coins and Medals at the British Museum.

Just before the accident, Robert Brown had set off for France to spend a month among his French colleagues in Paris, as he had done from time to time since the end of the war. From these visits, as Banks told Blagden on 22 August, he never failed 'to bring back a Plentifull Crop of Botanical Information'. At the same time Mudge and Colby, from the Ordnance Survey, had taken Ramsden's great zenith sector to Dunkirk at the special request of Arago and Biot to measure an arc of the meridian as had been done with the same instrument at Balta in the Shetlands, but as on the former occasion the French avoided any direct comparison with the results from thir own repeating circle. By the end of November 1818 Mudge and Colby were back in London with the sector ready for its loan to Heinrich Schumacher in Denmark. These were the last matters of survey with which Banks was concerned as a mediator.

There was, however, one more distant operation which stemmed from Soho Square over the same period. Dr Johann Tiarks was at work across the Atlantic as British astronomer on the American Boundary Line commission, an appointment which Banks had arranged for him in 1818, after a period of seven years as assistant librarian after the death of Jonas Dryander. His vacancy in the library was eventually filled by John Lindley for the last 18 months of Banks's life. Thus Soho Square briefly nourished another important seedling for the advance of nineteenth-century botany to be cross-fertilized with that other hardy transplant encouraged by Banks in the spring of 1820 – the new Regius Professor of Botany at Glasgow, William Jackson Hooker. What the course of botanical science and horticulture in Great Britain might have been had Robert Brown not refused the chair at Edinburgh made vacant by the death of Daniel Rutherford late in 1819 is fertile ground for debate. His decision to refuse was probably made during January 1820, when Banks was framing the terms of the codicil, signed on 21 January, which not only gave Brown his annuity of £200 a year but the use and enjoyment of the library, the herbarium and all the contents in the back buildings of the house at Soho Square, with reversion to the British Museum after Brown's death. He had enjoyed them all for the past 14 years and now Banks held out to him the prospect of an undisturbed future possession with accommodation and a sufficient competence. Having refused Edinburgh, Glasgow offered no greater temptation to Brown, and Banks was free to press Hooker into the chair which Robert Graham had so briefly occupied. With Robert Brown firmly anchored at 32 Soho Square and William Jackson Hooker induced to accept the Scottish challenge, Banks, with the imminence of his own death already clear had ensured the continuity of what his life had done so much to enrich in systematic botany and world horticulture. And with the provision for Franz Bauer of the annuity of £300 to continue unhampered his botanical art at Kew he had further strongly moulded the shape of things to come.

CHAPTER 25

A PUBLIC SPIRIT PASSES
1813–1820

As to the record of his own shape and substance, Banks was well known to have been an unwilling subject, certainly in his later years. The last portrait likeness captured from life was probably that taken by the young Francis Chantrey in the spring of 1816 as drawings for the bust commissioned by William Alexander who, with John Barrow, managed to induce Banks to submit. The plaster model was exhibited at the Royal Academy that year to become the marble presented by the artist to the Royal Society in 1819 and the source of other replicas such as that in the Linnean Society commissioned by its members. The Chantrey bust, finished in marble in 1818, was used in much the same way for replication as the Phillips portrait in oils which was painted in 1807 but finished in 1809. The original portrait was commissioned by Banks's good friend Joseph Mendoza y Rios in token of which Banks had the artist depict the Spaniard's paper to the *Philosophical Transactions* of 1801 on the table before him – 'On an improved Reflecting Circle'. But to mark the actual time when the portrait was painted, Banks nominated the paper held in his hand to be the Bakerian Lecture of 1807 by Humphry Davy, read on 19 November 1807, 'On some new Phenomena of chemical Changes produced by Electricity ...' From this Thomas Phillips produced other versions, but on 12 September 1808 Banks made his own views clear when the matter of an engraving was raised by the artist, with the suggestion that it be done by Nicholas Schiavonetti. Much as Banks admired the Italian he said he preferred William Sharp. In the end it was the burin of Schiavonetti that triumphed to add a fourth to that trio of portrait engravings that Banks himself had nominated as satisfactory likenesses, in this order – first, the mezzotint engraving by Dickinson of the Reynolds painting of 1772–73; next, the admirable mezzotint by the 21-year old John Raphael Smith of the long-lost (but now, at last, discovered) full-length and first authentic portrait of Banks by Benjamin West in 1771–73; finally, the 'most decided likeness', the stipple engraving by Joseph Collyer in 1789 of the pastel drawing by John Russell of 1788. How these had fared among the print-sellers he did not know but, he told Phillips

> ... I doubt whether any adequate Reward was Obtained by the artist for Either of the Large ones, a man like me who has never medled in Politics & who cannot of Course possess a Squadron of Enthusiastic Friends is not likely to Sell a dear Print, a Cheap one will answer better among the man of Science, many of whom have honord Russels Print with a Place in their apartments

Before he died there were, however, at least two other assaults on his vanity. In July 1819, as he lay ill at Spring Grove, a friend whose identity remains unknown proposed to deposit a portrait of Banks with his old college, Christ Church. Banks

Sir Joseph Banks, PC, KB, PRS. *aet.* 65. From the painting by Thomas Phillips, RA, 1809; engraved by N. Schiavonetti, 1812.

acceded to the idea so far as to confess that he would regard a place in the Hall 'Superior to what would accrue from a Place in the Picture Gallery' against the preamble that

> ... I am not much addicted to the Love of Posthumous Fame but I Confess the Idea of being Rememberd by those who in Future Receive intellectual nourishment from the milk of the alma mater by whom I was Fed is an Idea that Renders the natural Fear of Dissolution Less alarming ...

There is however today no known portrait of Banks in the collection at Christ Church.

After 41 years in the chair at the Royal Society he was elected again and for the last time unanimously on St Andrew's Day 1819 and soon after he heard through Blagden from Arceuil that Countess Rumford, the widow of Antoine Lavoisier, planned to have a Sèvres vase made to be decorated with illustrations of episodes in Banks's career on one side and with a portrait specially drawn of Banks himself seated in his study on the other. On 7 December Banks wrote to Blagden begging that he would do what he could to dissuade the Countess from the whole idea, though he took the precaution of correcting certain errors in the episodes she proposed to use. Protesting that he did not feel that vanity was a strong trait in his character, he said that he would stand to be convicted of it if, to decorate a Sèvres vase, he were

> ... to employ an artist to make a drawing of my room next the Library, with my Fauteuil, including my Battered Carcase ...

Two weeks later he hoped that Blagden had softened his remarks on the intended compliment the Countess had proposed but that nonetheless he had dissuaded her. There, as far as we know, the subject resting leaving Banks to die six months later, his memory unbesmirched by any porcelain artefact, however kindly meant.

II

In early June 1787 the 1st Earl Sheffield was busy in a minor literary way scribbling notes and comments on the draft by Banks of a paper intended to shed light on a troubled British wool trade in aid of the growers. Across the Channel, in his summer house by the shores of Lake Geneva Edward Gibbon was writing the last lines of the long *History* ... which was to seal his fame and whose manuscript sheets would come with him to join the Earl, his literary executor, in the library at Sheffield Place before the end of July. From here before mid-August 1787 the texts of the last three volumes of the *Decline and Fall of the Roman Empire* were sent to press to meet the acclaim of the world. But of the annotated paper returned from Sheffield Place to Banks two months before, there is only the silence of almost complete obscurity. Gibbon and Banks, the authors of these widely disparate literary works, would meet in London during the winter as mutual friends of Lord Sheffield and as fellow members of the Literary Club. Before this reunion both would suffer the agonies of gout in November. For Banks this was his first encounter with what would become his familiar demon and whose 'savage clutches' he told Sheffield on 22 November now chained him to his chair. It was cold comfort in return to hear from Sheffield Place of the waning of the 'Gibbonian Gout'. More warming to the heart from near at hand, if

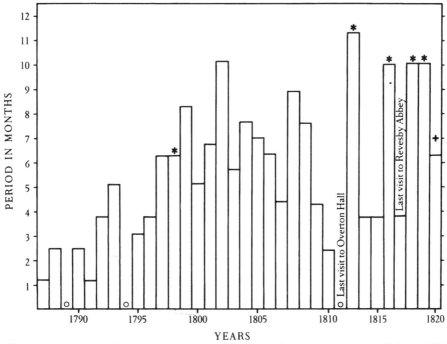

O: no apparent attacks   *:   no estate visits made that year   +: died 19 June 1820

The 'gout' history of Sir Joseph Banks 1787–1820

Periods of incapacitation per annum due to 'gout' or affiliated conditions in which he
was more or less bedridden or housebound.

no great easement to his right great toe, was the gentle condolence from the King
then at the Queen's House on 29 November:

> ... The King is sorry to find Sir Joseph is still confined; and though it is the
> common mode to congratulate persons on the first fit of the Gout, He cannot join
> in so cruel an etiquette ...

From this month to the end of his life, the rise and decline of gouty episodes form an
irregular punctuation in his activities and explanatory eddies disturbing the flow of
his correspondence. From it a clinical mosaic of the next 33 years can be formed as a
classic picture of the syndrome so common among Banks's contemporaries.

That there was a familial tendency to a 'gouty diathesis' among the men of the
Banks family is likely from the desultory evidence. His great-grandfather, Joseph I,
seems to have suffered in his late middle age to die at 62. His grandfather, Joseph II,
apparently fell victim at the age of 38 in January 1733 and took solace in the waters at
Bath during the last seven years of his life. His uncle Joseph III, died young at 26
without recorded evidence of the condition. His own father William, a chair-bound
cripple for some 16 years from another cause, left no evidence of gout in his medical
history from the little we know before his death at 42. His guardian-uncle Robert

lived to 70 when he succumbed apparently to the combined effects of a pleurisy and a kidney failure leaving his fond nephew the memento of a splendid cystic calculus, *post mortem*. Joseph IV alone lived out a span of days long enough with a trail of episodes sufficiently recorded from which some form of medical judgement can be shaped even though we cannot have the diagnostic weight of modern biochemistry and other aids in our support. In his case at least there is enough clinical evidence to interpret the 'diathesis' as a probably high level of blood urates with the syndrome of a classical gout broadly confirmed by the implicit response to colchicine buried under the terms *eau médecinale* of Husson and Vinum Colchici as extracts of *Colchicum autumnale* or kindred species. A 'diathesis' is one thing. An actual gouty episode is another. By what trigger mechanism an attack is launched is as much a mystery as it ever was. To the range of possible physical and physiological factors there have been added at various times those more particularly of a psychological significance, almost placing primary gout in the category of psychosomatic ailments. As the direct and indirect evidence gathers there is much to focus attention on Banks as a case in point. Although he would seem to have been a notable example of the 'gouty habitus' at his first attack – a middle-aged male of large physique, heavy set and over-weight – and as a subject in medical history an important instance of primary gout in a classical sense, there was certainly more to his case than will fit easily into the pattern of this syndrome alone.

For a year after his opening attack he was apparently free. Then in the autumn of 1788 he suffered his second bout as a more sustained but fairly short episode which had gone by the end of the year. For the whole of 1789 he was sufficiently well to merit congratulation from Benjamin Stephenson who had himself resisted the disease until the age of 55 but now after 30 years, badly crippled, warned Banks in January 1790 to expect a return of its pangs. These came in the late spring and lasted over the summer of that year preceded by a depression which left him with an aversion to his growing correspondence for some weeks. As Stephenson was soon to note, Banks in these early years of his gout history did not bear its confining grip well as he slowly learned the extent to which he had lost his physical freedom. The old man observed his tormented master during the last weeks of October 1790 at Revesby Abbey and Lincoln where, as Lady Banks reported, he had the gout 'very smartly in one Foot & for two or three days was a little afraid of it in the other' though it receded enough for him to attend the Stuff Ball in the city on Thursday 21 October. But after this brief remission his last month at Revesby Abbey was spent in bondage with a release just in time for the journey back to London to meet his Royal Society obligations in November.

In 1791 his attack marred the pleasures of summer at Spring Grove briefly and at the same season for a longer period of three months in 1792, his first bed-ridden illness for 22 years, that is, since his brush with death in Batavia in 1772. But in 1793 there occurred his longest and, to that point, his worst crippling series of episodes from January for some six weeks, a return in May and June, and a bout that laid him low in bed at Revesby Abbey from 24 October 'with both feet both Knees & both ancles bursting full of the Gout' as he described it to William Perrin on 4 November. He continued:

> . . . I have now some relaxation from Pain & yesterday I beleive I passed the
> Rubicon of increase today I am gently retreating or rather the Gout is gradually

withdrawing itself tho very Slowly I hope however in a few days more to begin to Crawl or hop about the house having been hitherto Confind to my bed and on an arm-chair incapable of Standing up much less of moving forward . . .

This was summed up next day by Lady Banks writing to Mary Heber that 'Sir Joseph being very Indifferent with the Gout' they would have to defer their return to London for another week:

. . . He don't like to fail attending the Royal Society if he can help it; this week it can't be help'd . . .

But in fact another month of rural isolation was to pass before he could take the chair again at Somerset House, a month moreover under the medical care of Dr Edward Harrison of Horncastle, a regime composed of pharmacy and physiotherapy. Harrison's local treatment of the affected limbs to restore tone and circulation was first 'a very gentle and long continued friction with fine old linen several times in the day when the tenderness of the parts admit of such an application'. Later this was to be followed by the cautious application of heat, immersing the legs in water as hot as could be borne for short periods. He even advised applying 'the electrical fluid' or a little mild galvanism.

Whatever the merits of this Lincolnshire medication, Banks was able to sustain his year as High Sheriff in 1794, a period of much travel and physical activity, without any recorded evidence of gout until the spring of 1795. Thereafter the attacks assumed a more regular and vicious pattern, extending at length over the autumn and winter of each year with shorter stabbing returns in the summer. In the spring of 1796 he was approached for his support in the Westminster election and by the Duke of Portland to appear on the hustings in favour of Sir Allan Gardner. He was constrained to refuse the Duke's request on Friday 27 May:

. . . I am but recovering from a Severe attack of the Gout which has left my body
Enfeebled in a great degree & my mind by no means in that state of Spirits
necessary for a man who means to oppose with any degree of success the Coarse
raillery of the Westminster mob
    I am able to move from Room to Room with difficulty & was so wholly
fatigued last night by taking the Chair at the R.S. which I did for the first time that
I with dificulty supported myself to Chelsea [his mother's house] where I slept
    I mention this merely to Shew how improper it would be for me to appear in
the Hustings Either for my own sake or that of my Freinds . . .

On 25 October at Revesby Abbey he was bed-ridden with an attack affecting his legs when the riots in Lincolnshire began and again there was a call for his physical presence but this time in a more dangerous and threatening situation. Although he had to demur until he could regain some degree of use of his legs, he rose from his bed and, with Thomas Coltman as the resident magistrate, moved about the county for more than two weeks, unarmed and by coach, concerting action to suppress the unrest aided by the military units sent for this purpose. When the main task was done he found himself under siege from the gout and forced to withdraw from the field, his fears being justified by his left knee becoming affected and demanding resort once more to his 'Flannells & Gouty Chair'.

Up to this period, while his legs had been severely affected in each episode, his hands had been left free. Now after ten years, this was to change. In 1797 during May and June his right hand was sufficiently crippled to impede his correspondence. There was no cheer in the prognosis. He cancelled the fishing party on the Witham for that year and never revived it. He withdrew from the tour of the county which he had hoped to make with Arthur Young in the autumn and wrote to him gloomily on 19 August:

> ... I am now like a Founderd horse lame when I go out, unsound when I come in & never likely to be any more an usefull animal . . .

This pessimism from the man who had but recently been appointed a Privy Councillor was almost the last cry of revolt from an ageing man of action nearly but not quite ready to accept the constraints of his changing physical state. The nadir came the next year, when during the spring and summer of 1798, Banks was for the most part immured at Spring Grove, mainly in his bedroom, and the autumn visit to Overton and Revesby Abbey was cancelled for the first time in his married life. Lady Banks was now clearly worried, declaring her husband 'a sad Invalid' tormented with rheumatism and gout alternately and leaving him only once for a few hours in a period of five weeks during August and September. So much was Banks apparently withdrawn from his ordinary good spirits that the gloom spread even to John Parkinson in Lincolnshire. It reached the point where he apologetically burdened Lady Banks with estate and county affairs in the form of questions, leaving her to judge the right moment to seek the invalid's opinion. By November Banks was well enough to engage in Royal Society business and to take the chair again as he was elected to the Presidency for the twenty-first time, but in January he relapsed and for the first three months in 1799 suffered an uncomfortable winter. This was followed by a short episode in June and July and then a long bout which started at Revesby Abbey in October to last, with fluctuations, for six months into the spring of 1800. The new century carried a modest comfort for Lady Banks in her impression that, though the complaint was long sustained and troublesome, Banks himself did not seem to be as ill as in the previous two years. There were in fact increasing signs that Banks was slowly achieving an accommodation with his ailment, gaining some sort of psychological ascendancy even though the ginger regime of Mr Pittonet and the milk regime of Dr Pitcairn may not have greatly eased his torments.

In 1802 he was free from gout for scarcely more than three months, and the fluctuations of his mood and of the syndrome itself flicker through his ordinary correspondence. To John Parkinson on 12 April his spirits rose a little after the long winter struggle:

> ... Altho my last illness did not give me much bodily pain, it producd a languor & debility I have not before been accustomd to, so much so, that business was irksome to me which is the reason I have so long delayd answers to your letters. Thank God however I now feel more as I usd to do, & have in the last three days gone through a good deal of business of course I have no doubt I shall speedily recover my usual spirits . . .

But the summer days were marred again by two months of illness. Both at Overton and Revesby Abbey from early September and for the rest of the year he was continuously tormented. From Revesby Abbey on 30 September his frustration is conveyed to Charles Greville:

> ... I am here Crippled & Crazy Obligd to go to bed before the Rest of the Family & to Lye Late in the morning I hope however for better Times & hope in which I am much inclind to indulge is Certainly one of our best Comforts in this Life ...

Later to William Aiton on 21 December he records another complication:

> ... I am very far from well, I have a Cough that tears me to Peices & prevents my Sleep & aches & cramps in most of my Limbs I look forward however with hope of being better before it is Long ...

Then in the summer of 1803, just past his sixtieth year, writing from Spring Grove to Lord Sheffield on 19 July, he begs to be excused from attending the wool meeting in Lewes:

> ... I am Sorry to Say with the Old woman in the Farce, that I'm not what I was 20 Summers ago; ... I become every day to my Greif more Stationary much as I struggle to Keep myself moving & I Foresee that the time when I shall Rest to a Point like the old weather Cock is not very far distant ...

From early December 1803 to the end of February 1804 he was largely bedridden at Soho Square, for much of the time deprived of the use of his right hand and subsisting on the milk diet prescribed by Dr Pitcairn, with Lady Banks from time to time writing to his dictation. In July and early August he was again prostrate at Spring Grove during the pressure of arrangements for 'the adventurous step' he had taken of offering the King's Spanish Merinos for sale by public auction. He was abroad for the sale itself on Wednesday 15 August 1804 but a month later was again in bed for five days with a sudden gout at Overton during September and a further attack in October at Lincoln and Revesby Abbey. For this, however, Lady Banks was inclined to attribute some benefit to Dr Pitcairn's increasingly strict dietary regime in the relative speed with which her husband seemed to recover from each episode.

Over the next five years only his formidable will seems to have kept him abroad and active, with little more aid than the management of his diet and the judicious use of a horse instead of a carriage. In this form of exercise he was perhaps mindful of what old Benjamin Stephenson had told him as far back as 31 January 1790, forecasting gout as 'a sad companion for old age', but finding in his experience that what he gained the most benefit from was 'geting on horseback'. On 31 May 1806 Banks commiserated with Lord Liverpool on the Earl's illness and described his own measures against their common enemy:

> ... I have of late taken much to Riding which I have not for several years been able to do & I find vast benefit from the exercise the only one I am capable of taking your Lordship accuses me of imprudently proceeding unattended through the Streets I wonder you should think me Capable of so absurd a measure I have always a Servant walking on the Pavement within a few yards of me who carries

my Stick without which I Could not go up my neighbors Stairs when I visit them as I mean only to walk my horse not being such a desperado as to trot fast over the Stones this is much more Convenient to me than a Servant on horseback as soon as I dismount he mounts & waits till I mount again . . .

His austerity in diet was well enough known, as Farington notes on 2 June 1806:

. . . Sir Joseph in the last 3 years has eat no animal food, no wine, no spirits, but lives on Pudding and vegetables, and has had better health from it . . .

But soon after this, as Banks told Dawson Turner on 28 June, he could not visit Holkham Hall for the Sheep Shearing that year as another attack struck him. The illness haunted his journey to Derbyshire and his stay at Overton but Lady Banks regarded this as mere teasing, for the attacks were lighter now and did not confine him to the house. By 18 September at Revesby Abbey she thought him 'vastly well again'. Two days later there is some trace in Banks's own opinion that the syndrome had somewhat eased in severity as he wrote apologetically on 20 September to Governor King in distant New South Wales

. . . I greive that I have been so often disappointed in my intention of writing to you by being confined by the gout at the time when opportunities offered. I have, in fact till this year been harassed in a degree scarce credible. I have not been two months from fit to fit, and of course, scarce clear of the first before the second placed me again in my bed. Last year [1805] ended with forty days in bed. This has been better I now live on vegetables entirely and drink nothing but water. Since this regime has taken place I have never been confined to my bed and I now hope to be better . . .

There is some evidence that the gouty episodes for the next three years were more widely spaced and on the whole less severe but there was a greater inclination now to seek some relief from sitting in the chair at Somerset House in the winter sessions of the Royal Society as Banks took rather more precautions with his prodromal warnings. However as late as 14 December 1809 he could write to Thomas Andrew Knight:

. . . Thank God I am at present free from the Gout; I feel better than I have done for some years, & begin to hope that my abstemious diet begins to produce an effect in my condition . . .

Two months later he was forced by a return of the disease on 14 February 1810 to ask William Marsden to take the chair at the Royal Society for him the following day. In the course of this episode three days later comes the well-recorded and dramatic turn in the clinical history of the Banksian gout.

On Saturday morning 17 February 1810, by the hand of her husband the 2nd Earl, Lady Spencer sent Banks at Soho Square a bottle of the French palliative – Dr Husson's *eau médicinale* – with Sir Henry Halford's instructions for its use. Lord Spencer, after some well-intended obstruction by the porter at the door, gained access to Banks abed upstairs in the grip of a severe fit of the gout. There ensued a

530

long debate with Lord Spencer pressing the virtues of the *eau médicinale* as something at least worth trying not for its curative but for its relieving effects. Banks despondingly recounted his long history of affliction against which nothing had availed him after trying every course then known to medicine. However he agreed to make the trial. Some hours later in the evening, Everard Home visited Banks as his regular physician. Banks shrewdly did not tell Home of his intention but asked him for a detailed clinical description of his present state. This was a pulse of 94, gouty lesions of his left side involving the great toe, ankle, heel, knee, hip, elbow, shoulder and hand, with signs of its imminent extension to the right hand and possibly the whole of that side as well. Home left Banks with the gloomy prognosis of an attack likely to last possibly a month in as severe a form as any he had observed. With such a vision of agonies to come Banks surrendered at last and took his first dose of the *eau médecinale* – half a bottle by one account, two teaspoonsful by the testimony of Banks himself. Next day, Sunday 18 February, Home found Banks as it was said at the time, 'in a very extraordinary state'. 'How? What's the matter?' asked Home. 'Why,' replied Banks, 'I have taken a quack medicine', and was forthwith scolded by Home for being so childish. However the alleviating effects which had begun during the night were now clearly apparent as Home directly ascertained much to his own astonishment – the pulse now 62 and all the joint pains relieved in inverse order to the sequence of their onset. On Monday 19 February, 48 hours after the first, a second dose of the *eau médecinale*, two teaspoonsful according to Banks, was taken. This time there were purging effects with five bowel evacuations over the next 12 hours. Apart from a slight nausea after the first dose, this was the only side effect from the new concoction and on 21 February Lord Spencer found Banks free from all gouty pains though still weak from his ordeal and in bed – the latest and one of the clearest examples of the power of the French medicine.

With his friend Major James Rennell as another notable case, Banks now entered the texts of British medicine in the pages of John Ring's *Treatise of the Gout ... and Observations on the Eau Medicinale*, 1811. Moreover his sceptical physician Everard Home was sufficiently stung by the evident success of the 'quack medecine' to begin a serious study of its properties and active principle. The same mystery also added a new zest to life for Banks in this last decade of his life as he sought the vegetable origins of the decoction whose composition Captain Nicolas Husson had kept as a close secret, from its first public use in 1783 and which remained a mystery as late as 1816 after its production in France had ceased. By this time however its relation to extracts from plants of the genus *Colchicum* had been suspected, as Dr James Want in 1814 had reported the successful use of an extract of *Colchicum autumnale* in the treatment of rheumatism. Everard Home by this time also had evolved his own recipe by extracting two pounds of macerated roots of the same plant with gentle heat in 24 ounces of sherry wine for six days before bottling the resultant fluid. Banks himself, by correspondence with his kinswoman Lady Hester Stanhope, had pursued the mystery of the plant hermodactyl of the ancients. He had received from her consignments of roots from Syria with French translations from Arabic texts in 1815, though by this time he was already convinced that the genus *Colchicum* at least harboured an active principle with effects similar to that in the *Eau d'Husson*, though the exact pharmacological relationship seems never to have been made clear.

From his first exciting experience in February 1810 Banks kept faith with the French medicine as long as he could obtain it. Strenuous efforts were made by his enemy-colleague Delambre, as perpetual secretary of the Institut, to secure 400 phials of the *eau medecinale* for which he received the approval of Napoleon on 15 September 1810. Despite the hostilities Delambre continued his efforts to obtain the medicine, for which Banks had already lodged a sum with the French banker M. Perregaux in Paris, but on 22 November reported his defeat on a point in police regulations. This was the requirement that secret formulae should be divulged to the Government before trade in the product was allowed. The purveyors of the *eau médecinale* preferred to keep the secret and supplies were no longer to be had. Delambre was deeply apologetic for not anticipating this obstacle though Blagden was evidently aware of the ban. Nonetheless on 31 December 1810 Berthollet read a letter from Blagden before the Institut extolling the virtues of Husson's water as a palliative in gout attacks in which Banks was now a case of some note. None of this brought a supply through the Institut however, though evidently another channel was found. Banks was able to use the *eau médecinale* for some years until he was finally convinced that its actions were effectively the same as the new *Vinum Colchici* which had become available in London. Banks then drew his supplies of the new tincture from a Mr Fisher, an apothecary of Conduit Street, after the end of 1816 or early 1817.

Banks was a chair-bound cripple from about 1810 with only the most limited and uncertain use of his legs even though his frequent use now of Husson's water released him from the worst agonies. The general change was noted by William Milnes writing to John Lloyd from Overton on 17 September 1811:

> ... Sir Joseph for several days complained a good deal of having the Gout flying about him and was obliged to have recourse to pretty strong doses of the french medecine ... I was sorry to observe that Sir Joseph appeared sometimes rather low and listless and seemed to have no inclination to stir out of his room, altho' the weather was extremely fine, he never once walked into the garden, nor rode upon the hill to look at the plantations ...

The year 1812 was his last experience of a life relatively free from gout or its complications but, from the early days of the New Year, 1813 was a stark contrast. This time the *eau médecinale*, even in immoderate quantities with all its unhappy side effects, could not relieve him. Everard Home became really alarmed and this state spread to his friends. Samuel Goodenough, Bishop of Carlisle, expressed their concern to Sir James Edward Smith on 25 February 1813:

> ... He is one that cannot be well replaced. I shall still hope that his strong constitution, as of iron, will carry him through ...

And it did; but even at the end of April he was still confined upstairs at Soho Square and only just able to use his right hand again for his letters. With the warmer weather he convalesced at Spring Grove where he was wheeled about the garden and from place to place, but here he stayed firmly anchored until the Royal Society and its affairs called him back to Soho Square in early November. For the second time since his marriage his county travels were cancelled. Other more general systemic changes were now becoming apparent, over-riding the gout which on the whole was still responsive to what he termed now his 'Faithfull Remedy'. There was some evidence of kidney dysfunction in the occasional calculus passed and the grosser signs of a periodic uraemia. If in the autumn of 1813 Queen Charlotte's observation that she found him 'looking like Ivory' be taken clinically, then perhaps there was also some evidence of anaemia. How much this was confounded by convalescent pallor after months in the bedroom and a measure of nutritional deficiency from his ascetic diet it is hard to say. The old theme of intermittent gout remained however, with Banks counting the intervals between bouts in days rather than in months. On 4 May 1814, to a close but unknown friend, he excused the delay of his reply to a letter received:

> ... under the influence of a Fit of the Gout which after an interval of 37 days chose to Return upon me with the usual Symptoms & in about 3 days to take away one arm one Leg & to Render my Loins so Sore I could not turn in bed without Exquisite Pain
> So circumstancd I Flew to my Faithfull Remedy which at once Releivd me & I am now Sound & whole again as Ever I was I have now as you Know taken the medecine for more than 4 years & am now fatter & of better liking than I was when I began ...

Each remission and note of optimism was inevitably checked now by an exacerbation and note of gloom. His correspondence with Thomas Andrew Knight was peppered now with agonized interruptions, as he noted for example on 15 January 1816:

> ... my Right hand was Seizd & held in Fetters by the Gout for near Two months which has Causd Such a Gap in my Correspondence as Cannot Easily be filld up ...

Later in the year, after a further succession of short attacks, withdrawn to Spring Grove but again in bed there, he reviewed his physical state in some clinical detail on 19 August to the medically receptive attention of Sir Charles Blagden now resident in post-war Paris:

> ... I Fear it is probable that I Shall be obliged to Spend the greater Part of my Future Life in a Prostrate Posture, Home will say nothing about the Future I fear that my case is not well Known to him in Practise, in Truth I am of opinion that the use of Husson's medecine has protracted my Life to a Period which Gouty Persons Seldom attain & that I am in Consequence suffering by /a Consequence/ an Effect of Gout which other people have not Lived to attain ...

He spoke more particularly of the increasing shedding of the epithelial layers or 'scarf skin' of his feet and legs after each attack, but also of the extensive oedematous swelling of his legs for some weeks after each episode. He noted especially that since his extended bout in 1813 this oedematous state in his legs had never to any degree receded and that he had been obliged to keep them bandaged ever since. For the third time during his marriage he was prevented from making his county rounds as he reported to Blagden on 3 October from Spring Grove:

> ... I am Still Confind here & prohibited from Proceeding to Lincolnshire or Even from visiting London I am however very much better I can go about the Garden in

my Little chair & am now able to Sit in my chair Resting my Feet on the Ground for some hours in the day So that I have no longer any doubt of being able to perform the Duty of my office for one year Longer at the Least . . .

But another more disturbing view of the man emerges during this month from the pages of the diary of Sylvester Douglas, Lord Glenbervie:

. . . [Fred North and I] found him in bed, his body and head swelled apparently with dropsy, but with all his accustomed energy and true politeness of manner of a sensible Englishman, now, and perhaps always so rare. I know not by whom he can be replaced . . .

Yet in the course of this protracted bed-ridden isolation out of London, as long as his right hand would permit, he continued the management of his affairs. The world perforce came to Spring Grove instead of Soho Square or Revesby Abbey where, despite his infirmities and bed-ridden state, Banks made all welcome. To Blumenbach on 3 March 1817 however he was forced to confess that he had in fact been almost disabled from public business, that his general debility was advancing fast under the impact of his chronic gout which was returning at intervals now of 14 to 21 days, though still held at bay by the *eau d'Husson*. He feared that when this medicine ceased to have an effect 'the first fit must finish my Carcass'. About this time he abandoned Husson's water in favour of the *Vinum Colchici* as a palliative using it at the same dose rate of 60 drops every 48 hours. Any greater quantity or frequency he found produced a gastric disturbance. By this time too he had convinced Everard Home that 'the *Eau médecinale* under the name of Vinum Colchici' was a useful addition to the available pharmacopaeia, whereupon his medical disciple proposed some improvements in its preparation. Late in the year, beyond the usual date of his autumn migration, Banks managed to get permission from Home to venture north to Lincolnshire for a month. He promised to travel in short stages, none so long as 40 miles in a day, and to take four days over the journey. This occupied the month of October and was apparently the last visit he was to make to the county or indeed anywhere away from the close neighbourhood of London.

Although 1817 passed with Banks in better health on the whole than he had enjoyed for several years he was again confined to bed with his right hand crippled early in 1818. In January both Robert Brown and James Roberts occasionally acted as amanuenses but in the main Banks painfully managed those letters he deemed most urgent as a matter of duty without excuse or comment on his handicap. This kind of extenuation he reserved only for the few intimates like Blagden, Knight or Lord Sheffield with whom correspondence was less a penance and from whom his health was a matter of continual enquiry. It was full summer in June 1818 before he could leave Soho Square to enjoy the pleasures of Spring Grove with a surcease from gout until the autumn. He wrote to Lord Sheffield on 29 June:

. . . I agree with your Lordship in thinking that I should have been dead & buried 5 or 6 years ago & I should have been so had I not taken the gout medicine, which we now make in London of the Root of the Meadow Saffron & find to be at least as Efficaceous as the *Eau medecinale*; I find it so who have taken it instead of the French Eau for more than a year.

534

I Find myself better this summer than I have been these three years & more inclind to exertion. I have therefore undertaken to act in two Commissions the one to Report on the Probability of introducing a more uniform System of weights and measures the other to Consider the Means of Preventing the Forging of Bank Notes. Two more dificult Questions you will not Readily Conceive. I have however men of my own choice for my colleagues & am not without hopes of Pleasing the Public . . .

His engagement with these two commissions, which mostly met at Soho Square, was a last burst of optimism. In August came that coach accident to shatter the close-knit domesticity with the death of his sister Sarah Sophia as a delayed consequence at the end of September, and soon thereafter the return of his gout. This was now marked by two worrying changes which he noted as a last paragraph in a letter to Blagden on 24 November, written in the hand of James Roberts:

. . . You ask after my health it is much as it was, 60 drops of Vinum Colchici now fails to drive away the Gout. my last interval was 17 days & this is the third since I took it. it came in my Right arm which is still sore & prevents me writing today. my worst ailment is an eruption of Chalk from my great Toe which makes it necessary for me to spend more time in Bed than I would wish to do . . .

This letter giving details of the recently returned Arctic expedition of Ross and Parry and the latest report of Phillip Parker King's survey of the northern coast of Australia sent from Timor was well dictated and clear, but the signature which Banks affixed was a feeble travesty of what it once was. 1819 was marked by the appearance of jaundice after his apparent recovery and he continued sick and mostly bed-ridden either at Soho Square or Spring Grove with this new symptom fluctuating for the greater part of this year. Beneath the more general systemic disturbance his gout as such seems to have lessened, at least in its frequency, as he noted on 5 May to Mrs Ann Winder in his advisory letter for her husband's benefit on the use of the *Vinum Colchici*:

. . . My intervals have of late been much longer than formerly, the last I had was 58 days. The present is now 31 & no fresh symptoms have been found. I suspect that age has worn out the disease as I am now 76 years of age . . .

Age however had other items on the debit side and there were now more frequent and extended periods of lassitude and inappetance. Occasionally a gouty twinge would, as he joked with Francis Douce, drive him to antiquarian studies even as late in the course as January 1820, and under the rigours of that severe last winter of his life.

His letters, though they had never been notably long, were now mostly limited to a few lines and of which Blagden was in these last weeks almost the only recipient as Banks sent across the Channel a last sequence of crisp items mostly of scientific relevance. This last line of communication, whatever the true nature of his feelings for Charles Blagden, evidently gave Banks a modestly sustained sense of purpose in a life that was all too clearly near its end. He had managed to occupy the chair at Somerset House three times in January, once in February, and for the last time on 16

535

March 1820. From this point, as Barrow has noted, his strength and spirits obviously faltered. His last letter to Blagden had been a brief hundred words on 1 March. On 27 March Berthollet wrote to Banks of Blagden's sudden death over the dinner table at Arceuil on the 26th. For Banks this may have been the snapping of a last vital cord and, for all practical purposes, after this month his pen seems to have been laid aside, except to submit and then to withdraw, under strong friendly pressure, his resignation from the chair of the Royal Society on 1 June 1820.

It was probably in April some weeks after the last appearance of Banks as President both of the Royal Society and of its Dining Club that he invited John Barrow to spend a day with him at Spring Grove. Here Barrow 'found him much altered in his looks, and more than usually languid', though he soon rallied and grew more cheerful to laugh and joke with Lady Banks and the others in the small party round him. This was a visit which Lady Banks told Barrow had roused him from what was becoming a state of persistent languor, a stoical acceptance of impending death. For this he found a few words in his last conversation with Sir James Edward Smith some weeks later. Alone together at Spring Grove about the middle of June he told Smith that 'he was quite easy about the event, which he knew could not be far distant, considering the state of his stomach'. Several days later, on Monday 19 June about three in the morning, he died.

III

When Banks died there passed from the English scene a stalwart Georgian country gentleman of independent means and a truly independent cast of mind. This was a character he was pleased to bear with some pride. From his adolescence he studied to preserve it, aware of the solid base of inherited property on which it rested and of the burdens of responsibility this implied; first, to his family as the custodian of entailed estates; second, to the counties in which these lay as the owner of large natural resources and the landlord of tenants from whose well-being the family wealth derived.

As a middle-class landed gentleman he was born into that segment of eighteenth-century society from which emerged and into which migrated increasingly the rising professional groups as they differentiated slowly from various educational roots in the church, the law, the liberal arts and medicine, with mercantile, industrial and financial pursuits the background to their wealth. For many the ranks of the nobility were opened by inter-marriage with consequent accretions of wealth and influence. For many this social change came by virtue of titles gained for services to King and country. Some few were achieving honours for professional or intellectual distinction.

In this social spectrum Banks had his place as the fourth-generation beneficiary of wealth accrued from modest origins in a county legal practice, quickened by shrewd property investments and profitable inter-marriage. Consolidated under an entail, these estates, after half a century, ensured his position as one of the larger landholders and more wealthy of the county esquires. At his majority in 1764 with property of some 9000–10000 acres, mainly in Lincolnshire, and an income of £5000–£6000 a year he ranked among the 300–400 most wealthy men in the kingdom. This status he had adorned with an education at school and university beyond that of all his forebears but without the final touch of an academic degree.

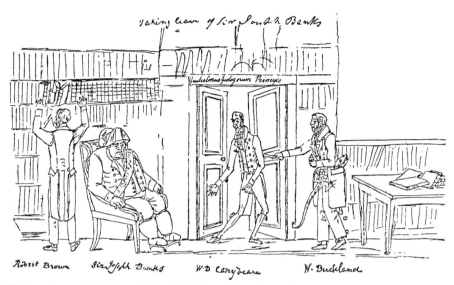

'Taking leave of Sir Joseph Banks.' A sketch by Count Breuner *c.* May 1820 of Banks in his study at 32 Soho Square with Robert Brown FRS as W. D. Conybeare, FRS and W. Buckland, FRS bid him farewell before leaving for France where Buckland heard the death of Banks announced at a meeting of the Institut.

This preparation for the world of affairs was more than enough to carry him as high and as far as any of his contemporaries in the power complex of his day had he wished. With an intelligence of a high order and a questing curiosity his energies were stored in a body of great strength and endurance – in his prime a handsome six feet and 13 stone in weight. A will of tempered steel was cloaked by an outward bearing of notable good humour and a patience rarely broken by events. Such was the young man at 21 who came down from his Oxford college seeking a purpose in life but already determined at least on one thing – never to enter Parliament.

To deny himself this tempting path to fame and influence set him down in his generation as perhaps a man of small ambition, extrovert and amiable, restless and dilettante, but certainly not profligate or careless with his patrimony. Behind the façade, whatever his deficiencies in the classics at Eton or the failings in the natural sciences offered at Christ Church, somehow a serious student had been born for whom a vision had been raised and a search begun. Matured a little further in the company of his elders at and about the British Museum in its first decade his learning in natural history evolved from the hobby of a cheerful youth as a lonely pursuit in the provinces into the semblance of a scientific occupation. Its extension as a life of adventurous travel into unknown seas was an aberration neither much approved nor wholly understood by his family or immediate friends.

After his voyage to Newfoundland and Labrador he had clearly reached a second conclusion of key importance – that natural history was now to be the vineyard of his labours. With little enough to guide him he had in fact by this time devised for himself a profession through which he could realise that other element in the vision – a service, as he defined it to himself in later years

537

for the advantage of the Public, without the Expectation, the Hope or Even a wish to derive advantage of any Kind from the Result of his exertions.

From the spring of 1767, as he settled in his own house as master for the first time at 14 New Burlington Street, can be dated the demise of the dilettante and the rise of the committed scientist and the wide-ranging scholar. The well-organized growth of the herbarium attests the one. The library and its effective use over a lifetime establishes the other. The welding of these two elements 'for the advantage of the Public' is evident enough after the autumn of 1777 in the history of 32 Soho Square.

However careless about his books the young Banks at 14 may have seemed it is certain that seven years later, as he probed the intellectual ramparts of London, much had changed. That he should have become Mr Joseph Banks, FR & AS at the age of 23, whatever the oddities of such elections then, implied something more than the qualities of 'a respectable tradesman', in the pejorative words of Barrow a lifetime later. That he should have been deputed by the Council of the Royal Society and accepted by the Lords of the Admiralty as a civilian scientist at 25 on his own terms for the *Endeavour* voyage suggests no failing in his intellectual stature or power to impress. With so much publicly at stake in the expedition something more than a mere ability to finance himself as a supercargo was demanded. That he was able to provide this extra aid in full measure is evident enough now from the history of Cook's first voyage.

In the brief *Resolution* rumpus and the withdrawal of 'Mr Banks the traveller', in his thirtieth year, from Cook's second voyage there was the pang of a temporary frustration but, more important, the elements of a third and far-reaching decision. A moment had come for some compromise to be found between the open-air attractions of nature in the raw and the probing curiosity of the scholar at his desk. The events of the next five years from 1773 seem to show that Banks had charted a course toward some form of scientific leadership. Whether he had chosen 'Newton's chair' as his ultimate goal may be argued but that he intended his own scientific ménage as a centre of influence is apparent from his assiduous devotion thereafter to a far-flung and various correspondence, a life of penmanship not easily endured by the hearty countryman that in character he remained.

His election to the chair at Crane Court in 1778 set the first shackles on a personal freedom of action that he valued highly. His marriage in 1779 completed the bondage to which he submitted with an outwardly amiable and conscientious good grace for the rest of his life. However, the very success with which he combined his public eminence as the long-serving President of the Royal Society with his more private and personal effectiveness as friend and adviser to the King and Queen and as consultant to successive administrations at Westminster and in Whitehall, certainly imposed strains, both physical and psychological. Almost as a last straw, flattering and useful as it was, came his appointment to the Privy Council in 1797. From this year the episodes of his medical history move steadily from the fairly tolerable well-spaced gouty spasms of the lower limbs, as they began with the rising pressures on his time and energies in 1787, to the more general and sustained bouts of real invalidism more common thereafter.

His serious engagement with public affairs as an unpaid civil servant of Whitehall may be dated from 1784 as the 'dissensions' in the Royal Society declined and the star of the younger Pitt ascended after the general elections in the spring, with the passage of the India Act and the appointment of the Board of Control in the late summer. Between the claims of his King at Kew and Windsor and of his country in Westminster the staunchly independent landowner of Lincolnshire was moulded into what William Eden neatly defined as 'His Majesty's Ministre des Affaires Philosophiques' or, with less polish but in more modern terms, his Minister of Science and – perhaps – Technology. In some such guise Banks served the state for the next 30 years or more, encompassing by degrees a wider field almost as a permanent secretary in a Ministry without Portfolio – or, indeed, as such a Minister himself. But whatever the historic pigeonhole, if any, that he came to fit this much was very clear – his services were at no time a burden on the Treasury. This point he made emphatically to a friend seeking his patronage for a 'place of Emolument' in 1798:

> I hold no such place myself nor do I mean to receive a Salary from Government. My independance of action & opinion I value beyond any thing that can be given to me and as I am not or ever have been in Parliament I have not even a Vote which I can give to a Minister.

There can have been few men who devoted so much of their time and personal fortune to the service of their country with quite the same measure of disinterested philanthropy and, on the whole, of beneficial common sense. Nor can royalty anywhere have enjoyed for so long such unselfish devotion from someone who stood, in effect, above the station of an equerry – a Gentleman, not of the Bedchamber, but in practice of the Botanic Garden and the Farm – with no drain on the Privy Purse for stipend or emolument otherwise. In Banks the King also had a friend who never exploited his place of favour in the Court either for himself or others, an attitude of integrity he kept unblemished whatever the doubts of a cynical world. His cold rebuke to a clerical friend seeking his influence toward a vacant bishopric in 1790 set his consistent stance on the subject plainly enough:

> You are not the only one of my friends who think I ought to use what you call my consuetudinous intercourse with his Majesty as an engine to promote your interests. Was I to ask from him a tenth part of the favors I am requested to do, I should in a week forfeit the whole of the good opinion I have the honor to enjoy. But I give the same answer to all. I do not ask for anything for myself or I have no doubts I might obtain both honor and profit. But I feel a spirit too independant to use the friendship even of a King as a ladder to ambition, and if I refuse to barter that independance of mind for advantage to myself it is not reasonable that I should sacrifice it to the wishes of others.

This strict code remained inviolate as far as any records tell. The single honour from his royal master in 1795 and nothing more beyond its elevation under the Regency into the Grand Cross of the Order bears cogent witness to the strength of his personal abnegation. His one conceit, if such it truly was, lay in his baronetage conferred in 1781.

It is difficult to assess how far this preferment to the lowest rank of the heritable peerage derived from his county status as an extensive landholder and how far from his academic status as a President of the Royal Society in his third year of office, a

539

notable savant in natural history with a private scientific establishment and collections to match. Only one of his predecessors as PRS will bear direct comparison. Sir Hans Sloane was raised to the baronetage as an eminent physician, natural historian, and landholder of Chelsea, but this was before his election to long service in the chair at Crane Court. As baronets the relative claims of these two men have much in common. The place of Sir John Pringle as a baronet in his own right differs by his inheritance of the title also. But however he stands as a baronet there still remains the conundrum of Banks the President of the Royal Society.

From his marriage in March 1779, during his first year in the chair, the routines of the Royal Society formed a rigid framework for his life very much in the university academic pattern until his death. It was seldom disturbed by exceptional events though intermittently by ill-health. The standard measure of this diligence is his record of attendance at 417 out of 450 council meetings during his long tenure apart from the ordinary occasions on Thurdsay evenings after sitting as host in the Royal Society Dining Club at the *Mitre* or the *Crown and Anchor*. He rarely left London for his county affairs before the last meeting of the Society in July and, with only three exceptions due to illness, was back for the opening of business well before the Anniversary Meeting on St Andrew's Day. Nor was the long summer vacation ever quite free as Secretaries or authors pursued him with problems of papers in press for the *Philosophical Transactions* or for the winter sessions to come. The welfare of the *Transactions* as a scientific journal lay close to his heart both for its content and as a specimen of British printing. Though never an author in its pages he is associated closely with some 243 papers at least published there in his lifetime – that is, a quarter of those in the relevant 42 volumes.

The criticism that during his presidency 'science and especially mathematics, physics and chemistry' were kept subordinate cannot stand, for under these heads nearly two-thirds of the 969 papers printed from 1781 to 1820 fall among nearly three-quarters which may be grouped as non-biological. Over these 40 years his own special field of general botany is represented by no more than 37, or less than 4 per cent. By contrast astronomy, mathematics, chemistry and physics, comprise some 585 or 60 per cent of the papers printed over the same period. Whether printed or not all those papers read before the Royal Society for this span of time form a continuous theme in the Banksian correspondence and, indeed, many would not have been published but for this stimulus.

How much the Royal Society gained as a focus of intellectual eminence by the open house in Soho Square is not easily judged but that the long association was important is beyond doubt. As a meeting place for the Fellows and their provincial or foreign visitors it augmented the conviviality of the Dining Club and the amenities of Somerset House with the more relaxed evenings over tea in the quiet of the Banksian library above Dean Street, attended for so long by the helpful services of Jonas Dryander. With the more frequent working breakfasts these were occasions of high value at no cost to the Society, open also to a broad band of the London intelligentsia in other fields. Beyond this role again, through 21 years of world war and foreign revolution by the astute diplomacy of its master, 32 Soho Square was a haven of comfort and a remarkable channel of international communication not only in science but also in the world of affairs. In this aspect of his life Banks risked at times the accusation of traitor at home and that of spy abroad but through it all kept alive at least one spark of civilized humanity in a dark and savage world.

After the transition years, with 14 New Burlington Street as a base from the spring of 1767 to the summer of 1777 including the trials and errors of the five years after the *Endeavour* voyage, the move to Soho Square heralded a regime which kept a remarkably stable and happy course thereafter. At the end of March 1773 Daniel Solander returned to duty at the British Museum as under-librarian, having for some four years and eight months worked as the paid associate and valued friend with Banks during the exciting years of the South Pacific and Iceland voyages. Another nine years of a loose collaboration centred round the *Endeavour* collections before the untimely death of Solander at Soho Square broke the partnership at last. By then the staff had already been strengthened for nearly five years by the appearance of Jonas Dryander in July 1777 and his immediate attachment to Banks as an assistant at 32 Soho Square. After the death of Solander in May 1782 Dryander thenceforward was beyond doubt the responsible curator, librarian, and Banks's veritable right arm, his field botanist also among the gardens of London and the home counties.

From 1772, for five years, Banks had the clerkly penmanship of Sigismund Bacstrom fully at his service with others, such as Frederick Walden and Alexander Scott, for lesser periods until the move to Soho Square. Thereafter the workaday copying was taken up by William Cartlich as the reliable scribe for nearly 40 years, occasionally aided by such as John Swan, serving more especially the office needs generated by his master, the industrious penman at the big desk in the small study on the ground floor behind the great staircase of the main house.

Then, until 1800, almost in view from the study across the courtyard, in the engravers' room below the herbarium there laboured that artist of the copper plate Daniel Mackenzie, for nearly 25 year another steadfast servant of Banks whose skills were applied beyond the special calls at No. 32. They had indeed been used to some effect, in a Banksian quirk of publication, to engrave those plates in 1797 which proclaimed Franz Bauer as 'Botanick Painter to His Majesty' without the qualifying phrase 'by courtesy of Sir Joseph Banks' as the mantle under which both men worked. Though further afield at Kew, from 1790 to the end of his life in 1841, Franz Bauer was no less bound to the service of Banks his paymaster, director and warm friend than were Dryander, Mackenzie and all those others who worked in the back premises at Soho Square. With Banks himself their various abilities were dedicated to the greater glory of the Royal Botanic Garden and thus to the advancement of botanical science at large. As such His Majesty was pleased to accept them but they were in no way a charge on the Privy Purse. In principle, Banks and his staff were as much at the service of the scientific public as any one of them ever was for the King. By this unwritten formula the two Aitons as members of the royal establishment in garden management and development had their share of help from Soho Square. So too from the same Banksian resources were the botanical education and artistic hobbies of the Queen and the royal princesses nourished and served.

Woven into the relations between Banks and the royal family – social and otherwise – the villa of Spring Grove was an important element under its successive head gardeners: John Smith from 1779–1803; Thomas Fairbairn, 1803–15, overlapping briefly with Isaac Oldacer who served from 1814 until the death of Lady Banks in 1828. In the flowering season, as with Kew, botanically it came under the watchful eye of Jonas Dryander. Horticulturally it supplemented the Royal Garden, some three miles away across the river, as a haven for exotic plants and as an experimental ground for species of likely market value as fruits and vegetables. As

541

such it bore the character, in practice, of a field station enhancing the work of the 'institute' at Soho Square for, in his day, perhaps no man more than Banks bestrode with such ease and authority the horticultural territory that lay between the dried specimens on the herbarium bench and the crop plants growing in the field or displayed on the market stall.

Some ten miles to the east and well within two hours on horse-back or by carriage from Spring Grove the Swedish connection at Soho Square, based on the early friendship between Banks and Solander, had been made solid from the summer of 1777 with the induction of Jonas Dryander as the first full-time curator and librarian. Beneath the flat copper roof of the 'back premises' this academic regime formed a small intellectual hotbed devoted to the natural sciences and their propagation. It was augmented from 1792–7 by another Swede, Samuel Toerner, as assistant to Dryander during the first pressures of organizing the *Catalogus Bibliothecae* . . . He was replaced by yet another Swede, Frederic Schutzen, from 1797–1801 until the last volume of the catalogue had been published. Thereafter the academic base was extended by the appointment of Karl Dietrich Eberhardt König, otherwise Charles Konig, from the University of Göttingen as assistant librarian from 1801–7. Within this period König, with John Sims, launched the *Annals of Botany* 1805–7 on its brief career before he joined Dr George Shaw at the British Museum as the first Assistant Keeper of Minerals.

Before Konig left Soho Square Robert Brown had entered, albeit on Admiralty pay, after his return in November 1805 with Ferdinand Bauer to work in the 'back premises' on the *Investigator* collections for the next four years until the death of Dryander in October 1810. Before the end of that year Brown had been installed as Dryander's successor in full charge of those rich scientific resources of which, after 1820, he would have the untramelled enjoyment until his own death on the same premises in 1858. In 1811 Brown was joined by Johan Tiarks, another alumnus of Göttingen, a mathematician who served as assistant librarian until 1818 when, with Banks's support, he left to join the United States–Canadian Boundary Line Commission as astronomer and to pursue a career in that field. His place was filled briefly by the young John Lindley in whom Banks had lit his last torch of the many kindled in the precincts of 32 Soho Square to illuminate the natural sciences and botany in particular. Through Brown the future of systematic botany in the British Museum was assured. Through Lindley the rescue and resurgence of the Royal Botanic Garden at Kew to meet the scientific destiny framed for it by Banks would be effected by the report of 1838 and the subsequent appointment of William Jackson Hooker as Director.

Apart from these accessions of personnel to the growth of science and scholarship at the British Museum there was at all times from as early as 1767 a steady flow of material gifts to the collections – manuscripts, antiquities, and items of importance in zoology and ethnology, especially in 1792 – all of them adding greatly to the material value of Banks's final bequest of his library and herbarium. In 1822 this last great founding benefaction was valued by the Trustees for the purposes of insurance at a round figure of £14000. This compares well with the estimate of £20000 for which the nation acquired the collections of John Hunter some 20 years earlier which had themselves also been enriched at intervals from Banksian sources.

Though botany was the leading science to which Banks had devoted the best part of his life and, by his own confession, the one for which he had voluntarily

Left Franz Andreas Bauer, FRS, FLS, *aet.* 76. Drawing W. Brockedon, 1834.
Right Charles Konig (formerly Carl Dietrich Eberhard Koenig), FRS, FLS, Keeper of
Natural History, 1813–37; Keeper of Minerals (including Fossils) 1837–51, British
Museum.

exchanged prospects of 'Parliamentary consequence & possibly of high office', there
is no doubt that he made skilful use of his plant hunting and the pursuit of natural
knowledge as a mobilizing theme for European, notably British, expansion in the
eighteenth- and early nineteenth-century world. The 'gentle science' was often the
small quiet note from which greater more political orchestrations grew and within
which it was almost invariably concealed. From the *Endeavour* voyage onward for
half a century until his death the association of Banks is an indelible, though seldom
easily apparent, element as an inspiration or active participant in the planning and
execution of the major British excursions of peaceful though hardly apolitical intent
beyond Europe and its close neighbours.

The far-flung origins of the specimens in his herbarium and the names of those by
whom they were collected form a rich testimony to the global range of his influence
as surviving evidence near at hand today. Less conveniently evident is the material
record of his correspondence among the nooks and crannies of modern history into
which his spider scrawl has made its way – the yellowed relics of his many thousand
friends, associates, and hopeful seekers after knowledge, news, or easement in
distress; the files of minuted official papers in record centres and libraries across the
world. Here and there a place name marks his status as a man to be remembered and
here and there a simple plaque. Here and there some plant or animal may bear with
taxonomic legality the commemorative *banksii* as a chance survival from time past or
in belated justice – though all too few within the scope of his historical merits.

Among the varied fragments, however, which remain to attest his existence some
two centuries ago, none more clearly invokes his memory than the map of the island-
continent in the south-west Pacific. None appeals with more historic force for the full

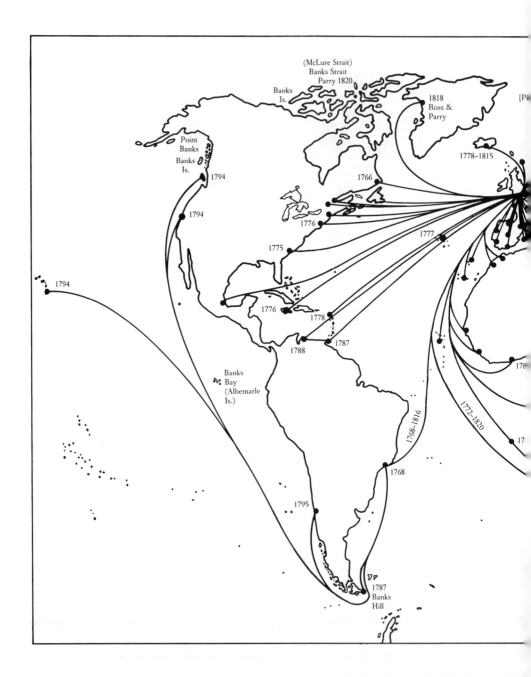

The general pattern of the Banks correspondence, 1766–1820, with some commemorative place names.

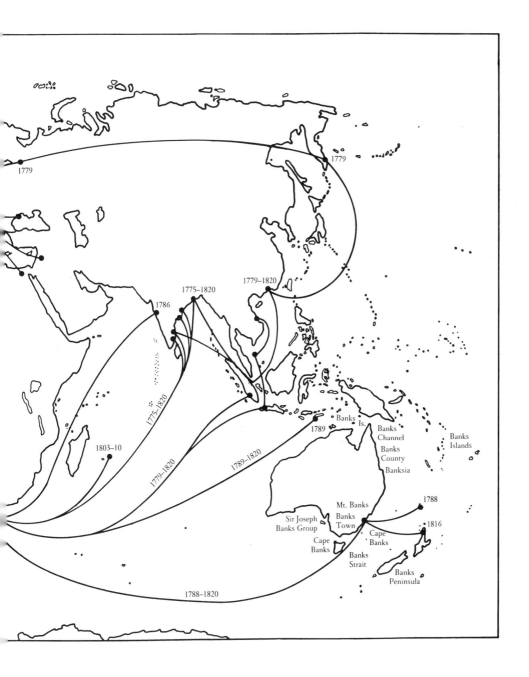

1779

1779

1779–1820

1775–1820

1786

1775–1820

1803–10

1779–1820

1789–1820

1789

Banks Is.

Banks Channel

Banks County

Banksia

Banks Islands

Mt. Banks

Banks Town

1788

1816

Cape Banks

Sir Joseph Banks Group

Cape Banks

Banks Strait

Banks Peninsula

1788–1820

545

and just commemoration of his life. A few names of places and plant species bestowed by his more discerning contemporaries record the young 'man of adventure' as he passed that way. Beyond this very little more. Yet there is no man of whom it can more truly be said that he was 'the father of Australia'. From before the sailing of the *Endeavour* in 1768 to the anchorage of the 'First Fleet' at Sydney Cove in 1788 the possibility of a white European settlement somewhere on its eastern shore survived on the firm intellectual support of Banks's geographical and biological insights, both instinctive and observed.

From the moment of its inception as a distant plan no man laboured more continuously or constructively to ensure the survival of that remote British outpost through the years of global war, uneasy peace and changing Ministries at home. No man was more steadfast as the ultimate support of successive governors with his advice and help in their lonely struggles facing the challenges of an unstable small society in an enigmatic vast new world. No man did more to ensure that the world map should include Terra Australis as a British settled region with 'sources of wealth of the utmost importance to the future wealth and prosperity of the United Kingdom'. Of wider import still to the modern world no other man, for over half a century at the vortex of this historic process, was so extensively involved in the discoveries, the patterns of European occupation and the understanding of the whole Southern Hemisphere as we conceive it now.

APPENDICES

APPENDIX I

Personnel of the various parties enlisted by Banks for the actual or intended voyages, 1766–72

HMS *Niger* Capt. Sir Thos. Adams 1766–7 (April 1766–January 1767)	HMS *Endeavour* Capt. Jas. Cook 1768–71 (August 1768–July 1771)	HMS *Resolution* Capt. Jas. Cook / HMS *Adventure* Capt. Tob. Furneaux 1772 (Party withdrawn June 1772)	*Sir Lawrence* Brig Capt. Jas. Hunter 1772 (Privately chartered July–December)
Scientist Joseph Banks, FRS & AS	*Scientists* Joseph Banks, FRS & AS Daniel Solander, FRS	*Scientists* Joseph Banks, FRS & AS, DCL Daniel Solander, FRS, DCL James Lind, MD	*Scientists* Joseph Banks, FRS & AS, DCL Daniel Solander, FRS, DCL James Lind, MD
Associate (friend/guest) Lt. Constantine Phipps, RN			*Associate* (friend/guest) Lt. John Gore, RN Uno von Troil, MA John Riddell Esq.
	Artists Sydney Parkinon* Alexander Buchan*	*Artists* John Zoffany, RA John Frederick Miller James Miller John Clevely	*Artists* John Frederick Miller James Miller John Clevely
	Secretary Hermann Dietrich Sporing*	*Secretaries* Sigismund Bacstrom Frederick Herman Walden	*Secretaries* Sigismund Bacstrom Frederick Herman Walden Alexander Scott
Servant Peter Briscoe	*Servants* Peter Briscoe } collectors James Roberts } Thomas Richmond* George Dorlton* Nicholas Young† Alexander Samarang†	*Servants* Peter Briscoe } collectors James Roberts } Nicholas Young Alexander Samarang John Asquith Peter Sidserf John Marchant } French Robert Holbrooke } horn players	*Servants* Peter Briscoe } collectors James Roberts } Nicholas Young Alexander Samarang John Asquith Peter Sidserf John Marchant } French Robert Holbrooke } horn players – Morland – gardener Anthony Douez – cook
	*died on voyage †recruited on voyage		

Appendix II

The voyage of HMS *Endeavour* round the world from Plymouth 25 August 1768 to Deal 13 July 1771

Summary of Collecting Regions

At anchor: [various harbours, anchorages, landing sites]

Madeira – Funchal	6 days
Brazil – Rio de Janeiro, Isle of Raza	24
Tierra del Fuego – Bay of Good Success	6
Society Islands – Tahiti, Huahine, etc.	106
New Zealand –	
Poverty Bay, Araura Bay, Tolago Bay, Mercury Bay, Bay of Islands, Queen Charlotte Bay, Admiralty Bay	58
East Coast of Australia –	
Botany Bay	6
Bustard Bay to Cape Grafton	7
Endeavour River	48
Lookout Point to Booby Island	6
East Indies – including New Guinea, Savu, Batavia, Prince's Island	96
Cape of Good Hope – Cape Town	31
St Helena	4

Total, days at anchor   398 days

At sea: [collecting excursions by Joseph Banks in his small boat for shooting sea-birds or netting marine fauna in calm weather]

North Atlantic – Madeira to Rio de Janeiro	7
South Atlantic – Rio to Tierra del Fuego	3
South Pacific – Tierra del Fuego to Tahiti	7
– Society Is. to New Zealand	10
Tasman Sea – New Zealand to coast of N.S.W.	3
East coast of Australia – to Torres Strait	5
Arafura Sea – New Guinea to Savu	1
North Atlantic – near the Scilly Is.	2

Total, days collecting at sea   38 occasions

Total, days at sea   653 days

TOTAL, days in the whole voyage   1051 days

Appendix III

Equipment prepared by Joseph Banks for his party at his own expense intended for the voyage on board HMS *Resolution* and HMS *Adventure*, 1772

Item			
Pocket time-keeper, Arnold No. 5 [John Arnold]	£100.	0s.	0d.
1 × Knight's Azimuth compass [Henry Gregory]	[£80.	0s.	0d.]
1 × Equatorial instrument complete [Jesse Ramsden]	£63.	0s.	0d.
2 × 4 ft. achromatic telescopes, barometers, etc. [Edw. Nairne]	£46.	5s.	6d.
1 × Barometer for measuring heights [Edw. Nairne]	£13.	13s.	0d.
1 × 15-inch sextant [Jesse Ramsden]	£8.	18s.	6d.
2 × portable barometers with stands	£11.	11s.	7d.
1 × 4-inch sextant	£6.	6s.	7d.
2 × best Ellis's microscopes [Jesse Ramsden]	£7.	7s.	0d.
Cleaning & repairing 4 × Ellis's microscopes, with magnifiers, watch glasses, thermometers, hydrometers, pluviometers [P & J Dollond]	£22.	19s.	0d.
2 × cases of instruments in Nurse[-shark] skin	£9.	9s.	0d.
1 × 15-inch sextant with new adjustment, plus cleaning and repairing telescopes [P & J Dollond]	£37.	12s.	0d.
	£405.	2s.	2d.

1. Instrumental Equipment as above	£405.	2s.	2d.
2. Guns, traps, cages etc.	£175.	1s.	2d.
3. Fishing tackle, nets, etc.	£100.	5s.	11d.
4. Equipment, miscellaneous	£41.	4s.	0d.
5. Glass bottles, various containers, etc.	£34.	15s.	6d.
6. Paper, drawing equipment, etc.	£53.	11s.	0d.
7. Sea charts, etc.	£48.	12s.	0d.
8. Sundry chemicals, etc.	£131.	16s.	3d.
9. Dietary extras (e.g. dried fish, fruit etc.)	£75.	19s.	6d.
10. Personal items (e.g. toilet articles)	£33.	0s.	6d.
11. General containers (e.g. chests, casks, kegs, etc.)	£66.	2s.	2d.
	£1165.	10s.	0d.

APPENDIX IV

Arthropod species in the Banks collection from the *Endeavour* voyage as classified by J. C. Fabricius and recorded in his *Systema Entomologica* 1775

REGION / FABRICIAN ORDERS	Madeira	Brazil	Tierra del Fuego	Society Islands	New Zealand	New Holland	East Indies	Cape of Good Hope	Saint Helena	TOTAL
I. ELENTERATA Beetles, weevils	2	22	11	1	22	78	1	33	6	176
II. ULONATA Earwigs, locusts	1	5	–	–	–	7	–	5	–	18
III. SYNISTATA Wasps, hornets, bees, ants	2	9	1	1	6	47	–	3	–	69
IV. AGONATA Scorpions, crabs, crayfish	–	1	2	1	1	1	–	–	–	6
V. UNOGATA Spiders	1	1	1	–	–	3	–	–	–	6
VI. GLOSSATA Butterflies, moths	1	11	2	1	2	44	–	1	–	62
VII. RYNGOTA Crickets, cicadas, bugs	1	9	1	2	3	25	–	3	–	44
VIII. ANTLIATA Flies, lice, acari	–	4	–	1	3	7	–	–	–	15
TOTAL	8	62	18	7	37	212	1	45	6	396

APPENDIX V

Summary of the botanical drawings of Sydney Parkinson, finished and unfinished 1768–71, on the *Endeavour* voyage; those finished by other artists in London 1773–84; and the copperplate engravings derived from all these, 1773–89, with those surviving to be printed for the *Banks Florilegium* 1980–7

ARTIST or ENGRAVER / REGION	Madeira	Brazil	Tierra del Fuego	Society Islands	New Zealand	Australia	East Indies	TOTAL
Sydney Parkinson, 1768–71, outline	2	1	1	15	174	408	72	673 } 942
finished	16	30	77	113	30	3	—	269 }
John Frederick Miller, 1773–6, finished	—	—	—	1	26	61	11	99
James Miller, 1773–7, finished	—	—	—	—	27	52	6	85
John Clevely, 1773–7, finished	—	—	—	—	4	20	2	26 } 594
Thomas Burgis, 1777, finished	1	—	—	—	1	—	1	3
Frederick Polydore Nodder, 1777–84, finished	—	—	—	—	56	198	17	271
Unattributable, unsigned, 1773–7, finished	5	7	2	—	61	28	7	110 }
TOTAL, 1768–84, finished	22	37	79	114	205	362	44	863

Copperplate engravings, 1773–84+							
Daniel Mackenzie	5	6	30	24	59	120½*	7	251½
Gerald Sibelius	4	3	10	17	60	93	8	195
Gabriel Smith	1	7	8	25	28	44	4	117
Charles White	—	2	5	7	2	15	3	34
William Tringham	—	1	6	3	11	10	—	31
Robert Blyth	—	—	—	—	5	20	—	25
Frederick Polydore Nodder	—	—	—	—	9	13	2	24
Jabez Goldar	—	—	4	—	5	11	2	22
– van Drazowa	—	4	—	1	2	5	—	12
Thomas Scratchley	2	—	—	2	2	4½*	—	10½
John Lee	—	—	—	3	1	3	1	8
Jean-Baptiste Michell	—	—	—	3	3	1	—	7
William Smith	—	—	1	—	1	1	3	6
Edward Walker	—	—	1	—	1	3	—	5
John Roberts	—	—	1	1	—	—	—	2
Thomas Morris	—	—	—	—	—	—	1	1
– Bannerman	—	—	—	—	1	—	—	1
Francis Chesham	—	—	—	—	—	1	—	1
TOTAL, recorded 1773–1784	12	23	66	86	190	345	31	753
recorded 1833, Rbt. Brown	:	:	:	:	:	:	:	743
recorded 1983, BM(NH)	11	23	65	89	183	337	30	738

Banksia ericifolia Linn.f. jointly engraved by Mackenzie and Scratchley

Appendix VI

The General Basis of the Herbarium of Sir Joseph Banks

1. *Original Plants collected by Banks himself:*
   E.g. Lincolnshire, Berkshire, Middlesex, Kent, Oxfordshire, Derbyshire, Carmarthenshire, 1754–65; Newfoundland, Labrador, Portugal, 1766–7; S.W. England, Wales, Midlands, 1767–8; Madeira, Rio de Janeiro, 1768; Tierra del Fuego, Society Islands, New Zealand, 769; New Zealand, East coast of Australia, East Indies, 1770; Cape of Good Hope, St H 'ena, 1771; Western Isles of Scotland, Iceland, Orkneys, 1772; Holland, 1773; S.W. England, South Wales, 1773; Lincolnshire, Derbyshire, Middlesex, Kent etc., 1773+

2. *Plants purchased by Banks from other herbaria:*
   E.g. William Houstoun and Phillip Miller, 1774; Moravian Brothers, 1775–8; Herbarium Helveticum (Dick's), 1775; Nicolaus Joseph Jacquin, 1777; Joseph Mutis, 1779; Jean Aublet, 1790; George Clifford, 1792; Paul Hermann, 1793; Nicolaus Laurens Burman, 1794; Jean-Francois Berger, 1814

3. *Plants from individual gardens, private and public:*
   E.g. Chelsea Physic Garden, 1762–92; James Lee, The Vineyard, Hammersmith, 1765–98; Botanic Garden, Edinburgh, 1766–1820; Revd John Lightfoot, Uxbridge, 1767–87; Royal Botanic Garden, Kew, 1773–1820; James Gordon, Mile End, 1776–81; Hon. Charles Greville, Paddington Green, 1778–1808; Dr John Fothergill, Upton, 1778–90; Dr William Pitcairn, Islington, 1778–86; Imperial Garden, Schonbrunn, 1777–1817; William Malcolm, Kennington, 1778–85; William Curtis, Bermondsey, 1785–9; Jardin des Plantes, Paris, 1779–1820; James Vere, Kensington Gore, 1790–1800

4. *Plants acquired by gift, exchange or commission from other collectors:*
   E.g. John and William Bartram, 1766–80; Peter Kalm, William Clifton, William Wright, Henry de Ponthieu, Roger Shakespear, John Greg, Olof Swartz, 1769–90; Franz Oldenburg, 1772; Francis Masson, 1772–1805; Constantine John Phipps, 1773; Joao de Loureiro, 1774–81; Johann Reinhold and Johann Georg Forster, 1775–8; Andrea Auge, David Nelson, 1776–89; James Robertson, 1772–6; William Anderson, 1776–9; Johan Gerhard Koenig, 1775–85; Carl Thunberg, 1778–90; Henry Smeathman, 1779–87; William Roxburgh, 1779–1815; Patrick Russell, 1781–9; John Duncan, 1782–9; Anton Hove, 1785–98; Captain Arthur Phillip, 1787–92; Captain Phillip Gidley King, 1788–1805; Alexander Duncan, 1789–95; Lt-Col. William Paterson, 1790–1810; William Brass, 1790; Captain John Hunter, 1791–1800; Alexander Anderson, 1789–1811; James Wiles, 1791–1806; Christopher Smith, 1791–1807; Archibald Menzies, 1791–5; Adam Afzelius, 1791–6; Sir George Leonard Staunton, 1792–4; Sir George Thomas Staunton, 1792–1817; Francis Buchanan[-Hamilton], 1794–1815; James Niven, 1798–1803; George Caley, 1800–10; Peter Good, 1801–3; Robert Brown, 1801–5; William Kerr, 1803–13; John Thompson, 1807+; John Reeves, 1812+; James Bowie, 1814+; Allan Cunningham, 1814+; Christen Smith, 1816; David Lockhart, 1816; Nathaniel Wallich, 1815+; John Ross and William Edward Parry, 1818.

APPENDIX VII

Summary of Plant Introductions recorded in *Hortus Kewensis* 2nd Edition in the name of Sir Joseph Banks 1767–1813*

YEAR / REGION	1767–70	1771–80	1781–90	1791–1800	1801–10	1811–13	TOTAL
North America	2	–	9	5	–	–	16
West Indies	–	2	3	19	2	–	26
South America	–	1	4	8	1	–	14
Cape of Good Hope	–	2	1	6	–	–	9
Australia[1]	–	3	46	30	15	–	94
New Zealand	–	8	2	1	–	–	11
East Indies[2]	–	21	25	69	42	1	158
China & Japan	–	1	11	9	2	–	23
Elsewhere[3]	–	8	8	35	37	–	88
TOTAL	2	46	109	192	99	1	449

(1) Mainly N.S.W.; (2) Including India and Ceylon; (3) Mainly Northern and Southern Europe, Middle East, North and West Africa.

* In the 3-volume 1st edition of *Hortus Kewensis*, 1789, Banks is credited with 47 introduced species among the c.5600 recorded; in the 5-volume 2nd edition of 1810–13, he is credited with 449 (as above) among the 11013 recorded. This, of course, takes no account of the long list of introductions attributed to those others who worked under his direction (e.g. Masson, Hove, Kerr, Cunningham, Bowie) or in his employment (e.g. Nelson, Caley) or under his influence (e.g. Phillip, Bligh, Paterson, the Duncans, Russell, Roxburgh, Menzies, Brown, Wallich, Reeves, etc.)

APPENDIX VIII

Associates of Sir Joseph Banks whose names are recorded for Plant Introductions in *Hortus Kewensis*, Editions 1 & 2

Gardeners and Collectors

Francis Masson	HMPP
David Nelson	Sir JB
Anton Hove	HMG
James Wiles	HMG
Christopher Smith	HMG; HEICo, India
David Burton	HMG
George Caley	Sir JB
Peter Good	HMG; HEICo
William Kerr	HMPP; HEICo, exp.

Officers of HM Services

Admiral Arthur Phillip	HMG
Admiral William Bligh	HMG
Colonel William Paterson	HMG

Personal Friends

Mr George Aufrere (uncle)	Pr
Mr William Philp Perrin	Pr
Hon. Charles Francis Greville	Pr
Sir George Leonard Staunton	Pr

Professional Men

Dr Daniel Solander	BM; Sir JB
Mr Jonas Dryander	Sir JB
Dr Robert Brown	HMG; Sir JB
Dr Johan Koenig	HEICo, India
Dr Patrick Russell	HEICo, India
Dr William Roxburgh	HEICo, India
Dr John Duncan	HEICo, China
Dr Alexander Duncan	HEICo, China
Dr Alexander Anderson	HMG
Dr Adam Afzelius	SLCo
Dr Archibald Menzies	HMG
Dr John Sibthorp	Pr; Un.Ox.
Dr Pierre Broussonet	FrG; Sir JB
Mr David Lance	HEICo, China
Mr John Reeves	HEICo, China
Dr Francis Buchanan	HEICo, India
Dr Nathaniel Wallich	HEICo, India

Source of income shown above:
HMPP = His Majesty's Privy Purse; Sir JB = Sir Joseph Banks's private income; BM = British Museum; HMG = public funds, various departments; HEICo = Hon. East India Company; SLCo = Sierra Leone Company; Un.Ox. = University of Oxford; Pr = private income; FrG = French Government

Appendix ix

Special Arrangements for the Transport of Living Plants organized by Sir Joseph Banks

1787–8   HMS *Sirius*, Captain Arthur Phillip
[living plants in the great cabin and officer's cabins]

1787–9   HMS *Bounty*, Lt William Bligh; gardeners David Nelson and William Brown
[special platforms for pots on the quarter deck and in the great cabin]

1789–90 HMS *Guardian*, Captain Edward Riou; gardeners George Austin and James Smith
[a glazed plant cabin on the quarter deck]

1791–5   HMS *Discovery*, Captain George Vancouver; surgeon Archibald Menzies
[a glazed plant cabin on the quarter deck]

1791–3   HMS *Providence*, Captain William Bligh; gardeners James Wiles and Christopher Smith
[special platform for pots as in the *Bounty*]

1794–5   HC Ship *Princess Royal*, Captain Henry Bond; gardener Peter Good
[a glazed plant cabin on the quarter deck with plants from Kew for Calcutta and *vice versa*]

1795–6   HMS *Reliance*, Captain Henry Waterhouse
[a glazed plant cabin on the quarter deck]

1795   Merchant Ship *Venus*, Captain Marmaduke Vickermann; gardener George Noe
[special platform for pots in the hold]

1800–1   HMS *Porpoise*, [No. 2] Captain Philip Gidley King; gardeners George Caley and George Suttor
[a glazed plant cabin amidships]

1801–5   HMS *Investigator*, Commander Matthew Flinders; botanist Robert Brown; gardener Peter Good
[a glazed plant cabin for the quarter deck, carried out dismantled in the hold]

1806   HC Ship *Thames*, Captain ——; Thomas Manning and a seaman in charge
[a glazed plant cabin with plants from Kew for China]

APPENDIX X

'Royal Botanic Garden, from Christmas 1801 to Christmas 1815' [with a note inside saying that the Royal Botanic Garden, Kew, was placed on the Household Establishment from Michaelmas 1801]. A bound account book.

Public Record Office. Records of the Lord Steward's Dept. L.S. 10/5

Examples of Mrs A. Layton's bills for water carriage to Kew for plant consignments from Sir Joseph Banks, 1801–7

p. 14	24 December 1801	parcel of plants	£0. 0s. 9d.
	27 April 1802	box of seeds	£0. 1s. 0d.
p. 27	17 September 1802	large case of plants	£0. 5s. 0d.
	23 September 1802	basket of plants	£0. 1s. 6d.
p. 34	29 April 1803	basket of plants	£0. 1s. 0d.
	28 June 1803	box of seeds	£0. 0s. 9d.
p. 48	7 December 1803	basket of plants	£0. 1s. 0d.
p. 60	9 June 1804	cases of seeds etc.	£0. 6s. 0d.
p. 79	6 November 1804	box of plants	£0. 1s. 6d.
p. 91	12 July 1805	large case of plants & box of seeds	£0. 6s. 0d.
	13 September 1805	box of seeds [from Dryander]*	£0. 1s. 0d.
	14 September 1805	box of seeds [from Dryander]	£0. 1s. 6d.
	13 December 1805	box of seeds [from Dryander]	£0. 1s. 6d.
p. 114	9 October 1806	basket of plants	£0. 1s. 6d.
	18 October 1806	large basket of plants	£0. 2s. 6d.
	31 October 1806	case of seeds	£0. 2s. 0d.
p. 115	5 December 1806	box of seeds	£0. 1s. 0d.
p. 128	31 January 1807	basket [of plants]	£0. 4s. 0d.
	11 February 1807	2 baskets of plants	£0. 6s. 0d.
	18 March 1807	2 parcels of seeds	£0. 1s. 6d.
	19 March 1807	basket of plants	£0. 4s. 0d.

*consignments by Dryander in the absence of Banks at Revesby Abbey and his illness in December 1805.

Some records of material despatched to and/or received by Sir Joseph Banks as the consignee, May 1787 to November 1793 (from the manuscript correspondence)

Date of Consigning Letter or Reference Document	Writer or Consignor	Ship and/or Ship's Captain	Nature of Consignment
1787 May 16	Francis Masson (Cape Town)	*Talbot* Indiaman *per* Mr Staples, Bengal consul	2 boxes containing 110 species of seeds
July 11	Do. Do.	*Barrington* Indiaman *per* Sir John McPherson	about 62 species of seeds
Sept. 2	Gov. Arthur Phillip (Rio de Janeiro)	[a southern whaler] *per* Mr Morton, late master HMS *Sirius*	Four different kinds of Ipecacuanha (i) from a Jesuit estate 36 miles from Rio de Janeiro called Ipecacuanha de Raio parda, in a bottle; (ii) and (iii) from the mines; (iv) the white sort called by the natives *poalha*; gum from a tree called *Jataby* said to make fine varnish; a small amount of Peruvian balsam
Nov. 13	Francis Masson (Cape Town)	*Treasurer Schimelman* Captain Heysel *per* Captain Cox	a box of about 90 species of seeds and bulbs
1788 Jan. 5	Francis Masson (Cape Town)	HMS *Vestal* frigate Captain Rodam *per* John Ewart	a box of 100 species of seeds
May 15	Gov. Arthur Phillip (Sydney Cove, N.S.W.)	[*per* Home Office and Lord Sydney]	Seeds; 'red gum from the large gum-tree by tapping, and the yellow gum which is found on the dwarf palm-tree'
July 10	Do. Do.	*Alexander* transport *per* Lt Shortland	1 case containing a stuffed kangaroo and several skins; 1 keg of gum; 1 keg with a young kangaroo and a fox-bat in spirits; 1 case with bottles of plants in spirits of wine; 4 cases of seeds and plants; 1 small box of gum; some feathers from the skin of the bird sent in spirits to Lord Sydney, July 11; some native flax

Date	Collector/Source	Ship	Contents
Nov. 16 [marked as received 12 May 1789]	Do. Do.	*Fishburn* transport Mr Browne Master	1 case with white clay used by the natives for marking themselves; 1 case with small box of sand from a well?; containing lead; some Norfolk Island 'pepper'; a square bottle with last plant of Ipecacuanha from Rio, a flower 'for its beauty' and 'sweet water'; some gum used by the natives on their spears and one small vial of essential oil from the leaves of a gum-tree which smells like oil of peppermint; 1 case of seeds; 1 keg with young kangaroo rats, birds, young kangaroos &c.
Nov. 16	Do. Do.	*Golden Grove* transport, William Sharp Master	4 tubs of flowering shrubs
Nov. 18	David Considen (Sydney Cove, N.S.W.)	Do. Do.	8 paroquets, prepared and stuffed; a nameless bird, prepared and stuffed; flying squirrel, prepared and stuffed; 2 American beetles; some seeds, all in one box; 2 live paroquets in a cage; 2 live opossums, male and female; 2 kangaroo skins, stuffed; some native spears
1789 Mar. 26	Francis Masson (Cape Town)	*Alexander* transport from New Holland *per* Lieut. Shortland	3 boxes containing 422 species; 2 boxes of seeds and some bulbs; 1 box with 25 pots of 'Liliceus Bulbs'
Dec. 21	Do. Do.	A Dutch packet boat, *per* Captain Bligh	a small box of about 60 species of seeds
1790 Feb. 12	Do. Do.	A Dutch ship *per* Mr Hayward late midshipman on HMS *Bounty*	a box containing 40 species of bulbs
Apr. 13	Gov. Arthur Phillip (Sydney Cove, N.S.W.)	HMS *Supply* [to Batavia] Lieut. Ball *per* Lieut. P. G. King on to London	1 Fern Tree [yellow flower] with seeds; Seeds of the Duchess of Cumberland Tree [Downy Clerodendron, *Clerodendron tomentosum*, introduced to Kew by Banks, 1794, *Hortus Kewensis*, 2d. ed. IV, 64]
May 27	Francis Masson (Cape Town)	A Dutch ship *per* Mr Fryer late Master on HMS *Bounty*	1 small box with 20 species of bulbs; 1 small box with 40 species of seeds; 3 seeds of 'an extra curious *Euphorbia*'

June 2	Francis Masson (Cape Town)	*Jackal* whaler Captain Raven	1 packet of 41 species of seeds; 7 seeds of *Strelitzia lutea*
Aug. 22	Do. Do.	*Neptune* transport [from New Holland]	6 tubs of plants

APPENDIX XIB

Date of Consigning Letter or Reference Document	Writer or Consignor	Ship and/or Ship's Captain	Nature of Consignment
1791 Feb. 25	Do. Do.	Princess Amelia Captain Millet	2 small chests of seeds and bulbs about 200 species
Feb. 25	Do. Do.	HMS Sphinx Captain Tripp	2 boxes with 386 sorts of seeds and bulbs; Strelitzia alba (growing plant), drawing of Strelitzia sp.; seeds of Geranium trifoliata 16 gals. White Frontiniac Constantia wine per Lieut. Riou; 1 box of 200 species of seeds and bulbs; seeds of Strelitzia alba; book of dried specimens
Mar. 7	Do. Do.	Princess Royal Captain Horn-castle	1 box of 200 species of seeds and bulbs; seed of Strelitzia alba; book of dried specimens
Mar. 8	Alexander Duncan (Canton)	Ceres, Abergavanny and Hillsborough East Indiamen	1 box of living plants; 1 packet of seeds; 1 cask of nuts
Mar. 24 [marked as received 23 April 1792]	Gov. Arthur Phillip (Sydney Cove, N.S.W.)	Waksamheyd Dutch snow per Lieut. Edgar	No. 1 a case 2ft. sq. with dried plants, 4 small boxes of seeds in paper and a small amount of yellow gum No. 2 a box 2ft. by 2ft. 4ins. with seeds in paper No. 3 a box 1ft. 9ins. by 1ft. 7ins. with seeds &c No. 4 a box of clay from which it is supposed lead may be extracted; 1 hogshead and 1 forty gallon cask of white clay; 1 eight gallon keg with a young kangaroo, a porcupine, a rat kangaroo in which the false belly is differently placed to what it is in the kangaroo and various other animals; a skin of the ma-ra-rong [the emu]
Apr. 13	Francis Masson	An East Indiaman in False Bay	1 box of 130 species of seeds and bulbs; about 10 books of dried specimens

May 23	Captain George Tripp RN (Portsmouth)	HMS *Sphinx* Captain Tripp	Seeds and bulbs including *Strelitzia alba* sent by Francis Masson Feb. 25 [see above]
June 25	Captain G. Keith (ex ship)	*Hillsborough* East Indiaman Captain Keith	1 cask of nuts called Lingos; drawing of Dwarf Plaintain; from Alexander Duncan, Canton, Mar. 8 [see above]
June 29	Captain O. Giodesen (ex ship)	*Disco* Captain Giodesen	1 box of growing plants from William Roxburgh, Calcutta; Fector & Minette, agents, Dover
July 17	Captain Trail (ex ship)	*Neptune* transport Captain Trail	2 boxes of growing plants, including 12 pots of *Euphorbia* spp. and *Oxalis* spp.
Nov. 10	Moses Marshall (Chester, Pa.)	*Pigou* Captain Loxley	1 box of growing plants
Nov. 24	Gov. Arthur Phillip (Sydney Cove, N.S.W.)	HMS *Gorgon* Captain Parker	*No. 1* one case about 6ft. long containing a skeleton of a kangaroo and an egg *No. 2* one case 2ft. 2½ins. by 1ft. 5ins. by 1ft. 7ins. deep containing seeds and dried plants *No. 3* a box of Norfolk Island clay or earth and four casks of clay Sixty tubs containing 221 shrubs and 8 pine trees
Nov. 26	Alexander Duncan (Canton)	*Albion* Captain Parker	Specimens of the stone used for polishing gems
Dec. 29	Do. Do.	*Britannia* Captain E. Cumming	Specimens of the stone used for polishing gems transferred from *Albion*; Lacquer trees; 1 box of Suchong tea for Lady Banks
1792 Feb. 9	Sir John Murray (Calcutta)	*Northumberland per* ship's surgeon	1 basket with 96 kinds of seeds
Apr. 20	Captain Edward Cumming (Isle of Wight)	*Britannia* Captain Cumming	2 boxes of plants from Alexander Duncan, Canton Dec. 29 [see above]; a boat [canoe] belonging to the King of the Palau Islands [now with British Museum]

June 30	John Lindsay (Jamaica)	...	1 flower pot full of young ferns
Aug. 22	Captain James Urmiston (London)	... Captain Urmiston	2 boxes of plants; a picture of three natives of the Palau Islands [? now in Univ. of Gottingen]
Sept. 2	Sir John Murray (Calcutta)	*Ganges* per Mr Macfarlan and a ship's officer	Seeds fro Rohilcund and Mysore
Sept. 12	Francis Masson (Cape Town)	*Crown Princess Maria* Captain Christmas	a parcel of seeds of 30 species of plants
Dec. 12	Dr Hugh Gillan [on board HMS *Lion*, Rio de Janeiro]	*Hero* whaler Captain Folger	3 Brazilian nopal plants covered with cochineal insects [*Dactylopius* spp.]; arrived Spring Grove 25 February 1793 alive
Dec. 30	Adam Afzelius (Freetown)	*Felicity* Captain Wickham	Seeds and growing plants

Date of Consigning Letter or Reference Document	Writer or Consignor	Ship and/or Ship's Captain	Nature of Consignment
1793 Jan. 1	William Roxburgh (Samul Cattah)	…	1 box of growing plants; notes on the Lacc insect
Jan. 2	Colonel Robert Kyd (Calcutta)	*Pitt* transport Captain Manning	1 mango tree; flowering ornamental trees called Ufsuck and Nagkissore; drawing of pappah [paw-paw]; packet of Nagpore wheat with a packet of the same for M. Thouin
Jan. 9	Do. Do.	Do. Do.	Seeds of Shiraz musk melon; seeds of the Guatemala and Manilla species of Indigo
Jan. 10	Sir John Murray (Calcutta)	Do. Do.	1 bag of grass seed called Neungla or *Typha* sp. 1 bag of paddy rice from the coast of Coromandel; 1 bag of beardless Bengal paddy rice
Feb. 25	Francis Masson (Cape Town)	*Albemarle* Captain Bowen	1 box of bulbs [ship captured by the French]
Feb. …	Do. Do.	*Swallow* packet	Seeds
Feb. 26	Colonel Murray [Calcutta]	*Tenter* packet	Seeds
Feb. 27	Francis Masson (Cape Town)	a Genoa ship *per* Mr Myers, passenger	Seeds
Feb. 28	Sir John Murray (Calcutta)	… *per* Lieut. Connyngham of the 76th regt.	Seeds

Date	Donor	Ship / means	Contents
Mar. 6	Adam Afzelius (Freetown)	*Good Intent* Captain Buckle *per* Mr Lowes, ship's surgeon	Seeds, dried plants and bulbs
Mar. 9	Sir John Murray (Calcutta	*King George* per Mr Tipton	1 basket of seeds collected in the Rajemal hills
Apr. 21	Gov. Arthur Phillip (London)	[*Atlantic* per Gov. Phillip, passenger]	Seeds from Norfolk Island
Apr. 22	Captain John Hunter (London)	[Returned by *Wakhamseyd* in April 1792]	Pine seeds from Norfolk Island
n.d. [but marked as received Apr. 25]	Sir John Murray (Calcutta)	*General Goddard* Captain Wakefield	1 basket of seeds from the Rohilla country
Apr. 26	Gov. Arthur Phillip (London)	[*Atlantic per* Governor Phillip, passenger]	1 packet of seeds from Port Jackson
May 8	Colonel Murray (Calcutta)	*Francis*	2 baskets of seeds
May 8	Mr Crisp	*Worcester* Captain Robson	1 *Dicksonia*
May 26	Governor Dawes (Sierra Leone)	…	Seeds
May 27	Francis Masson (Cape Town)	an American ship *Hercules per* Mr Bisset, passenger	Seeds
May 27	Professor Anderson (Glasgow)	…	Seeds from Siberia
June 12	Francis Masson (Cape Town)	*Crown Princess Maria* Captain Christmas	About 100 species of bulbs and plants
June 19	Drs Dancer & Broughton (Jamaica)	…	Seeds

July 19	[Adam Afzelius Freetown]	...	Bulbs from Sierra Leone
Sept. ...	Alexander Duncan (Canton)	*Triton, Hindostan, Ceres, Northumberland, Warren Hastings,* East Indiamen *Worley* Captain Wilson	Growing plants from China
Nov. 10	Dr William Withering (Lisbon)	...	*Andropogon hirtius*
Nov. 10	John Lindsay (Jamaica)	...	Seeds of ferns [cf. Lindsay to Banks, 30 June 1792]

APPENDIX XII

Summary of visits made by Jonas Dryander in and from London, 1777–1810

Place visited	Number of Occasions	Period of Years
1. Hammersmith [James Lee, The Vineyard]	659	1777–1798
2. Kew [Royal Botanic Garden; the Aitons]	161	1777–1809
3. Chelsea [Apothecary's Garden; J. E. Smith]	34	1777–1792
4. Paddington Green [Charles Greville]	50	1778–1808
5. Islington [Dr Wm. Pitcairn]	13	1778–1786
6. Kennington [Wm. Malcolm]	11	1778–1785
7. Upton [Dr John Fothergill]	8	1778–1790
8. Spring Grove [Sir Joseph Banks]	93	1779–1809
9. Heston [Robt. Banks-Hodgkinson]	10	1779–1787
10. Chiswick [Mr Berry]	48	1779–1782
11. Uxbridge [Revd John Lightfoot]	22	1779–1787
12. Chelsea [Mrs Wm. Banks]	55	1780–1803
13. Bermondsey [Wm. Curtis]	9	1785–1789
14. Dartford [Dr John Latham]	5	1786–1795
15. Chelsea [Mr George Aufrere]	13	1787–1802
16. Buckhurst Hill [Mr Warren]	33	1797–1808
17. Various [In London and the counties]*	102	1777–1810

*These include: to Oxford with Banks, 1783, 1788; to Leeds to R. A. Salisbury, 1789, and later at Mill Hill; to HMS *Providence* in the Thames with Banks 1791 and after Bligh's return, 1793; to Boston and Revesby Abbey and the fishing party with Banks, 1793; to Revesby Abbey via Boston by stage coach, 1800; to Narborough, Norfolk, with Banks, 1801; to Overton via Woodstock with Banks, 1803

It should be noted also, apart from these, that visits to certain places were often of several days' duration. For example those to Uxbridge included Cowley and Bulstrode at times; those to Kew with W. T. Aiton sometimes led to other Royal domains; those to Spring Grove, especially in summer, meant that Kew and Heston were often visited also. All five visits to Dartford were each of several days and, finally, from 1797 so were all the visits to Buckhurst Hill.

Appendix XIII

The Library of Sir Joseph Banks at 32 Soho Square in 1820 according to the inventory of the British Museum librarians, H. H. Baber, F. A. Walter and H. F. Cary [BL 460.g.1]

Main Subject Groups	Number of titles	
	Books	*Opuscula*
1. Travel, by land and sea	1225	135
2. Botany	1225	1516
3. Zoology, comparative anatomy, etc.	945	997
4. Natural History in general	485	264
5. Materia medica, toxicology, medicine etc.	585	456
6. Geology, mineralogy, palaeontology	580	777
7. Agriculture, livestock, hunting, fishing, falconry, fowling	495	441
8. Horticulture, gardening	230	—
9. Natural philosophy (physics), chemistry	230	214
10. Astronomy, navigation, surveying, microscopy	210	47
11. History, antiquities, classics, theology	540	81
12. Architecture, art, letters	225	76
13. Civil affairs, parliamentary reports, etc.	180	524
14. Library catalogues	135	110
15. Museum catalogues	110	52
16. Dictionaries etc.	95	—
17. Directories etc.	55	—
18. Miscellaneous, unclassified	275	401
19. Duplicates	110	—
Total number of titles counted	7935	6091

14026

APPENDIX XIV

An estimate of the published papers, 1780–1820, with which the name of Sir Joseph Banks is closely linked

PUBLICATION	As Author	Communicated to	Communicated by	As source of material or important assistance	TOTAL
Philosophical Transactions of the Royal Society of London	1	124	90	28	243*
Archaeologia	7	11	1	1	20
Transactions of the Linnean Society of London	2	2	4	51	59
Transactions of the Horticultural Society of London	12	8	–	13	33
Annals of Agriculture	17	–	–	–	17
Transactions of the Society for the Arts Manufactures and Commerce	1	–	–	–	1
Journal of Natural Philosophy, Chemistry and the Arts (Nicholson's)	1	1	–	2	4
Communications to the Board of Agriculture	5	–	–	–	5
Philosophical Magazine and Journal (Tilloch's)	2	–	–	–	2
Agricultural Magazine	2	–	–	–	2
Annals of Botany (Konig and Sims)	–	–	1	1	2
Gentleman's Magazine	1	–	–	–	1
TOTAL	51	146	96	96	389

* Out of 969 published in the period by 323 contributors

Appendix XV

Summary of papers contributed to the *Phil. Trans R. Soc. Lond.*, Vols LXXI–CX, 1781–1820, during Sir Joseph Banks's presidency

General Subject	Contributions		
	No.	Per cent	
Astronomy	167	17.25 } = 228 or 23.5%	= 580 or 60.0% — NON-BIOLOGICAL
Mathematics	61	6.30	
Chemistry	207	21.38 } = 352 or 36.4%	
Physics	145	15.00	
Meteorology	53	5.47	= 697 or 72%
Geology	35	3.61	
Geography	28	2.89	
Metallurgy	11	1.18	
Engineering	10	1.08	
General Botany	37	3.82	
General Zoology	35	3.61	
Comparative Anatomy	116	11.98	= 272 or 28%
Comparative Physiology	27	2.79	
General Medicine	29	2.99	
Oriental Studies	8	0.83	BIOLOGICAL
TOTAL	969	100.00	

APPENDIX XVI

Main social categories of the Fellowship of The Royal Society (1) as at 30 November 1780 and
(2) during the whole term of Banks's Fellowship from 1766 to 1820

	(1) 1780		(2) 1766–1820	
	no.	p.ct.	no.	p.ct.
1. Royalty (British and Foreign)	9	1.5	15	1.1
2. Dukes	8	1.4	12	0.9
3. Marquesses	2	0.3	9	0.7
4. Earls	26	4.4	55	4.0
5. Viscounts	7	1.2	15	1.1
6. Barons	10	1.7	49	3.6
7. Baronets	25	4.2	76	5.6
8. Knights	13	2.2	48	3.5
9. Younger sons of nobility (Hons etc.)	14	2.4	26	1.9
	114	19.4	305	22.5
10. Bishops	4	0.7	19	1.4
11. Other clerics	57	9.7	126	9.3
	61	10.4	145	10.7
12. Medical profession	64	10.9	160	11.8
13. Other professions	9	1.5	13	1.0
14. Royal Navy	2	0.3	18	1.3
15. Army	8	1.4	52	3.8
16. Landed gentry, merchants, trade etc.	218	37.2	547	40.4
17. Foreigners	111	18.9	116	8.5
	587	100.0	1356	100.0

Note: Among these categories in the 'Home' Fellowship as at 30 November 1780 [n = 476] there were: Fellows of the Society of Antiquaries, 131 (27.5%); members of Parliament, 24 (5.0%); Trustees of the British Museum, 15 (3.2%); academics of professorial status, 10 (2.1%); physicians to His Majesty, 13 (2.7%). Among the 'Foreign' Fellowship [n = 111] there were: from France, 40; Italy, 21; the German states, 12; Russia, 7; Switzerland, 6; Holland, 6; Spain, 5; Sweden, 4; Portugal, 3; Denmark, 3; Poland, 1; Austria, 1; Jamaica, 1; doubtful, 1.

Among the titled lay aristocracy up to the rank of Earl during the period 1766–1820, especially in the ranks of Baron, Baronet and Knight, a high proportion were honours for services of more or less distinction and therefore new creations or advances in status.

Meetings of the Royal Society 'rebellious' dining club, founded by Mr Joseph Banks at the *Mitre* tavern, 23 November 1775, and moved to the *Devil*, also in Fleet Street, on 26 February 1778; Banks elected 'Perpetual Dictator' 8 May 1777; the club disbanded 12 June 1784.

YEAR	DINNERS HELD	DINNERS ATTENDED BY THOSE MOST CLOSELY LINKED WITH THE DEVELOPMENT OF THE ORDNANCE SURVEY			
		Banks	*Roy*	*Calderwood*	*Shuckburgh*	
1775	4	4	4	–	–
1776	25	25	21	12	1	At the *Mitre* to 19.2.1778
1777	26	24	24	16	18
1778	31	30	21	23	23
1779	24	24	16	9	21
1780	20	18	9	–	17	At the *Devil* from 26.2.1778
1781	9	9	2	1	5
1782	1	1	1	–	–

[Banks receives Cassini's *Mémoire*, October 1783,

| 1783 | – | – | – | – | – |

& recommends to the King the English trig. survey]

| 1784 | 1 | 1 | 1 | 1 | 1 |

[Hounslow Heath base-line survey commences under Roy, 16 April 1784; completed 30 August 1784; the club disbanded 12 June 1784]

The Experimental Sheep Flock of Sir Joseph Banks at Spring Grove 1785–92

YEAR / BREED & CROSS	1785	1786	1787	1788	1789	1790	1791	1792
Spanish Merino	2	2	3	6	9	8	8	11
Scotch	2	2	2	3	3	–	–	–
Wiltshire	2	2	2	1	2	–	–	–
Sussex	7	7	6	1	6	–	–	–
Hereford	4	4	6	2	2	–	–	–
Lincoln	2	2	3	1	–	–	–	–
Shetland	–	–	–	–	–	–	4	–
Spanish Merino cross								
x Scotch	–	–	–	2	4	1	–	–
x Wiltshire	–	–	–	2	4	3	1	–
x Sussex	–	–	–	6	11	11	11	–
x Hereford	–	–	–	2	4	5	5	–
x Lincoln	–	–	–	3	3	4	5	–
x Shetland	–	–	–	–	–	–	–	2
Spanish métis	–	–	–	4	4	4	4	–
TOTAL	19	19	22	33	52	36	38	13

Sources: 1785 – *Spanish Merino*, original ram and ewe imp. *ex* L-J-M Daubenton, Montbard, France, *per* P-M-A Broussonet; *Scotch*, *ex* Sir John Sinclair, Caithness; *Wiltshire*, *ex* source unknown, Hounslow Heath; *Sussex* [= *Southdown*], *ex* Lord Sheffield, Sheffield Place, nr. Lewes; *Hereford* [= *Ryeland*], *ex* Robert Bakewell, Dishley, Derbyshire; *Lincoln*, *ex* Mr Fowler, Ketsby, lincolnshire; 1788 – *Spanish métis* [*ex* Daubenton] *ex* H.M. King Geo. III; 1791 – *Spanish Merino* ram, *ex* H.M. King Geo. III; *Shetland*, *ex* Sir Thomas Dundas, Upleatham, North Allerton, Yorkshire.

Dispèrsals: 1786 – *Spanish Merino* ram, to Lord Sheffield, Sheffield Place, nr. Lewes; 1789 – *Spanish Merino* ram, to Major John Cartwright, Marnham, Nottinghamshire; *Spanish Merino* ram, Mr Lambert, Woodmansterne, Surrey (brother-in-law of John Hunter, surgeon); from this year the flock consisted only of the pure Spanish Merinos and their ½ and ¾ bred crosses as shown above; 1792 – *Spanish Merino* ewes and rams, to Arthur Young, Bradfield Hall, Suffolk

APPENDIX XIX

YEAR	DAYS AT WORK [Lincs.]	SUMMARY OF PAYMENTS MADE BY BANKS			SUMMARY OF FINISHED DRAWINGS MADE			
		Salary & Expenses	Finished Drawings	TOTAL	Churches	Houses	Others	TOTAL
		£. s. d.	£. s. d.	£. s. d.	n =	n =	n =	n =
1789	48	36. 15. 0	54. 1. 6	90. 16. 6	25	1	–	26
1790	38	29. 8. 0	43. 19. 6	73. 7. 6	43	14	–	57
1791	34	27. 6. 0	64. 5. 0	91. 11. 0	86	7	17	110
1792	31	22. 11. 6	64. 5. 0	86. 16. 6	27	8	–	35
1793	31	29. 8. 0	21. 10. 0	50. 18. 0	38	26	16	80
1794	49	53. 6. 6	104. 8. 6	157. 15. 0	51	20	–	71
1795	19	23. 12. 6	36. 10. 0	60. 2. 6	31	13	11	55
1796	36	31. 10. 0	25. 10. 6	57. 0. 6	32	4	12	48
1797	18	14. 14. 0	25. 10. 6	40. 4. 6	21	5	3	29
TOTAL	304	268. 11. 6	440. 0. 6	708. 12. 0	354	98	59	511

A summary of the time spent in Lincolnshire by John Claude Nattes (1765?-1822) and the approximate number of drawings and water colours made by him under the direction and at the expense of Sir Joseph Banks of the county churches, associated monuments, houses and other buildings in the years 1789–97 at the rate of half-a-guinea per day with expenses when the artist was out of London and approximately a guinea for each finished drawing. Cf. Lincolnshire Archives Office, RA3/9 for original notes.

The majority of these drawings are now incorporated in four large volumes in the Strong Room of the Central Library at Lincoln with a manuscript preface in the autograph of Banks and the title: 'A Collection of Views/of the Seats of the Nobility and Gentry/of the Castles and Chapels and Churches/ The Ruins of Ancient Buildings/and other Objects/Executed at the Latter end of the Eighteenth Century/ by Claude Nattes & other Artists/under the Superintendance/of Sir Jos: Banks/The Whole Alphabetically arranged/according to the names of the respective Parishes/in Four Volumes'? n.d. but c.1815–20.

Appendix xx

Check List of the Fish Species caught in the River Witham between Dog Dyke and the Grand Sluice in the Fishing Parties of Sir Joseph Banks 1784–96

Pike (*Esox lucius*)	Esocidae
Perch (*Perca fluviatilis*)	Persidae
Eel (*Anguilla anguilla*)	Anguilidae
Bream (*Abramis brama*)	Cyprinidae
Chub (*Leuciscus cephalus*)	Cyprinidae
Tench (*Tinca tinca*)	Cyprinidae
Carp (*Cyprinus carpio*)	Cyprinidae
Barbel (*Barbus barbus*)	Cyprinidae
Burbot [= Burbolt] (*Lota lota*)	Gadidae
Flounder (*Platichthys flesus*)	Pleuronectidae
Salmon (*Salmo salar*)	Salmonidae
Herring (*Clupea harengus*)*	Clupeidae

*From its habitat in the Witham this was almost certainly a Shad (*Alosa* sp.) probably Twaite Shad (*Alosa fallax*), Family Clupeidae, similar to the herring but migrating into fresh water to spawn

Colloquial terms used:
Brewitt   – the silver eels that go to sea; a good eel**
Kemp   – the yellow-bellied eel that does not go to sea and is bad to eat; a bad eel
Butt   – a name for any flat fish, e.g. sole, turbot, plaice or flounder
White fish– a term used here mainly implying bream and chub

**Cf. Banks to Thomas Andrew Knight, Soho Square, 15 January 1816, referring to Knight's last letter on eels coming up from the sea; Banks discusses the two kinds of eels which he says he is able to recognize and says that the fishermen sell them at two different prices. Hereford Record Office 28/1/70/52–53

APPENDIX XXI

Summary of the Catch at the Annual Fishing on the River Witham 1788–96

YEAR	PIKE		PERCH		EEL Brewitt		EEL Kemp		WHITE FISH gross wt.	TOTAL WT.	REMARKS
	No.	Mean	No.	Mean	No.	Mean	No.	Mean			
1788	47	lb. 2.22	76	lb. 1.15	23	lb. 1.31	5	lb. 1.05	lb. 1502	lb. 1765	6 Flounders = 1lb. 1 Salmon, 18½lb.
1789	15	3.52	103	0.56	4	1.37	10	1.18	648	694	2 Flounders = ½lb. 1 Pike, 13½lb. 2 Perch, 2½lb. each
1790	33	2.82	98	0.60	13	1.85	29	1.00	1493	1712	18 Chub = 39lb. 5 Tench = 7¼lb. 1 Flounder, ½lb.; 2 Brewitts = 5½lb.
1791	29	1.84	130	0.45	11	1.85	19	1.26	680	843	14 Flounders = 2¼lb. 2 Burbot = ¾lb. 1 Tench, 1½lb.
1792	32	2.60	110	0.73	49	1.30	33	1.05	1124	1411	1 Salmon, 10½lb.; 1 Salmon, 6lb.; 1 Burbot, ½lb. 1 Tench, 2lb.; 1 Barbel, 3½lb., 22″ long 7 Flounders = 2¼lb.; 1 Chub, 1½lb.; 1 Herring [? = Shad]
1793	59	2.75	117	0.74	42	1.30	43	0.90	2331	2644	4 Barbels = 2¾lb.; 5 Flounders = 2½lb., plus 19, no wt. 4 Pike = 13lb.; 1 Pike, 2lb.; 2 Burbot = 1½lb. 3 Perch = 2½lb.; 142 Perch thrown back

578

1794	33	2.54	89	0.82	30	1.10	67	0.94	1050	1366	1 Pike, 2lb. 4 Burbot = 2¾lb. 9 Flounders, 1 Butt, no weight
1795	23	2.17	131	0.53	24	1.44	95	0.74	2332	2568	1 Pike, 1½lb. 1 Tench, 2½lb.; 1 Tench, 2¼lb. 12 Butts, no weight
1796	31	1.78	74	0.65	21	1.39	57	0.85	1365	1562	1 Barbel, 1½lb.; 6 Butts = 2½lb. 3 Flounders, 3 Butts, no weight 356 Perch thrown back

Appendix XXII

Income from the Lincolnshire estates of Sir Joseph Banks

YEAR	TENANTS n =	Area of Land ac.	Of which Woodland ac.	Income from Rent £	Income from Woodland £	TOTAL INCOME £
1791	403	} 14,300	1,000	5,500	1,500	7,000
1807	485			8,400	3,900	12,300
1820	523			16,000	[6,000]+	22,000+

Appendix XXIII

Summary of Income and Expenses Revesby Abbey, 1790–1

ITEM	£
General Estate Expenses	641
Servants	259
Labourers	185
Tradesmen & others	418
Corn & Stock	231
Housekeeping	84
Miscellaneous	161
Cash balance to Snow & Denne	5279
GROSS INCOME	7158

Appendix xxiv

Summary of Annual Expenses at 32 Soho Square (1785–90)

ITEM	1785	1786	1787	1788	1789	1790
	£	£	£	£	£	£
Taxes	145	165	171	174	170	106
Servants Wages, Cloaths &c.	251	236	269	262	301	318
Apparel	54	80	70	57	68	137
Travelling Expenses	86	60	89	97	79	86
Carriages & Horses	409	594	310	310	336	336
Furniture	136	53	33	104	86	43
Building & Repairs	230	74	32	33	57	41
Liquors	211	94	36	155	75	158
Coals and Woods	117	143	123	114	118	124
News Papers	11	8	9	11	16	16
Miscellaneous	175	46	37	95	68	88
TOTAL £	1827	1555	1178	1412	1374	1453

Appendix XXV

Summary of the Annual Expenses at Spring Grove (1782–91)

ITEM	1782	1783	1784	1785	1786	1787	1788	1789	1790	1791
	£	£	£	£	£	£	£	£	£	£
Tythes & Taxes	34	39	42	269*	279*	276*	278*	275*	278*	51
Farming Expenses	123	124	127	94	111	113	90	15	13	34
Garden Expenses	83	92	120	103	132	120	117	54	39	54
Building & Repairs	77	76	45	49	48	33	28	54	40	81
Malt, Hops, Grain, &c.	165	158	169	157	163	162	87	120	171	135
Coals	41	40	41	28	27	28	15	30	33	31
Miscel-laneous	86	51	43	25	32	20	46	3	4	49
TOTAL	609	580	587	725	792	752	661	551	578	435

*Elisha Biscoe, 1 year's rent; 4 July 1791, Biscoe's terms – Rent £200 a year; lease 21 years; the premises to be put into tenantable repair; leave to use the land at pleasure for 14 years. By an indenture dated 30 July 1791 Spring Grove was demised to Sir Joseph Banks at the yearly rent of £200 clear of all taxes and outgoings for the term of 21 years with provision for the purchase of the fee simple when a good and sufficient title had been made out by Biscoe for the price of £6000; Banks purchased the fee in 1808.

APPENDIX XXVI

A Plan of an Estate situated at Smallbury Green in the Parish of Heston & County of Middlesex, belonging to Sir Joseph Banks Bart. Surveyed by D. Todd, Hounslow, 1800

References		[Area]		
		A.	R.	P.
A.	Park	13.	3.	7
B.	Pleasure Ground	3.	0.	22
C.	Cold Bath Field	4.	2.	6½
D.	Thirteen Acre Field	13.	2.	9
E.	Pond Field	11.	1.	17½
F.	Gooseberry Garden	0.	2.	23
G.	South East Kitchen Garden	0.	1.	22
H.	South West Do. Do.	0.	2.	6
I.	North Do. Do.	0.	2.	56
K.	Court Yard			
	c Dwelling House	0.	2.	0
	e Stables			
L.	Cow Yard			
	Farm Buildings	0.	0.	30
M.	Rick Yard	0.	1.	30
		49.	3.	15

[Area on Plan of Smallbury Green on Spring Grove frontage to the eastern boundary as defined on Enclosure Award Map of 1818]

8.	1.	8
58.	0.	23

Appendix XXVII

Academic and Civil Honours and Memberships of Societies

1761 *Society for the Encouragement of Arts, Manufactures and Commerce*, London, 21 October – Member

1766 *Society of Antiquaries*, London, 27 February – Fellow
Royal Society of London, 1 May – Fellow

1771 Doctor of Civil Law, University of Oxford, 21 November
Freedom of the Borough of Boston, Lincolnshire, 3 December

1772 *Academie Royale des Sciences*, Paris, 11 March – Corresponding Member
Freedom of the Borough of Kirkwall, Orkney, 20 October

1773 *Royal Academy of Science*, Stockholm, 6 May – Foreign Member
Batavian Society of Experimental Philosophy, Rotterdam, 14 May – Foreign Member
Royal Society of London, 30 November – Member of Council

1774 *Society of Dilettanti*, London, 6 February – Member
Royal Society of London, 30 November – Member of Council

1776 *Royal Academy of Madrid*, 12 February – Foreign Member
Gesellschaft der Freunde vor Naturforschender (Société des Curieux de la Nature), Berlin, 27 February – Honorary Member
Physiographic Society of Lund, Sweden, 7 August – Foreign Member

1777 *Royal Society of London*, 30 November – Member of Council

1778 *Royal Society of London*, 30 November – President (and each year thereafter until his death, 20 June 1820)
Society of Dilettanti, London, 1 February – Very High Steward; March – Secretary and Treasurer to June 1794
The Literary Club, Turk's Head Tavern, Gerrard Street, London, 11 December – Member
The British Museum, London, 18 December (first attendance) – Trustee, *ex officio*, until his death 20 June 1820

1780 *Der Naturforschenden Gesellschaft*, Danzig, 13 January – Corresponding Member
Imperial Academy of Sciences, St Petersburg – June – Foreign Associate

1781 Baronetcy conferred, 28 March
Royal Academy of Science and Literature, Naples, n.d. – Foreign Member
Royal Society of Gotheburg, 6 December – Foreign Member

1782 *College of Physicians*, Edinburgh – December, Honorary Member

1784 *Royal Society of Medecine*, Paris – December – Foreign Member

1785 *Royal Society of Agriculture*, Paris, 31 January – Foreign Member
Royal Irish Academy, Dublin, 2 May – Original Fellow
Academy of Sciences, Munich, 8 November – Honorary Member
Literary and Philosophical Society of Manchester, 21 December – Honorary Member

1786 *Royal Society of Sciences*, Copenhagen – January – Foreign Member
Academy of Science and Literature, Mannheim, 8 May – Honorary Member

1787 *American Philosophical Society*, Philadelphia – August – Honorary Member
Royal Academy of Sciences, Paris – August – Foreign Member

1788   *Kentish Society* – February – Honorary Member
American Academy of Arts and Sciences, Massachusetts – 30 April – Fellow
Linnean Society of London, 7 March – Founding Fellow; 30 May – Member of Council; 4 July – Vice-President; first Honorary Member, 1788–1820
Association for Promoting the Discovery of the Interior Parts of Africa [The African Association], 8 July – Founding Member and Treasurer, 1788–1805; Acting-Secretary, 1795–7; Member of Committee, 1788–1820
American Academy of Arts and Sciences, New York – November – Honorary Member

1789   *Academy of Sciences*, Lisbon, n.d. – Foreign Member
Imperial Academy of Sciences, St Petersburg, 26 May – Foreign Member
Imperial Academy of Students of Natural History [Academia Imperale Naturae Curiosorum], Erlangen, 4 November – Foreign Member

1790   *Dutch Society of Science*, Haarlem, 21 March – Foreign Member
Literary and Physical Society, Danzig – March – Foreign Member
Natural History Society of Paris, 24 September – Foreign Member

1791   *Society for the Improvement of Naval Architecture*, London – April – Vice-President

1792   *Royal Society of Edinburgh* – January – Fellow
Natural History Society, Copenhagen, 8 June – Foreign Member

1793   *National Society for the Advancement of Science and Art*, Verona, 15 July – Foreign Member
Board or Society for the Encouragement of Agriculture and Internal Improvement [Board of Agriculture] 23 August 1793

1794   High Sheriff of Lincolnshire – May
Society of Dilettante, London – June – Secretary only until February 1797

1795   Knight of the *Order of the Bath* (K.B.), 1 July

1797   Privy Councillor, 29 March
Lieutenant-Colonel, Supplemental Militia, Northern Battalion, Lincolnshire, 3 April

1798   *Royal Society of Sciences*, Uppsala, 15 December – Foreign Member

1799   *Royal Institution of Great Britain*, 7 March – Chairman, first General Meeting of the Proprietors, 32 Soho Square; 23 March – Chairman, Meeting of Managers, 32 Soho Square; Member, Committee of Managers, 1799–1802
Imperial Academy of Sciences, St Petersburg – June – Foreign Member

1801   Privy Councillor, 14 January
Lycee du Departement du Gard, Nime – October – Associate Member
Dublin Society, Dublin, 5 November – Member

1802   *Institut National des Sciences et des Arts*, Paris, 5 January – Foreign Member (Class des Sciences, Mathematiques et Physiques)
Society of Agriculture and Commerce, Caen, 16 January
Society of Agriculture, Paris – March – Associate Member
Royal Institution of Great Britain, n.d. – Diploma as an original subscriber

1803   *Academy of Sciences, Arts and Literature*, Dijon, 20 May – Foreign Member
Cork Literary and Philosophical Society, Cork – June – Honorary Member

1804   *National Academy of Science, Literature and Fine Arts*, Turin, 28 February – Corresponding Member
Society for the Improvement of Horticulture, [Royal Horticultural Society], 7, 14 and 28 March – Original Member; 11 April – Chairman of Committee to frame the Rules of the Society; 4 July – Vice-President

1805   *Royal College of Surgeons*, London, 3 December – Patron
University of Vilna, 10 December – Diploma

1806   *Society of Naturalists*, Moscow, 31 January – Honorary Member
         Royal Academy, Berlin, 3 August – Diploma of Science and Law
         Imperial University of Moscow, 31 August – Diploma

1808   Recorder of Boston, Lincolnshire
         Wernerian Natural History Society, Edinburgh, 26 February – Member
         Wetterauische Gesellschaft fur die gesamt Naturkunde, Hanau, 30 November – Honorary
         Member

1809   *Zeeuwsch Genootschap der Wetenschapen*, Middelburg, 7 January – Foreign Member

1811   *The Merino Society*, London, 4 March – President (until his death 20 June 1820)

1812   *Royal College of Surgeons*, London – April – Honorary Fellow

1813   *Antiquarian Society*, Newcastle-on-Tyne, n.d. – Honorary Member
         Batavian Society of Experimental Philosophy – March – Honorary Member
         New York Historical Society, New York – October – Foreign Member

1814   *Academy of Useful Sciences*, Erfurt, Thuringia, 7 January – Honorary Member
         Holderness Agricultural Society, 25 March – Honorary Member

1815   *Physio-Medical Society*, Erlangen, 20 March – Honorary Member

1817   *Society for the Promotion of Natural Knowledge*, Marburg, 13 September – Honorary
         Member
         Massachusetts Society for Promoting Agriculture, Boston, 29 March – Foreign Member
         Natural History Society of Switzerland [Societas Naturae Scrutatorum Helvetorum], Zurich, 7
         October – Honorary Member

1818   *Academy of Sciences, Arts and Literature*, Dijon, 6 May – Honorary Member
         Royal Economic Society of Saxony, Dresden, 6 November – Foreign Member
         Agricultural Society of Saxony, Dresden, 1 December – Foreign Member

1819   *Pharmaceutical Society*, St Petersburg, 29 March – Honorary Member
         Lincolnshire Agricultural Society, Newark – August – Vice-President
         Imperial Agricultural Society of Steyermark, Austria, 1 September – Honorary Member

SELECT BIBLIOGRAPHY

This biography has depended for its main primary sources on the material to be found among the Banks papers in their widely scattered repositories. The necessary copies in various forms which I have gathered are now in the custody of the British Museum (Natural History) grouped in the chronological order established for all my transcripts as far as this can be done. I am therefore greatly indebted to the owners and curators of the various collections from which these have been drawn for their permission to use these documents in this way. A list of the repositories is given here but more details are to be found in *Sir Joseph Banks (1743–1820). A guide to biographical and bibliographical sources*, published by St Paul's Bibliographies in association with the British Museum (Natural History).

The Manuscript Collections

United Kingdom

Bodleian Library, Oxford
British Library, Bloomsbury, London
British Museum (Natural History), South Kensington, London
Buckinghamshire Record Office, Aylesbury
Central Libraries, Birmingham
Central Library, Lincoln
Derbyshire Record Office, Matlock
Earl Spencer, Althorp, Northampton
Fitzwilliam Museum, Cambridge
Herefordshire Record Office, Hereford
India Office Library and Records, Southwark, London
Kent Archives Office, Maidstone
Lincolnshire Archives Office, Lincoln
Linnean Society of London, Burlington House, London
Mr Victor Montagu, Mapperton House, Mapperton
National Library of Scotland, Edinburgh
National Library of Wales, Aberystwyth
National Maritime Museum, Greenwich, London
Public Record Office, Chancery Lane, London, and Kew, Surrey
Reference Library, Boston, Lincolnshire
Royal Astronomical Society Archive Centre, Churchill College, Cambridge
Royal Botanic Gardens, Kew, Surrey
Royal Society of London, Carlton House Terrace, London
Trinity College, Cambridge
University Library, Cambridge
University of Keele, Keele
University of London, Imperial College of Science and Technology, London
University of London, Library, Senate House, London
University of London, School of Oriental and African Studies, London

University of Reading, Reading
Whitby Museum, Whitby

United States of America

American Philosophical Society, Philadelphia, Pennsylvania
Hunt Institute for Botanical Documentation, Pittsburgh, Pennsylvania
Hyde Collection, Somerville, New Jersey
New York Historical Society, New York
Pierpont Morgan Library, New York
Public Library, Boston, Massachusetts
Public Library, New York
Sutro Library, San Francisco, California
University of California, Los Angeles, California
University of Wisconsin, Madison, Wisconsin
Yale University, New Haven, Connecticut

Other Countries

Alexander Turnbull Library, Wellington, New Zealand
McGill University, Montreal, Canada
National Library of Australia, Canberra, Australia
Niedersachssische Staats- und Universitäts Bibliothek Göttingen, Göttingen, Federal Republic of Germany
Royal Asiatic Society of Bengal, Calcutta, Republic of India
Royal Geographical Society of Australia (South Australian Branch), Adelaide, South Australia
State Library of New South Wales, Sydney, Australia
Stockholm Universitets-Bibliothek, Stockholm, Sweden
Uppsala Universitets-Bibliothek, Uppsala, Sweden

PRINTED WORKS BEFORE 1820

ABEL, C. 1818. *Narrative of a Journey in the Interior of China, and of a Voyage to and from that Country, in the years 1816 and 1817; containing an account of the most interesting transactions of Lord Amherst's Embassy to the Court of Pekin, and Observations on the countries which it visited.* London.

ACKERMAN, R. 1814. *The History of the University of Oxford, its colleges, halls, and public buildings.* 2 vols. London.

A CORRESPONDENT [GREGORY OLINTHUS]. 1820. A Review of some leading Points in the Official Character and Proceedings of the late President of the Royal Society. *Philosophical Magazine and Journal* **56** (269): 161–174, (270): 241–257.

A FRIEND TO DR HUTTON. 1784. *An Appeal to the Fellows of the Royal Society, concerning the Measures taken by Sir Joseph Banks, their President, to compel Dr. Hutton to resign the Office of Secretary to the Society for their Foreign Correspondence.* London.

AFZELIUS, A. 1794. *Account of the natural productions of Sierra Leone.* London.

AITON, W. 1789. *Hortus Kewensis.* 3 vols. London.

AITON, W. T. 1810–13. (2nd edit.). *Hortus Kewensis.* 5 vols. London.

ANDERSON, J. 1788. *Letters to Sir Joseph Banks, Bart. on the subject of Cochineal Insects, discovered at Madras.* Madras.

——. 1789. *Letters on Cochineal continued.* Madras.

——. 1790. *The conclusion of letters on Cochineal.* Madras.

ANON. 1771. *A Journal of a Voyage round the World in His Majesty's Ship Endeavour, in the years 1768, 1769, 1770, and 1771; Undertaken in Pursuit of Natural Knowledge, at the Desire of the Royal Society: containing All the various Occurrences of the Voyage, with Descriptions of several new discovered Countries in the Southern Hemisphere; and Accounts of their Soil and Productions; and of many Singularities in the Structure, Apparel, Customs, Manners, Policy, Manufactures, &c. of their Inhabitants. To which is added, A Concise Vocabulary of the Language of Otahitee.* London.

ANON. 1773 (1st edit.) 1774 (2nd edit.). *An Epistle from Mr. Banks, voyager, monster-hunter, and amoroso, to Oberea, Queen of Otaheite. Transfused by A.B.C., Esq., Second Professor of the Otaheite, and of every other unknown tongue. Enriched with the finest passages of the Queen's letter to Mr. Banks.* London.

ANON. 1774. *The journal of a voyage undertaken by order of his present Majesty, for making discoveries towards the North Pole, by the Hon. Commodore Phipps, and Captain Lutwidge.* London.

ANON. 1775. *An historical epistle from Omiah to the queen of Otaheite; being his remarks on the English nation. With notes by the editor.* London.

ANON. 1784. *An Authentic Narrative of the Dissensions and Debates in the Royal Society. Containing the Speeches at large of: Dr. Horsley, Dr. Maskelyne, Mr. Maseres, Mr. Poore, Mr. Glenie, Mr. Watson and Mr. Maty.* London.

ANON. 1778. *New Discoveries concerning the World and its Inhabitants . . . Related by Dr. Hawkesworth, Sydney Parkinson, Mr. Forster and Captain Cook.* London.

ANON. 1787. *Certain Particulars respecting the BREAD-FRUIT TREE; which it is wished to introduce, from the South-Seas, into the British West-India Islands, for the Use of their various Classes of Inhabitants, as an essential Article of Food; taken from the Accounts of the Voyages of Capt. Dampier, Lord Anson, and Capt. Cook.* London.

ANON. 1792. *An account of the Society for the improvement of Naval Architecture.* London.

ANON. 1801. Sir Joseph Banks *Public Characters of 1800–01.* London.

ANON. 1801. *A Compendious GAZETTEER; or Pocket Companion to the ROYAL PALACES, With a Description of the TOWNS, VILLAGES, VILLAS, and REMARKABLE PLACES, Within Sixteen Miles of Windsor: Pointing out Whatever is most Remarkable for Antiquity, Grandeur, or Rural Beauty: With Historical and Biographical Remarks.* Windsor.

ANON. 1820. *Memoirs, Historical and Illustrative, of the Botanist Garden at Chelsea Belonging to the Society of Apothecaries of London.* London.

BANKS, J. (ed.). 1791. *Icones selectae Plantarum quas in Japonia collegit et delineavit Engelbertus Kaempfer; ex archetypis in Museo Britannico asseveratis.* London.

BEDDOES, T. 1808. *A Letter to the Right Honourable Sir Joseph Banks, Bart. P.R.S. on the Causes and Removal of the Prevailing Discontents, Imperfections, and Abuses in Medicine, from Thomas Beddoes M.D.* London.

BLIGH, W. 1790. *A Narrative of the Mutiny, on Board His Majesty's Ship 'Bounty'; and the Subsequent Voyage of Part of the Crew, In the Ship's Boat, From Tofoa, one of the Friendly Islands, to Timor, a Dutch Settlement in the East Indies.* London.

BLIGH, W. 1792. *A Voyage to the South Sea, Undertaken by Command of His Majesty, for the Purpose of Conveying the Breadfruit Tree to the West Indies, in His Majesty's Ship the Bounty. Including an Account of the Mutiny on Board the Said Ship.* 2 vols. London.

BLUMENBACH, J. F. 1795. (3rd edit.). *De Generis Humani Varietate Nativa, Praemissa est epistola ad virum perillustrem Josephum Banks, Baronetum, Regiae Sociatatis Londini Praesidem.* Göttingen.

BOARD OF AGRICULTURE. 1796. *List of the Members of the Board of Agriculture.* London.

BOUGAINVILLE, L. A. Comte de. 1772. *Voyage round the world 1766–1769, in the frigate le Boudeuse and the storeship l'Etoile.* London.

BROWN, R. 1810. *Prodromus Florae Novae Hollandiae et Insulae Van-Diemen exhibens Characteres Plantarum quas Annis 1802–1805 per oras utriusque insulae collegit et descripsit Robertus Brown; insertis passim aliis speciebus auctori hucusque cognitis, seu evulgatism seu ineditis praesertim BANKSIANIS, in primo itinere navarchi Cook detectis. Vol. I.* London.

BURCKHARDT, J. L. 1819. *Travels in Nubia; by the late John Lewis Burckhardt.* London.

[CHALMERS, G.] 1782. *The Propriety of Allowing a Qualified Exportation of Wool Discussed Historically. To which is added An Appendix: Containing a Table, Which shews the Value of the Woolen Goods of every Kind, that were Entered for Exportation at the Custom-house, from 1697 to 1780 during all that Period.* [Prepared in collaboration with Sir Joseph Banks.] London.

COLLINS, D. 1798. *An Account of the English Colony in New South Wales.* London.

COLNETT, J. 1798. *A Voyage to the South Atlantic and Round Cape Horn into the Pacific Ocean, for the Purpose of Extending the Spermaceti Whale Fisheries . . .* London.

COOK, J. 1776. The Method taken for preserving the Health of the Crew of His Majesty's Ship the Resolution during her late Voyage round the World. *Philosophical Transactions of the Royal Society of London* **LXVI**: 402–406.

COOK, J. 1777. *A Voyage towards the South Pole and round the world, performed in His Majesty's Ships the Resolution and Adventure, in the years 1772, 1773, 1774 and 1775; written by James Cook, Commander of the Resolution In which is included Captain Furneaux's narrative of his proceedings in the Adventure during the separation of the ships. In two volumes Illustrated with maps and charts, and a variety of portraits ... and views ... drawn during the voyage by Mr. Hodges, and engraved by the most eminent masters.* London.

COOK, J & KING, J. 1784. *A Voyage to the Pacific Ocean, undertaken by the command of His Majesty for making discoveries in the northern hemisphere, to determine the position and extent of the west side of North America, its distance from Asia, and the practicability of a northern passage to Europe, performed under the direction of Captains Cook, Clerke and Gore, in His Majesty's Ships, the Resolution and Discovery, in the years 1776, 1777, 1778, 1779 and 1780.* London.

DANCE, G. jun. 1811. 1814. *A Collection of Portraits sketched from the Life since the year 1793 by Geo.Dance, esq., and engraved in imitation of the original drawings by Will. Daniell, A.R.A.* London.

DANCER, T. 1804. *Some Observations Respecting the Botanical Garden.* Jamaica.

DIBDIN, T. F. 1817. *The Bibliographical Decameron.* 3 vols. London.

DIXON, G. 1789. *A Voyage Round the World; but more particularly to the North-West Coast of America: performed in 1785, 1786, 1787, and 1788, in The King George and Queen Charlotte, Captains Portlock and Dixon.* London.

DODD, G. 1818. *On Steam Engines and Steam Packets.* London.

EDWARDS, B. 1794. *The History, Civil and Commercial, of the British Colonies in the West Indies.* London.

ELLIS, J. & SOLANDER, D. 1786. *The Natural History of many curious and uncommon Zoophytes, collected from various parts of the globe By the late John Ellis, Esq. F.R.S. Soc. Reg. Upsal. Soc. Author of the Natural History of English Corallines, and other works. Systematically arranged and described By the late Daniel Solander, M.D. F.R.S. &c.* London.

FABRICIUS, J. C. 1784. *Briefe aus London vermischten Inhalts.* Leipzig.

FAUJAS SAINT-FOND, B. 1799. *Travels in England, Scotland, and the Hebrides; undertaken for the purpose of examining the state of The Arts, The Sciences, Natural History and Manners, in Great Britain. Containing Mineralogical Descriptions of the Country round Newcastle; of the Mountains of Derbyshire; of the Environs of Edinburgh, Glasgow, Perth, and St. Andrews; of Inverary, and other Parts of Argyll; and of THE CAVE OF FINGAL.* 2 vols. London.

FLINDERS, M. 1814. *A Voyage to Terra Australis; Undertaken for the Purpose of Completing the Discovery of that Vast Country, and Prosecuted in the Years 1801, 1802, and 1803, in His Majesty's Ship the Investigator, and Subsequently in the Armed Vessel Porpoise and Cumberland Schooner. With an Account of the Shipwreck of the Porpoise, Arrival of the Cumberland at Mauritius, and Imprisonment of the Commander during Six Years and a Half in that Island.* London.

FORBES, J. 1806. *Letters from France written in the years 1803 and 1804.* London.

GAERTNER, J. 1788. *De Fructibus et Seminibus Plantarum.* Stuttgart.

GOLDSMITH, O. 1774. *An history of the earth and animated nature.* London.

GRANT, J. 1803. *The Narrative of a Voyage of Discovery, performed in His Majesty's Vessell The Lady Nelson, of sixty tons burthen, with sliding keels, in the years 1800, 1801, and 1802, to New South Wales.* London.

GOUGH, R. 1786–96. *Sepulchral Monuments of Great Britain applied to illustrate the History of Families, Manners, Habits, and Arts from the Norman Conquest.* London.

GOUGH, R. (ed.). 1789. *Camden's Britannia, translated from the edition published by the Author MDCVII. Enlarged by the latest Discoveries.* 3 vols. London.

HASTED, E. 1782. *The History and Topographical Survey of the County of Kent.* Canterbury.

HOME, E. 1814–28. *Lectures on comparative anatomy: in which are explained the preparations in the Hunterian Collection.* London.

HOOKER, W. J. 1811. *Journal of a tour in Iceland in the summer of 1809.* Yarmouth.

HOOKER, W. J. 1813. (2nd edit.). *Journal of a tour in Iceland in the summer of 1809.* 2 vols. London.

HUDSON, W. 1762. *Flora Anglica, exhibens plantas per regnum Angliae sponte crescentes etc.* London.

HUNTER, J. 1793. *An Historical Journal of the Transactions at Port Jackson and Norfolk Island, with the Discoveries which have been made in New South Wales and in the Southern Ocean, since the publication of Phillip's Voyage, compiled from the Official Papers; Including the Journals of Governors Phillip and King and of Lieut. Ball; and the Voyages from the first Sailing of the Sirius in 1787, to the Return of that Ship's Company to England in 1792.* London.

JEFFRIES, J. 1786. *A Narrative of Two Aerial Voyages.* London.

JENKINSON, C. 1805. *A Treatise on the Coins of the Realm; in a Letter to the King.* London.

JONES, E. G. 1810. *An Account of the Remarkable Effects of the Eau Medecinale d'Husson in the Gout.* London.

KIPPIS, A. 1784. *Observations on the late contests in the Royal Society.* London.

KNIGHT, R. P. 1786. *An Account of the Remains of the Worship of Priapus, lately existing at Isernia, in the Kingdom of Naples.* London.

LABILLARDIÈRE, J. J. H. DE. 1799. *Relation du voyage á la recherche de la Pérouse, pendant les années 1791 et 1792.* 2 vols. Paris.

LEE, J. 1810 (4th edit.). *An Introduction to the Science of Botany, chiefly extracted from the Works of Linnaeus; to which are added Several New Tables and Notes, and A Life of the Author.* London.

L'HERITIER DE BRUTELLE, C. L. 1788. *Sertum Anglicum, seu plantae rariores, quae in hortis juxta Londinum imprimis in horto regio Kewensi excoluntur.* Paris.

LINNAEUS, C. 1762–63 (2nd edit.). *Species Plantarum.* 2 vols. Holmiae [Stockholm].

LINNAEUS, C. 1766–8 (12th edit.). *Systema Naturae.* Holmiae [Stockholm).

LOW, G. 1813. *Fauna Orcadensis: or, The Natural History of the Quadrupeds, Birds, Reptiles, and Fishes, of Orkney and Shetland. By the Rev. George Low, Minister of Birsa and Haray.* Edinburgh.

LYSONS, D. 1792–7. *The Environs of London, being an Historical Account of the Towns, Villages, and Hamlets within twelve miles of that Capital.* London.

LYSONS, D. 1800. *An Historical Account of thos Parishes in the County of Middlesex which are not described in the Environs of London.* London.

MACKENZIE, A. 1801. *Voyages on the River St. Lawrence and through the Continent of North America to the Frozen and Pacific Oceans, in the years 1789 and 1793.* London.

MANN, D. B. 1811. *The Present Picture of New South Wales, illustrated with four large coloured views of Sydney with a plan of the Colony, etc.* London.

MARRAT, W. 1813. *Sketches Historical and Descriptive in the County of Lincoln.* Boston.

MASSON, F. 1776. An Account of Three Journeys from the Cape Town into the Southern Parts of Africa; undertaken for the Discovery of new Plants, towards the Improvement of the Royal Botanical Gardens at Kew. *Philosophical Transactions* **LXVI** (XVI): 268–317.

MISOGALLUS. 1802. A Letter to the Right Honourable Sir Joseph Banks, K.B. [dated London, 21 January 1802]. *Cobbett's Annual Register,* **I**: 327–331.

MYLNE, R. & RENNIE, J. (eds). 1812. *Reports of the late John Smeaton F.R.S., made on Various Occasions in the course of his employment as a Civil Engineer.* 3 vols. London.

NICHOLS, J. 1812–15. *Literary Anecdotes of the Eighteenth Century.* London.

NICHOLS, J. 1817–58. *Illustrations of the Literary History of the 18th Century, etc.* 8 vols.

OXLEY, J. 1820. *Journals of Two Expeditions into the Interior of New South Wales, undertaken by order of the British Government 1817–18.* London.

PARK, M. 1799. *Travels in the interior districts of Africa, performed under the direction and patronage of the African Association, in the years 1795–1797.* London.

PARKER, M. A. 1795. *A Voyage round the World in the Gorgon.* London.

PARKINSON, S. 1773. *A Journal of a voyage to the South Seas, in His Majesty's ship, the Endeavour, faithfully transcribed from the papers of the late Sydney Parkinson, draughtsman to Joseph Banks, Esq., on his late expedition with Dr. Solander, round the world; embellished with views and designs, delineated by the author, and engraved by capital artists.* London.

PARKINSON, S. 1784. *A Journal of a voyage to the South Seas, in His Majesty's ship, the Endeavour, faithfully transcribed from the papers of the late Sydney Parkinson, draughtsman to Sir Joseph Banks, Bart., in his expedition with Dr. Solander round the world; and embellished with twenty-nine views and designs, engraved by capital artists. To which is now added Remarks on the Preface, by the late John Fothergill, M.D., F.R.S. &c. and an Appendix containing an account of the voyages of Commodore Byron, Captain Wallis, Captain Carteret, Monsieur Bourgainville, Captain Cook, and Captain Clerke.* London.

PATERSON, W. 1789. *A Narrative of Four Journeys into the Country of the Hottentots and Caffraria.* London.

PENNANT, T. 1776 (2nd edit.). *A Tour in Scotland, and Voyage to the Hebrides; MDCCLXXII.* Part I. London.

PENNANT, T. 1784, 1787. *Arctic Zoology.* 2 vols and supplement. London.

PHILLIP, A. 1789. *The Voyage of Governor Phillip to Botany Bay; with an Account of the Establishment of the Colonies of Norfolk Island; compiled from Authentic Papers which have been obtained from the Several Departments; To which are added, The Journals of Lieuts. Shortland, Watts, Ball, & Capt. Marshall with an Account of their New Discoveries.* London.

PHIPPS, C. J. 1774. *A voyage towards the North Pole, 1773.* London.

PORTLOCK, N. 1789. *A Voyage round the World, but more particularly to the North-West Coast of America: performed in 1785, 1786, 1787, and 1788, in The King George and Queen Charlotte, Captains Portlock and Dixon.* London.

RING, J. 1811. *A Treatise on the Gout: containing the opinions of the most celebrated Ancient and Modern Physicians on that disease; and Observations on the Eau Medicinale.* London.

ROSS, J. 1819. *A Voyage of Discovery, made under the orders of the Admiralty, in His Majesty's Ships Isabella and Alexander, for the purpose of Exploring Baffin's Bay, and Inquiring into the Probability of a North-West Passage.* London.

ROY, W. 1785. *An Account of the Measurement of a Base on Hounslow-Heath.* London.

SAUER, M. 1802. *An Account of a Geographical and Astronomical Expedition to the Northern Parts of Russia.* London.

SCORESBY, W. 1820. *Account of the Arctic Regions and Northern Whale Fishery.* London.

SCOTT-WARING, J. 1774. *An Epistle from Oberea, Queen of Otaheite, to Joseph Banks, Esq. Translated by T.Q.Z., Esq., Professor of the Otaheite language in Dublin, and of all the languages of the undiscovered islands in the South Sea; and enriched with historical and explanatory notes.* London.

SCOTT-WARING, J. 1774. *A Second letter from Oberea, Queen of Otaheite, to Joseph Banks, Esq. Translated from the original, brought over by His Excellency Otaipairoo, Envoy Extraordinary and Plenipotentiary from the Queen of Otaheite, to the Court of Great Britain, lately arrived in His Majesty's Ship the Adventure, Capt. Furneaux. With some curious and entertaining anecdotes of this celebrated foreigner before and since his arrival in England. Together with explanatory notes from the Queen's former letter, and from Dr. Hawkesworth's Voyages.* London.

SHAW, G. & NODDER, F. P. 1789. *The naturalist's miscellany, or coloured figures of natural objects drawn and described immediately from nature.* London.

SHAW, G. 1794. *Zoology of New Holland.* London.

SMITH, J. E. 1793. *A Specimen of the Botany of New Holland . . .* Vol. I. London.

SOME MEMBERS IN THE MINORITY. 1784. *An History of the Instances of Exclusion from the Royal Society, Which were not suffered to be argued in the course of the late debates. With Strictures on the Formation of the Council, and other Instances of the Despotism of Sir Joseph Banks, the Present President, and of his incapacity for High Office.* London.

STAUNTON, G. L. 1797. *An Authentic account of an embassy from the King of Great Britain to the Emperor of China; including cursory observations made, and information obtained, in travelling through that ancient empire, and a small part of Chinese Tartary . . . Taken chiefly from the papers of his excellency the Earl of Macartney, Embassador . . . Sir E. Gower, commander of the expedition, and other gentlemen in the several departments of the embassy.* London.

THUNBERG, C. P. 1795. *Travels in Europe, Africa, and Asia, made between the years 1770 and 1779.* London.

TYTLER, J. 1797. Hessian Fly. *Encyclopaedia Britannica* (3rd edit.), **8**: 489–495.

WEBBER, J. 1808. *Views in the South Seas from Drawings by the late James [sic] Webber, Draftsman on Board the Resolution, Captain James Cook, from the Year 1776 to 1780.* London.

WILSON, J. 1806. *A Biographical Index to the Present House of Commons.* London.

WILSON, R. 1806. *Voyages of discovery round the world, successively undertaken by the Hon. Commodore Byron, in 1764; Captain Wallis and Carteret in 1766; and Captain Cook in the years 1768 to 1780 inclusive . . . selected, from the journals of the respective commanders by R.W.* London.

WOLCOT, J. [Peter Pindar *pseud.*] 1794–6. *The complete works of Peter Pindar.* 4 vols. London.

VANCOUVER, G. 1798. *A Voyage of Discovery to the North Pacific Ocean and Round the World; in which the coast of North-West America has been carefully examined and accurately surveyed. Undertaken by His Majesty's Command, Principally with a view to ascertain the existence of any navigable communication between the North Pacific and North Atlantic; and performed in the Years 1791, 1792, 1793, 1794, and 1795, in the Discovery Sloop of War, and Armed Tender Chatham, under the Command of Captain George Vancouver.* 3 vols. London.

PRINTED WORKS AFTER 1820

AGNARSDOTTIR, A. 1979. Ráðagerðir um innlimum Íslands í Bretaveldi á árunum 1785–1815.
Sérprentun úr Sögu, tímariti Sögufélagsins, **XVII**: 1–58, Reykjavik.

ALLAN, M. 1967. *The Hookers of Kew (1785–1911).*
London.

ALLIBONE, T. E. 1967. The club of the Royal College of Physicians, the Smeatonian Society of Civil Engineers and their relationship to the Royal Society Club.
Notes and Records of the Royal Society of London, **22**: 186–192.

ANDERSON, B. 1960. *Surveyor of the Sea. The Life and Voyages of Captain George Vancouver.*
Seattle.

ANDREWS, A. 1985. *The Devil's Wilderness: Caley's Journal of his journey to Mount Banks.*
Tasmania.

ANON. 1835. Sir Joseph Banks.
The Penny Cyclopaedia of the Society for the Diffusion of Useful Knowledge.
London.

ANON. 1901. *Report to the Lords Commissioners of His Majesty's Treasury of the Departmental Committee on Botanical Work and Collections at the British Museum and at Kew dated 11th March 1901. House of Commons Sessional Papers.* (205) lix: 511–758.

ANON. 1886. *The Brabourne Papers, Relating to the Settlement and Early History of the Colony; purchased from Lord Brabourne by Sir Saul Samuel, Agent-General [for New South Wales]: A Pamphlet containing a Summary of the Contents of these Important Papers.*
Sydney.

——. 1897 [A reprint of this pamphlet].
London.

ANON. 1940. (4th edit.). *The Record of the Royal Society of London for the Promotion of Natural Knowledge.*
London.

ARBER, A. 1945. Sir Joseph Banks and Botany.
Chronica Botanica, **IX**: 94–106.

ASPINALL, A. (ed.). 1962–70. *The Later Correspondence of George III.* 5 vols.
Cambridge.

AUSTIN, K. A. 1964. *The Voyage of the Investigator 1801–1803 Commander Matthew Flinders. R.N.*
London.

AUSTIN, R. H. 1966–67. Uranus Observed.
British Journal for the History of Science, **III**: 275–284.

AYLING, S. 1972. *George the Third.*
London.

BABBAGE, C. 1830. *Reflections Upon the Decline of Science in England, and on some of its causes.*
London.

BAKER-JONES, D. L. 1968. Edwinsford: A Country House and its families.
Carmarthenshire Historian **5**: 17–42.

BAMFORD, F. (ed.). 1936. *Dear Miss Heber: An Eighteenth Century Correspondence.*
London.

BAND, S. 1983. The steam engines of Gregory Mine, Ashover.
Bulletin of the Peak District Mines Historical Society **8** (5): 269–295.

BARRAU, J. 1961. *Subsistence Agriculture in Polynesia and Micronesia.*
Honolulu.

BARROW, J. 1849. *Sketches of the Royal Society and Royal Society Club.*
London.

BARRETT, C. (ed.). 1904–05. *Diary and Letters of Madame D'Arblay (1778–1840).* 6 vols. London.

BARTON, G. B. and BRITTEN, A. 1889. Sir Joseph Banks. *History of New South Wales* **I**: 78–85. Sydney.

BARTON, G. B. 1891. *The History of New South Wales from the Records, Volume I.* Sydney.

BATESON, C. 1959. *The Convict Ships, 1787–1868.* Glasgow.

BEAGLEHOLE, J. C. (ed.). 1962. *The Endeavour Journal of Joseph Banks 1768–1771.* Sydney.

BEAGLEHOLE, J. C. 1966 (3rd edit.). *The exploration of the Pacific.* London.

BEAGLEHOLE, J. C. 1974. *The Life of Captain James Cook.* London.

BEALE, E. 1964. Cook's First Landing Attempt in New South Wales. *Journal and Proceedings of the Royal Australian Historical Society* **50**: 191–204.

BEASELEY, H. G. 1927. Metal Mere. *Journal of the Polynesian Society* **36**: 297–298.

BEDDIE, M. K. (ed.). 1970. *Bibliography of Captain James Cook, R.N., F.R.S., circumnavigator.* Sydney.

BELL, F. D. & YOUNG, F. jun. 1842. *Reasons for promoting the cultivation of the New Zealand Flax.* London.

BENDYSHE, T. (ed.). 1865. *The anthropological treatises of Johann Friedrich Blumenbach.* London.

BENNETT, J. A. 1976. 'On the power of penetrating into space': the telescopes of William Herschel. *Journal of the History of Astronomy* **7**: 75–108.

BENTHAM, G. & LINDLEY, J. (eds). 1841. *Thomas Andrew Knight. A selection from the physiological and horticultural papers published in the Transactions of the Royal and Horticultural Societies; to which is prefixed a sketch of his life.* London.

BISWAS, K. 1950. *The Original Correspondence of Sir Joseph Banks Relating to the Foundation of the Royal Botanic Garden, Calcutta, and The Summary of the 150th Anniversary Volume of the Royal Botanic Garden, Calcutta.* Calcutta.

BLADON, E. McK. 1930. *The Diaries of Colonel The Honourable Robert Fulke Greville, Equarry to His Majesty King George III.* London.

BLAINEY, G. 1966. *The Tyranny of Distance.* Melbourne.

BLAXLAND, G. 1823. *A Journal of a Tour of Discovery across the Blue Mountains in the Year 1813, by Gregory Blaxland.* London.

BLUNDEN, G. 1968. *Charco Harbour.* London.

BLUNT, R. 1921. *By Chelsea Reach. Some riverside records.* London.

BLUNT, W. & STEARN, W. T. 1973. *Captain Cook's Florilegium. A Selection of Engravings of Plants collected by Joseph Banks and Daniel Solander on Captain Cook's first Voyage to the Islands of the Pacific with Accounts of the voyage xxx and of the botanical Explorations and Prints.* London.

BLUNT, W. 1978. *In for a Penny: A Prospect of Kew Gardens.* London.

BOAHEN, A. A. 1964. *Britain, The Sahara, and The Western Sudan, 1788–1861.* Oxford.

BONWICK, J. 1882. *The First Twenty Years of Australia.* London. Sydney.

BRETSCHNEIDER, E. 1898. *History of European botanical discoveries in China.* 2 vols. London.

BRIDSON, G. D. R., PHILLIPS, V. C. & HARVEY, A. P. 1980. *Natural History Manuscript Resources in the British Isles.* London. New York.

BERMAN, M. 1972. The Early Years of the Royal Institution 1799–1810: A Re-evaluation. *Science Studies* **II**: 205–240.

BERMAN, M. 1978. *Social change and scientific organisation: The Royal Institution 1799–1844.* Ithaca.

BRIEM, H. P. 1936. *Sjalfstaeoi Islands 1809.* Reykjavik.

BRIGHAM, W. T. 1900. *An Index to the Islands of the Pacific Ocean.* Honolulu.

BRISSENDON, R. F. (ed.). 1973. *Studies in the Eighteenth Century.* Canberra.

BRITISH MUSEUM (NATURAL HISTORY). 1904–12. *The History of the Collections contained in the Natural History Departments, etc.* London.

BRITTEN, J. 1900–05. *Illustrations of the Botany of Captain Cook's Voyage Round the World in H.M.S. Endeavour in 1768–71 by The Right Hon. Sir Joseph Banks, Bart., K.B., P.R.S., and Dr. Daniel Solander, F.R.S. Part I. Australian Plants.* London.

BRITTEN, J. 1920. Some Early Cape Botanists and Collectors. *Journal of the Linnean Society, Botany* **XLV**: 29–51.

BROCKWAY, L. H. 1979. *Science and Colonial Expansion. The Role of the British Royal Botanic Gardens.* New York.

BROUGHAM & VAUX, H. P. Brougham, 1st Baron, 1855. Sir Joseph Banks. *Lives of the Philosophers of the time of George III.* London.

BROWN, R. 1830. *Supplementum Primum Prodromi Florae Novae Hollandiae: exhibens Proteaceas Novas quas in Australasia legerunt DD. Baxter, Caley, Cunningham, Fraser et Sieber; et quarum e siccis exemplaribus Characteres elaboravit Robertus Brown.* Londini.

BROWN, R. 1960. *Prodromus Florae Novae Hollandiae et Insulae Van Diemen 1810 Supplementum Primum 1830 by Robert Brown With an Introduction by William T. Stearn. 1960 Facsimile.* New York.

BURRIDGE, J. 1824. *The tanner's key to a new system of tanning sole leather, of the right use of oak bark, &c, stating several most important discoveries and documents, in addition to Sir Humphrey [sic] Davy's experiments and the late Sir Joseph Banks' reports to the Honourable East India Company.* London.

BYNUM, W. F. & PORTER, R. (eds). 1985. *William Hunter and the Eighteenth Century Medical World.* Cambridge.

CALVERT, A. F. 1902. *The Discovery of Australia.* London.

CAMPBELL SMITH, W. 1969. A History of the First Hundred Years of the Mineral Collection in the British Museum with particular reference to the work of Charles Konig. *Bulletin of the British Museum (Natural History)* (Hist. Ser.) **3** (8): 237–259.

CAMERON, H. C. 1952. *Sir Joseph Banks, K.B., P.R.S.: the autocrat of the philosophers.* London.

CARR, D. J. 1983. The books that sailed with the *Endeavour.* *Endeavour* **7** (4): 194–201.

CARR, D. J. (ed.). 1983. *Sydney Parkinson: Artist of Cook's Endeavour Voyage.* London. Canberra.

CARTER, H. B. 1964. *His Majesty's Spanish Flock: Sir Joseph Banks and the Merinos of George III of England.* Sydney.

CARTER, H. B. 1974. *Sir Joseph Banks and the plant collection from Kew sent to the Empress Catherine II of Russia, 1795.* London.

CARTER, H. B. 1979. *The Sheep and Wool Correspondence of Sir Joseph Banks 1781–1820.* Sydney. London.

CARTER, H. B., DIMENT, J. A., HUMPHRIES, C. J., & WHEELER, A. C. 1981. The Banksian natural history collections of the *Endeavour* voyage and their relevance to modern taxonomy. *In* A. C. Wheeler & J. H. Price (eds). *History in the Service of Systematics.* London.

CARTER, H. B. 1981. Sir Joseph Banks: the cryptic Georgian. *Lincolnshire History and Archaeology* **16**: 53–62.

CARTER, H. B. 1987. *Sir Joseph Banks (1743–1820): A guide to biographical sources.* London.

CHALLINOR, J. 1971. *The History of British Geology. A Bibliographical Study.* Newton Abbot.

CHALMERS-HUNT, J. M. 1976. *Natural History Auctions 1700–1972.* London.

CHAMBERS, J. D. & MINGAY, G. E. 1966. *The Agricultural Revolution 1750–1880.* London.

CLARKE, H. G. 1848. *The British Museum: its Antiquities and Natural History.* London.

CLARK, R. W. 1983. *Benjamin Franklin. A Biography.* London.

CLOSE, C. 1969. *The Early Years of the Ordnance Survey.* Newton Abbot.

COATS, A. 1969. *The Quest for Plants: a history of the horticultural explorers.* London.

COHEN, E. W. 1941. *The Growth of the British Civil Service 1780–1939.* London.

COPEMAN, W. S. C. 1967. *The Worshipful Society of Apothecaries of London 1617–1967.* London.

CORNELL, C. (ed.). 1974. *The Journal of Post Captain Nicholas Baudin, Commander-in-Chief of the Corvettes Geographe and Naturaliste. Assigned by the Order of the Government to a Voyage of Discovery.* Adelaide.

COX, E. G. 1935. *Reference Guide to the Literature of Travel.* Washington, D.C.

CRAIG, J. 1953. *The Mint.* Cambridge.

CRANMER-BYNG, J. L. (ed.). 1962. *An Embassy to China: Being the journal kept by Lord Macartney during his embassy to the Emperor Ch'ien-lung 1793–94.* London.

CREASY, E. S. 1850. Sir Joseph Banks. *Memoirs of Eminent Etonians.* London.

CRITCHFIELD, H. J. 1951. *Phormium tenax* – New Zealand's Native Hard Fibre. *Economic Botany* **5** (2): 172–184.

CROSLAND, M. (ed.). 1975. *The emergence of science in Western Europe.* London.

CURREY, J. E. B. (ed.). 1967. *Reflections on the Colony of New South Wales: George Caley, Explorer and Natural History Collector for Sir Joseph Banks.* London.

CUVIER, G. L. C. F. D. 1821. *Éloge historique de M. Banks; lu à la séance publique de l'Académie Royale des Sciences, le 2 April 1821.* Paris.

CUVIER, G. 1827. Historical Eloge of the late Sir Joseph Banks, Baronet, President of the Royal Society. *Edinburgh New Philosophical Journal* **2**: 1–22.

DAVID, A. C. F. 1984. Cook and the Cartography of Australia. *The Globe* **22**: 47–59.

DAWSON, W. R. (ed.). 1958. *The Banks Letters. A Calendar of the manuscript correspondence of Sir Joseph Banks preserved in the British Museum, the British Museum (Natural History) and other collections in Great Britain.* London.

DEANE, Phyllis & COLE, W. A. 1967. (2nd edit.). *British Economic Growth 1688–1959.* Cambridge.

DE BEER, G. R. 1949. The malady of Edward Gibbon F.R.S. *Notes and Records of the Royal Society of London* **7** (1): 71–80.

DE BEER, G. 1960. *The Sciences were never at War.* Edinburgh.

DERMIGNY, L. 1964. *La Chine et L'Occident. Le Commerce a Canton ou XVIIIe Siecle, 1719–1833.* 3 vols. Paris.

DESMOND, R. 1977. *Dictionary of British and Irish Botanists and Horticulturalists: including Plant Collectors and Botanical Artists.* London.

DIBNER, B. 1964. *Alessandro Volta and the electric battery.* New York.

DICKINSON, H. W. 1936. *Matthew Boulton.* Cambridge.

DIMENT, J. A. & HUMPHRIES, C. J. 1980–7. *Banks' Florilegium: a publication in thirty-four parts of seven hundred and thirty-eight copperplate engravings of plants collected on Captain Cook's first voyage . . . gathered and classified by . . . Sir Joseph Banks and Dr. Daniel Solander . . . engraved . . . after drawings by Sydney Parkinson.* London.

DIMENT, J. A., HUMPHRIES, C. J., NEWINGTON, L. & SHAUGHNESSY, E. 1984. Catalogue of the natural history drawings commissioned by Joseph Banks on the *Endeavour* voyage 1768–1771 held in the British Museum (Natural History). Botanical. 1. Australia. *Bulletin of the British Museum (Natural History)* (hist. Ser.) **2** (complete): 183.

DIMENT, J. A. & WHEELER, A. C. 1984. Catalogue of the natural history manuscripts and letters by Daniel Carl Solander (1733–1782), or attributed to him, held in British collections. *Archives of Natural History* **11** (3): 457–488.

DIMENT, J. A., HUMPHRIES, C. J., NEWINGTON, L. & SHAUGHNESSY, E. 1987. Catalogue of the Natural History Drawings commissioned by Joseph Banks on the *Endeavour* Voyage 1768–1771 held in the British Museum (Natural History). Part 2. Brazil, Java, Madeira, New Zealand, Society Islands, Tierra del Fuego. *Bulletin of the British Museum (Natural History)* (hist. Ser.) **12** (complete).

DODGE, E. S. 1971. *Beyond the Capes: Pacific Exploration from Captain Cook to the Challenger (1776–1877).* London.

DRYANDER, J. 1966. *Catalogus Bibliothecae Historico-Naturalis Josephi Banks Baroneti, Balnei Equitis, Regiae Societatis Praesidis, Caet.* Amsterdam. London New York.

DUNCAN, A. 1821. *A short account of the life of the Right Honourable Sir Joseph Banks, K.B., President of the Royal Society of London.* Edinburgh.

DUNMORE, J. 1965. *French Explorers in the Pacific. Volume I. The Eighteenth Century.* Oxford.

DUNMORE, J. 1969. *French Explorers in the Pacific. Volume II. The Nineteenth Century.* Oxford.

DUPREE, A. H. 1964. Nationalism and Science – Sir Joseph Banks and the Wars with France. *A Festschrift for Frederick B. Artz* 37–51. Durham, North Carolina.

EDWARDS, E. 1870. *Lives of the Founders of the British Museum.* 2 vols. London.

EDWARDS, P. I. 1978. Sir Joseph Banks and the Botany of Captain Cook's Three Voyages of Exploration. *Pacific Studies* **2**: 2–43.

EDWARDS, P. (ed.). 1981. The Journal of Peter Good, Gardener on Matthew Flinders Voyage to *Terra Australis* 1801–03. *Bulletin of the British Museum (Natural History)* (hist. Ser.) **9**: 1–213.

EDWARDS, P. I. 1982. Botany of the Flinders Voyage. *[Proceedings of the XIII International Botanical Congress,* Sydney, August 1981,] pp. 139–166.

EHRMAN, J. 1969. *The Younger Pitt: The Years of Acclaim.* London.

ELLIS, A. R. (ed.). 1889. *The Early Diary of Frances Burney, 1768–1778.* London.

ESDAILE, A. 1946. *The British Museum Library. A Short History and a Survey.* London.

EVANS, J. 1956. *A History of the Society of Antiquaries.* Oxford.

FERGUSON, A. (ed.). 1948. *Natural Philosophy through the Eighteenth Century.* London.

FISHER, R. & JOHNSTON, H. 1979. *Captain Cook and his Times.* Vancouver.

FLETCHER, J. J. 1901. On the Rise and Early Progress of our Knowledge of the Australian Fauna [Presidential Address, Section D,]. *Report, 8th Meeting, Australian Association for the Advancement of Science (Melbourne 1900).* Melbourne.

FLETCHER, H. F. 1969. *The Story of the Royal Horticultural Society 1804–1968.* Oxford.

FOISSET, J. T. 1842. *Le Président de Brosses.* Paris.

FORD, T. D. 1967. The first detailed geological sections across England by John Farey, 1806–8. *Mercian Geologist* 2: 41–49.

FOTHERGILL, B. 1969. *Sir William Hamilton: Envoy Extraordinary.* London.

FOX, R. D. 1919. *Dr. John Fothergill and his friends. Chapters in eighteenth century life.* London.

FRANCIS, J. 1972. Sir Joseph Banks, Architect of Science and Empire. *Proceedings of the Royal Society of Queenlsland* 83 (I): 1–19.

FRIIS, H. R. (ed.). 1967. *The Pacific Basin: A History of its Geographical Exploration.* New York.

FROST, A. 1976. The Pacific Ocean: the eighteenth century's 'new world'. In *Studies on Voltaire and the eighteenth century, CLI–CLV*: 799–822.

FROST, A. 1980. *Convicts and Empire: A Naval Question 1776–1811.* Melbourne.

FROST, A. 1981. New South Wales as *Terra Nullius*: The British Denial of Aboriginal Land Rights. *Historical Studies: Australia and New Zealand* 19 (77): 513–523.

FRY, H. T. 1970. *Alexander Dalrymple (1737–1808) and the Expansion of British Trade.* London.

FURBER, H. 1974. *Rival Empires of Trade in the Orient 1600–1800.* Minneapolis.

GAGE, A. T. 1938. *A History of the Linnean Society of London.* London.

GAGER, C. S. 1937. Botanic Gardens of the world: materials for a history. *Brooklyn Botanic Garden Record* XXVI: 151–353.

GARLICK, K. & MACINTYRE, A. (ed.). 1978–86. *The Diary of Joseph Farington.* Yale.

GAZLEY, J. G. 1973. *The Life of Arthur Young 1741–1820.* Philadelphia.

GEIKIE, A. 1917. *The Annals of the Royal Society Dining Club: The Record of a London Dining-Club in the Eighteenth and Nineteenth Centuries.* London.

GEORGE, A. & ROSSER, Celia. 1982–8. *The Banksias.* Vols I–III. London.

GETMAN, F. H. 1937. Sir Charles Blagden F.R.S. *Osiris* 3: 69–87.

GILLEN, M. 1982. The Botany Bay Decision, 1786: Convicts and Empire. *English Historical Review* XCVII (385): 740–766.

GORDON. 1894. *The Life and Correspondence of William Buckland, D.D., F.R.S.* London.

601

GILBERT, L. F. 1954. The Election to the Presidency of the Royal Society in 1820. *Notes and Records of the Royal Society* **11** (2): 256–279.

GIBBS, F. W. 1965. *Joseph Priestley: Adventurer in Science and Champion of Truth.* London.

GIRAUDOUX, J. 1937. *Supplément au Voyage de Cook.* Paris.

G . . ., J. W. L. 1821. *A Letter to Sir Humphry Davy, Bart. &c. &c. &c. on his being elected The President of the Royal Society with some Observations on the Management of the British Museum, By a Fellow of the Royal Society.* London.
[The author is unidentified but was evidently someone who knew Banks and his household well.]

GONNER, E. C. K. 1888. The settlement of Australia. *English Historical Review* **3** (12): 625–632.

GRATTAN, C. H. 1963. *The Southwest Pacific to 1900: a modern history.* Michigan.

GREAT BRITAIN, PUBLIC RECORD OFFICE. 1963. *Guide to the Contents of the Public Record Office.*
Vol. I: Legal Records etc.
Vol. II. State Papers and Departmental Records.
London.

GRIFFITHS, P. 1967. *The History of the Indian Tea Industry.* London.

GUILDING, L. 1825. *An Account of the Botanic Garden in the Island of St. Vincent from its First Establishment to the Present Day.* Glasgow.

GUNTHER, A. E. 1980. *The Founders of Science at the British Museum 1753–1900.* Halesworth, Suffolk.

HALLETT, R. (ed.). 1964. *Records of the African Association 1788–1831.* London.

HALLETT, R. 1965. *The Penetration of Africa: European Enterprise and Exploration Principally in Northern and Western Africa up to 1830. Vol. I. to 1815.* London.

HAMILTON, H. 1967. *The English Brass and Copper Industries to 1800.* London.

HARLOW, V. T. & MADDEN, F. 1953. *British Colonial Developments, 1774–1834.* Oxford.

HARLOW, V. T. 1964. *The Founding of the Second British Empire 1763–1793.* 2 vols. London.

HARTLEY, D. 1969. *Thomas Tusser 1557 floruit. His Good Points of Husbandry.* Bath.

HAVILAND, J. B. 1974. A last look at Cook's Guugu Yimidhirr word list. *Oceania* **44**: 216–232.

HAWKEY, A. 1975. *Bligh's Other Mutiny.* London.

HAYWARD, J. 1825. *On the science of agriculture, comprising a commentary on and comparative investigation of the agricultural chemistry of Mr. Kirwan and Sir Humphry Davy, the code of agriculture of Sir John Sinclair, Sir Joseph Banks and other authors on the subject.* London.

HEDLEY, O. 1975. *Queen Charlotte.* London.

HENREY, B. 1975. *British botanical and horticultural literature before 1800.* 2 vols. Oxford.

HERMANNSSON, H. 1928. Sir Joseph Banks and Iceland. *Islandica. An annual relating to Iceland and the Fiske Icelandic Collection in Cornell University Library. XVIII.* Ithaca, New York.

HILL, J. W. F. (ed.). 1952. *The Letters and Papers of the Banks Family of Revesby Abbey 1704–1760.* Hereford.

HILL, F. 1966. *Georgian Lincoln.* Cambridge.

HOARE, M. E. 1982. *The Resolution Journal of Johann Reinhold Forster 1772–1775.* 4 vols. London.

HOLMES, M. 1952. *Captain James Cook, R.N., F.R.S.: A Bibliographical Excursion.* London.

HOME, E. 1822. *The Hunterian Oration in honour of surgery . . . delivered in the theatre of the [Royal] College [of Surgeons, London], February 14, 1822.*
London.

HOLT-WHITE, R. 1901. *The Life and Letters of Gilbert White of Selborne.*
London.

HOPE, F. W. 1845. The autobiography of John Christian Fabricius, translated from the Danish, with additional notes and observations.
Transactions of the Entomological Society of London **4**: i–xvi.

HOPKINSON, G. G. 1952. Lead Mining in 18th Century Ashover.
Journal of the Derbyshire Archaeological and Natural History Society **25**: 1–21.

HORN, D. B. 1967. *Great Britain and Europe in the Eighteenth Century.*
Oxford.

HOVE, A. P. 1855. *Tours for Scientific and Economical Research, made in Guzerat, Kattiawar, and the Conkuns, in 1787–88, by Dr. Hove. Published from the MS. in the Banksian Library, British Museum, under the care of Alexander Gibson, F.L.S.*
Bombay.

HUDSON, K. 1972. *Patriotism with Profit: British Agricultural Societies in the Eighteenth and Nineteenth Centuries.*
London.

HUNKIN, J. W. 1943. Bicentenary of Sir Joseph Banks.
The Fortnightly 271–275 (October).

HUNT, W. H. 1979. The Horncastle Navigation Engineers 1792–1794.
Journal of the Railway and Canal Historical Society **25** (1): 2–11.

HYAMS, R. & MARTIN, G. 1975. *Reappraisals in British Imperial History.*
London.

INGLIS-JONES, E. 1968. The Knights of Downton Castle.
The National Library of Wales Journal **15** (3): 237–264; **15** (4): 365–388.

INKSTER, I. & MORRELL, J. (eds). 1983. *Metropolis and Province: Science in British Culture 1780–1850.*
London.
Philadelphia.

ISAAC, P. C. G. 1984. *William Bulmer, 1757–1830: 'Fine' Printer.*
Cambridge.

JACKSON, B. D. 1885. Sir Joseph Banks. *Dictionary of National Biography* **3**: 129–133.
London.

JOURDAIN, M. & JENYNS, R. S. 1967. *Chinese Export Art in the Eighteenth Century.*
London.

JONES, B. 1871. *The Royal Institution: Its Founder and First Professors.*
London.

JOPPIEN, R. 1979. Die Gelehrtenbibliothek des Sir Joseph Banks.
Buch und Sammler, Privat und öffentliche Bibliotheken im 18 Jahrhundert.

KENNEDY, G. 1978. *Bligh.*
London.

KING, G. 1893. *Annals of the Royal Botanic Garden, Calcutta* **IV**: i–ix, preface.

KING, G. 1895. A Brief Memoir of William Roxburgh.
Annals of the Royal Botanic Garden, Calcutta **V**: 1–9.

KING, P. P. 1827. *Narrative of a Survey of the Inter-tropical and Western Coasts of Australia, performed between the years 1818 and 1822, by Captain Philip P. King, R.N.* 2 vols.
London.

KING, R. 1985. *Royal Kew.*
London.

KNATCHBULL-HUGESSEN, H. 1960. *Kentish Family.*
London.

LANDES, D. 1969. *The Unbound Prometheus.*
Cambridge.

LANYON-ORGILL, P. A. 1979. *Captain Cook's South Sea Vocabularies.*
London.

LARWOOD, H. J. C. 1962. Western Science in India before 1850.
Journal of the Royal Asiatic Society of Great Britain and Ireland: 62–76.

LHOTSKY, J. 1843. Biographical Sketch of Ferdinand Bauer, Natural History Painter to the Expedition of Captain Flinders, R.N., to Terra Australis.
Hooker's Journal of Botany **2**: 106–113.

LIGHTON, C. 1958. *Sisters of the South.* Cape Town.

LOVEJOY, A. O. 1942. *The Great Chain of Being.* Cambridge, Mass.

LYONS, H. 1944. *The Royal Society 1660–1940. A History of its Administration under its Charters.* Cambridge.

LYSAGHT, A. M. 1959. Some Eighteenth Century Bird Paintings in the Library of Sir Joseph Banks (1743–1820). *Bulletin of the British Museum (Natural History)* (hist. Ser.) **1** (6): 253–371.

LYSAGHT, A. M. 1971. *Joseph Banks in Newfoundland and Labrador, 1766: His Diary, Manuscripts and Collections.* London.

LYSAGHT, A. M. 1977. Banks's artists in the Endeavour. *In* Cook, J. *The Journal of H.M.S. Endeavour, 1768–1771.* Guildford.

LYSAGHT, A. M. 1980. Banksian reflections. *In* Banks, J. *The journal of Joseph Banks in the Endeavour.* Guildford.

LYTE, C. 1980. *Sir Joseph Banks: 18th century explorer, botanist and entrepreneur.* Newton Abbot.

LUBBOCK, C. A. 1933. *The Herschel Chronicle: the Life-Story of William Herschel and his Sister, Caroline Herschel.* Cambridge.

LUGARD, C. E. 1972. *The Saints and Sinners and the Inns and Outs of Ashover.* Leicester.

LUPTON, K. 1979. *Mungo Park the African Traveller.* Oxford.

MABBERLEY, D. 1985. *Jupiter Botanicus: Robert Brown of the British Museum.* Braunschweig.

MACALPINE, I. & HUNTER, R. 1969. *George III and the Mad-Business.* London.

McCORMICK, E. H. 1977. *Omai: Pacific Envoy.* Auckland.

McGILLIVRAY, D. J. 1970. A checklist for the illustrations of the botany of Cook's first voyage. *Contributions from the New South Wales National Herbarium* **4** (5): 112–125.

MACK, J. D. 1966. *Matthew Flinders 1774–1814.* Melbourne.

MACKANESS, G. 1930. Sir Joseph Banks and colonial currency. *Journal and Proceedings of the Royal Australian Historical Society* **16**: 263–267.

MACKANESS, G. 1936. *Sir Joseph Banks, his relations with Australia.* Sydney.

MACKANESS, G. 1951. *The Life of Vice-Admiral William Bligh.* Sydney.

MACKAY, D. 1974. Banks, Bligh and Breadfruit. *The New Zealand Journal of History* **8** (1): 61–77.

MACKAY, D. 1969. British Interest in the Southern Oceans, 1782–1794. *The New Zealand Journal of History* **3** (2): 124–142.

MACKAY, D. 1981. Far-flung Empire: A Neglected Outpost at Botany Bay 1788–1801. *Journal of Imperial and Commonwealth History* **IX** (1): 125–145.

MACKAY, D. L. 1985. *In the wake of Cook: Exploration, Science and Empire.* London.

McKAY, D. 1973. Great Britain and Iceland in 1809. *Mariners Mirror* **59** (1): 85–95.

MACOWAN, P. 1887. Personalia of Botanical Collectors at the Cape. *Transactions of the South African Philosophical Society* **4**: xxx–liii.

MADDISON, R. E. W. & MADDISON, R. E. 1954. Spring Grove, the country house of Sir Joseph Banks, Bart., P.R.S. *Notes and Records of the Royal Society of London* **11**: 91–99.

MAIDEN, J. H. 1909. *Sir Joseph Banks: The 'Father of Australia'.*
Sydney.
London.

MAINDRON, E. 1888. *l'Académie des Sciences.*
Paris.

MANDER-JONES, P. 1972. *Manuscripts in the British Isles Relating to Australia, New Zealand and the Pacific.*
Canberra.

MANN, T. A. 1845. *Lettres de l'abbe Mann sur les sciences et les lettres en Belgique, 1773–1788.*
Bruxelles.

MARKHAM, C. R. 1895. *Major James Rennell and the Rise of Modern English Geography.*
London.

MARSHALL, J. B. 1978. The handwriting of Joseph Banks, his scientific staff and amanuenses.
Bulletin of the British Museum (Natural History) (Bot.) **6** (1): 1–85.

MARSHALL, P. 1968. *Problems of Empire: Britain and India 1757–1813.*
London.

MARSHALL, P. J. & WILLIAMS, G. 1982. *The Great Map of Mankind: British Perceptions of the World in the Age of Enlightenment.*
London.

MARTIN, T. 1961. (3rd edit.). *The Royal Institution.*
London.

MARTIN, G. (edit.). 1978. *The Founding of Australia.*
Sydney.

MARTIN-ALLANIC, J-E. 1964. *Bougainville, navigateur et les Decouvertes de son Temps.*
2 vols.
Paris.

MATHIAS, P. 1969. *The First Industrial Nation.*
London.

MATHIAS, P. (ed.). 1972. *Science and Society 1600–1900.*
Cambridge.

MERCER, V. 1972. *John Arnold & Son Chronometer Makers 1762–1843.*
London.

MILLER, E. 1973. *That noble cabinet.*
London.

MILLER, D. P. 1981. Sir Joseph Banks: An Historiographical Perspective.
History of Science **XIX**: 284–292.

MINGAY, G. E. 1963. *English Landed Society in the Eighteenth Century.*
London.

MITCHELL, R. E. 1939. George Caley: His Life and Work.
Journal and Proceedings of the Royal Australian Historical Society **XXV** (VI): 437–542; **XXVI**: 186–7.

MITCHELL, T. C. (ed.). 1979. *The British Museum Yearbook 3. Captain Cook and the South Pacific.*
London.

MITCHISON, R. 1962. *Agricultural Sir John: The Life of Sir John Sinclair of Ulbster 1754–1835.*
London.

MOOREHEAD, A. 1966. *The Fatal Impact: An Account of the Invasion of the South Pacific 1767–1840.*
London.

MORSE, H. B. (ed.). 1926. *The Chronicles of the East India Company Trading to China, 1635–1834.* 5 vols.
Oxford.

MORTON, A. G. 1981. *History of Botanical Science.*
London.

MOUGEL, F-C. 1978. Une societe de culture en Grande-Bretagne au XVIII[e] siecle. La Societe des Dilettanti (1734–1800).
Revue historique **259** (2): 389–414.

MUKHERJEE, S. N. 1968. *Sir William Jones: a study in 18th century British attitudes to India.*
Cambridge.

MUSSON, A. E. & ROBINSON, E. 1969. *Science and Technology in the Industrial Revolution.*
Manchester.

NEWBURY, C. W. (ed.). 1961. *The History of the Tahitian Mission 1799–1830. Written by John Davies Missionary to the South Sea Islands.*
Cambridge.

NEWMAN, A. 1969. *The Stanhopes of Chevening, A family biography.*
London.

NICHOLSON, H. A. 1886. *Natural history: its rise and progress in Britain as developed in the life and labours of leading naturalists.*
London.
Edinburgh.

NIXON, F. 1957. The Early Steam Engine in Derbyshire.
Transactions of the Newcomen Society **31**: 1–25.

O'DONOGHUE, Y. 1977. *William Roy 1729–1790 Pioneer of the Ordnance Survey.*
London.

O'BRIAN, P. 1987. *Joseph Banks: A Life.*
London.

OLIVER, D. L. 1961. *The Pacific Islands.*
Cambridge, Massachusetts.

OLIVER, D. L. 1974. *Ancient Tahitian Society.* 3 vols.
Honolulu.

PARIS, J. A. 1831. *The Life of Sir Humphry Davy, Bart, L.L.D.* 2 vols.
London.

PARKER, R. A. C. 1975. *Coke of Norfolk: A Financial and Agricultural Study 1707–1842.*
Oxford.

PARKINSON, C. N. 1937. *Trade in the Eastern Seas 1793–1813.*
Cambridge.

PARRY, A. 1963. *Parry of the Arctic. The Life Story of Admiral Sir Edward Parry 1790–1855.*
London.

PARRY, J. H. 1971. *Trade and Dominion. The European Oversea Empires in the Eighteenth Century.*
London.

PAWSON, H. C. 1957. *Robert Bakewell: Pioneer Livestock Breeder.*
London.

PEARSON, W. H. 1973. Hawkesworth's Voyages. *In* Brissenden, r. f. 1973. *Studies in the Eighteenth Century* **2**: 239–257.
Canberra.

PERKINS, J. A. 1977. *Sheep Farming in Eighteenth and Nineteenth Century Lincolnshire.*
Sleaford.

PHILIPS, C. H. 1940. *The East India Company: 1784–1834.*
Manchester.

PORTER, R. 1977. *The making of geology: earth science in Britain, 1660–1815.*
Cambridge.

POWELL, D. 1973. The Voyage of the Plant Nursery H.M.S. *Providence*, 1791–1793.
Bulletin of the Institute of Jamaica, Science Series, **15** (2): 71.

RAISTRICK, A. 1950. *Quakers in Science and Industry.*
London.

RAUSCHENBERG, R. 1964. A letter of Sir Joseph Banks describing the life of Daniel Solander.
Isis **55**: 62–67.

RAUSCHENBERG, R. 1968. Daniel Carl Solander, naturalist on the Endeavour.
Transactions of the American Philosophical Society **58** (8): 1–66.

REED, M. 1983. *The Georgian Triumph 1700–1830.*
London.

REICHWEIN, A. 1925. *China and Europe, Intellectual and Artistic Contacts in the Eighteenth Century.*
London.

REINITS, R. & REINITS, T. 1963. *Early artists of Australia.*
Sydney.

ROLT, L. T. C. 1966. *The Aeronauts: A History of Ballooning 1783–1903.*
London.

ROTH, W. E. 1901. The structure of the Koko-Yimidir language.
North Queensland Ethnographic Bulletin **2**: 1–35.

ROTH, W. E. L. 1897. *Ethnological studies among the North-west Central Queensland Aborigines.*
Brisbane.

ROUSSEAU, G. S. & PORTER, R. S. (eds). 1980. *The ferment of knowledge: studies in the historiography of eighteenth century science.*
Cambridge.

ROYAL COMMISSION ON HISTORICAL MANUSCRIPTS. 1982. *The manuscripts/papers of British scientists 1600–1940.*
London.

RUDWICK, M. J. S. 1972. *The Meaning of Fossils. Episodes in the History of Palaeontology.*
London.

RYAN, W. F. 1966. John Russell R.A. and early Lunar Mapping.
The Smithsonian Journal of History 1: 27–48.

RYDEN, S. 1963. *The Banks Collection. An episode in 18th Century Anglo-Swedish Relations.*
Sweden.

ST JOHN, H. 1976. Biography of David Nelson and an Account of his Botanizing in Hawaii.
Pacific Science 30 (1): 1–5.

SANDEN, W. 1892. *Thomas and Paul Sandby, Royal Academicians: Some account of their lives and works.*
London.

SHAPIN, S. A. 1971. The Royal Society of Edinburgh: a study of the social context of Hanoverian science.
Thesis, Ph.D.: University of Edinburgh; University of Pennsylvania.

SCHEER, F. 1840. *Kew and its gardens.*
London.

SCHOFIELD, R. E. 1968. *The Lunar Society of Birmingham. A Social History of Provincial Science and Industry in Eighteenth Century England.*
Oxford.

SCORESBY-JACKSON, R. E. 1861. *The Life of William Scoresby.*
London.

SEALY, J. R. 1956. The Roxburgh Flora Indica Drawings at Kew.
Kew Bulletin 2 (2) & (3): 297–399.

SEALY, J. R. 1975. William Roxburgh's collection of paintings on Indian plants.
Endeavour 34: 84–89.

SHARMAN, G. B. 1970. Observations upon animals by the naturalists of the *Endeavour.*
Queensland Heritage 2 (2): 3–71.

SHAW, A. G. L. 1968. The Hollow Conqueror and the Tyranny of Distance.
Historical Studies: Australia and New Zealand 13: 195–203.

SHAWCROSS, F. W. 1970. The Cambridge University Collection of Maori Artifacts made on Cook's First Voyage.
Journal of the Polynesian Society 79 (3): 305–348.

SHERBORN, C. D. 1928–9. The earliest known geological section across England.
The Naturalist: 393–394.

SIM, K. 1969. *Desert Traveller: The Life of Jean Louis Burckhardt.*
London.

SKELTON, R. A. 1962. History of the Ordnance Survey.
Geographical Journal 128: 415–432.

SKEMPTON, A. W. 1971. The Publication of Smeaton's Reports.
Notes and Records of the Royal Society of London 26: 135–155.

SKERTCHLEY, S. B. J. 1877. The Geology of the Fenland.
Memoir. Geological Survey, England and Wales.
London.

SMILES, S. 1861. *Lives of the Engineers.*
London.

SMITH, J. E. 1821. *A selection of the correspondence of Linnaeus and other naturalists, from the original manuscripts.* 2 vols.
London.

SMITH, J. 1880. *Records of the Royal Botanic Gardens, Kew.*
London.

SMITH, E. 1911. *The Life of Sir Joseph Banks, President of the Royal Society with some notices of his friends and contemporaries.*
London.
New York.

SMITH, B. 1960. *European Vision and the South Pacific 1768–1850: A study in the History of Art and Ideas.*
Oxford.

SMITH, B. 1979. *Art as Information: Reflections on the Art from Captain Cook's Voyages.*
Sydney.

SMITH, H. M. 1974. History of the botanical exploration of the Society Islands. *In* M. L. Grant, F. R. Fosberg, and H. M. Smith. Partial flora of the Society Islands: Ericaceae to Apocynaceae.
Smithsonian contributions to Botany **17**: 54–69.

SPARROW, C. J. 1965. The growth and status of the *Phormium tenax* industry of New Zealand.
Economic Geography **41**: 331–345.

SPATE, O H.K. 1983. *Monopolists and Freebooters.*
Canberra.

STAMP, T. & C. 1976. *William Scoresby, Arctic scientist.*
Whitby.

STANBURY, P. & PHIPPS, G. 1980. *Australia's Animals Discovered.*
Sydney.

STANHOPE, E. 1894–5. Notes on Revesby.
Lincolnshire Notes and Queries **IV**: 129–137.

STEARN, W. T. 1960. Franz and Ferdinand Bauer, masters of botanical illustration.
Endeavour **XIX** (73): 27–35.

STEARN, W. T. 1961. Botanical Gardens and Botanical Literature in the Eighteenth Century.
Catalogue of Botanical Books in the Collection of Rachel McMasters Miller Hunt **II**: xliii–cxl.
Pittsburgh, Pennsylvania.

STEARN, W. T. 1968. The botanical results of the *Endeavour* voyage.
Endeavour **27** (100): 3–10.

STEARN, W. T. 1974. Sir Joseph Banks (1743–1820) and Australian Botany.
Records of the Australian Academy of Science **2**: 7–23.

STEARN, W. 1981. *The Natural History Museum at South Kensington. A History of the British Museum (Natural History) 1753–1980.*
London.

STEVEN, M. 1983. *Trade, Tactics and Territory.*
Melbourne.

STRAUSS, W. P. 1964. Paradoxical Co-operation: Sir Joseph Banks and the London Missionary Society.
Historical Studies, Australia and New Zealand **11** (42): 246–252.

STIMSON, D. 1949. *Scientists and Amateurs: A History of the Royal Society.*
New York.

SUTTOR, G. 1855. *Memoirs, historical and scientific, of the Right Honourable Sir Joseph Banks, Bart.*
Parramatta, N.S.W.

SWEETING, G. S. 1946. An outline of the geology of Ashover, Derbyshire.
Proceedings of the Geologists' Association **57**: 117–152.

TAILLEMITE, E. 1978. *Bougainville et ses compagnons autor du monde, 1766–1769.* 2 vols.
Paris.

TAYLOR, E. G. R. 1966. *The Mathematical Practitioners of Hanoverian England 1714–1840.*
Cambridge.

THISELTON-DYER, W. T. 1891. Historical Account of Kew to 1841.
Bulletin of Miscellaneous Information, Royal Gardens, Kew **60**: 279–327.

THOMAS, J. 1938. Josiah Wedgwood and his Portraits of 18th Century Men of Science.
Proceedings of the Royal Institution of Great Britain **XXX** (III): 142: 497–517.

THOMPSON, P. 1821. *Collections for a Topographical and Historical Account of Boston, and the Hundred of Skirbeck, in the County of Lincoln.*
Boston.
London.

TOMLINSON, C. 1844. *Sir Joseph Banks and the Royal Society: a popular biography, with an historical introduction and sequel.*
London.

TROIL, U. von. 1780. *Letters on Iceland: containing observations on the natural history, Volcanoes, Basaltes, Hot Springs etc. made in 1772 To which are added Professor Bergman's curious observations and chemical examination of*

the Lava and other substances produced on the island.
London.

TURRILL, W. B. 1963. *Joseph Dalton Hooker: Botanist, Explorer, and Administrator.*
Edinburgh.

URNESS, C. (ed.). 1967. *A Naturalist in Russia. Letters from Peter Simon Pallas to Thomas Pennant.*
Minneapolis.

VALENTINE, A. 1970. *The British Establishment 1760–1784: An eighteenth-century biographical dictionary.* 2 vols.
Oklahoma.

VAN STEENIS, C. G. J., VAN STEENIS-KRUSEMAN, M. J. & BACKER, C. A. 1954. Louis Auguste Deschamps, a prominent but ill-fated explorer of the flora of Java, 1793–1798.
Bulletin of the British Museum (Natural History) (hist. Ser.) **1** (2): 51–68.

VEIT, W. (ed.). 1972. *Captain James Cook: Image and Impact.*
Melbourne.

VILLIERS, A. 1967. *Captain Cook, the Seaman's Seaman.*
London.

VON ERFFA, H. & STALEY, A. 1986. *The Paintings of Benjamin West.*
New Haven & London.

WATERS, I. 1964. *The Unfortunate Valentine Morris.*
Chepstow, Monm.

WATT, G. 1889–96. *A Dictionary of the Economic Products of India.* 6 vols.
Calcutta.

WATT, J. 1979. Medical Aspects and Consequences of Captain Cook's Voyages. *In* R. Fisher & H. Johnston (eds), *Captain James Cook and his Times.*
Vancouver.

WEDGWOOD, B. & H. 1980. *The Wedgwood Circle 1730–1897.*
London.

WELD, C. R. 1848. *A History of the Royal Society, with Memoirs of the Presidents. Compiled from Authentic Documents.* 2 vols.
London.

WESTWOOD, A. 1926. *Matthew Boulton's 'Otaheite' Medal. Distributed by Capt. Cook on his Second Voyage to the Pacific Ocean, 1772.*
Birmingham.

WHEELER, A. 1985. The Linnaean fish collection in the Linnean Society of London.
Zoological Journal of the Linnean Society of London **84** (1): 16–76.

WHEELER, A. 1986. Catalogue of the Natural History Drawings commissioned by Joseph Banks on the Endeavour Voyage 1768–1771 held in the British Museum (Natural History). Part 3: Zoology.
Bulletin of the British Museum (Natural History) (hist. Ser.) **13** (complete).

WHEELER, W. H. 1896. *A History of the Fens of South Lincolnshire, being a description of the Rivers Witham and Welland and their Estuary, and an account of the reclamation, drainage, and enclosure of the fens adjacent thereto.*
Boston.
London.

WHEELWRIGHT, E. G. 1939. *The Physic Garden.*
London.

WHITE, W. 1856. *History, Gazetteer, and Directory of Lincolnshire, and the City and Diocese of Lincoln; . . . A General Survey of the County . . .*
Sheffield.

WHITE, J. 1889. *Ancient History of the Maori.*
Wellington.

WHITEHEAD, P. J. P. 1969. Zoological Specimens from Captain Cook's Voyages.
Journal of the Society for the Bibliography of Natural History **5** (3): 161–201.

WHITEHEAD, P. J. P. 1978. A Guide to the Dispersal of Zoological Material from Captain Cook's Voyages.
Pacific Studies Fall, 1978: 53–93.

WHITLEY, W. T. 1928. *Artists and their Friends in England.* 2 vols.
London.

WILKINS, G. L. 1955. A Catalogue and Historical Account of the Banks Shell Collection.
Bulletin of the British Museum (Natural History) (hist. Ser.) **1** (3): 71–119.

WILLIAMS, G. 1962. *The British Search for the Northwest Passage in the Eighteenth Century.*
London.

WILLIAMS, G. 1979. Seamen and Philosophers in the South Seas in the Age of Captain Cook.
The Mariner's Mirror **65**: 3–22.

WILLIAMS, G. 1981. 'Far more happier than we Europeans': Reactions to the Australian Aborigines on Cook's Voyage.
Historical Studies: Australia and New Zealand **19** (77): 499–512.

WILLSON, E. J. 1961. *James Lee and the Vineyard Nursery, Hammersmith.*
London.

WOOLF, H. 1959. *The Transits of Venus: a study of eighteenth-century science.*
Princeton, New Jersey.

WRIGHT, N. P. 1963. A Thousand Years of Cochineal: A Lost but Traditional Mexican Industry on its way back.
American Dyestuff Reporter **17** (52): 25–29.

SOURCES OF ILLUSTRATIONS

Frontispiece   Joseph Banks *aet.* 28 by Benjamin West, PRA. By courtesy of the owner, private collection.

PART I
Page

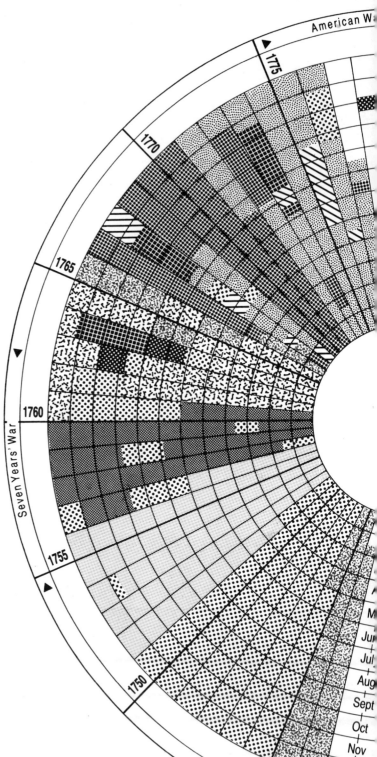

Sir Joseph E

American Wa

1775

1770

1765

1760

1755

1750

1745

Seven Years' War

M
Jur
Jul
Aug
Sept
Oct
Nov
Dec

A polar diagram of the life of Sir Joseph Banks and some important related events.